T0316855

Energy for Development

Advance Reviews

'*Energy for Development* is a book that should be mandatory reading for all government, industry and other stakeholder interests in global energy policy development and implementation. Its unbiased and comprehensive look at energy policy experiences and future constraints on both broad international and country-by-country bases provides critical information that should be used as the basis for creating an international sustainable energy strategy.'

Jack Siegel
Former Acting Assistant Secretary for Fossil Energy, U.S. Department of Energy
Chair, Fossil Fuel Working Party, International Energy Agency

'Dr Vedavalli through her wide experience, has edited an important book for the energy community worldwide. This book is essential reading for every one involved in global energy issues particularly those pertaining to developing countries.'

Dr Hisham Khatib
Honorary Vice Chairman, World Energy Council
Former Minister of Energy and Planning (Jordan)

'This book is a timely and comprehensive review of energy needs in non-OPEC developing countries with focus on access to affordable, efficient and reliable energy for development. In view of the rising share of developing countries in the world oil consumption, the book has aptly touched upon the issue of energy security by providing a lucid analysis on the achievements and failures of developing countries in the context of reforms in energy sector.'

YV Reddy
Governor of the Reserve Bank of India

Anthem Studies in Development and Globalization

Fullbrook, Edward (ed.) *Real World Economics* (2007)
Ringmar, Erik *Why Europe Was First* (2007)
Ellman, Michael (ed.) *Russia's Oil and Natural Gas* (2006)
Buira, Ariel (ed.) *Reforming the Governance of the IMF and the World Bank* (2005)
Ringmar, Erik *Surviving Capitalism* (2005)
Ritzen, Jozef *A Chance for the World Bank* (2004)
Fullbrook, Edward (ed.) *A Guide to What's Wrong with Economics* (2004)
Chang, Ha-Joon *Kicking Away the Ladder* (2003)

Energy for Development

Twenty-first Century Challenges of Reform and Liberalization in Developing Countries

Rangaswamy Vedavalli

Anthem Press

Anthem Press
An imprint of Wimbledon Publishing Company
www.anthempress.com

This edition first published in UK and USA 2007
by ANTHEM PRESS
75-76 Blackfriars Road, London SE1 8HA, UK
or
PO Box 9779, London SW19 7ZG, UK
and
244 Madison Ave. #116, New York, NY 10016, USA

British Library Cataloguing in Publication Data
A catalogue record for this book is available from the British Library.

Library of Congress Cataloging in Publication Data
Vedavalli, R. (Rangaswamy)
Energy for development : twenty-first century challenges of reform and liberalization in developing countries/Rangaswamy Vedavalli.
(Anthem studies in development and globalization)
Includes bibliographical references.

ISBN 1-84331-223-9 (hardback)
1. Energy consumption–Developing countries.
2. Power resources–Developing countries.
3. Energy policy–Developing countries.
I. Title. II. Series.

HD9502.D442V53 2006
333.7909172'4–dc22
2006011207

1 3 5 7 9 10 8 6 4 2

ISBN 1 84331 223 9 (Hbk)
ISBN-13 978 1 84331 223 9 (Hbk)

Printed in Singapore

To all who encouraged me to write
Energy for Development

CONTENTS

ABBREVIATIONS

AFDB	African Development Bank
APDP	Accelerated Power Development Program
APDRP	Accelerated Power Development and Reform Program
APM	Administered Pricing Mechanism
ADB	Asian Development Bank
AFR	Africa
AIC	Average Incremental Cost
Bcm	Billion cubic meters
Btu	British thermal unit
BJP	Bharatiya Janatha Party
BPCL	Bharat Petroleum Corporation Ltd
BOO	Build, Own and Operate
BOOT	Build, Own, Operate and Turnover
BP	British Petroleum
CDF	Comprehensive Development Framework
CEE/CIS	Central and Eastern Europe/Commonwealth of Independent States, Georgia and the Baltic States
CEA	Central Electricity Authority
CNPC	Chinese National Petroleum Company
CNOC	China National Offshore Corporation
DCs	Developing countries (all countries except OECD members and CEE/CIS)
CPEs	Central Government Public Enterprises
DGH	Directorate General of Hydrocarbons
DME	Department of Minerals and Energy
DOE US	Department of Energy
DPC	Dabhol Power Company
EDB	European Development Bank
EU	European Union
ECA	Eastern Europe and Central Asian Countries
EAP	East Asia and Pacific
EEHC	Egyptian Electric Holding Company
EGAS	Egyptian Natural Gas Holding Company

EGPC	Egyptian General Petroleum Company
EIA	Energy Information Agency
ERSAP	Economic Reform and Structural Adjustment Program
ESCOM	Electricity Supply Commission of South Africa
ESMAP	Energy Sector Management Program
FDI	Foreign Direct Investment
FERC	Federal Energy Regulatory Commission
FIPB	Foreign Investment Promotion Board
GAAP	Generally Accepted Accounting Principles
GDP	Gross Domestic Product
GNP	Gross National Product
GECC	General Electric Capital Corporation
GEF	Global Environmental Facility
GOI	Government of India
Gtoe	Gigaton of oil equivalent
GW	Gigawatt
GAIL	Gas Authority of India (Ltd)
HFO	Heavy Fuel Oil
HPCL	Hindustan Petroleum Corporation Ltd
IBRD	International Bank for Reconstruction and Development
IDA	International Development Association
IDB	Inter American Development Bank
IDBI	Industrial Development Bank of India
IEA	International Energy Agency
IFC	International Finance Corporation
IMF	International Monetary Fund
IIASA	International Institute for Applied Systems Analysis
IOC	Indian Oil Corporation
IOCs	International Oil companies
IPCL	Indian Petrochemicals Corporation Ltd
IPP	International Private Power Producers
IPO	Initial Public Offering
IRBID	Irbid District Electric Company
ICB	International Competitive Bidding
JNEPCO	Jordan National Electric Power Company
JEPCO	Jordan Electric Power Company
JPRC	Jordan Petroleum Refining Company
Kw	kilowatt
Kgoe	kilogram of oil equivalent
KERC	Karnataka Electricity Regulatory Commission
KPCL	Karnataka Power Corporation Ltd
KPTCL	Karnataka Power Transmission Corporation Limited
LAC	Latin America and Caribbean

LPG	Liquefied Petroleum Gas
LNG	Liquefied Natural Gas
LRMC	Long run marginal cost
M&A	Mergers and Acquisitions
MDG	Millennium Development Goals
MEE	Ministry of Electricity & Energy
MEMR	Ministry of Energy and Minerals
MIGA	Multilateral Investment Guarantee Agency
MNA	Middle East and North Africa
MNCs	Multi National Companies
MOP	Ministry of Power
MOEP	Ministry of Electric Power
MOU	Memorandum of Understanding
MSEB	Maharashtra State Electricity Board
Mtoe	Million tons of oil equivalent
MWh	Megawatt hour
NDA	National Democratic Alliance
NELP	New Exploration Licensing Policy
NFFO	Non-Fossil Fuel Obligation
NHPC	National Hydroelectric Power Corporation
NOCs	National Oil Companies
NPC	National Petroleum Company
NTPC	National Thermal Power Corporation
NPC	Nuclear Power Corporation
NGOs	Non-Governmental Organizations
NRC	National Regulatory Commission
OCC	Oil Coordination Committee
OECD	Organization for Economic Cooperation and Development
OIDC	Oil Importing Developing Countries
OLADE	Latin American Energy Organization
ONGC	Oil and Natural Gas Commission
OCC	Oil Coordination Committee
OEP	Organization for Energy Planning
OPEC	Organization of Petroleum Exporting Countries
PFC	Power Finance Corporation
PGC	Power Grid Corporation
PPA	Power Purchase Agreement
PRB	Petroleum Regulatory Board
REB	Regional Electricity Board
REC	Rural Electrification Corporation
RLDC	Regional Level Development Commission
ROACE	Return on Average Capital Employed
SAL	Structural Adjustment Loan

SAPP	Southern African Power Pool
SAR	South Asian Region
SEBs	State Electricity Boards
SDPC	State Development Planning Commission
SECAL	Sector Adjustment Loan
SERC	State Electricity Regulatory Commission
SETC	State Economic and Trade Commission
SOEs	State Owned Enterprises
SPC	State Planning Commission
SPEs	State Government Public Enterprises
SSTC	State Science and Technology Commission
SSA	Sub-Saharan Africa
T&D	Transmission and Distribution
TPC	Tata Power Company
Toe	Tons of oil equivalent
TWh	Tera watt hour
UK	United Kingdom
UN	United Nations
UNDESA	United Nations Department for Economic and Social Affairs
UNDP	United Nations Development Program
UNIDO	United Nations Industrial Development Organization
USEA	United States Energy Association
WB	World Bank
WBG	World Bank Group
WDR	World Development Report
WEA	World Energy Assessment
WEC	World Energy Council
WEO	World Energy Outlook
WTO	World Trade Organization
ZESA	Zimbabwe Electricity Supply Authority

LIST OF TABLES

LIST OF BOXES

PREFACE

15 years after developing countries embarked on energy sector reform and liberalization, the promise of quick energy market transformation to attract private sector has proven illusory even in countries such as Argentina, Brazil and East Asian miracle countries. Since the late 1980s, developing countries ranging from Argentina in Latin America and China and India in Asia, to countries in Sub-Saharan Africa (SSA), launched energy sector reform as part of their economic liberalization program to attract private investment in their energy sectors. Attempted reform measures in the energy sector include liberalizing energy prices, establishing independent and transparent regulatory institutions, restructuring/ commercialization/ privatization and creating an environment to attract private investment in energy.

As of 2005, developing countries continue to face energy shortages and power black-outs persist. As the demand for energy increased, non-OPEC net oil exporters such as China turned to become net oil importer. There is little reduction in the number of over 2 billion people, accounting for over 40 per cent of the population in the developing world, who lack access to commercial energy. Even with slower rates of growth, the world's population will increase from 6 billion to 8 billion in 2050. The share of population in developing regions will increase from 77 per cent today to 85 per cent in 2030 and to over 90 per cent by 2050. With rising populations and the required rates of economic growth, developing countries' share of energy demand in the global energy demand is expected to double from 30 per cent in 1998 to 60 per cent in 2050. Meeting the rising demand for energy to expand access to efficient, reliable and affordable energy in developing countries will be an increasingly difficult and urgent challenge. The pendulum shift solution since the 1990s towards private investment in energy has not delivered as expected. Even in the top ten developing countries where reform attracted investment in energy, the interest of private investors in energy has begun to wane. The problem is not with reform per se, but partly with the failure in managing the application of reform measures and partly with the expectations of the private sector's rates of return on their investment in energy for development. It also runs deeper to a misunderstanding of the fundamentals of the market transition process, the basics of an institutional reform process and the required standards of economic governance for effective reform implementation.

Developing countries cannot go back to the traditional 'command-control' system. Nor can they mobilize the required scale of investment in energy merely by crawling ahead on the path of reform. The decision-makers will need to face the facts to find systemic solutions rather than indulging in politically safe opportunistic behavior by tinkering around the edges of the problem. After 15 years of reform experience one ought to learn what works and what doesn't. Energy sector reform experience has also demonstrated that many challenges lie ahead. As developing oil importing countries are now at a crossroads in their energy market transition process, there is a need to incorporate the lessons of global reform experience, identify the challenges and plan for the way forward. A comprehensive energy for development framework is required to provide a basis for addressing the effects of the changing global energy industry since the 1990s, to reflect on lessons of energy sector reform and liberalization, to evaluate the impact of these events for developing countries since 2001 including that of power sector reform experience in developed countries, implications of practices of international energy companies, rising oil prices and energy security to confront the challenges of the future of energy.

Developing oil importing countries need to take the onus for an effective framework and the implementation of reform elements of energy for development. Lessons drawn from global experience indicate that critical elements for attracting finance include the rule of law and contract enforceability, creditworthiness both at macroeconomic and energy enterprise levels, sector policies including pricing based on reducing subsidies overtime to reflect full costs, transparent legal and regulatory frameworks to signal pricing/ tariff policies, bankability of investment, the creation of effective domestic capital markets and effective economic governance and government commitment to sustained action for long term planning and change.

However, reform experience and the events impacting the rising oil prices since May 2004 have also underscored the global interdependence of energy security and the future of energy in the twenty-first century. Today energy for development is part of the future of global energy. Implementation of a comprehensive framework of energy needs to be supported by mechanisms to push global action to a level mutually beneficial for energy stakeholders, governments, energy industry, private investors, energy technology developers and energy consumers. For ultimately, given the growing share of the potential market for energy in developing countries it is also in the interests of the global energy industry, energy technology developers and private investors to meet the growing energy demand to expand access to energy for development.

In writing this book I have drawn on my decades of experience working for the World Bank (WB) and World Energy Council (WEC), assisting several developing countries in Asia, Africa, the Middle East and Latin America to reform and liberalize their energy sectors. While managing the financing of energy projects and preparing oil, gas and power sector reform policy papers for the WB, from the post oil crisis period of the 1970s through the launch of energy sector reform in the 1990s, I have consulted and worked with various stakeholders, including representatives of energy industry, oil, gas, power and renewable energy companies, financing institutions, bilateral/ multilateral donors, and governments of developing and Organization for Economic Cooperation and Development (OECD) countries. I have attempted to reflect on my experience in this book.

I hope at best this book will open a debate among energy stakeholders at global, national and local levels on the issues of energy for development in the twenty-first century. At the very least, this book should provide facts about the reform experience. More information from comparative country reform case studies, analyses of reform experience and lessons learned from them will illustrate the challenges that lie ahead. I hope that this will lead to better policies and actions to deal with these challenges of energy for development and facilitate the way forward toward a better and sustainable energy future.

CHAPTER 1

THE CHALLENGE OF INCREASING ACCESS TO ENERGY FOR DEVELOPMENT

This book studies the increase of access to affordable, efficient and reliable energy for development in the twenty-first century with special reference to non-OPEC developing countries. In doing so the book evaluates energy sector reform and liberalization experience since the 1990s in non-OPEC developing countries and the impact of events since 2001 (including the spiking of crude oil prices to US $60 barrel in June 2005).

Over 85 net Oil Importing Developing Countries (OIDC) began to reform their economies in some form or other in the 1990s. The guiding principles of energy sector reform in developing countries were part of the overall 1990s globalization framework of market transition for developing countries widely known as the 'Washington Consensus'. It called for trade and financial liberalization, privatization, deregulation, openness to Foreign Direct Investment (FDI), a competitive exchange rate, fiscal discipline, lower taxes and smaller government.

In spite of the 1990s wave of globalization that prompted developing countries to liberalize and privatize their energy industry to finance the required investment for generating energy supplies for development, it is now clear that only a handful of developing countries were able to attract capital and grow rapidly. Also, in the initial years of the twenty-first century energy black-outs due to shortages of energy supplies for fuel development persist. While the total number of people without electricity has fallen by less than 500 million since 1990, over 1.6 billion people in the developing world (accounting for over 40 per cent of the population in Africa and South Asia in 2004) still have no access to electricity. In 2004, over 2 billion people in developing countries continued to use traditional biomass for cooking and heating.

Even with slower rates of population growth the world's population will increase from 6 billion in 2000 to 8 billion in 2030. The share of population living in developing regions will increase from 77 per cent today to 85 per cent in 2030 and to 90 per cent in 2050. The number of people lacking access to commercial energy will continue to grow in the developing world.

The twenty-first century began with an important series of events: the California energy crisis, economic slowdown in the USA after 9/11, the great black-out in the USA in 2003, the cancellation of the annual World Bank (WB) and International Monetary Fund (IMF) meetings, protest demonstrations against globalization and policies of the WB-IMF, Enron's debacle, Argentina's collapse, India's 2004 election outcome, the post Iraq war violence and lack of security in the oil rich region of the Middle East, terrorist attacks on an oil workers' compound in Saudi Arabia and the spiking of oil prices at a 'terrorist premium' since May 2004. Despite the OPEC's decision in June 2004 to increase its production by 8.5 per cent, the continuance of surging demand, shrinkage of excess capacity and terrorist threats were expected to affect the stability of the oil market.

The price spikes in oil markets have exacerbated concerns over the security of oil supplies. They have also added to the nervousness of governments and have raised questions on energy policies with continued dependence on oil. Access to energy has emerged as the overriding imperative of the twenty-first century. It has become the guiding geopolitical principle for all energy importing countries. The events in the initial years of the twenty-first century have a critical bearing on increasing access to energy supplies for development. They also underscore the reality that the globalization process of the 1990s in itself is not a panacea for alleviating poverty, increasing access to energy to fuel the growing economies of energy importing countries and the need to expand energy services to over 2 billion people living with no access to commercial energy.

The rapid and large oil price increases since 2004 have created growing concerns among OIDC regarding the impact on their economies and balance of payments. They have also raised questions on pursuing energy sector reform and liberalization policies to finance the investment required to increase access to efficient, reliable and affordable energy for development.

A number of studies on world energy undertaken in recent years by the International Energy Agency (IEA) [1],United Nations Development Program (UNDP)[2], World Energy Council (WEC)[3] and the World Bank[4] deal with

---

1. IEA, *WEO* (Paris, 2004); IEA, 'Energy Policies of IEA Countries', *Review* (Paris, 2004); IEA, *World Energy Investment Outlook* (Paris, 2003)
2. UNDP, UNDESA, WEC, *WEA Update* (2004); UNDP, UNDESA, WEC, *World Energy Assessment - Energy and the Challenge of Sustainability* (New York, 2000), p. 100-17

energy issues in developing countries to some extent. The IEA publications of 2004 and 2003 provide a world energy outlook and global energy investment requirements up to 2030 including those of developing countries, respectively. The UNDP/ ESMAP reports provide a generic scorecard for energy reform in developing countries in the 1990s and provide knowledge based general policy responses to higher oil prices.

But these studies are mainly prescriptive and of a 'one size fits all' nature. They have not addressed the effects of the changing energy industry of the 1990s, the 1990s reform-globalization-reform experience of developing countries, the impact of events in the post 9/11 world and the challenges for developing countries to increase access to affordable, efficient and reliable energy for development in the twenty-first century. They do not investigate energy pricing, regulation, commercialization, financial and investment reform experience in the energy sector of developing countries. They do not address the expectations and realities of the 1990s reform experience to finance energy for development, and are not informed by the lessons of over fifteen years of energy sector liberalization. They also fail to address reform implementation experience and issues at global and national levels impacting the future of reform as vehicles to finance the required investment in energy for development in today's changing world of energy.

Since reform and liberalization act as vehicles for public and private investment in twenty-first century global energy, understanding the financing of the required investment in energy for development requires several questions on sector reform and liberalization in developing countries to be addressed.

This book is a pioneering effort in this direction. It acknowledges earlier publications and goes further to discuss an important pair of issues — namely, the experience of energy market reform and liberalization in developing countries to finance the required investment in energy for development, and the increase of access to reliable, efficient and affordable energy to their population which lacks access to energy services.

15 years after embarking on energy market reform, OIDC face a number of challenges to increase access to energy for development in order to satisfy the growing demand, reduce dependence on imported oil, ensure security of energy supplies and shape reform policies for the future of energy in the changing world.

Energy demand is growing rapidly in several emerging developing economies including China and India. Between 1970 and the late 1990s,

---

3. WEC, *Energy for Tomorrow's World - Acting Now!* (London, 2000)
4. UNDP/ WB/ ESMAP, The *Impact of Higher Oil Prices on Low Income Countries and the Poor* (Washington DC, March 2005); WB/ ESMAP, *Energy and Development Report* (Washington DC, 2000)

energy use by developing countries has increased three to four times as quickly as that of countries in the Organization for Economic Cooperation and Development (OECD) reflecting the impact of rising income and higher population growth. Consequently, the share of developing countries in global commercial energy use increased from 13 per cent in 1970 to almost 30 per cent in 1998. Between 1990 and 2001, the average annual growth rate of primary energy use in industrialized countries was 1.5 per cent; in developing countries it was more than twice that at 3.2 per cent, with important variations among different regions of developing countries accounted for by population growth and levels of economic activity.

The varying growth rates in energy use have helped to reduce the gap in energy services between industrialized and developing countries. On a per capita basis however, the increase in primary energy use has not resulted in more equitable access to energy services between developed and developing countries.

Table 1.1 shows significant inequalities in annual per capita primary energy use among groups of countries. In 2001, industrialized countries used 4.7 tons of oil equivalent (toe) per capita, in contrast to developing countries which used only 0.8 toe per capita. Overall, per capita energy use in developing countries remains at 50 per cent of the world average per capita and less than 20 per cent of per capita use in the OECD countries. In Africa energy use has barely increased since 1971 and remains at less than 10 per cent of per capita use in the OECD countries. The same is true for Asia despite a near doubling in per capita energy use since 1971. This means that most Africans and Asians have no access to commercial energy. Latin America saw little improvement in energy use per capita.

Table 1.1. Primary Energy Use Per Capita by Region: 1971–2001 (kilogram of oil equivalent (kgoe))

Region	1971	1980	1990	1997	2001
OECD countries	3,484	4,248	4,344	4,656	4,680
Transition economies	2,976	3,960	4,344	1,694	2,980
Developing countries	480	600	696	816	790
Of which					
Latin America	864	1,008	960	1,128	1,070
Middle East	840	1,464	1,788	2,280	1,620
Africa	552	624	648	648	600
Asia non-OECD)	360	408	504	624	720
World Total	1,488	1,656	1,680	1,680	1,640

Sources: UNDP, *WEA*, Annex C, 'Energy Trends', p.458; UNDP *WEA Update 2004*, Table 2; WB *WDR 2000–1*, Table 10, pp. 292–3.

Energy demand outlook

Various sources, including UNDP, WEC, International Institute for Applied Systems Analysis (IIASA)[5], IEA and oil industry make short and long term forecasts for *World Energy Outlook* (WEO) including that of developing countries. Chapter 9 of the UNDP *World Energy Assessment* (WEA) has developed three cases out to the year 2100. Case A assumes high economic growth, Case B represents a middle course reference case and Case C includes ecologically driven scenarios. There are considerable differences in expected total energy consumption among the various cases. However, all point to an increase in the world's commercial energy consumption over this century. Today's consumption levels are roughly 2.5 to 5 times those of 2002 and there will be continued dependence of over 40 per cent of total energy on fossil fuels (coal, oil and natural gas) through 2100. Even with rising energy taxes and demand side interventions, world consumption of commercial energy in the Case B reference scenario is projected to double from 10.3 Gtoe in 2002 to 19.8 Gtoe by 2050. Table 1.2 shows projected demand for energy in the three cases.

Table 1.2. Global Primary Energy Consumption (Gtoe)

	A	B	C
2002	10.3		
2020	15.4	13.6	11.4
2050	24.8	19.8	14.3
2100	44.9	34.7	20.9

Source: UNDP, *WEA*, Table 9.1, p 338; IEA, *WEO* (2004), Table 2.1.

Even with the slower rate of population and economic growth, perhaps as many as 4–6 billion more people will require access to modern forms of energy over the next half century. Especially with most of the population increase in developing countries, large increases in world energy demand lie ahead in any scenario of economic growth and continued dependence of over 40 per cent of total energy on fossil fuel (coal, oil and natural gas) through 2100.[6] IEA's *WEO* (2004) reference scenario projection assumes continuance of policies in force as of mid-2004 in OECD countries. The projected rates of growth in Gross Domestic Product (GDP) and population are much lower between 2002 and 2030 compared with the second half of the 1990s and the historical annual average rate of growth between 1971 and 2002. This reflects slowing annual average rates of growth in population

5. IIASA WEC, *Global Energy Perspectives* (Cambridge, Cambridge University Press,1998)
6. UNDP, *Energy Scenarios*, chapter 9, (2000)

in developing countries, from 2 per cent between 1971 and 2002 to 1.2 per cent between 2002 and 2030. Oil price is assumed to increase less than 1 per cent in year 2000 dollars reflecting the increase in IEA's crude oil import cost to $29 per barrel in 2030 from $27 per barrel in 2003. Table 1.3 below summarizes IEA's assumptions for its reference scenario.

Table 1.3 IEA: *WEO* (2004) Reference Scenario Assumptions

1. Energy/ environment policies	No change in energy and environment policies through the projection period	
2. Technology	No new breakthrough technologies beyond those known in mid-2004 will be used before 2030	
3. Fossil fuel prices	2003* (in year 2000 dollars)	2030 (in year 2000 dollars)
IEA crude oil imports ($/barrel)	27.0	29.0
Natural gas ($/Mbtu)	5.3	4.7
Of which US imports	3.4	4.3
Japan LNG imports	4.6	4.8
OECD steam coal imports($/ton)	38.0	44.0
4. Population growth	1971-2002 (average annual rate in per cent)	2002-30 (average annual rate in per cent)
OECD	0.8	0.4
Transition economies	0.5	0.3
Developing countries	2.0	1.2
World	1.6	1.1
5. Economic growth	1971-2002 (average annual rate in per cent)	2002-30 (average annual rate in per cent)
OECD	2.9	2.2
Transition economies	0.7	3.7
Developing countries	4.7	4.3
World	3.3	3.2

* *Represents historical data*

IEA projects the world energy demand to expand by almost 60 per cent between 2002 and 2030, with an average annual rate of growth of 1.7 per cent. Global energy demand is projected to reach 16.5 billion toe in 2030 from 10.3 billion toe in 2002. Fossil fuels accounting for 85 per cent of the increase in primary energy demand will continue to dominate the energy mix (Table 1.4).

Table 1.4: World Primary Energy Demand (Mtoe)

Energy sources	1971	2002	2030	2002–30 (average annual growth-rate in per cent)
Coal	1,407	2,389	3,601	1.5
(of which) Developing countries	293	1,099	2,192	2.5
Oil	2,413	3,676	5,766	1.6
(of which) Developing countries	299	1,142	2,517	2.9
Gas	892	2,190	4,130	2.3
(of which) Developing countries	40	515	1518	3.9
Nuclear	29	692	764	0.4
(of which) Developing countries	0	30	135	5.6
Hydro	104	224	365	1.8
(of which) Developing countries	16	94	202	2.7
Biomass and waste	687	1,119	1,605	1.3
(of which) Developing countries	580	922	1,221	1.0
Other renewables	4	55	256	5.7
(of which) Developing countries	0	21	89	5.2
Total	5,536	10,345	16,487	2
Developing countries	1,1228	3,824	7,873	3

Source: IEA, *WEO* (2004), Table 2.1 and Annex A Table, 'Reference Scenario, Developing Countries'

Energy demand in developing countries

IEA's *WEO* (2004) projects that two-thirds of the increase in the world's primary energy demand between 2002 and 2030 will come from developing countries, especially those of Asia. Developing countries' share of world energy demand will increase from 37 per cent in 2002 to 47 per cent in 2030. The share of fossil fuels in developing countries in the total primary energy consumption will increase from 72 per cent in 2002 to almost 80 per cent in 2030. The share of commercial energy will rise from 80 per cent to 88 per cent over the same period. The replacement of traditional biomass by commercially traded energy will reduce the share of biomass from 24 per cent in 2002 to 16 per cent in 2030 (Table 1.4).

The main factors contributing to the strong increase in energy demand in developing countries include their economic growth, industrial expansion, population increase, urbanization, increased use of fuel in the transport sector and substitution of commercial fuels for non-commercial fuels. Low-energy prices in many developing countries also contribute, though this factor could become less significant as subsidies are reduced. The link between growing incomes and the demand for transport with high-energy use is evident in China and India. Affordability of motorized transport for population in China, Thailand, Malaysia and India has led to rapid growth in oil consumption.

Energy demand is growing rapidly in several emerging developing economies including China and India. Demand for energy and dependence on oil have increased since 2001. Oil's share of primary energy consumption varied among developing regions. Oil's share in Latin America remained at 46 per cent in 2002. Oil's share of total primary energy consumption in Africa was 21 per cent in 2002. Also, in 2002 the share of oil in total primary energy consumption in Asia was 40 per cent. However, the share of oil consumption in Asia varied widely from 25 per cent for China and India, to 50 per cent for the Philippines and 60 per cent for Thailand. However, Oil's share of total energy consumption in India and China will increase with the rapidly increasing transportation demand and increasing access of commercial energy to the rural population. China, the fastest growing economy which was the net oil exporter in the pre-1990s, became a major importer of oil since 1994. India's oil imports have increased to over 70 per cent of its growing demand.

While oil's share of the world primary energy consumption (accounting for 36 per cent in 2002) is projected to fall to 35 per cent in 2030, oil's share of primary energy consumption in developing countries is expected to increase from 30 per cent in 2002 to 32 per cent in 2030. Developing countries' oil consumption is projected to more than double from 1,142 Mtoe in 2002 to 2,517 Mtoe in 2030 accounting for more than 65 per cent of the net increase of 2,090 Mtoe in world oil consumption. The share of oil in total primary energy consumption for China and India is projected to increase from 20 per cent and 22 per cent in 2002 to 25 per cent and 26 per cent in 2030. respectively.

Increasing access to energy

For the first time, IEA's *WEO* (2004) measures the increase in access to energy in developing countries by developing an Energy Development Index (EDI) — a composite measure of energy use in developing countries and of their progress in modern energy use. The EDI is composed of per capita commercial energy consumption, the share of commercial energy in total final energy use and the share of population with access to electricity. A separate index for each of the three elements is created for 75 developing countries for 2002. Performance in each element is expressed as a value between zero and one. The index is then calculated as the arithmetic average of the three values for each country.[7]

According to *WEO* reference scenario projections for developing countries, the EDI index scores are expected to continue to rise in all developing regions. The index for developing countries as a whole is projected to rise from 0.48 in 2002 to 0.57 in 2030, with regional variations. The medium-income Latin American and high-income Middle Eastern countries are ranked high ranging from 0.60 to 0.99, reflecting the high rates of household electrification and their limited use of traditional biomass. East Asian countries range in the middle with EDI rankings between 0.60 and 0.70. South Asia is below 0.40. The SSA countries with uniformly low household incomes and electrification rates rank below 0.20. Ethiopia and Myanmar are the least developed countries in terms of energy with ranks of 0.037 and 0.091 respectively.

Despite regional variation in energy use, IEA's reference scenario projects access to energy in developing countries to rise over the projection period from 66 per cent of the population of developing countries in 2002 to 78 per cent in 2030. Except for South Asia and SSA, electrification rates are expected to reach 100 per cent in all other regions by 2030.

Despite the optimistic outlook projections, because of rising population in developing countries (albeit at a slower rate) the total number of people without electricity is expected to fall only slightly from the present 1.6 billion to 1.4 billion. In addition, the number of people relying entirely on traditional biomass for cooking and heating will also increase from 2.4 billion people in 2002 to over 2.55 billion in 2015.

Energy for development: Uncertainties

As with any attempt to project future energy developments all projections are subject to a wide range of uncertainties, including macroeconomic framework conditions, fossil fuel supplies and costs, energy policies, technological developments, environmental policies and twenty-first century supply shocks. IEA's projections recognize these uncertainties by undertaking a separate alternative policy scenario assessment on how global energy markets could evolve with the implementation of a range of new energy and environmental policies whose adoption OECD countries are considering. For non-OECD countries, where policy discussions are less advanced, energy efficiency and energy intensity are assumed to improve more rapidly than in the reference scenario as a result of future policies and faster technology transfer from OECD countries. Given that new policies and technologies would take effect only gradually, global energy demand in the alternative scenario is expected to be 0.4 per cent points less than in the refer-

7. IEA, *WEO*, *Energy and Development*, chapter 10 (2004)

ence scenario.

Sustained high oil prices which are not assumed in any projections could adversely impact economic growth in oil importing countries and reduce energy consumption. IEA's completed study with the OECD and IMF in 2004 indicates that a sustained $10 per barrel increase in oil prices from $25 to $35 (the average price for the first 8 months of 2004) would result in a loss of about 0.4 per cent GDP in the first and second years of higher prices to the OECD as a whole. Inflation would rise by half a percentage point and unemployment would also increase. IEA's separate analysis to examine the effects of high oil prices (assumed to average $35 per barrel in year 2000 dollars) show that fossil fuel demand for energy would fall sharply by 14 per cent in 2030 compared with the reference scenario. The use of nuclear power is projected to rise by 14 per cent and that of non-hydro renewables (excluding biomass) by 30 per cent. The impact on energy demand would grow throughout the projection period because new policies and technologies would take effect only gradually.

Implications of high oil prices for developing countries

The impact of high oil prices on net oil importing countries is different from that of net oil exporting countries in terms of reduction in GDP and energy consumption and impact on balance of payments. The WB/ ESMAP Report[8] estimates that the lowest income oil exporter group would enjoy 5.21 per cent improvement in GDP and a substantial improvement in its balance of payments. However, oil exporting countries in Africa, such as Angola and Equatorial Guinea, will continue to face challenges of combating corruption, transparency in the allocation of incremental oil revenue to development programs and effective program implementation to increase access to energy for development.

The adverse economic impact of higher oil prices on oil importing developing countries is more severe than on OECD countries because their economies are more energy intensive. One obvious factor that determines the impact of higher oil prices on oil importing countries is the ratio of net oil imports to GDP. Based on the ratio of net oil imports to GDP the WB/ ESMAP report estimates that for every sustained ten dollar increase in oil prices there will be a reduction of GDP by 1.47 per cent for the poorest 18 countries with GDP per capita of less than $300. The loss of GDP for 58 low and middle income developing countries with per capita income of less than $9000 ranges from 0.56 to 0.76 per cent. The estimated reduction in GDP for 21 higher income developing countries with over $9,000 per capita

8. WB/ ESMAP, *The Impact of Higher Oil Prices on Low Income Countries and on the Poor* (Washington DC, March 2005)

income is 0.44 per cent. Rising global oil prices will also impose an additional loss of 0.5 per cent GDP on OIDC as their exports begin to fall. In several OIDC the 2004–5 hikes in oil prices have caused oil imports to absorb a large share of their export earnings.

The impact of higher oil prices on the balance of payments and subsequent adjustments of exporting and importing developing countries will also depend on the exchange rate policies of individual countries. Countries directly linking their currencies to the US dollar may have to bear the full impact as oil prices are quoted in dollars. Francophone countries in West Africa linked to the Euro and countries linking their currencies to a basket of foreign currencies (dollar/ Euro/ pound sterling) may be partially affected subject to variations in exchange rates.

The share of OIDC in world imports of crude oil and petroleum products increased from less than 10 per cent in 1975 to almost 20 per cent in 2000. Net oil imports from OIDC increased from 8 million barrels per day in 1988 to over 10 million barrels per day in 2000. At an average of US $28 per barrel in 2000, OIDC spent US $280 million per day. For OIDC, the post Iraq war uncertainties resulting in terrorist attacks and violence in the Middle East have underscored the fragility of world oil supplies and have raised concerns about the volatility of oil prices and the rising cost of increasing oil imports on their balance of payment and economic development.

Table 1.5 shows net imports of crude oil and products for key OIDC.

Table 1.5: Net Oil Imports of Selected OIDC (Thousand metric tons)

Selected OIDs	1973	1978	1998	2000	2001
Brazil	32,735	44,075	37,108	20,023	21,987
Chile	3,466	3,772	10,764	11,484	11,083
Morocco	2,361	3,614	6,842	7,095	7,690
South Africa	14,198	15,490	17 996	12 710	13,365
Jordan	706	1,332	4,709	4,761	4,846
India	17,445	18,505	62,326	74,999	75,650
Philippines	9,092	11,011	18,390	16,803	17,932
China(Taipei)	8,844	9,211	39,433	39,194	38,644
Thailand	8,149	10,490	28,329	27,117	27,632
China, (People's Republic)			32,253	73,755	78,622
China,(Hong Kong)	4,861	6,187	11,667	12,020	11,906

Sources*:* IEA Statistics, (2003), *International Energy Agency, Oil Information, OECD, (Paris); UN Energy Statistics Yearbook* (2000)

When oil prices rose to US $50 per barrel in April 2005 compared with the US $22–28 per barrel through most of 2003, OIDC had to pay 80 per cent more at US $500 million daily for the same volume of oil (10 million barrels per day) imported in 2000. For every dollar increase in per barrel price of oil, OIDC incur an additional cost of over US $4 billion a year. Oil importing countries such as India and China that have recently liberalized their oil prices face increases in consumer prices for oil. In several OIDC the 2004 hike in oil prices caused oil imports to absorb a large share of their export earnings. Table 1.6 shows increasing oil import bill of OIDC in 2004 for the same volume of OIDC oil imports in 2000.

Table 1.6. OIDC Net Oil Imports

OIDC by region	2000* '000 Mtoe	$ 28/barrel Million US$	$35/barrel Million US$	$50/barrel Million US$
Africa	42,804	8,732	11,195	15,624
Latin America and Caribbean	89,992	18,358	23,478	32,847
Asia (include Jordan)	280,000	57,120	73,360	102,200
Total OIDs	412,796	94,200	108,033	150,671

*UN, *Energy Statistics Yearbook* (2000)

The inevitable price spikes in the oil market as a result of rising demand for oil, continued tension in the Middle East and the downward revision of oil reserves in 2004, have added to the nervousness of governments and have raised questions on energy policies with continued dependence on oil. As of 2005, access to a secure supply of energy has emerged as the overriding imperative of the twenty-first century. It has become the guiding geopolitical principle of all oil importing countries. Uncertainties of fossil fuel prices and the security of energy supply have implications for short and long term energy policies and investment requirements for increasing access to efficient energy for development. With the rising share of demand for energy in developing countries, they will have to become the largest capital investors in any energy scenario.

Capital requirements and financing

Because adequate and affordable energy supplies are critical for fuelling economic growth, capital investment is crucial for energy development. Any difficulties in attracting capital for energy investment can slow economic development, especially in the least developed countries where the majority of people (2 billion) without access to commercial energy live. Although energy investment accounts for only a small share of the global capital market, the availability of the capital needed for a growing energy sector cannot be taken for granted but depends on prices and regulations that permit investors to earn rates of return that compete with other opportunities offered by international capital markets.[9]

In any scenario of energy consumption capital requirements will be large relative to current standards. As a share of the GDP, global energy investments range from 1.5 per cent to 1.9 per cent. It is expected to grow at the same rate over the period 2001-30. During the early 1990s energy investments averaged just over 1 per cent of global GDP at $240–280 billion a year. The *WEO* (2004) estimates a cumulative global energy infrastructure investment of $16 trillion (in 2000 dollars) to maintain over 10 billion toe of existing supplies and increase over 6 billion toe of new energy supplies through 2030. In absolute terms, annual global energy investment requirements are estimated to be around US $568 billion a year through 2030, marginally higher than the estimate of $550 billion a year equal to 1 per cent of global GDP made by IEA's 2003 study on World Investment Outlook.[10] More than half of the investment is expected to be required to replace or maintain existing and future capacity. The electricity sector is projected to absorb about $10 trillion or over 62 per cent of total investment. Total investment in the oil and gas sector is estimated to be around $3 trillion or 18 per cent of the total global investment. Coal investment is projected to be around $400 billion, accounting for 2.4 per cent of the global energy investment.

Table 1.7: Cumulative Energy Investment by Region 2001–2030

Region	2001–10	2011–20	2020–30	Total: 2001–30
Total: OECD	2,093	2,238	2,231	6,552
Russia	269	391	389	1,050
Other transition economies	168	221	233	622
Total: Transition economies	438	612	622	1,672
China	578	787	888	2,253
Other Asia (including India)	489	689	876	2,055
Middle East	268	332	444	1,044
Africa	248	393	567	1,208
Latin America	339	440	558	1,337

9. WEC Report, *Financing the Global Energy Sector – The Task Ahead,* (London,1997)

10. IEA, *World Energy Investment Outlook* (Paris, 2003)

Region	2001–10	2011–20	2020–30	Total: 2001–30
Total: Developing countries	1,923	2,641	3,332	7,897
Inter-regional transportation	97	129	134	360
Total: World	4,551	5,610	6,320	16,481
Annual Average	455	561	632	549

Source*:* IEA, *World Energy Investment Outlook*, (Paris, 2003)

Although the projected global energy investment of $16.5 trillion equates to 1 per cent of global GDP on average through 2030, the share of energy investment in the GDP varies from a low of less than 1 per cent for OECD countries to a high of 3-5 per cent for developing oil importing and transition economies. The IEA study concludes that global financial resources are adequate to cover energy investments of more than $16 trillion, provided conditions in the energy sector are attractive for investment. The private sector is expected to play an increasing role in financing energy investments worldwide as governments retreat from direct ownership and intervention. Developing countries will have constrained access to long-term capital for energy projects, given the limitations of their financial markets. For developing countries therefore, FDI is expected to remain an important source of private capital.

An important aspect of future energy investment is that 70 per cent of the increase in world primary energy demand and almost all the growth in energy production between 2001 and 2030 will occur in developing countries and transition economies, and energy investment requirements will be greatest and increase most rapidly in those regions. Almost half of total energy investment, or $7.9 trillion will have to be in developing countries and 10 per cent ($1.7 trillion) in transition economies.

The challenge for OIDC in the twenty-first century will be to raise an increasing fraction of capital requirements from the private sector to increase energy supplies for meeting the growing energy demand. Because oil and gas are internationally tradable and generate revenues in hard currencies, oil and gas upstream projects in developing countries will be able to attract FDI with stable macroeconomic conditions and appropriate government policies. Consolidation in the coal industry and improved operational and financial performance in competitive markets will facilitate financing of coal projects. However, developing countries will find it difficult to finance the large-scale investments required in domestic electricity and downstream gas.

In this regard, critics[11] of the IEA's estimates of investment requirement for developing countries argue that because of uncertainties in the growth rates of GDP and population in developing countries, the IEA's estimate of annual investment requirements of $320 billion in 2030 for electricity infrastructure and maintenance and expanding access for energy services to the poor is overstated. The critics argue that except for the core financing challenge of $30 billion for minimum commercial electricity access in the world's poorest countries in Africa, developing countries in other regions should be able to finance the remaining $290 billion by raising operations and maintenance practices in existing power plants, realizing existing potential for end-use efficiency gains and ready access to the capital market.

While it is true that energy for development could be financed by realizing some potential savings, improving operational efficiency and creating a climate to facilitate access to the capital market, the ground reality is that despite launching energy sector reforms in the 1990s efficiency gains in the electricity sector in developing countries' existing plants remain yet to be improved. As for access to the capital market, the fact remains that only a handful of developing countries have been able to attract the flow of international capital in the 1990s. A number of the top ten developing countries attracting the flow of international capital in the 1990s also faced currency speculation, crony loans and capital flight leading to financial and economic crisis in East Asia in 1998 and Argentina in 2001, impacting investment in their energy sectors.

Developing economies were also hit by the global slowdown in the initial years of the twenty-first century and faced even more dire circumstances because of falling commodity prices, plunging economic activities, increasing distrust of big business energy corporations and the heightening jitters among international investors. Although the global economy has begun to re-emerge since 2004, developing countries need to recognize the challenge of sustaining the recent strengthening of capital flows and the risk of continuing fluctuations in the availability of external finance in the post 9/11 world.

Future energy investment needs will be determined by the rate of growth in energy demand and the amount and cost of supply capacity needed to meet the increase in demand and to replace old plants. These variables in the post 9/11 world depend on several uncertainties, such as macroeconomic fundamentals, energy prices, geopolitical factors, technological developments and government policies directed towards the energy sector.

Rising oil prices since 2004, the uncertainties associated with fossil fuel price, and their effects on resource availability and the effects of supply costs

---

11. WEC 2005 'Electricity Challenge in Developing Countries', *World Energy Fax* (1 February, 2005)

on energy prices pose new challenges to the increase of access to efficient and affordable energy supplies for development. These depend not only on production conditions and technological developments but also on geopolitical factors. Changes in government energy and environment policies and the need to address energy security could impact energy investment requirements and could have profound consequences on energy market reforms.

Countries' energy policies are closely linked and will have a substantial overall impact on global energy developments. Related issues include legal frameworks for energy markets, questions of supply security, pricing policies, infrastructure financing, FDI and technology transfer. While it is widely assumed that the global trend towards more market orientation, transparency and entrepreneurship will continue, the precise nature of the energy structure that will emerge is difficult to predict. Socio-political developments in the non-OECD countries will be particularly important because these countries will generate most of the increase in energy demand over the next 25 years and beyond.

The election outcomes since 2002 in democratic developing countries such as Argentina, Brazil and India reflect the growing divide between the winners and losers of globalization. The new governments in these countries have already reconsidered the concepts of reform, privatization and liberalization by adopting the principle of 'globalization with a human element' as they are faced with the realities of their experience in energy sector reform.

With rising shortages of energy for development and with more than one-third of the population in Asia and Africa lacking access to electricity, the promise of quick market transformation to attract private investment for increasing access to reliable, efficient and affordable energy has proven illusory. Developing countries are now at a crossroads regarding the progress of energy sector reform. The new democratic governments coming to office since 2002 in India, Brazil, Argentina and Bolivia are revisiting energy sector reform and liberalization policies. In the wake of rising oil prices since 2004, the new governments have adopted a revised pricing policy to continue with government intervention and subsidies, and have reverted back in part to administered energy prices.

The twenty-first century is fraught with the tension of reconciling developing countries' economic and social development with increased energy use and protection of the environment. The consequent uncertainties call for a fine balance between increasing access to energy supplies to alleviate energy shortages in the short term and continuation of reforms to promote investment and to maintain the fundamentals of long term economic growth. This requires reconsideration of concepts such as governance, efficiency, the role of the state, equity and social justice to formulate appropriate macro/ sector policies and to take actions to implement these policies.

Given that governments continue to play a big role in determining whether or not energy projects can be financed even when they are not directly involved in the financing, government policies are critical to set the general conditions for determining the extent of economic, political and legal risks. While limitations of the domestic financial market constrain local currency financing, access to international capital will be limited by the exchange rate risk, deficiencies in the legal and regulatory systems and economic and political uncertainties about the continuation of macro/ sector reforms and their effective implementation.

For developing countries, the major uncertainty lies in addressing doubts about the commercial viability of investment in energy and the required rate of return on energy sector investments to raise the necessary finance for future investments. Moving ahead on the reform path to create an environment that will attract both public and private investment in energy requires an understanding of the experience of energy sector reform and liberalization in developing countries. The following questions need to be addressed:

i. For developing countries what are the implications of the changing global energy industry since the 1990s?
ii. Compared to the 1970s and 1980s, how has the energy market transition changed financing energy development in developing countries since the 1990s
iii. What were the expectations from reform and liberalization in the energy sector in developing countries and what are the realities now?
iv. How have energy sector reform and liberalization impacted the finance of energy services to increase access for over 2 billion poor people?
v. What are the lessons learnt from the 1990s energy sector reforms in developing countries as vehicles to financial investment in energy?
vi. How have global events since the 1998 East Asian crisis and the events of 2001 (including energy black-outs in OECD countries, global energy company practices, rising oil prices, energy security issues and election outcomes in democratic developing countries) impacted energy policies and reform?
vii. In the light of the emerging geopolitical transformation of energy business with rising oil prices of 2004, growing energy demand in developing countries and security concerns of oil supplies, what are the challenges of increasing access to economic, efficient and affordable energy for development in the twenty-first century?
viii. How can such access be provided to the 2 billion who currently have no access to commercial energy?
ix. Finally, what is the way forward?

CHAPTER 2

CHANGING GLOBAL ENERGY INDUSTRY: IMPLICATIONS FOR DEVELOPING COUNTRIES

The global energy industry entered the year 2005 with rising oil prices, uncertainty about future trends in oil prices, rising shares of developing countries in the world energy consumption contributing to continued domination of use of fossil fuels in the energy mix and serious concerns about energy security.

Globalization and continued liberalization of international trade and investment since the 1990s, the political and economic transformation of Eastern Europe and the Former Soviet Union (FSU) and the events since 2001 are changing the global energy industry in the new millennium. The fall of the Berlin Wall in 1989 signalled the failure of the command and control economy. Most of the world recognized the need for the changing role of the state from being the owner to the facilitator of business. For the first time many world economies embarked on the path of liberalization by moving toward the market by opening up trade, by deregulating their economies and by privatizing public enterprises.

The waves of economic globalization and continued liberalization of international trade and investment are most evident in the global energy industry. All segments of the global energy industry from exploration and production (E&P), transportation, refining and marketing to the power utility sector, are being shaped since the 1990s by the emerging trends and influences of the new market dynamics. Given that developing countries started to reform their energy sectors modelled on developed countries since the 1990s, the changing international energy industry, (including the ongoing energy market reforms in OECD countries) has implications for developing countries.

This chapter, therefore, examines the changing global energy industry and energy market liberalization in OECD countries in the context of their implications for developing countries to attract investment and thereby increase access to efficient and affordable energy for development.

At the beginning of the 1990s the petroleum industry was poised for more structural changes. The oil glut of the 1980s and the consequent developments in the oil market created new possibilities for the oil industry and shaped the corporate strategies formulated by key players in the oil market, OPEC National Oil Companies (NOCs) and the international oil companies.

The international energy industry entering the twenty-first century is characterized by changing trends in the petroleum industry and energy liberalization in the OECD countries. The international oil, gas and power industries increased the use of natural gas, and the liberalization in natural gas and electricity segments and development of renewable energy created enormous opportunities for global energy companies. Natural gas has become the fuel of choice partly due to environmental concerns and partly due to economic and efficiency considerations and availability of supplies. The IEA, in the *WEO* (2004) forecasts natural gas's share of the world energy market rising from 21 per cent in 2002 to 25 per cent in 2030. Competition and environmental concerns are driving the need for technology and efficiency gains in the production, transportation and distribution of energy. These have implications for developing countries which are opening up to attract private investment in their energy sectors.

Emerging trends in international petroleum industry

In the 1980s when oil prices hit a low point, oil and gas companies were under pressure to achieve Return on Average Capital Employed (ROACE) to their shareholders comparable to those available elsewhere. Petroleum companies sought to expand their asset portfolios and mitigate the risk while seeking further cost-reduction through economies of scale. The corporate strategy of major oil companies in the USA and Europe was redefined in the light of developments in the world economy and the international oil market of the 1990s.

The 1990s decade of boom, energy complacency and optimism about plentiful oil supplies gave the oil and gas industries the luxury of gazing at the prospect of continued prosperity as they headed into the twenty-first century. With declining oil prices since the early 1980s and their collapse in 1986, structural changes in the private oil industry, particularly in the USA, included a wave of mergers, acquisitions, consolidations as well as geographic and functional concentration of operations, reorganization of non-energy and non-petroleum operations.

The closing years of the twentieth century saw the industry once again realign itself. The last few years will be remembered as the age of mega-mergers for the oil industry.

Geographic, political and reserves composition (oil versus gas) diversification acted as a key strategic driver for these mega-mergers. The emerging privatization and globalization of formerly state-owned oil companies is also driving the integrated companies to seek optimum mass to counter the threat from these new competitors.

The mega-merger activity was driven by the industry's acceptance in the 1990s of the likelihood of relatively low-oil prices over the long term. Most energy industry analysts believed that long-term increases in margins are expected to come primarily from cost-reduction efforts. This required the integrated company to seek economies of scale to lower and/ or spread their costs over a larger reserve base in the up stream sector and consolidate market share in the down stream sector. The need to rationalize operations, cut costs in the face of falling oil prices and increased competition is changing the dynamics of the oil industry demanding a focus on how to survive and maximize ROACE according to the new dictates of the global energy sector. The outcome was the emergence of today's distinctive three-tiered industry structure with different elements facing a variety of strategic pressures.

The three-tiered industry

The merger and acquisition activities since 1998 have redrawn the boundaries of the global oil industry by changing the twentieth century vertically integrated oligopoly structure. As of 2004, the merger activity has created a three-tier oil industry consisting of super-majors, middle-majors and independents[1].

Exxon Mobil, BP-Amoco and Shell have emerged as the top-tier super major companies. The second-tier companies include Elf, Total-Fina, Chevron-Texaco, Phillips and Conoco. The third-tier consists of the so-called 'independents'—smaller E&P companies. This tier can be divided into two groups—with the companies listed on the stock exchange at the top, and small ones at the bottom. Historically, in the USA independent E&P companies have often followed in the footsteps of the majors, picking up the properties the larger, vertically integrated companies have shunned or cast aside[2]. Now, the same pattern is emerging in other parts of the world.

Not all the independent producers are limiting their activities to picking up properties cast off by the majors. Some are focusing on developing new discoveries. For example, Houston's Newfield Exploration purchased three-

1. Petroleum Economist, *World Energy Yearbook* (2000)
2. Petroleum Economist, *North America: Independents* (London, January 2004)

dimensional seismic data on the UK North Sea's southern gas basin and is using that information to develop prospects and appraise undeveloped discoveries. It also acquired acreage in the 21st licensing round earlier this year and plans to capitalize on that prospect in 2004.

Independents have also moved into offshore West Africa when major oil companies shifted their operations. United Meridian, now part of Oklahoma's Devon Energy acquired some of the seismic data and made two small discoveries off the Ivory Coast. Spurred on by these successes, in 1992 it acquired the right to drill on three blocks off Equatorial Guinea adjacent to the Nigerian border and signed on Exxon Mobil as a majority partner and operator. Mobil's second well led to the discovery in 1995 of the Zafiro field which holds probable oil reserves estimated at as much as 1 billion barrels. Since the field's discovery, production has increased more than ten fold making it the country's largest producer.

Some E&P companies such as Cairn Energy and Premier Oil which have spearheaded exploration in the Indian sub continent, are becoming specialized recognizing that their value-added potential is at its greatest in the early stages. Shell has recognized the value possessed by Cairn and Premier in their local knowledge, their familiarity with local legislation and local players. The mutually beneficial approach for all involves Shell backing these companies through joint venture agreements and areas of mutual interest during the exploration and appraisal stages. As projects come on the stream, Shell increases its interest in the project. Within the third tier itself, companies may see the potential for joint ventures and even for closer tie-ups among themselves.

As they move into overseas energy basins that have been dominated by the majors, they are benefiting from their relatively low overhead and operating costs, their aggressive approach to doing business, their ability to respond quickly to promising opportunities and their adroitness at squeezing oil from properties that have been extensively explored. Through their relationship with service contractors, they also are able to take advantage of three-dimensional seismic and other state-of-the-art technologies that were once accessible only by the large energy companies.

High oil prices in 2004 have led to high valuations and the oil industry's top oil companies like Exxon Mobil, Chevron-Texaco, Conoco, Phillips Royal Dutch Shell, British Petroleum and Total Oil reported percentage net income increases in 2004 against 2003 of 18 per cent, 84 per cent, 72 per cent, 38 per cent, 35 per cent and 37 per cent, respectively[3]. Since the investment level of any individual company is influenced by each company's cash flow and its outlook for the industry, for independent explorers as well as for oil giants, the higher prices for crude oil, natural gas and petroleum

3. Petroleum Economist, March 2005:*Oil firms awash with cash,* London. p16–17.

products along with rising demand will give a substantial boost to industry cash flow to fund investments that are not feasible below $20 per barrel.

The significant improvement in the outlook for the petroleum industry could start a new positive period in the industry investment outlook. The openness of countries with large resources to FDI will be an important factor in determining how much and where up stream investments will be made. As of 2005, Kuwait, Mexico and Saudi Arabia remain closed to outside investment. Oil companies are having problems in Nigeria regarding corruption and conflict in the utilization of oil funds for development. Access to many others such as Russia and Iran are restricted.

OIDC will also have to compete to attract FDI in their upstream oil and gas sectors with countries endowed with a large potential resource base and outside investment in non-OPEC developing countries in Western Africa, Latin America and countries of FSU. In the oil and gas down stream sector attracting FDI depends on market size, pricing, fiscal and investment incentives and socio-political stability for creating a business environment.

The structure of the oil industry has changed from oligopoly and vertical integration into competition and again into reintegration, albeit in a different format in 2004. Furthermore, post 9/11 unfolding political realities of the Middle East and the cloud of the expanding war on terrorism exert pressures on the new course of the international petroleum industry. Developments in the international petroleum industry in the last 35 years confirm the volatility and cyclical nature of the oil market. The last 35 years of the world oil industry witnessed four major supply interruptions and four sharp price hikes. Crude oil and petroleum products that are increasingly viewed as 'commodities' included in their quoted prices for the first time in May 2004 a 'Terrorist Premium'.

Financial Times reported on 4th May 2004, a survey among industry members and observers by Seymore Pierce, a UK broker, found that more than 40 per cent thought that the sector was near or at the top of its cycle. However, the popular answer from those working in the industry was that there was no longer any cycle at all. Proponents of this school argue that the high oil prices are here to stay, breaking out of the ups and downs of the past 20 years. Sir Richard Giordano, Chairman of the British Gas (BG) group says that since 2001 a series of dramatic, inter-linked global and political developments have raised serious concerns for the first time in many years about petroleum industries' ability to continue meeting demand and ensuring the uninterrupted supply to their markets[4].

---

4. Richard Giordano, "Security of Supply-It's time to put energy policy at the heart of foreign policy" *International Petroleum Encyclopaedia 2003,* Tulsa, Oklahoma, Pennwell

Adequacy of oil resources in the twenty-first century

In 2004, the downgrading of 'proved' reserves of oil and gas by several oil companies raised the oil markets' concern of adequacy and sustainability of oil reserves. In January 2004, because of errors in classification of reserves in a number of fields discovered in the late 1990s[5] Royal Dutch Shell Company announced that it was revising its reporting of reserves, moving 3.9 billion barrels of oil equivalent from the proved to the probable category. Shell Oil Company's downgrading of its proved oil and gas reserves by 20 per cent to the probable category in January triggered a fall in its share prices, rocked investors' confidence in the management and prompted a debate on how oil companies should account for their reserves[6]. Following Shell's four subsequent downward revisions, Royal Dutch Shell reported in March 2005 that its controversial 2002 figure was overstated by 41 per cent. The amended report shows its proven oil and gas reserves equivalent to 13.72 billion barrels as opposed to 19.35 billion barrels.

Several other companies, including Canada's Nexen and Husky energy, El Paso of the USA and the US independents, Forest oil Vintage Petroleum and Western Gas Resources, have announced major reserve downgrades since the beginning of 2004. Petroleum Economist in its February 2004 issue article 'More reserve, Please' reported that major oil companies have been under enormous pressure from shareholders to perform, setting ambitious reserves replacement and production growth targets and pointing out that many companies have fallen foul of this pressure. The article stated that BP among others, had to downgrade production-growth forecasts repeatedly to the extent that it now prefers not to make such predictions as these can be easily disrupted by various factors.

Paul Roberts, the author of 'end of oil' argues that even optimists concede that non-OPEC, non- Middle East oil will peak between 2015 and 2020. After that point the Middle East's control, he says, will become irresistible. Roberts acknowledges that new suppliers have entered the market over the past 20 years, but he emphasizes the geological fact that the largest and cheapest deposits of oil on earth are located in the Middle East. With no documentary sources cited except two unnamed former government officials

---

5. The oil industry categorizes its reserves under 'proved', 'probable' and 'possible' reserves. Almost 90 per cent of the estimated 'proved' reserves can be profitably produced. The percentage of estimated probable reserves that could be profitably produced depends on the rate of success in further confirmation of these reserves from 'probable' to 'proved' category. The global oil companies are expected to conform to the industry standard definitions of reserves with regular up and down adjustments reflecting companies' improvement of technical knowledge.
6. Petroleum Economist, February 2004, '*More reserve, please*', London.

and two outside analysts, Roberts even argues that the undeclared aim of the Iraq war (2003) was not simply to capture Iraq's oil but to permanently break OPEC's power over global oil supply. Although Roberts' provocative thesis of 'the end of oil' may not mean the absolute exhaustion of the planet's petroleum deposits, it underscores subtler, scarcely less disruptive transformation, warning about an inevitable upheaval in the world's oil supplies.

Addressing the supply side issues the US Energy Information Agency (EIA) in its International Energy Outlook 2004, argued that the reserve revision by Shell turned out to be a reinterpretation of reporting conventions and had more to do with natural gas than oil.

The US EIA in its International Energy Outlook 2004 expects conventional oil to peak closer to the middle than to the beginning of the twenty-first century. The EIA bases its analysis on US Geological Survey's (USGS) April 2000 assessment of 3 trillion barrels of ultimately recoverable conventional oil resources worldwide.

The EIA's International Energy Outlook 2004 makes a distinction between conventional oil resources and non-conventional oil resources such as oil sands, ultra heavy oils, gas to liquids technologies, coal-to-liquid technologies, bio fuel technologies and shale oil and takes the view that pessimism about oil resources has been focused entirely on conventional resources. EIA further goes on to argue that while fossil fuels are subject to depletion, and that depletion leads to scarcity which in turn leads to higher prices, a combination of escalating prices and technological enhancements can transform the non-conventional resources to conventional oil. Non-conventional oil resources are expected to act as a buffer against prolonged periods of high oil prices well into the middle of the twenty-first century.

The unfolding geopolitical tensions, rising oil prices, supply disruptions and increasing dependence on oil signal that governments and the energy industry can no longer afford the complacency of the 1990s. Given that transparent and reliable reserves data are critical measures of the value of company assets and their future cash flows, uncertainty about reserves estimates may undermine investor confidence and slow investment. Governments are also concerned about the degree of accuracy of reserve estimates to ensure security of supplies. The future availability of hydrocarbons at reasonable cost has implications for decisions to be made on long-term energy policy. Energy is emerging as the determinant of economic growth and statecraft. The longer the failure to address emerging energy issues, the economic and political outcomes will turn out costlier.

Energy market reform and liberalization

Liberalization in the energy sector launched in the late 1980s shows great diversity. A variety of motives, policy driven, economic or practical (or a combination) has driven countries to launch energy liberalization. The energy sector —given its important role in a country's economic, political and social development—has traditionally been in the hands of the government. The extent of government involvement has varied between countries and energy industries and has been changing since the late 1980s. The trend towards market-based structures and competition has been growing while government's role is becoming more that of a regulator. In different countries and industries this trend has been driven by different motives but common to all of them appears to be the need to choose this market-oriented direction. In many cases (particularly in developing countries) it has been forced upon governments by different circumstances when financial constraints of energy sector development, further liberalization of trade and increasing globalization and competition have played a major role.

The overall objectives of Energy Liberalization include:

- Improving efficiency, and lowering costs
- Introducing competition and attracting private capital to improve efficiency and management
- Increasing access to energy supplies and improving reliability of supply by promoting private investment in energy
- Removing energy subsidies

Each country's experience is overlaid with the imperatives of its own peculiarities, local circumstances, economic and political philosophies, fuel sources, regional circumstances and inter-industry relationships. For example, in the USA and in most of the OECD Western Europe oil and gas industry the market has always played a dominant role in driving and shaping the industry, while a good number of the 'Top 20' oil companies, mostly in the FSU and among the OPEC, are under government control.

In the upstream oil and gas the common liberalization features include:

- Opening up of acreage to the private sector through new open international licensing rounds where the state company co-competes on equal terms with other private bidders and where the private bidders are not required to participate jointly with the state company
- Relaxing import and export restrictions on oil and gas
- Removing price control mechanisms and allowing unrestricted crude oil sales; enabling private sector participants to realize the value of their production at market prices. This has also included removal of fixed prices and subsidies
- Adopting a structural fiscal framework for upstream oil and gas

activities for rational division of economic rent-one that will be attractive to private investors and will encourage participation in the sector and its growth but will also provide government revenue from petroleum activity.

The highly complex and costly nature of natural gas projects necessitates a secure market outlet with long-term supply contracts to reduce risks and ensure an adequate return on large-scale investments. The issue of pricing and costs is a serious challenge to which the industry will always be exposed. Natural gas prices in international markets are still closely linked to the price of crude oil and products and are therefore vulnerable.

Given that new technologies, both gas turbine and combined cycle technology, are also making the economics of natural gas as fuel in power generation more attractive, oil companies such as Shell are pursuing the 'Fuel-to-power' strategy to move into the international power arena to grow its down stream operations. Market liberalization measures such as the unbundling of natural gas transportation from supply and establishment of open access will help create a new contractual framework for natural gas pricing, reflecting its own market conditions both in terms of the benefits and risks involved.

For the gas sector, market competition has continued to spread in the USA, European Union (EU) and IEA Pacific regions at different speeds and stages. With the progress in the opening of gas and electricity markets and the cost reductions in the liquefied natural gas (LNG) chain allowing more flexible LNG trade, gas-fired power generation has emerged as a new driver of gas demand worldwide. In the USA higher prices of natural gas have dampened consumer interest in alternative supply options and the number of marketers actively serving consumers dropped from 159 in the year 2002 to 92 in the year 2004. To improve the supply situation, the US government is moving quickly to encourage the construction of LNG terminals by adopting supporting regulation and streamlining the authorization process. In Europe 2004 has been a challenging year with the enlargement of the EU to 25 member states and opening of the gas market to all non-household customers. A directive on security of gas supply was adopted in April 2004, and a common position has been agreed upon by the Council on the legislation on regulation of access to gas networks. In IEA Pacific the Australian Productivity Commission of the natural gas access regime is proposing improvements to reduce regulatory costs. In Japan the Gas Utility Law was amended in June 2003 to expand the mandatory third-party access (TPA) to all gas supply pipelines and consider measures to allow a higher rate of return for TPA for a certain period of time.

Downstream oil liberalization includes:

- Enabling private sector participation in the refining and marketing businesses through joint venture or other contractual arrangements
- Introducing competition into oil distribution through the removal of the state monopoly on the distribution of refined products and the break-up of regional control
- Relaxing import–export restrictions on refined products by removing export quotas and permitting companies other than those with approved status or those with refining assets to import and export refined products
- Removing economic and fiscal subsidies to enable the private sector to participate on a more competitive basis.

The coal industry shows a strong contrast between a fully liberalized case like the USA and the state-owned and state-run, heavily expanding coal industry of China. Many other coal producing countries are in the process of restructuring their coal industries.

The common features of liberalization of coal industry are:

- removal of price controls;
- removal of price subsidies and cross-subsidies;
- elimination of guaranteed markets;
- formulation of programs supported by public funds for restructuring of former mining regions and re-employment of former miners hit by the closure of mines.

Electricity, because of its crucial importance for every country's economic and social development, was controlled and run by the state in almost all countries. In the 1990s the pendulum began to swing in the opposite direction when over 85 countries in the world began to consider reducing government involvement in running the power companies. The constraints of public ownership of electric power companies in terms of operational efficiency and financial viability are forcing changes on the electric power industry all over the world. Utility companies are undergoing the most significant transformation around the world.

Electricity liberalization includes:

- Unbundling of the former vertically integrated utility industry into generation, transmission and distribution;
- Regulating the natural monopoly elements such as transmission;
- Creating competition, either 'for the market' through competitive tendering, new entry and open access or 'within the market' through the establishment of a power pool (as in the UK, Norway, Sweden, Poland and New Zealand) or some other clearing market

in generation and in supply together with putting in place arrangements to coordinate operations and ensure transparency in the market;
- Phasing out of subsidies and cross-subsidies including removing the obligation to continue to supply customers who do not pay bills (in Eastern Europe and the Commonwealth of Independent States, Georgia and the Baltic Sates (CIS)).

There were a number of practical and policy motives and objectives for liberalization:

- an ideological belief that ownership and management of the electricity industry were best in the private sector;
- a belief that the introduction of competition would be the best stimulus for efficiency and the best promoter of customers' interest;
- the wish to maximize public revenues arising from the sale of state assets;
- an acknowledgement of the need to establish effective regulation of an industry with natural monopoly components;
- the need to ensure continuing security of supply and effective industry coordination.

Liberalization includes privatization. While privatization may not be an absolute requisite for liberalization, it was believed that it could greatly help to achieve efficiency by productivity improvements, competition and changes in service standards. Restructuring, even if this is restricted to functional unbundling, is often a prerequisite for privatization.

Electricity market reform in OECD countries

In the USA in the early 1990s, the privately owned electricity industry was subject to extensive government regulation. Prices remained high covering the cost of capital projects entered into during a time of high interest and inflation rates. Pressure for change came both from policy and business perspectives. Introducing competition and reducing the role of the government were seen as routes to greater efficiency. Increasing international competition and open access appealed to business.

In the USA reform has come on two levels. At the federal level moves towards competition in generation and the introduction of non-discriminatory transmission access have been effected through Federal Energy Regulatory Commission (FERC) orders 888 and 889. Order 888 mandated open access to the electricity transmission grid, set out new requirements on transmission access for electricity wholesalers and required utilities to apply the same rates and terms for them that it applies to itself. It also defined and allowed for the recovery of certain stranded costs. Order 889 requires utilities to electronic systems to share information about available transmission capacity.

The process of liberalization in Western Europe started in the UK in 1990 through launching of the England and Wales Electricity industry liberalization and privatization process. This process began on the principles of Thatcherite free market economics and privatizations. The electricity industry before liberalization was a mature one, split between 12 Area Boards with local supply and distribution monopolies and a central generation and transmission company. Particular features of the industry at the time included a surplus of generation capacity, plentiful supplies of relatively cheap natural gas from the North Sea fields and the use of expensive coal from a domestic coal industry in decline.

The liberalization process was also aided by national experience of other liberalization and privatization programs (inter alia the telecommunications, gas and transport sectors). The electricity sector was unbundled with the creation of independent generation, transmission, distribution and supply companies. A power pool was established, competition was introduced in the electricity generation market and over a staggered timetable, which has yet to be completed, supply markets and price regulation were established in the natural monopoly areas of transmission and distribution.

An office of Electricity Regulation, independent of government, was established to ensure that reasonable demands for electricity are satisfied, to license suppliers of electricity, ensure that they are financially viable and promote competition wherever possible.

The liberalization process in the 1990s spread to Scandinavia, Germany, Poland, the Czech Republic and France. As of January 2002, the UK, Norway, Sweden, Germany and Austria have opened their markets for distribution of electricity completely, while others including Greece, Italy, Spain and the Netherlands are less than 50 per cent liberalized. Nonetheless, the EU is sufficiently confident of progress being made that it has cut its deadline for completion of this leg of the project to 2005 from 2008. Outside the EU several central European states, notably Poland, Hungary and the Czech Republic are also moving gradually towards more liberalized and unbundled regimes.

Over the past few years, despite some benefits of improvement in efficiency, increased competition and in certain cases lower prices to consumers, electricity markets in the USA and Europe have faced serious difficulties. In the USA, following the rolling California power black-outs in 2001 the reform suffered a severe setback. The crisis was at its peak between mid January and late February 2001, but flared up at other times in the year. At the start of 2001, California's grid transmitted about 46.25 Giga Watt Hours

(GWH) over the peak demand period while 46.50 GWH was supplied by generation in the state or imports from nearby, giving it a 250 Mega Watt Hours (MWH) margin. A hot summer followed by a cold dry winter exposed fundamental flaws in the state's electricity sector which were compounded by the greed of Enron-like energy trading companies that resorted to energy price gouging.

California opened up its power market in 1996. In the decade leading up to 2000, California's population grew by 12.5 per cent, from 29.8 million to 34.0 million with the internet boom in the Silicon Valley. But in those ten years, not one power station was built in California. Environmental obstacles and the 'not in my backyard' syndrome have been blamed by many for this failure to develop capacity. Although the Californian Public Utilities Commission ordered the utilities to construct power stations before deregulation, they did not comply. In addition, after deregulation, insistence on a retail price cap proved a disincentive to new entrants in the market. The rate cap was imposed because its old utility industry produced power that was 50 per cent more expensive than the US average. So California was already a special case. Massive gas price rises (gas is the main generating fuel) kicked in at the wrong time.

The ill-conceived liberalization legislation accentuated capacity shortages and resulted in a 5 per cent drop in generating capacity between 1988 and 1998. Rolling power black-outs starting in December 2000, forced California to import electricity on a massive scale, beginning a political, corporate and regulatory nightmare. Hopes that imports could be funded by bond sales fell through when the bonds were shunned by investors, leaving the taxpayers to pick up the tab. The San Francisco based generator, Pacific Gas and Electric, went bankrupt. Other utilities struggled. While energy trading firms including 'Enron' were called 'pirates' by California's Governor, Gray Davis, in February, after warnings that California's energy bill for 2002 might rise by as much as ten times to $70 billion. The California power crisis also resulted in the recall of its Governor, Gray Davis. After California there is more reluctance in the USA to move ahead with deregulation. California mimicked the UK system of having a spot-market pool, which failed to work because of a lack of infrastructure and supply.

The antidote to the Californian nightmare—as far as the USA goes—can be found in Texas. Texas opened its market in 2002. In deregulating, Texas had many advantages over California. The wholesale market was liberalized in 1995. Texas had time to phase in electricity reform while also getting familiar with hedging techniques through the gas experience. By August 2003, 'Deregulation' has occurred in some form or other in 22 states, reports the Edison Electric Institute, the industry's trade group.

The largest supply disruption in North American history struck at about 4 p.m. on 14 August 2003, affecting eight US states and the Canadian province of Ontario. About 61,800 MW of electricity load was lost and 50 million people were disconnected. While most services in the USA were restored within two days, in some areas it took up to four days. Much of Ontario operated under power restrictions for over a week.

The US–Canada Power System Outage Task Force determined that the North American failure was due to lack of adherence to industry standards, deficiencies in corporate policies and inadequate management of reactive power and voltage (US–Canada Power System Outage Task Force, 2004). First Energy, a utility in Ohio, was singled out as having violated basic reliability procedures. The Task Force also described some standards and processes of the North American Electric Reliability Council as inadequate because they did not give sufficiently clear directions to the industry on preventive measures needed to maintain reliability.

Two severe disruptions involving failures of transmission services also struck Europe. The Nordic transmission system experienced its worst disruption in 20 years at 12.35 p.m. on 23 September 2003. Southern Sweden lost about 4,700 MW of supply, while Denmark lost about 1,850 MW. 4 million people were disconnected, including many in Copenhagen. Transmission services in southern Sweden were restored within an hour, with complete services restored within a few hours. The second supply disruption in Europe in 2003 struck Italy at 3.28 a.m on 28 September 2003 following a loss of about 6,400 MW imported into Italy from its northern bordering countries. The incident cascaded into a total loss of around 25,000 MW. Nearly 56 million people were disconnected, with services restored within 24 hours.

A report on the Scandinavian black-out by Elkraft system, the network operator in eastern Denmark, indicated that the disruption was caused by the simultaneous occurrence of mechanical faults at three different points in the southern Sweden power system. The report concluded that given the present design of the power system, a power failure could not have been prevented in the very unusual circumstances.

Three separate reports on the Italian black-out indicated the causes of outage from unresolved conflicts between the involved countries and companies on the one hand to technical requirements of the existing transnational electricity system on the other, bad communication by the operators and technical problems of the network system.

European electricity prices are rising, critical investment decisions have to be made and the European power sector is finding it hard to become more competitive.

For the market to function efficiently and to the greatest benefit of consumers, the ability to move electricity between countries for supply to meet demand at the lowest possible cost, is of key importance. Otherwise any one country will always be captive to its internal generation capabilities. That is largely the case, with only 7 per cent of electricity consumed in Europe in 2000 coming from cross-border trade.

Geography makes this a problem for Europe. The continent (including EU states) is split into separate groups as far as electricity is concerned. They are Central Europe (the Netherlands, Germany, Austria, France, Switzerland and the Czech Republic) and the five electricity 'islands'—Italy, Iberia, the Nordpool countries, the UK and the East European countries. These islands all have barriers to transmission links with a wider Europe. In the case of the UK the barriers are the English Channel and the North Sea, in Italy it is the Alps and France's grid—the most accessible—is particularly weak in the corner closest to Italy. There is a risk that real competition will be tainted if problems occur in Italy, but the Italian regulators were trying to speed up the process of approving power station construction. The time horizon involved is not necessarily incompatible with achieving the required generating capacity. Again, when it comes to developing both new capacity and transmission links the physical wires that transport electricity to distributors are expensive and unattractive. Politically, it has been easier for state-owned utilities not to invest in them any more than they absolutely have to and until recently there was no incentive to build them across borders.

Following the setback for electricity market reforms in the years 2000–2 the electricity market reform process in OECD countries seems to be picking up. The European Commission proposed a Directive in December 2003 to safeguard security of electricity supply and infrastructure investment. In North America the US FERC issued a new set of rules to standardize the interconnection of new generation facilities to transmission grids in July 2003. The Ontario government proposed an Electricity Restructuring Act in June 2004. In IEA Pacific, in December 2003 the Ministerial Council of Energy (MCE) in Australia agreed on a new electricity market reform package to improve regulatory efficiency by concentrating many regulatory responsibilities in one body instead of having different regulators in the states and territories. In Japan the Electricity Utility Law was amended in June 2003, stipulating a retail market opening of 40 per cent in 2004 rising to 63 per cent in 2005. In Korea, the planned separation of distribution assets of the Korean Electricity Power Corporation (KEPCO) was brought to a halt in June 2004[7].

Effects of liberalization

Globally, the distinct results of liberalization are often difficult to distinguish from the factors affecting the industry at the same time (technological development, effective use of cheaper fuel sources and the effects of

7. IEA:"*Energy Policies of IEA countries, 2004 Review*", Paris

exogenous economic factors.) Evidence from developed electricity markets in the USA, UK and Western Europe indicate that the effects of liberalization on achieving the objectives of creating competition and free market price for electricity are mixed.

A number of factors complicate any impact on liberalization of prices. End-user prices are affected by developments throughout the value chain and may be affected from both regulated and competitive markets. Regulatory frameworks designed to protect past investment and/ or imposing retail price cap would affect new entrants as in the case of California. The effects of flawed regulatory mechanisms created capacity shortage and reduced available supplies.

Competition and regulation led to decreases in prices in the 1990s in the end-user markets in Europe. In England and Wales domestic tariffs, affected by competitive generation costs and regulated in all other aspects, have fallen on average. Prices to intensive users have shown greater decreases, upto nearly 30 per cent in real terms since liberalization. In Norway, incentive regulation of transmission and distribution costs led to charges decreasing by 5–10 per cent.

Prices in many European electricity markets are being determined either through organized markets or through bilateral contracts. In markets such as those of England and Wales all generation is cleared through an organized market. The price in the spot market has a strong influence on the bilateral contracts. The spot price is also decisive for production planning.

With liberalization such a dominant force worldwide, national utilities are close to becoming global operators. In addition, utilities have started the process of consolidation by converging with other energy based companies. The industry has launched a 'Fuel-to-Power' strategy by going through considerable merger and acquisition activity as well as significant asset acquisition and divestiture activity. As a result, while electricity companies are buying natural gas, distribution and pipeline companies, natural gas producers have entered the electricity generation market by establishing independent power producer (IPP) subsidiaries and/ or by acquiring an electricity utility.

Deregulation essentially requires the old monopolists to sell some or all their power plants and transmission and distribution networks to other operators. Competition among power producers, the theory goes, will promote efficiency and reduce rates. Transmission and distribution networks will be open to all. But the theory has two big flaws. First, no one is responsible for reliability. There are multiple power producers and distributors. No one can ensure that the necessary plants and distribution systems gets built. Companies may sacrifice long-term reliability to maximize short-term profitability. As power is increasingly bought and sold across state lines—outside the service areas of oil monopolies—daily operational problems also multiply. In this regard the transition to competitive markets has raised valid concerns about continuation of voluntary compliance with reliability standards. Second, the idea of electricity 'deregulation' is misleading because—despite all the changes—electricity production remains highly regulated. Virtually every major decision (where plants and transmission lines are built, what fuels–nuclear, coal or natural gas are used, what companies can do) depends on government decisions.

The 14 August 2003 black-out in the north-east and mid-western states of the USA, considered the worst in the nation's history, demonstrated these flaws of deregulation. The August 2003 power outage shut down more than 100 power plants—including 22 nuclear reactors in the USA and Canada—in a lightning cascade that took nine seconds and plunged millions into darkness over a 9,300 square mile area from New England to Michigan. Analysts of the event were unanimous in their opinion that the event was perfectly predictable. The transition to a competitive electricity market and an increase in regional power transfers placed greater demands on a near stagnant transmission infrastructure.

Investing more in transmission, though widely seen as needed, has not occurred for a number of reasons. First, the governmental and legal obstacles to setting and constructing new high voltage transmission lines are often insurmountable and can delay major projects for years. No single government authority at either the state or Federal level can identify the need for multi-state transmission facilities and cause them to be built. A second problem is that historically regulators have given investors inadequate financial incentives to justify the risky investment of time and money needed to clear the bureaucratic hurdles for building new transmission lines. Although the FERC has begun to rectify this problem, finding the right level of investment incentives will continue to be a critical issue. Other steps including replacing the voluntary compliance with new mandatory enforceable reliability standards are being considered.

Deregulation puts market participants in a more uncertain environment than in the past. Companies face uncertainty and risk in several areas of business. Price volatility may be considerable following deregulation. Risk management becomes a key element of a company's activity, bringing with it a comprehensive need for new kinds of competence and decision-support systems.

Liberalization also has caused the industry to restructure within companies, both as a part of fundamental restructuring of the industry (where the different elements of a vertically integrated company are functionally unbundled into separate business centres) and as a response to external competitive pressures. Such restructuring is often expensive in the short term and may require significant upheaval within energy organizations. Ensuring that delivery of products and services to customers is not disrupted at this time is vital for the acceptance of the liberalization process. Successful corporate change, managing the transition to new operating arrangements and systems, establishing new reporting systems and legal and fiscal structures, make considerable demands on management.

Energy liberalization has had significant social consequences. Considerable reductions in utility manning levels have been in evidence in liberated markets. These reductions have been achieved in many cases through voluntary severance and redundancy schemes. While this approach avoids the confrontation associated with forced redundancies, the cost of attracting employees to voluntary schemes can be substantial.

Price liberalization has affected mostly the vulnerable groups. The need for regulators and/ or government to intervene to afford protection to vulnerable groups has been apparent, especially where implicit subsidies are being reduced.

Implications for developing countries

The waves of economic globalization and liberalization of international trade, investment and the global energy industry in the 1990s have impacted the political, economic and energy environment in developing countries. Some of the key features that have influenced energy sector in developing countries include the following:

- *Economic restructuring*: Most of the developing world has recognized the need for changing the role of the state from being the owner to the facilitator of business. Since the early 1990s governments are moving towards limiting their intervention in the energy sector and encouraging the private sector to invest in petroleum and power generation activities.
- *Changing petroleum industry*: In the 1970s and 1980s OIDC were concerned about security of oil supplies and the issues of structural and sector adjustment to high oil prices. In the wake of globalization and the emergence of the future market for oil since the 1990s, OIDC recognize that crude oil and petroleum products are increasingly viewed as 'commodities' that should be supplied through the most cost effective channels. Inclusion of a 'terrorist premium' in the price of oil in May 2004, continued concerns about the volatility of oil prices and supply disruptions impact increasing dependence on oil imports and OIDC's ongoing efforts of sector reform and liberalization.
- *Natural gas has become the fuel of choice*: Partly due to environmental concerns and partly due to economic and efficiency considerations, natural gas has become a popular fuel in developing countries. A large portion of gas is used for power generation where efficiency of

gas based combined cycle plants has increased considerably.

- *Power sector in transition*: Many countries in Latin America and Asia have tried moving away from the traditional state owned integrated utility model. The industry structure is being reshaped to allow competition where possible, alongside a trend towards testing the competitive forces in areas that have been traditionally considered to be natural monopolies (electricity transmission). In many developing countries this is giving rise to the IPP, an investor-owned enterprise dedicated substantially to generation. Financial constraints forced many reluctant governments and utilities in the 1990s toward the IPP model for expanding their generating capacity.
- *Renewable energy development*: The 1990s also witnessed countries in Asia and Africa focusing on development of renewable energy partly due to environmental concerns and mainly due to the need to provide access to energy supplies for nearly 2 billion people. China, for example, planned to meet at least 10 per cent of its energy requirement using renewable energy supplies by 2020.
- *Private investment flows in the 1990s*: Overall, the volume of private capital flows to developing countries has quadrupled in the 1990s. Given the expanding potential of energy markets, international investors looked to developing countries in the 1990s. However, over 75 per cent of private capital flows to the developing world are concentrated only in the top ten countries and mostly in non-energy sectors.
- *Official development assistance (ODA)*: ODA fell from $54.5 billion in 1990 to $48.5 billion in 1997, its lowest point in real terms. Net ODA to developing countries from members of the Development Assistance Committee (DAC) of the OECD increased to $58 billion in 2002, up from $53.7 billion in 2000. However, the rise in aid provided by donors does not translate directly into an increase in aid received by developing countries. Half of the $6 billion boost in ODA was generated by an increase in debt relief, which more than doubled in 2002. Administrative costs involved in managing donor agencies, also classified as ODA, remained at about $3 billion. Aid received net of debt relief increased only by $3 billion of which $1 billion went to Afghanistan and Pakistan. Thus, the rise in ODA excluding these two countries was only $2 billion[8].

The above features have important policy implications for developing countries as many changes that have occurred in the global economy are irreversible. On the macro front, advances in communications and transportation

8. WB, *Global Development Finance* (Washington DC, 2004), p.109.

mean that large segments of national economies are much more exposed to international trade and capital flows than they have ever been, regardless of what policy makers choose to do.

The changes underway around the world carry great opportunities for those countries with a political will to effectively formulate and implement the required policies to facilitate investment in energy. For developing countries with weak institutions following the models of liberalization of mature economies, the risks of failure of both formulating the right policies and their effective implementation are far greater. The experience of the USA and Europe's energy liberalization raises a number of issues relevant for developing countries trying to follow in their footsteps.

Issues of energy liberalization

The liberalization process is not smooth and inappropriate decisions complicate the process. There is no certainty that liberalization will be effected successfully in any particular country.

Significant challenges exist in the liberalization process in all countries. The California power crisis of 2001, the regulatory issues of the UK power market and major black-outs in the USA, Canada and Europe illustrate that even mature market economies with a tradition of liberalization and privatization face both short-term and long-term challenges.

Short-term issues

In the short term there are physical constraints to the integration of markets, in particular with electricity grids and gas transportation pipelines. These constraints can limit the geographical extent of the liberalized market. The very length, scope and complexity of the process of achieving wide ranging legislative, regulatory and operational change over a period of years, of balancing the demands of different groups and the risks and responsibilities they should bear (employees, customers, government, shareholders, local economies and the environment) and of devising and managing difficult transitional issues, poses a considerable challenge.

The interrelationship of the different segments of the energy sector, the existence of a long and complex chain with reliance and competition between segments, dictates that liberalization of the energy sector as a whole is required for the process to succeed. Difficulties arise where different parts of a physically integrated system or common economic unit are in different phases of liberalization.

Long-term issues

Concern exists as to how able liberalized markets will be to take a sufficiently long-term view for risks and rewards to be interpreted appropriately. Capital markets have come to be viewed as being interested in short- and medium-term performance and returns: the scramble to acquire electricity assets around the world up to 1997 shows appetite for investments with positive returns only in the medium term. It may be that only the 'easiest' slices of the energy sector—the upstream segments of oil and gas—have been exposed to markets. The liberalization process will not take on the most problematic areas first. In particular, the development of sustainable energy production—such as hydropower and nuclear energy in particular—has yet to be widely exposed to liberalization. It remains to be seen, therefore, whether a liberalized market will be able to support necessarily long-term investment.

Another area where the prospective long-term credentials of a liberalized market are questioned is that of environmental protection. It seems clear that the need to reduce total emissions of greenhouse gases as the energy market grows will only need to be addressed through government action on an international basis.

One final area exists where long-term consensus surrounds governance issues. Who should control companies and more importantly, the regulatory function and to whom should the regulator be accountable? The enduring authority of regulators cannot be ensured. The extent to which they should be accountable to government or to parliament (or to some other legislative body) and to which they are subject under the normal legal process cannot be predicted.

Liberalization entails inevitable local or inherent complications. Establishing workable and pragmatic compromises to provide the best realistic result will be a common characteristic. The process is a lengthy one, during which transitional arrangements will often be required to over come short-and medium-term challenges.

Liberalization places great challenges on those employed in the sector. This is particularly the case where the liberalization process involves a paradigm shift from a command-control public sector to a private-sector market mind-set. Support for the development and training of management and staff where changes are to be radical will be important.

External factors can often mean that the move to liberalization is an inevitable fact rather than a choice to be made. Pressure from international funding organizations or the severity of operational and financial crises may mean that liberalization is the only option for the government.

Technological developments can often play an important role in assisting or even enabling the liberalization process. The development of new technology can make private participation easier. In the electricity industry, for example, the development of relatively cheap and quick-to-build combined cycle gas turbines has presented opportunities for liberalization and has had a considerable effect on the possibilities of introducing competition in the generation market in a number of areas. Advances in information technology can make competition more easily possible through the increased sophistication of metering, billing and market-clearing operations.

A fundamental issue of liberalization to be addressed both in the short and long term will be how to strike an appropriate balance in the sharing of benefits of liberalization between different stakeholders. For developing countries it requires ensuring that the terms of privatization are such that public finances, customers, employees and shareholders all share in the benefits of the transfer of ownership. Future efficiencies will often be an issue. In developing countries, there will also be the issue of ensuring that the benefits of securing foreign investment reach parts of the population currently with few energy resources as well as providing developing industries and commerce with the conditions for economic growth.

Establishing the right sequence for elements of the restructuring process, particularly when this is accompanied by privatization, can be vital to the success of liberalization. The political will to carry out fundamental restructuring programs, which may need to overcome vested interests, is mostly exercised in the initial stages, when an industry remains in public ownership. At later stages, once the fundamental restructuring has been established, it may be politically attractive for further aspects of liberalization to be enacted through a separate regulator.

The international integration of markets for goods, services and capital and the changing global energy industry and liberalization in the 1990s are pressuring developing countries to alter their traditional practices. The rising trade and globalization of economies require world-class infrastructure services, particularly in energy and transport and has put unprecedented pressure to attract the flow of investment in energy for development.

For OIDC, financing increased energy supplies for development in the tense geopolitical environment of the early years of the twenty-first century transcends the limits of the transition to a liberalized energy market. Since 2001, the energy market, geopolitical developments and rising energy consumption have pushed supply security to the top of energy policy. This raises a new policy challenge of how to reform the legal, regulatory and policy framework to finance the required investment to secure energy supplies in the short and long term for development. The situation calls for a thorough review of financing energy for development in developing countries in the pre- and post-1990s, developing countries' experience with energy liberalization and the challenges they face in the twenty-first century to increase access to economic, efficient and affordable energy for development.

CHAPTER 3

ENERGY FINANCING IN DEVELOPING COUNTRIES IN THE PRE-AND POST-1990S: TOWARD ENERGY SECTOR REFORM AND LIBERALIZATION

Oil price increases of the 1970s, the debt problems of the 1980s, the globalization wave of the 1990s and the associated changing global energy industry have had profound effects on reforming and financing investment in the energy sector in developing countries.

This chapter examines the changing patterns of financing energy in developing countries in the pre and post 1990s. The chapter discusses the steps developing countries were required to take to reform and liberalize their energy sectors to integrate with 1990s globalization and attract finance for energy for development.

Energy financing in the pre-1990s period

In the pre-1990s period governments traditionally intervened heavily in the energy sector often through ownership of energy companies. During the 1960s and the early 1970s, external capital financed only a small share of total energy investment in developing oil importing countries. As a result the government budget and government sponsored borrowing were often the main sources of financing for energy investment, especially for coal, natural gas and electricity projects. With rising oil prices in the 1970s, two major shifts in international capital impacting financing energy have occurred. First is the shift from equity to debt and the second is from official to private finance.

Rising debt burden

The growth of borrowing since 1973 produced a corresponding rise in external debt. Between 1970 and 1984 the outstanding medium and long-term debt of developing countries as recorded in the WB Debtor Reporting System (DRS) increased from US $68 billion to US $686 billion, an average increase of 16.7 per cent a year. Debt service payments increased from US $9.3 billion in 1970 to US $100 billion in 1984. The average maturity of their total public debt shortened from 20.4 years in 1970 to 14.2 years in 1982 because loans from private sources (the fastest growing component) carried shorter maturities—an average of 8.2 years in 1973.

An Increasing debt burden and deteriorating terms of trade despite a break in oil prices in 1986 affected the creditworthiness of developing countries. Private lenders remained extremely cautious in their lending to developing countries. Some countries enjoyed continued access to bank loans at low spreads and a few East Asian countries—China, Korea and Malaysia—were able to tap bond markets. Most developing countries however, were unable to obtain new net lending from private sources, except under rescheduling agreements. Long-term net private loans to low and middle income developing countries fell from US $44.5 billion in 1982 to US $7.1 billion in 1990. Long-term financial flows to low and middle income economies fell from US $91 billion in 1982 to 81.5 billion in 1990[1].

Although dollar amounts borrowed for energy have increased dramatically over the 1975–84 period, energy's share in outstanding debt remained relatively constant. Table 3.1 summarizes energy-related debt outstanding compared to total debt outstanding by country income group between 1975 and 1984.

Table 3.1. Total Debt Outstanding and Disbursed for Developing Countries (in US$ billion)

	1975		1984	
	Total debt	*Energy as % of total*	*Total debt*	*Energy as % of total*
Low income oil Importers	41.0	10	80.0	12
Middle income oil importers	84.0	18	375.0	22
Middle income oil Exporters	66.0	20	232.0	19
Total	191.0	17	687.0	19

Source: World Development Report, 1985.

The important change in both the energy related and total debt pattern of

1. WB, *Annual Report 1992*, Washington D.C.

developing countries between 1970 and 1984 is the dramatic increase in private commercial flows.

Table 3.2 summarizes energy financing patterns by country income group between 1975 and 1984. The low income oil importers are much more dependent than the others on multilateral and bilateral concession flows for external financing of energy because they cannot attract much financing on commercial terms. For low income oil importers, multilateral and bilateral concession flows accounted for 79 per cent of the total public debt on energy. For middle income oil importers, export-related and private financial flows accounted for most (78 per cent) of their debt for energy. For middle income oil exporters the non-concession and private commercial share increased further to 83 per cent of the total.

The relationship between country income level and source of financing remains relatively constant within energy sub-sectors. For example, 95 per cent of the oil and gas loans and 72 per cent of the power loans to middle income oil exporters came from export-related and private commercial sources. These two sources also provided 94 per cent of the oil and gas loans and 75 per cent of the power loans to middle income oil importers. For low income oil importers, bilateral and multilateral lenders provided 66 per cent of oil and gas loans and 94 per cent of power loans. In all three income groups of the coal sector export-related finance has been the major source of external lending.

Table 3.2. External Public Debt for Energy: Source by Country Income Group 1975-84 (% of total)

Country group	*Export-related financial sources*	*Financial institutions*	*Bilateral/ multilateral sources*
Coal			
Low-income oil importers	70	0	30
Middle-income oil importers	44	43	13
Middle-income oil exporters	73	–	27
Oil and gas			
Low-income oil importers	11	23	66
Middle-income oil importers	45	49	6
Middle-income oil exporters	42	53	–
Power			
Low-income oil importers	15	1	84
Middle-income oil importers	35	40	25
Middle-income oil exporters	39	33	28

Source: *WB, World Development Report* (1985)

Official export credit programs evolved as national programs to support commercial export transactions. Export credit finance can be based either on suppliers' credit (extended directly to foreign buyers by the exporters), or buyers credits, where banks finance foreign buyer purchases of export products and services. Official support for these transactions varies by country and can include financial facilities (refinancing, interest rate subsidies, specialized funds) as well as insurance programs covering commercial and political risk. For the 1975–84 period official export finance for energy in developing countries accounted for about 35 per cent of total public capital flows for energy development. Overall, the power sector has received the bulk of official export credit financing, representing about 70 per cent of the global total. Oil and gas projects have attracted smaller percentages of total flows at 28 per cent, with 16 per cent for exploration and development phase and 12 per cent for refineries, LNG units, LNG tankers and pipelines.

In terms of sector distribution, power accounted for the largest share of the total external public debt. This is because power loans are publicly guaranteed debt to finance power expansion programs in developing countries.

In the 1970s and 1980s ownership of power supply facilities in developing countries was mostly consolidated into national or state utilities. These state-owned utilities which were directly or indirectly run by their corresponding governments became responsible for power generation, transmission and distribution. Governments were responsible for raising funds from the government development budget and official borrowing for public utilities. Power supply was considered a socio-economic and strategic matter with natural monopoly characteristics. National power companies in the developing countries did not have access to other sources of external private capital. Borrowing levels in the pre-1990 period therefore reflect country creditworthiness considerations, rather than project or sponsor attractiveness. Generally the public utility would borrow funds, with government backing usually in the form of government counter guarantee.

External financing for power

Table 3.3 below shows the pattern of external financing sources for power between 1980 and 1992 in developing countries. The values in Table 3.3 shows that in real terms the funding to the power sector fell from US $9.8 billion in 1980 to US $7.6 billion in 1992. However, only the multilateral assistance grew in real terms. In the early 1980s export credit financing represented more than 20 per cent of total funding. As official export credit programs have not generally encountered constraints of resources, export credit represents an important potential source of financing for developing countries. However, official export credit agencies take into account both country and project related risk in their evaluation process. Also long maturities can be difficult. This and the inability to meet local cost requirements could limit the usefulness of official export credits for projects which have high local costs, or in countries not creditworthy for further commercial borrowing or with other debt management problems.

By mid 1980s while the use of export credits still continued it was no longer a source of power sector financing in Africa and Latin America. The largest decline was registered in the 'other' category which includes development funds and other sources of non-guaranteed finance that are outside multilateral and bilateral agencies.

Table 3.3. External Financing Sources for Power in Developing Countries: 1980–92 (US$ million)

Region	*1980*	*1985*	*1990*	*1991*	*1992*
East Asia: Total	2,309	2,235	2,058	2,304	3,110
Bilateral	356	250	263	454	373
Export credits	844	766	679	557	633
Multilateral	304	488	751	837	702
Non-concession-bilateral	396	266	76	210	740
Other credits	409	465	289	247	662
Africa:Total	767	947	679	514	387
Bilateral	147	174	162	205	122
Export credits	235	505	71	9	11
Multilateral	143	200	419	277	216
Non-concession-bilateral	64	46	19	14	38
Other credits	179	23	7	9	0
Latin America	5,467	2,240	2,118	2,206	1,861
Bilateral	51	40	130	122	192
Export credits	905	342	302	295	24
Multilateral	578	972	958	994	1,065
Non-concession-bilateral	531	304	314	170	100
Other credits	3,402	581	414	625	480
North Africa and Middle-East:Total	826	889	1,113	1,262	1,356
Bilateral	247	213	301	172	305
Export credits	472	425	389	723	723
Multilateral	99	204	220	265	304
Non-concession-bilateral	6	45	75	91	25
Other credits	3	2	129	11	0
South Asia:Total	499	1,019	2,079	2,144	1,671
Bilateral	178	324	655	829	544
Export credits	21	13	83	227	204
Multilateral	288	511	1,125	810	722
Non-Concession-bilateral	12	22	93	125	118
Other credits	0	149	124	154	85
Total All Developing countries	9,868	7,330	8,047	8,430	8,385

Source: Donald I, Hertzmark, Financing Power Sector Expansion in Developing countries, 1980-1993, A Report to the World Bank, July 1994.

Region wise East and South Asia show significant relative growth. In East Asia while export credits fell from a peak of US $844 million in 1980 to US $679 million in 1990, multilateral flows more than doubled from US $304 million in 1980 to US $751 million in 1990. The South Asia region recorded both an absolute and relative increase in external funding from US $499 million in 1980 to 2,079 million in 1990. Both bilateral and multilateral aid increased for the South Asia region. For Africa while there was an increase in bilateral and multilateral funding for power between 1980 and 1992, the total external financing for power fell more than two-third in absolute terms from US $767 million in 1980 to US $387 million in 1992.

Petroleum financing

In contrast to the mainly state ownership of power projects, oil and gas projects in developing countries are owned and managed by both public and private foreign companies, including national subsidiaries of international parent companies and joint ventures with state/ public-owned energy companies. In addition, a further share of total financing for oil and gas projects has been channelled through foreign companies either as direct investment and/ or intra company borrowings and transfers.

After the rapid oil price increase in 1973 many developing countries began to pay special attention to developing domestic energy resources. Energy price increases improved the overall economics of many oil and gas projects, making them more attractive to both public and private sector sponsors. In the 1970s and the early 1980s, international oil companies (IOC) continued their active role in financing oil investments while governments in both oil exporting and oil importing countries began taking prominent roles in the petroleum sector.

In oil exporting countries government involvement was motivated by the incentive to preserve their national resources and ensure the security of their share of oil reserves. In oil importing countries interest stemmed from the concern that security of supply was essential for national economic stability. Government intervention enforced mainly through strengthened national oil companies (NOCs) was accompanied by flows of state funds into petroleum projects or state-sponsored borrowing into equity and debt financing of such projects.

In the 1970s and early 1980s IOC continued their active role in financing oil investments and preferred to fund projects from their own resources—including borrowing on their corporate accounts. Other sources of financing for oil projects during this period include governments, multilaterals, bilaterals and commercial banks.

The collapse of oil prices in 1986 and the continuing softness of prices thereafter, the debt problems of developing countries and the over-exposure of commercial banks to energy financing all resulted in limiting both the sources and availability of financing for energy in the second half of the 1980s and early 1990s. The lower and uncertain petroleum prices not only reduced the attractiveness of oil investments but also imposed financial hardships on most IOC. This hardship was exacerbated for some IOC with the evolution of greater government control over oil and gas resources, tightening of contract terms, the institution of production-sharing and other types of agreements.

The new environmental standards for existing facilities translated into significant costs for some IOC. As a result IOC restructured and adopted new, stringent investment standards. They increasingly preferred shared risks and faster paybacks than they required earlier. As a result IOC have become much more selective in undertaking investments and have sought to share project risks by involving other parties, particularly local partners. These preferences led to more financing arrangements addressing the constraints of countries or weaker or less creditworthy partners. Straight forward corporate financing is no longer fully applicable. Rather various sources of funds and guarantee instruments are needed.

IOC as project sponsors employed a variety of new instruments to fund oil and gas projects. IOC turned to borrowing both to improve rates of return on equity and to involve international lenders in the project, hoping their participation would reduce the risk of economic or actual expropriation. In addition, the magnitude of capital costs involved in developing new, often technologically more difficult and expensive oil, gas and coal reserves also prompted oil company sponsors to attempt to incur new debt on an off-balance sheet basis to preserve debt–equity ratios and overall credit ratings. All these factors led to the increased utilization of project financing approaches (as compared to equity investment or direct corporate borrowing) for financing of international oil and gas projects, including those in the developing countries. However non-recourse loans for energy projects in developing oil importing countries have been limited because of the requirements of strong private corporate sponsorship and concerns of political risk in all international lending.

In the pre-1990s financing of natural gas projects was similar in some ways to financing of oil and in other ways to that of power projects. Upstream gas development projects have been modelled on those of the oil sector. The important difference between gas and oil projects is that upstream gas investment is normally contingent on long-term contracts with downstream gas companies and large end-users, mainly electricity companies. Natural gas transmission and distribution in most developing countries have been viewed as constituting a natural monopoly and are treated like the power sector. Hence gas transmission and distribution investments have historically been undertaken by state entities. Gas development in the pre-1990s period was open to private companies or to joint ventures between the public and private sectors.

Coal

Coal has a long history of extensive government involvement in the 1970s and early 1980s, often in the form of ownership. Governments kept prices to consumers below the cost of supply. Administered low prices for coal did not cover costs and led to poor financial performance. Developing coal producing countries including China and India had to finance investment through government budget allocations and/ or indirect subsidies to keep prices below the cost of supply.

Energy sector reform and liberalization since the mid 1980s involved the closure or consolidation of small unprofitable mining, diversification of their activities and seeking of private investment. This development has been particularly progressive in South Africa, China and India. Major coal producing developing countries have also undertaken reforms to liberalize coal prices, improve efficiency and allow private investment to fill the gap between available domestic financial resources and investment needs.

Multilateral programs for energy

Following the oil price increases in 1973 and the corresponding macroeconomic difficulties of many of oil importing developing countries, several official/ multilateral development assistance programs were reoriented to emphasize the energy sector. New programs for renewable energy (oil, gas and coal) development were created in a number of institutions and priority was given to energy as a share of lending operations. The multilateral development institutions were unique in providing the developing countries with an important source of external capital for investment combined with longer term technical advice and assistance. The perspective of the multilateral institutions is based on long-standing country relationships, including an active macroeconomic dialogue. These factors made the multilateral development institutions an important source of assistance to the developing countries in the energy sector.

However, despite these efforts official and concession financing has met only a small percentage of total external capital flows for energy in developing countries. Between 1975 and 1985 multilateral and bilateral concession aid represented about 25 per cent of total public debt for energy in developing countries. In terms of total energy commitments however, multilateral institutions have accounted for only 16 per cent of the total. Still their role in project identification and preparation has helped to attract other sources of financing to the energy sector in developing countries.

Traditionally, the bulk of multilateral assistance for energy has been devoted to the power sector. However, after the 1973 rise in oil prices new programs were created in the petroleum sector, including lending for oil, gas and coal exploration and development projects. New programs were also started in the areas of energy conservation, including industrial retrofitting, and macroeconomic and sector policy work were stepped upto develop a better analytical and intellectual framework for energy lending programs. The multilateral development institutions played an important role in the identification of energy sector issues, preparation of energy sector reform and adjustment programs, the development of sector–project investment opportunities and the mobilization of necessary funds for capital investment through cofinancing and raising internal resources.

Another important feature of multilateral energy programs is the emphasis that has been placed on technical assistance and training in overall lending for energy investment. Traditionally, the multilateral institutions have been a special source of sector and macroeconomic analysis and advice for developing countries. These activities were expanded to include energy sector issues, including the strengthening of planning and institutional capabilities as well as measures to stimulate the development of domestic energy resources and to manage domestic demand. The systematic effort in this area has been the WB/ UNDP/ ESMAP donor financed programs of energy assessments.

Despite the efforts for diversification of energy lending practices, a feature common to all multilateral programs in the energy sector is the high share of power in total commitments although both the WB and Inter-American Development Bank (IADB) created special programs in the oil and gas sector. The power sector received the bulk of multilateral funds, ranging from a high of 100 per cent of energy operations in the African Development Bank and European Development Bank, to 93 per cent in the Asian Development Bank (ADB), 86 per cent in the IADB and 80 per cent in the WB. The WB did make an effort to diversify it energy lending program into oil and gas. However, WB lending for oil and gas fell after reaching a peak of over US $1 billion in 1985. In dollar amounts the WB has been the largest source of multilateral energy assistance, with total commitments of over $40.0 billion during the 1975–90 period of which the power sector accounted for US $31 billion.

Internal financing for energy in the pre-1990s

Even considering non-guaranteed borrowing and private direct investment which are not included in the flows of public debt for energy, over 50 per cent of the energy investment needs to be mobilized domestically to finance the local cost of energy operations. Limitations on borrowing from public and private sources and the importance of the local cost element in total investments, particularly in coal, hydro and power projects make raising adequate internal funding critical for energy investments. The mobilization of internal funding for energy investment has been constrained by several factors, some specific to the energy sector and others relating to the more general problems of macro economic adjustment in the aftermath of oil price increases in the 1970s and the debt problems of the 1980s.

The energy sector of the pre-1990s in developing countries, mainly the power sector, was dominated by public ownership. The governments were both the owners and operators of the power sector companies. In the early 1970s, in addition to government budget allocations many power utilities in developing countries were able to generate a portion of their needed investment from internal resources termed as 'self-financing' source. Following the oil price increases of 1973 and 1979, inadequate tariff increases, coupled with rising unit investment and fuel costs and the impact of macro-economic adjustment on the power sector severely drained power sector finances. Financial performance has also been weakened by low capacity utilization, slow collections, particularly from government agencies.

The real problem, however, has been the widening gap between power tariffs and real investment and operating costs. Efforts to reduce domestic inflation and maintain consumer satisfaction have made many governments reluctant to approve and implement regular power tariff increases. The increases which have been granted tend to be on an *ad hoc* basis, limiting the ability of the utility to plan and execute its financial operations on a viable basis. In many cases the impact of tariff increases has been wiped out by inflation and accelerating investment costs for the development of power facilities. An additional problem was the absence of any domestic long-term capital markets in developing countries.

All of these factors made it difficult for national power companies to generate internal and external funds for investment programs. In the WB experience, only 35 per cent of the countries were able to generate self-financing ratios between 15 per cent and 40 per cent over time. Shortfalls in local cost financing led some governments to create medium- and long-term local financing and increase contributions from the public budget for project financing and direct equity injections to the national companies.

In the pre-1990 period NOCs in developing countries also were owned and operated by governments. Many of the NOCs are integrated through exploration, development, refining, and marketing, including imports of crude oil and products. In general, their record of generating investment funds has been mixed. In cases where exports of domestic oil and gas are based on international prices, and domestic prices both cover costs and provide an adequate per barrel netback to the company, self-financing has contributed to new investment. Where the NOC supplies the domestic market at administered prices which do not cover total costs, self-financing has been limited.

NOCs, like public power utilities, experienced serious problems with overdue payments from government agencies, particularly from specialized funds established to stabilize prices or cover price differentials between international and domestic markets. This resulted in serious liquidity problems for the NOCs. Examples of this situation were found in Thailand and Turkey. In other countries such as China and India, the NOC is involved in all stages of oil exploration and production but administered prices for crude sales have been set high enough to allow the company to cover production costs and allow the NOC to finance a reasonable portion of its investment program. NOCs also continue to be an important source of tax revenue for the national budget through their generation of export earnings (for oil exporting developing countries), royalties, other production-related taxes and corporate income taxes.

Most coal projects in developing countries are designed to produce coal for domestic markets mainly for power generation. Domestic market coal projects with high capital costs, long gestation periods and administered coal and transport prices were not attractive to external equity investors. Many coal development projects relied on newly established institutions which normally rely heavily on borrowing to meet start-up costs for the long construction period before production begins. A shortage of funds for transport and handling infrastructure prolongs the construction period, further increasing the capital costs.

Internal funding for energy, particularly for power and coal, will continue to be difficult. Local sources will need to produce an increasing proportion of growing capital requirement if shortages are to be alleviated and access to energy for development be expanded.

In the pre-1990s governments have been bearing more of the burden of energy financing. Tax revenues, budgetary allocations and government borrowings accounted for over 90 per cent of energy financing in developing countries. Consequently the burden on public finances are enormous. On average, energy's share of total government investment was around 20 per cent of total government investment. In addition, maintenance, operating expenditures and subsidies command a high share of current expenditure[2].

Changing patterns of financing energy in the 1990s: Toward energy sector reform and liberalization in developing countries

In the 1970s and the first half of the 1980s energy importing countries were concerned about security of petroleum supplies and the risk of high prices. During the late 1980s and early 1990s the global political, economic and energy environments changed drastically. As discussed in Chapter 2, the international oil, gas and power industry also began to change in the 1990s. Crude oil and petroleum products in the 1990s began to be viewed as 'commodities' that should be supplied through the most cost-effective channels.

The wave of globalization in the 1990s required developing countries to liberalize their economies and open up to the private sector. The integration of developing countries into the global economy increased in the 1990s with improvements in their economic policies, the massive expansion of global trade and finance driven by technological innovations, communications, transport, information technology and data management.

The 1990s heralded a shift in financing energy in developing countries from the pre-1990s' heavy dependence on public financing to seeking more private sponsorship. The changing global environment of the 1990s, the collapse of the former Soviet Union in 1989 and the deficiencies of state enterprises as both owners and operators in developing countries made the governments recognize the need for redefining the role of the state as that of policy maker, facilitator and regulator to create an environment for both public and private investment.

Sector inefficiencies

Since the oil crisis of 1973 and 1979, both technical and financial performance of power utilities in a majority of developing countries deteriorated. The performance of power sectors was impaired by general economic difficulties, particularly the impact of high inflation rates, depreciation of exchange rates and acute foreign exchange shortages. Inadequate tariff levels impeded cost recovery and gave incorrect signals to energy-users. For many developing countries, utilities financial performance as measured by the rates of return, self-financing ratios and level of overdue accounts all declined in the 1980s. Mounting debt restricted access to foreign capital needs

---

2. WDR, *Infrastructure for Development* (Published for the World Bank, Oxford University Press, 1994)

of developing countries to increase their power supply.

Many developing countries impacted by the oil price hikes of the 1970s and the debt problems of the 1980s continued to experience macroeconomic difficulties requiring structural and sector adjustment of their economies. The changing structural and sector adjustments of developing countries was characterized by an increased awareness of the costs to the economies of inefficient public utilities and the inability of the state to raise the financial resources to meet the increasing demand for energy without increasing the already unacceptable fiscal burdens.

The deficiencies of state ownership were clearly evident in the energy sector, particularly the failure of governments to address the declining trend in electric power sectors' pricing, financial, technical and institutional performance. There are several examples of efficient state-run power sectors and many successful state owned individual projects. But as confirmed by a review of WB lending for electric power, a declining trend was clearly evident by 1988 in the sector's pricing, financial, technical and institutional performance. The result of inefficiency is low-quality and unreliable service and consumer dissatisfaction. The problems include both technical and financial inefficiencies in operations, inadequate maintenance, unresponsiveness to user demand mainly due to governmental failure to address the sector's fundamental structural problems[3].

In 1987 one quarter of the power utilities in developing countries had losses of electricity in the transmission and distribution network that were twice the size of those in efficiently operated systems. Inefficient use of labour and overstaffing and inadequate maintenance are also common in electric power operations. Inadequate maintenance of power generators result in capacity loss, output decline and substantial additional investments simply to sustain existing levels of service. Poor maintenance practices account for some of the low availability of power generating capacity, which averages less than 60 per cent for thermal plants in many developing countries compared with more than 80 per cent in systems operated at the best practice standards.

Sometimes problems of operation and maintenance are rooted in the initial design or construction of facilities. Operations and maintenance can be made more difficult by inappropriate design standards that increase the requirements for skills in short supply or involve heavy dependence on imported spare parts where foreign exchange is scarce. Poor construction and design of power plants and inappropriate location makes it difficult to carry out operations and maintenance.

---

3. WB, *The World Bank's Role in the Electric Power Sector, A World Bank Policy Paper* (Washington DC, 1993)

Procurement problems are often a factor in weak operational performance. Systematic delays in purchasing by sector entities and inadequate supervision of contracts are estimated to increase costs of imported materials to some African countries by 20 per cent to 20 percent.

During the 1980s, power tariffs in developing countries were on average about half the costs of new supply and were much lower than in OECD countries. Over the period 1979–88, average real power tariffs in developing countries declined from 5.2 cents to 3.8 cents/ KWH, quality of service deteriorated, technical and non-technical losses and fuel consumption continued to be high and poor performance of plants persisted. Inadequate metering, billing and collection were the result of a lack of enforcement of industry standards for commercial operations. While institutional building (training of power utility staff and modernization) continued to progress, conflicts between government's role as owner and its role as operator of utilities have affected sector performance. Opaque command and control management of the sector, poorly defined objectives, government's interference in daily affairs and a lack of financial autonomy affected productive efficiency and institutional performance.

Financial performance as measured by indicators such as the rate of return on revalued assets, self-financing ratios and the level of overdue accounts, also declined. On average, rates of return fell from levels averaging about 9 per cent before the mid-1970s to less than 5 per cent in 1991. Self-financing ratios on average were only 12 per cent of investment requirements in 1991, against targets of between 20 and 60 per cent; and the actual number of days receivable increased from 77 days during 1966–73 to 108 days in the 1970s to 112 days in the 1980s. The overall average of accounts receivable by 1991 was 96 days compared with the general WB target of 60 days. Poor financial performances by many power utilities caused them a loss of creditworthiness. It also resulted in low reliance on internal revenues to finance investment and an inability and lack of incentive to improve and expand service.

Developing countries' deteriorating macroeconomic situation and the debt overhang of the 1980s exacerbated these financial problems and worsened debt-service coverage. Budgets were tightened for macroeconomic reasons. The large share that energy represents in government investment led to proportionately sharp reductions in spending in this sector. Such sharp declines are appropriate where private investment is attracted or inefficient spending is reduced or where macroeconomic adjustment is needed. Under these circumstances it was evident by the mid 1980s that the pre-1990 pattern of financing energy, where the state played the predominant role, could not continue.

Given the large capital requirements and ingrained energy–power sector inefficiencies, neither developing countries nor their traditional sources of financing, including multilateral institutions such as the WB, could continue with a 'business as usual' approach to financing and managing the energy sector. The WB financed macro and sector adjustment reform required reduction of government budget deficit by liberalizing energy prices and creating an enabling climate for attracting private investment in energy.

Furthermore, the changing global environment of the 1990s and the competition for access to financial resources underscored the need for the efficient utilization of energy sector resources. Under these circumstances, redefining of the role of the state with enterprises distanced from excessive day-to-day government management was critical to create a suitable business environment.

Redefining the role of state

The worldwide move toward reliance on free-market systems since the early 1990s and globalization and liberalization of the international energy industry (Chapter 2) are changing the global environment where developing countries have to compete to access global financing for energy development. The low oil prices since 1986 and the debt problem of the 1980s raised the risks of energy investment in developing countries and the funding of energy projects became quite complex involving public and private investors and financiers. Where budgets have been tightened for macroeconomic reasons, the large share that energy represents in government investment led to proportionately sharp reductions in spending in this sector.

The public financing constraints affected energy investment both in power and petroleum public investment in energy (which accounted for 20-30 per cent of total investments in the 1970s), declined to less than 10–15 per cent in the 1990s. Such sharp declines are appropriate where private investment is attracted or inefficient spending is reduced or where macroeconomic adjustment is needed. Under these circumstances it was evident by the mid 1980s that the pre-1990 pattern of financing energy where the state played the predominant role could not continue.

Future investment requirements to meet the growing energy demand (as projected in Chapter 1) are massive and are driven by four factors. First is the urgent need to overcome current bottlenecks and make up for past under-investment, particularly in Africa and countries in transition (Cambodia, Laos, Mongolia and Vietnam) in Asia. Second, the need to sustain high economic growth rates in several countries in Asia and Latin America. Third, rapid industrialization throughout the developing regions raises the need for much higher investment in energy infrastructure. And fourth, the need to increase access to the estimated 2 billion people who are currently 'unserved' with commercial energy. All these require that developing countries' need for substantial increase in investment to GDP ratio from about 2 per cent to about 5 per cent to finance energy for development.

As explained in Chapter 1, the developing world is faced with a huge potential increase in energy demand which is quite likely to double in the next 20 years. In the coming decades over 90 per cent of the incremental growth in energy demand will come from the developing world. This reflects in part the widening access to commercial energy in the lesser developing countries where today some 2 billion people have no access to it.

The challenge that faces most developing countries is to mobilize the required financing of over US $300 billon per year for replacing and expanding their energy sectors even to satisfy modest rates of growth in their energy demand given that most of their funds are already earmarked for priority programs in education, health and other social services. There is a growing concern that many developing economies are unable to mobilize all the finance they require for energy investment because of inadequate public resources and/ or are unable to attract private sector investment. This has resulted in a widening of the financial resources gap that affects increasing access to required energy supplies in developing countries.

The industrialized countries, multilateral institutions such as the WB and the IMF and NGOs—including the WEC—therefore, began to emphasize the inevitability of developing countries to adopt a free market system and to liberalize their economies to facilitate public and private investment in energy. The WB in its policy papers[4] prepared in 1992 stated that it is changing the way it does business in energy and the Bank and its borrowers cannot keep using a 'business-as-usual' approach to lending when power utility performance was deteriorating in most developing countries. The papers made it clear that the future role of the Bank in the power sector is that of a facilitator to require developing countries to pursue pricing and institutional reforms to attract private investment. The WEC's study entitled 'Financing the Global Energy Sector—The Task Ahead' (1997)[5] concluded that global financial resources are more than adequate to meet all potential investment and finance needs for energy provided that countries meet certain conditions to liberalize their economies to facilitate private investment. An IEA study however, acknowledges that the situation in developing countries and the transition economies is less secure. Export oriented projects are expected to be more

---

4. WB, 'The Woeld Bank's Role in the Electric Power Sector, A world Bank Policy Paper' (Washington D.C. 1993)
   WB, 'Energy Efficiency and Conservation in the Developing World, A World Bank Policy Paper, (Washington D.C. 1993)
5. WEC, *Financing the Energy Sector—The Task Ahead* (London, 1997)

readily financed than projects to supply domestic markets in developing countries. Few governments in developing countries were expected to finance the large-scale investments required in domestic electricity and downstream gas. Borrowing from domestic markets will be constrained by poorly developed financial markets. Access to international capital will be limited by the exchange-rate risk, deficiency in the legal and regulatory systems and more general fears of government policy and political uncertainties.

The energy policy papers cited inefficient energy use on distorted energy-pricing policies, inappropriate control and regulation of energy enterprises and protection of energy-using industries from competition. Other legal, institutional and information barriers to efficient market operations also needed to be addressed. Developing countries were encouraged to reform their energy sectors by adopting four basic principles. These include economic energy pricing to promote competition, transparent regulation, commercialization–corporatization–importation of energy services/ privatization and institutional reform and restructuring and private investment. The policy paper linked future WB lending for electric power to countries that clearly commit themselves to improving power performance in line with these guiding principles.

In 1995 the WB[6] also re-examined its oil and gas lending strategy in consultation with member countries, representatives of the international petroleum industry and other sources of finance. The strategy was revised to take account of the changes since 1978. The new strategy emphasized helping developing countries to mitigate project risks and enabling governments to serve as effective regulators. The new strategy puts substantial emphasis on developing countries to create open and competitive markets to encourage private capital. In keeping with the principles of developing private sector the new strategy shifted away from lending for oil and gas in the upstream sector and focused on technical assistance to facilitate sector restructuring, privatization, private sector development and the establishment of environmental standards and monitoring institutions.

Financing energy in the 1990s: Guiding principles for energy sector reform and liberalization

Large capital investment requirements and higher risks, ingrained sector inefficiencies, dismantling of the supporting traditional pattern of financing governments and inefficient state owned energy enterprises generated pressures for new approaches. New approaches required liberalization of energy

---

6. Vedavalli, Rangaswamy, '*World Bank Oil and Gas Policy, Review and Recommendations*', *World Bank* (Washington DC, 1995)

prices, restructuring and evaluating sector management on the basis of commercial principles to attract and mobilize the changing pattern of financing energy sector investment in the 1990s. These approaches revolve around a new framework for addressing pricing and financial, regulatory and institutional issues to reform the energy sector to encourage and attract public and private investment.

Pricing

The first guiding principle of the reform approach focused on liberalization of energy prices. Between 1973 and 1988 energy prices in both oil importing and exporting developing countries generally did not cover economic costs except in the case of some petroleum products like gasoline. The fall in international oil prices since 1986 did improve the relation of domestic energy prices to economic cost, but significant distortion in energy prices including power tariffs persist. Specific inadequacies in price policies and structures include:

- Petroleum product prices while generally reflecting economic costs on average, involved cross subsidization with gasoline being above economic cost, and kerosene, LPG and feedstocks priced below. Ex-refinery prices have generally been set above border prices, but major petroleum price distortions persisted in some countries where product prices still remained well below border prices even after the fall in international oil prices in 1986.
- Natural gas prices have typically been pegged to the price of fuel oil. In countries with large domestic natural gas reserves (Algeria, Egypt and Yemen Arab Republic), economic value of natural gas fell below its fuel oil equivalent. Gas pricing is an important issue as key investment decisions to explore and develop natural gas are sensitive to the economic price of domestic gas and its use in power generation.
- Coal and lignite prices for domestic production were usually priced below average imported costs and domestic coal prices ranged from 25 per cent to 98 per cent of economic cost. In contrast, the prices of imported steam and coking coal were set at Cost Insurance Freight (CIF) costs. The concept of marginal pricing for domestically produced non-traded coal was waiting to win support.
- Electricity prices have generally been set below Long-run Marginal Cost (LRMC) and remained substantially lower except in a few countries. Governments were reluctant to increase electricity tariffs.

Resolution of the pricing issue has been complicated by the fact that energy price setting has been the responsibility of governments rather than the market. In setting energy prices governments gave greater weightage to industrial competitiveness, impact on household budgets and inflation, than economic efficiency, cost recovery or the financial viability of energy enterprises. Lower international oil prices since 1986 did narrow the gap between domestic energy prices and their economic costs. However, so long as the mechanism of administered pricing was practiced it perpetuated economic distortions and continued to be a barrier to mobilize public and private energy investments. Low energy prices encouraged excessive energy demand and, by undermining the revenue base, reduced the ability of energy enterprises to provide and maintain supplies.

Transparent regulation

The second principle of the reform approach required establishing a transparent and independent regulatory process to create an appropriate climate for investors by clearly articulating goals, reforming countries legal frameworks to make decisions more transparent and to allow a fair hearing for both consumers and the general public. Transparency of decision-making in a regulatory framework is a safeguard against corruption, patronage, waste and the abuse of executive authority.

A legal framework setting out clearly the rights and duties of the government and contractors and covering key issues such as ownership and taxation is a sine qua non for investment in the oil sector of any oil producing region. Acceptable framework legislation is now widely regarded as essential but questions remain concerning what form the legislation should take:

- Should legislation cover all resources or focus specially on petroleum?
- Should the legal regime be license-based, raising the spectre of unilateral withdrawal or revision of licenses by the government. Or should it be a contract-based regime that is mutually binding on the government and the investor?
- Should the parliament approve all contracts and amendments or should reasonable authority be delegated to the government?
- How should federal and regional interests and authority be balanced in such difficult areas by approving licenses and contracts, controlling operations, safeguarding the environment and sharing tax revenues?
- What special privileges, if any, should be granted, particularly for

natural gas to foreign investors?

Basic elements to be put in place with regard to a legal framework for the power sector include:

- A clear set of rules known in advance;
- Rules actually in force;
- Mechanisms to ensure application of the rules;
- Conflict resolution through binding decisions of an independent judicial body or through arbitration;
- Known procedures for amending the rules when they no longer serve the purpose;
- A framework of regulatory incentives (including the possibility of price-capping) to support competition and induce efficiency.

Commercialization/ Corporatization/ Competition and institutional reform

With independent legal status, transparent legislation and the right energy price signals, the third principle of the reform approach focused on getting energy enterprises to operate as commercial businesses to attract private investment. Commercialization requires energy enterprises to pay interest and taxes, earn commercially competitive rates of return on equity capital, and have responsibility for their own budgets, borrowing, procurement, pay and staff conditions. This means that the governments' relationship with the energy enterprises must be more transparent and must emphasize financial discipline together with the setting of overall policy frameworks and goals. This should also include overall reforming of the domestic financial sector to develop domestic capital market to finance energy investments.

Understanding the implications of launching parallel reforms in both the energy and financial sectors is essential for designing an energy sector reform program. The success of such a program requires that reforms in these sectors be linked and well integrated with the overall economy-wide reform process. Many developing countries had already launched adjustment programs in the 1980s that go beyond the correction of initial imbalances to the reform of economic policies and institutions. In many countries the beginning of the 1990s was the right time for launching inter sector reform program.

In some of the least developed countries, where there are weak public and private sectors, a relative lack of market forces and undeveloped capital markets, an early step in bringing about energy sector reform and increasing sector management efficiency required bringing local, developed country or more advanced developing country energy services into the sector.

Among the underlying causes of poor energy sector development and management is a country's level of economic, human and institutional development. Lack of qualified and trained manpower and weak institutions reduce the capacity of countries to provide sound development management.

In such weak situations a priority is to find innovative ways to draw on international hands-on experience as a means of developing local manpower, skills and institutional capabilities. Early steps in bringing about sector improvements also involved twinning arrangements or the contracting out of selected sector services to foreign entities that can provide in-country management services at reasonable cost and create local capacity in the sector.

Private investment

The above guiding principles partly aimed at helping countries establish a framework of policies and institutions that would result in a competitive and more efficient energy sector. Such a sector was considered able to attract private capital. The expectations of gains of private investment include shared financial and technical risk, accelerated development and shared technical and managerial ideas and practices. But getting energy prices right and putting in place an accountable institutional framework may not be sufficient. Private investors could still be understandably reluctant to make significant financial commitments because of the lack of experience with the operation, stability and reliability of the new policy framework. Governments on the other hand, are concerned that investors will try to compensate for the perceived risks by seeking high rates of return that could require unpopular increases in energy prices. Both parties thus have an interest in lowering the perceived risks.

It is in the early stages of the policy reform process that investors perceive the greatest risks. On the one hand most investors are prepared to bear the commercial risks associated with energy–power projects. They are also prepared to accept some country risks. In particular, they are willing to take the debt obligations under satisfactory conditions for being paid for their services. On the other hand, in many cases investors do perceive a financial risk in conjunction with the reform process. They are concerned that unavoidable bureaucratic difficulties of implementing new ways of doing business could result in an uneven and unpredictable cash flow in the early years of their investment. In most cases, some of the most prominent concerns are about price and availability of fuels, timely payment for power and natural gas purchased by the dominant state-owned public sector company and delays in obtaining the agreed conversion of local currency into foreign exchange. An additional source of uncertainty is government bureaucratic inexperience in dealing with the disputes that will inevitably arise between power companies, natural gas companies and private suppliers under complex power-purchase agreements.

To compensate for risks such as these, commercial lenders either require a larger equity investment from the project sponsors or pursue a larger package of public guarantees for their loans. Both requirements raise the cost of projects, although this increase could be more than offset by quick construction and subsequent operational efficiencies of the privately owned plants. Equity investors require a higher rate of return than the interest rate on the loans to compensate for their high exposure to risk, while public guarantees would divert the limited resources of the public sector from alternative uses.

Since some of the risks for private investors are linked to a government's timely implementation of its contractual obligations, a third party could help underwrite these risks. In many private financial transactions, one way in which third party guarantees can be obtained is by posting performance bonds, establishing escrow accounts, buying insurance policies or similar risk-covering mechanisms. Governments, of course, could take the initiative in mitigating these risks and thus reducing the prices demanded by private producers, by arranging risk coverage for their own performance. The credit support programs developed by the WB, International finance corporation (IFC) and Multilateral Investment Guarantee Agency (MIGA) to promote private financing of infrastructure have focused on covering some risks through partial guarantees to private investors. They require four broad actions: liberalizing energy pricing, applying commercial principles to energy operations, encouraging competition from appropriately regulated private sector providers and attracting public-private investment.

Financing mechanisms for energy in the 1990s[7]

The guiding principles for adopting new approaches to financing energy discussed above began to change the financing pattern for energy operations in the 1990s. Innovations and diverse financing techniques were employed to support an accelerating transition from public to private sector risk bearing in energy operations. Mechanisms for financing specific stand-alone projects were designed to contribute to the changing pattern as governments shift from being energy providers to becoming facilitators and as private entrepreneurs and lenders take a more direct role.

---

7. Vedavalli Rangaswamy, 'International energy financing', *WEC Journal*, London, (July 1994).

Private entrepreneurship in energy through the privatization of state-owned utilities and through policy reform that made possible the construction of new facilities in competition with or as a complement to existing enterprises began to evolve in the late 1980s. International companies began seeking business in energy in developing countries and often operated in association with local companies.

In the early 1990s foreign direct investment opened another route into international equity markets. For example, General Electric Corporation, an international conglomerate, took an active interest in developing power projects in developing countries. Its subsidiary, the General Electric Capital Corporation (GECC), issued securities on US and European markets and invested the funds in selected projects. For example, GECC participated as an equity investor in the northern Mindanao 108 MW diesel-fired power project in the Philippines. Backed by the group's total operations, the placement of securities issued by GECC was easier than it would have been in stand-alone developing country power projects.

In the energy–power sector several new financing approaches were used to finance major new energy–power developments in the 1990s. These include:

- Independent power producers
- Captive power plants
- Financial intermediaries
- Stock exchange listing
- Privatization
- Leasing
- Bond markets
- Project Financing: Build Own and Operate (BOO)/ Build, Own, Operate and Turnover (BOOT) Arrangements
- Extended credit operation
- MIGA
- IFC

Independent power producers (IPP)

Independent private power generation facilities are stand-alone, privately owned and operated electric power plants that sell bulk power to the national grid. Where governments are willing to change 'the rules of the command and control game' and allow private sector producers to sell power to existing utilities, the rules being changed include new laws which open up the power sector to competition (especially generation) by requiring utilities to buy power from producers at their avoided costs, i.e. the price that utilities would have to pay to produce their own additional requirements. Sometimes access to the grid is provided enabling new producers to sell directly to large consumers. This has happened in Chile where producers arranged long-term supply contracts with large industry at market (negotiated) prices.

These types of changes provide opportunities for investors to arrange their own financing to build new power plants. They obtain funding in conventional ways ranging from share issues, commercial and syndicated bank loans and bond issues. Often they attract public funds from banks, insurance companies, pension funds and private investors.

The best way to encourage these developments once the barriers to entry have been removed and the procedures have been established is to invite proposals from bidders for a specified amount of new plants. This will enable open competition and should lead to selection of least-cost projects. Independent producers however, will only survive if they can operate and maintain power facilities and continue to produce electricity at prices which are below the existing public supply system's avoided cost. Determining the avoided cost is often difficult since it is imprecise. As a result independent producers are likely to establish new plants only where they have access to reliable and cheap fuel, e.g. natural gas or water rights for existing hydro or new technology such as fluidized bed boilers using low-cost waste from coal washing.

Captive power plants

In many developing countries large potential consumers have found the public system so inadequate and unreliable that they have decided to build their own plants dedicated to their own requirements. This has been the case especially in India, Indonesia and Pakistan. The industries in these cases arrange their own financing. However, often their costs of production are higher than those of the public system, especially where the latter is subsidized. They also need to depend on the public system for stand-by facilities if their own plant becomes inoperable or is shut down for maintenance. The financial return from captive power plants can be increased by encouraging them to sell to the public system if prices are right, i.e., at least sufficient to cover short-run marginal costs of fuel and operations plus a contribution to fixed costs.

Financial intermediaries

The WB in the 1990s encouraged the development of financial intermediaries to provide local and foreign finances for power development. Government sponsored energy development funds were designed as transitional mechanisms to provide long-term finance until capital markets are better developed. Private funds serve the commercially useful function of diversifying investor risk. As transitional mechanisms these funds serve two purposes. They allow the leveraging of government resources or official development assistance by attracting cofinancing from private sources. They can also create credit histories for borrowers perceived as risky. In time these borrowers can secure direct access to capital markets.

The Private Sector Energy Development Fund in Pakistan and the Private Sector Energy Fund in Jamaica were designed to catalyse private financing for power projects. In response to perceived country risk and a lack of long-term financing compatible with the requirements of the power sector, the Jamaican government made long-term financing available through the energy fund (upto a maximum of 70 per cent of the project costs) as a means of attracting private investments. Investors in the fund include the WB and IADB.

Others include the Public Participation Fund in Turkey, the Power Finance Corporation (PFC) in India and Financiera Electrica Nacional (FEN) in Colombia. They operate like banks but appraise and supervise the new projects. No commercial creditworthiness tests were sought. Funds were provided from domestic and foreign sources for the exclusive use of the power sector. They are particularly useful where the sector is fragmented and there are a number of producers—state, regional, municipal or privately owned.

Often these intermediaries have been public-owned and been supported by government guarantees. In many developing countries specialized development banks such as the Industrial Development Bank of India (IDBI) and PFC of India are a conduit for funds used in energy/ power projects. Such specialized energy financing institutions suffer from all the negative features associated with government ownership, such as inefficient targeting and subsidization of lending, interference in operations and corruption. Inadequate diversification of risk has also led to periods of heavy demand followed by substantial slack. Moreover, the banks' traditional function as conduits of government funds is inconsistent with the trend toward less reliance on government budgets and increased use of private savings to finance energy operations.

Specialized energy financing intermediaries could play a catalytic role in capital market development. To ensure their own creditworthiness, financial intermediaries must set performance standards for borrowers to achieve. In the long run however, it is desirable for the sector entities to establish themselves as market participants able to borrow directly on their own right. Intermediaries can also be used to coordinate funding by multilateral development banks, export credits and other foreign sources.

Good design for such domestic funds require that they price their loans on market benchmarks. It is also important to incorporate incentives for private sponsors to seek commercial financing or to commit a larger amount of equity funds and to ensure that the fund manager or the operating intermediary has a stake in the success of projects financed. Appropriately designed funds could be useful instruments while capital markets are still developing. However, long-term financing of energy infrastructure requires reform of the financial sector and improved creditworthiness of borrowers.

A number of private funds in the early 1990s had been established to channel international capital for developing country infrastructure. They pool risks across projects and hence increase the availability as well as lower the costs of finance. These funds mobilize resources through private placements from institutional investors, including pension funds. As has been the practice of government-backed funds, private funds have concentrated heavily on power projects. Continued flow of resources into such funds will depend on investments being made in sound projects with credible sponsors as well as the pace at which regulatory restrictions on instituition investors are relaxed.

Stock exchange listing

Once local capital markets are sufficiently well established they should be able to provide finance for new power projects. However, existing energy producers in developing countries embarking on reforming their energy enterprises and looking to raise equity capital for their own investment needs had to first commercialize their accounts and adopt objectives and practices similar to those of private sector businesses. They then have to seek corporate status through adoption of the local companies code. This often required restructuring boards and management, reducing excess staff, phasing out subsidies and introducing the same taxes and dividend targets as private sector entities.

Before this becomes feasible, prices need to be set at levels that ensure adequate returns for investors. A reliable and transparent regulatory system must be in place that assures investors that returns will be sustainable. Given that it is not reasonable to expect that equity financing should be used to provide all the investment needs, it is desirable to see a reasonable mix of debt to equity. A prudent level of debt to equity for power development should not exceed 60:40. An adequate interest coverage is also considered essential to provide comfort to lenders. For the power sector based on US capital market standards, a coverage of three to four times is considered desirable. The rate of return on capital which investors should seek would normally need to be at least equal to returns investors in the country are seeking for similar investments and risks. This will vary according to country circumstances. Once a reasonable track record of profits is established, an approach to the local market can be considered through stock exchange listing. Audited financial statements based on application of international accounting standards will be a prerequisite.

Privatization

The privatization of energy operations has given a boost to local stock markets. Of the US $61.6 billion of revenue obtained by privatization of public enterprises between 1988 and 1992, about one-third ($21 billion) came from the privatization of infrastructure entities. Aggregate proceeds from infrastructure privatization have been highest in Latin America, with the most activity being in telecommunications some Asian countries have opted for partial privatization. Outside Latin America and Asia however, privatization in energy so far has had a limited impact.

Techniques for financing privatization have implications for the broadening of share ownership on stock markets and for the general development of capital markets. Chilgener in Chile illustrates the implications of privatization for financial markets.

- All except Chilgener sought a strategic (or core) investor in order to introduce management expertise and to create a commitment to further growth.
- A significant proportion of shares was sold to the general public and shares were allocated to the employees.
- Substantial proceeds from the initial stock offerings and subsequent rise in share prices have given these companies a dominant position in their domestic capital markets.

Leasing

In the 1990s leasing was introduced as another approach to independent power. Leases can provide an important source of capital for new project financing and have also been used by electric utilities for off-balance sheet financing. They may involve the formation of a financing company by interested investors who then lease the plant back to the electric utility that operates and maintains it. In Panama bids were sought in 1993 from the private sector to rehabilitate a 40 MW plant. The plant was leased to the private sector after it was rehabilitated for ten years.

Bond markets

Bonds can attract to energy/ power financing a whole new class of investors, such as pension funds and insurance companies seeking long-term stable returns. Generally, it has been the role of the government to foster the development of bond markets. Government bond issues establish the benchmarks—in terms of pricing and maturity structure—for bond markets overall.

In developing countries the use of bond financing is in its early stages. Revenue bonds (used for green field projects and paid back from the project's revenues) are new in energy finance in developing countries. They have been used to finance Subic Bay Power station in the Philippines. Corporate or municipal bonds, based on the credit of a company or government authority, have been used by infrastructure entities but the bonds have often been placed on international markets because domestic bond markets are underdeveloped.

Project financing: Boo/ Boot type projects

Many new energy projects in the private sector are built by 'special-purpose corporations' which bring together private sponsors and other equity holders. Despite their lack of credit history, several such ventures have successfully attracted equity and loan finance. Project financing, which permits sponsors to raise funds secured by revenues and assets of a particular project, is often used in new ventures that have no track records. This technique requires a clearer delineation of risk than in the case of traditional public projects. Allocating risk among participants has often been a difficult and time-consuming process, but new safeguards and conventions are evolving to deal with project risks and complexities. Privately sponsored and financed projects measure their success against contractually agreed targets for new capacity, construction costs, time overruns and indicators of service quality. The continuing role of government lies in ensuring the private investor against policy induced risks.

The most commonly adopted model of project financing in power in the 1990s is the BOOT approach. This approach involves use of limited recourse financing which means that they are financed on the basis of the cash flow and risks associated with each project and not on the credit of the project owners. Creditors and providers of debt financing have only limited recourse to the project owners. These arrangements require detailed analysis to ensure that all risks are satisfactorily covered and that there is an adequate rate of return and cash flow to attract private investment.

This approach has been successfully applied in the power sector in only a few developing countries. The best known are Shajiao in China, the Hopewell Project in the Philippines and the Hub River Project in Pakistan. Other countries to consider this approach are Jamaica, Indonesia and the Dominican Republic. Under the BOOT scheme private developers construct a power generation station and sell power to the utility for an agreed upon price and transfer the project to the utility at a nominal price once the project debt has been repaid. In the case of the BOO projects no transfer takes place.

Debt is commonly raised by the project company from commercial sources, often with the backing of export credit guarantee agencies or multilateral or bilateral donors. Lenders are typically not covered by direct full sovereign guarantees. Debt to equity ratios are typically in the range of 70–85 per cent (debt) and 15–30 per cent (equity).

Most BOO/ BOOT projects in developing countries' power sectors have been complex both from a legal and financial viewpoint because of the difficulty assigning risks to the participants in the project. As a result these projects have been very expensive to develop.

The project company typically consists of a consortium of project developers, foreign and local investors, equipment suppliers and contractors who will build the facility. Government support has been critical in guaranteeing the performance, especially payments by the power utility under the power purchase agreement and guarantees to cover foreign exchange, etc. Governments are also responsible for removal of legal and regulatory constraints.

The Hopewell–Pagbilao independent power project in the Philippines marked the first time that a loan from the export–import bank was not backed by a government counter-guarantee, placing the bank on the same footing as private lenders which encouraged them to improve their project appraisal, assessment of borrower creditworthiness and monitoring.

To attract international private capital to developing countries, several multilateral development banks including the WB and the ADB have developed guarantee schemes. The WB's capital market guarantees are used to facilitate the access of developing countries to the international capital markets by lengthening the maturity of relative borrowing. The proceeds from such loans can be used for power project investments. The WB also issues guarantees for project financing—through Extended Credit Operation and through its agency—the MIGA discussed below.

Extended credit operation (ECO)

This involves the use of an ECO guarantee to protect private lenders in the event the government fails to meet specific obligations approved by the WB (excluding commercial risks). The guarantee would cover up to 100 per cent principal and interest payments of the private lenders. In the event of a default, the WB would pay the lenders and the government would then be obliged to repay the WB. This technique was used in the Hub River project for power in Pakistan and is being used for financing some gas projects.

MIGA

The MIGA of the World Bank Group (WBG) seeks to promote the flow of international capital to developing countries by providing guarantees against the following non-commercial forms of risk:

- Transfer risk arising from host government restrictions against convertibility and transfer of foreign exchange;
- Loss risk resulting from legislative or administrative action of the host government that leads to loss of ownership, control or benefits;
- Contract repudiation risk when the outside investor has no recourse to an adequate forum, faces undue delays or is unable to force a favourable judgement and
- War or civil disturbance risk.

IFC

The IFC of the WBG can participate in private power projects through equity investments, direct loans or it can underwrite or syndicate commercial bank loans.

Energy financing prospects in developing countries

Moving from the pre-1990s heavy dependence on public financing to the post 1990s system of more private sponsorship is likely to be a long and sometimes painful process. From the menu of new financing approaches discussed above the options available to a country depend on its administrative capability and the state of its capital market. The structuring of standalone projects using project finance techniques may require considerable effort and technical assistance from international agencies. Where domestic capital markets are not well developed and financial intermediaries are weak the only other option may be to strengthen specialized energy finance institutions. Once financial intermediaries are well developed they can take on the task of catalyzing the development of domestic capital markets through appraisal and underwriting functions.

In theory, once credit rating and public regulation of financial markets are in place other options open up and the use of long-term savings of contractual institutions and the development of financial instruments should become possible. However, in practice, the working of the reformed financial sector given the environment of corruption and the required change in the mind-set put additional burden on governments' oversight and facilitator responsibilities.

Nonetheless, the 1990s heralded the movement of private enterprise into a number of developing countries and projects in the energy sector. Legal and regulatory reforms were launched in many countries. Energy enterprises were privatized in Latin America and East Asia.

The financial crises of 1997–99 from East Asia to Brazil impacted developing countries in many respects. In most developing countries, growth remained weak and well below pre-crisis trends. Most East Asian economies experienced virtually no growth in 1998. Since the onset of the East Asian crisis in 1997 the corporate sectors and financial systems in the crisis economies remained in severe distress. The banking systems' non-performing loans skyrocketed to unprecedented levels: in 1999 non-performing loans ranged between approximately 30 per cent of GDP for Korea and Malaysia to 60 per cent of GDP for Thailand.

The string of financial crises in developing countries since 1997 shook the confidence of many in global financial markets. The financial crisis underlined how globalization, especially financial integration, exposes developing countries to external shocks. It has demonstrated that capital inflows through their volatility can also impose significant costs.

The financial crises since 1997 and its effects on international capital flows have important implications for energy–power investment in developing countries. The financial crises affected power sector financing both by triggering massive macroeconomic downturns which resulted in a stagnation or decline in electricity demand and by drastically downgrading the risk profile of investments. These consequences have had a negative impact both on private investment in divested assets and on private incremental investment.

Private investment in divested assets continued on an upward trend in 1997 in East Asia and Latin America. In 1998 however, the level of divestitures dropped significantly in these regions: by 95 per cent in East Asia and by 50 per cent in Latin America. Prior to the 1997 crisis East Asia followed by Latin America led the worldwide boom in privately financed IPPs. Focused mostly on power generation, new green field projects in East Asia worth nearly US $40 billion accounted for 60 per cent of all such projects in the developing world between 1990 and 1997. The share of private capital in total incremental power sector investment peaked at 40 per cent in 1996 for all developing countries. It fell to 19 per cent in 1997 and to 11 per cent in 1998. Table 3.4 shows the regional breakdown between 1996 and 1998.

Table 3.4. Share of Private Capital in Total Incremental Power Sector Investment

Region	*1996 (%)*	*1997 (%)*	*1998 (%)*
East Asia	68	31	17
South Asia	38	9	5
Latin America and the Caribbean	86	55	34
All developing countries	40	19	11

Source: Energy and Development Report, 1999, Energy After the financial Crises, ESMAP; World Bank, Washington D.C.

These steep declines in the proportion of total incremental investment in the power sector, financed privately by over half in the case of Latin America and by over three quarters in the case of East and south Asia, show the negative impact of the reassessment of the country, currency, and sector-specific risks on the willingness of the private sector to finance incremental developing country power sector investment.

East Asia's heavy reliance on bank-based financial systems and the high-debt equity ratios of corporations made the economic distress especially acute. Weak firms in East Asia operated on thin margins in the years leading up to the crisis in 1997 and their inability to pay interest following the onset of the crisis added to their debt burden. They will continue to act as a drag on investment and growth until the financial claims on them are resolved and either their operations return to adequate profitability or their assets are redeployed.

The financial crises constituted a major reassessment of emerging market country risk: they also precipitated a far-reaching re-evaluation of many sector specific commercial and regulatory risks in the case of divestiture. By contrast, the increased cost of financing for green field investment could only be mitigated by extensive reforms to renew confidence in the macro-economic and sector environment. Vigorous corporate and financial re-structuring and addressing deeper structural problems are required to return to sustainable growth. If there is to be sustained private risk bearing and investment in energy, parallel and far-reaching actions are required to re-form legal and financial institutions and to develop capital markets that efficiently intermediate savings into investment. Government restructuring policies are focusing on an institutional structure for corporate and financial restructuring. Malaysia and Chile are examples of countries that have effectively used their energy sectors to mobilize domestic funds.

The challenge for the future is how the US $8 trillion that is expected to be needed in energy investments in developing countries through 2030 be mobilized? Although globally capital is available on the necessary scale, ease of access to capital varies among regions and sectors in developing countries. Access to capital for particular energy projects might be constrained by the expectation of inadequate returns on investment relative to the perceived risks, when compared to alternative use of capital.

Both foreign and domestic sources of capital will need to be tapped. In OECD countries domestic savings at 23 per cent of GDP, are more than 40 times higher than their energy investment needs. Outside the OECD, countries in Asia, especially East Asia, have high domestic savings rates which have underpinned high investment and rapid economic development over the past decades. China, with strong support from the government, makes use of its abundant domestic savings to finance very high rates of domestic investment (36 per cent of GDP) which have been a basis for its rapid economic growth in recent years. India's domestic savings rate of over 20 per cent of GDP entails high energy investment of over 2.2 per cent of GDP. Energy investments equal one-fifth on domestic savings in Latin America. Domestic savings are lower than total domestic investment in Africa where the demand for capital for energy investment will amount to almost half of total savings.

Even where domestic savings comfortably exceed the energy sector's investment requirements, energy companies will still have to compete with other sectors for domestic financial resources. Furthermore domestic savings needs to be mobilized through financial markets to route private savings directly to private risk bearers who make long-term investments in energy–power projects. Doing so will require institutions and financing instruments adapted to the varying needs of investors in different types of energy projects and at different stages in a project's life. The benefits of financing private initiatives in energy go beyond the projects involved. Because energy investments command such a large part of a country's investment, improving the efficiency of energy financing will spur the general development of domestic capital markets.

Reliance on foreign savings remains a necessity for many countries with inadequate domestic savings. But there are limits to the capacity of any economy to access funds from abroad, particularly for debt finance. Over-dependence on foreign investment flows can be volatile and currency depreciation can increase the debt burden of borrower countries in case of electricity and downstream gas sectors where the revenues generated are in local currencies. Furthermore, countries that already have a large external debt will face difficulties in securing additional external capital. Overall balance of payments constraints and the sheer size of energy investments imply for most countries that a sustained energy investment program will have to be accompanied by a strategy for mobilizing domestic funds. In turn, an increasing share of domestic savings will need to come from private sources as governments reduce their involvement in energy.

The lack of appropriate mechanisms in domestic financial markets tailored to the needs of energy projects is likely to be more important than the absolute level of funds in many developing countries. Countries with more developed financial sectors provide companies better access to equity, bonds and borrowing. Long-term debt which is more suited to capital intensive energy projects is usually available only in sophisticated financial markets. Companies with access to international markets have a better chance of attracting investors and lenders by signalling their commitment to higher standards of corporate governance, enabling them to lengthen their debt maturity outcome. However, for developing countries with less developed financial markets, long-term local currency financing which is often sought by many electricity and gas utilities is not always available.

Since the crises of the late 1990s, several adjustments to domestic economic balances have reduced demand for external finance. These adjustments in many cases reflect a reduction in debt leverage, particularly in the corporate sector, and the increasing reluctance of borrowers to expose themselves to the risks of borrowing in foreign currency.

Of equal importance has been the development in recent years of deeper domestic capital markets in countries such as Brazil, Chile, India, the Democratic People's Republic of Korea, Malaysia, Mexico and South Africa. Apart from helping reduce their dependency on external finance and thus their exposure to exchange rate and liability mismatches, the development of local bond markets serve several functions, among them mobilizing domestic savings, providing an operational tool for economic management policies and setting benchmarks for a variety of fund allocation functions in the economy. Pension reform has played an important role in developing countries, particularly in developing a large local institutional investor base. Domestic markets provide borrowers with access to financing in local currency, important for borrowers operating in the non-tradable sectors (such as power and renewable energy for domestic consumption) and for sovereign issuers seeking to avoid currency risk[8].

Although energy investments could be a major part of the asset base in capital markets the problem with many domestic markets is the lack of commercially viable investments. Provided the energy enterprises earn reasonable returns and are prudently managed, they can become an important asset in these markets, particularly for institutional savings.

However, as dominant owner and supplier of energy, governments will continue to be major users of funds. To meet the growing needs of energy investment, governments are also creating specialized energy funds, as a

8. World Bank, 2004, *Global Development Finance*, pp 42–3.

transitional measure to make long-term financing available where private financing is not likely to be sufficient.

Synergistic links can develop between private energy projects and domestic financial intermediation through capital markets. Energy–power project developers and private savers share a long-term horizon. Bringing savers and investors together is the task of capital markets. At the same time, the financing of energy projects improves appraisal capabilities and expands risk-diversification possibilities for local commercial banks, equity and bond markets and institutional investors such as insurance companies and pension funds. Exploitation of these links can be promoted through prudent regulation, improved disclosure and reporting standards and the development of credit-rating capabilities and credit risk insurance.

The long-term goal must be to broaden and deepen domestic capital markets so that they can serve as efficient and reliable conduits for energy finance. Getting there will require broad investor participation and a variety of market-making players (brokers, dealers, underwriters and a wide range of financial instruments). In addition, markets require adequate disclosure of information to ensure efficiency and effective laws to safeguard investors.

In most developing countries the informational and contractual preconditions are not in place for efficient private and commercial financing of energy projects. Private institutions such as credit rating agencies and public ones such as regulatory agencies are required to ensure an adequate flow of information to investors, to facilitate monitoring and to discipline management. Financial liberalization and policies to encourage the growth of the formal financial sector will in time help overcome such shortcomings.

What sort of energy systems will the developing countries possess in the early decades of the twenty-first century? The practical challenge in most developing countries is how to manage the transition from the command and control, monopoly and public ownership energy sector to the competitive supply of energy services and private finance. It must be recognized that the energy systems of developing countries remain quite heterogeneous and their economic structures and approaches toward reform and liberalization will continue to differ. Because of these differences in developing countries' economic structures and approaches to development, their energy and financing systems are likely to remain quite diverse over the early decades of the twenty-first century.

There are nevertheless pressures that are leading most developing countries to rethink their ways of doing economic and energy business. One is the internationalization of markets, particularly the globalization of the energy industry and another is the need to adopt to declining multilateral–government–public financing for energy. Consequently, the pressure is on the developing countries to move forward with energy sector reform and liberalization to attract foreign and domestic private finance for increasing access to energy supplies.

A number of developing countries have taken steps to liberalize their financial and energy systems. During the 1990s, many developing countries began to place greater emphasis on market determined pricing, private sector and institutional reforms. Chapter 4 will focus on energy sector reform and liberalization in developing countries in the 1990s, expectations and reality. Chapter 5 will focus on case studies of energy sector reform and liberalization.

CHAPTER 4

WHITHER ENERGY SECTOR REFORM AND LIBERALIZATION IN DEVELOPING COUNTRIES? A REALITY CHECK

Introduction

After 15 years of energy sector reform in OIDC it is now time to assess developing countries' record based on the established guiding principles of energy pricing, regulation, commercialization/ corporatization and privatization and private investment[1] and address the question: whither energy market transition in developing countries?

This chapter first presents the overall status of energy sector reform in developing countries. This is followed by discussions on the progress to date of four specific reform elements of pricing, regulation, commercialization/ privatization and financial reform and private investment in energy. Detailed

1. As discussed in Chapter 3 international development/ financial institutions formulated the guiding principles of energy market transition to facilitate developing countries to abandon the command and control system to embrace the free market. These guiding principles were set out in four publications in the 1990s. These include: *The World Bank's Role in the Electric Power sector; Energy Efficiency and Conservation in the Developing World* (1993); *Rural Energy and Development: improving Energy supplies for Two billion People* (1998); and *Fuel for Thought: a New Environmental Strategy for the Energy Sector* (1999). Together, these papers outline how the WBG has reoriented its energy sector assistance to client countries in its efforts to transition to liberalized global energy market. Regional multilateral financial institutions followed WB's guidelines. The energy practice of the international financial institutions evolved in the 1990s in line with the shift in their portfolio toward sector reform and adjustment.

discussions of selected case studies from East Asia, South Asia, Africa, the Middle East and Latin America to identify issues and lessons to be learned will be undertaken in Chapter 5.

Overall status of energy sector reform in developing countries

As of 2005, over 85 developing countries made energy policy announcements that they have launched energy sector reforms. However, at the global level it is not clear what elements of the four reform components are addressed, what steps have been taken to liberalize energy prices, to regulate energy monopoly segments, to commercialize energy operations and finally to attract private investment to increase access to energy supplies for development.

15 years after the beginning of energy sector reform in more than 85 developing countries, the picture is mixed. In the 1990s, at the top of the reform ladder were a few countries like Argentina, Jordan, China, Malaysia, Philippines and Thailand seriously committed to the reform process. A few other countries in SSA are at the bottom of the reform ladder making loose policy statements of intending to reform the energy sector. A majority of developing countries fall in the varying stages of the middle of the reform ladder launching one or several steps of the reform process.

Given that the international development institutions were the sponsors of energy sector reform and liberalization, by late 1990s they began to take stock of the reform progress and assess the impact of the East Asian financial crisis on the energy sector.

The WB, the main architect of energy sector reform and liberalization prepared a *Report on Energy and Development* (1999)[2] and compiled a scorecard by administering a sample questionnaire to WB staff with experience of the energy sectors covered. The focus of the scoreboard was to monitor six important steps in energy sector reform: four of which made possible the introduction of private sector capital into a sector which had previously been entirely state-owned and two of which actually constitute private involvement. Six central steps of the WB survey include corporatization and commercialization of the state-owned enterprises (SOEs), passage by parliament of an energy law which permits the unbundling and/ or privatization of the sector in part or in whole, establishment of a regulatory body that is separate from the SOEs and from the ministry, restructuring of the SOEs, private sector investment in green field sites and privatization of at least some of the existing SOEs.

---

2. WB/ ESMAP, *Energy and Development Report 1999: Energy After the Financial Crises, A scorecard for Energy Sector Reform in Developing countries* (1999), pp.50–55.

Based on the survey, the WB study finds that:

- Energy sector reform has a long way to go in all sectors except upstream oil and gas, developing countries on average have taken only one-third of possible reform steps.
- Developing countries with private participation in their energy sector are still rare and especially so in Africa and the Middle East.
- Variations between countries in the number of reform steps taken is large.

Table 4.1 presents the overall status of the reform process. It gives the percentage of countries that have launched the reform steps in each of the energy sub-sectors, as well as the overall reform indicator for the sub-sector. The reform indicator for all sub-sectors is around one-third except for upstream oil and gas where it reaches 50 per cent. The higher level of reform steps taken in upstream oil and gas reflects the impact of higher weight of Europe and Central Asia (ECA) countries. Given the risks the state cannot afford the cost of exploration and development, especially offshore oil, private finance has been recognized as essential and it has been allowed into the sub-sector through the use of concessions. This has required the law to be changed and state petroleum companies to be restructured.

Table 4.1 also shows that the reform process is spread unevenly between countries, with upstream oil and gas experiencing the most even pattern. In the power sector, more than one-third of the countries in the sample of 115 had taken none of the reform steps and half had taken only one step. Most reforming countries are less than 10 per cent and these accounted for 30 per cent of all the reform steps that had been taken. This pattern suggests that reform is not a uniform process, but it proceeds rapidly when conditions are favourable and does not even start when conditions are unfavourable.

Table 4.1. Percentages of Developing Countries That Have Taken Reform Steps (number of countries in sample)

Energy sub-sectors	*Commercialization (%)*	*Regulator (%)*	*Private investment (%)*	*Privatization (%)*	*Reform indicator (%)*
Power (115)	44	29	40	25	34
Upstream Oil and gas (49)	67	31	69	14	49
Downstream gas (55)	60	40	27	27	38
Downstream oil refining (57)	54		23	28	35
Downstream oil Wholesale/retail (72)	43			28	32

Source: *WB/ ESMAP, Energy and Development Report* (1999), Table 1, p.52.

Table 4.2 shows the regional picture of the status of reforms in each of the energy sub-sectors. It shows in percentages of the countries in each region which have taken each of the four steps and the reform indicator for each region. Table 4.2 (a) shows that prior to 2001 reform in power was much more advanced in Latin American Countries (LAC) than in other parts of the world with 71 per cent of the key steps taken. Africa, Europe and the Middle East and North Africa (MNA) lagged behind with 15 per cent and 17 per cent, respectively. East and South Asia fall in the middle of the reform ladder at 41 per cent and 50 per cent, respectively.

The regional picture of the reform status among the energy sub-sectors is different for upstream oil and gas and other sub-sectors. In all regions the overall indicator for upstream oil and gas is around 50 and in Africa it is 59, reflecting the willingness of oil and gas producing countries to allow private investment. In downstream gas the LAC region with a high overall indicator of 63 per cent reflects success of the reform process with the implementation of number of reform steps including privatization. Other regions show little private investment and almost no privatization of existing assets.

The reform effort in oil refining is low in Africa, MNA and LAC. The downstream oil market is different from the upstream oil sector. Nearly one-third of the developing countries have had private participation in this sector. Where this is not the case, the willingness to privatize oil downstream activity is low. This contrast with the pattern in the upstream oil and gas sector where LAC has the highest proportion of privatization. This is because of the perception that it is a 'strategic' sector and the governments' concern to safeguard security of oil supplies. In many other countries such as India, the private sector is allowed to enter the oil distribution business. However, with the liberalization of oil prices in these countries privatization of the profitable, revenue-generating state-owned distribution companies is still under debate.

Table 4.2: Percentages of Developing Countries in Each Region That Have Taken Reform Steps (number of countries in the region)

(a) Power:					
Region (no. of countries)	Africa (AFR) (48)	East Asia & Pacific (EAP)(9)	LAC(18)	MNA(8)	South Asia (SRA) (5)
Commercialization	31	44	61	25	40
Regulator	8	11	83	0	40
Generation-Privatization	4	22	39	13	40
Distribution Privatization	4	11	44	13	20
Private investment(IPPs)	19	78	83	13	100
Reform indicator	15	41	71	17	50

(b) Upstream oil and gas					
Region (no.of countries):	AFR(11)	EAP(5)	LAC(8)	MNA(5)	SAR(3)
Commercialization	73	80	63	80	33
Regulator	36	40	50	0	33
Privatization	9	0	38	0	0
Private investment (concession)	91	40	63	80	67
Reform indicator	59	47	50	43	50
(c) Downstream gas					
Region (no.of countries)	AFR(6)	EAP(4)	LAC(9)	MNA(6)	SAR(3)
Commercialization	33	100	56	50	100
Regulator	33	25	78	0	33
Privatization	17	0	56	0	0
Private investment	33	25	56	0	33
Reform indicator	31	38	63	11	50
(d) Oil Refining					
Region(no. of countries)	AFR(11)	EAP(4)	LAC(11)	MNA(6)	SAR(3)
Commercialization	55	75	45	33	67
Privatization	0	50	18	17	33
Private investment	18	50	9	0	33
Reform indicator	24	58	24	17	44
(e) Downstream oil					
Region(no. of countries)	AFR(17)	EAP(8)	LAC(11)	MNA(5)	SAR(5)
Commercialization	29	50	36	40	60
Privatization	24	0	18	40	20
Price liberalization	6	13	45	0	0
Reform indicator	20	21	33	27	27
(f) Global (39%) Percentage of maximum	(32%)	(41%)	(53%)	(23%)	(46%)

Source: *WB/ ESMAP, Energy and Development Report* (1999), Tables 2 and 4, pp. 53–5.

Despite the varying number of country responses to different sub-sectors, an aggregate picture obtained by pooling the reform indicator scores globally and by regions gives the 'overall' reform indicator expressed as a percentage of the maximum possible[3]. Table 4.2 (f) shows the global and regional overall indicator. The overall reform indicator for all countries including transition economies in ECA and all energy sub-sectors is 39 per cent, indicating that globally, less than half the key steps for energy sector reform have yet been taken. With the exclusion of the ECA countries, the overall reform indicator would be around 30 per cent, indicating less than one-third of the key reform steps have yet been taken in developing countries.

3. World Bank, ESMAP, 1999, *Energy and Development Report*, pp.54–5.

Ten years since the beginning of energy sector transition in early 1990s, only 10 per cent of the developing countries accounted for having taken most of the reform steps.

Despite the fact that the WB study on a scorecard for energy sector reform in developing countries provides a basis for assessing the energy sector reform status in developing countries, the WB survey has a number of limitations:

First, it is a sample survey and the samples vary for different sub-sectors—ranging from a high of 115 countries for power to 49 for upstream oil and gas, 55 for downstream gas, 57 for refining and 72 for downstream oil, both wholesale and retail. With the exclusion of transition economies in ECA, the number of developing countries surveyed falls to 78 for power, 32 for upstream oil and gas, 28 for downstream gas, 35 for oil refining and 46 for downstream oil, both wholesale and retail. The survey with the exception of power has a larger weight for ECA countries and exercises its influence on the reform indicator for developing countries.

Second, the sample survey reform scorecard focuses mainly on private capital and ignores the energy pricing policy element—the key driver for success of all the six steps making up the scorecard. As it will be shown in the following sections of Chapter 4 and Chapter 5, energy pricing continues to be the key ingredient for reform progress and liberalization of the energy sector.

Third, the WB energy reform scorecard documents taking of the six steps in percentages, which could simply mean making policy statements. For example, establishment of a regulatory body that is separate from the SOEs and from the ministry could be effected by a mere announcement by a government decree, but assessment of how the regulatory body is set up and how it is functioning and with what results on the ground are critical to reform the sector. The percentage documentation based on journalistic type staff survey fails to assess the status of the results of the launched reform elements in achieving the reform objectives.

Finally, the study assumes perfect correlation between reform and private investment in energy sector and fails to consider macro–sector linkage, financial sector and energy sector linkage, market failure and other barriers such as the market size and multinational energy companies' investment behaviour. Furthermore, each developing region, East Asia, South Asia, Africa, the Middle East and Latin America and each country in these regions started the course of energy market transition with a different history, a different energy resource base, different human skills and a different political and institutional setup. In addition, the severe bumps experienced by developing countries in the aftermath of the East Asian financial crisis in 1998 and events since 2001 raise questions on the impact of financial crisis on energy sector reform.

Although prior to 2000, Latin America, EAP and SAR achieved about 50 per cent, 41 per cent and 46 per cent of the maximum reform efforts respectively, countries in these regions are affected by the events since 2001. EAP countries are trying to recover from the financial crises of the late 1990s. Countries in LAC such as Argentina and Brazil are yet to recover from the macro-economic adjustment problems since 2001 to be on the path of successful energy market transition. Countries in Africa and the Middle East have lagged behind with less than 33 per cent and 25 per cent of the steps taken. Discussions of case studies in Chapter 5 will present some of these barriers in selected country experiences.

The failures of many developing countries to take the required reform steps go deeper to a misunderstanding of a market economy and the basis for institutional reform process. A process of energy sector reform modelled on shock therapy has underestimated the information problems, institutional reforms, bureaucratic barriers, human infallibility and opportunistic behaviour and politics of the reform process itself. The expectations of politicians that the preparation of rightly worded policy statements on energy sector liberalization would lead to the flow of private investment to increase access to energy supplies have proven illusory in many developing countries. Policy makers in developing countries expected that by waving the magic wand of policy statement, private investors would instantaneously facilitate the flow of private investment into energy sector.

Even countries in Latin America—for example Argentina, considered the best practice model in energy market transition—and East Asia face difficult challenges to move forward. Understanding these challenges requires addressing the key issues associated with energy reform in the context of broader principles of global energy market and the reform process. The following sections of Chapter 4 will discuss the status of four elements of energy sector reform—energy pricing, regulation, institutional and financial and investment reforms to date.

Energy pricing reform

Energy pricing continues to be the chronic issue for decision makers in developing countries. Lower international oil prices in the mid-1980s offered some short-term relief. However, the gap between domestic and international prices and/ or costs of the two oil price shocks of 1973 and 1979 and relative price distortions between different forms of energy have not been significantly altered. Governments have been reluctant to price energy to reflect its economic cost because of their concerns about the adverse effects of energy price increases on industrial competitiveness, house hold budgets especially those of low income families and on inflation in terms of both its direct economic effects and its longer term social and political ramifications.

Prices of energy products, both for appraisal of energy investment projects and for the market-place, are a central tool of energy policy. The optimum choice of project design and development strategy hinges upon using the appropriate price of energy inputs in the selection process. In the market-place, adequate price incentives must be provided to producers to attract investment to encourage exploration, development and production of domestic supplies of oil, gas, coal, hydropower and other energy resources. Energy prices should encourage energy consumers—many of whom are producers of other goods—to use energy efficiently and to have the choice to select the right form of energy for their particular needs.

Successful energy market transition in developing countries depends on implementing market energy pricing principles to encourage investment to increase access to efficient energy supplies. This section discusses the economic pricing principles of crude oil, petroleum products, natural gas and electric power in formulating energy pricing reform. It then sets out to examine the experience of developing countries in implementing energy pricing reform in the context of energy market transition[4].

Economic theory and energy pricing principles

'Price' in economic theory is of three kinds. First, the market price, which means the current rate of exchange of money against goods. Second, the 'competitive supply price' that needs to be paid to bring forth the stream of outputs. And third, the 'reference price' that measures the expected benefit of the investment against its cost. Under perfect competition, the price-production system is in complete equilibrium and there is no incentive to increase or decrease the output. The study of the real market is a study of how these prices diverge and of the forces generated thereby.

In the real world divergence occurs all the time due to human behaviour and changes in expectations and technology. Demand may be greater than expected, raising market price. Conversely, demand may be lower than expected, lowering market price. The second basic reason for divergence is market control and how the market structure functions. Whether it is a monopoly, or group monopoly, or oligopoly or a competitive market. Understanding of these pricing principles as applied to different forms of energy is critical for formulating energy pricing policies.

4. Vedavalli Rangaswamy, 'Domestic Energy Pricing Policies, *World Bank Energy Series Paper*, No. 13, Washington D.C. (April, 1989)

Crude oil pricing

For nearly 40 years after the end of World War II crude oil was priced in cargo lots free on board (FOB) point of shipment, leaving the buyer with responsibility for transport and insurance to the refinery. So each crude stream, defined in terms of specific gravity and sulphur content, had its own price. The original system whereby oil companies 'posted' their prices (which were subjected to discounting for quantity) was superseded in the 1970s by a structure of government sales prices, all fixed in relation to an OPEC-determined quotation for the 'marker' crude (Arabian Light). In fixing the relationship between a given crude and the marker, account was taken of location relative to main markets, product yield pattern and quality difference such as sulphur and wax contents.

The second stage in the price fixing process was that of agreeing differentials for all other crude oils. Ideally, these should accurately reflect the preference of refiners which change from time to time and vary between different markets. In practice, it was seldom possible to avoid a mismatch between the government administered price structure and the preference of refiners, a difference, which created marketing problems for some sellers. The difficulty of maintaining accurate differentials was aggravated by the excess supply, which was constantly pressing on the market. In the autumn of 1985 the traditional system was tacitly abandoned.

The situation in 1985 was that in the prevailing oversupply situation the attempt to maintain prices at too high a level had forced exporters to make production cuts that were deemed to be unacceptable. Under these circumstances a number of OPEC oil exporters adopted 'netback pricing', which relates the price paid for each consignment of crude oil to the value of products derived from it. In principle, the concept of netback pricing seemed simple but turned out to be complicated in application. Given the uniqueness of each contract, the agreed terms were generally confidential and the exporter did not know at the time of the sale what price he eventually receives.

From the buyers' (refiners') standpoint the new system removed the risk of loss that could previously result from a drop in the spot price of the crude while on its way from shipment port to refinery. With a guaranteed margin written into the contract, some loss-making refineries became profitable once again. The fact that the new system substituted term sales for spot sales was thought to be a stabilizing factor. But nothing could disguise the fact that the buyers' price gain was the sellers' loss. Netback pricing was essentially a sophisticated mechanism for price discounting to boost sales. It soon became apparent that the extra exports had been secured at a heavy cost in terms of reduced crude oil revenues.

As oil exporting countries competed with one another by offering more and more favourable netback arrangements—including substantially discounted netback prices—the market collapsed. Oil prices fell under US $10 in December 1998. In real terms prices were at their lowest levels since 1973. Nonetheless, since 1973 international crude oil prices have been kept well above the costs of production because of output restraint by OPEC countries. In 2001, OPEC established a price band of $22 to $28 per barrel for its crude oil and it then seemed determined to adjust output to keep prices within these limits.

However, the Iraq war of 2003 followed by terrorist attacks in post-war Iraq leading to volatility in crude oil prices in May–June 2004 have added terror premium in crude oil prices and have raised concerns on security of supplies and future price of crude oil[5]. The 28 June 2004 handover of sovereignty though a step in the right direction has still not contained the violence and security continues to be a major threat to Iraqi oil supplies. Uncertainties of events unfolding in Iraq including the success of Iraqi government to establish security impact the Middle East and will influence the world oil market and future behaviour of international crude oil prices for oil exporters and importers.

The refined products price structure: Basic economics of joint supply in refining

Refining of crude oil will be done so long as the 'refining margin', the receipts cover the total costs including the necessary return on investment are covered. A given price or margin may at any given time be temporarily below or above the level necessary to bring forth reliable supply of the product at the current rate of output. Individual petroleum products are joint products and therefore refining costs are joint costs at first cut of the refining operation. If and when a refinery is working at less than optimum capacity, an additional barrel can be refined at a lower cost below the average cost. Conversely, when a refinery is at maximum output the cost of refining of additional barrel rises higher than the average cost because of additional storage cost, lack of normal downtime for maintenance, clearing and repair and product quality differentials, etc.

In general, incremental cost rising with higher output gives the signal to plan for expanding of refining capacity. Thus, the reckoning of short-term incremental cost—that of making the optimum choice given the present capacity—is replaced by considering long-run incremental cost—that of adding the best type and amount of additional capacity either in a new refinery or expanding the capacity of the existing refinery. In an expanding economy its incremental cost is a mixture of short- and long-term and is

5. Chapter 2.

higher than the current or future incremental cost at optimum levels of output. But even with no pressure on the price of the whole output, there can surely be a surplus of any particular product available at a very low incremental cost.

When products are joint in variable proportions, the incremental cost of a single joint product does exist within certain limits even if its average cost does not. For example, heavy fuel oil (HFO) is a simple combustible which is worth no more than any other source of heat, allowance being made for handling costs a little lower than coal and a little higher than gas. All other refined products have higher value uses with no near substitutes. Therefore, the HFO price cannot go appreciably above the price of crude oil, for if it did consumers would burn the crude oil. But the HFO price can go to zero or even below (if natural gas were available at very low prices, HFO's value would be negative since there would be a cost of disposal). The incremental cost of more severe cracking would then be in part offset by saving in disposal cost, in addition to the value of higher products secured.

The prices of other petroleum products cannot go below the price of crude, for then it would not pay to refine them out. They would have only fuel value. Therefore, the basic rule where refining margins are competitively determined is that the more the prices of other products above crude oil, the more is HFO below it. Conversely, the nearer the prices of other products to their lower limit (the prices of crude oil), the closer is HFO to its upper limit. It is competition which keeps the price of HFO below that of crude in equilibrium in the long run.

Determination of ex-refinery prices[6]

Import Parity principle includes landed cost of products:

(i) FOB prices
(ii) Marine freight from the source of import to the ports
(iii) Marine insurance
(iv) Ocean loss
(v) Basic custom duties and surcharges
(vi) Wharfage or river dues
(vii) Other compulsory landing charges, such as charges for pumping, customs, supervision, etc

The total cost of all these items constitute landed cost. To this should be added transport, marketing and distribution charges to arrive at the selling

6. R Vedavalli, *Private Investment and Economic Development: a case study of India in Petroleum* (Cambridge University Press, 1976)

price, the advantage of import parity ex-refinery pricing is that it provides a reasonable incentive to maintain internationally competitive standards of efficiency in operating domestic refineries in developing countries.

There are two disadvantages. First, problems posed by the existence of inland refineries. Second, parity pricing could include elements that unjustifiably raise the ceiling of ex-refinery prices. The main thrust of the argument here is what actually imported is crude oil, while freight charges, which are higher for products than for crude oil are charged. Furthermore, import parity does not pay attention to the actual cost of production of domestic refineries. 'Cost-plus pricing' provides an alternative to import parity pricing. Cost-plus pricing includes cost of crude oil plus a refiner's margin to cover the operating cost as well as a reasonable profit margin. Cost-plus pricing raises two basic issues. First is the problem of deriving a price structure which ensures a reasonable profit margin to refiners ensuring compatibility between the pattern of refinery production and consumption. Given the joint-cost structure of the refining industry, the best that can be attempted is to relate total costs to the total value of products to ensure adequate profit margin. The relative price structure has to be set taking into consideration the actual consumption pattern in such a way that the ultimate price structure will minimize product imbalances and maximize the net-back value. Second problem with the cost-plus pricing is the tendency towards pushing costs and higher prices. A cost-plus system of pricing has an inherent defect in reducing the incentive to efficient costs, particularly if the demand for the product is relatively inelastic. From the economic efficiency considerations cost-plus pricing is not an effective substitute to parity pricing.

Modification to parity pricing

The main thrust of the argument against import parity pricing is that it contributes to an inflation of ex-refinery prices, because of the difference between freight rates, wharfage and other landing charges allowed for products in the calculation of import parity prices, while these charges actually incurred are for imports of crude oil. These over-pricing differentials can be eliminated by substituting the charges applicable to the importation of crude. In this way a modified parity formula may be retained to include FOB prices of products and all other elements in the parity formula fixed at the rates applicable to the importation of crude oil with the exception of custom duties.

The rationale for allowing domestic refineries to price their products ex-refinery on a modified import parity basis is that it would allow them to earn a refiner's margin similar to that applicable to the international refineries assuming comparable levels of efficiency in refinery operations. This would also conform to sequencing of the liberalization of petroleum product selling prices.

Natural gas pricing

An appropriate pricing strategy for natural gas should aim to maximization of net benefits to the country from the use of its exhaustible natural gas resources. This strategy has three important dimensions, each of which implies certain pricing principles. First, there must be adequate incentive to explore for and produce natural gas. Particularly, encouraging private investment to natural gas development and production requires the provision of an appropriate pricing and regulatory/contractual framework. Second, there must be an incentive to promote efficient use of gas. And third, natural gas market development in developing countries should be rapid to match supply and demand for gas.

The basic pricing principle that facilitates the achievement of all the above three objectives is that both producer and consumer prices should be set near the marginal opportunity cost of natural gas. Excess producers' or consumers' surplus ('excess profits') should be captured through profit taxation. In practice, this approach is complicated by uncertainties affecting size of gas reserves and growth of the rate of natural gas market. However, a first step is to focus on determining the opportunity cost of gas under assumed conditions of known (predictable) supply and demand. Marginal economic cost of supply provides a lower boundary to pricing of gas. In countries with a large gas surplus, prices would be close to the marginal cost, while in gas deficit countries prices would include a larger depletion allowance.

Marginal cost principle for pricing natural gas

Following gas discovery, the immediate concern in many developing countries has been whether or not the gas is exportable as the domestic market may not yet be explored and developed. In developing countries generally natural gas development to meet domestic demand has been slow. The major reasons include lack of strong regulatory/ institutional setups to integrate the activities of production, transmission and distribution companies and consumers. Exploration and development have also been delayed due to the lack of a pricing agreement with producers. Furthermore, the analysis of gas supply, demand and delivery costs to domestic markets in developing countries has been limited. Countries began in the 1990s to appreciate that natural gas can be supplied to domestic markets at costs that compete with other fuels.

Since gas is not directly tradable in many developing countries and it could be used in the domestic market either as a substitute for imported fuel and/ or for new uses, it may need to be priced on the principle of the long-run marginal cost (LRMC) that could be below the opportunity cost of alternative fuels. The pricing of gas, however, requires extensions to the LRMC to allow for the exhaustible nature of natural gas and meet financial cost coverage, and income distribution objectives. They can also be used for inter-fuel cost comparisons to decide whether it is economical to develop natural gas. The LRMC of gas is useful in negotiating prices with producers and transmission companies and consumers. The LRMC approach is therefore an explicit framework for investment decisions regarding natural gas supply.

Characteristics of natural gas marginal costs

In principle, LRMC is the incremental cost of optimum adjustments in the gas system operations to meet small increments of demand. This approach estimates marginal costs of serving different consumers at different times in different regions. In practice, the major difficulty in the analysis of gas costs is that natural gas development and transport is subject to economies of scale and requires large and indivisible investments. Investments in gas infrastructure, following gas discovery are incurred at discrete stages. Costs of initial field development such as drilling and equipping gas fields, gas processing facilities and transmission are a high proportion of the overall lifetime costs.

A gas supply system can be divided into four interrelated stages. First, the exploration stage which establishes the level of proven reserves and their commerciability. Exploration costs include an estimate of finding cost of natural gas. Second, the development and production stage requires large indivisible investments for development drilling, field preparation, field gathering, compression, separation of natural gas liquids and treatment of gas to produce pipeline quality gas to meet contract volume, quality and pressure requirements. The third stage is the transmission of gas from the field of gas treatment plant to the city gate. Investments in transmission facilities are lumpy and costs are subject to significant economies of scale until the maximum capacity of pipeline is reached. The fourth stage is distribution to end-users.

Production of the first increment of gas thus requires a large initial expenditure in exploration, development and transmission. Production of additional volumes requires additional investment expenditures until maximum capacity is reached. Thereafter, indivisibilities and diminishing returns in providing gas to meet demand lead to additional discrete investments and raise marginal costs.

The characteristics of investment in natural gas development and transport for a given field imply that the marginal cost curve falls sharply for relatively low volumes of recovery and rises as cumulative production increases to over 60 per cent of estimated recoverable reserves. Because of capital indivisibilities, costs will be marginal at some time and non-marginal at others. The resulting large cost fluctuations could cause price changes over time that would not be acceptable to consumers. Therefore, a definition of LRMC that fits the structure of investments in gas development and transport is required. Costs must be estimated within a sufficiently long-run framework to incorporate the investment process.

The Average Incremental Cost (AIC) concept

The AIC definition of marginal cost provides a framework for pricing of non-tradable natural gas for domestic consumption in developing countries. The AIC smoothes out the indivisibilities in expenditures. It also reflects the general level of and trend of future costs that will have to be incurred as gas consumption increases. The AIC takes a longer view of costs and looks beyond the next increment in capacity. This is important as many developing countries are still at an early stage of gas development and expect a large potential shift in demand for gas.

The AIC is estimated by discounting all incremental costs that will be incurred in future to provide and maintain the estimated amount of natural gas required over a specified period and dividing it by the discounted volume of incremental output over this time. The time stream of expenditure for providing, maintaining and running the system corresponds to a set output over time[7].

$$AICo = \frac{\sum_{t=1}^{T} (It + (Rt - R0)) / (1 + i)t}{\sum_{t=1}^{T} (Qt - Q0) / (1 + i)t}$$

'It' is the capital costs in year *t*; Qt is the natural gas production in year t resulting from the investment; Rt is the operating and maintenance costs in year *t*; *i* is the opportunity cost of capital; *T* is the time horizon for development as well as a 20 year production life ($t = 0$) is the base year.

---

7. For producing fields with a declining production profile the formula has to be adjusted to estimate the incremental production due to the investment as the difference between the two production profiles with and without the investments (Qt-Qt1), where Qt is the production without the investment; the operating and maintenance costs should also be similarly adjusted.

Determination of marginal cost of supply requires agreement on the production profile in the denominator based on credible demand forecasts and supply potential to plan the least cost investment plan. In addition, the crucial question is what system of expansion should be designed to deliver gas to consumers at the least possible cost. The numerator is the present value of the least cost investment stream as well as incremental operating and maintenance costs necessary to start production and to increase production to the optimum capacity and maintain it at that level. This least cost expansion plan to meet projected demand is determined assuming a target level of system reliability. Once the price of gas is determined and the gas system begins to operate, actual consumption may be different from demand estimates and consequently costs will have to be revised.

The AIC, however, is only one of the criteria used to determine the price of natural gas. Appropriate pricing strategy for natural gas must allow for distortions because of externalities, taxes, monopoly practices, duties and subsidies as well as the objectives of financial viability and income distribution. It must also be adjusted because gas is an exhaustible resource and therefore has a depletion value that should be reflected in its pricing.

Marginal economic cost of supply provides a lower boundary to prices. In countries with large gas surplus, prices would be close to the marginal cost while in gas deficit countries prices would include a larger depletion allowance.

Three basic principles can be used to delineate appropriate range of gas prices. First, the upper limit of delivered prices should be set equal to the economic costs (at shadow prices) of the next best alternative fuel delivered to the particular user. Second, gas should not be sold at a delivered price lower than its full marginal economic cost of supply. Third, revenue flows to both gas producing and supplying companies or agencies should be high enough to cover their full accounting costs, including depreciation and sufficient return on capital to keep them financially viable.

These principles set forth price ranges but do not determine specific prices *per se*. They help in setting the outer bounds, which are basically determined by the opportunity cost of alternative resource uses and availabilities and the principles of economic and financial viability. As applied to natural gas pricing, these pricing principles provide a viable approach to ensure that the benefits of expenditures in the sector exceed costs.

The gas transmission and distribution services are similar to other utility services where the use of marginal cost pricing is prevalent. Regulatory or institutional institutions are required to rational pricing of monopoly segments of gas industry and to encourage competition in natural gas supply.

Electric power pricing[8]

LRMC was used as a concept to provide price signals in electric power sector in developing countries. LRMC as a concept aimed to provide price signals for an effective tariff structure and for identifying new investments in the electricity sector. However, in practice, price setting in the electric power sector rarely fully reflects LRMC principles. At best, electricity tariffs are often targeted only to reflect an average of the power system's LRMC. Pricing distortions in the electric power sector continue to exist because of cross subsidies and failure to reflect economic fuel costs or the real cost of capital that do not reflect the costs of supply. Consequently, many power utilities continue to be economically and financially nonviable and a drag on the national budget.

Mobilizing additional resources for investment, facilitating a competitive environment, improving efficiency and developing financially viable power sectors require that electricity pricing be moved toward commercial practices. Pricing policies should be flexible so that power enterprises can respond to changes in competition, economic activity and resource costs.

The regulatory authority must provide power enterprises with clear pricing guidelines that reflect the sometimes conflicting objectives of (a) a commercially based allocation of costs among consumers according to the burdens they impose on the system; (b) assurance of a reasonable degree of price stability; (c) power tariffs that generate sufficient revenues to meet the financial requirements of the sector and (d) a tariff structure simple enough to facilitate metering and billing.

Power entities need to be encouraged to be more market oriented in setting prices and to offer a variety of pricing and service options that reflect the actual costs of providing service to customers. Aggressive load management programs should be put in place with peak-load and time-of-use pricing, as well as prices that reflect different voltages, consumer classes, and levels of reliability and availability. Large consumer needs to be given the opportunity to negotiate prices and service options directly with power suppliers. Cross-subsidies that make competition more difficult, promote inefficiencies and lessen accountability should be eliminated. Countries with relatively undeveloped power markets are required, at a minimum, to put in place long-run incremental cost-based pricing that incorporates simple time-of-use elements to meet the financial objectives of utilities.

A framework of regulatory incentives can include price capping to support competition and induce efficiency. Multipart (declining block) tariffs above short-term marginal costs could be considered for the non-

8. WB, *The World Bank's Role in the Electric Power Sector, A World Bank Policy Paper*, (Washington D.C. 1993).

competitive segments if the greater revenue requirements for financial viability would cause unacceptable welfare losses under linear tariffs. Pricing of electric power should be regarded as a commercial issue and governments need to legislate fair entry conditions for private entities to supply power and related services.

Implementation of energy pricing reform

Given the context of globalization and the need for transition to a liberalized energy market, governments in developing countries have addressed the issue of reforming energy prices at macro, sector and end-user levels. At the macro-level energy pricing reform becomes part of the macroeconomic adjustment process requiring elimination of subsidies and generation of revenues reflecting market prices.

At the sector level, energy pricing reform objectives include achieving economic and financial viabilities and encouraging public–private investment in energy sub-sectors to increase access to energy supplies. Pricing reform needs to address both absolute and relative prices of different forms of energy, such as petroleum, natural gas and renewables, with special emphasis on interactions among different sub-sectors and their linkages. Finally, at the disaggregated end-user level, energy pricing reform needs to focus on economic-efficient energy pricing ensuring access to reliable energy supplies.

Formulation of appropriate pricing policies reconciling efficiency, financial viability and equity objectives and their effective implementation require interaction at all three levels. Energy pricing reform in developing countries is complicated by the fact that energy price setting has been typically the responsibility of the government rather than energy enterprises. In setting energy prices governments have given greater weight to industrial competitiveness, impact on household budgets, socio-political objectives and inflation, than economic efficiency, financial viability and market considerations. Lower international oil prices since 1986 have narrowed the gap between domestic energy prices and their economic costs. However, energy pricing reform continues to be the major issue of energy market transition to attract the flow of private investment.

The primary challenge in developed countries in terms of energy pricing reform is usually to bring prices down to the competitive cost of service. However, in developing countries the challenges are to set energy prices to reflect the full economic cost of delivering efficient and reliable service and to ensure collection of payments from all consumers of energy. Successful transition to global energy market requires liberalization of energy prices. As discussed in the foregoing sections of this chapter, by the end of 1990s, 45 per cent of the countries in LAC, 13 per cent in EAP and only 6 per cent in

AFR took steps to free petroleum prices[9]. Less than 40 per cent of the developing countries took steps to set up regulatory agencies to reform pricing of power and natural gas. The following section presents developing countries' experience in energy pricing reform and identifies critical issues of energy pricing reform process.

Developing countries' experience to date

Following the oil price increases of 1973 and 1979, OIDC began taking steps at the macro-, sector and end-use consumer levels to adjust energy prices, particularly those of some petroleum products to reflect market prices. Since the 1990s, more than 50 per cent of all developing countries took steps to reform energy pricing in some form or other. Despite falling oil prices since 1986, with the exception of a few, energy prices in both oil importing and exporting countries still do not cover economic costs[10]. Cross-subsidization of petroleum products and electric power persist. Some progress has been achieved in pricing of natural gas by pegging gas prices to the price of fuel oil. In major coal producing developing countries such as China and India, steps are being taken to price domestic coal to reflect its economic cost.

Oil exporting developing countries in general continued to price energy below the market price. For example, as of 2000, energy prices in the Islamic Republic of Iran were below border prices. Energy prices are still substantially below market prices and do not meet the macro/ sector objectives of eliminating subsidies and financial viability[11]. Other oil exporters such as Indonesia and Mexico discussed below show a similar pattern.

Latin American countries such as Argentina, Brazil and Chile liberalized and deregulated energy prices. Argentina privatized most of its assets, including its largest oil and gas company, its electricity generation plants and most of its gas and electricity distribution grid. In the electricity market, generation, transmission and distribution were unbundled and government took steps to promote competition.

The residential customers in Argentina experienced price decreases and an improvement in their services since the liberalization of the sector in the 1990s. By the mid-1990s, Argentina served as the showcase of best practice for energy liberalization in developing countries. However, the collapse of the Argentine economy in 2001 and the renewed struggle to rebuild the economy have raised critical issues for energy sector pricing reforms and financial viability of energy enterprises. The effects of the crisis in Argentina

9. See Table 4.2 above in Chapter 4.
10. See Chapter 3,
11. WEC, *Pricing energy in Developing countries* (London, June 2001) p.47.

have also been felt throughout the Mercosur community[12].
Brazil's efforts to liberalize energy prices and its removal of subsidies contributed to inflation, which was exacerbated by the electricity crisis of 2001 caused by severe draught. Electricity prices became extremely volatile. The Spot price for electricity was more than $200 per MWH in July 2001, but fell to less than $4 per MWH in May 2002. Brazil continues to stay on the course of energy pricing reform. Prices for all energy products are expected to reflect international price trends more closely.

Mexico's energy policy aims to achieve a competitive pricing policy. However, in practice public sector firms dominate the energy sector in Mexico as it needs to address the challenge of liberalizing energy prices to attract private investment. Energy prices are not set based on the cost of supply, but based on their impact on inflation and national budget constraints. Although energy prices continue to be adjusted (almost every month in some cases) these prices do not fully reflect trends in market prices.

Mexico's efforts to restructure its electricity industry require tariffs to be determined by the market. Generators are expected to submit their offers for sale of electricity one day prior to dispatch and the minimum price they are prepared to accept for their supplies. These offers will be used to form a supply curve. The accepted offer (at which demand equals supply) determines the price payable to all generators.

In case the system faces transmission constraints, the prices will be determined for each of the locations depending on the cost at which a generator can produce for a particular location. The government is also proposing a capacity payment for generators to make sure that the country has sufficient capacity for meeting the peak demand.

Mexico continues to offer subsidies estimated at US $3 billion to certain customer segments. Energy pricing reforms intend to make them transparent and identify the level of subsidies for each segment specifically. The government plans to provide customers with information about the level of subsidies through their monthly bills.

A major issue facing Mexico in its efforts to liberalize energy prices is that of linking domestic prices of energy to the prices in the USA The main problem in linking Mexican energy prices to those in the USA is that in many situations the consumers feel that they end up paying higher energy prices that will not reflect the cost of its surplus domestic energy resources. Mexico's challenge to successful energy market transition will be that of reconciling the welfare objectives with those of liberalization of energy prices to attract much needed investment.

In the EAP region, about 13 per cent of the countries actually took steps

---

12. The common market of South America, Mercousur's members are Argentina, Brazil, Paraguay, with Chile and Bolivia as associated members.

between 1992 and 1998 to free petroleum prices. More than 50 per cent of EAP countries have taken steps to reduce subsidies for power and natural gas. The financial crisis of late 1990s and its impact on EAP economies have affected energy pricing reform in EAP countries. Results to date of the status of energy price liberalization varies among EAP countries.

China has a long tradition of energy subsidies. However, the pricing system evolved in recent years reflects better the underlying costs and prices on international markets although government authorities are still responsible for setting most of the fuel prices. Coal prices were largely deregulated in 2002. The price of coal from small municipal mines as well as state and provincial mines is now determined by negotiations between competing producers and industrial end users and distributors.

Oil prices are more aligned with international levels. Since 1998, domestic crude oil producers and refiners have been free to negotiate the price of crude delivered to refineries. When they cannot reach agreement, the State Development Planning Commission (SDPC) intervenes to set the price. SDPC also sets base prices for retail sales of gasoline and diesel. Since October 2001, these prices have been based on spot prices on the Singapore, New York and Rotterdam markets. Oil companies are allowed to set retail prices within a range of 8 per cent either side of the base prices. All controls over oil pricing are expected to be removed by 2010.

There is a dual-pricing system for natural gas. Wellhead and retail prices are fixed for gas from projects launched before 1995. In principle, prices for gas from projects begun after 1995 vary from project to project according to development costs, including a 12 per cent rate of return. These prices are adjusted periodically in line with the prices of competing fuels and inflation. SDPC is considering further reforms to allow prices to reflect more accurately the difference in demand profile among buyers, changes in market conditions and project-specific costs.

Retail electricity prices are set by the electricity distributors but must be approved by the government. Up to the early 1980s, they were controlled directly by the government and covered only a small percentage of supply costs. To date, they are in line with or higher than LRMC in most cases. However, pricing is still inefficient. Wholesale tariffs paid by distributors to independent generators under long-term agreements take no account of seasonal or time-of-day variations in system load. As a result, generating capacity is not always dispatched in an economic way[13]. Transmission is not priced as a separate service and costs are not fully reflected in consumer prices. This has restricted power trade among the provinces and encouraged over-building of generating capacity. China expects to remain on the course of energy pricing reform to reflect fully the economic costs of supply and

13. WB, *Fostering Competition in China's Power Markets* (Washington DC, 2001)

follow trends in international energy prices by 2010.

In Indonesia, energy prices are still heavily subsidized. Macro economic reforms negotiated with the IMF have reduced the subsidies on oil products and electricity. Domestic prices of petroleum products, like gasoline, kerosene and industrial diesel oil were on average, 43 per cent of international prices in 2000. In January 2002 an automatic price adjustment system was introduced. Under the system, Pertamina, the state-owned oil company, resets domestic oil products prices at 75 per cent of international prices every month. The price of kerosene for households is an exception. It is set at around 63 per cent of the international price. Natural gas prices are also kept below economic costs. Fuel switching to gas has been limited.

Since the economic crisis, as part of the macro/structural adjustment program the state-owned electricity company has received direct subsidies from the government and electricity consumers have been paying less than actual cost. Energy pricing reform is expected to continue through 2010.

In the South Asian region over 50 per cent of the countries have taken steps to adjust electricity tariffs to reflect costs. However, cross-subsidization between different categories continues and problems of business fundamentals, such as collection of tariff payments and electricity thefts, continue to undermine the commercial viability of state electricity entities. As of 1998, none of the South Asian countries took steps to free petroleum product prices[14]. However, since 2000 India has taken important steps towards removing price controls on oil, coal and lowering subsidies to energy. Coal prices were decontrolled in 2000 and there are no longer any direct subsidies to coal production or consumption. Delivered coal prices, nonetheless remain below market levels due to continuing subsidies on rail transportation. In April 2002 the Indian government completed the dismantling of the Administered Pricing Mechanism (APM) for oil products and natural gas and the removal of all subsidies, except for those on kerosene and LPG used by households. Consumer prices for coal, oil products and gas are expected to follow international prices.

Indian electricity sector is heavily subsidized. On average, retail electricity tariffs cover less than 70 per cent of real costs. About half of electricity sales are in fact billed, and only about one-third of the bills are regularly paid for, mainly because of theft and corruption. The central and state governments are making announcements to address these problems as part of the broader restructuring of the power industry. But electricity pricing reform has been blocked mainly because of politics of power in the states.

In the African region, although about 60 per cent of the countries have taken reform steps in the oil/ gas upstream sector, less than 10 per cent of African countries have taken steps to liberalize petroleum product prices.

---

14. WB, *Energy and Development Report* (1999), Table 2, p.53.

Access to commercial energy in many African countries is limited. With a few exceptions, cost recovery in SSA countries is inadequate and electric power utilities are generally not financially viable.

Several African countries, such as Ghana, Mali and South Africa are taking steps to reform energy pricing to reflect costs. South Africa has implemented a reasonably elaborate process of determining the cost of service at different points of value chain in the electricity supply industry. Generation costs are determined by estimating the total revenue requirements (cost of supply plus an appropriate return), including the cost of imported energy. As for distribution, there is no national standard for determining the cost of service. The distribution activity in the South African Electricity Supply industry is highly fragmented. Consequently, the country has over 2000 different tariffs. Another distortion in the pricing process comes from monopoly pricing by some of the municipalities for their industrial and commercial consumers. This practice imposes unequal burdens on these segments, which could lead to distortion in the customer cost structure.

Prices of petroleum products are linked to import parity at the refinery gate. The profitability at wholesale and retail levels is controlled by fixing margins at these levels.

South Africa's coal industry has operated as a competitive market since 1992. Coal production and beneficiation is in the hands of the private sector. The government's role is restricted to monitoring of the industry's performance to determine whether coal resources are used optimally to meet national priorities.

The Experience of developing countries to liberalize energy prices thus far indicates that the governments are clearly aware of the cost of inefficient energy prices, but have been reluctant to correct pricing distortions for a variety of reasons. The governments are concerned because, first, an increase in the price of energy and particularly of electricity and kerosene would adversely affect the welfare of the poor. Second, the increase in energy prices would erode industrial competitiveness of their exports and would, in the case of use of substitute fuels like kerosene and fuel wood, contribute to severe deforestation problems with undesirable ecological effects. Third, raising energy prices would be inflationary and this would adversely affect economic growth. Subsidized energy prices are used as tools for poverty alleviation and inflation controls and in democracies such as India they serve as a vote catching tool by granting exemption to political interest groups including wealthy farmers.

Furthermore, the experience of countries in EAP following the financial crisis of late 1990s, that of countries such as Argentina in LAC since the economic crisis of 2001 and continued spikes in crude oil prices since 2004 have raised doubts on the benefits from embarking upon globalization and liberalization for developing countries. They have also raised several questions on staying the course of the energy pricing reform process. These include:

(a) What are the implications of a specific energy pricing regime for the future market shares of primary energy fuels and secondary energy supply (such as electricity) in the total energy supply mix?
(b) At what rate should domestic non-renewable energy resources in developing countries be depleted and does the price applied to any given resource satisfy the objectives of the depletion rate?
(c) Should energy prices be used as a mechanism to achieve the objectives of income distribution in a society? If so, how to reconcile this objective with that of free energy prices?
(d) How to balance the objectives of energy price liberalization at macro-, sector and end-user levels in the aftermath of financial/ macroeconomic crisis?
(e) What are the implications of energy price liberalization on increasing access to efficient energy for over 2 billion poor in developing countries? What are the options for energy price liberalization? Is shock therapy—moving domestic prices suddenly to world market levels—a better option than incrementalism? Or adjusting prices gradually in increments over a period of time? And, finally,
(f) How to continue to stay the course on energy price liberalization and minimize government interventions during periods of global oil price spikes witnessed since August 2004?

The complexity of the above questions is such that answers can only be provided in a country-specific setting. Nevertheless, the pricing principles discussed earlier in this chapter should provide appropriate guidelines to price different forms of energy. Tradable energy forms should reflect their opportunity costs defined as their respective border (export or import) prices. For non-tradable forms of energy, prices should be set to reflect the LRMC of production and distribution.

Subsidies despite being socially justifiable severely distort demand patterns for energy and encourage wasteful consumption, inefficient energy use and loss of much needed revenue receipts to the national budget and in the case of energy exporters there is a loss in export earnings. Subsidized energy prices also entail costs associated with putting in place administrative and bureaucratic mechanisms necessary to ensure the operation, maintenance and monitoring of the price control regime. It is, therefore, important that while formulating energy pricing policies a thorough evaluation of economic costs of perpetuating the subsidized energy pricing status with that of costs and benefits associated with eliminating price distortions should be made.

Developing countries are moving in this direction by identifying the categories of consumers receiving subsidies and reflecting the costs in their budgets at the centre, state/ provincial levels.

A policy option to eliminate subsidies would be to administer 'shock therapy'—the standard western device—by raising domestic energy prices suddenly to world market levels and simultaneously recycling the revenues to energy consumers in the form of a temporary subsidy to income proportional to the initial energy consumption. The income subsidy could then be phased out gradually along a path linked to the ability of producers and consumers to adjust capital and durable inputs. The advantage of this option is that it would provide an immediate incentive to replace capital stock and durables with energy efficient units. So the move to energy efficiency would be completed after one turnover of the capital stock beginning from the time when the policy is implemented. Also, the immediate jump would forestall any further speculation on energy prices and would release any existing energy hoards into productive use. A basic question, however, is the administrative feasibility and costs associated with such a program. Furthermore, given the weak institutional set-up and prevalence of corruption and political concerns of social unrest, implementation of 'shock therapy' to increase energy prices in one jump was not considered as a serious option.

A gradual phasing out of the subsidy as consumers and producers are able to replace existing capital into energy efficient units would serve exactly the same purpose as a gradual price adjustment permits a smooth transition. Developing countries have realized that energy prices must eventually reflect their opportunity costs. For tradable forms of energy the relevant opportunity cost reflect the world price. For non-tradable forms of energy such as electricity and natural gas, marginal and opportunity cost pricing provide a rationale for appropriate tariff/ price structures. Given that electricity and gas enterprises in many developing countries are owned and operated by public monopolies, governments have taken steps to set up regulatory agencies as part of the energy pricing reform process. The following section discusses the status of regulatory/ institutional reform in developing countries.

Regulation and institutional reform

Institutional reforms generally focus on restructuring, commercialization, corporatization, privatization and regulatory reform. For improving the performance of energy sector privatization/competition/and deregulation are the standard prescriptions. However, important segments of power and gas sub-sectors such as power transmission and gas pipelines continue to be natural monopolies and impact the performance of energy supply and service providers. Furthermore, creating a competitive environment in the energy market depends on the industry structure, conditions of market entry and the price and non-price terms and conditions of access to energy network facilities for competitive suppliers. The nature and form of regulatory institutions that are developed will affect both the performance of the existing monopoly segments and their ability to create the environment for competition to increase access to efficient energy supplies.

As discussed in Chapter 3, the standard principles for good regulatory institutions include independence, transparency, accountability, expertise and credibility. However, in practice, implementation of these principles in setting up regulatory institutions and their effective functioning depends on the existing legal, political, administrative and social realities of different countries. In large countries such as India, it also differs between different states within the country.

The role of regulation[15]

The dual role of the government as operator and owner of utilities has drawn governments into day-to-day interventions in developing countries. There is, therefore, a need to set up some form of regulatory body as part of a broader governmental effort to redefine the respective roles of government, utility and consumers. This implies a shift away from the monolithic command and control type of governmental management and toward more decentralized and market-based systems. The Government would retain responsibility for setting objectives and articulating overall policies and for planning and coordinating sector development. It would also establish the legislative and legal framework to protect the interests of the various stakeholders and the public. But regulatory approaches need to be established that appropriately balance protection of the public interest with the need for enterprise autonomy. This requires regulatory entities to be independent of both government ministries and enterprises themselves.

With more independent and transparent regulatory agency, consumers, investors and environmentalists could all have a say in policies related to investment programs, pricing, access to service, reliability of service, energy conservation, plant location and environmental issues. Such a regulatory framework should instil investor confidence and facilitate at least some competition among suppliers. Regulation, therefore, affords a means of fostering an environment that not only enables potential new entrants access to the market, but also provides a means of replicating the effects of competition as closely as possible. The role of regulation is mainly to prevent abuse of dominant market position by a private or public monopoly against new entrants.

In the electricity sector there is broad agreement that it is relatively simple to introduce competition in generation, unlike the transmission and distribution systems where there is a natural monopoly. Many countries embarking

15. WB, *'Infrastructure and Development'*, *World Development Report* (1994)

on the process of unbundling the power sector by the separation of transmission and distribution services from the supply of electricity aim to allow competition in supply, at both the bulk and retail level. Competition is generally limited to wholesaling to the bulk supply points. Beyond competition in generation and bulk supply, competition at the retail level entails the right on the part of generators and other distributors to supply end users connected to the distributor's system, thereby, allowing the end user to bypass the monopoly of the local distributor.

The development and application of 'use of system agreements' (being contracts that permit the use of another person's transmission and/ or distribution assets to wheel electric power) is central to the development of genuine competition in the electricity sector[16]. They provide suppliers the means of access to end-users who are embedded in a competitor's physical system and who would otherwise be captive customers of that supplier's competitor. If competition is only introduced at the wholesale level, these contracts will be limited to the use of the transmission system to allow direct purchasing from generators. If retail competition is to be included, even when limited, a form of use of system contract for the utilization of distribution assets will be necessary.

An important feature of the natural gas industry is the marked variation in prices at the wellhead. Because of the high risks and capital investment associated with bringing a gas field on stream, the price is also a function of the level of the take-or-pay commitment and the length of the contract. These long-term contracts with producers reflect the prevailing market conditions at the time. The level of take-or-pay risk is often a key determinant in industry structure since the risks will need to rest with those most able to bear and manage them. This factor may of itself preclude or limit the degree of possible competition for a considerable period. The possibility for full separation of the gas trading function from transportation and distribution in a natural gas market is quite likely to be limited by the risks inherent in large long-term gas purchase contracts.

Nevertheless, like electric power, competition in natural gas may be introduced at two levels-bulk supply and retail. Large industrial users or gas-fired generation stations directly connected to the high pressure network may be entitled to purchase quantities of gas direct from producers for delivery. Competition may also be introduced at the retail level and the issues of connection and open access, as in electricity, become paramount to effective competition.

Although regulatory regimes are diverse, there are certain common features which make it possible to classify them by the framework adopted and

16. Martin C, Stewert-Smith, 1995, *Industry Structure and Regulation: World Bank, Policy Research Working Paper 1419*, pp 16–17.

the functions they perform. These common features are: first, the establishment of an autonomous regulatory agency which is charged with administering economic regulation and consumer protection, usually on a sector basis. Second, the law empowers the regulator by delegating authority. The duties of the regulator are also spelt out and security of tenure conferred. Third, the basis for economic or price regulation is established although the particular form of economic regulation adopted may differ markedly. And fourth, the authority to review the terms upon which industry participants operate is clarified, such as the policing of license terms for interconnection and other matters affecting competition.

Regulation is categorized by structure, expertise/ staffing, procedure and price control methodology.

(*a*) ***Structure, expertise and staffing***

The structure of the industry which is adopted will have an impact upon the effectiveness of the regulator in the performance of its duties. Experience has shown that full vertically integrated utilities are the most difficult to regulate, largely due to lack of information flows from regulated enterprise to regulator, but also due to the limitations on the opportunities made available to competition. Competition assists the regulator in performing its functions.

The regulator may be constituted as a commission or panel of regulators or may be a single appointee with the appropriate staff. In any event the importance of 'the right person for the job' is not to be overlooked. The regulator should also have access to advisors with strong expertise in the industry in order to permit quicker resolution of debates and to facilitate efficient operation of the regulator as a whole.

The security of tenure to be afforded to the regulators is clearly an important issue and since the regulator often is quasi-judicial in its functions and powers, appointment and removal procedures akin to those for the judiciary provide a possible model, assuming that the judiciary is sufficiently separated from the other branches of government. The number of years of appointment and the parameters within which they are to operate should be clearly stated within the law. In addition, the law should lay down in what circumstances the regulator may be removed from the office. Typical grounds for removal are bankruptcy, crimes of dishonesty or gross misconduct, similar to those in relation to the judiciary. If the extent of tenure is left as a matter of ministerial discretion with no clear legal rules, the independence of the regulator will be undermined. Equally, these rules and procedures should be publicly known. To ensure credibility of the regulator the terms should also specify the nature of disclosure requirements to the legislature and the general public as to the outside interests of the regulators, with a prohibition of any financial interest in the regulated enterprises.

Promoting or at least facilitating competition should be part of the terms of the regulator. New entrants need to be convinced that the regulators have sufficient commitment and capacity to facilitate competition before they agree to enter the market. Equally, investors in the privatization of the state enterprise need to be confident as to the ability of the regulators to withstand, within the law, the pressures placed upon them by politicians to focus on political rather than commercial objectives. A commitment to competition in the relevant sector is important not only at the ministerial level but also on the part of the regulators.

A fear of loss of accountability is usually the main argument put forward for not establishing an autonomous regulator. The necessary balance between accountability and independence can best be achieved by a combination of judicial review of individual decisions and of transparency in the regulatory function. The regulator should operate under a procedural framework, which allows any interested party, including the government or consumer groups, to provide inputs into the decision-making process. The regulator should prepare a written statement of reasons for its decisions, both to enhance public confidence in the transparency of the process and also to facilitate judicial review. The regulatory scheme should also include opportunities for review by the legislative of the work of the regulator. A useful approach is to require the regulator to submit a report, preferably annually, to the legislature on its activities and on any significant competition issues that may require legislative actions. In this way there is an opportunity for public discussion of the performance of the regulator while at the same time preserving the independence of the regulator on a day-to-day basis.

In certain cases the regulator may deliver its report to the legislature through the sector ministry. To ensure that the relevant ministry acts as a 'conduit' rather than a 'filter', the law should also require that regulators publish a full unabridged copy of any annual report submitted to the ministry and that written instructions from the ministry may be referred to the public. Whatever the legal safeguard, in practice, the personalities involved will materially affect the true functional independence of the regulator and its accountability to the legislature.

(*b*) ***Procedure***[17]

The nature of the procedures to be adopted and utilized by the regulators will impact greatly upon their efficiency in carrying out their functions. The approach of due process, open hearings and rights of appeal adopted in the USA has advantages in that all interested parties have an opportunity to participate and there is transparency in the decision-making. The disadvan-

17. WB, 'Industry Structure and Regulation', *Policy Research Working Paper 1419* (1995)

tage of this approach is the cost of decision-making, both in terms of money and time (aside from costly lobbying on the part of interest groups and regulated enterprises), although the gains obtained from transparent decision-making procedures are seen by many as outweighing those costs. Conversely, in the UK, the view taken is that expeditious decision-making is paramount, resulting in procedures that are more discretionary, involving closed negotiation and limited rights of appeal. Nevertheless, the strong impartial judiciary provides recourse under the existing procedural and substantive rules governing judicial review of administrative decisions.

The availability of judicial review by courts will depend not only on legislative enactment, but also upon the internal administrative procedures adopted and published by the regulator. Where these procedures lay down in great detail the consultation process (for example, the number of days to elapse between one step and the next) or where there are detailed rules as to the content of decisions, the decision-making process is more transparent. However, judicial review is easier to instigate on the basis of the failure to comply with a procedural step, which may result in a decision being overturned. As a result, procedural steps undertaken thereafter based on that decision may then be declared void. Conversely, an absence of administrative procedures is quite likely to result in legitimate interests complaining of being denied the opportunity to make their views known when a decision does not favour their interests. The courts will also have greater difficulty in carrying out a judicial review the wider the discretionary nature of the regulator's powers. Clearly, there is a trade-off involved between the speed of decision-making and procedure and balance need to be struck in context.

(*c*) ***Price methodology***

The crucial role of economic regulation is the control of prices paid by the end use consumer as well as by the different businesses or divisions that make up the regulated company where those divisions relate to third party users of their systems or services. Two main types of price control are generally adopted. One approach, with a long track record in the USA, is that of regulating the rate of return, or being essentially a 'cost-plus' approach. The key feature of this approach is the periodic review of the tariffs, which the utility wishes to bring into effect. This involves the examination of the utility's operating costs, capital employed and cost of capital during an agreed test period to determine a fair rate of return. This information, together with assumptions as to demand, is used to calculate the total revenue requirement and from this requirement the level of tariff is determined. To avoid discrimination, an examination of each tariff for each category of service takes place involving the allocation of common costs. Once approved, the tariffs generally remain in force until the utility seeks a review. There are many variations on the principle of cost plus, but these are the fundamentals of rate of return regulation.

Managing a reasonably good cost-based regulatory system places an enormous information burden on the regulator. It requires putting in place a good accounting and auditing system. Methodologies for measuring the firm's cost of capital and evaluating its behaviour through management audits and benchmarking studies need to be implemented. These tasks are challenging in the context of developing countries where the utility/ company remains a monopoly with little competition.

These are capabilities that a new regulatory agency is unlikely to be able to acquire instantly and it may take years to develop the necessary capabilities and experience. These considerations confirm that without institutional reform newly created regulatory agencies are unlikely to have the capability to function effectively.

The main criticism of the rate of return price regulation being essentially a 'cost-plus' approach is that the regulated enterprise has little incentive to make efficiency gains. As a result, the UK has adopted a modified form of rate of return regulation. This modified form, referred to as RPI-*x*, allows the utility to make any changes it wishes to its prices during a predetermined period of four to five years, provided that the average price of a specified basket of services does not increase at a rate greater than RPI-*x* (where RPI is the rate of inflation and *x* is a factor determined as representing the projected efficiency gains over the predetermined period).

The relative advantages of the RPI-*x* approach/ price cap mechanism over rate of return regulation are threefold. First, RPI-*x* is less likely to result in inefficiency from cost-push practices since the utility may retain gains that are made above *x*. Since part of the efficiency gain is passed on to consumers in *x*, prices tend to be lower than they would be under rate of return regulation. Second, RPI-*x* affords the utility greater flexibility to adjust its pricing structures within the limits of the basket of regulated services. Services outside the basket are generally not regulated. And third, RPI-*x* is generally simpler to operate on the part of the regulator and the utility since it does not require the detailed calculations and verification of inputs associated with calculating the total revenue requirement in rate based regulation.

Despite these advantages there is some doubt about the transferability of the British price regulation model to developing countries, given the weaker institutional features. The main problem of the price cap mechanism in the UK has been that distributors have achieved much larger productivity improvements than were anticipated by the productivity factors in the initial price caps, allowing them to earn high profits. High profits have led to public criticism of the system and enormous pressures on the regulator to reset prices and tighten productivity targets, which have been done. It was difficult to find the right productivity adjustment factor ex-ante and this has conflicted with rent extraction goals. But the provision built into the regulatory design for periodically resetting the price level based on actual performance and the productivity factor going forward made it possible to adjust price levels and their future trajectory as more information and experience were obtained by the regulator.[18]

Status of regulatory reform in developing countries

While regulatory setups and price mechanisms in developing countries are modelled on the experience of industrialized countries, the economic and institutional attributes of developing countries create special challenges for the choice of effective regulatory institutions and pricing principles. Differences in development and performance in energy sub-sectors and differences in basic market, legal and political institutions limit benefits from the one-size-fits-all approach in setting up regulatory mechanisms. It is important to recognize that the balance of costs and benefits of alternative price mechanisms, the rate of return/ cost-plus or the price cap mechanisms, differ significantly from country to country based on the initial economic/ financial conditions of the sector, the legal and political environment and the information available to and technical expertise of the regulator.

Latin America is much more advanced in the areas of passage by parliament of an energy law permitting unbundling and/or privatization and establishment of a regulatory body that is separate from the SOEs and from the ministry. Over 83 per cent of the countries in Latin America had taken steps to establish a regulatory body in power sector compared with just 11 per cent in EAP and 8 per cent in Africa. In downstream gas the LAC again are more advanced with 78 per cent of the countries taking steps to set up regulatory agencies as against 33 per cent of those countries in Africa and South Asia and 25 per cent in EAP. Table 4.3 below shows the overall status of regulatory reform in developing countries.

Table 4.3: Percentages of developing countries taking reform steps in power, oil and gas

(a) Power Region (no. of countries)	AFR (48)	EAP (9)	LAC (18)	MNA (8)	SAR (5)
Law	15	33	78	13	40
Regulator	8	11	83	0	40
(b) Upstream oil and gas	AFR (11)	EAP (5)	LAC (8)	MNA (5)	SAR (3)
Law	91	60	63	60	67
Regulator	36	40	50	0	33

18. Paul L. Joskow, 1998, *World Bank: Annual World Bank Conference(ABCDE) on Development Economics:: regulatory Priorities for Infrastructure Sector Reform in Developing countries*, p.211.

(c) Downstream gas	AFR (6)	EAP (4)	LAC (9)	MNA (6)	SAR (3)
Law	33	50	78	0	67
Regulator	33	25	78	0	33

Source: WB, *Energy and Development Report* (1999), Table 2, p.53.

Many LAC countries have legislated reforms and set up a regulatory body with legal and regulatory frameworks to provide equitable and transparent operating and pricing rules for all participants. They have all initiated pricing schemes using competitive, market-based pricing at the bulk-power level, retaining regulated tariffs mainly for monopolistic transmission and distribution functions. The LAC countries are also taking steps to strengthen the authority of the regulatory entity over the sector. The countries, however, differ in the structure and framework of regulatory authority in the sector and in the use of different pricing mechanisms. Argentina, Chile, Colombia and Peru have opted for a sector with mostly separate generation, transmission and distribution functions. These countries use contracts between generators on the one hand and consumers and/ or distributors on the other, to establish market prices for electricity at the bulk level. They have reserved price regulation for open access transmission and distribution grids and for retail tariffs applied to most residential and other 'captive' end-consumers.

Argentina enacted reform laws in 1991 and 1992, which incorporated lessons from Chilean and UK reforms. Between 1991 and 1998, Argentina was credited to have established the most competitive and deregulated wholesale power market in the LAC region. Argentina served as a model of best practice in power and gas regulation. The new National Regulatory Commission (NRC) was entrusted with considerable political and fiscal independence and was functioning effectively. Its key duties are to set rates for the regulated transmission and retail distribution markets, set technical, operating and quality of service standards, oversee the functions and activities of regulated areas and players and protect consumer interests[19].

Chile's extensive power sector reforms targeted and successfully transferred almost all generating, distribution and transmission operations to the private sector during the course of the 1980s. The Chilean reforms were often cited as an example of the worldwide reform movement and provided a model for subsequent power reforms in Latin America and other developing countries.

Peru enacted a reform law in 1992 and following closely on Argentina and Chile's footsteps, planned to open its power sector to market competition and private investment. The sector was divided into separate operating

19. WB, '*Reforms and Private participation in the Power Sector of selected Latin American and Caribbean and Industrialized Countries, Report No. 33*' (Washington DC, 1994)

functions. Non-discriminatory open-transmission and distribution access are provided for in the new system. Most sector entities require a concession to establish generation, transmission or distribution enterprises.

Deregulated pricing is to be applied at the wholesale generating level, and large consumers have access to this market. Regulated transmission tariffs are based on the cost of service, using capacity charges for access to the system, and entry–exit nodes on the system to determine tolls for the use of the system. Benchmark regulation for transmission and distribution tariffs use an efficient enterprise model. Investment factors and a fair return on capital investments are included in the pricing formula, which will be reviewed every 4 years.

The Jamaican experience of regulation recognizes the small size of its power market to enable full competition as in the Argentine and Chilean models. In 1993 Jamaica took steps to establish a new, politically independent Office of Utility Regulator (OUR), to set standards and oversee the quality of service, define technical and financial criteria, set cost-based tariffs for transmission and distribution services, and provide for equitable operating conditions for both regulated transmission and distribution (T&D) and self-regulating (generating) entities. The tariff policy in Jamaica is being restructured to align retail tariffs and transmission fees and tolls on cost-of-service criteria. Increasingly, new generating capacity is expected to be added under the competitive solicitations, which will offer power from BOO and IPP schemes at competitively bid market prices to the T&D entity.

The LAC region's experience of regulation indicate that in most cases establishing a more independent regulatory authority was viewed as necessary to implement, oversee and enforce reforms in the sector. Therefore, an important feature of the new regulatory framework was to give the regulatory authority functional independence accomplished through the selection process for regulators, support by high-level professional staff, adequate compensation, autonomous budget authority and competition in the hiring of consultants—to insulate it from political pressures exerted by the central government and by regulated companies and thereby ensure rate-making functions followed pre-determined economic criteria. However, the results are far from certain as to the effectiveness and autonomy of the regulatory entity.

Chile has failed to achieve a strong, independent regulatory entity. The Ministry of Economy retains final authority over rates. The Commission Nacional de Energia (CNE), an integrated political composition which initially enabled it to undertake major sector reforms in the 1980s, has become a liability over time, lacking a core of unified support from its council members. It currently lacks the ability to independently analyse issues and make non-partisan decisions concerning the sector (WB, *Report no. 33* (1994), p.10).

It is not clear that other countries of the LAC region besides Chile, enacting regulatory reforms, are functioning with effective regulatory independence. In some of these countries, laws constrain staffing levels and budget provisions. In many countries the selection process for the regulators appears too closely associated with political sponsors to foster independent perspectives.

As of 1998, Argentina offered the most viable regulatory independence. The regulatory entity was given considerable independence from other political agencies. It was partially funded by fees collected from generating, transmission and power purchasing entities and it prepared and submitted its own budget. Adequate professional staffing levels and competitive salary levels were provided to make the entity self-sufficient in carrying out its duties. However, the macro/ financial economic crisis of 2001 has affected Argentina's energy sector. It has raised serious doubts on staying the course of market liberalization.

In the case of Africa, just 8 per cent of countries have taken steps to set up some form of regulatory agencies. Separation of responsibilities between the regulating authorities and the operating companies is deficient in all the SSA countries. Even in the small percentage of countries taking steps to set up regulatory entities, the legislative and organization steps are mainly theoretical. In practice, the government retains control of the selection process and appointments[20].

Prior to the financial crisis of 1998, independent power projects (IPPS) have become widely accepted in East Asia as the main instrument for reforming the power sector by promoting competition. In the case of EAP, about 11 per cent of the countries have taken steps to set up regulatory entities. Although several countries in East Asia have taken steps to reform energy sector by separating the regulatory functions from that of ministry and energy enterprises, in practice, government control is exercised in price setting. For example, in China, following the energy reforms of 1998, energy bureaus and a department for power were created within the State Economic and Trade Commission (SETC) that included policy and regulatory tasks. However, the precise scope of their regulatory responsibilities and independence were not clarified.

In South Asia about 40 per cent of the countries initiated regulatory reforms mainly to conform to the requirements of international financial institutions such as the WB and ADB. In contrast to the coherent strategy conforming to the basic elements of regulation outlined above in this chapter, countries in South Asia opted for a piecemeal process of regulatory reform required as a condition of eligibility for borrowing from WB.

India took steps to set up regulatory institution both at the centre and some of the states. However, the selection of regulator is generally a political process with little attention paid to expertise and capabilities to reform the

20. WB, *Lending for Electric Power in Sub-Saharan Africa* (Washington DC, 1995)

sector. For example, the state of Karnataka in India announced in 2000 the establishment of a regulatory authority, Karnataka Electricity Regulatory Commission (KERC), to comply with WB requirements. It was staffed with two civil service employees and one power engineer. With little expertise in regulation, KERC functions mainly by holding public hearing on required tariff increases and bargaining tactics with the state power enterprise.

Since KERC was formed in 2000, three tariff increases are implemented mainly to residential consumers. Residential consumers' tariffs have gone up to US $0.08/kwh, for low quality, interrupted power supply including blackouts and burnouts. The state government in its budget for 2003–4 is incurring US $500 million in subsidies in the electric power sector because of over 35 per cent technical/ power theft loss, less than 40 per cent of accounts receivable, ever increasing cost because of technical, business and financial inefficiencies of the state power generating enterprise and the near bankrupt status of state-owned monopoly power enterprise. The state of Karnataka generally represents the status of regulatory reform in India. With a few exceptions, in India, the state regulatory authorities have not been able to enforce the standard commercial practices in the regulated state power monopolies. The financial non-viability of state electricity boards because of not conforming to the fundamentals of commercial business practices has increased subsidies, with implications for the centre and state governments' budget and financing of private power projects. Chapter 5 discusses India as one of the case study countries pursuing energy sector reform and liberalization.

Experience of developing countries in regulation confirms that effective regulatory institutions cannot be created overnight. The establishment of a regulatory function for power/ natural gas became a central theme of the policy dialogue between the multilateral financial institutions and their member countries since the early 1990s. It has become a feature of many technical assistance and reform loans. Given the complexities of not only establishing regulatory institutions but also adopting in practice the principles of independence, transparency, accountability, expertise and credibility cited to guide the regulatory arrangements, transformation takes time. An important question is the extent to which these principles are actually achievable in the context of developing countries. For example, there are particular problems that arise with attempting to create an autonomous regulator in developing countries.

The nature of developing countries' energy sector structure is closely related to the political and economic history of that country, which in turn influences the view of regulation and regulators within each country. Sector arrangements have historically followed those adopted in industrialized countries. For example, in the electricity sector the role of regulation depends on whether the US, British or French system is adopted and whether the system is a national monopoly or diversified. Since the legal traditions are likewise influenced, the legal tradition itself may prove to be an impediment to the establishment of a regulator. Further, difficulties arise when in practice a mixture of different regulatory regime features are applied to a mixed structure of the industry with public ownership and some competition in the generation segment.

Broadly, the British approach provides for the electricity industry to carry on its activities under license and the role of government, in general terms, is confined to regulation. There is no direct participation in operations. Conversely, many developing countries adopting the British model of regulation are still evolving from public ownership of electricity sector through ministry or as public corporation. Even where the system is being diversified, generation and distribution activities continue to be separate public sector companies and their operations remain within the scope of government activity.

In some francophone countries, the terms of the constitution require any authority that is exercising government functions, such as the sector regulator, to be an integral part of the government organizational structure (Martin C Stewart-Smith, p.42)[21]. The law thereby precludes the possibility of autonomous regulator. Nevertheless, even while the concept of an autonomous regulator may be achievable legally and acceptable politically, putting the concept into practice will be difficult given the environment of lack of interagency coordination in developing countries where a multiplicity of agencies with overlapping functions already exists.

Establishing and building effective regulatory institutions is an integral part of the sector reform process. These institutions must develop to protect consumers from abuse of public/ private monopoly power. They must promote efficient supply behaviour by firms providing monopoly services, such as transmission and distribution and pipeline transport services, subject to public regulation. Regulation needs to police open access and interconnection in electricity and natural gas sectors, thereby allowing new entrants into the market. Experience in developing countries thus far shows difficulties in effective regulation which have as much to do with inadequate attention to sector structure as they do with the institutional capacity of the regulator itself. Effective regulation must facilitate competition by implementing appropriate terms and conditions for access to network facilities. Competition allows the sector to respond to market forces and often results in market driven sector restructuring.

A number of developing countries at various stages of development are beginning to evolve better frameworks for managing their energy sectors. The new compact entails unpleasant political choices. Governments will

---

21. Martin C, Stewart-Smith, *Industry Structure and Regulation, Policy Research Working Paper 1419*, p.41, World Bank, Washington D.C.

have to shift away from central planning and control toward decentralization and market-based incentives, regulated by an independent authority. Governments, however, need to retain responsibility for setting the overall policy for sector development, establishing the legal and institutional framework to protect the interests of the various stakeholders, including the public. Reforming the legal framework and building effective regulatory institutions should improve sector accountability by making decision-making transparent and allowing greater participation of both the consumers and the general public.

Effective regulatory institutions cannot be created overnight. Even in the LAC region, where reform was more advanced than in other regions, building effective regulatory institutions with principles of independence, transparency, accountability, expertise and credibility is still work-in-progress. Given that the regulatory practices being adopted in developing countries are modelled after industrial countries, care should be taken while designing a regulatory framework that works. Regulatory agencies could be started with simple objectives, rules and procedures and developed as information and experiences are gathered while staying the course on the reform process. In this way, governments will be much more vigilant on the learning curve and will be much better equipped to take positive steps towards building efficient and independent regulatory institutions that perform well over long periods, following the introduction of competition, sector restructuring and commercialization/ corporatization.

Commercialization/ corporatization and privatization

The removal of SOEs from direct government control and their establishment as independent legal corporations with the goal of behaving like commercial companies is the first step in the reform process. This step makes it more likely that costs can be reduced, efficiency improved and tariffs raised to cover costs so that the company would attract private participation. Without this step private sector companies would not be able to compete with SOEs on equal terms and in the power sector, where state-owned electricity companies despite government subsidies are virtually bankrupt such as in India, private investors would demand favourable conditions at a cost to the economy before they enter the market.

Under a policy of commercialization of electric utilities, governments would act more like shareholders and less like managers, receiving dividends and taxes and holding utility management accountable but relinquishing direct control over pricing, budgets, procurement, borrowing and personnel. Power sector functions—from raising capital to producing a product to bill collection—are essentially those of a large capital-intensive industry that sells products to a mass market. Commercialization can be accomplished with autonomous publicly owned utilities or through privatization. Commercialization would insulate management of the power sector from short-term political influences.

The transition plans for moving from the 'command and control model' of the vertically integrated public utility to that of commercially operated business corporation involves introducing commercial and corporate principles into the industry. These steps may include a degree of private generation and would lay the ground for an increase of private investment subsequently. The following box summarizes some key elements for the situation where the enterprise is initially state-owned and government intervention is intrusive:

Box 4.1 Key steps in commercialization/ corporatization and privatization

Commercialization of State Enterprise

- Autonomy given to Board and management
- New (arm's length) regulatory structure with focus on profit
- International accounting standards adopted
- Subsidies and non-commercial practices phased out
- Commercial salaries adopted with full responsibility for staffing
- Private generation on system is invited

Corporatization

- Conversion of SOEs to a company under corporate law
- Regulatory arrangements redefined
- Existing staff may transfer to new company
- All rights, assets and obligations of former state enterprise are assumed
- Articles, objectives and functions of enterprise set out
- Restructuring balance sheet to determine capital structure
- Share capital and bonds issued to owners

Privatization

- Access to stock and bond markets and public shares issued
- Independent power generation introduced
- Board and management accountable to shareholders and regulators
- Franchises (on distribution)

The list serves only to highlight the main elements. The initial preference may be to go for commercialization/ corporatization, the utility operating on commercial principles, but with competitive procurement of new generation followed in some cases by privatization. All the steps in Box 4.1 reflect the redefinition of government's role requiring a strong and sustained political commitment. Corporatization of utility functions, defined as a process of making an enterprise operate according to a profit-oriented, competitive commercial framework, is seen as an effective means (short of privatization) to remove political considerations from the decision-making process. Through corporatization, the government's role is redefined to let management direct the company on a commercially oriented basis, and redirect operations to be viable under competitive market conditions. Countries in the LAC, such as Chile and Jamaica, have taken the approach of corporatization as a logical step for preparing government-owned companies to compete in the market place and to facilitate their transition to private ownership if the enterprise is targeted for divestiture. Corporatization before privatization is seen to demonstrate the enterprises' competitiveness and thus allow a better basis for evaluating its sales value, for both sellers and prospective buyers.

Corporatization allows a smooth transition to different forms of ownership. Corporate legislation establishes the general legal environment the sector carries out its activities. In many cases these changes are first steps toward privatization. Organizational changes to be made by unbundling the vertically integrated energy enterprises aim to improve performance and encourage competition. Regulatory changes will be introduced to reduce the level of government involvement in the operations of enterprises and establish mechanisms by which boards and managers are held accountable for performance.

In a number of developing countries, governments in the 1990s opted for privatization to increase efficiency, reduce debt and administrative and financial burden of the energy sector on the budget. Privatization occurs through such methods as auctions, stock offers, stock distributions, negotiated sales, management-employee buyouts and voucher or coupon exchanges. Other methods include leasing, joint ventures, management contracts, concessions, BOO, build-operate-transfer (BOT) and BOOT arrangements.

In the 1990s privatization revenues in developing countries and former centrally planned economies of Eastern Europe and Central Asia in power, oil and gas together totalled US $95.226 billion and accounted for over 30 per cent of total privatization revenues of US $315.712 billion[22]. Privatization revenues in oil and gas of US $45.074 billion between 1990 and 1999

---

22. WB, *Global Development Finance* (2001), p.189.

were generated almost entirely by oil and gas sales in Argentina, Brazil, India, Poland and Russia. Privitization revenues in power totalled US $53.412 billion in the 1990s. In 1999 power sector deals generated US $3.9 billion in the LAC, $968 million in Eastern Europe and Central Asia, $522 million in the EAP, $114 million in SSA and $37 million in South Asia.

Privatization has not necessarily involved the sale of an enterprise to private owners, but it has encompassed a wide variety of activities that have increased private sector involvement in ownership and/ or operation of government-owned energy businesses. They range from partial or full privatization through issue of shares by private placement to institutions or to the public, sale of assets, contracting services for construction, operation or management to removing barriers to entry for encouraging competition.

In the initial phases of privatization public enterprises issued shares, some of which were bought by non-resident investors. However, as privatization deepened non-residents purchased more and more shares. The 10 per cent-ownership threshold that divides portfolio equity from FDI was crossed in many cases resulting in reclassification of portfolio equity as FDI, as a large part of equity was purchased by multinational companies for the purpose of acquiring control over the privatized enterprises, especially in the oil and gas sector such as privatization of Argentina's oil company Yacimientos-Petroliferos-Fiscales (YPF).

In the global context, nearly 50 per cent of developing countries are taking steps to commercialize/ corporatize their energy enterprises compared with about 25 per cent of developing countries taking steps to privatize their existing assets in energy enterprises as reform efforts are spread unevenly both across energy sub-sectors and among different regions. Except for SAR, commercialization efforts in the upstream oil and gas experienced the most even pattern. The regional picture of commercialization efforts is different for oil, gas and power. Less than one-third of the African countries took steps toward commercialization in power, downstream gas and downstream oil. In those African countries where there is oil production, private concessions have been allowed and efforts have been made to corporatize the state oil company.

In the power sector the LAC region is more advanced in commercialization with 61 per cent of countries taking steps. Commercialization efforts vary between 25 per cent and 44 per cent in other regions with MNA and AFR at the lower end. Table 4.4 shows the status of energy sector commercialization/ corporatization/ privatization in developing countries in percentage terms.

Table 4.4. Percentage of Countries in Developing Countries Taking Commercialization-privatization Steps (no. of countries in region)

(a) Power					
Region (no.of countries)	AFR(48)	EAP(9)	LAC(18)	MNA(8)	SAR(5)
Corporatization	31	44	61	25	40
Generation-privatization	4	22	39	13	40
Distribution-privatization	4	11	44	13	20
(b) Upstream oil&gas					
Region (no.of countries)	AFR(11)	EAP(5)	LAC(8)	MNA(5)	SAR(3)
Corporatization	73	80	63	80	33
Privatization	9	0	38	0	0
(c) Downstream gas					
Region (no.of countries)	AFR(6)	EAP(4)	LAC(9)	MNA(6)	SAR(3)
Corporatization	33	100	56	50	100
Privatization	17	0	56	0	----
(d) Downstream oil-refining					
Region (no.of countries)	AFR(11)	EAP(4)	LAC(11)	MNA(6)	SAR(3)
Corporatization	55	75	45	33	67
Privatization	0	50	18	17	33
(e) Downstream-wholesale-retail					
Region (no.of countries)	AFR (17)	EAP(8)	LAC(11)	MNA(5)	SAR(5)
Corporatization	29	50	36	40	60
Privatization	24	0	18	40	20

Source: WB, *Energy and Development Report* (1999), Table 2, p.53.

It cannot magically be assumed that private finance will be forthcoming once a new electricity law is in place and the industry has been corporatized. Even where governments have accepted in principle that private greenfield investment alleviates the claims on scarce public and multilateral funds for system expansion and privatization of existing assets reduces the need for subsidies, experience has shown that there is bound to be a long period of adjustment in the process of energy market transition. Cost recovery in publicly owned power utilities has often been poor and heavy public subsidization has been required. System expansion had to be financed publicly at the expense of expenditure on the other sectors.

The inheritance in most countries, as the WB policy paper on electric power (1993) documented, continues to be one of capacity shortages, (except in some East Asian countries following the 1998 macro/ financial crisis when energy demand declined), overloaded distribution systems, large losses, theft of supplies often amounting to over 35 per cent of electricity produced, non-payment of electricity bills over 60 per cent of electricity supplied, much generating capacity in disrepair and numerous managerial inefficiencies. This will deter private investment in green field investments and private acquisition of existing assets. Furthermore, new investors are more attracted to supplying new capacity than to acquiring and rehabilitating the existing system.

The fundamental change required in reforming the energy sector has been the better recovery of costs from end-users. Without pricing energy services to reflect the cost of provision-tariff reform and without the elimination of non-payment on a large scale, no schedule of investments either to maintain or to expand the energy sector can ultimately be sustainable, whether financed privately or publicly.

The institutional reform elements of independent regulation, commercialization/ corporatization and organizational restructuring should result in an increase in the sector's creditworthiness to attract public or private capital. While these elements are all necessary to facilitate private investment, they need to be supplemented in parallel with financial reforms and rational investment policies.

Private investment

The entry of the private sector into the ownership of new investment has been seen as a crucial first step in the reform of the energy sector. A country that is willing to allow some private sector participation, even though it does not address directly the inefficiencies of the existing industry, may be more open to consideration of extensive reform and the state-owned company may be encouraged to improve its own operations, partly by the example set by the private sector operator.

One strategy advocated for the power sub-sector in early 1990s was to encourage the entry of IPPs, on the grounds that this might be less problematic for the government since it did not involve the sale of national assets or the immediate redundancies which a private sector owner might require. It was hoped that IPPs would both set an example of good performance to the rest of the sector and also eventually force the sector to become more efficient and to be willing to embrace privatization of existing assets.

In the power, downstream gas and refining sub-sectors, the presence of private sector investment on a greenfield site is associated with a higher proportion having taken other reform steps including privatization of existing assets. The difference in proportions between those with private sector investment and all countries is around 20 per cent for power and 30 per cent for downstream gas and refining. In these sectors, countries which have admitted IPPs and the private sector, have been substantially more ready to take other reform steps. In upstream oil and gas the presence of a concession is associated with only a slight increase in the proportion having taken other reform steps, and with virtually no increase in the proportion that have privatized existing assets.

The steps of commercialization, law reform, regulation and unbundling of the sector are all necessary to facilitate the entry of the private sector. However, these reform steps are not sufficient to attract private investment. Many potential private investors are concerned about addressing commercial, financial, economic and political risks.

A suitable environment for oil and gas production requires contracts as a risk-mitigating tool. Many potential power investors are concerned about security and price of fuel supplies, timely payments for purchase of power by a dominant state-owned power company and delays in the agreed conversion of local currency into foreign exchange. Developing appropriate financial mechanisms for mitigating these risks is required to interest private investors. Table 4.5 shows the percentage of developing countries with private green-field investment that have taken other reform steps.

Table 4.5. Percentage of developing countries with private greenfield investment that have taken other reform steps

	Commercialization/ Corporatization	*Law*	*Regulator*	*Privatization*
Power				
With IPPs	63	57	50	50
All	44	33	29	25
Upstream oil and gas				
With concessions	74	79	38	18
All	67	69	31	14
Downstream gas				
With private investment	80	67	67	60
All	60	40	40	27
	Commercialization/ Corporatization	Law	Regulator	Privatization
Refining				
With private investment	92	n/a	n/a	62
All	54	n/a	n/a	28

Source: WB, *Energy and Development Report* (1999), Table 3, p.54.

The experience of developing countries to interest private investment in new greenfield investment and in acquisition of existing assets is different between regions and across energy sub-sectors. Table 4.6 shows percentage of developing countries with private investment and privatization.

Table 4.6: Percentage of Developing Countries with Greenfield Private Investment and Privatization

Energy sub-sectors	*Global*	*AFR*	*EAP*	*LAC*	*MNA*	*SAR*
Power						
IPPs	40	19	78	83	13	100
Privatization	25	6	33	50	13	40
Upstream oil and gas						
Concessions	69	91	40	63	80	67
Privatization	14	9	0	38	0	0
Downstream gas						
Private investment	27	33	25	56	0	33
Privatization	27	17	0	56	0	0
Downstream oil						
Private refinery investment	23	18	50	9	0	33
Privatization:refinery	28	0	50	18	17	33
Privatization-wholesale	28	24	0	18	40	20
Overall energy % of maximum (weighted)						
New private investment	40	40	48	53	23	58
Privatization	24	11	17	36	14	19

Source: WB, *Energy and Development Report,* Table 5, p.55.

Table 4.6 shows that only 24 per cent of countries have yet allowed any form of privatization of existing assets in the energy sector and only 40 per cent have the private sector to be involved in new investment. There are large regional differences. Even in the two regions with advanced reform experience—EAP and LAC—only about 17 per cent and 36 per cent, respectively, have allowed privatization. There is a notable difference between the willingness to permit private sector participation in greenfield sites and the willingness to privatize existing assets in all regions.

A notable feature is that in power and oil the percentage of countries permitting the entry of private investors into greenfield sites is much larger than the number that have introduced formal regulation. Such countries appear not to be preparing for privatization and the creation of competitive markets so much as augmenting the existing system by admitting private investment in new sites. The low proportion of countries that have privatized existing assets confirms this interpretation, especially for upstream oil and gas.

Ten years after the beginning of energy market transition even those countries in EAP and LAC considered to be more advanced than others (Malayasia, Philippines, Thailand and Argentina) face severe obstacles on their path of transition. The East Asian financial crisis since 1998, and macroeconomic/ financial crisis in the countries of Latin America, Argentina, Brazil since 2001, have impacted the flow of private investment in energy sector.

Prior to the crisis, East Asia led the worldwide boom in privately financed IPPs. Focused mostly on power generation, new greenfield power projects in East Asia worth nearly US $40 billion accounted for 60 per cent of all such projects in the developing world between 1990 and 1997. Four countries in East Asia—Indonesia, Malaysia, Philippines and Thailand—accounted for over 90 per cent of negotiated IPPs amounting to over 60 per cent of all the investment in their infrastructure.

The core response to troubles with honouring long-term power purchase agreements is for cash-strapped state-owned monopoly utilities to ask their private IPP suppliers for re-negotiation of power purchase agreements. Most affected were Indonesia, Malaysia and Thailand, but so was Philippines. Private generators were asked to lower tariffs and/ or guaranteed off-take levels. Private parties, including project lenders, in turn try to invoke government guarantees or request other forms of government support. Cash-strapped governments try to stall, raise consumer prices a little and start considering privatization of older state-owned generating plants and sometimes also distribution and transmission assets belonging to their state-owned utilities. The utilities in turn try to resist this loss of 'power'. But while they lack cash, investment programs are slashed.

Table 4.7 shows private investment in developing country power sectors between 1994 and 1998. It is clear from Table 4.7 that private investment in both new greenfield sites and privatization peaked in 1996 at US $44.5 billion and fell over 60 per cent to US $18.7 billion in 1998. Table 4.7 also confirms that in 1998 the flow of private investment to developing country power sectors fell in all regions with no private investment in the Middle East and North Africa.

Table 4.7. Private Investment in Developing Country Power Sectors, 1994–98*
(US $ Billion)

Region	*1994*	*1995*	*1996*	*1997*	*1998*	*Total: 1994–8*
Sub-Saharan Africa	0.2	0.5	0.9	0.5	0.2	2.3
East Asia and the Pacific	12.4	22.4	27.0	18.4	6.9	87.1
Latin America and the Caribbean	3.4	9.5	9.7	21.0	10.3	54.0
The Middle East and North Africa	0.3	0.2	1.7	1.1	0	3.2
South Asia	3.1	6.1	4.0	1.6	0.9	15.7

Region	1994	1995	1996	1997	1998	Total: 1994–8
Europe and Central Asia (ECA)	0.6	1.6	1.2	1.7	0.4	5.5
Total for developing countries including ECA	20.0	40.3	44.5	44.3	18.7	167.8

**Includes investment in new greenfield sites and privatization.*
Source: WB, *Energy and Development Report* (1999), Table 2, p.12.

Energy sector reform in the 1990s: Conclusion

The energy sector reform agenda of the 1990s ranged from energy price adjustment and setting up of regulatory institutions to unbundling of power sector and attracting independent private investment in power generation. On balance developing countries made policy changes to open up their energy sector to private investors. Progress has varied by regions, countries and policy instruments for implementation. During the decade, over 85 developing countries embarked on energy sector reform as part of their macroeconomic liberalization. By 1997, several countries in East Asia and Latin America, notably Argentina, carried out rapid macro and sector reform. South Asian countries despite making progress in macroeconomic liberalization and announcing a big-bang opening of policy in energy sector made a few small policy steps in energy sector reform implementation. South Africa, the Arab Republic of Egypt and Jordan announced bold policy statements to reform the energy sector. However, despite announcing to reform energy sector a number of oil importing Sub-Saharan countries made little progress in implementation.

Even countries successfully implementing sector reform in East Asia and Latin America were impacted by the 1998 and 2001 East Asian and Latin American financial crises. Following the 1998 crisis, GDP in East Asia declined by an average of about 8 per cent in 1998. Consequently power demand declined. Consumers were hard put to pay for electricity. Private power producers faced financial difficulties and bankruptcies.

Countries in Latin America such as Argentina, which served as a model in the energy market liberalization face structural adjustment problems following the macro/ financial crisis of 2001. The major adjustment process of continuing stresses has become political raising doubts about the benefits of liberalization and blurring of lines of private, public and political responsibilities.

Developing countries continue to face politically difficult and contentious fiscal adjustment to re-emerge from the crisis. Energy market transition has not proceeded in the way it was predicted a decade ago. The WB's, '*Energy and Development Report*[23] 1999 titled 'Energy After the Financial Crises" concluded that despite encouraging trends in many developing countries' energy sectors, none of the players in the energy industry, financiers, NGOs or policy makers have yet got the right institutional and financial formula. The report candidly acknowledged the WB's failure to bring various actors together to reform the energy sector to facilitate increased flow of both public and private investment in energy particularly in poor developing countries.

The Operations Evaluation Department (OED) of the WBG, in its report on 'Power for Development: a review of WBG's experience with private sector participation in the electricity sector' concluded that the outcomes of WBG experience with private sector development depend on country's commitment and effective implementation of reforms. The report went on to comment that the 1993 policy enunciated what to do, but because of the limited experience in implementing such policies it was not accompanied by a strategy on how to do it. In most countries the report finds reforming the power sector for private investment remain in the early stages[24].

The Bank anticipated that the necessary experience would be obtained through 'learning-by-doing' and was accompanied with 'fly-by-night' travel by western advisors across the globe and 'one-size-fits-all' recipes for quick transition to global energy market. This technocratic view did not give adequate weight to the time required for building of institutions for effective transition and to the intricacies of the political economy of the reform process. The result was that the initial euphoria of private power interest in the early to mid-1990s in the power sector waned following the 1997 Asian financial crisis. The power sectors of developing countries continue to be in crisis, particularly in terms of their finances and their ability to meet demand, at least cost, on an environmentally sustainable basis.

WB lending for energy sector dropped sharply after 1998. Energy sector lending fell from the peak period average of 15 per cent of total lending during 1992–7, to 3 per cent of total WB lending in 2003. The WB merged both energy and mining together in its annual reporting since 2002. During (FY) 1992–7 the Bank's energy sector's annual average lending was US$ 3.2 billion. Thereafter, it continued to decline from US$ 1.3 billion in 1998–9 to US$ 1.2 billion in FY 2000 and dropped to its lowest level of US$ 593.2 million in FY2003. Oil and gas lending fell from its annual average peak of $551 million during FY 1992–7 to a low of $78.8 million in FY 1998–9 and to $1.5 million in FY 2003 (Table 4. 8).

In the power sector, the WB's lending for the expansion of generation capacity dropped from a peak of US $2.6 billion in 1992 to almost nothing in

23. *Energy and Development Report 1999: Energy After the Financial Crises.*

24. WB-OED, *Power for Development: a review of World Bank's Group's Experience with Private Participation in the Electricity Sector* (Washington DC, 2003), pp.xviii–xxiii

2003. It was substituted for support by sector reforms, transmission and distribution, where still much remains to be done.

Table 4.8. World Bank Energy Sector Lending Fiscal 1992–2003 (Millions of dollars)

Energy sub-sector	*FY1992–7 (annual average)*	*FY1998–9 (annual average)*	*FY2000*	*FY2001*	*FY2002*	*FY2003*
Total: Energy	3,098.1	1,332.4	1,161.2	906.0	1,259.6	593.2
Power/ Energy	2,547.2	1,253.6	994.2	824.4	1,076.6	591.7
Oil and gas	550.9	78.8	167.0	81.6	183.0	1.5
Total:World Bank Lending	21,543.1	*28,795.0	15,276.2	17,250.6	19,519.0	18,513.0

**1998–9 figures are consolidated*
Source: *World Bank Annual Reports,* 2001, 2002 and 2003.

The WB's 2001 Energy Business Renewal Strategy (EBRS) attributed its failure to poor portfolio performance in the 1990s, the decline in sector lending and the pressure to include poverty alleviation and environmental sustainability. However, as shown in Table 4.8 energy sector lending is on its decline since 2001. Oil and gas lending has almost disappeared.

The IFC's power investment approvals also reached a peak of $872 million in FY 1995 accounting for 16 per cent of IFC's total approvals, but dropped to US $335 million or 6 per cent of its total approval in FY 1999. Cumulative gross approvals totaled US $4.4 billion over the 1990s compared to US $177 million before the 1990s. The level of support for energy from other multilateral development banks is small on a comparison of their overall programs. The ADB approved 40 loans in the energy sector between 1995 and 1999, representing 11 per cent of ADB loans. More than 50 per cent of the active projects of the IADB are in the energy sector.

Improving energy access for the poor through private sector investment was overshadowed in the 1990s by the urgent and overriding need in many countries to add generation capacity. However, lagging reforms in transmission and distribution, lack of progress in commercialization of state electricity boards and continued deterioration of their financial viability over the 1990s have constrained power delivery and made expansion of access, especially for the poor all the more challenging. Investment and operating costs of rural energy projects are high relative to revenue potential, making returns unattractive to private investors.

High dependency on coal for electricity generation is expected to continue. At the end of the 1990s, overall progress for power sector reforms in developing countries had clearly fallen short of the expectations that had been set by the WBG's 1993 Electric Power Lending Policy. The OED review (2003) attributed this to the poor investment climate for attracting private investment in energy in many low to middle income countries, reluctance on the part of some governments to tackle the political decisions involved in eliminating subsidies and a drying up of interest in emerging market investment. With the exception of a few countries in Latin America and Asia, many developing countries are reported to be either undecided or are stalled in their privatization attempts and some have reversed privatization plans.

Even a small percentage of countries such as Argentina and Brazil, with all of their successes prior to 2000, face hard challenges ahead. The economic crisis in Latin America has impacted private sector participation in Argentina, Bolivia, Brazil, Ecuador and Peru. It is ironic that after a decade of embarking on reforms Brazil is back to square one and has once again been the recipient of US $455 million loan in FY 2002 from the WB for supporting pricing, regulatory and investment reforms in its energy sector.

Chapter 5 will discuss the experiences of selected developing country case studies, from EAP, SAR, AFR, MNA and LAC regions, in implementing the four elements of energy sector reform, which will form the basis for lessons to be learned for correcting the reform course and to identify the challenges for moving forward on the course of energy sector reform to increase access to efficient energy supplies in developing countries in the twenty-first century.

CHAPTER 5

WHITHER ENERGY SECTOR REFORM AND LIBERALIZATION: CASE STUDIES

Introduction

In the 1990s many developing countries faced with the inefficiencies of public sector energy enterprises and the adverse impact of increasing energy subsidies on their budget, embarked upon an extensive program of energy sector reform within the framework of macroeconomic reform and liberalization. Developing countries expected that the reforming of the energy sector by reversing the pre-1990s command and control strategy of monopoly of public energy enterprises would promote competition, improve energy enterprise efficiency and attract private investment to increase energy supplies for development. While the number of countries on the reform path increased in the 1990s, not all of them were equally successful. At one end of the reform spectrum, countries such as China and Argentina were considered to be successful reformers. Democratic Argentina, embracing a US style free market was considered (until the economic crisis that started in 2001) to have successfully completed its energy sector reform and was put forward as a model and the best practice to other developing countries embarking on a similar reform process in the 1990s. Other countries in East Asia seemed to be succeeding until before the 1998 crisis and are now trying to get back into the reform process. Many other countries at the other end of the spectrum in SSA burdened by economic and political difficulties continue to struggle along with little success.

As discussed in Chapter 4, the review of energy sector reform and liberalization in developing countries shows mixed performances with inter-regional and inter-energy sub-sector variations. A better understanding of this mixed performance requires a review of the reform program in country-specific settings to evaluate the outcome of energy sector reform and liberalization policies since the 1990s, aimed at increasing access to energy for development.

The methodology of this chapter is eclectic. Unlike much generalizing and model-building in academic development economics, this chapter is not based on the experience of one or a few countries. Nor does it take an econometric approach that conceives of a few representative countries. In the last several years the academic literature on macroeconomic reforms has blossomed. Yet all this literature is primarily focused on analyzing the processes of energy pricing polices and subsidies. Broadening the scope of evaluation by giving more attention to the disconnect between reform principles and practices of policy implementation is critical for understanding how the reform experience impacts energy for development.

This chapter attempts to take into account the detailed and diverse experience of seven large and medium size countries, representing high, medium and low income from Asia, Africa, Latin America, the Middle East and countries from the SSA region. The objective of this country case study evaluation is to understand what lessons we can draw from over 15 years of energy sector reform experience, to provide guidance to shape policies for a better energy future.

The case studies are heterogeneous. Each case study country/ region represents its unique features of energy resource base, policy objectives and design, macro-sector and inter-sector linkages, market size, approaches to reform policy implementation, political commitment/ governance and institutional set up. Their diversity poses a challenge not only for evaluating individual reform elements and for deriving cross-cutting lessons, but also to develop an effective strategy for shaping the future of energy for development.

Case study countries vary widely in size. They range from big energy consumers like China and India with over 100,000 MW of electric capacity to small energy consumers of SSA with less than 150 MW. The case study countries also vary in reform design, approaches to reform implementation, governance and institutional setup for effective reform implementation. Furthermore, energy sector reform often has an implicit or explicit objective, that of coordination of approaches and practices in the energy sector and the country and activities practiced at the macro and global level. The extent to which sector policies are linked to the fundamentals of macroeconomic and global finance and the role of reforming institutions is critical in determining the outcome of sector reform.

To gain some insights into this subject, Section I of this chapter presents case studies of seven countries—China, India, Argentina, Brazil, Egypt, Jordan, South Africa and SSA—most of which have gone through some form of energy sector reform.[1] Each case study consists of four sections: sector context, energy sector institutions and policy, energy market reform status and future direction. Energy policy considerations include measures to address short-term goals in the energy sector, and long-term policies to reform the sector. These include the four main elements of energy market reform, energy pricing, regulation/ institutional reform, commercialization/ corporatization/ privatization and private investment.

Section II of this chapter attempts an assessment of energy sector reform experience and its implications on energy for development in each of the case studies. The findings of these specific country experiences underline the major impediments and factors enabling the reform process. They are used to identify the key issues and challenges for increasing access to efficient energy supplies for development.

CHINA

As of 2005 China is the world's most populous country and the second largest energy user in the world after the USA. In 2003 China's oil consumption at 5.56 million barrels a day (b/d) surpassed that of Japan. China was estimated to have accounted for over 35 per cent of the global oil demand growth in 2003. The US EIA expects China's oil consumption to almost double to 10.5 million b/d in 2020, making China a major factor in the world oil market.

Sector context

China has abundant energy resources and ranks within the world's top five energy producers of coal, oil products and electricity. It has vast resources of coal. It ranked second in the world's production and consumption of coal, second in the production of electricity, second in the capacity of its refineries and seventh in the production of crude oil.[2] Despite a temporary stagnation in energy demand in 1998–9, China is the world's second largest consumer of energy, accounting for more than 10 per cent of the world's total primary energy demand and over one-third of the total energy consumption in developing countries. China's explosive demand for oil has resulted in an increasing gap between its domestic production and consumption and China has become a net importer of oil since 1994. The share of oil imports account for

1. Discussion of case studies in this chapter draws from the author's extensive experience working in these countries as WB task manager and principal economist for energy sector projects and programs (1991–97), Director of Energy Facilitation Programs at the WEC (1997–98) and follow up since 1998.
2. Philip Andrews Speed, 'China's Energy Policy in Transition: Pressures and Constraints', *The Journal of Energy Literature* (2001)

over one-third of its oil consumption. Increasing oil imports makes China a strategic buyer in world energy markets.

China's interest in FDI in energy as a vehicle for transfer of capital and technology has enabled it to begin to sell energy equipment and services overseas. China's expanding energy market, the rate of growth in China's energy demand, the large investment requirements to meet the growing energy demand and China's entry into the World Trade Organization (WTO)—all these factors could attract global energy investors. These factors also empower China as a key player in the global energy market to play an increasing role in global energy geopolitics.

China's main fuel is coal. China's total coal reserves—proven, probable and possible—is estimated to be as high as 4 trillion short tons, about 12 per cent of the world total. It is the world's largest consumer of coal, with 30 per cent of world consumption in 2000. Coal meets nearly 70 per cent of China's energy needs. It represents almost 90 per cent of the fuel used in the electricity sector. Primary coal demand has increased by 4.3 per cent per year since 1960. Demand for coal has declined since the mid-1990s due to a combination of factors, including the impact of energy conservation measures, switching from coal to oil products and gas and consolidation and restructuring of inefficient coal mines. However, with abundant domestic coal supply, China's high dependency on coal for electricity generation is expected to continue to reduce dependence on oil imports and to maintain low electricity tariffs. The demand for coal is expected to grow at an average rate of 2.3 per cent from 2002 to 2030.

China, as of 2002, has about 18.3 billion barrels of proven oil reserves. Much of the domestic oil production of around 3.4 million b/d comes from old fields in the eastern onshore basins, which are in slow decline. China has been a net importer of products since 1993 and of crude oil since 1996. In 2003 oil imports reached almost 2 million b/d, accounting for 35 per cent of China's oil consumption.

China's efforts to reduce dependence on oil imports include increasing domestic oil production and securing direct control over foreign oil resources through its state-owned oil companies. Despite China's frantic efforts since 2000 to locate new reserves both at home and abroad and to diversify to alternative energy sources, especially natural gas, the situation is expected to deteriorate and oil imports are expected to rise to 4 million b/d by 2010 and to 8 million b/d by 2020.[3]

Proven gas reserves were 1.5 trillion cubic meters (TCM) in 2002. Total gas resources including mean undiscovered gas are estimated to be large, at around 50 TCM, 25 per cent of which is likely to be recoverable. Nearly 60 per cent of gas resources are located in the western and central provinces.

---

3. *Petroleum Economist* (December, 2003)

Connecting the producing fields in the west to the main potential markets in the east will require the construction of long-distance transmission lines and the expansion of distribution networks.[4]

China has abundant hydroelectric resources. The Three Gorges Dam will have a total of 18 GW when completed. Doubts and uncertainties about the environmental and social impact and about the cost of building the transmission lines that would be needed to bring electricity from dams in the remote western areas to markets in the east limit the potential expansion of hydropower capacities.

China's Ministry of Electric Power (MOEP) in its renewable Energy Development Plan for China, aims at a rapid expansion of power related renewable energy capacity. The aim is to provide power to remote off-grid locations. Wind power, solar, geothermal and biomass supplies are expected to grow rapidly, especially after 2010 when the cost of renewable energy sources is expected to fall due to improvement in renewable technologies. But their share in generation will continue to be small.

Primary commercial energy demand in China grew by more than 6 per cent per year from 1990–6, but stagnated from 1998. In the middle and late 1990s China experienced two major shifts in its energy balance. First, in 1994 China's oil consumption exceeded domestic production for the first time. China became a net importer of oil in 1993 and the level of net oil imports has steadily increased since then. This situation is caused by a substantial rise in demand for oil products, mainly in the transportation sector, combined with a failure to raise the level of domestic oil production.

The second shift occurred in 1998–9 when energy consumption in China fell for two successive years. The fall in energy demand was due to a combination of general economic slowdown related to the Asian economic crisis, a decline in output from energy-intensive industries, closures of inefficient state factories and a general increase in end-use efficiency. Demand for oil and electricity flattened temporarily before picking up again in the year 2000. Electricity consumption surged over 9 per cent annually in 2001 and 2002. In the summer of 2003 an unexpected spike in electricity demand wiped out the surplus from China's power grid. When actual growth jumped to 15 per cent, as many as two-thirds of China's provinces suffered from severe power outages.

By 2003 China's oil consumption reached 5.56 million b/d and oil imports topped 2 million b/d. Increasing demand for energy with the double-digit growth of the Chinese economy was considered a contributing factor in triggering the spike in oil prices in May 2004.

Projections for future energy demand in China depend on a number of factors

4. Philip Andrews Speed, 'China's Energy Policy in Transition: Pressures and constraints', *The Journal of Energy Literature* (December, 2001), Vol. VII, Number 2.

such as the rate of economic growth, the structure of the economy and the level of end-use efficiency. Based on China's Tenth Five Year Plan's assumption of 7.5–8 per cent of GDP growth, a review of most projections indicate that China's primary energy consumption will more than double by 2030.[5] Projections of oil consumption vary from a low of 7 million b/d in 2010 to a high of 13 million b/d. In 2004, with per capita income rising above the $1,000 mark a consensus emerged that China had reached a crucial 'inflection point' and was poised for explosive growth in energy demand.[6]

Compared with the historical rate of growth of over 9 per cent in electricity consumption, China's planned projections of electricity demand are conservative. The ADB's March 2003 paper on electricity demand in the People's Republic of China acknowledges that China's planned forecast of electricity demand of 5 per cent per year and ADB's forecast of an annual average of 5.8 per cent for 2002–10 are lower than the historical trend of 9 per cent in the period 1978–2001. The surge in electricity consumption since 2001 has already created a power shortage in 2004. Even with a low rate of growth in demand for electricity at 5 per cent per year, the total capacity incremental is estimated to be 187 GW between 2002 and 2010, with the required investment of $193 billion.[7]

The critical issue is the future energy mix rather than the absolute level of energy consumption. Table 5.1 shows IEA projections of total primary energy demand in China between 1971 and 2030:

Table 5.1 Total Primary Energy Demand in China (Mtoe)

Energy sources	*1971*	*1990*	*2002*	*2010*	*2030*	*Average annual growth 2002–30 percentages*
Coal	192	365	713	904	1,354	2.3
Oil	43	90	247	375	636	3.4
Gas	3	23	36	59	158	5.4
Nuclear	0	---	7	21	73	9.0
Hydro	3	---	25	33	63	3.4
Other renewables	0	--	0	5	20	--
Biomass	164	190	216	227	236	-0.3
Total primary energy	405	478	1,242	1,622	2,539	2.6

Source: *IEA, WEO* (2004); WB, Energy Demand in china (1995)

5. IEA, *WEO* (2004)
6. Clay Chandler, 'Can China Keep the Lights On?', *Fortune Magazine* (23 February, 2004), p.120.
7. Bo Q Lin, 2003, *Electricity Demand in the People's Republic of China. Investment Requirement and Environmental Impact, Asian Development Bank (ADB)*, ERD Working Paper Series No.37, March.

Recent trends indicate a rise in proportion of oil and gas consumption. The IEA forecast on China shows declining share of coal in China's energy demand from 57 per cent in 2002 to 53 per cent in 2030. While the share of coal in the overall Chinese energy consumption is projected to fall, coal consumption will still be increasing at 2.3 per cent per year in absolute terms. Primary consumption of oil and gas has grown steadily. In China's largest cities passenger car sales leaped by 55 per cent in 2003. Industry experts predict continued growth through 2010 as car prices fall and Chinese banks and foreign car makers expand financing programs for would-be drivers.

In the absence of new oil discoveries and peaking of domestic oil production, China would have to increase the share of oil imports from 35 per cent in 2003 to over 80 per cent of its oil requirements in 2030. The use of natural gas is expected to expand rapidly. Nonetheless, it is projected to meet only about 6 per cent of the total energy needs in 2030.

Biomass remains an important source of energy in the Chinese residential sector in poor rural areas, although its share in total energy use has been declining. In 2002 biomass use accounted for 17 per cent of the total primary energy demand, almost equivalent to primary oil consumption. This is expected to remain flat until 2010 and then start to decline due to replacement by commercial fuels.

Based on its 2004 Energy Demand Outlook (Table 5.1), IEA projects that China's energy investment requirements will amount to $2.4 trillion through 2030, equivalent to 15 per cent of the world's annual energy investment needs[8] of over $760 billion.

Energy sector institutions

The structure of institutions and their effectiveness in operations are crucial for rational reform policy formulation and their successful implementation. Unlike Russia's 'diving in' approach where the collapse of the communist party led to an institutional vacuum, China preserved the old structures of institutions and permitted the gradual introduction of market reforms against a background of sustained economic growth. The communist party continues to be a political force, which permeates almost every aspect of China's economic and institutional reform process.

The institutional structure of China's energy sector has undergone a number of reorganizations since the 1980s. In the 1990s there were two reorganizations, one in 1993 and the other in 1998. The structure of the energy sector institutions on the eve of the 1998 reforms had been in place since 1993. As part of the reorganization, the Ministry of Energy was abolished in 1996. Prior to the 1998 reform, the energy sector was under the State Coun-

---

8. *World Energy Investment Outlook 2003 Insights*, 2003, IEA, Chapter 2, p.48.

cil headed by a Premier acting as the executive of the Chinese National Peoples' Congress. The State council coordinated the work of the government, commissions, ministries, bureaus, offices and state-owned corporations and acted as the highest organ of the government.

The various commissions under the State Council were in charge of planning government projects in their respective areas. The ministries were in charge of implementing and managing the projects. The State Planning Commission (SPC) reporting to the State Council was in charge of policy, planning and budget approval for large infrastructure projects. The other two relevant commissions, the SETC and the State Science and Technology Commission (SSTC), played minor roles in the energy sector.

Each of the main energy industries was dominated by a single institution which was either a state corporation or a ministry, namely China National Petroleum Corporation (CNPC) for petroleum exploration and production (E&P), Sinopec for oil refining and distribution; the MOEP and the ministry of coal industries for coal. These large institutions dominated their respective industries both due to their sheer size and due to their dual role as government agency and commercial enterprise. They were involved in policy formulation, regulation and enterprise management, though certain regulatory tasks such as investment approval and pricing were retained by the SPC.

The objectives of the 1998 institutional reorganization were threefold. First, separation of government and enterprise functions. Second, energy industry restructuring and introduction of competition and third, reduction of civil service overemployment and streamlining of energy policy and regulatory functions.

The institutional reforms since 1998 nominally separated the functions of the government and the energy enterprises, abolished some of the administrative bureaus of the SETC and gave SETC a role in the energy sector by creating two energy bureaus within it, one for petroleum and petrochemicals and another for coal. A new department for the power industry was also set up. Furthermore, the continued important role of the SDPC in the energy sector resulted in overlapping of functions between SETC bureaus and SDPC. The SDPC was therefore restructured. The infrastructure bureau oversees planning and investment in the energy industry. The Pricing Bureau retains responsibility for energy prices.

Prior to 1997, the MOEP acted as policy maker, regulator and enterprise manager for most of China's power industry. Under the MOEP, the provincial power bureaus held monopoly power over transmission, distribution and supply within their respective areas. Some of these bureaus were consolidated into regional Power Groups for the purpose of inter-province transmission of power. In 1997 the State Power Corporation of China (SPCC) was established to take over the enterprise management functions of the MOEP. The MOEP was abolished in 1998 and its government functions were transferred to the newly expanded SETC under its Department of Power. The provincial and lower level bureaus were renamed as companies.

The SPCC has started a number of institutional reform measures including corporatization of provincial companies, the separation of generation and transmission and the corporatization of generation companies in selected provinces. Efforts have been made to introduce competition in generation in some provinces since 2000.

Reforms to the coal industry in 1998 were aimed at decentralization to improve efficiency and resulted in the consolidation and closure of small mines. The Ministry of Coal Industries was abolished and its government functions were transferred to the new State Administration for Supervising Production Safety, created in 2001 within the SETC. The SDPC retains control over major investment decisions and the Ministry of Land and Natural Resources has taken over responsibility for licensing.

Ownership, operation and much of the regulatory responsibilities of the state mines were transferred from the ministry of coal industries to the provincial governments. No single institutional model was imposed on the provinces. Some provinces created a single coal mining group to incorporate all the state-owned mines in the province. Others allowed each of the major mines to become a company in its own right or created a number of groups. Following the general government policy of encouraging mergers between state companies, a smaller number of large coal companies are taking over smaller companies in other provinces. In addition, most provinces with coal mines have set up provincial coal transport and trading companies.

The outcome of the two major reorganizations of the institutional structures in China's energy sector in 1993 and 1998 include: first, the creation of a new Ministry for Land and Natural Resources with clear powers over licensing and land management consolidates the licensing authority under one ministry; second, the abolition of MOEP, the Ministry of Energy and Ministry of Coal Industries appears to separate government departments and enterprises. Nominal separation and renaming have taken place; third, the SETC is now given a role in the energy sector, with the transfer of government functions from the abolished power, energy and coal ministries to the newly created petroleum and coal bureaus and the department of power within the SETC (however, SETC still plays a limited role in energy policy making and implementation);
fourth, the companies continue to play a major role in national energy policy making and in some cases, have been made directly responsible for developing reform strategies for their own industries (e.g., the SPC plays a central role in developing reform strategy and conducting its own experiment in competition); fifth, some reduction in government employment due to consolidation,

closure and general streamlining has taken place. This has led to understaffing in SETC's capacity to carry out its role in the energy sector. The symbol of a planned economy, the State Planning Commission, changed its name to the SDPC and was given the responsibility of long-term development planning. The SDPC continued its role in making long-term plans for the power industry and in giving approvals for large project financing and price setting. However, fragmentation of planning and policy across several agencies and lack of clear definition of roles and responsibilities makes the SDPC continue to retain its dominant institutional role in the energy sector.

Finally, China's entry into the WTO and its selection as host to the next Olympic Games have motivated the government to launch a new phase of institutional reforms in the power sector to encourage competition to continue further restructuring of the SPC and creation of a national regulatory commission under the State Council.

The government may consider that it has been successful in achieving its objectives of institutional reorganization. The objective of separation of government and enterprise functions appears to be the reallocation of ministerial functions to the SETC while the SDPC retains its dominant role in the energy sector. Corporatization of enterprises has renamed them as companies. Whether these power and coal companies are commercially operated and financially viable is not clear. Some reduction in civil service employment has occurred. Encouraging competition will not be easy given the government ownership of power plants and transmission assets. China has continued its incremental institutional reform process adhering firmly to its political communist philosophy of retaining the ultimate control of its energy institutions with the State Council. This has implications for formulating energy policy.

Energy policy

Consistent with the centrally planned economic system, China's energy policy was mainly a document of aggregate targets to be achieved for investment, production and consumption. Given the continued importance of SDPC, the government's policy priorities for the sector are a part of the Five Year Plans. Although target planning practices of the 1980s in the energy sector achieved some of the goals, they failed to address economic, efficiency and energy market transformation issues. The government priorities in the early 1990s gave equal importance to energy exploitation and energy conservation, and rationalization of consumer and producer prices.

The Ninth Five Year Plan (1996–2000) addressed some of the sector and energy mix issues. Having turned a net importer of oil, China began to emphasize increasing efficiency of energy production and conservation. Increasing energy production included stabilizing oil production in the east of China and developing new fields in the west, increasing domestic natural gas E&P targets and promoting overseas oil and gas exploitation. Other priorities for increasing domestic energy supply included large-scale hydroelectricity projects, renewable energy and coal-bed methane. Domestic and international pressures on reducing pollution resulted in a joint effort from SPC, SETC and SSTC and China put forward its policy on environment and renewable energy — 'China's Agenda 21: White Paper on China's Population, Environment and Development in the Twenty-first Century' — and a National New and Renewable Energy Development Plan for the period 1996–2010 was released.

The Tenth Five Year Plan announced in 2001 recognized the future reliance of China on increasing oil and gas imports to meet the rising demand and the need of conservation to contain the growing demand for oil products by developing a new transport strategy. Petroleum is clearly viewed as having strategic importance and construction of a strategic oil reserve to ensure security of oil supplies is envisaged in the Tenth Plan. The main objectives are to diversify energy mix, to ensure the security of energy supply, to increase the efficiency of energy production and utilization and to facilitate the flow of funds to energy projects and government revenue from the energy sector.

To diversify the energy mix, the government plans to promote development of gas and renewables. The new renewables will represent 10 per cent of China's power generating capacity by 2010 and 12 per cent by 2020, despite an expected doubling of electricity demand during this period. The Tenth Five Ykear Plan also calls for development of nuclear power. It sets numerical targets, including reduction in the share of coal in the primary fuel mix to 64 per cent and increasing the share of gas to 5 per cent by 2005. The government plans to establish a petroleum storage system to provide a cushion in the event of supply disruption and also plans to establish stronger links with the international energy market to encourage foreign investment in upstream projects. Investment in the energy sector is also intended to contribute to the development of western provinces as part of the larger effort to reduce income disparities. This 'Go West' policy was officially endorsed at the March 2000 session of the National People's Congress and is expected to impact long-term development of the Chinese energy market. The West–East gas pipeline project, connecting the Tarim basin in Xinjiang with markets in Shanghai, is a major element of this program.

China's energy policy in the 1990s recognized China's dependence on petroleum imports, increasing the share of oil in the relative energy mix and formulating a set of objectives to increase energy supply targets and to improve efficiency. How these objectives are going to be achieved is not clear.

---

9. Chapter 6 discusses China's renewable energy development in the context of increasing access to energy.

The evolution of China's energy policy mirrors the incremental and *ad hoc* process of institutional reform. It reflects the fragmented institutional structure of the energy sector, overlap of energy policy functions across agencies, short-term focus and a piecemeal approach to address the problem at hand. For example, in the electricity sector, except for the 2002 announcement of separation of the SPC and a statement permitting competition in generation there is no supporting policy framework of market reform steps required to be implemented.

In the natural gas sector, development and utilization of natural gas is being used as an instrument for China's important domestic policy initiative to 'Develop the West'. The gas pipeline project from west to east involves the construction of a network of pipelines to take gas from northern and western China to the energy poor provinces of eastern China. In promoting this project the government has decided to exploit domestic gas resources in preference to importing gas, regardless of the fact that these domestic gas resources may have a higher direct cost (Andrew Speed). By 2007 the project will ultimately carry up to 12 billion cubic meters a year (cm/y) from inland fields in Shanxi and Zinjiang to its prosperous coastal provinces. The initial phase of the pipeline, between Jingbian and Shanghai, is complete with the first gas delivery in January 2004.

The decision to construct the west to east gas pipeline is based mainly on political considerations rather than on a reflection of the economic cost benefit considerations. The political considerations include enhancing the status of the 'Develop the West' Program, providing clean energy supply to the eastern provinces and empowering China's State oil companies, primarily Petro China, to invest in and earn revenue from major gas production and transportation projects. Actual benefits to western China will depend on their realized share of revenues from production royalties and gas pipeline tariffs.

In conformity with the persistent central planning mind-set, energy policy formulation in China continues to be an array of policy statements and objectives to strengthen the state energy companies to be internationally competitive in global energy business operations. The explosive growth in China's energy demand since 2002, increasing oil imports and power shortages testify to the complexities of managing China's economic transformation. China's government in recent years liberalized much of the economy, allowing markets to determine how much factories can produce and at what price, with individuals and businesses to consume as much as they can afford. But the supply of energy has remained tightly regulated.

Inadequate understanding of the critical issues to be addressed in the energy policy framework including the linkages between economic growth, liberalization and their impact on energy demand led to misjudgement of energy demand. As discussed above, the government's planned projections of energy and electricity demand turned out to be too conservative. In 1998 the government was forecasting a 3 per cent growth in demand for electricity. Since then, growth has been in double digits with a jump of 15 per cent in 2003. The Tenth Five Year Plan, which started with a power surplus, is heading towards a power shortage. A major exporter of coal and oil in the early 1990s, China in 2004 is consuming all of its production of coal and importing over 40 per cent of its oil consumption, putting pressure on the global supply.

The biggest casualty of the energy shortages in China so far is the momentum for reform. Opting for the incremental approach to reform the energy sector, it was difficult for the government to predict the impact on energy demand, which has sown doubts about the virtues of its reforms. The government-provided tariff incentives to encourage electricity consumption in many provinces with an electricity supply surplus contributed to a surge in demand, leading to energy shortages in 2003–4. Much needed reforms in China's electric power have largely taken a back seat compared to measures that address current electricity shortages. Over two-thirds of Chinese administrative regions have experienced black-outs or shortages since 2003. Shortages peaked in the summer of 2004, with cities like Shanghai, Nanjing, Beijing and Guangzhou implementing emergency measures to control peak load. Given these shortages, government officials are paying attention to demand-side issues in shaping the overall energy policy. Nonetheless, given the growing demand for all forms of energy and the security of supply concerns, the mind-set of China's institutions that are responsible for energy policy is focused mainly on securing supplies and storage targets to be reached.

Energy price liberalization

Energy pricing reform in China has evolved in the 1990s to reflect better the costs and prices on international markets. Coal prices were largely deregulated in 2002. The price of the coal originating from small municipal mines is now determined by negotiations between the competing producing and industrial end-users and distributors. Recent reforms have brought oil prices more in line with international market levels. Since 1998, domestic crude producers and refiners have been free to negotiate the price of oil delivered to refineries. When they cannot reach an agreement, the SDPC intervenes to set the price. The SDPC also sets the prices for retail sales of gas and diesel. Since October 2001, these prices have been based on spot prices on the Singapore, New York and Rotterdam markets (IEA, *WEO* (2001)). Oil companies are allowed to set retail prices within a range of the base prices. Oil prices are expected to become fully deregulated by 2010.

There is a dual pricing system for natural gas. Wellhead and retail prices are fixed for gas from projects launched before 1995. Fertilizer producers pay the lowest prices, while commercial and industrial customers pay the highest. In principle, the pricing of gas from projects that began after 1995 vary from project to project according to development costs, including a 12 per cent rate of return. These prices are adjusted periodically in line with the prices of competing fuels and inflation. The SDPC is considering further reforms to allow prices to reflect the differences in demand features among buyers, changes in market conditions and project-specific costs more accurately.

In a fully deregulated power industry, tariffs for electricity at both the wholesale and retail levels are determined by the supply and demand for power. However, in practice, the addition of generating capacity is a lengthy process as new power plants take years to develop, construct and finance. The Power Law of 1996 formalized the power pricing system in practice by confirming the distinction in three prices—'the power purchase price from the power production enterprises by the power network, the mutual-supply electricity price among interconnected power networks, and the electricity sale price of the power networks to the users.'[10] Since 1996, the original policy, 'new price' for 'new power', was gradually replaced by a single price based on the Power Purchase Agreement (PPA). PPA prices are decided on the basis of 'cost plus profit' and vary according to their locations in a particular transmission grid, generation capacity, type of power (to meet normal demand or peak hour demand), or type of generation—hydro, thermal or nuclear.[11]

Retail electricity prices are set by the electricity distributors but must be approved by the government. Compared with the long tradition of power subsidies and government direct control of pricing prior to the mid-1980s, electricity pricing today reflects the LRMC of supply in most cases. However, it is estimated that average power prices are 10–15 per cent below the LRMC in coastal provinces and below the LRMC by 30 per cent or more in interior provinces.[12] In addition, a number of inefficiencies in power pricing still exist. Wholesale tariffs paid by distributors to independent generators under long-term agreements take no account of seasonal or time-of-day variations in system load. As a result, generating capacity is not always dispatched in an economically efficient way. Transmission is not priced as a separate service and costs are not fully reflected in consumer prices. This has restricted power trade among the provinces.

---

10. *China Electric Power Press, Electricity Law of the People's Republic of China* (Beijing, 1997), p.14.
11. Xu Yi-Chong, *Powering China: Reforming the Electric Power Industry in China* (England, Dartmouth Publishing Company, 2002), p.217.
12. Yi-Chong, *Powering China*, p.219–20.

China expects to continue to phase out energy subsidies gradually through 2010. By 2010, prices are expected to reflect fully the economic cost of supply and to follow trends in international energy prices. China has come a long way in reforming energy prices. However, the government retains its authority to set prices. The SDPC plays a major role in energy pricing decisions which could limit the benefits of energy price liberalization, those of encouraging competition and of attracting private investment.

Regulation

In the 1990s, China's energy sector went through a series of organizational/ institutional changes in line with the 1993 and 1998 reforms to rectify the underlying weaknesses. The four basic institutional problems of centralized organization, direct government management of China's energy/ power sector enterprises, lack of a transparent legal and regulatory system and absence of incentives for efficiency had to be addressed. Recognizing these underlying problems, the government launched the 1993 and 1998 structural and institutional reforms to transform the energy/ power sector from a centrally planned entity to adapt to a socialist market economy. The successful working of the reform process, including separation of government from energy enterprises, corporatization/ commercialization and the introduction of competition, needed to be accompanied by reforms in how the government regulates the sector. A new regulatory system was considered a critical component of energy/ power sector reform.

As part of energy sector reform, it was necessary for China to set up regulatory institutions to transform from plan to market. It required the enactment of laws to abolish the monopoly of the state oil and power companies, strengthen capital markets to support private entrepreneurs and define the rules of how privatization will take place. The legal framework is important because most private investors will look for clear rules of sector operation that make investment attractive. A basic legal framework covers contract law, the status of organizations such as joint ventures and stock companies, freedom of property (i.e. selling shares and assets, expatriating profits and so on) and a mechanism for dispute resolution.

Oil and gas regulation

Principal regulatory responsibility is spread among three national level government agencies—the National Development Reform Commission (NDRC), the Ministry of Commerce (Mofcom) and the Ministry of Land and Resources (Molar). In addition, the State Council has jurisdiction over upstream projects where foreign investment exceeds $0.5 billion. No ministry or government body has exclusive regulatory jurisdiction over oil and gas.

Responsibility for foreign investment in the oil and gas sector in China is shared among government bodies which perform a regulatory role and the NOCs which carry out commercial and/ or production functions. Through its Energy Bureau, the NDRC determines the oil and gas blocks made available for foreign investment based on the relevant NOC in the area. It is also charged with the approval of the operator's Overall Development Plan for upstream oil and gas exploration, development and production, whether onshore or offshore. In addition, the NDRC reviews any overseas investment projects proposed by an NOC.

Mofcom has broad responsibility for the formulation of industry policy and for approving production sharing contracts (PSCs) and other industry joint venture arrangements with foreign enterprises.

Molar's principal area of authority in the upstream oil and gas sectors include identification of location and acreage of contract areas for exploration, the approval of geological reserves reports and the review, issuance, registration and assignment of licenses to the NOCs for oil and gas E&P. It is the PSC that gives a foreign investor an interest in the activities and production arising from the NOC license.

In addition to Mofcom, Molar and NDRC, other governmental agencies control certain aspects of PSC. The State Administration for Industry and Commerce registers all incorporated entities that conduct business in China, including PSC companies; the State Administration of Foreign Exchange oversees foreign capital investment in China and the remittance of profits under the PSC; the State Administration of Taxation supervises tax payments under the PSC regime; and the Customs General Administration handles any duty exemption issues with respect to the materials used in petroleum operations.

CNPC, China Petrochemical Corporation and China National Offshore Oil Corporation (CNOOC) are the three NOCs authorized to manage PSCs with foreign enterprises. They also have the authority to operate independently. Each has a public listed subsidiary through which it performs many of its petroleum activities.

The PSC embodies as contractual terms and conditions, a number of the basic requirements of China's petroleum laws and regulations and the provisions of the relevant E&P licenses. It determines the sharing of production from a successful endeavour, including the formula by which the contractor (foreign investor) recovers its risk investment made during the exploration phase.

Under the PSC regime in China, the contractor bears all risks, costs and expenses during the exploration, evaluation and development phases, although once a discovery is made, the Chinese NOC partner has the right to take up to a 51 per cent participating interest in the block. After the payment of value added tax and royalty, the contractor is entitled to recover the development costs and exploration investment out of production. Thereafter, the operating costs are shared between the NOC and the contractor according to a formula that tracks the parties' production share.

The remaining value of the production stream is divided between the contractor and the NOC. Royalty is paid on a sliding scale that ranges from 0 to 12.5 per cent for oil and 0.3 per cent for gas, each based on production. The contractor has the right to export its share of oil to any destination, although the NOC has the right to exclude destinations that are contrary to the interests of China.

The central government continues to encourage stronger contractual compliance by providing a framework for legal dispute resolution. China is a member of both the International Centre for Settlement of Investment Disputes and the UN Convention on the Recognition and Enforcement of Foreign Arbitral Awards (New York Convention). Even so, other model form contracts (including PSCs) propose arbitration under the rules and procedures of the China International Economic and Trade Arbitration Commission (Cietac). Foreign investors have mixed views of Cietec's procedures and effectiveness, given the availability of well developed international arbitration rules frequently used by the oil and gas industry.[13] The structure of the upstream foreign investment regime may well be a reflection of China's perceived need to minimize its supply deficit by increasing domestic supply.

Power sector regulation

China's regulatory system in the power sector has been evolving in several stages since 1993. In the context of China's prevailing government's command and control system, there was much confusion in the discussions on regulation. The concept of regulation as a government's control of an enterprise's activities required clarification and a distinction between the prevailing old Chinese method of governments' direct control of operations and ownership and the new style of regulation, with separation of government and enterprise functions that allows power enterprises to manage as financially viable business operations.

By the mid-1990s, the government made the decision to move from the old system of command and control to the new regulatory system of oversight and supervision of autonomous commercially oriented enterprises with necessary legal safeguards to ensure that all parties comply with the terms of the regulatory system. In China's power sector, the term *legal framework* refers to a coordinated structure of laws and other legal instruments that together define the regulatory system within which the power regulatory commission and power enterprises must operate.

---

13. China, 2004, *Petroleum Economist*, December.

On 28 December 1995, the Standing Committee of the National People's Congress enacted a comprehensive new law that applies to every aspect of the power sector. The Electric Power Law became effective on 1 April 1996 and is intended to support reforms that are necessary to introduce the socialist market economy to the power sector.

Consistent with the direction of reforms for the Chinese economy, the Electric Power Law's objectives are:

- To encourage the development of the power industry in a manner consistent with development of a socialist market economy and the environment
- To encourage development of poor and rural areas
- To encourage private investment in power generation, but not in other power sector activities, such as transmission and distribution (T&D)
- To protect the legal interests of power enterprises, investors and power consumers
- To encourage development of renewable resources and new technology
- To safeguard power facilities and installations

The Electric Power Law covers the construction of power facilities and the supply of power in China (except Hong Kong, Macao and Taiwan) and applies to both Chinese and foreign companies. This law provides the basic legal framework for regulation of the power sector by establishing the general principles that will govern decisions. It provides the required legal basis to establish and reinforce the new regulatory system.

The Electric Power Law broadly addresses the overall design of the industry, authority of the electric power administrative departments under the State Council and principles for making regulatory decisions. It provides the broad principles of a new pricing system linked to the cost of supply of electricity. The law does not include specific provisions relating to the creation and precise authority of the national and provincial regulatory institutions, the allocation of regulatory responsibilities among different government institutions and the standard procedures for appeals of regulatory decisions. However, a number of these matters could be adequately addressed through State Council regulations.

The new regulatory system has been entrusted with the following eight potential tasks:

- To define the specific service obligations and establish high quality of service standards of regulated power enterprises

- To determine and supervise tariff levels for power enterprises consistent with general principles laid down by the Electric Power Law and State council regulations
- To approve the investment plans of regulated power enterprises to the extent that those plans are consistent with national and provincial plans
- To establish an accounting system for power enterprises within the guidelines established by the Ministry of Finance
- To oversee the financial planning of regulated power enterprises
- To oversee industry structure, including coordination and power pooling agreement among power enterprises
- To make and enforce regulatory requirements and decisions
- To resolve disputes involving power enterprises

Consistent with China's gradual and incremental approach to reform in the institutional structure discussed earlier in this chapter, the government adopted a four-staged implementation of the new regulatory system and legal framework. Stage 1 (1996–7) focused on the separation of government from power enterprise management. It involved the elimination of MOEP, allocation of government functions previously performed by MOEP to SETC and other central government institutions and adoption of legal instruments that are a precondition to further reform of the power sector. Stage 2 (1997–2000) took steps towards the concentration of power regulatory functions at the central and provincial levels within the respective government institutions. It also provided national and provincial regulators training in those regulatory techniques deemed appropriate for a socialist market economy. Steps were also taken to adopt the required legal instruments to define the regulatory relationship between power enterprises and the government.

It was decided to create a national regulatory authority called the National Power Regulatory Commission (NPRC) that is separate from other government institutions. The Commission would be under the supervision of the State Council. It was to be created through a State Council decree at Stage 4 of a four-stage, multi-year implementation process.[14] In Stages 3 (2000–5) and 4 (2005–7), the Commission would be given substantial operational autonomy. Similarly, provincial power regulatory commissions would be created in each province. To ensure coordination between the national and provincial regulatory authorities, provincial regulatory commissions would be supervised by the NPRC.

The national and provincial regulatory authorities to be established are

---

14. WB, *China: Power Sector Regulation in a Socialist Market Economy* (Washington DC, 1997)

expected to be responsible for tariff approvals. Tariff approval authority is to be split between provincial and national regulatory authorities. Under the guidance of the national regulatory authority, the provincial regulatory authorities would be responsibile for reviewing tariff filings for producer, bulk and consumer sales. The national regulatory authority would also have direct authority over tariff filings for separate transmission service and inter-enterprise power sales.

In March 2003, the State Council of China established the State Electricity Regulatory Commission (SERC), the first supervisory body for China's power industry. The SERC is slated to carry out a structural reform of the power industry. It will also accelerate the introduction of laws and regulations and develop an electrical supply trading market. In February 2005, the State Council of China promulgated the Electricity Regulatory Rules to take effect from May 2005.

Funds for both the national and provincial power regulatory commissions are allocated from the central government budget. The central government could also raise funds through a small levy on the prices paid by customers and an annual license fee paid by regulated power enterprises.

Tariff regulation

As discussed in the previous section on energy price liberalization, since the 1990s China has travelled a long way towards reforming its pricing system and adapting it to emerging market conditions. The power pricing system has improved, especially in the area of resource mobilization through the 'new plant-new price' policy. However, the tariff reforms in practice were introduced in a piecemeal fashion rather than as part of a systematic long-term price reform program.

The prices of power purchased by provincial power companies are determined on a plant-by-plant (sometimes even on a unit-by-unit) basis, depending on the origin of investment funds and the construction date of the plant. Power sale prices from virtually all power plants constructed before 1985 (primarily with government allocations) and from plants—or shares of plants—constructed with subsidized government loans between 1985 and 1992 are based on catalogue price tables issued every year by the government. These prices cover direct operating costs, especially labour, fuel and maintenance. They do not cover capital costs (depreciation, interest and return on investment).

The prices of power purchased from power plants not financed by the central government between 1986 and 1992 and from all power plants built after 1992 are based on the 'new plant-new price' policy. Under this policy, power is sold to provincial power companies at debt-repayment prices to provide sufficient revenues for the repayment of loan capital with interest, generally within ten years. These prices are determined annually by the provincial power companies and submitted for approval to the provincial power bureau. The 'new plant-new price' policy produces significantly higher producer prices. On average, the prices of electricity from the most recent plants are 65 to 100 per cent higher than those from old power plants. This reflects in part the fact that the capital costs are being recovered over a relatively short period.

At the generation level, the implementation of the 'new plant-new price' policy has led to contractual arrangements between purchasers (usually provincial power companies) and the generators, based on 'take-or-pay' provisions providing for a minimum use of the power plants (equivalent to a capacity factor of 57 per cent) charged at an energy (kWh) price covering variable costs (fuel and maintenance), repayment of debt (capital cost and interest) and a reasonable profit. The same price is applied to electricity purchased in excess of the minimum 'take-or-pay' provision.

The disadvantage of this combination of a minimum 'take-or-pay' provision and a one-part tariff is that it leads to over-investment in base generation capacity, because it is difficult to recover investments in peaking capacity. It leads to uneconomic dispatch because provincial power companies (dispatchers and purchasers) faced with higher prices from new and efficient power plants limit power purchases to contractual minimum amounts and rely more on old, inefficient power plants to minimize their financial costs. The current producer tariff policy fails to achieve the basic goal of producing electricity at the lowest cost to the economy.

In most parts of China, two types of consumer tariffs remain. Administered prices, or in-plan prices, are based on the catalogue prices issued annually by the government and differentiated at the provincial level. Additional fees and surcharges are often added to the administered prices by provincial, municipal and county authorities. These administered prices plus fees and surcharges are charged for electricity supplied to enterprises under in-plan quotas, generally set at 1985 consumption levels. *Guidance Prices* or 'out-of-plan' prices include administered (or state catalogue) prices, mark-ups for the higher cost of power purchased from new plants, plus additional fees and surcharges. Consumers pay guidance prices on any consumption that exceeds their 1985 consumption levels.

The various surcharges and fees added to the consumer tariffs played a role in increasing the mobilization of investment resources for building new power plants. However, it compounded the failure of the sector to take full advantage of economies of scale and increased its fragmentation because of the propensity of local governments to build their own power plants rather than invest in the state companies' power plants. It also created transmission bottlenecks because most of the surcharges funded new generation capacity not matched by the required investments in transmission networks due to the poor financial situation of the provincial power state companies.

Despite incremental tariff reforms, power prices in China are still set and controlled by the government at the central level (catalogue prices), provincial level (guidance prices, surcharges) and even municipal and county levels (surcharges). It still does not meet the major objectives of power sector reform to increase investment in the sector to alleviate shortages and improve efficiency. This results in delays in tariff adjustments and further deterioration of the financial situation of most provincial power companies and drastic reduction of their self-financing capabilities.

The Electric Power Law provides the broad principles of a new pricing system linked to the cost of supply. Consistent with this law, this approach requires (WB 1997):

- Two-part or multipart tariffs
- Non-discrimination among customers
- Recovery of full supply cost at all delivery levels
- Charging customers according to the characteristics of their demand, not just their total usage of electricity

If deviations from these principles are required to meet financial and social objectives, these should be undertaken in a way that will minimize the distortions in the structure of tariffs. A new Electricity Law, superseding the one established in 1995, is expected to address minimizing the structural distortions in tariffs.

Implementation of tariff reforms requires establishing tariff principles at different levels to move towards market-based prices in the competitive segment of the industry (generation) and regulated prices based on marginal cost principles (both for the structure and level of tariffs) in the monopolistic segments of the sector. Table 5.2 summarizes the principles of the tariff reform.

Table 5.2 Tariff Reforms for Implementation

Type of tariff	*Reform principle*
Producer	1. Switch from a one-part to a two-part tariff
	2. Acquire new generating supplies through competitive procurements
	3. Focus on prices, not profits
	4. Do not establish uniform producer prices based on administratively determined estimates of LRMC
Separate transmission	1. Use two-part transmission tariffs based on LRMCs
Bulk	1. Use two-part tariffs based on LRMCs
	2. The tariff should include generation and transmission

Type of tariff	*Reform principle*
Consumer	1. Use one or multi-part tariffs based on marginal costs
	2. Separate taxes and fees from the electricity price
	3. Unify the prices charged to customers with similar cost and demand characteristics
	4. Change prices to reflect the cost of providing service at different voltage levels
	5. Impose a capacity charge on customers when the expected benefits exceed likely metering costs
	6. Accelerate the movement of the seasonal and time-of-day tariffs for larger customers based on estimates of the supplying system marginal cost
All	1. Tariffs should always recover the full economic costs of supply
	2. Tariffs should not favour affiliates over non-affiliates

Source: WB, *China: Power Sector Regulation in a Socialist Market Economy* (1997), Table 5.1, p.74.

Commercialization/ Corporatization

In the Chinese context where government ownership and control pervades all levels, commercialization aims to take the required steps to focus on commercial objectives and to increase the profitability and efficiency of use of the enterprise's assets. Corporatization is defined as specifying the rights of parties with a stake in the profits earned on assets ('stakeholder') and improving the financial performance through capital market pressures.

The institutional reforms launched in 1993 and 1998 took steps towards commercialization/ corporatization as part of the energy sector reform process.

The objectives of the 1990s reform on commercialization involved:

- Establishment of managerial autonomy to separate energy enterprises from the government and to reduce government interference in day-to-day operations, leaving it to the management.
- Reform of pricing policy to reflect cost and international energy prices
- Adoption of Generally Accepted Accounting Principles (GAAP) of internationally recognized standard and valuation of assets
- Raising outside finance by diversification of investment funds
- Adoption of commercial principles for taxation and dividend payments
- Split-off of non-core and non-productive activities into separate enterprises, each with its own budget and a responsibility to operate

on a commercial basis.

- 'Socialization' of social welfare responsibilities and social objectives. For example, power enterprises in China carry extensive social welfare responsibilities for their labour forces, such as providing housing and running hospitals and clinics. In keeping with the decisions of the State Council on the reform of housing and the social security system, as part of commercialization it would be required to specify the character and cost of such social activities and to have to commit to paying for such costs from the budget.

In the process of corporatization, the energy enterprise is transformed into a company with rights and liabilities of the company law. The company may be a limited liability company or a joint-stock company. Corporatization requires articles of association specifying the company's main areas of activity, objectives, procedures for the appointment of senior managers and rights and responsibilities of owners and the management. Corporatization also involves a clarification of ownership claims on the assets and profits of the company.

For the petroleum sector, the reorganization of 1998 resulted in removing the government functions from the state companies and assigning them to the SETC. Prior to 1998, China's petroleum industry was dominated by three state petroleum companies, namely the CNPC, which was responsible for onshore oil and gas exploration, Sinopec, which undertook much of the oil refining and distribution and China National Offshore Corporation (CNOOC).

Following the 1998 reorganization, the Chinese government categorized most state-owned oil and gas assets into two vertically integrated companies—the CNPC and the Sinopec. This reorganization created two regionally focused companies—CNPC in the north and west, and Sinopec in the south, though CNPC is still tilted toward crude oil production and Sinopec toward refining. They retained their regional monopoly powers except in the retail marketing of oil products where competition is emerging. Other major state sector firms in China include the CNOOC, which handles offshore E&P and accounts for more than 10 per cent of China's domestic production and China National Star Petroleum, a new company which was created in 1997. Now, regulatory oversight of the industry is the responsibility of the State Energy Administration (SEA), which was created in early 2003.

The objective of the restructuring was to make these state oil companies more like similar vertically integrated global corporate entities. In connection with this process, the companies have been spinning off or eliminating many unprofitable ancillary activities such as running housing units, hospitals and other services near company facilities. Massive downsizing to correct SOE overstaffing has also been undertaken.

Further modifications to the structure of the three main oil companies

(CNPC, Sinopec and CNOOC) were implemented in preparation for their initial public offerings (IPOs) in 2000 and 2001. The drivers of change for the CNPC were primarily the company's need to raise external funds, a government reform program and the fact that China turned a net importer of oil. The specific objectives of CNPC's corporatization are to develop reserves and increase production, raise external funds, develop management skills, implement a regulatory framework for the oil and gas industry, and transform the company into a commercially operating entity.

The three largest Chinese oil and gas firms—Sinopec, CNPC and CNOOC—all have successfully carried out IPOs of stock between 2000 and 2002 bringing in billions of dollars in foreign capital. The productive assets of these companies to be offered were separated to form new companies. Unproductive and controversial assets remained with the respective parent companies, which were converted to holding companies. In the case of CNPC while unproductive and overseas investments were held in the hands of CNPC which remained the holding company, productive assets were included in Petro China, the vehicle for the IPO which carried out its IPO of a minority interest on both the Hong Kong and New York stock exchanges in April 2000. The IPO raised over $3 billion, with British Petroleum (BP) being the largest buyer at 20 per cent of the shares offered. Sinopec carried out its IPO in New York and Hong Kong in October 2000, raising about $3.5 billion. Like the PetroChina IPO, only a minority stake of 15 per cent was offered. About $2 billion of the IPO was purchased by the three global super majors—Exxon Mobil, BP and Shell. Higher oil prices and cost-cutting measures have contributed to successful operations and increase in profitability of these companies since 2001. CNOOC held its IPO of a 27.5 per cent stake in February 2001. Shell bought a large block of shares valued at US $200 million.[15]

There are two important features of these stock offerings. First, they all involved only minority stakes. Second, they have not given the foreign investors a major voice in corporate governance. The Chinese government still holds majority stakes in all three firms and the foreign investors have not received seats on their boards of directors. Industry analysts see these investments as attempts by the super majors to gain a foothold in China, which will necessarily involve partnerships with the Chinese majors. Even with the opening to foreign investment envisioned in China's commitments for membership in the WTO, it is still likely that almost all major oil and gas projects in China will involve one of the Chinese majors. All three of the global super majors, BP, Exxon Mobil and Shell, are planning to enter the Chinese retail market in partnership with CNPC, Sinopec or both.

As a net importer of oil since 1994, China's restructured petroleum indus-

15. USEIA, *China* (July 2004)

try is focused on meeting domestic demand by securing oil and gas assets abroad. China's drive into foreign oil and gas operations is led by China National Offshore Oil Corporation Limited (CNOOCL), the Hong Kong listed company in which CNOOC has a 70.6 per cent interest. Within a year of its listing, in January 2002, CNOOCL completed the acquisition of part of Repsol YPF's upstream assets in Indonesia for US $585 million. At the time of the deal the fields had a net production of 70,300 barrels of oil equivalent a day, with 79.2 per cent of that being liquids.[16] In addition to CNOOCL, the other three big state-owned oil and gas companies—China Petrochemical Corporation (Sinopec Group, the main asset of which is a 55 per cent holding in the New York, Hong Kong, London and Shanghai exchanges—listed Sinopec Corporation), the Petro China unit of CNPC and Sinochem—are all seeking foreign assets, with varying degrees of success.

The government is also seeking to secure through CNPC acquired interests in E&P in Indonesia, Kazakhstan, Sudan, Iraq and Peru. China is increasingly looking outwards in its energy policy. The most significant deal thus far is CNPC's acquisition of a 60 per cent stake in Kazakh oil firm Aktobemunaigaz, which came with a pledge to invest significantly in the company's future development over the next 20 years. The Kazakh and Chinese governments signed an agreement in May 2004 for the construction of a $700 million pipeline to export Kazakh crude oil into western China.

The new policy even extends to an agreement with the association of Southeast Asian Nations to open discussions on joint development of resources in the South China Sea, much of which is claimed by China. China and Vietnam signed an agreement in December 2000 which settled their outstanding disputes over sovereignty and economic rights in offshore areas near their border. CNOOC opened a tender for 10 new exploration blocks in May 2004.

In the power sector, commercialization/ corporatization process has been ongoing since 1985. The Chinese government is in the early stages of formulating a fundamental long-term restructuring of their electric power sector. The National Power Industry Framework Reform Plan promulgated by the State Council in April 2002, embodies the unbundling of generation, T&D assets. As per the government plan agreed in 2002, China has broken up the dominant SPC to five power generation companies and has unbundled the generation and transmission segments. The generation assets of SPCC are being transferred to the five nation-wide generation companies, namely China Huaneng Group, China Datang Group, China Guodian Group, China Huadian Group and China Power Investment Company. No generation company will be allowed to have more than 20 per cent market share of any regional or provincial power market. Each generation company will compete

16. China: Overseas, 2003, *Petroleum Economist*, December.

with the other for signing contracts with the power grid operators.

The T&D network has been reorganized into two national companies covering the south (Southern Power Grid Company) and the north (State Grid Corporation of China). These companies will be allowed to choose generators from whom they buy electricity.

Commercialization and corporatization in China has proceeded since 1985 in a piecemeal fashion as part of the 1980–90s institutional reform process of reallocation of government functions. The objective of commercialization/ corporatization of petroleum and power industries was to create large companies able to compete effectively on the international stage to gain access to energy resources.

Table 5.3 summarizes the key developments in these areas.

Table 5.3. Key Steps in Commercialization/ Corporatization, 1985–2002

Year	*Regulation or Directive*	*Significance*
1985	State Council:' Provisional Regulations on encouraging Joint-Investment Power Development"	Establishment of Huaneng International Power Development Corporation (HIPDC)
1988	State Council, 'On Management System Reform Directions for the Electric Power Industry'	First attempt at commercialization through establishment of power companies alongside government power bureaus
1992	State Council, 'Regualtions on Transforming the Management Mechanisms of SOEs'	Established the basis for SOEs to operate as commercial entities
1997	State Council	Establishment of the State Power Corporation of China
1998	State Council	Abolition of the Ministry of Electric Power and transfer of Government functions to SETC
2000	State Council	Introduction of 'competition in generation'
2002	State Council Plan	Separation of generation and transmission and reorganization of transmission network; sharing out major generation assets among four companies in addition to the State Power Grid Company which will retain peak-load plants
2003	State Council	Established State Electricity Regulatory Commission (SERC)

Sources: R Vedavalli, *Report on Institutions and Policies for Renewable Energy Development in China,* (WB 1996); *IEA, WEO* (2004)

Privatization/ Private investment

As part of the sector reform process, the Chinese government has opened the sector and is encouraging private investors to play a role in its development. Financing schemes explored by the government include:

- Privatization through stock offers, stock distribution and negotiated sales and leasing
- Promotion of joint venture and fully foreign financed IPPs through BOO, build-operate-transfer (BOT) and BOOT arrangements
- Issuance of stocks on overseas stock exchange markets to create shareholding companies and around one or more existing power plants. Some energy investment companies of the special economic zones have also been authorized to raise equity capital. Following its gradual approach the government designated Shandong province and Shanghai Municipality as pilot cases to test these new financial schemes. In addition, HIPDC has been authorized to list some of its power plants on foreign financial markets. Implementing the corporatization reforms is expected to facilitate listing companies to attract private capital. The share capital of listed Chinese companies comprises of two kinds of shares□local shares (A shares) restricted to Chinese nationals and foreign shares (B and H shares) restricted to foreign investors. B shares are listed on the two official stock exchanges in China (Shanghai Securities Exchange and ShenZhen Stock Exchange). H shares are listed in Hong Kong (China), and traded and settled in foreign currencies (such as US dollars)
- Establishment of a power development fund based in Hong Kong, which would float bonds in international capital markets or engage in commercial syndicated loans.
- Between 1991 and 2000 China's total privatization proceeds were about US $30 billion, accounting for over 55 per cent of the privatization proceeds in East Asia. In 1997 China reached the peak in privatization revenues and accounted for 90 per cent of total privatization revenue in the EAP (10.4 billion). It raised more than US $9.1 billion, mainly with the public offerings of H and B shares. Although China contributed to over 90 per cent of privatization revenues in the EAP region in 1997, the share of the energy sector was less than 8 per cent of the total privatization revenues at US $710 million through equity sale in the power sector. In 1998 following the East Asian crisis, privatization activity in East Asia including China declined considerably and started picking up in only 1999.

> Preliminary estimates for 2000 show that privatization proceeds increased significantly (surpassing the 1997 peak of US $10.4 billion) in the region, mainly as a result of Chinese divestitures in the oil and gas, telecommunications and power sectors (World Bank, 2001, Global Development Finance).[17]

Since the 1990s, China is the major recipient of FDI in the developing world and the rate of growth of FDI has been phenomenal. FDI includes greenfield investment to build new capacity and the acquisition of assets of existing local firms. China topped the list of the top ten recipients of the total FDI flows in the 1990s. Net FDI flow to China increased from US $11.2 billion in 1992 to peak at US $44.2 billion in 1997 and to US $42 billion in 1998. FDI to China continued its surge since 2002 to US $49.5 billion. China's share in regional FDI rose to 94 per cent at US $53.6 billion in 2003.[18]

Private investment in coal

China is becoming increasingly open to foreign investment in the coal sector, particularly in modernization of existing large-scale mines and the development of new ones. The China National Coal Import and Export Corporation is the primary Chinese partner for foreign investment in the coal sector. Areas of interest in foreign investment concentrate on new technologies recently introduced in China or with environmental benefit, including coal liquefaction, coal-bed methane production and slurry pipeline transportation projects. China has expressed a strong interest in coal liquefaction technology and would like to develop liquid fuels based on coal substitute for some of its petroleum demand in transportation.

Coal-bed methane production is being developed with BP, Chevron Texaco and Virgin Oil. Chevron Texaco is the largest foreign investor in coal-bed methane, with activities in several provinces. Far East Energy of the USA received approval from Chinese authorities in April 2004 for a farm out agreement with ConocoPhillips, under which it would undertake exploratory drilling for coal-bed methane in Shanxi province.[19] Over the longer term, China plans to aggregate the large state coal mines into seven corporations to seek foreign capital through international stock offerings.

17. WB, *Global Development Finance* (2004)
18. WB, *Global Development Finance* (2004)
19. USEIA, *China, Country Analysis Brief* (July 2004)

Private investment in oil and gas upstream

Although overall FDI inflows into China are the highest in the world, investment in the energy sector, especially in E&P, has typically lagged. Foreign investment in China's oil and gas sector, like investment in other industries, is subject to government guidelines and monitoring. There are two principal governing documents—the Foreign Investment Provision (Guidelines) and the Foreign Investment Industrial Guidance Catalogue (Catalogue).

The Guidelines divide investment activities into four categories (encouraged, restricted, prohibited and permitted) and thereby determine the acceptability of foreign investment enterprises and activities in China. The Catalogue describes the specific industries or activities that are included in the encouraged, restricted and prohibited categories, while any not mentioned are deemed to be permitted. The assignment of investment categories to various industries and activities is a reflection of China's commitment to certain WTO accession principles, as well as to encouraging the growth of its economy, which in the oil and gas sector includes enabling its NOCs to compete with foreign companies once China's energy markets are fully opened.

The principal guidance for foreign investment in the oil and gas sector is found in the PRC Exploitation of Offshore oil resources in cooperation with Foreign Parties Regulations (1982, amended in 2001, Offshore Regulations) and the PRC Exploitation of Onshore Oil Resources in cooperation with Foreign Parties Regulations (1993 amended in 2001, Onshore Regulations).

The Onshore and Offshore Regulations (joint regulations) are nearly identical and provide a starting point for foreign investment in the upstream sector. Under the regulations, CNPC and Sinopec are responsible for conducting onshore exploitation and CNOOC for offshore exploitation, each with exclusive responsibility for negotiating and performing contracts with foreign entities in their respective geographical areas. Onshore PSCs entered either as a result of public tender or negotiation. However, for offshore blocks a public tender must precede any contract award.

Much of the known oil and gas deposits are onshore, an area still largely off limits to foreign investors. Onshore exploration remains the domain of the domestic players, notably Petro China and Sinopec, although certain areas such as tight gas development and deep gas exploration are being promoted. But there is growing attention to the offshore, especially with the gradual opening of the country's gas market. Offshore oil output in 2004 accounted for 0.5 million b/d of total production, up by more than 200 per cent since 1995. The CNOOC, leading the country's offshore research, is in the midst of an active exploration program across four main areas covering Bohai Bay, Western South China Sea, Eastern South China Sea and East

China Sea. The company's oil and gas production is rising sharply following a series of discoveries in these areas.[20] Since 2001, CNOOC has shown greater flexibility in partnering with foreign firms including Chevron-Texaco, BP, ConocoPhillips, Statoil, Devon Energy and Burlington Resources.

Western oil companies have long angled for a role in China's domestic energy markets. The foreign oil company with the highest Chinese oil output, Chevron Texaco has interests in the South China Sea and the North China Basin, with a total net output in 2002 of 26,800 b/d from two areas. CNOOC's joint venture with Chevron Texaco and Agip produces 72,000 b/d in block 16/08 Pearl River Mouth Basin (PRMB) and 35,000 b/d in Bohai Bay.

ConocoPhillips comes a close second with a net output of 25,000 b/d. It is carrying out a two-phase development of China's largest offshore discovery, in the Penglai 19–3 area. Joint production with CNOOC is expected to reach 45,000 b/d in 2004, with a second phase due to start operations in 2008, reaching 200,000 b/d. Several medium sized players such as Devon Energy, Kerr-McGee and Burlington Resources, have also gained a foothold in the upstream.

Among the largest foreign investors are BP, which has committed US $4 billion in various Chinese projects since the 1980s—plus a further $1billion for a 2 per cent stake in the Petro China and Sinopec IPOs of 2000—and expects to invest a further US $3 billion in the next five years through 2008.[21] Warren Buffett, of US Berkshire Hathaway Inc., a diversified holding company spent an estimated US $500 million for a 13 per cent stake in Petro China in 2003.

The importance of the offshore sector is likely to grow given the relative success in locating oil and gas reserves by foreign and local firms and the higher costs and technical challenges associated with deep water exploration. In contrast with the slow decline in onshore oil production, offshore oil production has accelerated by more than 200 per cent since 1995 to reach 0.5 million b/d in 2003.

Despite an extensive and generally well developed legal regime, foreign investment in China's oil and gas sector has lagged behind expectations. Oil industry observers suggest that this is because China's best blocks have not been made available for foreign investment and that foreign investment regime does not provide sufficient incentives for foreign participation for investment in other blocks.

The laws regulating foreign investment in the oil and gas upstream sector place numerous requirements and in some cases, restrictions on foreign

---

20. China, 2004, *Petroleum Economist*, December.

21. China: No going back, 2003, *Petroleum Economist*, December.

participation, which reflect China's still-cautious stance on foreign trade and economic activity in this area. The burden of these requirements is compounded by the various levels of government involved in the approval process, which requires a concerted effort by newcomers to ascertain the specific approval procedures for an upstream project, including the authority and jurisdiction of the relevant bodies.

An evolving upstream regime produces inevitable inconsistencies in the enforcement of regulations, particularly when delegated to the various provincial (or even lower level) governments and industry bureau. Furthermore, although the government has launched campaigns to address corruption these encouraging efforts have been hampered by the lack of truly independent investigative bodies.

In addition to complex regulatory system, a foreign investor may also have to contend with the lack of full legislative transparency although this is not a challenge unique to China. Under the terms of its WTO accession agreement, China agreed to enforce only those laws and regulations related to trade, intellectual property and foreign exchange that have been published and were available for public comment. The practice of soliciting comments on newly drafted laws and regulations does not appear to be consistently employed and even when the regulations are released for comment, the periods are often brief. Furthermore, the effect that public comments have on the final regulations is unclear.[22]

The development of the gas sector has taken on huge importance as an alternate and cleaner source of fuel to compete against oil and coal. A number of international companies, including Shell, are working on coal gasification projects to convert coal into synthetic gas, in joint ventures with Chinese partners. The centrepiece of the government's aggressive gas policy is the West-East pipeline. The project is expected to ultimately carry up to 12 billion cm/y by 2007 from inland fields in Shanxi and Xinjiang to its prosperous coastal provinces. Three foreign majors—Shell, Exxon Mobil and Gazprom—are looking to take a 15 per cent shareholding each, although negotiations drag on. In 2002, three companies signed a framework agreement with lead partners Petro China and Sinopec, but questions including who will buy the gas remain unanswered given the uncertainties over pricing.

The prospect of international oil and gas pipelines from Russia and Kazakhstan is expected to involve some form of foreign participation. China and Japan are both courting Moscow in a bid to influence the direction of the pipeline. China is seeking competition and expertise where oil and gas companies can help them in the more efficient production of gas. Although there is a general acceptance of foreign investment in the energy business,

22. China, 2004, *Petroleum Economist*, December.

the industry is of the view that it will always have to be on China's terms.

Foreign companies have taken the chance to participate in the development of China's fledgling LNG industry, which has lagged somewhat behind the rest of Asia. BP is the foreign partner, with a 30 per cent stake, in the joint venture developing China's first LNG import terminal and associated pipeline network near Shenzhen, Guandong province. The 3.3 million tons per year (tpy) project is led by CNOOC and is expected to begin imports in 2006. LNG will be supplied from the Australian North West Shelf project, in which BP also has an interest. Earlier in 2003, the government approved a plan for a second LNG import terminal at Fujian. The 2.6 million tpy facility will be supplied by the Tangguh gasfield, in Indonesia, in which BP has a further stake. It is due to come on stream in 2007.

Private investment in petroleum downstream

The opening of the Chinese market, rising income levels in the cities and a robust automobile market have raised the interest of multinational oil companies in downstream and retail operations.

China's Guangzhou refinery was slated for expansion under a proposed agreement between Exxon Mobil and Guangzhou Petrochemical Corporation which would form a joint venture to increase capacity to 10 million tons per year (tpy) by 2005 and possibly to 18 million tpy in later years. BP has made its single biggest investment in a joint venture through Shanghai Secco Petrochemical, in which it holds a 50 per cent stake alongside Sinopec and Shanghai Petrochemical. The joint venture is building a $2.7 billion integrated petrochemicals and polymers complex at Caojing, near Shanghai, centred on a 0.9 million tpy ethylene cracker, due on stream in 2005. Ultimately, the plant is expected to have a total capacity of 2.3 million tpy of various petrochemicals.

BP, which has licensed chemicals technology in China for years, is making other equity investments including operation of retail sites. BP has a joint venture with Petro China to operate 500 retail sites in Guandong province and expects to expand this to 1,000 outlets across several coastal provinces by 2007. In October 2003, BP also signed a joint venture with Guangzhou Development Industry Holding to establish a new US $86 million oil products plant at Nansha, Guandong province. BP China's chief executive, Gary Dirks, says the joint venture will operate in an increasingly deregulated market and will work to establish itself both as the rental facility and as the supplier of choice to the local market.[23]

Shell is also planning to set up its own joint venture with Sinopec for gasoline stations in Jiangsu province, eastern China. Shell's flagship Chinese

---

23. China: No going back', *Petroleum Economist* (December 2003)

investment is the $4.3 billion Nanhai petrochemicals project, in Daya Bay, Guangdong, in association with CNOOC. It will produce 2.3 million tpy of petrochemical products. Construction has commenced in May 2003 and is due for completion at the end of 2005. The project team includes Bechtel, Foster Wheeler and Sinopec Engineering.

The Nanhai development illustrates the increasing availability of money for big Chinese energy projects. Not only is there a greater ability to pay within China itself, given the high liquidity of the banking sector, but third party financing is also more accessible. Shell's project attracted $2.45 billion in debt financing in August 2003 from a consortium of Chinese and international lenders, with support from five export credit agencies. Significantly, it marked the first major private financing in China by the US Exim Bank. Other potential US suppliers to the Nanhai project include Stone and Webster, Kellogg, Brown and Root and Triconex.[24]

Strong Chinese growth will continue to attract an increasing number of global and regional energy players as well as private financiers as the search for new upstream reserves gathers pace and the gas market develops. The advance of the giant Chinese consumer market has excited the interest of marketers and refiners and the increased requirement of oil and petrochemicals products looks to rocket in through 2010. Opportunities for private investment in the fast growing power sector are also emerging.

Private power investment

Power generation remains dominated by state-run firms, which receive state funds because of the industry's strategic importance and are subject to tariff controls. But since the late 1990s, in terms of greenfield development, private investors have been involved in developing power projects through three main methods—joint ventures (JVs), IPOs on stock exchanges and BOT agreements. This diversified approach allowed investors to adopt their corporate strategies to the particular problems and difficulties encountered in different parts of China and to choose the most appropriate risk mitigation methods. The vast majority of private power investments (amounting to about $15 billion) in China have been JV agreements to develop greenfield projects with limited recourse financing. One of the most successful investments, the Zhuhai (2×700 MW) coal-fired plant sponsored by Cheung Kong of Hong Kong, was the first JV project utilizing limited recourse financing in China without a multilateral or government guarantee. The initial JV was signed in 1993, reaching financial closure in 1996, with commissioning of the second unit in mid-2000. The total JV period is 20 years, with a total of

---

24. China: No going back', *Petroleum Economist* (December 2003)

six units (4,200 MW) planned.[25]

Second, IPO listings have raised almost US $2 billion in equity investment in the Chinese power sector through international and domestic listings. The third major project development in China was the official award in 1997 of the 700 MW Laibin B project in Guangxi Zhuang. This project represents China's first international competitive bid for a 100 per cent foreign-owned BOT project formally approved by the SDPC. It is considered a model for future projects in China. The project includes a 2×360 MW coal-fired power station in Guangxi province for a concession period of 18 years (operation of 15 years), and a total cost of US $616 million. Total equity was US $154 million (25 per cent), with commercial debt of US $159 million and a COFACE loan of US $303 million, including a $120 million standby and contingency facility. It has the added interest of risk being taken by a province, Guangxi, without a central government guarantee. This means export credit agencies are taking provincial risk for the first time.

Electricite' de France and GEC Alsthom, the sponsors, won through international competitive tendering with financial closure less than two years after the issuance of tender documents. Key success factors include establishment of the BOT legal framework, availability of government support via SDPC, ECA participation and favourable terms, allocation of foreign exchange to service the debt, clear tariff approval process and provincial government credit. The Laibin B project has been put forward as a model before the passing of the BOT laws.

The Asian crisis of 1998, despite the fact that China is obviously in a very different situation to the rest of Asia, had an indirect effect on foreign-financed IPPs. Although China's currency, the Renminbi, is stable, tariffs are more reflective of costs and China has been more careful about its reliance on foreign-funded IPPs. The Asian crisis has affected China by increasing the sensitivity of project developers and foreign financial institutions to certain project risks, including unilateral reforms of the power sector and abrogation of contracts. Despite the attractiveness of the growing Chinese market and the apparent interest of foreign power producers—more than 100 Memoranda of Understanding (MoUs) have reportedly been signed—the number of actual IPP deals is insignificant and the number of successful IPP deals that have actually begun construction is showing a surge only since 2000. As of 2002, China recorded 16 private power projects under construction, representing a total of 15,731 MW.[26]

Project developers and international financial institutions have expressed their main concerns about the project approval process, tariff approval and

---

25. WB, *The Power Sector and Power Generation in China*, Discussion Paper No. 406 (Washington DC, 2000)

26. *Platts International Private Power Quarterly*, 2002.

adjustment process, creditworthiness of the offtaker, contractual compliance and enforceability, foreign exchange risk and Renminbi financing, and clear and transparent regulation.[27] The government's approval for any projects financed by overseas investors is often seen as a major obstacle for attracting private investors. Overseas investors need to go through at least a five-step approval process starting from approval of preliminary feasibility study with letters of intent and project proposal to that of preparing and submitting negotiation, and signing of specific contracts and articles to that of the final step involving applying for a business license. Approvals at all stages are required from the SPCC, the SDPC and local governments.

The second reason for slow progress in IPP deals in the 1990s' is lack of a comprehensive, transparent and competitive framework clearly formulated in regulations and law. As a result, provincial authorities have consummated MOUs through bilateral negotiations rather than competition and the central government authorities, unsure about market rates of return on equity, appear reluctant to ratify agreements. At the same time, the authorities have signalled to producers that they wished to maintain ownership control, have Chinese contractors as turnkey constructors and vetoed rates of return higher than 15–17 percent. Restrictions on foreign exchange convertibility, inadequate fuel supply and power sales agreements and difficulties in enforcing contracts have compounded the disincentives of entering the Chinese market.

Concerns about tariff approval and adjustment process include the length of time it takes to obtain initial tariff approval and subsequent annual adjustments based on the cost-plus approach to reviewing tariffs and the requirements to have such tariffs approved on an annual basis. Developers expect an urgent need for a transparent and well-defined regulatory regime for determining tariffs, while China emphasized the need for developers to follow Chinese regulations regarding tariffs. The government stressed that emerging problems stem from the developers' reliance on approvals and assurances given by local authorities, who sometimes went beyond their decision-making power.

The overall performance of China's economy and the size of its market make the country a good credit risk but some foreign investors still retain questions about the long-term potential for unexpected policy or regulatory changes. More specific policy risks in the power sector relate to possible difficulties in price adjustments to reflect higher costs of fuel, general inflation and devaluation of the local currency.

Project risks are normally borne by project sponsors if they are of a commercial nature. However, the regulatory and other conditions prevailing in

---

27. WB, *The Private Sector and Power Generation in China*, Discussion Paper 406(2000), pp.15–7.

China and the perception of these largely affect the degree of commercial risks and, to that extent, change them into sovereign risks. Such risks relate to the prevailing local conditions for timely completion and smooth operation of the project and domestic input supply uncertainties. Consequently, project sponsors are either not prepared to take such risks or ask for a very high return on their investment as compensation.

China has been a late entrant in allowing IPPs and privatization and has drawn conclusions from what other countries have done when formulating its regulations. The reform measures since 1986 have succeeded in expanding and diversifying sources of finance. Contributions from the State Budget dropped from 60 per cent in 1986 to about 6 per cent in the 1990s. Provincial and municipal funds accounted for 47 per cent of total investment in the mid-1990s and private investors are increasingly involved in developing IPPs. China is now in the process of assessing the results from its experience since 1997 in the passing of the BOT laws and implementing stage 3 and 4 regulatory and institutional reforms through 2007. Foreign developers are expected to play only a minor role at least through 2010, because China's power companies have easy access to capital and do not need to look overseas.

Deeper sector reforms and their sequencing are required to create more opportunities for FDI, both in new (greenfield) investment projects and through privatization of existing state assets. This requires removing the major distortions and constraints in the financial and energy sectors. The financial intermediation to the power sector could be improved through development of appropriate policies and instruments to channel more domestic savings and/ or foreign investments to the power sector.

Despite the steps taken to separate generation from transmission and setting of state regulatory commission, China is still in the early stages of formulating a fundamental long-term restructuring of its power sector.

The major steps required to effectively implement the power sector reforms will include:

- Implementing further sector reforms in a transparent process, where the scope, direction and schedule of reform can be assessed by potential investors in the Chinese power sector
- Streamlining of the process for obtaining power project and tariff approvals
- Developing mechanisms to increase access to Renminbi financing for all power projects
- Commercializing various power companies that will be offtakers from private power projects
- Corporatizating power enterprises to rationalize electricity tariffs (especially power sales/ exchange prices to ensure adequate return

to investors)
- Developing an adequate legal and regulatory framework to support further introduction of market-oriented mechanisms to increase self-financing of power utilities to improve their financial viability, to facilitate their access to domestic and financial markets and to attract more private investors
- Providing power developers direct access to customers so that they are able to bear more market risk in the future

China's energy market transition: Status

China's energy sector reform, like its approach to macroeconomic reform, reflects China's pragmatism as summarized in Deng Xiaoping's statement, 'Black cat, white cat, it doesn't matter, so long as it catches mice'. In the Annual World Bank Conference on Development Economics (1999), Joseph E. Stiglitz, in his keynote address as senior vice-president of the World Bank on ' Whither Reform? Ten years of the transition' [28] concluded that China's transition has been a success. He credited the success for China's wisdom in choosing a path of gradualism to the market economy ('crossing the river by groping for stones') and non-ideological pragmatism. He went on to say that Chinese policy makers had the wisdom to know that they did not know what they were doing, so they did not jump off a cliff after being assured by experts that they would clear the chasm in one or more great leap forward. Between 1981 and 2001, China lifted 400 million people above the $1-a-day line and quadrupled the average income of more than 1 billion people. To meet the terms of its accession to the WTO, China abolished or amended 2,600 legal statutes and regulations.

Nonetheless, China continues to face the persistence of absolute poverty and the rural-urban divide with growing resentment between the urban technocrat *noveau* rich and suburban and rural poor. From China's perspective, there is no question that the acceptance of a greater degree of inequality was a necessary element of the reforms started in the early 1980s. Ironically, this is a variant of China's managed capitalism wherein the reform induced *noveau* rich represent the new China, motivating ordinary Chinese to the possibility of becoming rich by exercising their entrepreneurship, taking risks and working long hours.

---

28. Annual Bank Conference on Development Economics (ABCDE), 1999, World Bank, Washington DC. Stiglitz credits China 's successful transition to not only charting their own course, but to many of their policies (and the order in which reforms occurred) differing markedly from the advice the IMF was prescribing elsewhere with far poorer results.

Given that access to energy for development is critical, China pursued its pragmatic approach to focus on increasing energy supply by pursuing its policy of investing in its public sector energy enterprises. Between 1990 and 2000, China's net installed capacity of electricity generating plants more than doubled, from 98,600 MW to 235,170 MW. Its per capita energy consumption increased from 569 kilogram of oil equivalent (kgoe) in 1990 to 685 kgoe in 1997. By 2002, over 80 per cent of China's population had access to electricity.

Energy liberalization measures have been incremental. Energy policy continues to be a vehicle to achieve the strategic objective of security of energy supply and empowering of state energy enterprises in both domestic and international energy operations. Examples include China's delayed decision on 100 per cent foreign ownership for IPP in the late 1990s, and the decision to opt for BOT which entails transfer of the power company assets to the government after a specific period.

Energy prices are allowed to reflect cost and international price trends. However, the government continues to retain its control on determination of prices and energy trade. Competition in the energy sector exists only in marginal activity, such as gasoline retailing and power generation. Despite the decision to establish a national regulatory commission and a decade of stages of implementation, effective functioning of the regulatory system remains to be achieved.

Institutional reforms and commercialization/ corporatization have resulted mainly in the abolition of MOEP and Ministry of Energy and the creation of a new ministry of land reforms and reallocation of government functions to other government agencies, renaming of government agencies and energy companies. The energy-financing pattern has achieved diversification in the 1990s when direct government budget allocation fell to less than 10 percent. The share of provincial and municipal level financing has increased.

Although China topped the list for FDIs in the 1990s, the energy sector accounted for less than 10 per cent. A large part of FDI has come largely for labour-intensive manufacturing and service industries that earn their own foreign exchange and have a relatively short payback period. In the energy sector, China's willingness to encourage private investment is linked with assured realization of benefits from new capital and technology transfer to empower its state energy enterprises in domestic and international energy operations.

The energy sector is capital intensive and has a long payback period. The power sector in particular normally does not earn foreign exchange. As a result, foreign investors, despite substantial interest, are cautious to commit their funds. Investors are concerned about foreign exchange balancing requirements and persistent tight availability, followed by the commercially less developed legal system that may make enforcement of contracts very difficult. Other concerns include prolonged negotiations with multiple counterpart agencies, a multilayered and complicated project approval process, ambiguous information on various project conditions, limited availability of local currency funds and uncertainty about the local partner's legal status and financial condition. Box 5.1 summarizes the status of energy market transition in China.

Box 5.1 China: Energy market transition to 2004

Energy Pricing

- Deregulation of coal prices
- Oil prices in general in line with international market levels
- Dual-pricing of natural gas
- Retail electricity prices set by distributors subject to government approval
- Wholesale tariffs under long-term contracts
- Subsidies will be phased out gradually by 2010 and prices will reflect costs and follow trends in international prices.

Regulation

- Established National Regulatory Authority
- Tariff allows cost recovery principle
- Limited competition in generation
- Regulatory reforms in four stages from 1996–7 to 2006–7
- Stage 3 and 4 regulatory reforms to continue.

Commercialization/ Corporatization

- Energy enterprises renamed as companies/ corporations
- A few energy companies listed on stock exchange
- Permitted to raise finance by issuance of shares
- Further reforms to continue as part of institutional reforms

Privatization/ Private Investment

- Limited efforts since 1999 in power and oil and gas
- Private investment in a few IPP power projects
- Cautious, 'go as you learn' approach

Future directions

After almost two decades of transition, China has become a mixed economy with a combination of state-owned and private companies. The new infatuation with the Chinese economy began in the early years of the twenty-first century. Two key themes of the 2004 World Economic Forum in Davos, Switzerland were the remarkable durability of the US economy and the inexorable rise of China as a global economic superpower. Chinese policy makers have realized that economics overrides politics, especially in the post-Cold War period. In 2004 China took a significant step to alter its political economy through the decision to legalize private property. China registered a sharp rise in private enterprises with individuals owning almost 3 million business ventures with an investment of over US $40 billion. Private enterprise contributed to an equal share in national economic growth in 2003 of over 11 per cent.

For the past decade, China has been the world's fastest growing economy, lifting millions out of poverty and creating an industrial powerhouse producing virtually everything from toys and clothing to the most advanced microelectronics. Until July 2005 China pegged the value of its currency to the US dollar, which encouraged foreign investment and made its exports more competitive in the world markets. China kept the currency peg by buying dollars, which expanded Chinese money supply by more than 20 per cent in 2003.

The swift expansion fuelled by enormous injection of state spending on capital works projects and easy credit from state controlled banks has done much to create work at a time when millions of jobs are being eliminated with China's transition from communism to free market. It has also erected the infrastructure for an increasingly industrialized economy, from the roads and rails that carry products to the ports that have helped enable an export boom.

China's state banks sharply increased lending since 2001 and the legacy of bad loans of over US $500 billion have heightened concerns that they could be vulnerable to an economic shock. Such a shock could come from the bursting of the real estate bubble as China's cities have sprouted skyscrapers and suburban-style villas. Should prices drop, developers would be unable to repay depositors—the most commonly foreseen beginning to any potential Chinese financial crisis. Although insolvency is a problem for China's banks, they also remain the only place for China's people to park their savings. China's government continues to take aggressive action to slow real estate expansion, increasing the minimum that capital developers must have in hand to borrow for new projects, while lifting the ratio of deposits that banks must hold as a percentage of loans. Chinese banks are seeking foreign strategic investors to help them upgrade their technology, including risk-management systems and management expertise.

Under outside pressure from the USA and internal pressure to slow rapid growth and hold down the money supply, China announced in July 2005 that it was ending the dollar peg. Instead, the value of China's Yuan will be tied to a basket of currencies that will remain a secret, effectively allowing the government to set the value anywhere it wants. Consistent with its cautious approach, in July 2005 China revalued its currency against the dollar by 2.1 per cent and stated that no further moves were on the way.

China's transition has been far from easy. The future of China's energy sector is closely linked to that of China's booming economy with a real GDP growth of 9.5 per cent in 2004 and the course of its future direction. The government of China is trying to slow the growth to a 'soft landing' before what some analysts see as a 'bubble' economy, fuelled by foreign investment and a huge construction boom, explodes. A soft landing by the increasingly weighty Chinese economy is far more important today than it would have been in the 1990s. The fast growing economy, with increasing demand for resources is being seen to impact worldwide inflation in oil, steel and other commodities.

The Chinese government has encouraged foreign investment in energy, mainly in partnership with the government. The government continues to maintain in varying forms control and ownership over most of the energy sector, introducing reforms at the margin when it was expedient to do so. China is committed to pursuing the path of incrementalism and making the changes at the margin only when convinced of achieving its strategic objective of security of energy supplies by modernizing its state energy enterprises to gain access to advanced technologies. Foreign capital might finance the extensive network of pipelines needed to transport gas from western provinces to eastern factories. However, as a number of private investors have experienced, China will allow private investment on its terms where it requires capital and technology to increase oil and gas supplies in joint ventures and minority stakes where the most important shareholder will continue to be the Chinese government.

China's entry into the WTO in November 2001 will have both short-term and long-term implications for China's energy sector and consequently, on its transition reform path. The most immediate impact of the WTO will be in the trade and retail of oil products. In the energy sector this will mean the lifting or sharp reduction of tariffs associated with imports of classes of capital goods and the eventual opening to foreign competition of some areas such as retail sales of petroleum products. This could bring pressure on Sinopec as its assets are heavily weighted to the downstream. As discussed earlier, Sinopec has allowed foreign companies such as Exxon Mobil, BP and Shell to operate some retail outlets.

China's objective to become a major exporter may also come under pressure due to the WTO's rules on subsidies. The rest of China's energy sector may see little immediate impact from China's membership of WTO. Production of oil, gas and coal, as well as electricity generation could all be protected by the judicious use of new licensing procedures. Gas and electricity transmission and supply could well be protected by the ongoing stages 3 and 4 of regulatory reform. Membership of the WTO may even cloud the energy sector by the need of the government to pay more attention to those sectors directly impacted, such as agriculture, textiles, telecommunications and financial services.

Power generation remains dominated by state-run firms, which receive state funds because of the industry's strategic importance. Despite a few cases for foreign participation in independent power projects, there has been little privatization in China's power sector, although a small number of power companies and equipment manufacturers have listed on local and foreign stock exchanges. The foreign listings are carried out mainly to provide a mechanism for raising foreign capital and gaining access to advanced technology. Chinese enterprises will continue to dominate much of oil, gas and electricity operations.

As demand for energy, particularly oil is exploding in the country, China is rationing energy and limiting production in industrial areas. The turning point in energy strategy was the Iraq War in 2003 when China recognized the need for diversifying its oil and gas supply sources. Following rising oil prices since 2004 and increasing concerns regarding security of energy supplies, access to world energy resources along with new technologies, management methods, information and technical skills is a vital part of managing China's market transitions and opening up to foreign investment where China sees the need for technology and management methods and buying foreign companies as part of its two-pronged 'all options open' and 'go global' energy strategy.

Globally, China is set to become a significant player in the international oil market and in Asian oil and gas networks, both as a purchaser of oil and gas and as an investor. China's energy market transition so far shows that reform measures are used as instruments to achieve the government's objectives of self-reliance, security of energy supplies and increased participation of Chinese enterprises in global energy business. China's increasing dependence on oil imports and its growing demand for other forms of energy poses far-reaching challenges for both China and the global economy. In 2004, China is already competing with the USA, Japan and Europe for oil from the Middle East. Market analysts in the USA cited surging Chinese demand as the 'primary factor' driving world oil markets.[29] This new oil competition

29. In June 2004, General Motors (GM) said it will spend $US $3 billion in China over the next three years in a challenge to Volkswagen for dominance of the world's fast-

is fostering new alliances. China is pursuing new oil alliances in West Africa, South America and in the Middle East with Iran, Iraq and Saudi Arabia. The shift towards import dependency has pushed the country into a program of international oil diplomacy and investment in a bid to secure oil supplies. Chinese firms have taken upstream stakes in Algeria, Libya, Sudan and the United Arab Emirates (UAE).

In addition to efforts on the supply side to boost domestic production, China has begun to establish an overseas resource base and to diversify sources of oil imports.

The government has long viewed the widening gap between domestic production and the country's energy needs as a matter of national security. More than half of China's oil imports in 2004 came from the Middle East and the post-Iraq War 2003 situation in the region has raised the government's concerns about the dependence of the country's economic stability on access to oil in the world's most volatile region. The prospect of fast-rising import dependency to meet basic energy requirements has compelled China's government to give the NOCs a new mandate to acquire access to oil and gas reserves around the globe to provide China with secure sources of energy under its 'Go Global' strategy. In 2003 the Chinese President Hu Jintao called on the country's oil companies to 'continue to implement the overseas expansion strategy so that China will gradually establish some energy and resource bases outside China'.

China's NOCs, CNPC, Sinopec and CNOOC are targeting different geographical areas to avoid competition among themselves. Since 2003, CNPC has signed 20 contracts to explore or purchase production facilities securing a broad global portfolio covering North and South America (Canada, Peru and Venezuela), Central Asia (Azerbaijan, Kazakhstan, Russia and Turkmenistan), Africa (Angola and Sudan), Asia (Indonesia, Myanmar, Cambodia and Thailand) and the Middle East (Oman, and Syria). CNPC is the largest shareholder in a consortium of the oil areas in Sudan. CNPC's overseas production in 2003 was already 197 million b/d with the firm aiming to boost this to 275 million b/d. CNPC has made overseas expansion one of its main priorities. It wants its overseas oil and gas output to make up about half of its total production.[30] Sinopec operates in some of the same countries (Azerbaijan, Oman and Indonesia) but also has operations in Iran, Libya, Nigeria, Algeria, Tunisia and Yemen in its portfolio.

CNOOC operates primarily in Australia and Indonesia. It has also secured a contract to develop Saudi gas—not for the gas itself but to deepen relations with the world's largest oil producer. It is also seeking to diversify

---

est growing automotive market. GM is expected to set up an autofinancing venture with its Chinese partner, Shanghai Automotive Industry Corporation.

30. *The Insatiable Dragon', Petroleum Argus* (3 May 2004), Vol. XXXIV, 17, pp.1–2.

its market sources—about a third of its imports in the first two months of 2004 came from Africa. On 23 June 2005, CNOOCL made its $18.5 billion first unsolicited takeover bid for California energy firm Unocal Corporation. However, the US Congress got in the way of the Unocal bid partly because it feared that Chinese control of a US oil company would harm US national interest. The US Congress resented the idea that the Chinese bid was partially financed by cheap loans from the Chinese government. The US Congress passed a House resolution by 398 to 15 expressing national security concern about the deal and threatened to delay and possibly block the deal.

China's failed attempt by the state-owned Chinese energy company CNOOCL to purchase US based Unocal Corporation in its quest to lock up supplies of oil and gas underscores China's approach to economic reforms over 20 years focused on creating a Chinese variation of the US economic/business system by harnessing market to build the world's super economy. CNOOC's chief executive tried to sell its takeover bid purely as a business deal and independent from the Chinese government. CNOOC's board included two Western businessmen. It retained an expansive army of American takeover advisors and lobbyists. Nonetheless, China's Unocal bid failed because of the Chinese government's statements on the US Congress objections as 'meddling in commerce' which provoked an unfriendly US Congressional backlash. CNOOC withdrew its Unocal bid after six weeks on 2 August 2005, saying that the opposition in Washington was 'regrettable and unjustified'.

China's NOCs are no doubt learning from this 'Go Global' experience in their relentless focus on securing the required energy resources. Although CNOOC's decision ended a politically explosive takeover fight, it has raised serious questions about the divergent values of competition and selective application of free market principles by both China and the United States. It could have larger implications too for access to secure energy resources for development. They are centred on the competition for energy resources.

China has started to pursue an 'All options open' policy to deal with the long-term threats to its future shortage of energy and the growing dependence on imports of oil. China's oil and gas reserves satisfy less than half of its demand. With declining onshore production, as discussed earlier in this chapter, China has made efforts to develop its offshore oil and gas by building huge expensive pipelines from its oil rich western provinces to its heavily populated east. Since 1990, China has raised domestic production from 2.8 million b/d to 3.2 million b/d and is expected to maintain its domestic oil production. At the national level, while total production is increasing at 2 per cent a year demand for oil is growing at 7 per cent a year with rising oil imports to fill the growing gap between domestic supply and demand.

China's energy sector is presently between the plan and the market. Given the close energy–economic–institutional and political linkages of

China's energy sector, further progress in energy market transition will depend on the evolution of a wider context of China's socialist market economy. Energy sector reform has taken place within the context of economic reform. The swift expansion and industrial development has outstripped China's power supply with 10–15 per cent power shortage in key manufacturing areas including Shanghai. China's overheated economy began to face its worst and most widespread power supply crisis in June 2003 with severe shortfall of available generation capacity due to rapid economic growth, coal supply shortages, drought and high temperatures and electrification. By the end of 2003, 22 of China's 31 mainland provinces were experiencing rolling brown-outs or black-outs and extended wide area peak power outages.

In January 2004 the SDRC promised to resolve the power crisis by rapid construction of 13 major coal production bases around the country. The government forecast an estimated $108 billion worth of generating capacity to close the gap and expects to resolve the 2004 power crisis in two years.[31] In 2004 China is in the midst of a building boom in power plants, most of which will be completed before the 2008 Olympics. The Three Gorges Dam—the largest hydroelectric project in history—is beginning to provide power and is expected to be completed before 2008. China will continue to pursue economic growth in its efforts to showcase its economy to the world in the 2008 Olympics.

China has launched a multi-pronged power infrastructure development scenario, tapping all sources of energy—oil, gas, LNG, coal and nuclear power. More than 80 per cent of China's electricity is produced in coal-burning plants. But as coal shortages have emerged, the government has reinvigorated mining. China's energy industry has proposed seven LNG terminals along the coast for completion by 2010. Several major pipelines are also being planned and/ or constructed to boost the share of natural gas in China's total energy consumption from 3 per cent to 6 per cent by the year 2010.

China has also launched a vast, nuclear power-oriented industrial modernization program to include construction of more than 30 large reactors over the next 16 years by 2020. The scheme is in response to the dual challenge of growing electricity shortages and the increasing energy demand of an accelerating national economy, which has led to the shortfall. In the long term, China aims to become self-sufficient in reactor design and construction as well as in uranium supply and fuel production. Its energy planners want to increase nuclear power generation from 6,200 MW in 2004 to 32,000 MW by the year 2020. China has set out to revise the entire national energy economy in order to exploit to maximum effect their relatively modest available resources.

---

31. Peter S Goodman, '*China's Dark Days and Darker Nights*', *The Washington Post* (5 January 2004)

Although China is making efforts to conserve energy to reduce demand and to address environment pollution, China's economic growth is absorbing energy at a higher rate than many large industrial economies. According to China's State Energy Research Institute, to produce $1 million in GDP China needs two-and-a-half times as much energy as the USA, five times that of the European Union and nearly nine times that of Japan. Given an industrial base that includes power plants and factories built in the 1950s, the smog blanketing most Chinese cities and the black smoke spewing from factory stacks testifies to the continued role of low-grade coal and the use of antiquated technology in powering China's industry.

Power plants operated by municipal and provincial governments face pressure to buy coal from local mines—even when costs are higher than other sources—to support jobs and local taxes. The involvement of provincial governments has also deterred the creation of rational generation and transmission grids. The transmission grid is poorly coordinated and saddled with old technology, with as much as one-tenth of the load being lost along the way. While the state has allowed private and foreign investors into the power generation business, the grid remains controlled by two giant state firms. The state-owned distribution companies that carry power to residential consumers and businesses have traditionally kept a percentage of their revenues and hands the rest to the local government, limiting their incentive to upgrade.

Environmentalists worry that to reduce dependence on foreign oil, China will increase its reliance on coal accompanied with rising carbon emissions and the real question is not whether China is going to use its coal but whether China will use its coal cleanly. Installing sulphur 'scrubbing technology' adds 30 per cent to the cost of a new power plant—the difference between building four new power plants and building only three. Since energy costs affect the cost of producing goods and services and also hurt consumers buying power, the choice is expected to be to build a larger number of cheaper power plants to supply power at affordable prices by waiving emission requirements for coal power plants unless carbon capture technology costs are lowered. Such short-term considerations to increase electricity supply to relieve shortages would adversely impact the environment.

Despite the fact that China's per capita carbon dioxide (CO_2) emissions are just one-eighth those of the USA with its per capita electricity consumption less than a tenth of the average industrialized countries, China is already the second leading emitter of CO_2 right behind the USA. Given China's current energy trends, it is expected to occupy first place by 2010. Once China starts to approach western levels of energy use, its energy needs are expected to exceed the capacity of any global system that currently exists.[32]

32. Paul Roberts, *The End of Oil: On the Edge of a Perilous New World* (Boston and New

China is trying to improve its energy efficiency as part of its policy to improve environment by successive turnover of its capital stock, by planning to increase the use of natural gas and other alternative energy resources and by taking actions to address fuel efficiency in its growing transportation sector. In 2004 the NDRC, a powerful policy setting body, released a conservation plan calling for China to more than triple its use of natural gas by 2020 to minimize the use of coal, the source of 75 per cent of China's electricity in 2004. China has adopted clean air standards to persuade automakers to develop more fuel efficient and therefore less polluting cars and trucks. Automakers are being encouraged to build ultra compact vehicles for quick urban commute. Shanghai has also invested in passenger rail and new bus systems. In January 2003 Shanghai inaugurated the world's first commercial magnetic levitation, or 'meg-lev' train, a sleek, energy efficient train (capable of reaching speeds of 260 miles per hour) that links the city's financial district with its airport, 19 miles away.[33]

Energy security has become central to China and it is a matter of national significance. The struggle to maintain access to adequate energy supplies and the current efforts to keep the oil flowing have become one of the government's critical missions. In the wake of twenty-first century terrorism threats posed by regional conflicts or war, China has pursued a strategic approach to let its state-owned Chinese oil companies on overseas production. China's energy policy is focusing on short-term policy measures that are driven by energy security and supply considerations. For the longer term, despite the array of strategic objectives for the energy sector in its tenth plan, it has failed to address issues of the changing structure of the energy sector and the influence of a range of factors including political, economic and institutional factors. However, China's approach has been more strategic, keeping 'all options open' rather than adopting a market based approach. Thus far, energy sector reform was part of economic reform and liberalization. But as the twenty-first century is unfolding energy is emerging as a critical determinant for China's long-term economic growth in the foreseeable future. The future course of China's social capitalism depends on how it addresses the issues of the changing energy sector to formulate an integrated and coherent long-term energy policy balancing strategic and market considerations.

While keeping the reins on political liberalization, China has thus far followed the Chinese version of managed capitalism by moving forward in accordance with Deng Xiaopong's famous dictum that the colour of the cat does not matter as long as it catches mice. The new Chinese Premier, Wen

---

York, Houghton Mifflin Company, date?)

33. Roberts, *The End of Oil on the Edge of a Perilous New World, Houghton Mifflin Company Boston, New York*, p 161.

Jiabao, speaking in November 2003 as he prepared for a visit to the USA, defended the Chinese political system and its evolution over the past two decades arguing that the Chinese are freer now to travel, to find work, to seek information and to practice religion. He invoked the size of China's population to justify the government's decision to take 'resolute measures in a timely fashion to safeguard social stability. Our development over the past years has proven that stability is of vital importance for China' he said. 'As premier of this country, I think the most important issue for me is to ensure stability and development'.

Wen appealed for understanding from people who are eager to see political change catch up with the economy, which has tripled in size since market reforms began in 1978. He argued that a country with 1.3 billion people is just too big to move forward rapidly with political liberalization. 'Conditions are not ripe for direct elections at the highest levels', he said. 'The first hindrance in my view is the inadequate education level of the population'.[34] The world may or may not agree with the view of the Chinese premier, but it is clear that the government will stick to its political philosophy of gradualism in political change.

Equally evident to the government are China's domestic challenges. The most fundamental of these has been the impact of layoffs as part of the restructuring of the state-owned enterprises (SOEs) as many were severely overstaffed. Between 1997 and 2004, 50 million Chinese workers lost jobs in state-owned and collective firms. While there have been major gains in market-based productivity and income increases, this has created unemployment and has also been a burden on the government budget as the government has had to provide social benefits which were previously the responsibility of the SOEs. The government is also facing the impact of this high speed growth and the geographic concentration of privately owned industry in the urban centres along the coast on economic inequality between rural and urban population and associated social strains. China is splitting into a twenty-first century 'dual economy'. The cities are developing under the policies of 'managed market capitalism' that have been adopted by China's communist rulers. Nearly 200 million rural workers have migrated to non-farm jobs in towns and coastal areas from remote interior regions. Their competition for jobs and housing is a constant source of social tension, while back on the farm loss of rural land to non-farm investment have often triggered local conflict.

While ambitious young people from remote rural areas leave for the cities if they can, to pursue education or careers, those left behind remain poor and ill-schooled. The deadweight of two-thirds of the population still stuck

---

34. Pomfret, John, and Pan, Philip P, 2003, Wen Defends Chinese System, *The Washington Post*, 23 November.

in the rural past, unemployed and underemployed with the associated costs of anger, social tension, demonstrations and riots has the potential to shape the socio-political outcome of the future for democracy in China. The growing gap between the haves and the have nots and the perception of the have-nots of rampant government corruption at provincial and local levels are triggering almost daily demonstrations. In July–August of 2005, China faced a steady rhythm of violent protests. The Chinese government acknowledged that the number of 'mass incidents' was rising fast across China. In 2004, 3.76 million Chinese were reported to have taken part in 74,000 demonstrations. Most of these protests erupted over specific economic issues rather than political demands. Demonstrations and protests often serve as one avenue of recourse.

Rural protesters often cite farmland seizures by local governments working with developers or pollution of fields and irrigation sources by locally licensed factories or mines as reasons for their uprisings. Other protests have erupted over clashes between factory managers and the millions of youth who leave their villages to work in assembly plants in big city suburbs. Provincial, municipal and county governments have often proven unable to handle these complaints because local officials, eager for economic growth in partnership with businessmen, regard the aggrieved people as obstacles to success. Chinese authorities try to defuse most of these protests by working out some meaningful response to the grievance. Organizers and ringleaders are frequently arrested when there is violence. Managing these side effects of market reform causing increasing disparities between the rich and poor continues to be a daunting challenge not only for communist China but also for all reforming developing countries. For China, rapid economic growth, relentless commercial drive, loosening of lifestyle strictures and political tight-fist repressions so far seem to have maintained stability. However, given the lack of transparency in the political decision making process, it is hard to predict how China plans its long-term success to balance its focus as a global economic superpower with its need to address the increasing rift between the haves and the have nots.

INDIA

In 2003, India, the world's largest democracy was the world's sixth largest energy consumer and a net energy importer. India's pre-1991 planned approach to the development of its energy sector was influenced by the twin goals of achieving self-reliance and providing cheap energy to all consumers. India followed the path of what was known as a 'mixed economy' where private investment was allowed in petroleum sector. Three private refineries were set up in the 1950s. The three were privately owned and operated until they were nationalized in the 1970s.[35]

There was broad consensus within the government that the state could and should provide for the energy needs of the growing population. By capturing economies of scale, the government developed a large energy supply system. Recognizing the critical importance of energy for development, the government in the pre-1991 period invested almost 25 per cent of public resources for expansion of power generation, T&D.

The public sector model achieved many of its social objectives such as increasing access to energy services and generating employment within the sector. However, it also led to an over-extended public sector and guaranteed the supremacy of publicly administered monopolies in almost every aspect of the energy system. The strategic importance of energy sector provided justification for the government to exercise discretionary power to intervene in the governance of the public sector utilities. The public sector enterprises were required to achieve social goals without the freedom to manage them as financially viable companies.

The non-commercial operating procedures combined with politically permitted price distortions encouraged wasteful consumption and caused the insolvency of public sector coal and electricity enterprises, began to affect the quality and quantity of the domestic energy supply and increased the country's need to import energy. The energy tariff subsidy also imposed a huge burden on the state governments, which finance the bulk of the state electricity boards' operational losses and bill collection shortfalls. By 1991 the state electricity boards' commercial losses were over US $1 billion. With rising oil imports accounting for over 25 per cent of total imports, the energy sector affected India's economy, trade and the national budget.

In June 1991, in the midst of severe fiscal and external imbalances which had generated double-digit inflation and put the country on the verge of defaulting on its external debt obligations, a new government undertook the major task of stabilizing and liberalizing the economy. Over the years, reform of investment, exchange rate, trade regimes and the financial sector and the tax system have initiated a quiet economic revolution.[36] With energy sector reform and liberalization within the framework of the macroeconomic reform program, India joined the group of countries adopting the gradual approach to take measures to deregulate their domestic markets, to increase their integration with the global economy and to reduce the role of the government.

---

35. R Vedavalli, *Private Foreign Investment and Economic Development: A case study of petroleum in India'* (UK, Cambridge University Press, 1976)
36. WB, *India: Five years of Stabilization and Reform and the Challenges Ahead* (Washington DC, 1996)

Sector context

India's primary energy demand has grown over 3.6 per cent between 1971 and 2002. In 2002, India's total commercial primary energy consumption reached 538 mote tons of oil equivalent (mtoe). Yet India's overall energy use of roughly 317 kgoe of oil equivalent (kgoe) (in 2000) is low even when compared with other developing countries (per capita energy consumption in 2000 in China was 561 kgoe, 700 kgoe in Brazil). Despite the low per capita energy consumption and excluding biomass which accounts for about 40 per cent of total primary consumption, in 2002 India accounted for more than 3 per cent of the world's total demand for energy.

India has relatively modest endowment of energy resources to increase access of energy services to its growing population and to fuel economic development. Coal and hydroelectricity are India's main primary energy resources. Coal accounts for 55 per cent of the total energy demand and oil for 34 per cent. Gas, hydropower and nuclear power make up the remainder. In 2002, India was the world's third largest coal producer after China and the USA. Coal production increased from 36 mtoe in 1971 to about 178 mtoe in 2002. Proven coal reserves are estimated at 82 billion tons of which 70 per cent is concentrated mostly in the eastern region. Indian coal is high in ash, low in sulphur and of low calorific value.

Hydroelectric potential is estimated in the order of 150,000 MWe, of which less than 15 per cent is developed. Another 90,000 MWe is estimated for possible pumped storage capacity. Environmental concerns, costs and political factors have prevented increased harnessing of hydro potential.

India's oil and natural gas resources are limited compared with the need of meeting the growing demand. Revaluation of India's resources in 2002 led to increases in estimated proven reserves of oil to 5.37 billion barrels and natural gas reserves to 723.5 billion cubic meters.[37]

A major development in December 2002 was the announcement by Reliance Industries of its discovery of a large amount of natural gas in the Krishna–Godavari Basin offshore from the state of Andhra Pradesh along India's south-east coast. New reserves from this find are estimated at 7 tcf. Cairn Energy also reported finds in late 2002 offshore from Andhra Pradesh as well as Gujarat, which contain reserves estimated at nearly 2 tcf.

Biomass fuels—primarily fuel-wood, animal dung and crop residues—used mainly in the residential sector account for up to 40 per cent of India's total primary energy supply. Its consumption reached almost 208 mtoe in 2002. The share of biomass in total energy supply is expected to decline due to increased substitution by commercial fuels.

Projections of future energy demand scenarios both by the government

---

37. *International Petroleum Encyclopedia* (2003), p.163.

and other private and public organizations in India assume alternative rates of GDP growth, population and energy conservation and reform measures. Even with a slower rate of population growth India's population is expected to reach over 1.5 billion by 2030, requiring minimum energy consumption to more than double to over 1026 mtoe in 2030.

This case study considers the minimum requirements of a base case scenario of energy through 2030. India's primary commercial energy demand in a base case scenario is expected to increase at 2.3 per cent per year between 2002 and 2030—well below the 3.6 per cent rate between 1971 and 2002. The slowdown reflects, in part, lower GDP growth and population growth through 2030 and rising energy prices, reflecting cost and international trends in energy prices. Table 5.4 shows the total primary energy requirements in 2030.

Table 5.4. India: Total Primary Energy Demand to 2030 (mtoe)

Energy Sources	*1971*	*2002*	*2030*	*Average annual growth (per cent)*
Coal	36	178	362	2.6
Oil	22	119	267	2.9
Natural gas	1	23	90	5.0
Nuclear	0	5	29	6.4
Hydro	2	5	18	4.3
Other renewables	0	0	3	10.2
Biomass and waste	121	208	258	0.8
Total primary energy	182	538	1,026	2.3

Source: *IEA, WEO* (2004)

Even with the base line or reference case projections in Table 5.4, India's primary commercial energy supply needs to more than double to reach 1026 mtoe through 2030.

Coal and oil will continue to account for over 60 per cent of the primary energy demand in 2030. Natural gas use is expected to more than double from its share of 4 per cent in 2002 to 9 per cent in 2030. The share of nuclear energy supply is expected to more than triple from 1 per cent in 2002 to 3 per cent in 2030.

The growth in coal consumption requires substantial investment in coal production and new transport capacity. In coastal areas, higher quality imports are increasingly likely to be preferred to low quality domestic coal. In addition, India's coking coal reserves are limited and importation of coking coal for metallurgical purposes is expected to continue. Despite India's large coal reserves, India faced a demand-supply gap of about 40 million tons in 2002–3, which is expected to widen to almost 100 million tons by 2010.

Increased use of coal in power generation from the existing 67,000 MW coal based power generation plants to 200,000 MW in 2030 would require more than doubling of thermal power generating capacity and large-scale expansion of coal fields.

Given the regional concentration of coal deposits with high ash content and severe environmental implications, there is a need for fundamental restructuring of the coal sector to access new clean coal technologies and approaches to increase efficient coal utilization in the power sector. Productivity in Indian coal mines is well below international standards because of low levels of mechanization and poor mine design. Investment is urgently needed along the whole coal chain from production to use. The bankrupt financial condition of many state electricity generators—the main users of coal in India—is affecting investment in coal-fired stations. Although the government recognizes the fact that the coal industry stands at a crossroads requiring decisive actions towards fundamental restructuring, there appears to be little political support within the coalition government. Given the new government's emphasis on protection of employees and employment creation and the fact that it depends on support from the left parties, it is unlikely that decisive actions will be taken to reform the coal sector.

India's oil imports grew from 13 mtoe in 1971 to 114 mtoe in 2004. In 2004, oil imports accounted for 65 per cent of India's total consumption and will continue to grow because of in increasing demand for oil and declining production of domestic crude oil and natural gas liquids. Reported additional oil discoveries as of 2004 could possibly slow the pace of declining oil output. But based on the currently proven reserves, India will need to depend increasingly on oil imports. Increasing domestic demand for petroleum products also requires expansion of domestic refining capacity with substantial investment.

India's natural gas production reached 28.5 billion cubic meters (bcm) in 2004. Gas production is expected to more than double to 58 bcm by 2030 by better exploitation of the western gas fields and possible development of recently reported offshore gas discoveries in the deep water of the Krishna–Godavari basin. Imports of gas as LNG are expected to reach 8 mtoe in 2010. Problems with financing LNG import projects have dimmed some of the previous prospects for explosive growth in natural gas consumption. Financial problems in the power sector, the main consumer of natural gas, have also had a negative effect. India's first LNG terminal at Dabhol was to supply a power plant in which the bankrupt Enron company held a 65 per cent share. Disputes over power tariff and the future of the power company following the Enron collapse have delayed the completion of the project.

The prospects for both LNG and pipeline gas imports are uncertain. Although a number of proposals for gas imports from Iran, Qatar or Central Asia were studied, prospects from any of the gas pipeline projects are complicated by security considerations of the gas pipeline through Pakistan and Afghanistan. Some of the proposed LNG terminals have yet to secure gas supplies and financing for terminal construction and the purchase of ships.

Electricity demand forecasts indicate that India will have to add 300,000 MW capacity through 2030 to meet the growing demand for electricity. Although about 80 per cent of the population has access to electricity, power outages are common and the unreliability of electricity supplies is severe enough to constitute a constraint on India's overall economic development. The government has targeted capacity increases of 100,000 MW by 2012.

The power sector faces formidable challenges in mobilizing the required investment to provide reliable service to meet the rising power demand. A lack of peak-load capacity and the poor performance of the T&D system cause frequent, widespread black-outs and brown-outs. Plant load factors are often low, due to the age of generating units, poor quality coal, defective equipment and insufficient maintenance. The lack of inter-regional grid connections accentuates local power shortages. Power theft, non-billing of customers, non-payment of bills and free power for wealthy farms and lack of meters are common. Poor network performance as a result of under-investment and widespread theft has led to high T&D losses of almost 40 per cent, which is extremely high by world standards. Tariffs for most customer categories are below the cost of supply. State Electricity Boards (SEBs) are saddled with debt and are unable to make required investment. Many of the state electricity boards continue to be poorly managed and are bankrupt. The slow pace of structural, fundamental management and pricing reforms constitute a major source of uncertainty for India's electricity supply prospects.

The cumulative investment needed to meet the projected increase in generating capacity of 300 GW through to 2030 is estimated around $270 billion. Additional investment of US $130 million is needed for transmission and $300 billion in distribution and maintenance. India's public electricity sector today has insufficient resources to finance power development or even to mobilize financing needed for operations and maintenance. Unless measures are taken to mobilize both domestic and foreign private capital, improve state electricity board performance and manage demand, India's electricity gap will continue to widen.

Energy sector institutions

Among the agencies that oversee energy policy in India are the Ministry of Petroleum and Natural Gas, the Ministry of Coal, the Ministry of Non-Conventional Energy Sources, the Ministry of Environment and Forests, the Department of Atomic Energy, and the Ministry of Power. Within the Ministry of Power, the Central Electricity Regulatory Commission (CERC) works closely with individual SEBs, and utilities in power generation, T&D of electricity. Under the Department of Atomic Energy, the Atomic Energy Commission was established as the policy making body for the development and utilization of atomic energy for peaceful purposes. The ministries that oversee transportation of fuels are also important. The Ministry of Shipping Transport is responsible for the importation of energy aboard ships of the state-owned Shipping Corporation of India. The Parliamentary Committee on Energy and the Energy Policy Division of the Planning Commission also are involved in steering policies concerning energy.

India's energy sector is almost totally in the control of the government. The publicly owned Coal India Ltd. and its seven subsidiaries produce more than 90 per cent of India's coal. Through the Ministry of Coal, the Planning Commission and the Public Investment Board, the government controls all facets of coal operations. In addition, the Ministry of Coal oversees the Neyveli Lignite Corporation (NLC), Singareni Collieries and the Coal Controllers Organization which was established to monitor coal quality and distribution.

In the petroleum sector, with the exception of two joint refining ventures the government owns and manages the entire oil and gas activities. The Oil and Natural Gas Commission (ONGC) accounts for roughly 90 per cent of total crude oil upstream production and Oil India (OIL) produces the remaining 10 per cent. While six separate companies handle the refining and marketing of petroleum products, the Indian Oil Corporation (IOC) carries out all refining and distribution operations and is the main importer of crude oil and refined products. Most gas distribution is owned and managed by the Gas Authority of India Ltd (GAIL).

In the power sector, both the central and state governments share responsibility for supplying electricity. Since the 1970s, the government of India (GOI) has been actively involved in power development and establishing its own utilities which complement state efforts. GOI currently owns (among others) the National Thermal Power Corporation (NTPC), National Hydroelectric Power Corporation (NHPC), the Nuclear Power Corporation (NPC) and the Power Grid Corporation of India (POWERGRID), a transmission company and grid operator. As amended, the National Electricity Supply Act of 1948 puts the Central Electricity Authority (CEA) in charge of national power policy and planning, coordinating and regulating sector development. Through the Ministry of Power (MOP), the government approves national power plans and makes rules for carrying out CEA functions.

India's largest public petroleum companies—the ONGC and the IOC—following a series of sector reforms and deregulation of oil prices between 1990 and 2002, have the highest market capitalization and are listed under India's highly profitable, commercially run nine companies called "Nava

Ratnas' or Nine Gems". However, India's coal and power sector institutions continue to suffer from problems of government micromanagement, lack of enterprise autonomy, unclear lines of operational and regulatory authority and the unclear division of central, regional and state authority.

In the democratic political settings, India's public energy enterprises are ultimately accountable to the Parliament and government ministers exercise specific control over them. Members of Parliament allied with trade unions are able to influence public enterprises in personnel matters and to push social goals. Except for top management posts, public sector energy employees enjoy civil service security of tenure. Top power company officials are government appointees, many of these are from the civil service and others are on contract basis. Many of the top officials of power companies shy away from making tough commercial decisions for fear that they may be transferred and/ or their contracts will not be renewed. With the government firmly in the driver's seat, political concerns rather than commercial interest presently run India's state power sector companies, with a few exceptions.

Managed by government appointees and responsible to Parliament rather than to their customers, energy sector enterprises have little operational or managerial autonomy. Although laws such as the Electricity Act appear to grant state entities considerable autonomy, in practice these enterprises must obtain approval of state governments—and often from the highest political level—for most decisions affecting financing, tariffs, borrowing, salaries and personnel actions. State governments—guided by their political considerations—keep tariffs low and allocate the bulk of their sector investments to power generation. Where some reform-minded state governments such as Andhra Pradesh made efforts to stay the course on tariff reforms, they faced continued political opposition. As power enterprises have no operational autonomy and incentive to manage efficiently, their financial dependence on government increases. The SEBs' inability to pay for coal has exacerbated Coal India's—another public enterprise—cash flow problems.

Under the energy sector's current institutional setup, the roles of various government agencies in policy formulation, operation and regulation are not clearly defined. Regulation is carried out by various departments of the central and state governments, the CEA and the SEBs themselves. In each of India's five regions, a Regional Electricity board (REB) and associated Regional Level Development Commission (RLDC) oversees the operations of the regional grid.

The REBs manage the operation and promote interconnection among each region's constitutive power systems. Central regulation of the power sector however has conflicts between Centre Utilities and SEBs. Tariffs for the NTPC and the bulk supply to the SEBs are centrally set and not mutually agreed upon. States often feel that the CERC favours central utilities over state needs. NTPC has received large injections of government equity, which financed investment that helped it earn satisfactory rates of return.

As observed earlier, India's energy sector treats energy demand forecasts and investment planning as sequential rather than interdependent steps in the planning process. Planning continues to be predicated on demand forecasts extrapolated from past consumption trends with alternative scenarios. No attempt is being made to assess the crucial problems of unmet demand and the impact of price on demand. Planning efforts therefore fail to adequately address major constraints—particularly the serious shortage of resources.

Investment planning is now generally focused on optimizing the mix of new generation projects, yet where large shortages in capacity exist these are only marginally beneficial. Investment planning has failed to consider the substantial benefits from efficient operations such as plant rehabilitation and loss reduction, which are far less sensitive to such supply side uncertainties as fluctuations in world oil prices, the availability of natural gas and construction delays.

Planning arrangements also systematically focus on generation projects which has resulted in under-investment in much needed T&D which in turn jeopardizes least cost operation and encourages higher reserve margins. In addition, the Indian power market (interstate, centre-to-state, regional and inter-regional) has significant problems requiring near-term solutions; over- and under-use, lack of adequate metering, generation shortages, inadequate transmission facilities, poorly documented agreements and regional conflicts of interests.

Restrictive government institutions and government imposed barriers such as tariffs, licensing requirements, government control of the import sector and foreign exchange controls rarely take commercial considerations into account and impede both energy trade and investment. Even with the power supply contracts determined by the MOP, the current institutional setup through the government-approved fuel allocation schemes, tariff notification and coal linkages with electric utilities impede efficient operations and investment. For example, because of government-approved gas allocation the main Hazira-Bijaipur-Jagdishpur (HBJ) gas pipeline was not used to capacity.

The institutional structure in the energy sector is in transition since the 1990s with the setting up of the regulatory bodies at the federal and the state levels. CERC at the federal level and SREC at the state level have been set up. These commissions are assigned with the task of regulating tariffs and promoting competition and efficiency in India's electricity supply industry. Coal and oil sectors continue to be regulated through various government departments which are part of the Ministry of Coal and Ministry of Petroleum.

Energy policy

India's energy policy has evolved in the context of Five Year Plans consisting of objectives, plan strategies and targets of production to be achieved. Since energy sector development in the pre-1990s was based on government support and public fund allocation, the basic objectives of energy policy in the pre-1990s were to achieve self-reliance by reaching energy production targets set out in the Five Year Plans. Development of domestic energy resources, oil, coal and hydropower were the basic policy objectives. During the period between the two oil price increases (1973–9), the energy situation was reviewed under the aegis of fuel policy and energy policy committees.

The energy policy formulated in the post oil shock period of 1973–9 emphasized the importance of coal as the principal source of energy, the need for reducing reliance on imported oil and its substitution, including development of renewable energy. Energy strategies are outlined at regular intervals and at the time of formation of the Five Year Plan programs for the economy and continue to be part of the macroeconomic stabilization and reform program in the 1990s.

The main objectives of the Ninth Five Year Plan, 1997–2002, aimed to improve efficiency by adopting energy efficient technologies, to rationalize energy pricing to reflect real costs and phase out energy price controls over four years, to strengthen and to reform the institutional structures to implement energy reform policies by an overhaul of the Petroleum Law and Electricity Law and modernize the regulatory framework to promote private sector investment, both domestic and foreign, in the energy sector and to encourage joint ventures.

In the hydrocarbon sector, the government allows private sector investment in exploration and refining activities. In the coal sector, the government has amended the Coal Mines Nationalization Act to promote private investment, including 100 per cent foreign investment in the mining industry. In the power sector, private investment is allowed in generation and distribution and allows 100 per cent private ownership of transmission. However, the operational responsibilities of transmission services rest with SEBs and the Powergrid Corporation.

The government's energy policy for the Tenth Five Year Plan (2002–7) includes continuing the energy sector reform as part of the next phase of economic reform. The Tenth Plan which began on 1 April 2002, envisages economic growth of 8 per cent a year, compared with 5.6 per cent from 1997–2002. At present, the rate of oil consumption at 2.13 m b/d oil consumption is expected to more than triple to 7.3 mb/d by 2024–5. With declining domestic oil production at 0.64 m b/d, the widening gap implies dependence on oil imports of over 90 per cent of total oil consumption.

The highlights of the Tenth Plan in the energy sector include addition of

41,000 MWe in electricity capacity and focus on tackling import dependence by reducing India's crude oil requirement and taking greater care of the environment. In 2002, the government released 'Hydrocarbon Vision 2025', which aims to reduce crude oil imports by increasing domestic and overseas oil and gas production, to liberalize the energy sector and to address environmental issues by new technologies, particularly in relation to LNG and gas-to-liquid (GTL) projects. To diversify the energy mix, the government plans to promote the use of gas and renewables.

As part of the energy policy, the government is planning to set up a strategic petroleum reserve equal to 15 days of the country's oil consumption. The state-owned IOC is to take the lead in the development of the reserve.

As in China, India's energy policy in the form of objectives and targets to be achieved continues to be a part of governments' Five Year Plan priorities to address the prevailing situation of increasing dependence on oil imports. The fragmented and layered institutional bureaucracy at different levels—centre, region and state—continue to affect energy planning, policy and effective implementation of reform measures. In the petroleum sector, the Ministry of Petroleum and Natural Gas is responsible for policy formulation and oversees the entire chain of the oil and gas industries—E&P of crude oil and natural gas, refining, distribution, marketing of petroleum products and natural gas. The Ministry of Coal has the overall responsibility of determining policies and strategies relating to E&D of coal and lignite reserves. The Ministry of Power is responsible for power policy and for oversight of the electricity industry. Several authorities and agencies operate centrally under the Ministry of Power, among them the CEA, which assists the Ministry of Power in all technical and economic matters, the Rural Electrification Corporation, which finances electrification programs for rural areas and the Power Finance Corporation which guarantees financing for new power plants or the electricity grid.

The prevailing fragmented and multi-layered bureaucracy of energy institutions has not been able to formulate a comprehensive national energy policy that could identify the challenges, outline a vision for the future and propose strategies for implementation. For example, while much uproar is being generated to make a major shift in the structure of energy sources from fossil to renewable resources and expanding rapidly the use of nuclear and hydro sources of energy to reduce dependence on oil and gas, there is little attention to address the required challenges to make this required shift. As of 2004 the production of nuclear electricity in India is about 5 mtoe. It will require a ten-fold increase in nuclear power generation capacity to 50 mtoe that could provide less than 5 per cent of base line energy requirement in 2030.

The domestic energy source with the greatest potential is hydroelectric, although not in the conventional format of turbines built into large dams on rivers. The Brahmaputra River and its tributaries form one of the greatest sources of hydropower for India. The flow in the river varies from a minimum of 3,280 cubic meters a second (cm/s) to a flood peak of 72,460 cm/s, with an average of 20,000 cm/s. The total potential at the head is 5,000 cm/s and a significant part of this can be trapped to utilize the hydro potential by channelling the down-flowing water directly into turbines. Some experts envisage that a generation potential of 1 Terra Watt (TW), or 0.7 btoe a year can be conservatively realized.[38] However, there is still a vacuum in formulating the required strategy to exploit this hydro potential.

Both hydro and nuclear energy generation have high fixed and low operational costs as compared to coal generation or combined cycle gas generation. With India's decision to move towards commercial exploitation of nuclear electricity, electricity generation companies need to consider the implications of security, access and environment on the economic viability of all available options for generating electricity.

Harnessing the potential of solar energy is widely discussed and its potential for massive applications in the agricultural sector depends on breakthroughs in nanotechnologies to increase solar cell efficiencies currently averaging 15–50 per cent levels. Bio-fuel has significant potential for substitution of oil in the transport sector. Given that energy resource development, both conventional and non-conventional, needs decades of lead time, India's efforts in making progress in changing its future energy mix including expanding the use of renewable energy and bio-fuel require a focused action oriented program to access renewable technologies that bring down costs, to address all issues relating to generation of energy through wind, solar and biomass to meet the needs of a diverse range of applications and customers.

Given disjuncture between government policy statements and the record of the government's consistent efforts to achieve policy goals in a time-bound manner, it is doubtful that a major shift in India's future energy mix is achievable. Energy policy statements at the ministerial level without the required coordinated policy measures of action to effectively implement on the ground remain disjointed, particularly in the power sector. The poor quality, mounting losses of power and arbitrary pricing of electricity have been the greatest deterrents to India's economic growth and power development. As a result, the power sector has been the centrepiece of energy policy and regulatory reform in India since 1991. However, policy approaches to achieving adequate capacity, reliability of supply and rational rates have entered their second decade with little quantifiable progress to show for disjunctive policy approaches.

Under the Indian Constitution electricity is on the 'concurrent list', meaning that the state legislature's authority is comparable to that of the central

38. *Indian Energy, Petroleum Economist* (March 2005).

government regarding the country's power sector, although the Federal parliament can exercise pre-emptive power in the event of a conflict. The Constitutional underpinnings of the state level entities along with their vulnerability to political influence and bottlenecks in centre-state relations have delayed implementation of policy reforms and perpetuated market distortions caused by politically motivated subsidies to households and farmers. Lack of comprehensive and coordinated energy policy objectives and clear policy measures involving oil, gas, coal, power, transport, environment and finance continue to be barriers to mobilizing the required investment.

The new government which took office in May 2004 is mainly focused on dealing with the rising oil prices and shortages of electricity supply by announcing triple power generation capacity by 2015 to over 350,000 MW. The Prime Minister, in July 2005, set up an Energy Coordination Committee which is a step in the right direction to enable a systemic approach for policy formulation in the area of energy planning and security. However, given that the committee members are mainly drawn from the political establishment at the central and state governments, this committee's focus is on providing bureaucratic institutional support to decision making in the short term. India still lacks a comprehensive national energy policy that could identify the challenges, outline a vision for the energy future and formulate an integrated national energy policy and strategies for its implementation to achieve the government's repeated goal of energy security.

A first step in formulating a forward-looking energy policy for India's twenty-first century energy future requires drawing on the best domestic and global talent to undertake technical, economic, financial and environmental evaluation of all of its domestic energy resources. Based on the comprehensive evaluation of its domestic energy resources, the government will have to prepare its medium- and long-term energy planning, policy and strategy framework. An energy policy package must cover both conventional and non-conventional sources of energy and address energy security, access and availability, affordability and pricing, efficiency, environment, technology and financing issues. Given the fragmented nature of institutions responsible for energy policy and the government's short-term focus on handling day-to-day spikes in world crude oil prices, formulating an integrated energy policy and appropriate strategies for effective implementation to address the twenty-first century realities of the energy world will be a major institutional challenge of reforming the energy sector for development.

Energy price liberalization

In the pre-1990s, India's energy pricing structure was distorted as pricing practices were influenced more by political, social and economic factors than by market considerations. Prices did not reflect costs or international energy prices. The price of coal was administered by the government on a cost-plus basis. However, in reality, coal companies could not recover even the average production costs and price adjustments did not reflect the increase in supply costs.

Domestic crude oil and natural gas prices were set by the government well below the international price for oil and the supply costs. Petroleum product prices were set on the basis of the Administered Price Mechanism (APM), which had been in practice since 1977. The Ministry of Petroleum and Natural Gas through the Oil Coordination Committee (OCC) administered the scheme. The OCC undertook a cost updating study for each of the oil companies every three years to determine whether they were earning the stipulated revenues. Oil product prices remained distorted even after the government's macroeconomic stabilization reform started in 1991. With taxes, subsidies and adjustment through pooled accounts, petroleum product prices did not reflect fluctuations in international oil prices. Kerosene, diesel and LPG were heavily subsidized.

In the electricity sector, the problems of inadequate peak load capacity, inadequate transmission systems, below average load factor of the thermal system have all created a supply shortfall and widened the gap between growing demand and available supply. Electricity prices do not reflect market conditions and remain highly distorted. While each state sets its own prices and tariff structure, there is no standard method for establishing the prices charged to various categories of customers. While the domestic and commercial customers do not pay any demand charges in most states (West Bengal, Orissa, Karnataka and Kerala being a few exceptions), the industrial customers do pay demand charges depending on their connected load. The per kWh varies significantly across states as well as customer categories within a state. Tariffs in India are not structured to consider the time of usage and voltage level of supply. In addition to base tariffs, some of the SEBs have additional recovery from customers in the form of fuel surcharges and electricity duties.

Part of the government's resistance to market-oriented reforms of the power system stems from genuine concern about the effect of higher electricity rates on the poor. But it also reflects the clout of key constituencies, notably farmers, who are among the largest beneficiaries of power subsidies. Politicians' political and social concerns are reflected in heavily subsidized prices to agriculture and the poor. Politicians want to give free electricity to the agricultural sector or universally undercharge agricultural consumers at less than one US cent/kWh, which is less than 10 per cent of the actual LRMC of supply. The state government's efforts to increase agricultural tariffs have been met with stiff resistance. Electric power for rural pump set usage is subsidized by all the states in India. The Indian economic survey of 2003 estimated that rural subsidies accounted for 1.1 per cent of GDP. The farmers say that government set prices for staple crops do not reflect the cost of production and that increases in monthly electricity bills will force them deeper into debt.

India's high agriculture tariff subsidies universally undermine the financial viability of the SEBs and their ability to provide reliable service. In 2000–1, power subsidies reached US $5.8 billion, accounting for 1.3 per cent of India's GDP. The average rate of subsidy expressed as a proportion of the estimated full cost of electricity supply was 93 per cent for farmers and 58 per cent for households. Industrial and commercial consumers and urban above-life-line consumers in many large cities and the railways pay above-cost prices. About 55 per cent of electricity generated is billed and only 41 per cent is paid, mainly because of theft, non-metering and corruption.

The average tariff levels are below the average cost of supply for most of the Boards and the situation has deteriorated over the 1990s. Table 5.5 shows the cost recovery of electricity supply in India's states.

Table 5.5. India: State Electricity Board cost recovery in the 1990s.
(sales realization as a ratio of cost)

State Electricity Board	*1992–3*	*1995–6*	*1998–9*
Andhra Pradesh	94.2	62.2	80.6
Assam	47.4	57.1	63.3
Bihar	63.7	70.6	78.4
Delhi Vidyut Board	81.7	72.9	71.1
Gujarat	68.4	63.6	85.9
Haryana	54	98.8	64.1
Himachal Pradesh	88.5	13.2	90.2
Jammu and Kashmir	21.3	74.9	16.2
Karnataka	96.5	69	89.9
Kerala	84.7	79.5	75.1
Madhya Pradesh	84	91.2	72.3
Maharashtra	98.5	72.7	90.5
Meghalaya	81.3	77.1	38.7
Orissa	78.1	69.7	85.5
Punjab	57.6	67.8	60.9
Rajasthan	76	67.8	74.5
Tamil Nadu	86	97.1	92
Uttar Pradesh	70.6	70.7	69.8
West Bengal	71.5	78.5	78.6
Total	82.2	76.1	78.6

Source: *Planning Commission, Annual Report on the working of State Electricity Boards and Electricity Departments, Power and Energy Division, Government of India, New Delhi,* (1999).

The deteriorating operating performance of the SEBs and their inability to recover their costs are estimated to have cost them on average of US $7 billion a year in 1999. In order for the SEBs to achieve commercial viability the subsidies will have to increase by 25 per cent of the state government revenues or US $12 billion.[39] The gap between average revenue realization and average cost has been constantly increasing. During the year 2000–1, the average cost of supply was US $6 cents/kWh and average revenue was US $4 cents—a gap of 2 US cents for every kWh power supplied. As of February 2001, the total dues owed by the SEBs amounted to Rs 41,473 crores or US $10 billion, of which 60 per cent represents principal and 40 per cent interest.

By 2002 it was evident to the government that most of the SEBs were bankrupt. As part of the 2002 budget, the GOI took a major decision to bail the SEBs out of their staggering dues by announcing a one time settlement scheme under the Accelerated Power Development Program (APDP) to systematically work towards cutting T&D losses and commercializing electricity operation. As part of the APDP program, the GOI decided to waive 60 per cent of the interest amounting to an equivalent of US $2.5 billion and surcharge and securitize the remaining outstanding through tax free bonds at 8.5 per cent interest.

The GOI 2002–3 budget allocated US $700 million under the APDP to improve the electricity sector at the state level. The GOI made it clear that the availability of funds would be linked to the implementation of reforms by the states and the APDP was redesigned as the Accelerated Power Development and Reform Program (APDRP). Further progress in electricity pricing reform has been blocked by fierce resistance from some consumers and political leaders following the election of the United Progressive Alliance (UPA) government into power in 2004. The new ministry's programs and priorities would now revolve around the mission of 'power for all by 2012 and electrification of all villages and households by 2009'. Electricity pricing reform is expected to be slow and gradual in bringing prices up to cover full costs.

The GOI, since 2000, has taken important steps towards removing price controls on oil and coal and lowering subsidies to energy. On 1 April 2000, the pricing of coal became fully deregulated with the Colliery Control Order. This supersedes the Colliery Control Order (1945) of the Essential Commodities Act (1955) by which the central government had been empowered to fix the prices of coal by grade and colliery; there are no longer any direct subsidies to coal production or consumption. Delivered coal prices, nonetheless, remain below market levels due to continuing subsidies on rail transportation.

---

39. WEC, *Pricing Energy in Developing Countries* (London, June 2001), p.34

In March 2002 the government budget announced deregulation of petroleum products from 1 April 2002. The 2002–3 budget confirmed the government's efforts to move forward with what was called 'second generation reforms'. In the energy sector the government announced taking several steps to deregulate petroleum product prices. The OCC was abolished and the oil pool account of the APM was dismantled. The outstanding balances are to be liquidated by issue of oil bonds to the concerned oil companies. Dismantling of APM would also free domestic crude oil prices for oil produced by ONGC and OIL. Domestic crude oil prices are to be market determined.

With the dismantling of the Administered Pricing Mechanism (APM) for most of the petroleum products with effect from 1 April 2002, India seems to be moving towards liberalization of petroleum prices after a gap of three decades since the nationalization of oil majors Caltex, Esso and Burmah Shell in the early 1970s. Along with the dismantling of the APM, the complex system of Oil Pool Accounts, under which the prices of cooking gas (LPG) and kerosene were being subsidized, has also been discontinued.

The dismantling of APM is also being viewed as a major step towards reform in the key petroleum sector. Petrol, diesel and other petroleum products are sold at market determined prices by the oil companies. The government however continued to provide a subsidy of Rs 3 (US cents 7) a litre for consumption of the poor—supplied through the Public Distribution System (PDS) and Rs 90 (US $2) for cooking gas per cylinder.

Price deregulation of petroleum products was expected to let competition determine market prices and consequent fall in retail product prices. However, retail product prices have not fallen since April 2002. Following the dismantling of the APM there was expectation of reasonable stability of oil prices once a proper and effective regulatory system to oversee the petroleum sector is put in place. The government in 2002 announced the setting up of a Petroleum Regulatory Board (PRB) to oversee the downstream petroleum sector. As part of its functions the PRB was to be entrusted with authorizing marketing rights to private companies who have invested or propose to invest over US $400 million in oil infrastructure and would be permitted to market petrol, diesel and aviation turbine fuel.

Although the government officially ended the APM for petroleum products in April 2002, oil price reforms have not completely removed government influence on petroleum product prices. Subsidies have been maintained on some products such as kerosene and LPG, which are commonly used as cooking fuel.

Changing over to the deregulated market was expected to be smooth. However, the rising trend of retail petroleum product prices and the takeover of the newly elected UPA government following the 2004 election have raised questions about the new government's intention to allow market forces to determine the prices of petroleum products. Following the spikes in crude oil prices since May/ June 2004, the UPA government seems to be striving towards working out a political consensus over the need for an across-the-board 'moderate' hike in the prices of petroleum products.

Given that the UPA government was obliged to respect the 2004 election mandate, it has tried to address the concerns of the 'common citizen' by pursuing rather a 'burden-sharing' pricing agenda. Besides, considering the political sensitivity over pricing of petroleum products the government made the decision that it cannot remain indifferent to the phenomenon of rising petroleum prices by allowing the market to determine the prices. Deregulation was modified to reflect ground realities by allowing the oil companies to adjust price within 'socially acceptable limits' and to determine prices within a 10 per cent free-pricing band for gasoline and diesel. As for LPG and kerosene, oil firms would be advised to raise the price in a phased manner to avoid any shocks. The decision was taken to restrain oil companies from raising fuel prices that would have increased inflation. The finance and petroleum ministries dealing with rising international oil prices introduced a price band system of within 10 per cent for future price increases for gasoline and diesel and extended the phase-out period for the subsidy on kerosene and LPG.

Rattled by rising international oil prices and two consecutive weeks of mounting inflation, the government on 18 August 2004 announced its decision to cut customs and excise duties on gasoline, diesel, kerosene and LPG to share the burden of rising oil prices by the government and oil companies.While customs duty on petrol, diesel, kerosene and LPG was cut by 5 per cent, excise duty on petrol and diesel was reduced by 3 per cent and excise on kerosene was cut by 4 per cent. This decision was intended to give the consumers a temporary reprieve from the monthly price increases which reflect rising international crude oil prices.

Consequently, the IOC reported Rs 5,500 crores (US $1.2 billion) under recoveries from LPG and kerosene in August 2004.

The finance ministry also considered the introduction and setting up of a price stabilization fund. The monies from the fund would be used to moderate the impact of any abnormal rise or fall in international prices. Setting up of a price stabilization fund will turn out to be part of the problem rather than the solution given the administration and coordination issues and corruption practices associated with the historical experience of operations of such stabilization funds.

Furthermore, the solution is no longer limited to cyclical behaviour of oil prices, which necessitate correction by establishing a stabilization fund.

With the continued upward swing in oil prices since August 2004, the government declared in August 2005 that it would continue to adopt the pricing principle of equitable burden sharing between the government, consumers and oil companies, focusing mainly on minimizing the short-term impact of rising prices on consumers and on inflation. Even if oil prices were to stabilize, the government is expected to revert to fixing the prices every fortnight within the limits of the price-band mechanism.

The government continues to operate on the crisis management mode on a day-to-day basis by trying to balance the economics of reflecting real cost of energy by state intervention and the politics of staying in power.

Like China, India has come a long way in reforming energy prices. Three decades after the first oil shock, finally the GOI in 2002 had a plan to dismantle the administered pricing of oil. The price of natural gas is linked to the international basket of fuel oil prices comprising a mix of low and high sulphur fuel oils. Since 1999, the wellhead price for domestic natural gas was US $1.69 /mBtu, to which up to $1.00 /Btu was added for royalties, taxes and transportation charges. Compared with naptha and fuel oil around $7–8 /mBtu, gas was cheaper. Domestic gas supplies were sold to the agriculture and power sectors at subsidized prices, under the government's APM. Following the government's decision on petroleum price liberalization in 2003, the government wanted to link gas prices to 100 per cent import parity prices of fuel oil, removing floor and ceiling prices. The price of gas to the consumer has been linked with the calorific value.

In 2003 GAIL began to adopt market based prices. In April 2003 it signed its first contracts for gas at market rates from the satellite Rawa fields in the Krishna–Godavari Basin. Final delivered rates inclusive of taxes and transportation charges have been agreed with customers in Andhra Pradesh at $3.62 /mBtu, a significant step up from the standard post-tax price of around $2.50 /mBtu. The main customers are fertilizer and power firms.[40]

With deregulation of oil prices, the price of gas was expected to be in parity with international oil prices. Nonetheless, the events of 2004, change of government and spiking oil prices and rising oil imports all seemed to have set the clock back for liberalization of energy prices, particularly oil and power prices in India.

Power pricing processes are more often historical cost based and subject to bargaining in some states between the regulator and the electric utility. The pricing practices in India in the electricity sector, despite being based on the principle of cost-plus, have not been able to reflect costs to achieve the objectives of eliminating subsidies, increasing efficiency, increasing access to electricity to the poor segment of the population and mobilizing investment. There is very little incentive for a large segment of users to either use energy efficient equipment or alter their use to lower the demand for additional investment in building peak capacity.

Despite the progress made in pricing of oil, gas and coal, energy price

---

40. *Price Blocks LNG Progress, Petroleum Economist* (August 2003), p.27–8.

liberalization has suffered a serious setback with spiking oil prices since 2004. Given the inter-sector and macro-sector linkages of energy pricing, appropriate sequencing of pricing reform in agriculture, industry, energy and infrastructure sectors are required for progress. Furthermore, with rising energy prices since 2004 India's political and regulatory institutions continue to face the challenges of reforming energy pricing to improve efficiency, to promote competition and to attract investment in energy.

Regulation

Coal and oil sectors continue to be regulated through various government departments. In the hydrocarbon sector, the establishment of a Directorate General of Hydrocarbons (DGH) is entrusted with the responsibility of promoting private participation in the upstream sector. Downstream, the OCC was set up to provide technical and operational support in the implementation of regulatory policies. The OCC was abolished with the dismantling of APM and oil price liberalization. The government in 2003 announced setting up of a regulatory authority to oversee the petroleum sector downstream, including granting of licenses. The draft Petroleum Regulatory Board Bill as of 2004 was still pending because of discussions on the scope of the Bill to cover the gas sector. In September 2003, the government issued a draft policy for the development of a gas pipeline network that foresees the construction of a future gas transportation network on a common carrier principle with requirements for third-party access under public ownership and management. GAIL was nominated as monopoly builder and operator of cross-country gas pipelines. The draft policy triggered substantial debate among industry players and the private sector raised questions about a conflict of interest resulting from the different roles of GAIL as producer, transporter and retailer of gas. The new UPA government which took office in 2004 is expected to consolidate the pending multiple bills within the integrated national energy policy.

Economic Regulation of the Indian Power Sector is carried out by the central government, state governments, CEA and the SEBs themselves. There are a number of other regulatory bodies that control aspects of the power sector, such as the Ministry of Environment and Forests and the Reserve Bank of India (RBI). The central and state governments have several types of powers, which they can use to exercise regulatory control over the SEBs.

Electricity is a 'concurrent' subject under the Indian constitution. This means that both the central and state governments have powers to enact legislation affecting the power sector. The central government has taken the lead in defining the main legislation, the 1948 Electricity (Supply) Act (E(S) Act), and in providing the policy framework through the MOP. State governments have focused on specific issues relating to the generation and supply of electricity in their states.

The main purpose of the E(S) Act was to create the SEBs. These are statutory organizations responsible for the development of the power sector in their respective states. The Industrial Policy Resolution of 1956 reserved generation and distribution of electricity almost exclusively to the state sector in the form of SEBs. In the Union territories and in a few states in north-eastern India, however, power development is the responsibility of the electricity departments or municipal corporations.

The E(S) Act comprehensively covers the constitution and composition of SEBs, their powers, operation, staffing, and their financial accounting and auditing procedures. The Act also gives powers to the central and state governments in matters such as approval of investments and borrowings and gives wide powers for state governments to issue directives. The E(S) Act also created the CEA, which is administratively responsible to the MOP. The CEA became a full-time organization in 1974. It develops power sector policy and has wide powers to approve investment projects.

REBs were established in 1963 as associations of the constituent SEBs and other power utilities in the respective regions. The REBs are under the administrative control of the CEA. They are charged with the responsibility of coordinating the generating schedules of the power utilities, monitoring system operations and helping to arrange inter-state exchanges of power.

In 1976 the E(S) Act was amended to provide for the establishment of central and state generating companies to augment power availability and to achieve a more efficient utilization of national resources cutting across state boundaries. Five central generating companies were established. These include NTPC, National Hydrelectric Power Corporation (NHPC), North Eastern Electric Power Corporation (NEPC), NLC and Nuclear Power Corporation (NPC). Some of the state governments have also established power corporations responsible for power generation. However, in most of the states these corporations construct and commission power plants which are generally handed over to the respective SEBs upon completion.

As part of the energy sector reform program, in 1991 the relevant parts of the E(S) Act were amended to allow a generating company to be formed in the private sector as well. The Amendment also provided statutory powers for effective control to the REBs. According to the amendment of the E(S) Act of 1991, every license and generating company shall follow all directions of the REBs, including compliance with the instructions of the Regional Load Dispatch Centre to ensure integrated regional grid operations.

The Powergrid Corporation of India Ltd. (PGC) was established in 1989 with a view to formation of a national grid and integrating the grids in the five main regions of India. Powergrid has the legal form of a 'Generating Company' under the provisions of the E(S) Act although it does not have a direct involvement in generation *per se*.

Two power sector financial institutions exist; the Rural Electrification Corporation (REA) and the Power Finance Corporation (PFC). Both are under the administrative control of the MOP.

The GOI enacted an Electricity Regulatory Commission Act in July 1998. This Act provides for establishment of CERC and SERC at the national and state levels in an attempt *inter alia* to depoliticize the tariff-setting process. The CERC has been established and the commissioners appointed. It is responsible for approval of tariff for central sector utilities and tariff review/ setting of multi-state IPPs. By 2001, 14 SERCs had been set up. These commissions were assigned with the task of regulating tariffs and promoting competition in the electricity supply industry.

The legal and policy framework has also been established for rationalization of the tariff structure. Promoting competition in a market where public monopolies coexist with private entrepreneurs puts tremendous demand on the regulatory authorities. Beyond overseeing establishing a tariff that is fair to the consumers and curbing excessive rent-seeking, regulators must pressure public enterprises to improve their performance in technical and operational management and increase efficiency by commercializing the operations in the new competitive environment.

India's utilities pricing system use cost-plus mechanism that guarantee power companies a certain rate of return as long as they operate above a minimum level of efficiency. The 1978 Amendment to the E(S) Act requires SEBs to earn at least a 3 per cent return on historic cost asset base. Subsequent studies carried out in 1980 by the Rajyadyksha Committee on Power recommended that the SEBs should generate a gross annual rate of return of 15 per cent or a net return of 6 per cent on the average capital base.

Tariff determination by SEBs is carried out in three stages. First, the total cost of meeting a given level of demand is estimated. Operating costs include the cost of fuel, power purchase, operation and maintenance, establishment, administration and miscellaneous expenditures. Capital costs include depreciation, interest on debt and return on equity if the SEB has an equity capital. Depreciation is based on the straight-line method and is applied to the net capital stock (at book value) at the beginning of the year.

In the second stage, the costs at the extra high tension (EHT) and low-tension ends (LT) are estimated. The estimated cost of per kWh power includes both the cost of net generated power and purchased power. The costs at various transmission ends are computed using information on T&D costs after taking into account T&D losses. Some SEBs for their internal decisions, classify voltage end costs into capacity costs and energy costs. The joint and common costs of the SEBs are allocated at the different voltage ends on the basis of fully distributed cost method. A weighted average of these two costs is estimated for arriving at unit costs of power supply at these voltage ends.

The final stage is the fixation of tariff. At this stage, socio-economic and political considerations play an important role. Though the cost of electricity supply in rural and remote areas is higher than in urban areas, most states supply electricity to the rural areas at prices well below costs in order to achieve balanced development and remove rural-urban disparity mainly due to political compulsions. Similarly, SEBs charge lower rates for domestic lifeline customers and agricultural users who are supplied high cost power at the LT end.[41]

The PPA between public generating stations and public distributors are vague and do not make allowances for the risks involved. These include the risk of non-payment by SEBs, which have a monopoly on distribution, the risk of low offtake of power and the risk of non-availability of fuel when the power producer is required to buy it from specified locations owned by a public monopoly. Private power producers wanted PPAs with SEBs that allocate these risks within a commercial framework.

In the policy for private investment in power announced in 1992, private investors were offered a remunerative tariff based on a cost-plus formula with potentially attractive returns on equity linked to levels of capacity utilization. The new PPA were very different from existing arrangements in that the power tariff was expected to reflect explicit pricing of risks. This approach created differential tariffs for public generating plants where tariffs were based on the old pricing formula, while new private plants are guaranteed higher returns and protected against risks.

The SERCs' power to approve SEB tariffs is subject to state government approval. Pricing for different consumer groups is also effectively controlled by state governments. There are no restrictions on cross-subsidization. Absence of standardized tariff structure across states and the level of cross-subsidies have prevented the achievement of efficient standard industry practices. The tariff adjustment process is usually complex and reflects the preference for bureaucratic process wherein committees sit in judgement on what is a reasonable cost to be passed on to the customers and what is not, with hardly any benchmarking of standard costs.

Despite establishing the SERCs, it is the state government and not the regulator that makes the decision about subsidies. The state governments have exclusive authority in establishing social policy, subject to the limits established in various laws. The regulator does not make social policies but instead implements them. For example, the government of Karnataka acknowledged in its 2003 budget that despite a government subsidy of US $500 million and three tariff increases since establishment of the Karnataka

41. Govinda Rao, M Kalirajan, K P and Ric Shand, *The Economics of Electricity Supply in India* (Delhi, Macmillan India, 1998)

Electricity Regulatory Commission (KERC) in 2000, the power sector is inefficient. Tariff reform for SEBs is focused mainly on passing on rising costs due to technical, business and financial inefficiencies to 40 per cent of consumers who actually pay the bills. The average urban consumer in Karnataka pays over US cents 7/kWh from April 2003 for low quality, interrupted power supply including black-outs and brown-outs.

The KERC was established in 2000 to meet the requirement of the WB. Between 2000 and 2003, the KERC consisted of a civil service employee as commissioner, and two members, one drawn from the civil services and another a power engineer. Although on paper the KERC is to be independent, in practice it is run as a subservient bureaucracy subject to the political will of the government. The setting up of regulatory institutions in states such as Karnataka is more a matter for media/ TV show and advertisement than as an effective vehicle to set competitive market-based tariffs to reflect commercial viability of SEBs, to promote competition and to attract private and public investment to increase access to efficient and reliable power.

India's regulatory reform practices in the power sector both at the central and state levels have been that of catering to the emerging situation with required swings across the situation pendulum. Although electricity tariffs are based on the cost-plus principle, costs are based more often on historical costs of SEBs and LRMC has a very limited role. The differential rates of return policy for SEBs and private investors under the 'old' and 'new' pricing methods has failed to provide a level playing field and failed to encourage SEBs to commercialize their operations.

Regulatory reforms are required at the entry point to stimulate competitive conditions and also maintain a balance among different generating units. Regulation at the operational level needs to ensure the smooth and safe functioning of the grid at both the national and state level until tariffs evolve towards merit order operations. Regulatory reforms needs to be implemented as an important component of the power sector reform along with appropriate sequencing of industry restructuring, commercialization, privatization and private investment reform components.

SEB restructuring will require the government to redesign the regulatory relationship among centre, regions and states. With the ongoing reform of the power sector, India will need to demarcate clearly which regulatory functions belong to which institutions among the regions, the centre, and the states. The main purposes of regulation are to resolve conflicting interests, ensure competitive behaviour and protect consumer interest. In a segment where monopoly elements persist, competitive elements need to be stimulated through benchmark pricing schemes.

The GOI was well aware of the prevailing inefficiencies in the power sector and the need for making rapid progress to reform. In 2003, the GOI estimated that cumulative losses of the SEBs reached over US $6 billion in

2001–02 and warned that in future losses could more than triple to US $20 billion per year. The GOI called for states to come down hard on rampant power theft. The GOI attempted to rationalize power tariffs in a phased manner over a period of time and proposed the Electricity Bill 2000 which was passed by the Indian Parliament in May 2003. The Electricity Bill seeks to replace the three existing Acts, namely The Indian Electricity Act (1910), The Electricity Supply Act (1948) and the Electricity Regulatory Commission Act (1998).

The Electricity Act (2003) is a legal framework capable of adapting to the changing situation in the sector and providing long-term legal certainty to potential investors. The Act replaces and consolidates all existing provisions for the power sector. The main elements of the Bill include mandatory constitution of regulatory mechanism, restructuring the SEBs, freeing generation from licensing, the vertical unbundling of the SEBs, the commercialization and corporatization of sector entities and the need to pursue rural electrification outside the main grid through decentralized supply systems, licensing of private transmission companies by appropriate regulatory authority, providing open access of transmission lines to all licenses/ generating companies, providing open access to consumers in a phased manner and separating electricity supply from and requiring separate licenses for supply and trade.

The 2003 Electricity Act seeks to effectively insulate the tariff-setting process from political considerations. Accordingly, regulatory responsibility for the sector is to be vested in the CERC and the SERCs, whose establishment is to be mandatory. As of end 2003, 20 states had established SERCs. The Act also allows for the introduction of a multiyear tariff framework. In April 2004, CERC announced a five-year tariff order stipulating a flat 14 per cent return on equity for all central public sector undertakings and mega private projects. The Act seeks to drastically bring down loss relating to generation, T&D of power and would help the country to add 100,000 MW of new capacity by 2012.

The Indian private sector reacted positively to the opportunities under the 2003 Electricity Act including recognition of transmission as a separate entity and permitting private sector participation. At the end of December 2003, the first transmission license under the Act was awarded to a joint venture between the state-owned Powergrid Company and the privately owned Tata Power, with the latter being the majority shareholder, making it India's first interstate transmission project in the private sector. CERC operationalized open access in interstate transmission with effect from 6 May 2004.

In a major effort to boost power sector reforms at the state level, Section 172 of the 2003 Electricity Act called for unbundling of the SEBs by 10 June 2004. Section 39 laid down that all state transmission utilities would cease to engage in the business of trading, i.e. bulk purchase and sale of electricity to distribution companies after 10 June 2004. In 2003 the GOI created a US $8 billion package to provide performance-linked assistance to state governments by bringing down the technical and financial losses of the SEBs. This package was expected to be implemented through a six-level intervention strategy that encompasses initiatives at national, state, SEB, distribution and consumer levels. The package, spread over five years, would focus on accountability, deliverability and performance at all levels to rejuvenate the distribution sector.

The strategy involved technical, commercial, financial interventions, organizational and restructuring measures and incentive mechanisms for cash loss reduction. The total loss reduction would be the parameter to be monitored for providing incentives by way of grant in the ratio of Rupee One for every Rupees Two of reduction by the SEBs and power utilities. Given the social and political difficulties associated with implementation of the reform process, particularly following the 2004 election and adoption of the National Common Minimum Program (NCMP) of the new UPA government, the main concern is one of slow progress. Immediately after taking over the office, the new government in the first week of June 2004 issued a gazette notification extending the 10 June 2004 deadline for one year till 10 June 2005 of Sections 172 and 39 which required unbundling of SEBs and cessation of state transmission utilities in the business of electricity trading. An advisory body under Sonia Gandhi, the Chairman of the Congress party was formed to look into the bottlenecks in the implementation of the 2003 Act.[42]

By August 2005 it was evident that the Union power ministry was dragging its feet on unbundling, common carrier principle and effective implementation of elimination of subsidies by commercialization of SEBs. The SEBs were left to their own discretion to take decisions on cross-subsidization and commercialization. The momentum of reform seemed to have suffered under the politics of coalition.

Commercialization/ Corporatization

Commercialization of public enterprises was an essential element of the Fiscal Adjustment Strategy of GOI's 1991 macroeconomic stabilization and reform program. The reform program's areas included privatizing and commercializing Central Government Public Enterprises (CPEs) and reducing non-statutory central government transfers to the states (in the form of grants and loans). It required the states to improve cost recovery and reduce power subsidies by increasing tariffs, improving collection rates and adjusting

42. No more tinkering electricity law, *Indian Express* (16 June 2004)

public employment by commercializing state public enterprises (SPEs).

The economic liberalization reform program launched in 1991 and the subsequent governments of 1996 through 2003 reduced the number of industries reserved exclusively for public sector enterprises from 17 to eight in July 1991 and further slashed it to 6 in 1993. It now includes nuclear energy, certain defence industries, rail transport and some mineral sectors.

By the mid-1990s, the general macroeconomic situation improved and there was an increase in competition both from domestic firms and multinationals. In general, corporate attitudes began to change, domestic companies began remodelling their operations to become niche players, manufacturing partners or strategic allies with a view to strengthening their competitiveness. Restructuring began to take place along several lines. First, some firms started consolidating around core competencies and selling off units unrelated to their core activities. Second, mergers and acquisitions continued to increase in an effort to increase capacity quickly and consolidate market share. Third, a number of companies entered into strategic partnership, mostly with foreign companies, to acquire new technologies, management techniques and access to outside markets. Fourth, taking advantage of financial markets and increased access to international capital markets, firms started to reduce their interest costs by retiring high-cost domestic debt. Finally, companies began strengthening management and reducing excess labour through training programs and voluntary retirement schemes.[43]

Changing corporate attitudes got further boost in the energy sector with the liberalization of coal and oil prices. The state coal, oil and gas corporations began positioning themselves to successfully retain their lead role and in the case of oil companies, by mergers, acquisitions and expansion of their business operations.

The GOI recognized that the coal industry stands at a crossroads while it is poised for substantial growth. It requires large infusions of both capital and technology to commercialize its operations and to expand rapidly to meet the growing demand requirements of coal in electric power generation. The Coal Mines Nationalization Act has been amended to permit coal washing in the private sector. Recognizing the virtue of contracting out services in the coal industry, the GOI approved 13 contracts by 1995 with private companies for the development of coal mines associated with investments in power plants and three contracts for mines associated with investment in steel plants. Coal India entered into commercial contracts with NTPC and several private investors in power plants for the supply of coal. The government also allowed private participation in coal mining, building up of washeries by private agencies as agents to the power stations and construction of

43. WB, *India, Five Years of Stabilization and Reform and the Challenges Ahead* (Washington DC, 1996)

washeries on a BOO basis.

However, there is no comprehensive coal sector reform and investment strategy to mobilize the required investment and technology to commercialize coal operations. In the coal sector, commercialization measures include rationalization of manpower, decontrol of prices of all non-coking superior grade coals and coking coals, closure of uneconomical mines, capital restructuring packages for collieries, reduction of import duty on equipment and spares, parity for distribution of imported coal and domestic coal and implementation of cash and carry system for coal supplies. A draft legislative bill, the 'Coal Mines (Nationalization) Amendment Bill' that would allow private sector participation in commercial mining beyond captive usage has been pending in parliament since 2000. The Ministry of Coal also considered introducing a Coal and Lignite Regulation and Development Bill to introduce competitive bidding in the allocation of mining blocks, create an independent authority to oversee competitive bidding with the aim of creating a level playing field between the public and private sectors, and broaden the eligibility of BOO Projects for coal washeries. However, given the new UPA government's emphasis on employment creation, once again, passing of these bills to commercialize coal sector seems unlikely in the prevailing environment of coalition politics. Consequently, the required major structural changes in the coal sector are unlikely to be instituted.

India's oil and gas sectors have emerged as commercially oriented. Major policy developments since the 1990s have tried to deregulate the sectors. Commercialization measures in the oil sector include corporatization of public sector companies, private participation in the exploration, production and marketing activities of crude oil and the marketing of specific oil products in selected areas, joint ventures in the exploration and drilling of new wells. Deregulation of oil prices and the natural gas sector are aimed at encouraging private participation in exploration, production and transportation of oil and gas.

The ONGC was corporatized in 1994. This change in legal status enables it to raise money on the capital markets. Following the deregulation of oil prices in April 2002, ONGC posted a net profit of US $880 million for the first half of the financial year (April–September). Since corporatization in 1994, ONGC has adopted a growth strategy to increase its oil production from domestic and external sources by acquiring overseas assets.

ONGC planned in the 2002–3 fiscal year to invest US $1.24 billion to acquire oil equity abroad, mainly in Sudan, Iran, Libya and the US. ONGC's overseas arm, ONGC Videsh Ltd (OVL) took a lead in the acquisition effort, motivated by declining domestic oil output and the absence of major discoveries in India to gain some leverage on its huge growing import demand. OVL floated a special purpose vehicle, Nile–Ganga Pte, to buy a 25 per cent equity stake in Sudan's Greater Nile Oil Project from Talisman

Energy Inc (Calgary). In June 2002 OVL spent US $750 million in this effort. Partners include China's National Petroleum Corporation (40 per cent), Malaysia's Petronas (30 per cent) and Sudan's Sudapet (5 per cent).

OVL has a 40 per cent stake in Vietnam in a consortium that includes BP, Statoil and PetroVietnam. Box 5.2 shows ONGC's upstream assets as of May 2004.

Box 5.2 India—ONGC Videsh's upstream assets

Country	*Project*	*Type*
Sudan	Greater Nile Petroleum (25%)	300,000 b/d
Vietnam	Nam Con Son (40%)	Producing gas
Russia	Sakhalin (20%)	Production 2005
Myanmar	Block A-1	Exploration
Iran	Farsi Block (40%)	Exploration
Syria	Block 24 (60%)	Exploration

Source: *'India and China seek overseas expansion', Petroleum Argus,* (3 May 2004), Vol. XXXIV, p.5

ONGC is also a joint-venture partner with Petronet, IOC, GAIL and Bharat Petroleum, which was formed to manage future LNG supplies to the Indian market. To mitigate the inherent risks in being just an upstream player, ONGC entered the downstream market by acquiring a 37.5 per cent stake held by the Aditya Birla group in Mangalore Refinery and Petrochemicals.

ONGC expects to fund most of the expansion from its own balance sheet. The eventual removal of government controls on natural gas pricing will also help increase revenues. It is conducting a major restructuring program, which include rationalized systems and procedures, benchmark costs and practices, access to new technology and streamlining costs, transparent pricing and best practice policy based on being accountable. With corporatization and liberalization of oil prices, ONGC is one of the 'nine gems' of India's commercially viable public sector companies and is positioning itself to play an important role in increasing domestic and overseas oil and gas supplies. However, under the burden sharing pricing in 2005 ONGC was forced by the GOI to give a 20 per cent discount on its crude oil to public sector refineries causing it to lose over US $1 billion in revenues between July and December 2005.

ONGC is planning to diversify its business into the power generation sector. It already generates 1,000 MW for its own use but is now planning the construction of several large natural gas-fired wellhead power plants. In June 2004 it announced its plans to generate cheaper power from gas at Rs 2.5 to Rs 3 per unit (between US cents 5.5 and 6.6 /kWh) utilizing its gas resources in comparison with the going rate of Rs 4 per unit (US cents 10.8

/kWh). The company has coined a phrase 'well head to wire (WtoWi)' whereby, rather than transporting the gas from its offshore oil and gas fields, power would be generated and wheeled on the existing grids.

The state-run gas company GAIL is also corporatized and like ONGC, is teaming up with ONGC and IOC both within India and overseas for gas projects. GAIL is planning city gas projects in several countries to expand its international operations. GAIL has a 10 per cent stake in the A-1 gas field off Myanmar's northwestern coast. GAIL has also been offered 19 per cent equity by Shell in the Fayum Gas Company and Shell CNG Company, both in Egypt. The Fayum Gas Company supplies piped natural gas for domestic consumption while Shell CNG retails Compressed Natural Gas (CNG) for automobiles in Cairo. BG has offered GAIL equity participation in its gas distribution company in Brazil.

At the downstream level, India's largest oil firm, the IOC has been successfully playing in a competitive environment in respect of deregulated products. IOC is positioning itself to retain the lead status in the industry and will do all it can to defend its turf. IOC has swallowed up fellow state product marketer, Indo-Burmah Petroleum (IBP) and has forged a key deal with private refiner Reliance Petroleum to market its products.

IOC had been facing competition from other public companies even before deregulation. It completed an organizational restructuring in 2002 to ensure customer friendly relations. Its corporatization/ restructuring program has embarked on diversification and integration plans and restructuring of its marketing setup. It has a sprawling infrastructure in terms of refineries, pipelines, storage points and retail outlets which new entrants will take time to build. It is preparing itself to operate effectively in a deregulated and competitive environment with quality and availability of products, brand image and the standard of customer service.

Under the ongoing Tenth Five Year Plan, IOC has an investment plan of US $6.27 billion. Taking into account the current investments of US $2.73 billon, in various projects under implementation, IOC'c total investment for the Tenth Five Year Plan period 2002–7 could exceed US $9 billion. IOC has sought GOI's permission to offload equity held by ONGC and GAIL to raise funds to meet its investment requirements. IOC has also sought GOI's permission to go for Initial Public Offering (IPO).

IOC tops the list of India's 'nine gems'; it is one of the commercially viable public sector companies in India. IOC improved its position to 189 in 2004 from 191 in 2003 in the Fortune 500 list of global majors. IOC's ambitious plans are set to explore the entire hydrocarbon value chain and venture into E&P, petrochemicals, power, information technology and communications, gas and GTL, collaborative research and development, shipping, training and consultancy, engineering, construction and transnational operations. In June 2004 IOC unveiled a mega plan to diversify into oil exploration, gas marketing, petrochemicals and overseas refinery and retailing business to become a US $50 billion company by 2012 from US $25 billion in 2004. IOC is trying to synchronize its refining expansions with demand and investments. Like ONGC, IOC envisions transformation into a major, diversified, transnational, integrated energy player.

IOCs diversification operations include:

- Diversifying into power generation to improve productivity by setting up projects close to its refineries to use residual fuels wherever feasible through joint ventures. IOC has formed a joint venture with Marubeni for a 360 MW power project at Panipat, which will use petroleum coke from the refinery as fuel.
- Diversifying into gas-based alternative fuels such as LNG and dimethyl ether (DME) to supply power plants and other industrial consumers. IOC has a collaboration agreement since 1998 with Amoco (now BP) and GAIL to manufacture and market DME under its power strategy. In 2001 IOC signed an MOU with NTPC to set up power plants utilizing refinery residue. IOC is also studying the feasibility of setting up a 500 MW combined cycle power plant close to the CPCL refinery at Manali, Chennai.
- Venturing into the petrochemicals business through the production of speciality products and by implementing two major grassroot projects—for integrated paraxylene and PTA at Panipat and a linear alkyl benzene project at the Gujarat refinery. To consolidate its position in petrochemicals, IOC is acquiring equity in Indian Petrochemicals Corporation and Haldia Petrochemicals.
- Marketing its SERVO brand of lubricants in various countries in the Middle East. South Asia and the CIS region. IOC has a franchise agreement in Kuala Lumpur and Lube distributorship in Bangladesh, Nepal and Sri Lanka. IOC is planning to market petroleum products in Mauritius where it is setting up a bulk storage terminal, retail outlets and LPG plants.
- Pursuing overseas upstream opportunities in E&P jointly with OVL. The IOC–ONGC consortium is evaluating opportunities for equity oil and gas in Sudan, Algeria, Venezuela, Qatar, Iran, Oman, Vietnam and Bangladesh.

In the power sector, the GOI's fiscal adjustment program recognizes the need for commercializing SEBs and giving them autonomy as a prerequisite for improving sector operational and financial performance. In the central sector, public enterprises like NTPC, NHPC and PGCIL continue to be commercially viable corporations.

Power sector restructuring in the states has focused on unbundling the vertically integrated monopoly and separate generation, T&D activities for commercializing their operations. The State Reforms Act was passed to unbundle and corporatize SEBs and privatize distribution, a process started by the state of Orissa. States like Andhra Pradesh, Rajasthan, Uttar Pradesh and Karnataka have unbundled their SEBs since 2001. Delhi also has unbundled the Delhi Vidyut Board into generation, transmission and three distribution companies. The process of unbundling of generation, T&D, and establishment of regulatory commissions and re-adjustment in the existing industry structures are at different stages of implementation in different state utility systems.

While governments at the centre and state levels have made efforts to restructure power utilities to put them on a commercial basis, these attempts have not produced the expected improvements in public enterprise commercial performance. In many cases, unbundling is just a change of organization structure on paper without any effective implementation of measures to improve efficiency of operations. As discussed in foregoing sections on regulation, the weak financial situation of the SEBs as of 2001–2 and their commercial non-viability status have increased subsidies and continue to be the barrier to attract private investment in the power sector.

In 2004 the Credit Rating Information Services of India Ltd. (CRISIL) and Indian Credit Rating Agency (ICRA) reported declining performance of the states' power sector due to low scores in the T&D activities and commercial viability. Even the state of Andhra Pradesh, which ranked first in leading the reform in power sector, was lagging behind in performance. The new state government coming to power after the 2004 election announced free power to farmers, putting an extra financial burden of around US $80 million annually in the state budget to meet the subsidy bill.

The Bangalore Electricity Supply Company (Bescom) in Karnataka state, despite several tariff increases had a revenue deficit of almost US $100 million in 2004. Since industrial and commercial consumers cannot be expected to continue paying hefty power bills, which is also counter-productive to the economy, the centre under the CMP is likely to review and consider a central budgetary support to help states meet the power subsidy burden. Under the new government's CMP, reforms will have to continue with a human face. Tariff subsidies are expected to continue for several years as many SEBs remain commercially non-viable and financially bankrupt. Further progress in the commercialization of SEBs with effective implementation of The Electricity Bill passed by Indian Parliament in 2003 is being held in abeyance since 2004 under the new UPA politics of coalition government.

Privatization/ Private investment

The commercialization/ corporatization policy for public enterprises and privatization of energy sector provides for divestment of the government's share in public energy enterprises and attracting both domestic and foreign private investment. Coal mining sector provides for FDI limit of 74 per cent and coal washeries' projects allow 50 per cent of FDI. In the hydrocarbon sector and in oil exploration, declining domestic output and increasing dependence on imports have compelled the GOI to work out an enhanced exploration program and to invite private oil companies to explore for oil and gas. The New Exploration Licensing Policy (NELP) was launched in 1997 with a follow-up of three licensing rounds. In the third NELP licensing round, 23 blocks were awarded out of the 27 originally offered, with bids from ONGC and Reliance Industries accounting for 22. Cairns Energy of UK was the only foreign company to sign the NELP contract. No blocks were awarded to international oil majors.

The fourth round of NELP in 2003 offered 12 deep-water blocks—11 onland blocks and one shallow water block. The GOI claims that in the first three rounds of NELP, contracts for 70 blocks were signed with an estimated investment in 3 phases of over US $3 billion. The state-run ONGC and its partners, OIL, Bharat Petroleum Corporation Ltd. and Hindustan Petroleum Corporation Ltd. have committed a minimum investment of US $412 million in the mandatory first phase of exploration in these blocks.

Government efforts to encourage international participation in oil exploration in India's offerings have failed to attract international interest, with a few exceptions such as UK's Cairns Energy. In January 2004, UK's Cairn Energy announced a major onshore oil discovery in India's Rajasthan's Basin; the resource is estimated to contain 50–200 million barrels of oil. Although bidding is now open year-round, the same blocks are offered repeatedly and these continue to evoke unsatisfactory response. It also points out the fact that the GOI is offering acreage in areas where prospects are still to be evaluated and in areas such as deep sea exploration where it requires new technologies.

India's Foreign Investment Promotion Board (FIPB) had approved 12 prospective LNG import terminal projects in the mid-to-late 1990s. However, barriers of lack of confirmed demand for LNG supply from prospective LNG users, pricing and payment issues and financial viability of proposed LNG projects have delayed project development. Payment problems at the Enron-backed Dabhol Power Plant in Maharashtra state led many to question the financial viability of some of the LNG import projects. The Dabhol LNG terminal was nearly finished at the time the construction was halted in June 2001. Two American firms involved in the project, General Electric and Bechtel, purchased Enron's 65 per cent stake in the project. In the wake of the problems with Dabhol, firms backing several other LNG projects including CMS Energy, Unocal and Total pulled out of India in the second half of 2001. The government froze approvals of new LNG terminals in

2001.

India's first LNG import terminal project is a joint-venture between ONGC, IOC, GAIL, NTPC and Gaz de France. Each of the state firms owns a 12.5 per cent stake, the Gujarat state government owns a 5 per cent stake and the rest is owned by private investors, including a 10 per cent stake held by Gaz de France and Malaysia's Petronet. The import terminal at Dahej began operation earlier in 2004, receiving India's first cargo of LNG on 30 January 2004. The Dahej terminal has the advantage of being tied in with the main state-owned natural gas company, GAIL and the existing HBJ pipeline network.

Even Shell has begun construction of its LNG import terminal at Hazira in Gujarat and has contracted LNG supplies from Oman. Like the Petronet Dahej terminal, it is to be linked into existing natural gas pipelines.

In the downstream sector, the domestic oil companies have formed joint venture companies with foreign partners. Hindustan Petroleum Corporation Ltd. (HPCL) and Bharat Petroleum Corporation Ltd. (BPCL) have joined hands with Exxon and Shell respectively in each case, holding 51 per cent the equity. As of 2003 these joint companies are limited to marketing. IOC has a 50 per cent stake in a joint company with Shell. IOC has also formed an alliance with Reliance Industries to market its products.

GOI pursued the disinvestment program as part of the economic reform program to raise resources from the sale of public enterprise units (PSU). The GOI's disinvestment plan by the NDA government, which included the public issue of ONGC's 10 per cent share, was reported to being oversubscribed within ten minutes after the bidding started on Friday, 5 March 2004. The highest bidding of US $1 billion, which worked out to half the issue size, was received from Warren Buffett, the CEO of Berkshire Hathaway of USA. Domestic institutional investors, particularly mutual funds and insurance companies were reported to be among other bidders. The NDA government claimed that the ONGC IPO was a great success. It reaffirmed the fact that private foreign investors would be interested to invest in companies with proven oil reserves.

The NDA government's disinvestment plan included privatization of both HPCL and BPCL and allowing foreign investors to participate in the IPO of 10 per cent of its equity share in the ONGC and GAIL, two of the country's largest commercially viable companies. The IPOs went ahead in March 2004, were quickly oversubscribed and brought almost $2.5 billion in revenue to the government. The GOI sold Indian Petrochemicals Corporation Limited (IPCL) to India's market leader Reliance Industries. This practice of disinvestment and state sale of profitable oil enterprise to a strategic partner were questioned by the political parties in the ruling combine of the National Democratic Alliance (NDA) who demanded a review of disinvestment policy.

The key coalition partner, the Samata Party Chief, George Fernandes, questioned the policy that gives birth to monopolies such as the sale of IPCL to a strategic partner. He also expressed concern that complete privatization in strategic sectors like oil could threaten the nation's oil security. Persisting differences between the Bharatiya Janatha Party (BJP) and its coalition partners on various aspects of disinvestment forced the GOI to defer decision on the controversial proposal of the strategic sale of two profit-making oil firms, HPCL and BPCL. The new government taking office in June 2004 decided against the divestment of profitable state-owned oil companies.

The power sector being faced with an unprecedented power supply deficit, the GOI since 1991 evolved a fundamental transformation of the policies and institutions to attract private investment. In the early 1990s the primary concern of the government was to increase installed capacity by promoting private investment. The government opened the power sector to private investment in 1991 and offered a number of incentives for prospective investors. New guidelines released in October 1995 focused on private sector participation in the renovation and modernization (R&M) of existing power plants. Shortly thereafter, MOP issued a liquid fuel policy for power generation to facilitate the rapid installation of diesel engine generating (DG) units by the private sector. At the same time, MOP suggested that states facilitate the entry of captive power units into the system. This could be done by offering private investors an appropriate tariff for the purchase of surplus power by the grid and third party access for direct sale of power to the other industrial units.

To further enlarge the scope for private investment, the GOI proposed in November 1995 to facilitate the implementation by the private sector of *Mega Power Projects*. These are defined as private power generation projects with capacity of 1,000 MW or more, which supply electricity to more than one state. The premise is that, given the regional concentration of coal resources in India and the enormous difficulties of transporting coal over long distances, it would be more efficient to locate power generation closer to the source of fuel supply than to the load centres. The promotion of such projects need to be accompanied by a significant expansion and reinforcement of transmission infrastructure, most probably under the auspices of the Power Grid Corporation of India (Powergrid). In February 1996, the MOP announced the encouragement of private investment in the barge-mounted power plants as a possible option for coastal areas.

The process of liberalization and making the sector investor-friendly has continued over the years with the streamlining of procedures, delegation of authority and removal of the cap on FDI in the power sector. Since 1998 the government has taken steps to simplify the development of private sector projects, including preparation of model supply agreements for State governments and SEBs, increasing the threshold above which CEA authorization of capital expenditure needs to be sought and permitting 100 per cent foreign capital participation in generation. T&D guidelines for private sector participation in transmission segment have been issued. Transmission activities have been given independent status after the amendment of electricity laws in 2003. A Crisis Resolution Group (CRG) in the MOP was created in 1999 to resolve the 'last-mile' problems of power projects so that they could achieve financial closures and start construction.

The State Reforms Act was passed to unbundle and corporatize SEBs and privatize distribution. The GOI launched a massive power sector reform program to restructure the sector, and establish a regulatory mechanism for setting rational and fair tariffs to enable commercialization of power utilities. The state power sector reform program was launched first in the State of Orissa and was followed by several other states including Andhra Pradesh, Maharashtra, Haryana, Tamil Nadu and Karnataka.

With the passage of the Electricity Regulatory Commissions Act in 1998, the CERC became operational the same year and by 2003, 14 SECs had been set up in as many states. The legal and policy framework has also been established for rationalization of the tariff structure. With the unbundling of the power sector, the government expected to place greater accountability and discipline in the distribution sector to improve non-technical losses.

By 2001, the Mega Power Projects Policy was reviewed and revised. Additional fiscal concessions were given to Mega Power Projects to make the tariffs cheaper, including the duty free import of capital goods, and an income tax holiday for a ten year period. The Power Trading Corporation (PTC) was incorporated for the purpose of buying power from the Mega Projects under the long-term PPAs and selling to the beneficiary states. The GOI also established an Investment Promotion Cell in the Ministry of Power to provide guidance and support to the interested parties and to encourage foreign investment in the sector.

The drive to increase the country's generating capacity along with the general trend towards economic liberalization in India in the 1990s led to much interest among foreign investors in setting up IPPs in India. The private power development initiative launched in 1991 by the GOI aroused significant interest among potential private developers and investors, both domestic and foreign. More than 150 MOUs were signed.The first official US cabinet level visit to India in August 1994 envisaged a huge potential market for western investment, particularly in the energy area in the development of India's oil and natural gas reserves, the modernization and possible private sector participation in its coal industry and investment in the power sector. The then US Secretary of Energy, Sandra O'Leary, leading the US mission met with the Prime Minister P V Narasimha Rao and his Finance Minister Dr Manmohan Singh, the architect of India's economic liberalization policy.

O'Leary's delegation, which included senior officers from some of the fast-track developers such as AES, CTIS and Enron, gave a clear and well-coordinated message to India to get the first wave of deals out the door quickly and work on power system reforms designed to turn the SEBs into financially viable and commercially responsible entities in the longer term. This message received a high level of general acceptance from key Indian leaders. The GOI agreed on the necessity of counter-guarantees for the fast-track projects and the need for fundamental reforms of the SEBs that would remove the long-term need for such guarantees.

The finance minister proposed that in future, state governments would have to demonstrate visible progress in reforming their SEBs before GOI would counter-guarantee their guarantees of the SEBs' PPAs. The reform of the SEBs was the GOI's top priority. This was demonstrated by GOI's acceptance of several WB funded state power restructuring projects including Orissa, Andhra Pradesh, Maharashtra and Karnataka.

The most visible concrete achievements were the signing of 11 private sector agreements and about as many government-to-government agreements, most of them in renewable energy, energy efficiency and environmental areas and several in the clean coal technology and coal gasification areas. The focus was on the first wave of seven fast-track power projects, valued at over US $6 billion in 1994, for which the GOI announced in principle that it would provide financial counter-guarantees. Less visible, yet more immediately important was the misson's effort to accelerate the Indian government approvals necessary to get the incipient IPPs off the ground. Following the US cabinet mission to India in August 1994, Enron's Dabhol Power Project (Phase 1), the first fast-track IPP power project for 1,600 MW capacity, received GOI's counter-guarantee in September 1994, after 38 months of signing the MOU with the GOI in June 1992.

Faced with unprecedented power supply deficit that could severely undermine its macroeconomic stabilization program and development prospects, the GOI was genuinely concerned about removing barriers to promote private investment. The finance minister stated 'we are going through a difficult process of transition as we move from an over-regulated and over-protected economy to an internationally competitive economy'. Fast-track power projects were considered engines to fuel the development prospects and the pendulum of government's policy caught in the globalization/ liberalization wave shifted towards promoting the private sector.

A large number of project proposals were considered and a few of those moved towards the conclusion of PPAs. In addition to Enron, several domestic and foreign companies expressed their interest to invest in India's power sector. Domestic private sector power project proposals included the Tata Group's 240 MW Jojobera Power Project in Jharkhand, Reliance Industries' 450 MW Patalaganga and Jamnagar projects and the Birla Group-promoted

Bina Power Project.

Foreign investor sponsored fast-track projects of over 30,000 MW capacity that were proposed included the following: GVK Industries and CMS Generation sponsored 235 MW, natural gas and naphtha fired project in Andhra Pradesh, US Mirant sponsored 3.96 GW Hirma power plant in Orissa and 500 MW Balagarh project in West Bengal, Electricite de France (Edf) sponsored 1.08 GW Central India Power Project, US Cogentrix sponsored a 1 GW joint venture, Mangalore Power in Karnataka state and UK's PowerGen sponsored 580 MW thermal plant in Madhya Pradesh. In addition, the Enron Group consisting of Enron (65 per cent), General Electric (15 per cent) and Bechtel (10 per cent) proposed that in addition to its two-phase Dabhol project with 2144 MW capacity, it would install additional LNG fueled 7500 MW capacity in subsequent phases.

During the 1991–5 period, the selection of the project sponsors in most cases, including Enron, has not been on a competitive basis. Many of the MOUs issued in the initial batch of projects were issued without adopting any competitive or screening process. In several cases, the MOUs were not based on well-developed project proposals. Investors and lenders to these projects would find it difficult to support projects of promoters lacking in financial, technical and managerial capabilities or to fund projects which have not been properly appraised.

While the government was keen on attracting private investment in the power sector, its proposed guidelines assumed that all private power projects would operate as base-load stations and the tariff structure had been designed to help ensure project viability in such circumstances. Given the continuing problem of meeting the peak load, flexible government guidelines on the tariff to accommodate peak load and intermediate load factors in project design would have provided alternative options for private investment.

Widespread debate on the array of complex issues arising out of private power policy and financing of IPP projects on a limited recourse basis, has led to a better appreciation of the concerns of developers, investors and lenders by the SEBs and state government. Given India's democratic political system, the experience in the early 1990s of MOU projects and the lack of competition until 1994 has led to a public debate involving the SEBs and its state governments —accountable to the public and its elected representatives—on the terms and conditions (particularly the tariffs) under which private power proposals were approved and whether these were the best projects available (as evidenced by a fair competition).This has led to reopening of a few project deals, significant delays in reaching financial closures and the resulting negative effect it has had on investors' confidence.

Learning from its MOU experience, the GOI announced in January 1995 that competitive bidding is now required by the government for all private power projects and will be administered by the states (for their purchases) and by the centre (for mega projects for example). The government's decision to make competitive bidding its official policy is clearly a major step forward in the implementation of its private power development initiative. The Guidelines issued by MOP for screening the MOUs resulted 'in principle' in clearance for about 99 projects in 1996. By 2001 a total of 57 projects with a cumulative capacity of 30,000 MW were cleared by the CEA of which only 18 projects with a total capacity of 6,542 MW accounting for less than 25 per cent of the projects cleared have achieved financial closure. Of these, ten projects including Enron's Phase 1 with a total capacity of 744 MW were commissioned and eight projects with a 2,860 MW capacity are under construction.

The Tenth and Eleventh plans 2002–12, aim to achieve 100,000 MW of additional capacity from private sector projects. As of 2002, 30 IPPs with a total capacity of 17,715 MW having CEA clearance were struck due to tariff, financial guarantee and particularly problems pertaining to non-availability of escrow from the state governments and implementation problems.

Given that the GOI and the state governments were on the learning curve of the transition process, several key policy issues regarding the financing of these projects remained to be resolved —such as foreign exchange cover for return on capital equity or the provision of government guarantees for backstopping the obligations of SEBs or in respect of sovereign risks.

The crux of the problem facing the power sector is management and financing at the state government's level as electricity supply is the shared responsibility of both the central government and the states. SEBs, in continual and severe financial distress, have amassed billions of dollars in debt over the years because of mismanagement, subsidized tariffs to residential and agricultural consumers, low investment in T&D systems, inadequate maintenance, high levels of distribution losses, theft and uncollected bills.

Prospective sponsors are concerned because of non-payment problems even in the states of Orissa and Maharashtra which were considered to be pioneers of reform. Orissa was the first state to reform its power sector under the World Bank prescription. Orissa unbundled its power sector into generation, distribution and transmission and allowed privatization of generation and distribution.The WB lent US $350 million to the state to enable it to restructure its power sector. But non-payment problems ensued, and the generation companies were owed US $300 million in January 2002 from the sole buyer GridCo, the state-owned transmission company formed from Orissa's unbundled SEB.

The problem is the massive increase in tariffs of over 200 per cent, while the privatization of the various networks became mired in local politics. The state government's appointed Kanungo Committee to assess the performance found that in the ten years following privatization, tariff increases at the rate of 15 per cent every year reached a cumulative tariff increase of 279 per cent.

The Committee also found that despite tariff increases there was little improvement in techno-commercial loss or improvement in customer service. T&D losses, which were 46.94 per cent in 1995–6, remained almost the same (46.63 per cent). Costs had not been contained and performance had not improved. The private company had not been more successful than its public sector predecessor in collecting revenue. The private sector company defaulted in its payment to the grid company. Besides, rural electrification was a casualty. Increasing tariffs with little improvement in the quality and reliability of service led to growing public discontent over reforms. The Committee concluded that in Orissa, privatization was a failure. The management contract did not last even for six months. Nonetheless, the government of Orissa went ahead with outright privatization and sold three out of four distribution zones to the same firm with whom GridCo annulled the management contract.

With the exception of private sector distributors operating for a long time in Mumbai, Calcutta and Ahmedabad, where the distribution loss is significantly less than in the SEBs, unbundling of the SEBs into separate entities for generation, T&D has not resulted in privatization of distribution assets and has added to the complication of some IPPs.

In the march to reforms in the power sector, the state of Karnataka corporatized Karnataka Electricity Board (KEB), into Karnataka Power Transmission Corporation Limited (KPTCL) as a first step. Breaking up KPTCL into four distribution companies is the second and privatization the third step. The state government of Karnataka wanted to privatize not only to meet the requirement of the World Bank, but to avoid paying subsidies of over US $500 million per year for the SEBs' cost of inefficiencies and agriculture sector cost-recovery. In the absence of meters for agriculture, the government is unable to determine separately the cost of non-recovery in the agriculture sector and the cost of the SEBs' inefficiencies including power theft and T&D losses.

The Karnataka government appointed consulting consortium consisting of Deloitte Touche Tohmatsu, Cameron McKenna, Rothschild and Infrastructure Development Finance Corporation (IDFC) carried out an investor survey and found that no investor was interested in taking up distribution. This was a sequel to the Orissa privatization where the conventional belief that the private sector would be better able to reduce theft and improve collection was belied.

The fundamental obstacle to private sector investment in the power sector continues to be the weak financial position of the SEBs. For states in the process of restructuring, the IPP contracts and security arrangements including escrow, have had to be amended to cater to the restructured entities.

Lenders have, however sought escrow arrangements as a practical form of security, regardless of the availability of a counter-guarantee or SEB restructuring, but this has caused delay because the level of escrow that each state can sustain is, in almost every case, insufficient for the number of proposed IPP projects. Furthermore, even where escrow accounts are provided by the state governments, they are unreliable, since the state governments are no longer in a position to bear the burden of SEBs. The SEBs' poor financial situation has led to the cancellation of Industrial Development Bank of India's (IDBI) US $35 million assistance to ten power projects.

The delays in clinching a suitable security mechanism have forced many major high profile international power sponsors cited above, including CMS Energy, PowerGen, Edf, Cogentrix and Enron to exit the Indian power scene. Furthermore, the PPAs formula for pricing based on cost-plus basis was subject to alternative interpretations and emerged as the central issue between the government and the foreign investor. The forced closure of Enron Group's controversial US $2.9 billion Dabhol Power Company (DPC) project in June 2001 underlines the issue of the unbalanced PPAs resulting in high tariffs of about US cents 15 /kWh and non-payment of the financially non-viable Maharashtra state SEB.

It was Congress-I in the mid-1990s which approved the original first phase, only to be turfed out of office by the precariously balanced BJP–Shiv Sena coalition in a state election, which then threatened to cancel the first Dabhol project. Three years of litigation and a renegotiated tariff and fuel supply for the first phase revived the DPL.

The dispute centred on the Maharashtra State Electricity Board's (MSEB) refusal to pay some of its bills for the purchase of the electricity output of the 744 MW Phase 1 of the scheme —Phase 2 of 1444 MW, was almost ready in 2001 to go online but work on it was stopped. Dabhol remains idle after work stopped on the second phase of the mult-billion-dollar 2,184 MW project in Maharashtra state. The failure of its main customer, the MSEB, to pay bills forced it to close down.

The Dabhol dispute reached its nadir following a '*force majeure*' notice being served by the DPC on the MSEB, on the state government and on the central government on 7 April 2001. The DPC also launched a lawsuit in London landing it in international arbitration. Enron claimed that the defendants have been in breach of contract, that is, the PPA between DPC and the MSEB, which is backed by sovereign guarantees from the state and the central governments. Enron also warned that it could withdraw from the US $3 billion Dabhol power project. Since then Enron's bankruptcy following its collapse in November 2001 kept the plant and its LNG Facility mothballed.

As of mid-2004 the state of Maharashtra faced a huge shortfall of over 1,000 MW power and the ruling Maharashtra state's Democratic Front (DF) government was under pressure to allow MSEB to restart drawing power. The Indian lenders to DPC, led by IDBI, appointed Rothschild to study the revival of the project. The rupee lender's consortium favoured the sale of DPC's assets, which were in the custody of the Bombay High Court receiver since 2002.

The domestic lenders to Enron's stalled US $3 billion power project, backed by the NDA government offered to buy in April 2004 US $600 million in foreign creditor loans at a large discount. The Indian lenders were willing to pay around 50 cents for every dollar the foreign creditors lent to the project.

General Electric and Bechtel filed arbitration claims worth over US $6 billion at the London panel for breach of investment protection agreements. The arbitration that took place between GE, Bechtel and the GOI concluded with a consent award on 19 July 2005 in London. In July 2005, GOI finally reached agreement with both Bechtel and General Electric, who own 85 per cent of the DPC. In July 2005, the Supreme Court of India approved an out-of-court settlement between the DPC's shareholders GE, Bechtel (85 per cent) and MSEB (15 per cent). As per the terms of settlement, the promoters and the overseas lenders to the project were to drop all claims once the dues were cleared. The settlement amounting to US $2.5 billion reached in July 2005 with GE and Bechtel will clear the restarting of the mothballed 2,184 MW DBC by a Special Purpose Vehicle (SPV) to be known as 'Ratnagiri Power' floated by NTPC, GAIL and IDBI.The MSEB would be the sole buyer of the plant's power priced at Rs 3 /kWh (7 US cents) at a plant load factor of 80 per cent, which is far more affordable for MSEB than the Rs 7 /kWh (15 US cents) it was expected to pay the Enron Dabhol project. Electricity generation from the gas-based plant is expected to begin by July 2006. Box 5.3 gives the chronology of events of Enron's Dabhol Private Power Project.

Box 5.3 Chronology of Dabhol

June 1992
MOU signed between Enron and the Maharashtra state government

April 1993
Project cleared by Cabinet Committee on foreign investment

November 1993
The CEA clears the first phase

May 1994
The Union cabinet agrees 'in principle' to provide second level of guarantee

September 1994
First phase of project receives counter-guarantee

April 1995
New government in Maharashtra state orders review of the project

August 1995
Maharashtra state government decides to stall the first phase and scrap the second phase

October 1995
Maharashtra state government forms committee to renegotiate the project

January 1996
Maharashtra state government clears project

February 1996
Maharashtra state cabinet approves final PPA

May 1996
New United Front (UF) government at centre approves renegotiated PPA and counter-guarantee

July 1996
UF government extends counter guarantee; amended PPA signed between Enron and MSEB

December 1996
Enron's Dabhol Power Company (DPC) announces financial closure. The debt-equity ratio was about 60:40 versus the originally planned 70:30 because of equity infusion to pay for suspension costs. The expected rate of return was in the range of 18–20 per cent; DPC considered the first and only success story of FDI in India's power sector

September 1998
744 MW Phase 1 commissioned and financing for Phase 2 begins
Enron presents a ten year investment proposal with a series of power projects and associated domestic gas development and production and imported LNG projects

July–December 2000
Dispute brews between MSEB and DPC over MSEB complaint of high tariff and its refusal to pay some of its bills. MSEB refuses to pay DPC bill of US $21.70 million for December 2000 and says that the bill should be adjusted in light of a Rupees 4 billion (US $85 million) penalty equivalent to two weeks of non-power supply slapped on the DPC by the MSEB provided under the PPA provisions.

April 2001
DPC serves a 'force majeure' notice on the MSEB, the Maharashtra state government and the central government for failing to fulfill PPA contractual obligations. Enron warns to terminate the US $3 billion project and claim compensation under the provisions of the

PPA. The Maharashtra state government supported the MSEB's position of adjustment of DPC bill against the penalty that it was asked to pay. The central government also favoured the state position. The DPC was told by the central government implicitly that it does not intend to honour the counter-guarantee till the penalty issue was resolved.

June 2001
MSEB, the sole customer of Dabhol as per the PPA, stops drawing power due to high wholesale tariff of Rs 7 /kWh (US cents15 /kWh). Neil McGregor, the DPC's president and CEO quits following expiration of his contract in June. DPC stops its operations and remains idle.

17th July 2001
Enron's Chairman Kenneth Lay visits India and wants a quick resolution to the dispute. The Federal-owned Power Trading Corporation (PTC) offers its willingness to take over from the MSEB if the wholesale tariff is slashed from Rs 7.0 /kWh to Rs 2.7 /kWh (from US 15 cents /kWh to about US 5.5 cents /kWh).

November 2001
DPC's parent company the US Enron Corporation collapses following accounting improprieties and crashing of its stocks

May 2003
DPC continues to remain idle.

April 2004
Domestic lenders offer to buy

July 2004
India's Supreme Court reopens Dabhol Case.

Bechtel and GE file arbitration claims worth over US $6 billion at the London panel for breach of investment protection agreements

July 2005
The arbitration between GE, Bechtel and GOI concludes with a consent award in London. India's Supreme court approves out-of court settlement between DPC's shareholders, GE, Bechtel and MSEB.
India's state-owned NTPC, Gail and IDBI-led Indian lenders to Dabhol power project will restart the 2,184 MW power project by a Special Purpose Vehicle (SPV). Dabhol is renamed as 'Ratnagiri Power'

July 2006: Electricity generation to begin July 2006

The forced closure of Enron's $3 billion Dabhol power project in the state of Maharashtra has underlined problems of directly sponsored 100 per cent FDI power projects, lack of competitive bidding for the project resulting in high wholesale tariffs of US 15 cents /kWh, institutional weaknesses both at the centre and state levels, poor institutional and financial conditions of

SEBs and continued interference of state and local politics. The tariff dispute between the MSEB and DPC is the re-enactment at the state level, the GOI's dispute on petroleum pricing with foreign direct investors (Burmah-Shell, Esso and Caltex in the 1960s and early 1970s) in India's downstream petroleum operations resulting in the GOI acquiring the majority share in the 1970s.[44] The collapse of Enron's investment in the first large IPP also affected the FDI in India's LNG project, which faced issues of LNG pricing. Several proposed LNG import projects foundered because end-user prices were too high.

Given that multinational companies' (MNCs) investment in energy projects in developing countries remain tethered to profits with risk premium, tariffs charged are bound to reflect these risks. Whether the tariff levels charged reflect market realities depend on the institutional capabilities of the host government at the centre, state and local levels in creating competitive conditions and effectively monitoring and regulating them. The academic and bureaucratic process oriented cost-plus format failed to recognize the practical implications of the cost-plus formula. The fact that the original Enron deal was considered to be rather murky to begin with and ended in collapse coupled with the fact that the government institutions at centre, state and local levels were not equipped to deal with the complexities of liberalizing the energy sector have raised issues crucial to future FDI in India's power and natural gas sectors.

First, the closure of DPC for over five years, the adverse impact of electricity shortages on the economy of Maharashtra state, the payment of arbitration award and additional investment to restart the moth-balled 2,184 MW power plant have more than tripled the cost of reverting to public ownership of DPC power project. Second, the closure of DPC affected 40 international and domestic lenders who participated in the financing, implicitly placing faith in the government's guarantees. Third, the impasse affected domestic lenders such as IDBI, ICICI, IFCI, SBI and Canara Bank, all government financial institutions who have carried the greatest risk on the deal as they were unprotected with US $1.4 billion in debt.

Fourth, the failure of the first 90 per cent foreign company owned FDI in India's power project and the collapse of Enron in November 2001 have reconfirmed the suspicions of the host government both at the centre and state levels of MNC pricing and accounting practices and have raised questions about the FDI ownership of future power projects. The state governments, faced with growing power deficits into the election year of 2004, the withdrawals of several FDI sponsors and a lack of success in commercializing their SEBs reverted to state sponsored generation projects. They are

44. R Vedavalli, *Foreign Private Investment and Economic Development: A case Study of India in Petroleum* (UK, Cambridge University Press, 1976)

getting the quotes for projects from IPPs and SPCs and are opting for the cheap quotes of the latter.

For example, at the state level, the government of Karnataka's chief minister S M Krishna welcomed private investment and said when he took office in 1999 that he had laid a red carpet for private investors. However, after several years of bureaucratic wrangling, private investors including US Cogentrix left. The chief minister on 16 March 2002[45] squarely placed the blame on private investors and remarked 'it is illusive to think that the power situation will improve only after private players enter the arena of power production' and ridiculed IPPs by stating that they did not have a firm ground on the power sector.

The chief minister attributed the IPPs with high cost compared with the quotes given by the state KPCL. He cited the example of the 290 MW Alamatti Dam Power House Project. He said that as against the IPP quote of US $300 million, the state KPCL quoted US $140 million for the project and he therefore decided to go far the state-owned cheaper cost option. Given that 2004 was an election year for the state, the chief minister was making power policy a show for the media to get votes.

Fifth, the impasse has confirmed the frustrations of several high profile foreign companies who have withdrawn their proposed projects and international sentiment in India's private power has ebbed considerably. Under the circumstances it is doubtful that the GOI's Tenth and Eleventh Five Year Plans 2002–12 projections of a total of about 50,000 MW of additional private power capacity would be financed from majority FDI investment. The circumstances of collapse of the Enron Corporation and the corporate greed factor may cast doubt on the full culpability of the MSEB and leave a window of opportunity for future FDI in India's power sector.

Finally, the collapse of Enron's Dabhol FDI power project affected the future demand profile for both domestic gas and LNG imports. Given that the states' inability to pay for power has led to the failure of planned IPPs, the government's political will to implement power sector reforms will be critical for gas market development.

The most encouraging IPP development has been the Andhra Pradesh State government's signing of a new security mechanism agreement, linked to certain performance targets for the state (such as reducing transmission losses, improving revenue collection), which marks a step forward in power sector reform implementation. It paved the way for the financing of the GVK/ CMS's 235 MW Jegurupadu fast-track power project, which began generating power with one of its turbines in August 1996.

The government attempts to reform, started in the 1990s by encouraging IIPs to deal with growing power shortages, have been sporadic. The government

45. *Deccan Herald* (Bangalore, 16 March 2002)

concentrated too much on generation, leaving low-voltage T&D systems totally neglected. This resulted in quality deterioration, rising costs of maintenance and technical inefficiencies. Even in generation, of the 2000 IPPs original proposals in the early 1990s only 12 have come to fruition.

The Association of IPPs estimated that of a total of US $30 billion the IPP initiative was intended to attract, only $8 billion has been forthcoming. Even among these successful IPPs, India's largest showcase of foreign investment in power ($3 billion) and LNG collapsed because of pricing and contract enforcement issues. Overall commercial losses of the SEBs have risen from Rs 30 billion in 1992 to Rs 300 billion ($6.5 billion) in 2002.[46] In the power sector, during the 1990s reform period less than 5,000 MW of private power capacity was added of which over 40 per cent remain idle. India is doing all the right things on paper to encourage private investment in power generation and distribution and 20 states have set up regulatory commissions. However, the chronic problem of the bankrupt situation of the SEBs with increasing losses as of 2003–4 demonstrates the states' lack of political will to commit to the fundamentals of commercial viability of the SEBs.

Attempts to raise tariffs drew particularly heated protests from the agricultural sector, which for many years received its power free. Meanwhile, the distribution companies remained bankrupt because of negligible revenue collection, theft and corruption. The resulting shortage of power has caused continued blackouts in several states and impeded economic growth. To deal with the power shortage situation the government in 2002 unveiled a ten-year plan with a pledge of 'Electricity for all' by 2012. After a decade of piecemeal and sporadic reform in the 1990s, the government's ambitious 2002 ten-year plan aimed at expansion of the electricity sector by adding 100,000 MW new capacity and construction of the required T&D systems to fulfil its pledge. This would require a total investment of over US $180–200 billion over the next ten years with an annual average investment of about US $20 billion.

By 2003, there were promising signs in India that determination was forming at high levels of the central government to reform the electricity sector. The passing of the new Electricity Bill by the Indian Parliament in May 2003 involved further liberalization of generation with open access to captive power and no requirement for licensing (except for hydropower), offer of free access to transmission lines to distribution license holders and generators, open access to distribution to encourage private participation, mandatory metering requirement and performance linked financial assistance to SEBs.

However, market-oriented reforms in the electricity sector have been resisted by state and local politicians, worried that enforcing unpopular modernization

---

46. 'Getting a grip on power', *Petroleum Economist* (London, August 2003), p.28–9.

policies would cost them votes. The change of government following the 2004 election partly reflected voters' dissatisfaction with the reform process. The new UPA government coming to power in 2004 has retained the previous governments' plan of 'electricity for all' by 2012. The 2004 budget has also made provision for Rs 400,000 crores (US $9 billion) for financing public power projects. However, following the review of Electricity Act (2003), the new UPA government in 2004 decided to continue subsidies in the power sector and did not require states to commercialize their SEB operations. The pace of reform at the state levels will be rather slow.

Future FDI participation in India's power projects will depend on the states' commitment to reform with tangible achievements. The Electricity Bill passed by the Indian Parliament in 2003 recognizes that the SEBs' commercial viability is fundamental to privatization and the flow of private investment in the electric power sector. In the power sector, success would impinge on effective enforcement of reforms to commercialize SEBs reflecting efficient cost recovery. The key bottleneck for commercialization faced today is the enforcement of efficient industry standard user-charges in distribution and the inadequacies of regulatory institutions to effectively address issues of commercialization in tariff regulation. The new institutional mechanism of regulation is still in its infancy to grapple with the prevailing politics of tariff-setting and has been ineffective in requiring SEBs to achieve industry standard technical and operational efficiency.

Captive power in 2004 is estimated to account for an installed capacity of more than 25,000 MW. SEBs which bank on these consumers meeting a part of the subsidy bill are facing a threat as paying and high-ended industrial and commercial consumers tend to move out of the net. Phasing out cross-subsidies will have an adverse and direct impact on domestic consumers who would be loaded with very high power tariffs. Although it is felt that there should be a transparent budgetary support to the subsidies, the state finances are not in any shape to sustain the growing subsidies. The centre will have to probably review and consider options for a central budgetary support mechanism to help states meet the power subsidy burden linked to industry efficiency improvements and hold the states accountable. Furthermore, following the 2004 election the new UPA government's socio-political necessities of requiring to meet the NCMP and the centre-state issues of ownership of power sector will result in continuation of power subsidies and possibly stall the progress of reforming the SEBs.

India's energy market transition: 1991-2005

India's energy market transition since 1991 has been a part of its macroeconomic stabilization and liberalization program. In June 1991, in the midst of severe fiscal and external balances which had generated double-digit inflation and put the country on the verge of defaulting on its external debt obligations, the government undertook the major task of stabilizing and liberalizing the economy. By 1996, investment reforms, exchange rate and trade regimes of the financial sector and the tax system initiated a quiet economic revolution.[47]

India launched the stabilization program in 1991 on a cautious path maintaining a mixed economy as a 'middle way'. India followed the 'Middle Path' between socialism and capitalism which the Prime Minister P V Narashimha Rao called 'reforms with a human face' to avoid social problems and popular unrest in a secular and plural democratic political system.

With the stabilization and reform measures introduced since 1991, India joined the group of reforming countries to integrate with the global economy and to reduce the role of government. Within five years of implementation of the stabilization program, the economic recovery helped by good monsoons was rapid and robust. Inflation declined and external accounts improved and structural reforms to liberalize the investment regime were implemented. The reforms created the preconditions for India to grow at a stable 6–7 per cent annual growth.

In the energy sector, oil exploration, coal and power sectors were opened up for private investors. The liberalization efforts to attract private investment in oil exploration and power generation and distribution were mainly the result of a desperate situation to increase self-sufficiency in oil and to improve and increase power supply to fuel the growing demand for energy. Institutional and commercialization reforms of coal companies opened up coal and lignite mining and distribution to private sector participation ending 25 years of state monopoly. Indian companies were to be selected through competitive bidding for coal mining. Foreign companies would be allowed to carry out mining operations only through equity participation with a national company to be cleared by the Foreign Investment Promotion Board (FIPB) on a case-by-case basis.

A decision was also taken to amend the Mines and Minerals (Regulation and Development) Act 1957 to frame rules for setting up of an independent body to step up exploration of coal and lignite resources and to allocate blocks on the basis of competitive bidding process. With the opening up of the economy to the private sector, there has been a reduction in the public investment in coal and electric power. Public investment in coal declined from 0.5 per cent of GDP in the 1980s to 0.3 per cent in the post-1992 period. Public investment in power declined from 2.4 per cent in the pre-1990 period to less than 2 per cent in the post-1992 period. Following the oil price liberalization and corporatization of public sector oil companies, public investments in

---

47. WB, *India, Five years of Stabilization and Reform and the Challenges Ahead* (Washington DC 1996)

oil and gas exploration, oil refining and gas supply increased from 0.7 per cent of GDP in the Sixth Plan to 1.5 per cent of GDP post-1992. Box 5.4 summarizes the highlights of India's energy market transition to 2004.

Box 5.4 India: Status of Energy Market Transition to 2004

Energy Pricing

- Decontrol of coal prices in 2000; no direct subsidies to coal production and consumption
- Dismantling of Administrative Pricing Mechanism (ADM) for oil products and natural gas in 2002 and removal of all subsidies except for those on kerosene and LPG used by households
- Consumer prices for coal, oil products and natural gas to follow international prices
- Electricity subsidies continue; passing of Electricity Bill by India's Parliament in 2003 calls for commercialization of SEBs by reducing losses and efficient cost recovery
- Re-emergence of government control on pricing petroleum products since 2004 on equitable burden-sharing principle between oil companies, government and consumers

Regulation

- Established the Central Electricity Regulatory Commission (CERC) by passing the 1998 Electricity Regulatory Commissions Act
- Established State Electricity Regulatory Commissions (SERC) to regulate retail tariffs
- SERCs in 20 states were established by 2004
- The amended Electricity Law in 2003 requires states to establish regulatory commissions which would set retail tariffs on the basis of full costs and promote competition

Commercialization/ Corporatization

- Separation of generation from transmission functions
- Creation of PowerGrid, the newly created central transmission utility with responsibilities for inter-state transmission and centralized dispatch
- Continuation of SEB commercialization reforms as per the New Electricity Bill (2003) to include six-level strategy for distribution reforms envisaging an expenditure of US $8 billion during the Tenth

Plan (2002–7) period under APDRP scheme under implementation
- Since May 2004 SEBs are no longer required to unbundle their electric power operations. SEBs are no longer required to reach the goal of elimination of cross-subsidies

Privatization/ Private Investment

- Divestment of shares in state-owned profitable oil and gas companies halted
- Privatization of a few power distribution companies
- Private investment in coal and lignite mining and coal washeries
- Private investment in a few IPP power projects and joint ventures
- Continuation of promotion of private investment in oil and gas exploration through New Exploration Licensing Promotion (NELP) efforts and coal mining. Private investment allowed in oil downstream and distribution
- Promotion of private investment in power generation, T&D by passing New Electricity Bill in 2003 by easing licensing restrictions for new power projects (other than hydroelectric projects); granting open access transmission and obligating the states to set tariffs reflecting full cost recovery and requiring states that any subsidies on electricity retail sales be paid out of state budgets rather than through cross-subsidies. Since May 2004, implementation of these measures stalled.
- Dabhol Private Power Project (DPC) after lying idle since 2001, reverted to public ownership.

After a decade of transition, reform measures introduced since 1991 have considerably improved India's growth prospects. Pricing reforms in the coal, oil and gas sectors seemed to reflect international prices. However, the spiking oil prices since 2004 impacted new decision of the coalition government of the United Progressive Alliance (UPA) to continue with market pricing of energy mainly because of the need of coalition politics to balance staying in power and staying on the course of pricing reform.

It took 30 years since the 1973 oil crisis for successive governments to finally dismantle the administrative pricing mechanism for oil and liberalize oil prices even where the central government is mainly responsible for the sector. Oil price liberalization enabled the private and public oil companies to improve their financial viability by increasing profits. In the aftermath of generating increasing profits, the public oil companies are able to finance their investments from their balance sheets. The major state oil and gas corporations began to expand and diversify their operations both domestically and overseas. However, the UPA government's decision to revert to administered pricing by introducing equal burden-sharing pricing for oil prices have impacted the oil companies revenues. With continued increase in global oil prices in 2005, the state-owned profitable oil companies were expected to suffer losses of over $4 billion in 2005.

Public enterprises still dominate India's energy sector. In the power sector, government control and interference continues at varying levels. Given the sharing of responsibilities for power between centre and state governments, reforming of the SEBs is unlikely to be any time soon. Despite significant measures being taken to improve investment and trade regimes, India lags behind in overall FDI inflow despite the surge in FDI to the Information Technology sector and Enron Group's FDI inflow to DPC in the 1990s. In the 1990s, while China topped the list of top ten net FDI inflows in developing countries by attracting over US $40 billion, India with US $2.5 billion in the same period, was not within the top ten list. India's share of global FDI remains poor at less than 1 per cent compared with China's 12 per cent. China has received a cumulative FDI inflow of US $480 billion since 1990 compared with US $33.1 billion in India, a gap of a whopping US $446.9 billion. In 2001 India's FDI inflows accounted for a mere 0.5 per cent share of the world total against China's 6.4 per cent, 3.1 per cent for Hong Kong and 1.2 per cent for Singapore.

The Tenth Five Year Plan which began in April 2002 clearly set its objective to mobilize huge resources from strategic sale of public sector enterprises and attracting FDI. The Tenth Plan envisages raising US $15 billion from sale of government equity in public sector enterprises. The Steering Committee on FDI for a liberal investment regime submitted its report in September 2002 to attract at least US $8 billion per year of FDI to achieve the Tenth Plan objective of 8 per cent per year of GDP growth.

The committee preferred FDI to other forms of external financing options because they are non-debt creating, non-volatile and their returns depend on the performance of the projects financed by investors. The Committee also recognized that FDI facilitates international trade, transfer of knowledge, skills and technology. The committee called for attracting foreign investment of US $8 billion per year. The Committee's road map for foreign investment policy for the Tenth Plan period (2002–7) recommends 100 per cent FDI in oil refineries, oil marketing and petroleum exploration and doing away with current barriers on exit conditions. The Committee's recommendations call for radical changes on the policy regime and have raised serious issues for political debate.

After a decade of reforms, the political parties have accepted the need for reform and the fact that the change has been for the better. However, the main obstacles for implementing the reform are first, the difficulty of achieving consensus among different political parties in a pluralistic democracy and second, the process oriented nature of the reform process. Given that India's energy market transition is process oriented, there is lack of focus on achieving the results to reach the goal. This contrasts with the discipline of social capitalism's goal oriented approach in China with Chinese leaders' authority to demand results and China's flexibility to adapt to new process to reach its desired goal. China set the goal clear right from 1949, even before its 'liberalization' in the 1980s. In the 1990s China changed the process and adopted a different approach to reach its desired goal. For example, in 1950, both China and India started with identical installed capacity in electric power of 1,500 MW each. In 2001, after 50 years, India has around 100,000MW, whereas China has about 250,000MW.

Replying to the debate in March 2002 on the President's address to the Parliament on the budget session calling for consensus on economic reforms, A B Vajpayee, the National Democratic Alliance (NDA) government's Prime Minister said, 'We will have to leave the beaten track. We are trying to join both popularity and pragmatism and we are succeeding only sometimes. The coming into prominence of coalition politics where regional parties with their own limitations were tying up with national parties, which also had a bearing on the reform process'.[48] The Prime Minister's words turned out to be prophetic.

Future directions

The fall of the NDA coalition led by A.B. Vajpayee's BJP, despite positive outcomes of integrating India into the global economy turned out to be the surprise of the world's largest democratic election outcome of May 2004. Markets, industry and foreign institutional investors evidently disliked the electoral results.

India's stock market experienced the worst crash on May 17 2004 following the defeat of the NDA government. Shares on the Bombay stock exchange plunged as much as 17.5 per cent, the worst fall in its 129 years. Investors feared that the leftists, led by the Communist Party of India (Marxist) the third largest party in the parliament with 43 seats, would block or slow key reforms, especially privatization of public enterprises.[49] By voting out the NDA and by bringing in the left, the classic definition of socialism seemed to prevail, involving public ownership, public sector enterprises and no privatization. However, the left also has a more broadbased concern about equity. Hence the underlying message of election results was also interpreted as one where the growth process of the 1990s had been inequitable and that was a message that could not be ignored by the new coalition

48. *Deccan Herald* (Bangalore, 18 March 2002)
49. *AOL News* (17 May 2004)

government.

The Indian media interpreted the election results as popular rebellion. India's election outcome demonstrated that electorates punish leaders for failing to deliver results on the ground on the 1990s overblown promises of globalization. Failures in the institutional mechanisms at the centre, state and local levels affected the implementation of reforms. The future direction of reform continues to be the battle between one quarter of industrialized India, with the high-tech outsource centres reaping the benefits of globalization and three quarters of struggling countryside India, waiting for the trickling down of the benefits of globalization.

It is no accident that the ruling alliance lost heavily in Andhra Pradesh, Karnataka and Tamil Nadu, states that attracted information technology giants and transformed their cities into new-tech boom centres. The transformation has yet to reach most of the population. The entire information technology industry employs fewer than one million people, compared with 40 million registered unemployed and double that number of unregistered and unemployed. While policy reforms have helped to restructure the economy, they are yet to help an increasingly struggling agricultural sector, which supports some two-thirds of the population. Even the states such as Andhra Pradesh and Karnataka, that attracted the new-tech boom in the cities and adopted the so-called e-governance, failed to address the problems on the ground outside the tech boom centres.

The crucial outcome of the 2004 election is the return of Dr. Manmohan Singh of the Congress Party, the former finance minister (1991–7) and the architect of the reform process in India as the Prime minister of the new coalition government of UPA. In his address to the nation on June 24 2004, the prime minister spoke about the people's clear verdict to change the processes and focus of governance that economic growth has to be accompanied by equity and social justice. Seeking the consensus of coalition partners, the new government adopted UPA's National Common Minimum Program (NCMP).The NCMP was reported to seek to accelerate the tempo of social and economic change while paying particular attention to the needs of farmers, agricultural labour, workers and other weaker sections of society.

While several features of the NCMP — the promise to enact a National Employment Guarantee Act, comprehensive protective legislation for agricultural workers and the pledge to raise public spending to 6 per cent of GDP via a cess on central taxes and remove communalization of the school syllabus—were in keeping with the UPA's 'secular and progressive' credentials, issues relating to privatization, fiscal policy, capital markets and economic reforms were also addressed. On the controversial issue of privatization of PSUs, the NCMP promised to retain existing 'Navaratna' (Nine Gems) companies in the public sector. It emphasized that all privatizations 'will be considered on a transparent and consultative case-by-case basis'.

In order to revive industrial growth the NCMP promised incentives to boost private investment, to actively encourage FDI and to strengthen regulatory institutions to ensure competition. The NCMP declared that FDI will continue to be encouraged, particularly in the areas of infrastructure, high technology and exports. The essence of the NCMP is the recognition that economic reform is not only about freeing private enterprise from the shackles of bureaucratic control but also about making the government more effective. Privatization and disinvestment also are at the centre of discussions about economic policies of the new UPA government. It was clear that privatization, particularly that of profit making oil companies listed under the 'nine gems' companies, had not been very popular even in the previous NDA coalition government. In the case of profitable NOCs, concerns of security of supplies in addition to the general fear that private investors would seek profits ahead of or even at the cost of larger national interests and hurt public welfare influence political decisions in a democracy.

The Prime Minister, on May 27 2004, disbanded the Ministry of Disinvestment and said that the Department of Disinvestment would remain under the supervision of the finance ministry. Promising selective privatization following a transparent process of evaluation, Dr.Singh said 'normally privatization will not take place. In case of profit making public sector undertakings (PSUs), other options will be exercised only under certain conditions. For instance, we will be looking at other options if a company is earning excessive profits due to monopoly conditions and cannot sustain this trend in competitive conditions'. But PSUs making 'decent' profits in competitive conditions would be 'encouraged to grow and expand'. Dr. Singh said that the country would be taken into confidence whenever a PSU was disinvested. 'People must be told why privatization of a certain PSU is a superior alternative. People must also be convinced about the manner in which a PSU has been evaluated.'[50]

With regard to the power sector, following the review of the 2003 Electricity Law decisions on extension of unbundling of states' power sector, reforming the T&D segments and extension of power subsidies to fill the growing gap between revenues and costs of the SEBs will stall the commercialization and discourage private investment. To meet the UPA government's mission of 'power for all by 2012' and electrification of all villages and households by 2009, the government has launched a two-pronged approach of adding 50,000 MW hydroelectric initiative (aimed at developing 162 projects across 16 states) and 100,000 MW thermal power initiative for developing 62 power projects at pitheads, coastal locations, along gas pipelines and load centres. The power ministry expects to commission 41,000 MW by 2007, claiming that around 6,800 MW is already commissioned

50. 'Ministry of Disinvestment disbanded', *The Hindu* (28 May 2004)

while 27,500 MW is under construction and another 8,000 MW is close to achieving financial closure. To support funding of public power projects the UPA budget calls for the formation of an inter-institutional group formed by India's financial institutions and banks (IDBI, ICICI Bank, State Bank of India, LIC, Bank of Baroda and Punjab National Bank) and pooling of their resources on a callable basis, a sum of Rs 40,000 crores (US $9 billion) to be made available as and when necessary.[51] The budget also announced to piggyback on the public issue of NTPC included in the 'nine-gem' companies to disinvest approximately 5 per cent of its holding to yield about Rs 4,000 crores (US $900 million).

The power investments of about US $9 billion have been under consideration for some time and they are mainly for capacity additions and do not include the much needed investments in T&D segments. Following the UPA government's review of the 2003 Electricity Act, decisions of the UPA government allowing continuation of subsidies to cover the growing gap between revenues and costs including costs of technical and operational inefficiencies of SEBs and not requiring SEBs to commercialize their operations have adversely impacted the financial viability of SEBs with little prospects for attracting private investment.

The reform experience in India, the world's largest democracy carrying the deadweight of two-thirds of its impoverished population suggests that it faces multiple complications to move forward the economic and sector reform process. Several economic, political and social issues will affect the future of India's energy for development in the twenty-first century. In contrast with the discipline and focus on economic reform of the single party totalitarian rule in China which also faces the problem of inequity between the globalizing *noveau* rich cities and the rural poor, India is confronted with the need to build consensus on economic reform in a pluralistic democracy of often unruly coalition politics.

Reform of the energy sector and particularly that of the power industry started in the early 1990s within the general economic context and as part of the structural adjustment of the Indian economy. Removal of subsidies of petroleum products and economic pricing of energy were conditions to be fulfilled for seeking IMF/ WB assistance for structural adjustment. It took India three decades from the 1973 oil crisis to eliminate administered pricing of oil products in 2002. Even after the announced liberalization, the government approval was required for market price adjustments and subsidies on kerosene and LPG continued. The new government's policy to continue cross-subsidization of kerosene and LPG, establishing the oil price stabilization fund and burden-sharing petroleum product price adjustments have reinstated partly government intervention and has stalled back oil price liberalization

51. 'Full Text of Union Budget', *The Hindu* (8 July 2004)

reflecting market economics. The adoption of burden-sharing pricing has satisfied none of the partners. While the consumers continue to complain of rising oil prices, oil companies and the government are faced with revenue losses. In August 2005, with continued shortfall in revenue that could affect the macroeconomic balance, the finance ministry declined to share the burden of oil marketing companies (OMCs) through frequent cuts in excise duty on petrol and diesel. It also rejected returning to the Price Band Mechanism.

India's new government in 2004 sent conflicting but mainly negative messages about the ongoing power sector reform process. IPP projects in several states face renegotiation of their PPAs on grounds of alleged corruption in their original award. Several state governments including states such as Andhra Pradesh and Maharashtra ordered the state power utilities to provide free or below cost power to farmers and other groups in line with their election pledges.[52] Although these moves were retracted in 2005, they have necessarily set back India's power sector reform.

Facing acute shortages of power in March 2005, the Maharashtra state government announced its policy for private investment in the power sector providing incentives for setting up projects for 500 MW and above using combined fuel cycle of coal and gas. The incentives offered include total exemption from stamp duty, registration charges, excise duties and getting land from the government at a concessional rate. The state also offered to cooperate with investing companies for raising the necessary infrastructure like approach roads, water availability and transportation of the fuels. The projects can be set up by private companies on their own or in collaboration with the MSEB. The state will guarantee 200 MW or 50 per cent of the power offtake by the MSEB for the first five years.

Although the state has announced incentives of local cost savings, it has not addressed the critical factors of rate of return to the private investor and the tariff formula for power purchase from the private investor. Given MSEB's 15-year record in its partnership with Enron's private power Dabhol Project, it is doubtful that foreign investors would be interested in taking up Maharashtra's offer. Thus far, the only interest expressed is by domestic private investor Anil Ambani, who separated from Reliance Capital Inc. in June 2005. The newly formed 'Anil Dhirubhai Ambani Enterprises' announced in June 2005 a massive public-private expansion plan in gas-based, coal-based, hydro, nuclear and non-conventional power generation.

An important aspect of political and economic change is the quality of bureaucracy. In the power sector, which in India is the shared responsibility of the centre and states, implementation problems are magnified with turf control, political and ideological differences between institutions at the centre,

52. 'India states revisit PPAs', *Energy Economist* (July 2004), p.42

state and local levels. Several interested foreign investors in power projects left after years of unsuccessful effort trying to resolve economic governance issues. Despite oft-repeated policy statements to open up for FDI in power, neither the bureaucracy in the centre nor the state bureaucracies were equipped professionally to deal with issues of project implementation, fuel supply and regulatory issues with regard to pricing. Government's repeated statements on opening up of power sector for FDI failed mainly because of deficiencies in the economic governance of institutions.

Finally, energy is central to India's economic development. It has now become a matter of national significance. With growing energy shortage, and being unable to increase domestic production of oil and gas to meet its rapidly rising demand, India, like China is concerned with securing the required energy supplies. Like China, India is 'keeping all its options open with regard' to energy supplies. As discussed in the foregoing sections, India's NOCs have started strategic partnerships between influential state-controlled energy companies and bilateral governments on large-scale energy cooperation. India's ONGC is estimated to have invested over $3.5 billion since 2000 in overseas exploration and development.

As Indian companies have begun to invest overseas, they have made substantial investments in the Russian energy sector. 50 years ago, India and the then USSR embarked on a close relationship in the discovery of the Bombay High oil and gas field and India imported crude oil from Russia.[53] India's state oil and gas company, ONGC, is a participant in the huge Sakhalin-1 oil and gas development on the north-east shelf of Sakhalin island, with a 20 per cent stake, having made a $2.5 billion investment. Besides Sakhalin-1, currently under development and the company's biggest investment so far, ONGC has shares of gas production from Vietnam (7.5 million cft/d from block 6.1) and oil production from Sudan (300,000 b/d from GNOP), where an investment of $0.7 billion was made in 2003 and a gas field in Myanmar (Block A1). ONGC also has exploration interests in Sudan, Ivory Coast, Libya, Syria and Iran, where it has 40 per cent of Farsi offshore and Australia.

Following an historic four-day visit by Chinese premier Wen Jiabo to India in April 2005, India and China signed an agreement that sets a target for an annual trade of $30 billion by 2010. India has also expressed its interest in cooperating with China in the energy sector while bidding to acquire overseas oil and gas assets. China however, is keen on pursuing its own interest to acquire its oil and gas equity assets particularly after it faced a setback in its bid to acquire Unocal of USA. In August 2005, in a cut-throat competitive effort China's CNPC raised its earlier bid, trailing behind India's ONGC to

53. R Vedavalli, *Private Investment and Economic Development: A case Study of India in Petroleum* (UK, Cambridge University Press, 1976)

$4.18 billion to outbid India's ONGC-Mittal consortium's bid of $3.6 billion to acquire the Canadian oil firm, Petrokazakhstan Inc., operating in Kazakhstan, Central Asia.

The intense competition between India and China for overseas oil and gas equity positions ranging from Kazakhstan in Central Asia to the Middle East, Africa and Latin America raises critical issues of geopolitics for access to energy for development. China's aggressive pursuit of an 'all options open' policy to access energy resources could also impact geopolitics on the home front for India's exploitation of its domestic energy resource potential of the Brahmaputra river and its tributaries to generate electricity and large oil shale deposits in north-east India. In the initial years of the twenty-first century, energy has emerged as the central issue of development for India. It is no longer an appendix to the macroeconomic Five Year Plan document. Energy for development for India has emerged as both a security and geopolitical issue in the twenty-first century.

India's major strategic issue over the next 25 years is ensuring energy security to sustain growth and it is looking at all possible options to secure its future energy supplies. As of 2005, faced with stagnant domestic production and rising demand for oil, India imported 70 per cent of its requirement (95 mtoe/ year). Options being pursued by India to bridge its supply-demand gap include boosting domestic production by attracting foreign investment and technical expertise into domestic deep offshore oil and gas exploration, expanding the share of nuclear energy option by building commercial nuclear reactors that could generate up to 40,000 MW of electricity by exploitation of domestic thorium resources, developing alternative domestic sources of energy including large-scale hydro potential, investing in overseas oil and gas assets and oil and gas pipelines.

In June 2004 India signed a deal with Iran to import 5 million tons per year of LNG starting in 2009, over a period of 25 years. The buyers GAIL, IOC and BPCL agreed to pay $3.251 per million BTU (FOB). The agreement is part of a package in which Indian companies will be allowed to participate in developing two oil fields and one gas field in Iran. India's OVL will get a 10 per cent share in the development of Iran's biggest onshore oil field, Yadavaran (translating into 30,000 b/d of crude oil to India) and also 100 per cent development share in Jufeyr (another 30,000 b/d).

Energy sector reforms in India since the 1990s have been an appendix to macroeconomic considerations, piecemeal, slow and disjointed. Between 1990 and 2000, although India and China started with almost similar installed electricity capacities, India's installed electricity capacity increased over 50 per cent from 76,000 to 114,500 MW, while that of China almost tripled from 98,000 MW to 235,100 MW. In 2002 China's electrification index at 0.990 was more than double that of India's 0.444. The future direction of energy for development in India will depend more on the new government's capacity to achieve political consensus with a paradigm shift to install effective economic governance to survive in the twenty-first century than on exhortation of economic and market fundamentals. Development at the start of the twenty-first century requires reconsideration of concepts of governance, efficiency and social justice. The integration of the global energy world is a complex process involving changes in the role of government institutions and structures, laws and regulations, governance and politics, behaviour and expectations.

Success in transforming a plan for the integration of the global energy market in the twenty-first century world depends on the effectiveness of economic governance to reach the lowest level while thinking globally and acting locally. Effective economic governance depends on the success in changing the design, functions and capabilities of governance of institutions reflecting the shifting ideological paradigm towards action. No political statements of economic reform will work without transforming the institutions of economic governance at central, state and local levels. There is cause for concern that coalition politics in a pluralistic democracy could reverse the reform path leading to inadequate energy supplies and inefficient energy use.

Because of India's growing energy shortage, it could be faced with serious political problems. With planned economic growth to continue at 7–8 per cent and with an expected population of 1.5 billion by 2025, energy requirement could vary between a base case of over 1 billion toe/year to a high of 2.25 billion toe/year by 2030. As world crude oil prices began to increase since 2004 to reach $67 a barrel in August 2005, India's oil import bill for 2004 hit over $27 billion. India's President A P J Abdul Kalam, addressing the nation on 14 August 2005, the eve of Independence Day, defined a new goal for India's energy policy—of energy independence by 2030. In his vision of energy security by striving towards energy independence in the next 25 years to 2030, Kalam observed that the end of the fossil fuel era is fast approaching and called for energy independence in electric power generation.

The strategic goals for energy security and energy independence in electric power independence by 2030 call for a major shift in the future energy mix from oil and gas through increased utilization of domestic coal, hydro and thorium resources in nuclear power, massive application of solar power in agriculture, increasing the share of renewable energy to 20–25 per cent and through enhanced bio-fuel production to substitute oil in transportation sector. As discussed in the foregoing section on India's energy policy, energy self-sufficiency and electricity generation independence are lofty goals requiring long-term commitment to result oriented action requiring transformation of the economic governance of institutions. Translating policy to practices requires changing the culture of bureaucracy at the centre, state and local levels to commit to take actions to get results on the ground. It requires visionary leadership to complement economic globalization with effective governance culture to achieve the objectives of development.

What is required at the least is that India needs to take stock of where its energy industry stands. What are its major energy-economics-finance-geopolitics issues in the twenty-first century? How can India evolve a political consensus in a transparent and pluralist democracy to transform its institutions to address these issues to achieve its goal of energy for development? Shaping the direction of reforming India's policies for better energy for the future and formulating strategies for their effective implementation depends on the GOI's success to address these questions.

ARGENTINA

Argentina was a showcase model of the successful 'Diving-In' US-style free-market approach. In the 1990s, Argentina was a 'best-practice' model of the emerging market for Latin America and for developing countries in Asia, Africa and the Middle East. Argentina embarked on a reform program of macroeconomic and energy market liberalization in the late 1980s supported by the pro-market outsiders including the WB and the IMF. The government dealt with hyperinflation by pegging its currency to the US dollar, privatizing electricity, rail and oil and gas companies and opening its financial system to foreign-owned banks. Between 1991 and 1998, the Argentine economy grew at an average of 5.7 per cent a year. Having demonstrated its success in reforming its economy and energy sector, Argentina was chosen to host the XVIII World Energy Congress (WEC) in the new millennium in 2001.

Although Argentina suffered a severe financial crisis in 2001–2, the country is recovering to pre-crisis levels. In 2004 Argentina's real GDP grew at an estimated rate of 8 per cent. Despite strong economic growth, Argentina continues to deal with the 2002 default on its sovereign debt. In January 2005, the government initiated a program to exchange some $100 billion in old bonds for $50 billion in newly issued debt. This debt restructuring is critical for Argentina to regain its ability to borrow for necessary domestic programs and infrastructure projects.

Argentina's financial and economic crisis that began in 2001 critically affected the energy sector. The recession, devaluation of the peso and massive foreign debts hampered the ability of energy companies to invest in exploration and development. Power cuts and energy rations have occurred in 2004 for the first time in a decade.

Sector context

Argentina is one of Latin America's biggest energy markets, with a consumption of 397,000 barrels per day (b/d) in 2004. In 2004, Argentina was the fourth largest hydrocarbon producing country in Latin America at 692,600 b/d, after Mexico, Venezuela and Brazil. Argentina's oil production has steadily declined after peaking at 916,00 b/d in 1998. With around 2.7 billion barrels of proven oil reserves and with net oil exports of 295,600 b/d in 2004 primarily to Brazil and Chile, Argentina is a significant player in the Latin American oil market.

Argentina has proven natural gas reserves at around 21 trillion cubic feet (tcf). Natural gas production in Argentina has steadily increased in the 1990s and surpassed Mexico in 2000 as Latin America's largest natural gas producer. Despite a 3 per cent decline in 2002, natural gas production increased 6.8 per cent in 2003.

Argentina has very limited coal resources of about 474 million short tons of coal reserves and coal is not a major component of the country's fuel mix.

Hydroelectricity plays a major role in Argentina's energy sector. The Yacyreta hydroelectric dam, with its 3,200 MW of installed capacity, is the largest plant in Argentina. In 2002 the hydropower plant accounted for 16 per cent of the country's total electricity production and 33 per cent of production from hydropower plants.

Argentina has two nuclear power plants in operation: the 357 MW Atucha I and 648 MW Embalse. A third plant, the 745 MW Atucha II plant remains under construction. After the government's unsuccessful attempts to privatize it, work was halted in 1994. However, in December 2003 the government announced that it plans to spend $300 million to complete the project. Construction is expected to be completed by 2008.

Oil accounts for more than 51 per cent of Argentina's primary energy supply. Natural gas is the next largest source of energy, accounting for nearly 40 per cent. Hydroelectric power contributes over 7 per cent. A modest amount of coal and nuclear power makes up about 2 per cent of the country's total energy supply. Between 1990 and 2000, the total energy demand increased more than 40 per cent. Oil and gas constituted over 75 per cent of final demand, electricity accounted for over 20 per cent and other fuels, 5 per cent. The energy sector accounted for about 7 per cent of GDP prior to 1990.

Sector institutions and policy

Prior to 1990, Argentina's government was involved at all levels in every aspect of the oil, gas and electric power sectors. Many policies evolved in the form of laws, decrees and regulations. The overlapping responsibilities of numerous bureaus of the government contributed to institutionalized sector inefficiency. Among the agencies and ministries involved in setting policies, approving budgets, fixing prices, appointing top level personnel and approving contracts were the Ministry of Economy (ME), Ministry of Work and Public Services (MOSP), Finance Secretariat (SH), Energy Secretariat (SE), and the National Executive Authority (PEN).

In the petroleum sub-sector, the operating entities were dominated by two state companies, Yacimientos Petroliferos Fiscales (YPF) and Natural Gas del Estado (GdE). YPF was a state corporation (Empresa del Estado), having a corporate structure similar to a private corporation, but the only shareholder was the government. In practice, YPF controlled all E&P of hydrocarbons in Argentina, with the exception of some small old mining concession areas. YPF also controlled the majority of refining and marketing activities. Excluding the small concession areas, all private companies, both local and international, which participate in the exploration for or production of hydrocarbons performed their activities under service contracts with the YPF.

GdE was established in 1946 as a government enterprise to provide natural gas distribution services as a public service. GdE purchased natural gas from YPF in producing areas located primarily in the Northwest, Neuquen and Austral. Imported natural gas was also received from Bolivia. From the producing areas, GdE processed the natural gas and transported it to consuming centres from where it was distributed to the individual end-users. GdE also was responsible for producing and marketing LPG (propane and butane).

Prior to 1990 Argentina's power sector was fragmented, with a complex organizational structure. National utilities were in charge of development, production, transmission and distribution of electricity as well as development of bi-national hydro resources. There were over 20 provincially owned utilities mainly in charge of electricity distribution. There was neither a comprehensive electricity law nor a regulatory body in Argentina prior to 1990. Legislation was dispersed among various laws and decrees which overlapped and at times left important aspects of the electricity industry unregistered.

The Energy Secretariat had overall responsibility for planning and operations at the national level and for the collection and distribution of electricity funds. In practice, the MOE retained final authority since the government perceives electricity rates to have important political consequences. As the provinces in Argentina enjoy a great degree of autonomy, the forum for discussing relationships between the government and the provincial utilities was the Federal Electricity Council, a coordinating body which cannot make decisions. As a result, provincial governments had absolute independence for defining development policies and tariffs that may not be consistent with national policies and priorities.

Since this overly complex institutional framework was in part responsible for the sector inefficiencies, the Argentine government and the WB agreed on a plan of action for improving the legal/ regulatory framework. A commission formed by experienced professionals with legal, planning, engineering, operational and financial backgrounds prepared a diagnosis of the issues affecting the sector and a set of recommendations to address them in 1989. Implementation of legal/ institutional framework was required for WB support to the energy sector in Argentina and was closely linked to the Bank's lending operations to Argentina.

As part of the reform program in the beginning of the 1990s, Argentina evolved a deregulation and liberalization policy of its energy sector involving all its sub-sector energy activities. Argentina's energy policy features included liberalization of energy prices, institutional reforms included unbundling of electricity sector and regulatory reforms, privatization and promotion of competition to enhance efficiency and to attract private investment. The initial step for reorganization of the sector was to divide the electricity sector into distribution, transmission and generation and to establish regulatory agencies to ensure fair competition within the market.

Energy price liberalization

Argentina pursued energy price liberalization as part of its competitive free market reform program. Since 1992 the petroleum product market has been freed and oil prices reflect international price levels. Natural gas prices linked with petroleum product prices on a competitive basis. The price structure for natural gas in Argentina is based on wellhead prices (different in each basin and inversely proportional to the distance to Buenos Aires), transport tariffs (firm *vs* interruptible) and distribution tariffs. Distributors offer their clients full services (residential, commercial, industry and power) and clients can opt for a commercial or geographic bypass to get more competitive prices. The tariffs for natural gas T&D in the regulated areas are set by the state regulatory agency Enargas. Every six months they are adjusted according to a US index and with a correction factor for seasonal fluctuations.

The development of the residential gas prices in Argentina since 1990 shows a steep increase in the first years of restructuring and privatization. After 1993 the prices increased steadily from US 50 cents /MMBtu in 1990 to US $2 /MMBtu in 1997, the year when they first started to drop. In 2000 the average gas price per basin was US $0.90 /MMBtu, $1.20 /MMBtu, and $1.40 /MMBtu for the Austral, Northwest and Neuquen basins respectively, with an average city gas price in Buenos Aires of $1.90 /MMBtu.[54]

The new electric regulatory structure for power sector created in 1992 allows generation, T&D to be carried out by any private company. Under the law, generating companies are not regulated as to price (which is determined by the forces of supply and demand) but distributors are regulated based on an assumed fixed spread over the cost of power. Generators are used in inverse order of marginal cost (lowest cost first). The marginal cost of the last generator used determines the spot market price for electricity. The price-based tariff structure for the distributor provides an incentive for efficient delivery. As in the Chilean system, the costs paid for the marginal units of power (the most expensive of the private producers) signal the market prospects for investment.

In 1999 there was a significant gap between the electricity prices in the spot market and the contracts market. On average, the electric power in the contract market was 11 per cent cheaper than power in the spot market. Since 1995, the year when contracts for large users started to gain weight, the average purchase prices for electricity in the contracts market dropped by 27 per cent in real terms until 1999.

The spot market however, remained more volatile with several peaks, one in 1992 and a severe one in 1999. The bad conditions of precipitation and low water levels of hydro basins were responsible for the 1999 peak. It shifted a large part of the hydro generation to more expensive thermal plants. The peak in 1992, just after the liberalization, was a combination of low hydro flows and the low availability of the thermal plants. However, the general trend shows a substantial decline in the spot market prices since 1992 and a still steady decline from 1995 to 1998.

The electricity distribution sector in Argentina faces a double challenge. On the one hand it has to compete with generators who can sell electricity directly to large customers or to an increasing number of commercial electricity providers who buy the power on the spot market and sell it directly to large customers. On the other hand, it still has a social and economic function which is to provide electricity services to all its clients, especially to the poorer segment of its population.

Furthermore, municipal and regional taxes apply to the tariffs of the customers of the distribution companies, whereas commercial agents and generators only have to pay the fees raised by the regulatory agency and the T&D charges. In 1998 around 18 per cent of the delivered electricity was sold in the 'by pass' mode, thus flowing directly from the commercial agents or generators to large consumers.

Before liberalization, equity aspects dominated the pricing structure of distribution companies. The tariffs increased in blocks according to the

---

54. *Oil and Gas Journal* (15 October 2001), p.72.

amount of consumption. Consequently industrial customers were charged a relatively higher amount for the service. Since the liberalization, privatized distribution companies like Empresa Distribuidora y Comercializadora Norte, S A (Edenor.), which is responsible for the northern part of Greater Buenos Aires, have converted to a tariff system that decreases with the amount of sold electricity. The tariff structure applied by Edenor starts at a level of US 18 cents /kWh and decreases to US 5 cents /kWh for larger customers.

The regulated distribution sector does not permit the application of cross-subsidies or any rate schedule discrimination. However, the distribution companies that are still under municipal or cooperative administration, mostly in rural areas, have only in parts adopted the new pricing scheme. In addition to the tariff, residential customers in the city of Buenos Aires (Capital Federal) have to pay a further 28 per cent of the tariff in the form of municipal taxes. For customers in the region of Greater Buenos Aires the taxes even rise to 44 per cent due to special funds for improving the electricity infrastructure. For an average tariff of US $82 /MWh in 1999, residential consumers in the city of Buenos Aires paid another US $29 /MWh and in Greater Buenos Aires US $44 /MWh.[55]

Argentina's successful transition to a competitive energy market, particularly the power sector, resulted in a decrease in wholesale electricity prices. The price of electricity dropped from US $55 /MW in 1991 to US $22 /MW in 1998. The residential and industrial consumers with highest level of consumption have experienced price decreases of 71 per cent and 44 per cent respectively and an improvement of their services since the liberalization of prices in 1992. Intense competition within the privatized generation market accounts for this reduction, where market entrants increased from 13 in 1992 to 44 in 1997. However, household consumers with the lowest level of consumption experience a small percentage of 1.6 per cent decline in their prices. Between 1992 and 1998, the total service interruption time fell from 22 hours of outage per customer per year to 8 hours of outages and the frequency of such interruptions fell from 13 per year to 4.5.

Following the economic and financial crisis in 2001, the 2002 devaluation of Argentina's peso has adversely affected Argentina's energy prices. Government imposed caps kept energy prices low which drove a dramatic increase in energy demand that outstripped supply leading Argentina to face energy crisis in 2004. The government's imposed caps on natural gas prices led to a surge in natural gas usage exceeding the country's gas supply.

The peso devaluation since 2002 has affected the electricity sector. Until January 2002, private electricity companies operating in Argentina made sales in US dollars, to which the Argentine peso had been pegged since the

---

55. WEC, *Pricing Energy in Developing Countries* (London, June 2001)

1991 Convertibility Law. When this was abandoned and the peso was allowed to float freely in the market, it collapsed and lost approximately 70 per cent of its value. Consequently, the electricity companies (the majority of whom are foreign owned) suffered significant losses, especially those with dollar-denominated debts. As unemployment and poverty rates soared in the aftermath of the economic crisis, the government froze all utility tariffs at their peso-denominated rate making worse the financial situation for the companies. Electricity companies have essentially frozen investment, reduced service quality and dropped maintenance to a strict minimum to cut costs. Soon after, official negotiations between the government and the industry began over possible tariff adjustments. This process has continued since 2002. By 2004 demand for power outstripped supply plunging the country to power rationing. The government is now trying to reintroduce energy pricing reform with a goal to eventually liberalize energy prices over a period of time.

Regulation, institution reforms and industry restructure.

Until 1989 the oil and gas exploration activities in Argentina were conducted by the publicly owned companies Yacimientos Petroliferos Fiscales Sociedad del Estado (YPF SE) and Gas del Estado (GdE). In addition to that, a number of private companies, most of them Argentine companies, participated in the exploration. They held a share of 38 per cent in the upstream oil sector and 15 per cent in the natural gas sector and delivered their products under long-term contracts to the state-owned companies.

The reform in the oil sector between 1989 and 1991 included the restructuring of YPF SE into a society (*asociacion*) called YPF SA. As a first step in its privatization, YPF began a full-scale reorganization in early 1991 that led to its conversion to a public limited liability corporation. The law allowing YPF to privatize was approved after considerable delay in congress in September 1992. This permitted YPF to go ahead with its program to divest non-strategic assets. Following its privatization and a public offering of YPF SE the new ownership structure included a shareholder participation of 46 per cent private shareholders, 20 per cent of the central government, 12 per cent of provinces and 10 per cent of employees. In June 1999 YPF merged with Spain's Repsol. Repsol acquired YPF for US $13.5 billion, creating the largest oil and gas company in Argentina.

The acquisition of YPF was a good strategic fit for Repsol. Prior to the merger, most of Repsol's profits came from refining and marketing and the company had limited reserves. Adding YPF quadrupled the Spanish company's hydrocarbon reserves from 978 million barrels of oil equivalent (mboe) to 4.23 billion barrels of oil equivalent (bboe). It strengthened Repsol's position in Latin America, especially in integrated gas and electricity distribution. Repsol-YPF holds nearly 60 per cent of the country's oil reserves and about 50 per cent of the oil production. Repsol-YPF plans to expand its oil and gas production from 1 million b/d in 1999 to 1.5 million b/d by 2006. Much of the increased production will come from Repsol-YPF's operations in Bolivia, Trinidad and Tobago.

Under terms of divestiture arrangement Repsol made with the Argentine government when acquiring YPF, the company has to reduce its share of the retail gas market. Repsol-YPF owns about 3,000 service stations in Argentina, with 'constituting' nearly 50 per cent of the market share. The company plans on complying with the divestiture deal by swapping some of its downstream assets in Argentina with Brazil's Petrobas for some upstream and downstream assets in Brazil. The Argentine government changed its policy on gas supply contracts and will not renew third-party contracts when they expire, forcing Repsol-YPF to reduce its share of the gas market from 60 per cent to 44 per cent.[56] The company also had to dispose of crude refining capacity equivalent to 4 per cent of its domestic capacity as of 31 December 1998, cut domestic LNG sales by 4 per cent by 2002 and cancel the no re-importation clauses on LPG export contracts.

The other two largest oil producing companies in Argentina are Perez Companc producing 100,000 b/d and Petrolera Argentina San Jorge producing 80,000 b/d. The latter was acquired by Chevron in 1999. Other companies looking to expand their presence in the upstream oil sector include Argentina's Pluspetro, Brazil's Petrobas, Pan American, a joint venture between BP Amoco and Argentina's Bridas, Unocal and France's TotalFinElf.

In May 2003 Brazil's PetroBras acquired a majority stake in Argentina's other large, independent company, Perez Companac, which was renamed subsequently as PetroBras Energia. Four companies, Repsol-YPF, Pan American Energy, PetroBras Energia and Chevron San Jorge accounted for an estimated 77 per cent of oil production in Argentina in 2002.

The downstream oil sector is dominated by three companies, Repsol-YPF, Esso and Shell. There are 12 refineries in Argentina with a combined capacity of 665,900 b/d. Repsol-YPF's La Plata (176,000 b/d) and Repsol-YPF's Lujan de Cuyo (120,000 b/d), Shell's Buenos Aires plant (121,700 b/d) and Esso Compana (88,100 b/d) together account for over 86 per cent capacity. The smaller EG3 consortium consisting of Astra, Isaura and Puma control 14 per cent of the retail fuel market. Most of these refineries have been significantly upgraded in the 1990s, mostly to meet new environmental standards and streamline operations but also to be able to produce lighter products.

Oil and gas industries were privatized and deregulated in the 1990s. The

---

56. EIA, DOE, *Country Brief* (2003)

government realized over US $10 billion from the divestiture and privatization of the state oil company, YPF and the state gas company, Gas del Estado (GdE). Three refineries and miscellaneous assets belonging to YPF were sold and what remained was divested through international public offerings (IPOs).

GdE was an integrated monopoly for natural gas T&D, with no upstream activity or production. The company bought gas from YPF as well as from Bolivia for subsequent resale to industry, power stations and households. In June 1992, Argentina's Congress passed a law providing the framework for the new industry and the terms under which the company was to be sold.

The 1992 Gas Act established a regulatory entity responsible for licensing activities, price regulation at the retail consumer level, including a regular five-year review of overall tariff structures, regulation and inspection of safety and environmental protection standards, approval of significant mergers between units and prevention of monopolistic or anticompetitive practices. In particular, the law set out a new structure aimed at promoting competition in the supply/ delivery of natural gas and improving the operation, reliability and utilization of gas transportation and distribution facilities in an open access framework. The law also provides for the regulation of gas transportation and distribution to ensure that tariffs are equitable and reasonable.

This new system is being put in place following the breakup and privatization of GdE's operation. The natural gas industry was privatized in 1992 and is now a competitive market. The Gas Law split state monopoly GdE into two pipeline companies and eight distributors operating within a regulated monopoly. The transmission companies are obliged to provide free access to their pipeline, but are not allowed to sell natural gas. Large users can freely choose between distribution companies or buy directly from the producers. The trunk pipeline system of 12,600 km has been divided into two independent business units. The existing 9,400 km of secondary pipelines and 48,100 km of distribution network—including gas treatment, separation and compression plants, storage and harbour installations—have been organized into eight independent corporations.

The new regulations attempt to establish arm's length relationships between the various entities and to limit controlling cross-ownership among producers, transporters and distributors. Distributors were also limited to a maximum of two areas out of the eight. In late 1992 concessions were awarded for the operations of all ten of the new business units.

The Argentine gas market is growing and producers are interested in profitable gas projects through additional exports of natural gas and development of GTL or LNG projects.

Argentina has 750 billion cubic meters (bcm) of proven natural gas reserves. In 2000 production reached a volume of 45 bcm. Argentina has four main producing basins, Northwest, Neuquen, Gulf of San Jorge and Austral. The main producers are Repsol-YPF SA, with a 44 per cent share followed by PanAmerican Energy LLC, TotalFina Elf SA, Perez Companc SA and Pluspetrol SA.

In 2000 demand totalled 37 bcm (32 bcm domestic and 5 bcm exports), representing an increase of more than 100 per cent over the consumption levels of 1990. The greatest share of Argentine consumption growth is accounted for by the new gas-fired cogeneration power plants, followed by expansion in petrochemicals—notably at Bahia Blanca complex, expansion of aluminium plants, greater production of urea, increased LPG fuel usage in gas processing plants, growth in residential demand and strong growth of exports mainly to Chile, followed by Brazil and Uruguay.

The gas market is currently composed of five participants with different scopes and responsibilities. Producers (private concessions) under the scope of the Department of Energy with free market pricing; transporters (private concessions) whose sole activity is the transportation of gas through the existing systems under the scope of Enargas, the gas regulatory agency; distributors (private and regional concessions) whose responsibility is to distribute gas; traders, controlled by Enargas and offering gas and transportation or gas resale services; and clients include residential, commercial and industrial consumers.

Argentina's gas regulatory agency, Enargas, aims to obtain a more transparent and competitive natural gas system. The distinctive characteristics of this system include open access for transportation, the opportunity for implementing geographical and commercial distribution bypasses and dominant vertical integration restrictions. Prices for natural gas until 2001 were set in line with that of petroleum but tariffs on natural gas are adjusted every six months in relation to a US index and seasonal fluctuations.

In the early 1990s Argentina's electric power system was experiencing severe financial and operational difficulties. There were constant problems with black-outs, which worsened during dry periods due to the large proportion of hydroelectric generation in the system and many consumers were stealing electricity. Since 1992 Argentina's electric power sector has been privatized and deregulated following the passage of the State Reform Act in 1989 and is now competitive with numerous producers, three transmission companies in a regulated monopoly, regional distributors and a set of municipal utilities. Generators are free to serve any part of the country. Generation, T&D have been split into separate markets. The functions of generation, transmission and distribution are open to the private sector but there are restrictions on ownership of more than one function within the industry. The law guarantees access to the grid to create a competitive environment and to allow generators to serve customers anywhere in the country. Argentina has electricity interconnections with Chile, Brazil and Uruguay.

Argentina now has open access to the wholesale electricity market guaranteed by law and dispatch of electricity based on production costs of available generators, lowest cost first.

Argentina's open bulk power market, the Mercado Electrico Mayorista (MEM), started operating in 1992 with spot market prices set basically according to the short-run marginal costs of the system. Individual firm power contracts were negotiated between sellers and distribution companies and deregulated large users. T&D tariffs are set by a new federal regulatory entity, using cost-based energy and capacity charges set at the various nodes of the system plus the added value of the service. Distribution retail tariffs included the value-added of the distribution service plus the cost of the power purchased and factor in investment costs and a fair return on investment.

A new corporate entity, the Compana Administradora del Mercado Mayorista Electrico Sociedad Anonima (CAMMESA), a non-profit institution, administers the whole sale market. The COMMESA is owned equally by generators, carriers, distributors, major users and the Energy Secretariat, which represents retail customers is responsible for setting the dispatch guidelines and performing dispatch functions for the MEM. Fees are collected from system users to cover the costs of the dispatch services. The MEM uses a system of penalties and fines applicable to power generators or to power purchasers in cases where there is insufficient supply due to unavailability of generation or due to underestimated demand respectively.

The government agency responsible for overseeing Argentina's electricity sector is Ente Regulador de la Energia Electrica (ENRE). ENRE also serves as a mediator of industry disputes

The New National Regulatory Commission (NRC) has considerable political and fiscal independence. Its key duties are to set rates for the regulated transmission and retail distribution markets, set technical, operating and quality of service standards, oversee the functions and activities of regulated area and players and protect consumer interests. The Secretary of Energy, under the Ministry of the Economy, is responsible for policy-making for the power and other energy sub-sectors.

Private investment/ privatization

Argentina's liberalization program promoted foreign investment. The 1989 Economic Emergency Law, the 1989 Reform Law and a 1993 amendment to the Foreign Investment Law were combined in an act called Decree 1853 which allows foreigners to own 100 per cent of most Argentine companies and to fully repatriate profits and capital. Although the 1989 laws permitted foreign companies to invest in Argentina, the 1992 Bilateral Investment Treaty provides an additional incentive for US companies by ensuring that US firms can invest on terms at least as favourable as those accorded to domestic investors.

Argentina's energy sector has been undergoing privatization since 1991. Government policy for the electric power industry, the natural gas industry and the oil industry were targeted at encouraging investments and creating competitive markets. Most electric power companies have been privatized since 1991. In the oil and gas sector, domestic prices reflect international prices. Prior to 1992 the government set prices and volume production limits for oil and foreign producers were not permitted to export crude oil. These restrictive trade and investment policies were lifted in 1991.

Between April 1992 and June 1995, over 25 state operated power companies were privatized, essentially becoming IPPs. This privatization process is continuing at a slower pace as the government sells off its remaining power companies and the distribution services. 30 year concessions were awarded for hydroelectric plants while thermal plants were sold off. Over 2000 Mwe of natural gas-fuelled power plants are being installed. The power matrix has been diversified since 1992. While hydroelectricity dominated in 1990, as of 2000, Argentina has a balanced power matrix, with 45 per cent gas-fired, 45 per cent hydroelectric and 10 per cent nuclear power. Total installed capacity increased from 17,000 MW in 1990 to almost 26,000 MW in 2001.

Under the 1990s liberalization program, foreign and domestic companies had equal access to all economic sectors and were eligible for incentive programs and state procurements. Foreign investors do not need prior approval for investments. Between 1992 and 1999, net FDI flows to Argentina totaled US $43.5 billion. FDI exceeded $11 billion in 1999, up from more than $6 billion in 1998. In the 1990s Argentina ranked fourth among the top ten net FDI receiving developing countries.

Policies of energy market transition in Argentina focused on creating competition and deregulation of the energy industry. Since 1991 the hydrocarbons sector has been deregulated and liberalized. Private companies have been allowed unrestricted participation in the oil industry and private operators are guaranteed access to explore in areas of acknowledged potential and the right to develop discoveries on a concession basis, disposing of their production at prevailing international prices.

Implementation of the program started in January 1991 when producers were allowed to set oil prices at market levels and to export crude oil production without restriction. As the next step, four central areas with reserves estimated at 255 million barrels were opened to private participation. The 'Plan Argentina' for the oil industry was launched by the government later in 1991, letting a further 1.4 million square kilometers on land and the remainder in the continental shelf. This process has continued for most of the remaining potential oil field. More than 25 international oil and gas companies have entered Argentina. Competition was introduced into oil and gas production and refining. Argentine oil companies have been expanding into other Latin American markets.

Deregulation of the electric power industry created opportunity for gas-fired power generation. There is strong competition among producers of cutting edge combined-cycle power plants in the Argentine market. The market for electric power generation and transmission equipment was over US $1 billion per year in 1999 and 2000. Plans for installation of additional capacity of 8,000 MWe by the year 2007 represents a total investment of over US $10 billion in additional capacity installation and network upgrades.

Many US companies became active in Argentina's energy sector. Table 5.6. lists the active US companies in Argentina's energy sector.

Table 5.6. US Investors in Argentina's Energy Sector

Oil and Gas Exploration and Production

- Amoco Corporation
- Exxon Corporation
- LG&E Corporation
- Mobil Corporation
- Pioneer Natural Resources Company
- Santa Fe
- Unocal

Natural Gas Pipelines

- AES Corporation
- Amoco Corporation
- CMS Energy
- El Paso International

Oil and Gas Service Companies

- Baker Oil Tools
- Christensten International
- Hughes Tool Company
- Parker Drilling Company
- Weatherford International
- Western Geophysical

Electricity Generation and Transmission

- AES Corporati
- Amoco Corporation
- Cinergy Global
- Citicorp Capital Investors
- CMS Energy
- Dominion Resources
- Duke Power
- Enron
- Entergy Corporation
- Houston Industries, Inc.
- Kansas Power and Light
- LG&E Energy Corporation
- Northeast Utilities
- PSEG Global
- PSI Resources
- Southern Electric

Source: DOE, *Argentina Country Brief* (2003), *Energy Information Administration*

Argentina's energy market transition: Status

Argentina went all the way to embrace US style capitalism with open markets and unfettered foreign investment. By 1998 Argentina was viewed as successfully completing its energy market transition and served as a show case for 'Best Practice' to be adopted by developing countries. Box 5.5 lists the highlights of Argentina's successful completion of energy market transition in the 1990s.

Box 5.5 Argentina: Highlights of Completion of Energy Market Transition in the 1990s

Energy Pricing

- Decontrol of all energy prices
- Oil prices reflect international levels
- Natural gas prices linked to oil prices
- Electricity prices in the liberalized market segments of generation include spot market and the contract market. Prices reflect short-term marginal cost
- Substantial decline in the spot market prices since 1992 and a steady decline from 1995 onwards.

- Since 1995, the year when contracts for large users started to gain weight, the average purchase prices for electricity in the contracts market dropped by 27 per cent in real terms until 1999
- T&D tariffs are set by a regulatory entity
- Transmission tariffs are cost-based energy and capacity charges set at the various nodes of the system plus the added value of the service
- Distribution retail tariffs include value-added of the distribution service plus the cost of power purchased and factor in investment costs and a fair rate on investment
- The regulatory law does not permit the application of cross-subsidies or any rate schedule discrimination

Regulation

- The new 1992 new gas act established a regulatory entity for natural gas to promote competition in the gas market and set gas tariffs
- 1991 and 1992 reform laws established the competitive and deregulated wholesale power market
- Argentina's open bulk power market, the Mercado Electrico Mayorista (MEM), started operating in 1992, with spot market prices set basically according to the short-run marginal costs of the system
- Established National Regulatory Commission (NRC) to set rates for the regulated transmission and retail distribution networks

Commercialization, corporatization and privatization

- 1991 YPF Reorganization followed by its privatization. YPF was merged with Spain's Repsol Company
- The 1992 law provided a framework for breakup and privatization of GdE. GdE's operations were reorganized into ten companies which were privatized
- Since 1992 the electric power sector has been privatized and deregulated. Generation, T&D are split into separate markets. Open access to the wholesale electricity market is guaranteed by law
- Competitive generation market; generators are free to serve any part of the country
- Three transmission companies in a regulated monopoly, regional distributors and a set of municipal utilities
- Three federally owned electricity companies privatized—Segba, serving Buenos Aires, Ayee, serving most of the rest of Argentina and Hidronor, which oversaw hydropower in the south, produced about 80 per cent of Argentina's hydropower
- Between 1992 and 1995, over 25 state operated power companies were privatized, essentially becoming IPPs
- 30 year concessions were awarded for hydroelectric plants, while thermal plants were sold off

Private Investment

- 1993 amendment to the Foreign Investment Law combined in an act called Decree 1853, removed restrictions on foreign investment
- 1992 Bilateral Investment Treaty provides additional incentives for US companies
- Foreign investors do not need prior approval for investment
- Private companies allowed unrestricted participation in the oil and gas industry

- Deregulation of the electric power industry created opportunity for gas-fired private investment in power generation
- Between 1992 and 1999 Argentina ranked fourth in the top ten net FDI inflows in developing countries, totalling US $43.4 billion
- Annual FDI flows to energy sector to 2007 is estimated to be over US $2 billion
- Over 25 foreign oil, gas and power companies entered Argentina in the 1990s

Sources: DOE, *Energy Information Administration* (2003 and 2005);
WB, *Argentina Country Brief* (1999, 2000, 2001, 2002);
WB, *Global Development Finance* (Washington DC, 2004)

Future directions

For much of the 1990s Argentina experienced solid economic growth and macroeconomic stability by adopting monetary, fiscal, trade and investment reforms, which included privatization of nearly all state-owned enterprises including energy companies. Exports nearly doubled between 1992 and 1999 from US $12 billion to 23.2 billion. Imports increased from US $15 billion to over US $25 billion.

Argentina was the poster child of neo-liberalism and became the model for the notion that free markets would ensure prosperity. Free market programs included selling off state-owned companies, lowering of import barriers and adoption of 'convertibility system'— the decision to rigidly fix its currency against the dollar—one peso for one dollar. Adopted in 1991, the system appeared to be working for eight years to help Argentina tame its notorious hyperinflation.

However, a series of external shocks, mainly the Asian financial crisis spreading to Russia and then to Brazil, led to higher interest rates, reduced foreign investment and a general weakening of the economy.

Dr Joseph Stiglitz, the former Senior Vice-President of the WB and 2001 Nobel Prize Winner in Economics said that 'Argentina's experience is being read: This is what happens to the A-plus student of the IMF. The disaster comes not from *not listening* to the IMF, but rather from listening.'[57] Stiglitz argues that Argentina's move to the bottom of the class has much to do with the exchange rate system when Argentina listened to the IMF, adopted the fixed exchange rate system and pegged its peso to the US dollar. While much of Argentina's trade was with Europe and Brazil, Argentina could not sustain its trade deficits by pegging its peso to the dollar as the dollar strengthened.

With the collapse of the Brazilian currency, Argentina could not compete with its neighbour's cheaper exports. A falling Euro made it harder for Argen-

57. Joseph Stiglitz, 'Argentina shortchanged: Why the nation that followed the rules fell to pieces?', *The Washington Post* (12 May, 2002)

tina to export to Europe and low prices for the commodities Argentina exports further strained the economy. The peg to the rising dollar made Argentina's exports uncompetitive on world markets. The fixed exchange rate led to a vicious circle. As it became clear that devaluation was inevitable, lenders in pesos insisted on even higher interest rates to compensate them for this exchange rate risk. Argentina suffered under the strain of its debt and the global financial crisis of 1997–8 raised the risks further and the interest rates that Argentina paid to the foreign and domestic creditors soared. Given the high volatility of international financial markets the fixed exchange rate system could not survive and it broke.

The higher interest rates not only heightened the risk of devaluation but contributed to a new risk of default, which in turn led to even higher interest rates to compensate for this risk throwing the country to recession. Since the third quarter of 1998, Argentina's economy has been stalled in recession. While other countries in Latin America have rebounded from the 1999 economic downturn, Argentina recorded a 3.4 per cent drop in GDP in 1999 and a further decline of 0.5 per cent in 2000. When the economy did not turn around, lenders became more cautious and demanded ever-increasing interest rates.

The higher interest rates drained even more money from the economy, causing still more unemployment and slower growth. Since the Argentine economy had been dollarized, much of the debts of government and businesses and households were in dollars, as were most of the household savings. Argentina had piled up US $142 billion dollars in debt accounting for over 50 per cent of its GDP that was literally impossible to pay back. With just 37 million people, Argentina's debt at $142 billion represents 25 per cent of all emerging market debt and is widely held by financial institutions in the United States.

In the weeks leading up to the crisis in December 2001, the Argentine government's attempts to fiscal reforms to reduce budget deficit targets with IMF pulled the country deeper into recession. On 5 December 2001, the IMF decided to withhold a critical US $1.3 billion loan instalment to Argentina when it failed to meet its fiscal targets on a multi-billion dollar bail-out. IMF's pressure for more austerity from Argentina before releasing the needed loans triggered the financial crisis and the chain reaction of government's collapse.

Challenge of restarting

The collapse of Argentina has raised the question on benefits of adopting US style capitalism which entailed privatization, open markets and unfettered foreign investments. It has also raised criticism of the consequences that Argentina had to face listening to IMF's policies on exchange rate and its continued advice to follow contractionary fiscal policies when the country was facing downturn.[58] Eduardo Duhalde, who took office as Argentina's fifth president in two weeks on January 2, 2002, said, 'We must abandon this economic model, that is why the people are in the streets today'. In January 2002, Argentina faced its worst financial and economic crisis since opting for free a market in the 1990s. The Argentine peso lost nearly two-thirds of its value, faced US $142 billion in debt, 25 per cent unemployment, 44 per cent poverty rate—double the rate before it adopted market reforms in 1991 and continuing economic recession.

The free market reforms of the 1990s are widely credited with curbing inflation and producing short-lived economic growth. The reforms were followed by heavy spending, charges of corruption, a default of Argentina's foreign debt and an unprecedented financial collapse. Although many government-owned companies were privatized, Argentine industries remained uncompetitive. While trade barriers were lowered, trade flows remained relatively low. Government deficits continued with little coordination of federal-provincial financial relationship. Provincial governments continued to indulge in profligate spending and charging the national treasury with the bill. While public spending continued to rise, widely practiced tax evasion practices failed to boost the much needed revenues to match the rising expenditure. In 2001 the budget deficit was US $11 billion accounting for more than 10 per cent of its GDP. Argentina's economic hardship reached a peak in December 2001 when it defaulted on its US $140 billion debt to commercial banks and bondholders and lost access to private foreign credit. In November 2002 Argentina defaulted on WB debt.

The group of seven leading industrial countries, the G7, were worried about the consequences of Argentina's growing arrears for the credit ratings of the WB and the IADB. With US support, the G7 in January 2003 intervened and strong-armed the IMF into signing an interim agreement that would roll over $6 billion of Argentina's debt. The IMF dubbed the package 'transitional financial support' as it was aimed at tiding Argentina until a new government took power following the presidential election in April. The support included a $3 billion loan plus a deferral until 2002 of $3.8 billion more to 'cover all payment obligations to the IMF through August 2003'.

Argentina's economy has now embarked on stabilization. In January 2003, Argentina cleared its payment arrears to the WB and IADB. Combined with the approval of IMF's package, it paves the way for resumption of loans by development banks. The WB in January 2003 approved US $600 million loan to support unemployment relief in Argentina.

In April 2002 the peso tumbled about 65 per cent against the US dollar

---

58. Joseph Stiglitz, 'Argentina shortchanged: Why the nation that followed the rule fell to pieces?', *Washington Post* (12 May, 2002)

since the government devalued in January 2002. The fall out from Argentina's financial crisis affected its oil and gas industry and power utilities. Oil production that was rebounding slightly in 2001 declined in 2002 as producing companies were wary of investment. Natural gas companies continued to be hurt by policies adopted by the government during Argentina's financial crisis in late 2001. In 2002 many companies posted losses as a result of currency devaluation and a freeze of natural gas rates for residential consumers. Wellhead natural gas prices in Argentina dropped to about 35–45 US cents per million Btu from around $1.40 per million Btu before the crisis. Due to low natural gas prices many natural gas producers have been wary of investing in the sector. Examples include TotalFinaElf's postponement in 2002 of a US $400 million development of a natural gas project in Tierra del Fuego. Companies warning the government that Argentina could potentially face a natural gas shortage in 2004 became a reality. Since 2004 and into mid-August 2005, Argentina continued to face energy shortages.

Government switched electricity prices to pesos from dollars (a process known as pesofication) and prohibited rate increases following the devaluation, a move to keep inflation at bay. As a result, generators and utilities could not raise prices to compensate for losses caused by devaluation. Instead, the depreciating peso wiped out their revenue in dollar terms and nearly tripled the cost of running their plants and servicing their debts.

Prior to January 2002, power utility companies operating in Argentina made sales on the domestic market under the country's 1991 Convertibility Law. With the abandonment of the Convertibility Law in January 2002, foreign owned companies suffered sizable losses as the value of the peso fell dramatically. Simultaneous with drawl of tariff adjustments in April 2002, holding them at their peso-denominated rate passed the cost of devaluation on to power utilities.

Increases in fuel oil prices added to the problem of generators. Given that 95 per cent of power generation companies' costs in 2002 were in US dollars, 'pesofication' plus a rate freeze made it very hard for generators to make payments on their debts. In April 2002 Argentina's biggest generation company, Central Puerto, which is majority owned by TotalFinaElf, stopped repayments on its US $307 million of debt and started renegotiating with its creditors. Other big utilities, including natural gas distributor Metrogas, also halted debt payments. Most generators borrowed heavily during the heyday of Argentina's economic and monetary stability in the 1990s to build plants and equip them with the latest technology. Of the US $6 billion invested in the 1990s in the power sector, US $3.5 billion was borrowed in dollars from the financial markets. The government placed restrictions on the flow of foreign capital into the country and proposed cancelling contracts of privatized utility companies that fail to improve the delivery of services.

Faced with a looming energy crisis on 1 October 2003, the Lower House of Congress approved legislation giving the government the power to negotiate new contracts with natural gas, electricity and other utilities to make interim price increases previously barred under the Economic Emergency Law. The legislation allowed time for the government until 31 December 2004, to negotiate new contracts and pricing structures.[59]

The IMF has been pressing the Kirchner administration for increasing energy prices including for gas and electricity on the grounds that deteriorating energy infrastructure could slow economic growth and force it to use public funds to bolster the sector. Investment in new gas well drilling, building of power plants and pipeline capacity expansion have been at a minimum since the December 2001 crisis. A gas shortage in Argentina in early 2004 is shifting and diversifying energy flows throughout Latin America. Falling gas output, saturated distribution systems and a rebound in demand have led to gas rationing for large industrial users and power stations. Furthermore, without higher energy rates for gas and power, Argentina is heading into an energy crisis since 2004, with demand for power and gas rising at about 8 per cent a year. The energy crisis has threatened to stifle Argentina's economic recovery

The power market is also facing a potential shortfall. According to industry calculations, each percentage point of economic growth requires 1,000 MW of new generating capacity. Installed capacity in 2003 was around 23,000 MW, with only 16,000 MW available due to limited transport capacity. In January 2004 peak demand reached 14,350 MW.

The major problem remains depressed prices, with the spot price for electricity running at US $13.50 MWh—far less than the US $26 /MWh considered necessary for profitably building power plants. Moreover, gas prices at the wellhead in January 2004, averaged US $0.40 /MMBtu, less than the US $1.20 /MMBtu that producers require to restart drilling and exploring for fresh gas reserves.

In an effort to leverage the rate hikes for gas and power toward limiting supply disruptions, the government on 16 February 2004 introduced several new regulations for gas and power.

First, it created a differential pricing scheme for gas at the point of entry to the transport grid, which should enable producers to gradually charge higher well-head prices in fixed term contracts to large consumers while keeping prices unchanged for residents and small businesses. The new regulations would force many big users to return to the costlier contract market to buy gas—a number of large users had let contracts expire after the freeze on gas rates to take advantage of the lower cost of buying from distributors.

Second, in brokering the contracts the government would also set a refer-

59. EIA, DOE, *Argentina Country Analysis Briefs* (Washington DC, January 2004), p.14

ence price, although the final cost would be agreed upon between buyer and producer. It is expected that contracts would incorporate a gradual increase in price based on the wellhead price, with the goal of producers charging 80 per cent of the pre-devaluation price of US $1.20 /MMBtu by the end of 2006. By building a strong contract market, authorities also expect to provide producers with an additional incentive to invest in drilling for fresh reserves of gas.

Third, the government decree announced the creation of a trust fund to finance expansion of distribution and transportation networks. According to the decree, the fund would be built through the addition of a surcharge on users, credits from local and foreign lenders and monies from the companies contracted for extensions.

Fourth, the government has also authorized the creation of a real-time spot-market for gas and secondary markets for distribution and transport capacity.

Fifth, the government decrees have set up a new system for categorizing the sale of compressed natural gas (CNG), which is used to fuel about 20 per cent of the country's 7 million vehicles. Prior to the 2001 crisis all service stations selling CNG received deliveries on a non-interruptible basis, while some will now buy under interruptible contracts that would help defend against supply cuts during peak times of demand.

Finally, the government has reworked the seasonal rates adjustment system to create a pay-through mechanism, which facilitates higher payments from large users as compensation for the rising costs faced by generators. Since 2002 the government suppressed seasonal adjustments to rates, even though generating costs were rising.

The government of Nestor Kirchner announced on 27 February 2004, new regulatory changes including rate hikes of 12–35 per cent for natural gas and power, the first rate increase in more than two years. The government avoided increasing rates for small natural gas users and residential power users. Users of 9,000 cubic meters of natural gas or more would face a 12–25 per cent increase in rates. Power users who consume 10–300 kW will pay 15 per cent more for electricity, while consumers with loads of 300kW and above will pay 35 per cent above prevailing rates. The government also faces lawsuits opposed to the hikes, with opponents arguing that the hikes are outside the legal framework established for raising rates. That framework states that rate increase must come after the contracts of utility concessions are renegotiated.

The higher rates for power and gas mark the first major move by President Nestor Kirchner in addressing the price freeze since 2002. The rate increase was designed to quell any public outcry, with the higher rates falling on big business rather than on residents. More than half of Argentina's 36 million people live in poverty that is largely a result of the country's 2001–

2 economic crisis. In January 2004 the WB recommended that Argentina introduce lower natural gas, power, and other utility rates for the poor, an idea already under study by the government and utility companies. The move would protect the lower income households from 'the impacts of a pending rates increase' and preserve their access to gas, power and other public services.

In an announcement on 13 February 2004, Cabinet chief Alberto Fernandez, flanked by Planning Minister Julio De Vido and Energy Secretary Daniel Cameron, unveiled the increases saying, 'People won't suffer any type of extra increase (in rates). This time, it is those that have earned the most that will endure the increases'.[60] As Argentina in 2004 had just began to show signs of economic recovery and the general public was still suffering, this was probably a political necessity. The potential of supply shortfalls and the pressure exerted by the IMF impacted the government's decision to provide some relief to power and gas producers. The government's decision in February 2004 to increase gas and power rates was a balancing act of sparing its people from rate hikes and the need to conform to normalizing relations with international creditors and investors.

Argentina's president Nestor Kirchner continues to negotiate a new payment plan with the IMF with US support. After a decade of launching free market reforms, Argentina is once again back to basics in negotiations with the IMF. The lessons from Argentina's collapse are first, adopting a free market model requires a rational choice of exchange rate mechanism, adherence to economic fundamentals including fiscal discipline and the changing role of the government oversight function and strengthening of government institutions. Second, adopting the 'diving-in' approach to the free market without the basic economic fundamentals including the inability to control deficit spending of provincial governments and inadequate institutions to address governance issues of cronyism, corruption and inefficiencies could be dangerous. Third, the East Asian and Latin American financial crises since 1997–8 have underscored the fact that given the volatility of international financial markets the transition to free market is a 'learn as you go' process.

Fourth, one of the outcomes of the Argentine government's disagreements with foreign creditors and companies since the 2001 crisis is that there has been a notable change in attitude towards foreign private investors not only in Argentina but also in Latin America. The economic reforms and liberalization needed to promote private sector development and investment are no longer a popular proposition among voters. With rising global crude oil prices and foreign companies acting to increase domestic oil prices, Ar-

---

60. 'Argentine government to raise gas, power rates', *Platts Power in Latin America* (27 February 2004), Issue 130

gentina's government is concerned about the inflationary effect of domestic fuel price rises. The arguments between private sector investors who have been pushing for price increases to restore the profitability of their investments and the government accusing private investors of taking advantage of the country during the 1990s to siphon profits away instead of investing in new production capacity have continued to fracture their relationship. Despite the anti-foreign investment rhetoric, the administration has moved to increase gas and power prices gradually to pre-crisis levels.

Since 2001, because of the disillusionment of the benefits of globalization in the energy sector, anti-foreign private investment in oil and gas sector is gaining ground in several Latin American countries. For example, in October 2003, the Dominican Republic, one of the Caribbean countries that liberalized its economy during the 1990s, re-nationalized two privatized electricity distribution companies. Mexico's Congress has repeatedly blocked electricity liberalization. Costa Rica is still clinging to the idea of state monopolies for both the electricity and telecom industries. Uruguayans voted on a referendum to block private sector participation in the state oil company, even as the country's gas prices remain among the most expensive in the region. Bolivians continued demonstrations set on a collision course with its oil and gas sector that would impose a substantial taxation on the sector has impacted investment in oil and gas sector. The November 2005 Americas' Summit in Mar del Plato, Argentina, failed to reach an agreement on holding discussions on Free Trade for Americas.

Finally, an important outcome of Argentina's experience of transition to free market is that there has been a swing in WB lending towards the need for linking economic and social change. The WB was instrumental in showcasing Argentina's transition to free market energy and advocating market pricing of energy in the 1990s. In January 2004 the Bank recommended lower energy prices for the poor (over 50 per cent of Argentina's population). Argentina was a frontrunner of WB loans in the 1990s for energy sector reform and liberalization. After a decade of free market experience, ironically, Argentina has re-emerged as the frontrunner for a total of five WB loans of US $735 million in 2002 and US $1.1 billion in 2003 for structural adjustment, provincial reform adjustment, family strengthening and social capital promotion learning and innovation, economic and social transition structural adjustment and Heads of Household specific investment.[61]

Argentina's collapse shows what happens when the government just opts to copy the free market style without taking responsibility to adhere to economic fundamentals, to build effective institutions for market and to continue to allow corruption, cronyism and self-interest to prevail. Future directions in energy market transition in Argentina depends on the new government's will-

61. *The World Bank Annual Report* (2002 and 2003)

ingness to learn lessons from its 1990s market liberalization experience and to take actions to stabilize the economy, to calm investors' fears and to spur new investment in Argentina's energy sector and to address the institutional issues of corruption and inefficiencies.

The new government, in the midst of energy crisis in 2004, unveiled a new energy plan for the country by creating a new state controlled company, Energia Argentina (Enarsa) and includes US $3.8 billion investment to expand the country's natural gas and electricity infrastructure by 2009. The country's president Nestor Kirchner outlined a number of specific projects to boost generation and transmission capacity, increase supplies of natural gas and make a call for bids for the supply of 500 MW from Brazil. The political will of the Argentine government to learn from its experience of their 1990s' transition to free market to address the macro-sector linkage issues and success in building efficient institutions for economic governance will impact future directions of energy market transition.

BRAZIL

Brazil is Latin America's largest energy consumer, accounting for 36 per cent of the region's consumption in 2000. As the sixth most populous country (and the most populous country in South America) and possessing large and well-developed agricultural, mining, manufacturing and service sectors, Brazil accounts for almost half of central and South America's economic output and is expanding its presence in world markets. The sharp oil price increases of the 1970s and the debt crisis and inflation in the 1980s affected Brazil's economy and discouraged foreign investment. In its efforts to stabilize the economy, Brazil launched the Plano Real (Real Plan) in mid-1994.

However, the economic crisis that hit the emerging markets in South East Asia and Russia in 1998 endangered the confidence in emerging markets and impacted Brazil. Brazil's international reserves fell almost US $20 billion in September 1998. Brazil's efforts to tighten fiscal policy by raising short-term interest rates to slow down the capital flight failed as it had a trading ban on its currency and had to spend its foreign reserve to defend its currency.

Brazil turned to the IMF and other financial organizations to help in meeting debt obligations in the fall of 1998. The 1998 US $18.1 billion IMF line of credit provided help to stabilize Brazil's economy. On 15 January 1999, Brazil allowed its currency to float freely and the exchange rate fell from 1.20 to 1.99 real per US dollar by end January. The IMF agreement also required that Brazil cut spending to 3.5 per cent of GDP by 2002. As part of its stabilization plan Brazil began to institute reforms in the energy sector.

Sector context

Brazil's energy mix is dominated by oil (63 per cent) and hydropower (19 per cent). It has large renewable (hydro and biomass) resources, significant oil and gas resources and limited coal reserves. Total primary energy consumption in Brazil has increased at an annual rate of 3 per cent in 1992–2002, despite a drop in consumption in 2001. Since the early 1990s Brazil has made progress in increasing its energy production, particularly with regards to oil. In the beginning of the 1990s it was a large net oil importer, but by 2003 domestic production of oil accounted for over 90 per cent of its consumption. It expects to be self-sufficient in oil production by 2006, with output eventually reaching 2.3 million b/d by 2010. Since the early 1990s Brazil has been trying to promote the use of natural gas to diversify its energy mix, in particular to reduce its dependence on imported oil and hydropower. Brazil has also made considerable progress in developing bio-fuel to reduce the dependence of oil in the transport sector. Despite these encouraging developments, Brazil's energy sector has been hampered by the 2001 energy crisis, which forced the government to implement a power rationing program. The crisis highlighted Brazil's dependence on hydropower and its need to diversify the country's fuel mix.

Brazil has the third largest proven oil reserves in Latin America after Venezuela and Mexico, with 8.5 billion barrels as of January 2004. Total oil production has been rising steadily since the early 1990s, with an average of 1.88 MMbd in 2003. Oil consumption also increased in the 1990s, but oil consumption dipped to an estimated 2.12 MMbd. Although Brazil's oil production is increasing, the country still needs to import lighter crude oil which domestic refiners mix with Brazil's predominantly heavy crude oil to refine petroleum products.

Brazil's natural gas reserves were estimated to be around 8.5 trillion cubic feet (tcf) as of 2004. In 2002 natural gas accounted for 5.7 per cent of Brazil's total primary energy consumption. Following the 2001 energy crisis brought on by prolonged droughts, Brazil thought of making efforts to increase the use of natural gas in power generation to diversify its power supply and to lessen its dependence on hydropower. However, these efforts failed to materialize with resumption of rainfall facilitating to revert to hydro power. Brazil's natural gas market still faces the problem of expanding domestic demand for natural gas.

Brazil has proven coal reserves of 12 billion tons, mostly of steam coal quality. Coal however, plays only a small role in Brazil's energy mix, accounting for just 7 per cent of the countries total primary energy demand in 2002. Brazil produced 7 million tons of hard coal in 2002 and imported over 13 million tons. Its steel industry will continue to rely on coking coal imports.

Brazil has large hydroelectric resources. In 2002 its hydroelectric capacity was about 63 GW, which accounts for about 83 per cent of its electricity generation. It has enormous unexploited hydroelectric potential. It also has other renewable energy production in addition to hydropower. In 2002 Brazil produced 46 mtoe of energy from renewable sources other than hydroelectricity (mostly from firewood, sugar cane products and other biomass resources). Biomass demand represents nearly 25 per cent of Brazil's primary energy demand.

Energy demand projections for Brazil are subject to uncertainties about the rate of growth in the GDP, the future directions of reforms in the gas and electricity sectors and the rate of gas penetration in the power sector. Raising the share of gas in Brazil's energy mix in the near term will depend on securing the investment to build transportation and distribution infrastructure. The rate of increase in oil production is subject to attracting investment in Brazil's mainly offshore and deep water. A review of several projections including IEA's *WEO* (2004) indicate that between 2002 and 2030, including biomass, Brazil's energy consumption will grow at a lower rate of 2.5 per cent per year compared with 3.2 per cent for 1971–2002. Table 5.7 shows Brazil's energy demand outlook for the period 1971—2030.

Table 5.7: Brazil: Energy Demand Outlook: Reference Scenario (Mtoe)

Energy sources	*1971*	*2002*	*2030*	*1971-2002 percentage annual growth rates*	*2002-30 percentage annual growth rates*
Coal	2	13	22	5.5	1.9
Oil	28	88	172	3.8	2.4
Gas	0	12	59	16.4	5.8
Nuclear	0	4	6	--	2.0
Hydro	4	25	45	6.3	2.2
Biomass and waste	35	46	65	0.9	1.2
Other Renewables	0	0	2	--	42.9
Total	70	188	372	3.2	2.5

Source: *IEA, WEO* (2004)

Total primary energy supply including biomass is expected to double to 372 mtoe in 2030. Oil consumption is expected to increase from 88 mtoe in 2002 to 172 mtoe in 2030, natural gas consumption from 12 mtoe in 2002 to 59 mtoe in 2030, coal consumption to from 13 mtoe in 2000 to 22 mtoe in 2030.

Sector institutions and policy

As of the beginning the 1990s, the Federal Government's control in the energy sector was pervasive. The Federal Government was responsible for the coordination of energy policy, through the Federal Ministry of Mines and Energy (MME) and its National Energy Commission (CNE). The 1988 constitution gave the Federal Government a monopoly in exploration, development, production, refining, transportation and import and export of oil and gas. This monopoly was exercised through Petroleo Brasilerio, SA (PetroBras), which was established in 1953. Legally, the government must hold at least 51 per cent of PetroBras' voting shares. In 1989 the government held its minimum legal quota of shares, with the remainder held by private individuals and companies through publicly traded shares (26.4 per cent), other entities (12.3 per cent) and the National Development Bank (BNDES, 10.3 per cent).[62]

Apart from its major involvement in exploration, development, refining and transport, PetroBras has extended its operations into other areas through six subsidiaries to cover the production and sale of petrochemicals (Petroquista), the retailing of petroleum products (BR), the overseas E&P of hydrocarbons and the provision of services and technical assistance (Braspetro), the production and sale of fertilizers and raw materials (Petrofertil), the import and export of commodities (Interbras) and the evaluation of the hydrocarbon and mineral potential of sedimentary basins (Petrmisa). While PetroBras is not protected by monopoly in these activities, it dominated both the petrochemical and fertilizer markets in 1990 (over 80 per cent of market share) and is a major participant in the domestic retail distribution of petroleum products (40 per cent market share).

PetroBras has been actively pursuing projects to promote the use of natural gas by expanding the natural gas infrastructure. The first pipeline to connect Brazil to a foreign gas source was the Bolivia-to-Brazil pipeline, with a capacity of 11 bcm/year. It was inaugurated in July 1999. The second operational pipeline, Transportadora de Gas del Mercosur (TGM),[63] links Argentina to Brazil.

The state governments have the exclusive right to distribute gas directly or through state natural gas retailing companies. Gas distribution networks have been in Rio de Janeiro and Sao Paulo for many years. In Rio de Janeiro the distribution network is operated by a state-owned company, Companhia Estadual de gas do Rio de Janeiro (CEG). In Sao Paulo the Sao Paulo State Gas Company (COMGAS) operates gas deliveries.

Brazil's Ministry of Mines and Energy is responsible for the electricity sector and acts through the Department of Water and Electrical Energy (DNAEE). Electrobras is the government controlled holding company that

---

62. WB, *Brazil, Energy Pricing and Investment Study* (Washington DC, 1992)

63. The Common Market of the South, Mercosur's members are Argentina, Brazil, Paraguay and Uruguay, with Chile and Bolivia as associated members.

was created in 1961 to promote the development of projects to generate and transmit electricity in all of Brazil. It operates generation and transmission of electric energy throughout the Brazilian territory through its subsidiaries. In addition, Electrobras owns 50 per cent of the assets of Itaipu hydroelectric power plant, funds and conducts energy research at its CEPEL research centre and operates a number of federal energy programs. Distribution of electricity is generally left to various electric utility companies which, prior to 1995, was mainly state-owned.

Brazil has approximately 185,000 km of electric transmission lines, mostly owned by the major state companies. Brazil has two large transmission systems, one covering the south, south-east and parts of the central west, the other, the noth-east and parts of the north. These two main systems were joined with a 1,277 km, 500 kV line, called the 'North-South Interconnection'. However, the national transmission system still fails to reach many regions in the north and northwest, notably the state capitals Manaus, Macapa, Boa Vista, Rio Branco and Porto Velho. These state capitals, as well as dozens of smaller cities, receive power from regional stand-alone systems normally supplied by undersized diesel generators.

Towards the end of 1990, the government launched an important initiative to improve energy sector planning under the coordination of the Ministry of Infrastructure by setting up the Energy Matrix Commission (CRRME) which assesses energy sector strategies, policies for energy pricing, energy conservation and the environment and investment planning and related policies regarding major supply sectors, such as electric power, oil, gas, alcohol, coal and biomass. Energy policy initiatives in the 1990s were a part of Brazil's macroeconomic stabilization efforts to reduce the overall public sector deficit. The objective was to reduce the energy sector's claim on scarce public sector resources, which accounted for a significant share of total investment.

On 9 November 1995, the Brazilian Congress amended the Brazilian constitution, authorizing the Brazilian government to contract with any state or privately owned company to carry out activities related to the upstream and downstream segments of the Brazilian oil and natural gas sector. The main goal of opening up the oil sector was to increase oil production to reduce dependence on oil imports and eventually to achieve self-sufficiency. This amendment eliminated government-granted monopoly. The amendment was implemented by the adoption of the Oil Law, which revoked the country's initial Oil Law of 1953. The new Law also created a National Petroleum Agency (Agencia Nacional do Petroleo, ANP) charged with issuing tenders, granting concessions for domestic and foreign companies and monitoring the activities of the oil sector including establishing rights to explore for and develop oil and natural gas in Brazil

In July 1997 the Brazilian government approved the full text of the Brazilian

Petroleum Investment Law that limits Brazilian Treasury holdings in its national oil company PetroBras to 23 per cent. The new Law defines a new energy policy with the creation of the ANP, the National Council for Energy Policy (CNPE) and a presidential advisory council on integrated energy policy matters. Brazil's national environmental policy encourages the use of renewable power sources. Procel, the Brazilian program for energy conservation, was launched in 1995. The objectives of Procel are to promote the rational utilization of electricity and to secure an overall reduction in costs and investment needs.

In April 2000, a ten-year expansion plan (Plano Decenal de Expansao, PDE 2000–9) which outlines the growth of the public companies operating in the generation, transmission and distribution of electricity was added to the National Electric Energy Plan. This ten-year plan is used as a basic reference for setting the priorities of work in progress and corresponding investments in expanding the power systems and to indicate which projects shall be put to bid to guarantee continual increases in power supply for the country.

The 2001 drought induced electricity supply shortages led to an eight-month power rationing program to avoid black-outs. The energy shortage was blamed on lack of government planning, underinvestment in the energy sector and a severe drought that lowered reservoirs to alarmingly low water levels. The impact of the 2001 electricity crisis is still the greatest threat to Brazil's economic recovery. The crisis raised inflation because the government increased electricity prices to restore the financial capacity of power companies. This crisis has also raised questions on diversifying Brazil's electricity supply mix from its dependence on hydroelectricity as its main source.

A key determinant of Brazil's energy policy is its linkage with its macroeconomic stabilization program to fight inflation, to reduce public deficit by reducing the dependence of the energy sector on scarce public resources, which is needed in its stabilization program to reduce the inequality and dealing with issues of alleviating poverty. Brazil started with its program of energy transition in the mid-1990s. In conjunction with the creation of the National Council for Energy Policy in the late 1990s, the government has provided a basis for reducing the intervention of the Federal Government in the energy sector, expansion of natural gas supply and encouragement of greater participation of the private sector. The important policy features include liberalization of energy prices, institutional reforms, privatization and promotion of private investment.

Energy price liberalization

As of 1990, Brazil's energy prices did not reflect its economic costs. The domestic price level for liquid fuels was generally at or above border parity, but the structure of petroleum product prices was distorted, leading to economic subsidies of US $1.1 billion to consumers in 1989. Natural gas found it hard to compete with subsidized fuels despite its low cost and environmental advantages. The price of ethanol/ alcohol was close to the LRMC, but a substantial implicit economic subsidy of US $1.8 billion in 1989 existed due to the difference between ethanol/ alcohol's LRMC and the economic cost of gasoline, its close substitute.

In the petroleum sector, distortions in the price structure fostered an increased consumption of alcohol, diesel and LPG. Brazil embarked on a policy of manufacturing alcohol vehicles, greater dieselization of the truck fleet and increased imports of LPG. Low fuel oil and LPG prices made it difficult for natural gas to compete. Greater consumption of diesel and alcohol necessitated refinery investments to increase the yield of diesel and the search for suitable export markets to sell growing gasoline surpluses. Brazil had weathered an energy crisis in 2001 and suffered persistently weak or negative economic growth during 2002.

The low level of electricity prices affected the power sector's self-financing capability and forced the government to contribute increasing resources from its overstretched budget or risk underinvestment. The deteriorating financial situation of the sector became incapable of mobilizing the required resources for its development, which in turn imposed an increasing burden on the government's fiscal resources and aggravated Brazil's macroeconomic problems through higher public investment, debt and a larger public sector deficit.

The Energy Matrix completed in 1991 under the auspices of the Ministry of Infrastructure and the subsequent reform efforts in the 1990s started the energy price liberalization in the late 1990s. Early in 2003 the government opened Brazil's market to refined product imports and linked domestic prices to the fluctuation of international prices through a price trigger mechanism. Competing fuel prices including natural gas are close to international levels. However, in August 2003 the government reinstated oil price controls, ordering the ANP to curb hikes in oil products' prices, particularly that of LPG, used in Brazil mainly for cooking.

Power tariff reforms in Brazil are linked to liberalization of the electricity market and are still evolving. Some of the areas slated for reform are the overhaul of the wholesale energy market (MAE) including an end to its self-regulation and putting it under the control of national regulator (ANEEL), restructuring the Mines and Energy Ministry to strengthen its role in policy setting, replace postage stamp transmission pricing with distance-based tariffs encouraging industrial users to become 'free' customers through the gradual elimination of industrial tariff subsidies and rethinking the valour normative system of caps on purchased power prices that distributors can pass through in retail sales.

The 2001 drought induced electricity supply shortage forced the administration to implement an energy rationing program for eight months from June 2001 and to adopt a command and control approach to holding down power costs and retail tariffs to fight inflation. Following the end of restrictions in March 2002, Brazil found itself facing a power glut. This pushed many electricity companies deep into debt and has reduced incentives for companies to begin construction of thermoelectric power plants.

In July 2003 Brazilian energy minister put forth a new model for the electricity sector with the goals of ensuring reliable supply, stabilizing prices to consumers and attracting long-term investment to the sector. One of the proposed reforms includes pooling cheaper hydroelectricity prices with more expensive thermoelectric plants (natural gas). By pooling the various sources, Brazil hopes to reduce the electricity tariffs and to ensure power is purchased from the newly constructed thermal plants which are yet to be fully amortized.

Regulation and institutional reforms

After decades of PetroBras state monopoly, Brazil's petroleum and gas industry entered a new phase in 1995 when the Constitutional Amendment No. 9 of 1995 abolished its exclusivity for basic activities in the industry. A Hydrocarbon Law was passed in 1997 to open the sector to private participation and competition. This Law also created the ANP, the Hydrocarbon Sector Regulatory Agency to regulate the sector. The structure of the new institutional framework was finalized in 1998. It was given wide-reaching powers in regulating, contracting and controlling the petroleum and natural gas sector activities.

Since opening up the oil industry in 1998 ANP announced that more than 92 per cent of the nation's sedimentary basins were to be put up for bidding by other oil companies. This marked the end of PetroBras' petroleum monopoly. Majority private ownership is allowed in all areas of the natural gas business. Since opening up the oil industry ANP has held five bidding rounds as of 2003. The first round of tendering for exploration, development and production of petroleum and natural gas was announced by the ANP in June 1999. PetroBras won five of the 12 blocks. In the successive three bids PetroBras won many bids in partnership with foreign companies.

In mid-2002 diminished interest was shown by oil and gas companies in the ANP's fourth round of exploration licenses. Industry officials cited a shift in focus to onshore licenses, the paucity of significant discoveries on previously awarded acreage and Brazil's burdensome fiscal regime. Companies that won fourth-round licenses will invest US $1billion in the next nine years. Once again, PetroBras acquired the largest number of licenses in a Brazilian sale—eight blocks, including four in partnerships. However, one highlight of the fourth round was the debut of a number of foreign companies, notably independents—Australia's BHP Billiton Ltd. (Melbourne), Oman's Partex Oil and Gas (Holdings) Corporation, Devon Energy and Newfield Exploration Company (Houston). Cementing its participation in Brazil's exploration and development scene with a successful bid was a new Brazilian independent, Starfish Oil and Gas Co. which acquired 100 per cent of Block BT-REC-7.[64]

The 2003 fifth round did not attract the interest from oil companies as ANP envisaged. PetroBras was the main bidder with no oil majors' participation. Lack of interest of oil companies was attributed to uncertainties about taxes, lack of recent commercial discoveries and the geological challenge of oil recovery in deep waters.

In addition to opening up exploration and development to the private sector, the government also sold 28.5 per cent stake in PetroBras in August 2000. In January 2002 the company lost its monopoly on importing oil and refined products. However, PetroBras continues to be the largest petroleum company in Brazil. As of 2002, of 13 crude oil refineries in Brazil, PetroBras owns 11 of them as comprising almost 99 per cent of refining capacity. It plans to invest US $5.5 billion by 2007 to increase domestic refining capacity by 300,000 b/d to 1.9 million b/d and to upgrade many of its refineries.

Like the NOCs in China and India, PetroBras aims to become a transnational corporation and an important regional player and is making efforts to evolve from an oil company into an energy company. PetroBras in its ten-year plan outlines three major objectives—first, to consolidate and maintain its leadership in the oil and derivatives market, second, to establish a natural gas market in Brazil and third, to expand its international activities to diversify its risks and export its technology and services. It expects to finance two-thirds of its US $3 billion annual investments from its balance sheet and the rest to be raised by project finance and loans. It has signed 33 joint ventures with 20 companies in E&P.

PetroBras' overseas production target is set at 300,000 b/d by 2005 and is expected to come from its operations in West Africa, Gulf of Mexico, Bolivia, Argentina, Venezuela and Colombia. It holds 35 per cent of the equity in Bolivia's natural gas operations. It purchased assets in Argentina in mid-2002, including a controlling interest in Perez Companc and Petrolera Santa fe. It holds 70 per cent of equity in two of Bolivia's refineries.

The government's efforts in the 1990s to restructure the power sector included renegotiation of energy companies' debt in 1993, enacting constitutional amendments in 1995, introducing the possibility of direct private investment in Brazil's power market and creating in 1999 a new regulatory entity, ANEEL, responsible for regulating Brazil's electric power sector. In 1999 a federal law defined the new legal framework for the sector. Since

---

64. *Brazil, International Petroleum Encyclopedia* (2003), p.57–60

1999 ANEEL has extended its authority to inspect economic-financial aspects, quality of service and technical generation standards of all utilities. It also consolidated the decentralization of the various existing activities, allocating them to the newly created state agencies. In 2000 there were a total of 64 companies operating concessions (most of them private) to provide electricity distribution services to nearly 47 million households across the country. These companies operate under the jurisdiction of the Ministry of Mines and Energy whose ANEEL controls and regulates all power companies in Brazil.

Since 1995, 70 per cent of the concessions for power distribution in Brazil were transferred to private companies. However, 80 per cent of the Brazilian generation capacity and 95 per cent of the transmission network remain government-owned. The state-owned Electrobras executes the national electric power policy. This includes coordinating and supervising the expansion and operation of the generation, T&D systems, which are critical to the power sector given the large number of power companies in Brazil. Federal utility Electrobras controls about half of the country's installed capacity and most of the large transmission lines. In addition to executing the power policy, Electrobras finances the expansion of the power sector, making it the second largest agency for long-term financing in the country.

Electrobras is also a minority stakeholder in the remaining power utilities that are controlled by their respective state governments and by one city government. It holds 50 per cent of the capital of Itaipu Binacional (the world's largest hydropower plant, co-owned with Paraguay), controls Electrobras Termonuclear SA (Electronuclear), the Brazilian nuclear power entity created in May 1997 as a successor to the previous nuclear energy company, Nuclen and funds most of the energy research conducted at the Electric Energy Research Centre (CEPEL), in addition to operating a number of federal energy programs.[65]

While demand for electricity in Brazil rose 45 per cent in the 1990s, generation capacity grew by only 28 per cent in the same period. This mismatch was further exacerbated by a lack of investment in non-hydroelectric power sources. As a result, the country faced a severe energy shortage in 2001 when rainfall in the country was significantly below expectations.

To meet the country's energy needs, the government implemented an energy rationing program in 2001–2. The rationing called for consumers to lower their electricity consumption by 20 per cent in certain regions. The government also set up an emergency plan to increase the electricity supply by private sector investments. Electrobras' ten-year plan (2001–10) estimated a total investment of US $34 billion to be mobilized to finance electric power projects to meet the growing demand for electricity. The plan

---

65. EIA, DOE, *An Energy Overview of Brazil* (Washington DC, July 2003)

included construction of several hydro and thermoelectric power plants, and the expansion of transmission lines. These measures aimed not only at increasing supply but also at reducing the domestic dependence on hydroelectric generation sources.

The results were mixed. While there was an increase in generation capacity and diversification away from hydroelectric sources, power consumption was slow to recover following the lifting of the rationing in 2002. With resumption of rainfall, thermoelectric plants constructed during this time remained idle because of their higher production costs in favour of fully amortized and cheaper hydropower plants.

Following the lessons learned in 2001–2, the Brazilian government in July 2003 unveiled a new model for the country's electricity sector, with goals of ensuring reliable supply, stabilizing prices for consumers and attracting long-term investment to the sector. This new model was introduced in March 2004 with the creation of two energy trading markets—a regulated pool which buys power from generators and shares the cost between distributors at set prices and a free market environment where distributors and generators can negotiate their own contracts. The model restored power to the Federal Ministry of Mines and Energy (MME) to plan and tender power generation concessions, a role that the country's independent energy regulatory agency ANEEL delegated to Electrobras.

Three new bodies were created—the Company of Energy Research (Empresa de Pesquisa Energetica, EPE), responsible for long-term research and planning of the power sector, the Chamber of Electric Energy Commercialization (Camara de Comercializaco de Energia Electrica, CCEE), a body that will oversee trading in the pool, replacing the electric wholesaler Mercado Atacadista de Energia Electrica and the Electric Sector Monitoring Committee (Comite de Monitorramento de Sector Electico, CMSE), responsible for overseeing the security of supply in Brazil. Finally, the plan calls for electricity pricing to be determined by pooling cheaper hydroelectricity with more expensive natural gas based plants. By pooling the various sources, the government hopes to reduce electricity tariffs and to ensure power to be purchased from the newly constructed thermal plants. All of Brazil's 64 distributors will buy power at a single price generated from the new pricing formula.[66]

The new electricity model establishes two markets for the sale of power—a free market and a regulated market. In the free market, generating companies will be permitted to sell power directly to 'free consumers' entities that consume more than 3 MW as well as with traders. The generating companies and the free consumers will enter into bilateral contracts with limited oversight from the regulatory entities. Contracts can be negotiated

66. EIA, Brazil, *Country Analysis Brief* (Washington DC, August 2004)

for price, volume or term. Free consumers can purchase either through bilateral contracts or through distribution companies. Distribution companies are forced to purchase electricity in the regulated markets. The new model establishes a pool concept whereby generators sell into the pool and distributors contract to purchase power out of the pool at a market price. The pool is governed by an auction coordinated by CCEE.

On an annual basis, distribution companies will determine their power needs for the next five years. The distribution companies will be required to contract 100 per cent of their projected power demand. Generating companies will sell into the pool and will be required to sign contracts with all of the distribution companies in an amount equal to the distribution company's proportional share in the pool. The end result is that each of the distribution companies will have the same cost of power when purchased from the pool in each auction.

MME has established two sets of auctions—those for 'old' power and another for 'new' power. 'Old' power includes power from generating plants built before 2000. The majority of these plants has been fully amortized and thus has a lower cost base. 'New' power includes plants built after 2000 and those plants that are yet to be built.

Brazil held its first energy auction on 7 December 2004 of 'old' power. The auction sold enough power to meet 99.7 per cent of the demand of the distributors with realized prices significantly lower than the predicted price of R$70 /MW. The final prices in the auction were R$57.5 for deliveries in 2005, R$67.33 for 2006 and R$75.46 for 2007. The auction had a disproportionate effect on power generation—public companies with amortized costs and lower debt loads fared better than privately held companies with higher debt loads and acquisition costs. Following the auction, the stock prices for many of the generating companies fell significantly while the stocks of distribution companies rose.[67]

As of 2005, the reaction to the new power model has been mixed. Many foreign and private companies see the new regulations as the government consolidating its hold on Brazil's electricity sector, where generation is dominated by state-owned utilities. As the Brazilian economy grows, its power needs are expected to more than double, from 345 Terrawatt (TWh) hours in 2002 to 611 TWH in 2020 to 808 TWH in 2030. Just to keep supply and demand in balance through 2020, Brazil will need to finance over $80 billion between 2005 and 2020.

---

67. Susana Vivares and Jan Weiss, 'The Power of Brazil and Mexico', *International Power and Utilites Finance Review* (UK, Euro-money Year Books, 2005–6)

Privatization and private investment

In parallel with government efforts in the 1990s to restructure the energy sector, create regulatory agencies and define the new framework for the sector, Brazil started the privatization process in the energy sector. The Federal Government offered incentives to the states by anticipating the revenues to be realized from privatization. As a result of the sale of state distribution companies, by 2001, 65 per cent of all electricity distribution was in the private sector. Losses in the power distribution sector diminished by 9 per cent during 1995–9 while productivity jumped 136 per cent as distributing companies, as a group, moved from a 3 per cent return on assets in 1993 to a 4.3 per cent return in 1999.

In the power sector major multinationals have entered the market, such as France's Electricite de France, Spain's Endesa SA and Iberdrola SA and the US based AES Corporation, Enron Corporation and Reliant Energy. However, the privatization experience in distribution was not reproduced with electric power generation companies. Only four generation companies were sold from September 1996 to October 1999—Cacheira Dourada in the state of Goias, Gerasul in the state of Santa Catarina and Paranapanema and Tiete in the state of Sao Paulo.

The federal government lost momentum as the political opposition to privatization in the sector mounted. The 1999 devaluation of Brazil's currency and the economic crisis slowed the process before it picked up again in 2001.

The 2003 new electricity model discussed in the foregoing section seemed to have benefited the distribution companies undergoing major financial restructuring through a recapitalization program since several distribution companies defaulted on loans in 2001–2. If stock values of distribution companies continue to rise in future auctions, the credit quality of distribution companies could improve. The government's plan to auction nine licenses to build 3,400 km of transmission lines to provide universal access to power could interest private investors due to the lower construction costs and shorter amortization periods required to pay back debt. However, the new electricity model and its first two auctions are yet to convince private investors in generation regarding the auction process and their impact on securing adequate rates of return on their investment.

In the oil and gas sector, new concessions have allowed new investors including Texaco Inc., Royal Dutch Shell, Agip, Exxon Mobil Corporation, Repsol Ypf Amerada-Hess, Kerr McGee and Unocal winning bids to explore for oil and gas. Gas distribution concessions have been granted to private investors and are regulated by each state.

Several US companies have been active in Brazil's energy sector privatization. Companies such as Amerada Hess, British Petroleum (BP), Amoco,

Enron, Shell, Exxon (Esso), Kerr McGee, Texaco and Unocal have all participated in one way or another, by acquiring stocks in operating companies, or obtaining the right to explore in the petroleum sector.

After two 1995 laws restructured the industry and laid the groundwork for private investment, net direct investment flows to Brazil rose from US $4.9 in 1995 to $28 billion in 1998. Between 1995 and 1998, with net FDI flows totalling $59.8 billion Brazil was the second leading recipient of FDI after China. Private investors in 2002 owned 26 per cent of electricity generation, compared with 0.3 per cent in 1995 and 64 per cent of distribution, compared with 2.3 per cent in 1995.[68]

The 1988 constitutional distinction between national and foreign capital constitutes a denial of national treatment to foreign investors. The constitution also permits the Brazilian government to offer temporary protection and benefits to national companies in the procurement of goods and services by the government. The constitutional provision also gives the state the right to intervene to protect the domestic industry's market share. Foreign investors also point to other weaknesses such as onerous compulsory licensing provisions, stringent local working requirements and explicit authority for parallel importation.

Brazil's energy market transition: Status

Brazil's energy market transition since the 1990s has been a key feature of its macroeconomic stabilization program. A key need of Brazil's macroeconomic policy since the 1990s has been to reduce overall public sector deficit. The three-year IMF agreement (1998–2001) required Brazil to cut public spending to ensure a public sector surplus of 3.5 per cent of GDP by 2002. Given that Brazil's energy sector exerted a major claim on Brazil's public resources, the government took measures to privatize its energy sector and attract private investment. Box 5.6 summarizes the status of Brazil's energy market transition.

Box 5.6 Brazil: Energy Market Transition Status as of 2004

Energy Pricing

- Oil prices on average reflect international levels with exception of LPG
- Natural gas prices regulated
- Regulated electricity tariffs reflect cost under open-ended regulated price contract system

Regulation

- 1997 Petroleum Investment Law created the ANP to regulate the oil and gas sector

68. IEA, OECD, *Quarterly Statistics* (Paris, 2002)

- ANEEL, the regulatory entity, was created in 1999 and is entrusted with responsibilities to regulate Brazil's electric power companies, to enforce market competition and to ensure compliance with concession contract conditions
- Wholesale Energy Market (MAE) established to gradually replace the open-ended regulated price supply contracts from 2002. Generators, customers, retailers and resellers to negotiate PPAs through bilateral contracts with clearly stipulated prices, amounts and duration. Additional power requirements and surpluses to be traded on the new spot market
- Following the 2001 electricity shortage caused by severe drought and escalating spot prices, a new model in July 2003 created a regulated and free energy trading market
- In March 2004 the new electricity model came into effect. The new model establishes a pool concept for electricity pricing in the regulated market
- On 7 December 2004, Brazil held its first energy auction of 'old' power

Corporatization/ Privatization

- The 1997 Brazilian Petroleum Investment Law limits the government's share in the state oil company, PetroBras, to 23 per cent; 28 per cent of government's share in PetroBras sold in 2001
- ANP opened up 92 per cent of Brazil's hydrocarbon prospects since 1999. Between 1999 and 2002, four rounds of bids inviting foreign investors in oil and gas E&P are held. Several multinational oil companies in joint venture with PetroBras have entered Brazil
- Brazil's state oil company, PetroBras, is transforming into transnational Corporation with overseas investments in Latin America, Gulf of Mexico and Africa.
- By 2002, in the power sector 26 per cent of generation and 65 per cent of distribution are privatized
- New transmission lines are also being constructed by new privately owned companies

Private Investment

- Between 1995 and 1999, with US $59.5 billion net FDI Brazil was the second lead recipient of direct private investment
- Several multinational oil, gas, power and service companies have entered Brazil in the 1990s.

Brazil's experience illustrates that the specifics of each country's situation should guide reforms in its energy sector, particularly with regard to privatization in the power sector. Brazil followed the British model of separating distribution and transmission from generation, which would then be privatized. Unlike the UK, Brazil's generation is predominantly hydroelectric with huge upfront/ sunk costs and negligible marginal/ operational costs. Given that the gas network and domestic market for gas are still to be developed, even the long-run average cost of efficient combined cycle-gas power stations are higher than the amortized hydropower plants. Brazil's power sector with a large share of hydro system with unpredictable rainfall would make private investment even in the base load coal-fired and/ or peaking combined cycle gas turbines unprofitable without special reserve/ emergency capacity payments. Consequently, the private ownership of generation in Brazil has brought few efficiency gains. The new electricity model of 2003 allowing pooling of 'old' and 'new' power to price power is yet to convince private investors that they would receive adequate return on their investments.

Following liberalization of the hydrocarbons sector, foreign oil companies have been allowed to participate since 1999. However, obstacles to attracting international companies to Brazil's oil sector remain. PetroBras, the National Oil Company, is the only company making significant oil and gas discoveries and continues to be a major oil and gas producer

Future directions

Brazil made its decision to shift to the market in the 1990s. Privatization and promotion of private investment increased net FDI.The changes benefited Brazil. Hyperinflation exceeding 1000 per cent annually was brought under control. The anti-inflationary monetary policy, a flexible exchange rate and an austere fiscal policy produced budget surpluses, if interest payments on the national debt are excluded. But with the debt of the country's public sector having risen from 34 per cent of gross domestic product in 1997 to 54 per cent in 2002, the burden of paying interest and principal on the debt would continue to rise and would put pressure on creditors to accept debt restructuring.

By 2002 Brazil suffered a fourth year of economic stagnation with increasing unemployment and inequality where the richest tenth of the population controls 47 per cent of the national income, compared with 34 per cent in India and 31 per cent in the United States.

The election of Luiz Inacio Lula de Silva (Lula) in October 2002 as president of Brazil marked a return of the left to power after 38 years. It seemed that Lula's populist message had finally resonated beyond the labour unions, landless peasants and urban poor who have long been his political base. Promising a sharp change of track from president Fernando Enrique Cardoso's eight-year experiment with free trade and free market reforms, Lula has outlined a populist agenda that calls for new spending on social programs and promises millions of jobs.

Brazil's presidential election represents a final unravelling of the expected benefits of adopting free market and free trade policies that promise faster economic growth for developing countries. Many analysts portrayed the election of the leftist candidate as president as the most dramatic manifestation of a building backlash against free market policies in the developing world. It raised investors' nervousness about the political future of the country. Contrary to conventional wisdom, six months after assuming the office of president in January 2003, the leftist Lula has not thus far produced significant changes in economic policies. He has pledged to abide by the terms of US $30 billion IMF emergency loan to stabilize Brazil's economy. The new government has accepted that the state's role is not to manage companies but to plan, stimulate development with incentives and, if necessary, provide funding in partnership with the private sector.

However, in the energy sector the new government is showing signs of reversing some of the privatization policies of the previous administration since taking office in January 2003. The new government is attempting to reshape its policy for new investment in the oil and gas industry to generate employment for the Brazilian population. The government now requires companies which are awarded oil and natural gas leases to allocate a percentage of their investments to purchase goods and services provided by Brazilian firms. In July 2003, PetroBras launched a bidding round for the building of P-54 platform that requires between 60 and 75 per cent of the parts to be constructed locally. Unlike the previous administration, the new government wants hydroelectricity to remain Brazil's main source of power.

The main concern for the Brazilian energy sector under the new government include resolving the fundamental issues around guarantees to be provided to private sector partners and the terms of the bid process. The government's policies also need to focus on issues of price controls, simplification of the tax structure, investment incentives, upgrading the electricity sector and Brazil's role as a key player in the volatile political and economic scene. After a decade of economic sector reforms, Brazil is trying to address energy sector issues under the IBRD Energy Sector Reform Investment Loan in 2002 of US $454.6 million. The loan is expected to benefit Brazil by improving the investment climate and promoting economic growth by supporting reforming power tariffs, regulatory changes and expansion of access to power. In 2003 Brazil secured from the WB a second loan of US $12.1 million for technical assistance in energy sector for market development and regulation and long-term expansion planning to provide 2.5 million poor rural households with electricity.[69]

Future directions in energy market transition are closely linked with Brazil's macroeconomic adjustment efforts. Although Brazil is a country with great potential, 50 million people (30 per cent of Brazil's population) live below the poverty line. Brazil is a country like China and India with social inequities. Staying on the course of energy market transition depends on the success of the government in careful balancing of the state's role to fulfil its populist mandate to create better opportunities for its 50 million poor and pursuing sound economic policies to increase economic growth.

---

69. *The World Bank Annual Reports* (2002, 2003)

JORDAN

Jordan depends more than 95 per cent on energy imports for meeting its domestic energy requirements. Since the oil price increases in the 1970s, Jordan vigorously pursued a policy to explore and exploit oil, gas, oil shale and renewable domestic energy resources to decrease its reliance on imported oil. Despite its success in promoting oil exploration by a number of international oil companies in the 1980s, no significant oil resources were discovered. Some gas discovery was made in 1987. Jordan does possess a significant quantity of oil shale resources, possibly as much as 40 billion tons.

Macro-sector context

Jordan's economy is vulnerable to changes in world oil prices because income, employment and domestic investment are directly related to income levels in the neighbouring oil-producing countries in the region. Jordan experienced high rates of growth in energy consumption. Between 1975 and 1984, total energy consumption grew at 13.7 per cent to reach 2.8 mtoe in 1984. High growth rates of energy and electricity consumption prior to 1985 were a reflection of high rates of economic growth, rapid population growth, rising incomes stimulated by remittances from Jordanians abroad, increased public access to electricity; the establishment and growth of large energy intensive industries such as cement, potash and phosphate and the expansion of the service sector.[70]

The rapid decline in oil prices and the subsequent slowdown in the regional economy beginning in 1983 affected Jordan's economic growth prospects. Coupled with lower rates of economic growth since 1984, the government's pricing and conservation policies have reduced the rate of growth in energy consumption drastically to 2.5 per cent since 1988.

The future rate of growth of energy and electricity demand is influenced by the overall GDP and sector growth prospects and government's energy market liberalization policies. Jordan's demand for energy is expected to grow between 3 and 5 per cent per year to 2020 given that despite tensions in the Middle East, Jordan's real GDP grew at 2.8 per cent in 2003 and is projected to recover to 5.3 per cent in 2005. Much of the recent growth stems from expansion in the country's manufacturing sector. This has been driven in part by the US-Jordan Free Trade Area agreement, which was ratified by the US Senate in September 2001.[71]

Jordan has no significant oil resources of its own and relies on Iraqi oil for

---

70. WB, *Jordan: Energy Sector Study* (Washington DC, 1990)

71. US Energy Information Administration, DOE, *Jordan: Country Analysis Brief* (March 2003)

nearly all of its needs. In 2003 Jordan imported around 107,000 b/d. The March 2003 Iraq war caused major changes in Jordan's energy supply situation. Prior to 2003, Jordan's oil imports from Iraq were permitted by the UN under a special dispensation from the general UN sanctions regime on Iraq. In the wake of the war, Jordan had to seek alternative sources of supply. Kuwait, Saudi Arabia and the United Arab Emirates were Jordan's main oil suppliers in the last nine months of 2003. Supplies have come in mainly by tanker, through Jordan's port of Aqaba. Exports of goods to neighbours Iraq and Saudi Arabia also are important to Jordan's economy and growth in regional exports is helping to further Jordan's economic recovery.

Energy sector institutions and policy

Following the oil price increases in the 1970s, the share of oil in overall import of goods to Jordan rose from about 5 per cent in 1973 to about 22 per cent in 1984. Concerned about the impact of future increases in demand for energy on Jordan's balance of payments, the government set up the Ministry of Energy and Mineral Resources (MEMR) which is responsible for formulating energy policy with the objectives of reducing the cost of energy to the economy and to reduce Jordan's dependence on imported oil.

Established in 1984, the MEMR evolved through the 1990s and is responsible for overseeing the energy sector, defining and implementing policy, fixing tariffs and regulating the energy and electricity sectors. In the 1990s MEMR's responsibility included encouraging domestic and foreign private investment through BOO and BOT arrangements in power generation. Private investment was promoted in power generation and distribution, refining capacity expansion, oil and gas E&P and investment for exploiting renewable sources of energy.

Jordan's energy companies, both public and private, are under MEMR's oversight. These include the Natural Resources Authority (NRA) for mineral and hydrocarbons exploration and development, the Jordan Petroleum Refinery Company (JPRC) responsible for refining transport, storage and distribution of petroleum products in Jordan, Jordan National Electric Company (NEPCO), Jordan Electric Power Company (JEPCO) and Irbid District Electrical Company (IRBID) for electricity generation and distribution. NEPCO also operates the bulk power network in Jordan. The transmission system is structured on the north-south axis of Jordan. The distribution systems are served off this system at 132 kV.

Jordan's energy policy in the 1980s focused on first, the development of domestic energy resources through identification of exploration for oil and gas and exploitation of economically feasible renewable energy resources such as solar and wind energy. Second, the improvement of energy efficiency and encouraging energy conservation to reduce oil imports, to reduce pollution and to defer additional investments in energy production. Third, the diversification of fuel use from oil to other fuel sources. Fourth, the adoption of economic energy pricing policies and finally, protection of the environment from toxic emissions.

Following the fall in oil prices in 1986, the Jordanian economy faltered as a result of the decline in exports to the Arab oil producing countries of the Middle East, decline in remittances of its migrant workers working in the oil exporting countries and in financial assistance from other Arab countries. The combination of these forces led to a major decline in per capita income by 37 per cent in 1991 to US $1,000 over the 1982 level. These developments led the government to embark on a major economic reform program to address Jordan's macroeconomic imbalances, remove distortions in the trade balance and to promote economic growth by market-based economic reform to attract private investment.

Reforming Jordan's energy sector[72]

As part of its economic reform program, the government embarked on energy sector pricing, institutional, regulatory and investment reforms. The objectives of the reform process were first, to supply efficient energy reflecting cost; second, to ensure that energy sector ceases to be a burden on government's budget by commercializing the sector to mobilize financial resources required for upgrade and expansion; third, to establish an enabling regulatory environment to promote competition and to attract private investment to the energy sector.

To implement these reform objectives, the sector reform program pursued policies to attract private investment, to restructure and privatize government owned utilities and companies to make them financially viable commercial corporations, to implement a regulatory regime that provides transparent, stable and objective ground rules for all participants in the sector and to promote environmental and safety standards, energy efficiency and loss reduction.

Jordan adopted energy pricing policies to reflect cost and improve efficiency by removing subsidies to petroleum products and power. Prior to the 2003 Iraq war, Jordan's oil imports from Iraq were significantly below market prices. The weighted average prices of petroleum products reflect import parity. However, some oil products such as LPG and fuel oil for electricity production continued to be subsidized.

Cost-recovery pricing of electricity vary with the level of consumption and

---

72. WB, *Jordan Energy Sector Study* (Washington DC, 9 February 1990), Report No. 7984–J0, Washington DC, 9 February. The author managed the preparation of this study.

time of usage. Cross-subsidization of electricity tariffs of about 10 per cent for small industry, 20–40 per cent for water pumping and agriculture and over 90 per cent for street lighting continued in the 1990s. The level of subsidies for oil products have come down. Differences in rates based on time of usage help lower investment in building peak-load capacity.

The government's policy to encourage foreign oil companies to explore for oil and gas attracted several companies in the 1990s. In parallel, NRA continued its oil and gas exploration activities in its own areas where foreign oil companies were not active. NRA made some small oil and gas discoveries. Following the launching of the reform program in 1992, Jordan restructured its NRA. In October 1995 Jordan set up the state-owned National Petroleum Company (NPC) to handle upstream oil and gas exploration and development. In mid-1999 NPC divested its oil-drilling operation, oil and gas exploration and development, which now operated as Petra Drilling Company.

NPC is also active in natural gas activity. It developed its gas field at Risha, which has modest reserves of 230 billion cubic feet (bcf). The current output of 30 million cubic feet per day (mmcf/d) from the Risha field is used to fuel one power plant nearby in the eastern desert, which generates about 10 per cent of Jordan's electricity. Jordan has also signed an agreement with the Egyptian state-owned firm EGAS to import 100 mmcf/d of natural gas from 2003. EGAS was awarded a contract by the government of Jordan in August 2002 for construction of the Jordanian section of the gas pipeline, from Aqaba to power plants near Amman which was completed in mid-2003, allowing gas delivery to begin to one power plant in Aqaba. In August 2003 Jordan began imports of natural gas from Egypt.

The power sector reform program included unbundling of the power sector, institutional/ regulatory reform, privatization and promotion of private investment through IPPs. Given the already active private sector in electricity distribution where the private sector holds 77 per cent of JEPCO's share and 11 per cent of IDECO's share, the reform fosters 100 per cent private participation through sale of NEPCO's share 23 per cent and 89 per cent in JEPCO and IDECO respectively.

The power sector reform program launched in 1992–3 was planned to be implemented in three phases. The first phase started in April 1994 was completed in September 1996 and included amendment of the general electricity law to allow for the required restructuring and privatization. Jordan Electric Authority (JEA) was converted into a public shareholding company under the Companies Law. JEA, the state utility, owned the two main generating facilities, namely the Zarqa power plant, with a capacity of 400 MW and the Aqaba power plant, with a capacity of 650 MW, main transmission networks and distribution facilities. The new company called the National Electric Power Company (NEPCO), wholly owned by the government, retained the ownership and control of the national grid, existing generation plants and JEA's distribution assets. The corporatized NEPCO is no longer subject to the civil service regulations and is operating on a commercial basis.

The second phase which started in 1997 focused on unbundling of NEPCO into three or more companies by separating NEPCO's generation, T&D operations.

The government established a power sector Regulatory Commission under the General Electricity Law in 1999. The Commission is accountable to the Prime Minister. The Regulatory Commission's responsibilities include the issue and enforcement of licenses, protection of rights and interests of the consumers, establishment of performance standards, approval of investment programs and electricity tariff design and review.

The third phase started in May 2000 when Jordan awarded its first contract for an IPP to Tractebel of Belguim. The plant will have a capacity of 450 MW and will be located near Amman. It is to be fuelled with natural gas from Egypt. Jordan's reform program in the third phase involves completing the unbundling of NEPCO, whereby it will maintain ownership of transmission assets and privatize its existing generation and distribution assets.

Jordan's basic plan for the future of its electric utility system involves having NEPCO maintain ownership of transmission assets, but relying on private power generation and privatizing existing generation assets. NEPCO's distribution subsidiary, the CEDC, is to be privatized along with the Central Electric Generating Company (CEGC). Under a decision adopted by the Jordanian cabinet in March 2004, CEDC will be sold off, along with a 60 per cent stake in CEGC. NEPCO will also divest its share in two other private distribution companies—JEPCO in the Amman area and IDECO covering the area around Irbid. Box 5.7 summarizes the status of energy market transition in Jordan.

Box 5.7 Jordan Energy Market Transition as of 2004

Energy Pricing

- Weighted average price of petroleum products reflect import parity
- Subsidies on heavy fuel oil and LPG continue at a lower rate
- Electricity tariffs reflect cost; but cross-subsidies to agriculture low income consumers.

Regulation and Institutional Reforms

- Amendment of General Electricity Law in 1996 to allow for restructuring and privatization.
- Established Power Sector Regulatory Commission accountable to the Prime Minister. The functions of the regulatory commission include the issue and enforcement of licenses, protection of the rights and interests of the consumers, establishment of the performance standards, approval of investment programs and establishment and review of electricity tariffs.

Commercialization/ Corporatization

- Restructuring of NRA to set up state-owned NPC in October 1995 to handle upstream oil and gas exploration and development
- NPC divests its oil drilling operation to Petra Drilling Company
- Corporatization of JEA in 1995 to form NEPCO
- Unbundling and separation of NEPCO's generation, T&D assets and functions
- NEPCO to remain a state-owned company with ownership of transmission assets and responsible for transmission operations

Privatization/ Private Investment

- Plans for privatization of NPC and NEPCO's generation and distribution operations
- All future power generation open to private investment. First IPP for 450 MW capacity signed with Tractebel of Belgium in 2000 to start generation in 2004

Jordan's power reform program encourages potential regional cooperation involving integration of individual national power transmission grids into a regional power network. Such a network would allow power companies to take advantage of differences in peak demand periods, reduce the need for (and the costs associated with) installation and maintenance of reserve power generating capacity, and provide outlets for surplus generating capacity.

The first step in regional integration, linking the Egyptian and Jordanian power grids via an underwater cable between Aqaba and Taba (across the gulf of Aqaba in Sinai), was completed in October 1998 and formally inaugurated in April 1999. Syria and Jordan too have linked their grids. The reconstruction of Iraq opens up prospects for linking the Iraqi-Jordan grids.

Future directions

In the post-Gulf war 2003 period, Jordan occupied a strategic location in the Middle East, and was at a crossroads for regional energy integration. The post-war reconstruction efforts in Iraq and settlement of Israel-Palestine conflict would facilitate Jordan's economic growth prospects and would increase its demand for energy. Until the mid-1990s, Jordan financed its energy/ power sector investments from international and bilateral development institutions, bilateral concession lending or aid and commercial loans. With changes in international development institutions' role focusing mainly on investment in social infrastructure, Jordan adapted to the liberalization wave of the 1990s by giving priority to attract private investment in the energy sector. Jordan's privatization strategy in the power sector is a mix of 'strategic sales' and 'management contracts'. The decision to use a strategic sale or a management contract for a particular transaction is made on a case-by-case basis.

Jordan's energy sector has now reached a stage where sector development requires greater comprehensive planning, more in-depth analysis, and effective regulation, coordination and monitoring of energy sector activities. At the ministerial level, major issues include the adequacy of institutional arrangements to secure alternative oil supplies and the effective coordination of MEMR and the line energy operating companies. Jordan's oil imports from Iraq since the 1991 Gulf War were permitted by the UN under a special dispensation from the general UN sanctions regime on Iraq. In December 2002 Jordan's government renewed its agreement with Iraq on oil supplies. Under the agreement, Jordan receives half of its crude oil free of charge and receives steeply discounted prices for the rest. In addition to the crude oil imports, Jordan also imports about 20,000 b/d of refined petroleum products from Iraq at discounted prices.[73] In the wake of the Iraq war in 2003, Jordan had to seek potential alternate suppliers in the Persian Gulf from Kuwait, Saudi Arabia and the United Arab Emirates to diversify its future oil supplies.

Future directions in energy market transition will be influenced by Jordan's macroeconomic policies and regional developments in the post-2003 Gulf war period. Jordan was admitted to the WTO in April 2000 after agreeing to a package of trade and investment liberalization measures, as well as improvement in protections for foreign-owned intellectual property. As of 2003 Jordan's efforts to reform its energy sector, its active role in regional power-grid linkages and its successful efforts to attract private investment have established a proven record in adapting to successful energy market transition requirements.

Nonetheless, given Jordan's geographic location, the post Iraq 2003 situation and Jordan's role in a comprehensive settlement of the Arab-Israeli conflict, regional developments influence Jordan's economic and energy market transition prospects.

EGYPT

Egypt is a net oil exporter and a rapidly growing natural gas producer. Despite declining net exports of crude oil and petroleum products in recent years, higher crude oil prices in the world market have generated increasing oil revenues. Egypt also began exports of LNG from its first terminal in January 2005, which is expected to expand in late 2005 with the completion of the second LNG export terminal. Energy will continue to play an important role in Egypt's economy in the coming years.

Egypt embarked on its economic transition in the late 1980s when its centralized economy reached a crisis point. Egypt was burdened with a bloated public sector, low productivity, rising population growth, high inflation and

73. USEIA, DOE, *Jordan, Country Analysis Brief* (April 2004)

urban overcrowding. It was unable to service its debts, the currency was in a free fall and foreign exchange reserves could barely cover the country's import needs for a month. In 1991 members of the Paris Club, an organization of donor countries, which also belong to the Organization of Economic Cooperation and Development (OECD), agreed to reduce the net present value of Egypt's official debt by 50 per cent provided Egypt complied with an IMF stabilization program.

The government embarked on an Economic Reform and Structural Adjustment Program (ERSAP) to stem the decline in the GDP growth rate and to stimulate growth. In support of the ERSAP, an IMF Stand-By Arrangement (SBA) and a WB Structural Adjustment Loan (SAL) were approved in May 1991 and June 1991 respectively. Egypt has since been in the process of implementing the economic and structural adjustment program.

Macro-sector context

The energy sector is an important base for Egyptian economic development. At the end of the second five-year plan (1991–2), energy sector accounted for 12.2 per cent of GDP, 22.2 per cent of total investment, 56.1 per cent of commodity exports, 6.8 per cent of public revenue and 1.0 per cent of total employment.[74] Egyptian development policy sought to make the most of petroleum and natural gas resources as a basis for growing industrialization and export earning capability. However, with increasing domestic energy use Egypt faced a trade-off between maximizing growth on the one hand and expanding investment in energy for domestic use and for export markets on the other.

Although Egypt is an oil exporter, tripling of Egypt's energy consumption between 1980 and 2004 and rising energy consumption needs are outrunning increases in domestic energy production. In 2004 Egypt's oil production averaged 594,000 b/d, down from a peak in 1996 of 922,000 b/d. Domestic oil consumption increased rapidly from 501,000 b/d in 1996 to 585,000 b/d in 1999 and has been relatively flat since 1999, mainly due to increased use of CNG and reductions in subsidies of petroleum products. A combination of rising domestic oil consumption and declining production resulted in reduction of exports by 40 per cent in 1999. The Egyptian government has attempted to arrest declining oil production from maturing fields by encouraging increasing exploration, enhanced oil recovery and substitution of oil by natural gas for domestic consumption.

Egypt expects that exploration activity, particularly in new areas, will

---

74. Arab Republic of Egypt: Energy Sector Assessment: Challenges for the Egyptian Energy Sector, 1995, *World Bank ESMAP Report*, Washington DC, September. The author managed this project.

discover sufficient oil in the coming years to slow the decline in oil output. A new oil discovery was reported in October 2001 by Canada's Cabre Exploration in the Gulf of Suez which tested 8,000 b/d. A larger new discovery in the Gulf of Suez was announced by BP in May 2003. A peak production of 40,000–50,000 b/d is expected from the newly discovered Saqqara field. Saqqara represents the largest new crude oil discovery in Egypt since 1989. These new oil discoveries in the Gulf of Suez could slow the fall in overall Gulf of Suez production

In the absence of further large discovery of oil to compensate for decline in production, even moderate assumptions about Egypt's economic growth and energy demand projections indicate squeezing petroleum exports and eventually even turning Egypt into a net importer of energy as early as 2007–10. Consequently, energy market transition policies raise a number of key issues in the relationship between macroeconomic performance and energy for development.

The implications of faster economic growth on the energy sector suggest, on the one hand that faster growth is possible in view of energy related and balance of payments constraints, and on the other hand, the policies that are required to sustain a faster growth. Questions on energy development, energy sector institutions and policy, energy pricing, efficiency and conservation, regulation/ commercialization, private investment and energy sector liberalization are central to Egypt's ongoing transition to free market as a vehicle to sustained long-term development and growth objectives. The structural adjustment and improved development performance call for numerous microeconomic sector adjustments involving pricing, investment incentives, financial restructuring and regulatory and institutional reforms in the energy sector.

Energy sector institutions and policy

The government agency responsible for energy in Egypt is the Organization for Energy Planning (OEP). The OEP is an autonomous organization under the Supreme Energy Council (SEC) which includes all cabinet ministers concerned with production and consumption of energy. The OEP is responsible for energy planning, formulating energy policies, preparing energy balances and energy supply-demand projections and implementing energy conservation programs. Government ministries relevant to the sector are the Ministry of Petroleum and Ministry of Electricity and Energy. The Egyptian Environmental Affairs Agency (EEAA) manages the country's environmental activities.

The OEP was initially responsible mainly for implementing energy conservation programs. Although it evolved to be entrusted with the responsibilities for energy planning and policy formulation, the concerned petroleum and electricity and energy ministries are the main institutions in charge of planning, demand projections and policies in their respective sub-sectors. In the 1990s the OEP functioned mainly as an agency of energy data collection to prepare historical energy balances.

The state-run Egyptian General Petroleum Company (EGPC) controls the petroleum industry. It is active in upstream, downstream and petrochemical sectors. EGPC has full responsibility for all aspects of the Egyptian petroleum industry. It is the only company authorized to import and export crude oil and petroleum products. It issues licenses for oil and gas exploration and is the national partner with an international oil company (IOC) and forms joint-venture agreements with private companies under the standard production sharing agreements. EGPC controls all refinery operations, gas transportation and distribution through its state-owned subsidiaries. Through the public sector companies, MISR and COOP, the EGPC controls the wholesale petroleum products market and is virtually the monopoly supplier of all petroleum products in the country.

The Ministry of Electricity and Energy and the Ministry of Administrative Reform, Business Sector and Environment oversee the power sector. The principal institutions operating in the power sector include: Egyptian Electricity Authority (EEA), a state-owned enterprise responsible for all generation (through seven generation zones or GZs), dispatch (one national dispatch/ control centre and three regional dispatch centres) and transmission; the Rural Electrification Authority (REA) responsible for construction and distribution networks in urban and rural areas; the holding company for Electricity Distribution (formed under Law 203, known as Public Enterprise Law) which has the eight distribution companies or DCs organized as stock corporations (owned by the government) and responsible for all electricity distribution in the country.

The management of power sector operating companies is directly linked to the government and to the Ministry of Electricity and Energy. The links between the EEA and the government are strong in the areas of planning, tariff setting and policy making. The various organizations participating in the supply and distribution of electricity lacked a commercial focus in the 1990s as the government continued to be both the owner and operator of the electricity sector. The power sector enterprises lacked the incentive to operate with a commercial focus and financial discipline. The tariff setting procedure was not transparent and did not involve the participating power entities in the decision making process.

Energy pricing

Historically, the government's conception of abundance of petroleum, natural gas and hydropower allowed it to price energy below their economic costs. Low energy prices gave wrong signals to the consumers and resulted in inefficient use of energy, high rates of growth in energy consumption, depletion of the domestic energy resource base and diminished export potential.

The late 1990s Egyptian economic crisis and signing of an agreement with the IMF in 1987 required the government to take steps to rationalize energy prices. Following the IMF agreement, the WB resumed lending for Egypt's power sector in 1989. Under the WB US $165 million loan in a total investment of US $845 million for 1080 MW capacity combined cycle power plant at Faraskur (Damietta) signed in 1989, the government of Egypt agreed to make progressive annual increases of domestic prices of petroleum products, natural gas and electricity to reflect their economic levels by June 1995.[75]

The Egyptian government's decision to make progressive annual increases in energy prices eliminated the subsidies by 1995. By this time, the weighed average price of petroleum products and natural gas increased from 15 per cent in 1985–6 to 100 per cent, while electricity tariffs at an average of 16 per cent of LRMC in 1985–6 reached an average of 100 per cent by 1995.

Viewed from the low level of energy prices in the mid 1980s, energy pricing reform progressed by eliminating subsidies on a weighted average price basis. However the methodology adopted to carry out the comparison between domestic and international prices reflected FOB Italy/ northwest Europe and did not include transportation cost. Cross-subsidies among the products continued. Reaching the target that domestic prices reflect 100 per cent of international levels on the basis of a pricing formula did not constitute a decision to liberalize petroleum product prices as the government continued to exercise control over end user petroleum product prices. The government determined the final selling prices for all core products to both large and small customers, including gasoline and diesel and they remained at uniform levels throughout Egypt in the 1990s.

Government/ EGPC also determined the distributors' margins. The margins are determined in discussion with each of the marketing companies and are based on average operating costs and average return on capital. The maintenance of a pan-Egyptian pricing policy leads to significant misallocation of resources and consumer cross-subsidization. The price setting mechanism also masks the price levels at the refinery gate—a measure of the efficiency of petroleum processing and marketing operations.

In the 1990s government linked natural gas prices to 85 per cent of the price of the internationally traded fuel oil. This incentive led to major gas

---

75. WB, *Egypt: Fourth Power Project*, Report No. P-4665-EGT. The author was the task manager for this project.

discoveries and increased gas utilization. Gas pricing has played and will continue to play a key role in Egypt's gas development strategy. The major user of gas in Egypt is the power sector as per the government's decision that all future thermal fuel requirements will be met by natural gas. However, fuel oil will continue to be used in some plants not connected to the gas network until the gas network is completed by 2013. With increased gas availability, the government considers the option of moving towards LRMC for gas pricing for power projects.

Egypt has come a long way in reflecting the LRMC on average electricity tariffs by mid-1995. However, tariff levels are still referred to their economic cost. Reforming electricity prices to move towards commercial and market based tariffs requires that the tariffs reflect the financial cost of supply to put suppliers on a commercial basis and remove barriers to attract private investors. Future progress in tariff liberalization will be incremental and will depend on Egypt's ongoing experience with commercialization and attracting IPPs.

Regulation, commercialization and institutional restructuring

The upstream oil and gas sector is governed by PSCs and the downstream operations by laws and decrees that determine the rights and obligations of the key players. EGPC continues to function as both the regulator and operator. Law No. 20 (1976) established EGPC as a Holding Company. EGPC is responsible for coordinating the work of Petroleum Pipeline Company (PPC) which was established as a joint stock company in 1968 and Petrogas. The Ministerial Decree No. 15 (1988) gives Petrogas responsibility as the sole marketer of gas in Egypt.

The integrated nature of EGPC's operation in the 1990s kept a tight control on the players operating in the petroleum sector, operating policies and procedures as well as the prices. In the upstream segment, EGPC operates in joint venture with private oil and gas companies. Oil in the Gulf of Suez is produced mainly by the Gulf of Suez Petroleum Company (GUPCO), a joint venture between BP, Amoco and EGPC. Egypt's second largest oil producer, Petrobel, is a joint venture between EGPC and Italy's ENI-Agip. Other major companies in the Egyptian oil industry include the Badr-el-Din Petroleum Company (a joint venture between Shell and EGPC), Suez Oil Company (EGPC and Deminex) and El Zaafarana Oil Company (EGPC, British Gas and Shell).

EGPC has also formed joint ventures with private companies in gas E&P by providing the incentive to pay the world price for gas from any discoveries. This incentive led to more active exploration for natural gas in Egypt by foreign oil companies and major discoveries in the Nile Delta and Western

Desert. The gas price incentive required the Egyptian government to pay the going market price for gas that it was not using. It was unable to export this unused gas because it lacked the necessary infrastructure to liquefy or export any surplus natural gas. In November 1999 the Egyptian government decided to allow private producers to export the gas.

The decision promoted more joint ventures between the government and the private sector. As of December 2000 the top six foreign energy companies involved in Egyptian gas E&P in terms of reserves include ENI-Agip, BP, British Gas, Shell, Edison International SpA, and Repsol-YPF. Repsol sold its Egyptian interests to Apache Corporation. Between 1999 and 2002 natural gas production in Egypt doubled to nearly 2 bcf/d and is expected to rise to 5.0 bcf/d by 2007, with much of the increased volume to be exported as LNG.

Due to major recent gas discoveries, natural gas is likely to be the primary growth engine of Egypt's energy sector for the foreseeable future. As of November 2004 the Egyptian Government's proven reserves of natural gas are estimated 66 tcf based on several new finds. The rapid rise in natural gas reserves has led to a search of export options, which has become particularly important to Egypt's future international balance of payments due to the decline of oil exports. In late 1999 the Egyptian government announced that natural gas reserves were more than sufficient for domestic needs and that foreign firms producing gas in Egypt should seek export customers. The government also announced in September 2000 a new pricing policy, which includes ceiling and floor prices, designed to protect consumers and producers from the risks of prices indexed to oil.[76] The Egyptian government formed a new state-owned entity in 2001 to manage the natural gas sector, Egyptian Natural Gas Holding Company (EGAS), separating those assets out from EGPC.

The EGPC continues to be a monolithic organization controlling the activities of its various downstream oil operating entities. It continues both as regulator and operator as a holding company of petroleum refining, transportation, wholesale marketing and distribution activities through its specific roles of issuing licenses and setting level of margins and commissions. Its integrated nature of operation does not allow its eight refineries and various transportation facilities to operate as commercial subsidiaries. None of the subsidiaries operated in the 1990s are structured as cost and profit centres. The refineries do not have a choice in selecting crude oils to optimize their product patterns. The government controlled end-user prices including subsidies and cross-subsidies, poor utilization of refining assets and lack of commercial focus have resulted in inefficient refinery and transport operations. As a result, revenues earned in the upstream activities are lost through

---

76. USEIA, *Egypt, Country Analysis Brief* (February 2004)

inefficiency in the downstream sectors (refining, distribution and marketing), which in turn cause loss of tax revenues.

In May 2000 Egypt announced its plan to privatize parts of the oil industry by selling a 20 per cent stake in state-owned oil refineries and 30 per cent stake in state-owned oil distribution companies. While the retail marketing/distribution is largely operated by the private sector, there are no firm restructuring plans to make each of the refinery, transport and wholesale marketing and distribution as separate commercial cost centres.

Restructuring of the power sector was part of the broad overall framework of the economic reform and structural adjustment program. The main elements of the power sector restructuring program included tariff increases to reduce budget deficit and improve the financial viability of electric power companies, public enterprise reform, promotion of private sector and competition.

A restructuring plan for Egypt's electricity sector established a committee in 1995 by joint decree from the Minister of Electricity and Energy and the Minister of Public Enterprise Sector to study the establishment of an independent regulatory board for electric utilities.[77]

Egypt's power sector, as part of the restructuring, plans to separate the generation, T&D activities by forming five generation and seven distribution companies. In July 2000 the Egyptian Electricity Authority (EEA) was converted into the Egyptian Electric Holding Company (EEHC). The government plans to spin off the distribution operations to private investors and retain ownership of the transmission lines and power generation facilities. EEHC-owned power projects that are currently under construction include the 1,500 MW plant planned at Nuberia in the Western Nile Delta near Alexandria, a 1,500 MW addition to the Cairo North Power complex and smaller hydroelectric projects at Nag Hammadi and Asyut.

The addition to Cairo North is moving forward after several years of delays, now that funding has been secured from multilateral donors. It was scheduled to be operative in 2004. The first 750 MW generating unit at Nuberia is scheduled to begin operation in 2005. The 64 MW Nag Hammadi hydropower project too is under construction, with European Investment Bank financing and is scheduled for completion in 2006. A contract has been awarded to Russia's Power Machines Group for the refurbishment of the turbines at the Aswan High Dam. The project will extend the operational life of the turbines by about 40 years and increase generating capacity at the dam from 2,100 MW to 2,400 MW. In addition, funding for four gas-fired new power plants have come from the private sector under Build, Own, Operate and Transfer (BOOT) scheme that will sell power to the

77. Speech by H E Eng. Mohamed Maher Abaza, Egypt's Minister of Electricity & Energy, World Bank ESMAP sponsored Workshop, (Cairo, 5–6 June 1995)

EEHC.

Work on the interconnection of Egypt's electric transmission grid with other countries in the region has been completed The Five-Country interconnection of Egypt's system with those of Jordan, Syria and Turkey was completed in 2002. Egypt also activated a link to Libya's electric grid in December 1999.

The government completed several studies funded by USAID and other multilateral financial institutions to restructure the power sector and establish a regulatory board. Competition at the generation level has been introduced through IPPs. The distributing companies are no longer part of the Ministry of Electricity and Energy (MEE). They are now under the Ministry of Public Business Sector. However, they continue to be part of the EECC, the newly created Holding Company, with little change in instituting autonomy and commercial focus. Previous privatization plans for distributing companies have stalled.

Privatization / private investment

The Egyptian government began overall privatization efforts with the Public Enterprise Law 203 in 1991, under a series of macroeconomic and structural reforms it implemented to stabilize the economy. This law established the framework for the sales of public enterprises to private investors and allows foreigners to buy shares with no limits or restrictions on percentage ownership. Privatization remains a central component of the government's economic reform program. The process has proceeded slowly as the government has focused on selling less attractive firms with greater attention of social issues related to employment. The 1991 program targeted 314 firms and as of January 2000, 42.7 per cent of those companies have been at least partially sold. The government's majority stakes in 89 firms have been sold; of these 37 were sold through the equity market, 22 went to anchor investors and 30 were sales to labour unions.[78]

In the power sector, the government in 1996 approved plans to open power generation to IPPs. BOOT projects are used to fund large-scale public infrastructure without affecting the country's debt profile. Private developers are allowed to recover their costs of construction through ownership and operation of the plant for a fixed period before handing it over to the state. The first BOOT project was a gas-fired steam power plant with two 325 MW generating units, located at Sidi Kerir on the Gulf of Suez, which began commercial operation in late 2001. The plant cost US $450 million. Electricity from the plant is priced at 2.54 cents /kWh. This competitive price is largely due to the availability of cheap natural gas to be supplied

78. USEIA, DOE, *An Energy Overview of the Republic of Egypt* (2003)

from EGAS. US based Inter Gen (a joint venture of Bechtel Enterprises and Shell Generating Ltd.) along with local partners Kato Investment and First Arabian Development and Investment, have the 20-year BOOT contract for Sidi Kerir.

The second BOOT power project award went to Electricite de France (EDF) for two gas-fired plants to be located near the cities of Suez and Port Said. Each plant will have an installed capacity of 650 MW and the project cost will total around US $900 million. The price for power from the EDF plants will be 2.4 cents /kWh, the lowest price yet offered for a BOOT plant. The project reached financial closure in April 2001. Both plants began commercial operations in 2003. The future of BOOT financing in Egypt is unclear except for the plan to build a part-solar power plant at Kureimat as a BOOT project, which will have 30 MW of solar capacity out of a total planned capacity of 150 MW. The WB will provide a financing package from its Global Environmental Facility, which will offset the cost difference between the solar capacity and the thermal capacity.

While no new private sector BOOT projects are likely in the near future, the state-owned EEHC has undertaken construction of several power projects. These include the completion of 1,500 MW capacity expansion at the Cairo North Power in mid-2004, the 1,500 MW plant planned at Nuberiya in the Western Nile Delta near Alexandria and the 64 MW Nag Hammadi hydropower project.

Egypt recognizes the need for foreign investment in the energy sector but has no plans to privatize EGPC. The government improved incentives for oil and gas exploration to attract private investors by offering smaller and more manageable blocks, increased cost-recovery allowances and increased agreement periods. The government's incentive to price natural gas discovered at world gas price levels attracted several foreign companies and have resulted in major gas discoveries and significant additions to proven gas reserves.

The rapid rise in natural gas reserves has led to a search for export options, which has become particularly important to Egypt's future international balance of payments due to the decline in oil exports.

A smaller export pipeline to Jordan began commercial operation in July 2003, making possible Egypt's first exports of natural gas. Egypt was responsible for building the section from an existing pipeline terminus at El-Arish to Aqaba in Jordan, with a sub-sea section in the Gulf of Aqaba bypassing Israeli waters. Construction of the section of the pipeline from Aqaba to northern Jordan is being undertaken by a Jordanian firm, Al-Fajr Company for Natural Gas Transportation.

Egypt's other option for exports is LNG. Two LNG projects with foreign private investors are currently underway. The Spanish firm Union Fenosa is building a two-train liquefaction facility at Damietta, which shipped its first cargo in January 2005 upon the completion of its first train, with a capacity of 268 bcf per year. Union Fenosa has contracted with EGAS for supply of natural gas from its distribution grid, and will take 60 per cent of the LNG output itself for use at the company's power plants and distribution to other users in Spain and elsewhere in Europe. ENI also is involved in the project, purchasing a 50 per cent stake in Union Fenosa's natural gas business in December 2002. BP signed an agreement for sales of natural gas from its offshore fields to supply the second train at Damietta in July 2004.

The second LNG export project (Egyptian LNG) at Idku is to be built by British Gas (BG) in partnership with Petronas. The project is tied to natural gas reserves from BG's Simian/ Sienna offshore fields and began production ahead of schedule in March 2005, with a second liquefaction train operational by 2006. Gaz de France is to be the main offtaker for the Idku LNG project's first train, having signed a contract in October 2002 for 127 bcf per year beginning in 2005. An agreement to purchase a similar quantity of LNG from the second train was signed in September 2003 by BG LNG Services.[79]

Egypt is trying to increase its domestic gas consumption by substituting oil with natural gas in power, industry and residential customers. Egypt supplies natural gas at cheaper prices to fuel gas fired BOOT power projects and is trying to improve the availability of natural gas for residential consumers by allocating service areas to several private companies, beginning in 1998. BG heads a Group that includes Orascom (an Egyptian construction firm) and Edison International SpA, that plans to invest $220 million in a distribution network to serve Upper Egypt down to Assyout, an area with no existing gas service. The network is planned to expand as far as south as Aswan.

While the investment climate has become more open to private investors in upstream oil and gas distribution, there is little direct foreign investment in the downstream oil operations. The government owns all its eight refineries and plans to expend $2.5 billion to build five additional refineries and petrochemical plants. In July 1997 the Egyptian government awarded a contract to an Egyptian-Israeli private sector joint venture for construction of the 100,000 b/d Midor refinery at Sidi Kerir, near Alexandria. The refinery started trial production in April 2001 and includes a 33,400 b/d hydrocracker and a 22,800 b/d coker. In May 2001 Israel's privately held Merhav MNF Ltd. sold its 20 per cent stake in Midor to the National Bank of Egypt (NBE), putting the refinery entirely in the Egyptian government's ownership.

79. EIA, DOE, *Egypt: Country Analysis Brief* (Washington DC, February 2004)

Egypt's energy economy market transition: Status

Egypt has come a long way in its transition from a centralized, command and control system to a free market economy. Since 1991 Egypt has enacted structural reforms that included privatization of state assets, trade liberalization, liberalization of banking and capital markets, reductions in price controls and subsidies and strict fiscal and monetary policies to reduce the budget deficit. These measures have brought inflation under control, cut budget deficits and allowed Egypt to build up its foreign reserves. Consequently, Egypt's foreign debt burden eased substantially under the Paris Club arrangements. This reduction coupled with the US government's decision to forgive $6.8 billion in military debt has lowered the country's debt service ratio from around 50 per cent in 1989 to less than 9 per cent in 1998.[80]

In the energy sector the main reform measures included raising of oil and gas prices and electricity to reflect their economic costs, providing additional incentives by pricing natural gas to reflect world prices linked to oil to attract private investment and the opening up of the electric power generation to IPPs. Box 5.8 summarizes the status of Egypt's Energy Market Transition as of 2004.

Box 5.8 Egypt: Energy Market Transition Status, 2004

Energy Pricing

- Petroleum product prices reflect international prices on weighted average basis
- Electricity tariffs reflect LRMC on average
- IPP power prices determined on international competitive bidding (ICB) for BOOT projects
- Natural gas prices linked to world fuel oil prices. In 2001 government introduced a floor and ceiling price for natural gas

Regulation, Institutional Reforms and Commercialization

- EGPC, the petroleum holding company, carries out regulatory oversight, issuing of licenses and fixing of margins and commissions for its subsidiaries in downstream operations
- EGAS created in 2001 by separation of natural gas assets from EGPC to oversee natural gas pricing and operations.
- EEA converted as EEHC in July 2001
- Electricity Regulatory Board established
- Restructuring of power sector by separation of generation, T&D as separate companies.
- Plans to eventually privatize distribution

80. USEIA DOE, *An Overview of the Republic of Egypt* (Washington DC, 2003)

Privatization/ Private Investment

- Upstream oil and gas operations undertaken as joint venture with foreign and local private companies. Several international oil and gas companies active in oil and gas E&P
- Joint ventures with private companies in gas distribution
- Government plans to sell 20 per cent share of refining and 30 per cent of oil distribution assets
- Retail oil distribution in private sector
- IPPs invited in power generation BOOT by International Competitive Bidding (ICB). US and French companies active

Future directions

Following the implementation of economic reform measures under its ERSAP since 1991 and the debt relief provided under the Paris Club arrangements, Egypt registered strong GDP growth in the late 1990s, reaching 6.0 per cent in 1999. However, the pace of reform measures, particularly commercialization, privatization and structural reform, slowed in 2000. Egypt's government plans to accelerate its program for the privatization of state-owned enterprises (SOEs) have moved slowly due to the large debts of SOEs and severe overstaffing. The private sector percentage of overall Egyptian GDP has been growing by around 1.5 per cent per year, with 110 SOEs having been privatized since 1994.[81] Egypt's economic growth has slowed markedly since 2001. Real growth in Egypt's GDP was 3.3 per cent in 2001, compared with 6.0 per cent in 1999. The GDP declined to 1.6 per cent in 2002.

The post 9/11 situation of fear of war, terrorism and regional tensions have impacted Egypt's sources of foreign exchange earnings. The tourism sector has been hit hard and revenues from the Suez Canal too have declined. Egypt's main challenge continues to be matching employment growth to the nearly 800,000 new job seekers coming into the labour market each year. Over the long term, Egypt needs to maintain a high rate of GDP to lower its unemployment levels.

Egypt's economy is continuing its gradual recovery from the sharp downturn of 2002, but with a growth rate still far below that of the 1990s. Egypt's real GDP grew 2.9 per cent in 2003, with tourist arrivals up 30 per cent over 2002 level of 1.6 per cent. Real GDP growth is forecast with an upward trend towards 5.3 per cent by the end of the current decade.

Energy will continue to play an important role in Egypt's economy. Egypt's reform measures for its energy market transition were part of Egypt's ERSAP. The ERSAP's macroeconomic reform measures focused on

81. USAID DOE, *Egypt Country Analysis Brief* (2003)

controlling inflation, reducing the current account and budget deficit, liberalizing domestic prices, reducing subsidies and giving the right price signals to consumers and investors. The reform measures also included promotion of competition and private investment and public sector reform to improve efficiency by introducing competition, restructuring of public enterprises as well as commercializing and privatizing public enterprises.

The energy sector is closely linked with all of these macroeconomic reform elements. Egypt's actions to reform its energy sector in the 1990s are linked to meeting the ERSRP objectives. The government's decision to price oil, gas and electricity to reflect their economic costs in the 1990s have partly contributed to the budget deficit reduction. However, with the disconnect between economic and financial cost in the power sector, public power companies are yet to become financially viable. Government continues to control the level of prices of oil products and electricity tariffs and cross-subsidies between products and categories of consumers continue. Reaching economic energy price levels was necessary to meet the IMF and the WB requirements of SBA and SAL. However, this has not been sufficient to move forward with energy price liberalization. The future policy of the government towards energy price liberalization remains uncertain.

Public enterprise reform of energy sector enterprises includes converting the state-owned oil and power into holding companies. The power distribution companies have been removed from the MEE and placed under a holding company along with other public sector enterprises. With increasing growth in natural gas activities, natural gas assets from EGPC have been separated to a new natural gas holding company created in 2001. The government's future plans to target 'strategic' areas for privatization include telecommunications and power distribution companies. The EGPC and the new natural gas holding company EGAS, remain off limits. With declining oil exports, the government has provided improved incentives to promote oil and gas E&P. The decision to price natural gas to reflect world fuel oil price and permit private companies to export gas have resulted in major gas discoveries and additions to proven gas reserves. Natural gas exports are expected to become a major source of foreign exchange earnings over the next decade.

Egypt's energy market transition consists of implementing the minimal changes required to qualify for debt relief under the Paris agreement and meeting IMF-World Bank conditions under the ERSAP. Egypt's approach to energy market transition is that of selective adjustments required to allow private investment where the government perceives net benefit to economy in earning foreign exchange. Improved incentives to private investors in oil and gas E&P, natural gas pricing to reflect world prices and allowing private investors to export gas are all measures that reflect Egypt's selective approach to market reforms.

Egypt's selective market adjustment approach, with confirmed benefits to the economy, is demonstrated by its late entry to allow private investors in power generation. Egypt pursued ICB for BOOT power projects by providing cheap natural gas prices and has obtained the cheapest price for power generated at 2.4 cents /kWh compared with 15 cents in India under the Enron project and 6–8 cents /kWh in China's IPP.

Egypt represents a development model that has attempted to blend the precepts of a market economy with those of a highly socialist orientation given the persistence of poverty and high unemployment. It reflects the distrust of Egypt's policy makers to pursue a complete shift to the market as a panacea for full employment. Egypt embarked on structural adjustment with selective liberalization of incentives and redefining the institutional structure. Egypt's selective approach to economic energy market transition represents an export generation and import substitution strategy blended with a continuation of the dominant state ownership and control in key areas of the economy. The state is in the process of reducing its role as owner and producer in the tradable sectors of the economy.

Centralization of the control structure over state energy enterprises in the face of selective liberalization is considered necessary to maintain the state's welfare function of redistribution. This has led to a dual economy where state-owned energy enterprises that are being converted to holding companies are not allowed to operate as commercial entities and to respond to market signals.

Commercialization of state-owned enterprises beyond segments of natural monopoly such as electricity and gas transmission requires the government to let the state-owned companies become autonomous and operate as financially viable corporations. While the Law 203 of 1991 and the attached executive decree helped to separate direct supervision of public enterprises by individual ministries and the ministry of planning, it is not clear that the creation of holding companies by itself has resulted in the separation of business and state control functions. The incomplete status of regulatory reform and decentralization have obstructed commercialization and the creation of a competitive environment and raised the transaction costs in the oil downstream and public power sectors.

Future progress in Egypt's energy market transition is mainly linked to the progress in economic liberalization. Egypt's strategic position in the region, its links to the western economies, its favourable macro indicators including low inflation rate with the implementation of ERSAP and a favourable standing in the international investment community are positive factors for the future course of Egypt's economic transition. However, in the post 9/11 period, Egypt is concerned about the negative impact of regional tensions, war and terrorist threats on its growing population. A daunting challenge for Egypt is achieving a balance between staying the course of market transition, reducing the rising unemployment and improving living standards.

THE REPUBLIC OF SOUTH AFRICA

South Africa is one of the three upper-middle income countries of SSA along with Mauritius and Gabon, with a per capita income of over $3000. Since the installation of a democratic government in 1994, South Africa has made significant progress in making major institutional transformations of the judicial, educational, health, housing and governance sectors to close the gap between historically privileged (white) and disadvantaged (non-white) groups. However, despite the progress, wide income inequalities and a high official unemployment rate of over 30 per cent for black South Africans persists. The government is focusing on creating jobs, improving the overall standard of living and increasing exports.

Macro-sector context

In 1994 South Africa launched a Program of Reconstruction and Development of Growth, Employment and Redistribution. The new macro strategy focused on promotion of growth through exports, investments and redistribution by creating jobs and reallocating budget resources. South Africa's economic growth averaged 1.8 per cent in the period 1980–2000. Its real GDP grew at 2.6 per cent in 2004. Given the need for improving economic growth prospects, it began focusing on improving efficiency in various sectors of the economy. The development of competitive and efficient energy sector is seen as contributing to economic growth and employment creation.

South Africa has enormous reserves of coal of over 50 billion tons. It has historically relied extensively on this resource for its energy needs. South Africa was the world's fourth largest net exporter of coal (76.3 million short tons in 2001). Owing to its wealth of coal, South Africa has been slow to develop its petroleum and natural gas. Its modest petroleum reserves are currently estimated to be about 29.4 million barrels. South Africa's natural gas reserves are currently estimated at 780 bcf. But the gas fields off South Africa's west coast and neighbouring Namibia are estimated to contain as much as 12 tcf of natural gas.[82] South Africa is a regional leader in petroleum refining. It also has Africa's only nuclear power station. Since South Africa has supplies of cheap coal, liquid fuels provide only 21 per cent of the energy requirements of the country. A significant portion of liquid fuel needs is met through production of synthetic fuels from coal, natural gas and condensate. It has a highly developed synthetic fuel industry, which takes advantage of the country's abundant coal resources and offshore natural gas

---

82. USEIA DOE, *An Energy Overview of the Republic of South Africa* (Washington DC, 2003)

and condensate production in Mossel Bay. The two major players are Sasol (coal-to-oil/ chemicals) and the Petroleum Oil and Gas Corporation of South Africa (PetroSA), formerly Mossgas (natural gas-to-petroleum products). Sasol has the capacity to produce 150,000 b/d and PetroSA, 50,000 b/d.

Energy sector institutions, regulation and policy

The South African Constitution requires the government to establish a national energy policy to ensure that the national energy resources are managed efficiently to meet the country's needs. The Energy Policy White Paper of 1998 stresses the importance of Growth, Employment and Redistribution (GEAR) and emphasizes promotion of exports and investment and wealth redistribution. The importance of promoting wealth redistribution arises from the economic problems remaining from the apartheid era, especially those of poverty and the urgent need for economic empowerment among the disadvantaged population.

The objectives of the Energy Policy White Paper, 1998 include increasing access to affordable energy services, improving energy governance, stimulating economic growth, managing energy related environmental impact and securing supply through diversity. To meet its energy policy objectives of providing increasing access to efficient energy supplies, the government is encouraging the electric supply industry to restructure, to improve efficiency and to ensure adequate level of investment in expansion of generation, T&D capacity.

The government's initiatives are also focused on giving customers the right to choose their supplier, introduction of competition (especially in generation), allowing for open, non-discriminatory access to the transmission system and encouraging private participation in the industry. The government also set up the Electricity Restructuring Inter-Departmental Committee (ERIC) to recommend actions required to meet the energy policy objectives.

On the recommendations of the ERIC, the government has decided to consolidate the distribution activity into viable regional distributors to introduce a cost-effective tariff, an independent electrification fund and a capped tax for part funding of municipal services. The government has set up a full time restructuring team to examine issues relating to and involving major stakeholders in the planning and transformation process.

The Department of Minerals and Energy (DME) is the main regulatory body overseeing the energy sector in South Africa. Under the jurisdiction of DME are several important entities which carry out the government's oversight role, including the National Electricity Regulator (NER), which is the regulatory authority over the electricity supply industry in South Africa and the National Nuclear Regulator and the Council for Nuclear Safety, which are the regulatory agencies for the nuclear industry. The Department of Public Enterprises is the government apparatus handling the privatization program.

The NER was established in April 1995 as the successor to the Electricity Control Board. It is a statutory body, established in terms of the Electricity Act, No 41 of 1987, as amended by the Electricity Amendment Acts of 1994 and 1995. The Department of Minerals and Energy appoints board members but once appointed, the NER acts independently and reports to the parliament. The NER is funded from a levy imposed on generators of electricity which is passed on to all customers of electricity. Customers of electricity therefore pay for the protection that they receive from the NER and the general body of tax-payers is relieved of this obligation.

NER is responsible for the licensing of electricity generators, transmitters and distributors in South Africa. NER is also overseeing the restructuring of South Africa's electricity supply industry (ESI) in accordance with the existing legislation and the 1998 Energy Policy white paper.

The government is involved in the energy sector through state-run companies. The Central Energy Fund (CEF) is the government's holding company in the petroleum industry. Each of the companies within the CEF has its own board, which is appointed by the Minister of Minerals and Energy. South Africa has a developed synthetic fuels industry, which uses the country's abundant coal resources, offshore natural gas and condensate production in Mossel Bay. Sasol was created to produce liquid fuels from coal via gasification and subsequent liquefaction. It was privatized in 1979 and remains a major producer of synthetic fuels in South Africa. In 1996 Sasol began an upgrade and expansion program at its Secunda facilities to reduce costs and help it remain competitive. The project was completed in 2001 following the installation of the ninth new synthetic fuel reactor.

In early 2000 Sasol launched a study of the feasibility of replacing coal with natural gas as the synthetic fuel feedstock, utilizing natural gas reserves in neighbouring Mozambique. Sasol's switch to natural gas is expected to reduce investment in its coal mining operations and the high costs of compliance with environmental regulations associated with coal. The 536 mile transport pipeline from the gas fields in Mozambique to Secunda will be owned by a joint venture between Sasol, South Africa's government (SAG) and the government of Mozambique. The parties have made provision for the future inclusion of black empowerment shareholders as well as privatization initiatives.

Mossgas, the synthetic fuel company producing petroleum products from natural gas with a 45,000 b/d capacity, began its production in 1993. It is a state-owned company. The company is part of the CEF group of companies through which SAG's interest in the liquid fuel industry is owned, developed and managed commercially. In 1999 the DME decided to merge the CEF's commercial interests into a national company, in accordance with the 1998 Energy White Paper. Mossgas, along with Soekor Exploration & Production (Soekor) and the elements of the Strategic Fuel Fund (SFF) joined to create the Petroleum Oil and Gas Corporation of South Africa (PetroSA). The PetroSA was established as an independent subsidiary of CEF on 1 November 1999 by merging Mossgas (Pty) Ltd, Soekor E&P and elements of the Strategic Fuel Fund (SFF).[83]

South Africa has the second largest refining capacity in Africa. South Africa's total refining capacity (excluding synthetic fuel plants) of 489,547 b/d is surpassed only by Egypt's. Its refined products are sold in the local market and exported, mainly to other parts of southern Africa. Shell and BP, the co-owners of South Africa's largest refinery, plan to invest US $100 million in the facility in the next five years. The Sapref refinery, located in Durban, will be upgraded to meet environmental requirements. Durban's other refinery, the 125,000 b/d Engen facility, plans to increase its capacity by 25 per cent to 150,000 b/d. Multinational energy companies including BP, Shell, Caltex and Total are major participants in South Africa's downstream petroleum markets. Several domestic firms are also involved.

The government is trying to diversify away from its heavy reliance on coal to natural gas. In 2001 the South African Parliament passed a natural gas bill which set up a regulatory system and provided incentives to try to spur investment in the natural gas industry. Competitiveness of natural gas is promoted by price discounts to small businesses and large greenfield customers.

The major coal mining companies are the principal members of the Chamber of Mines of South Africa, which also includes operators of gold mines and other mineral commodities. BHP Billington subsidiary, Ingwe Coal (Ingwe), Anglo American's coal division, Anglo Coal (Anglo) and Swiss-based Glencore's Enex Resources (Enex) are the largest coal producing companies in South Africa. In 2000 South Africa's coal production was 225 million metric tons. It was the world's sixth largest coal producer.

The government owns the Electricity Supply Commission of South Africa (Eskom), the major player in the electricity sector. Eskom is a government owned statutory body and was set up under the ESKOM Act 1987. It is governed by the Electricity Council and a 35 member Management Board. The Council determines policy and objectives and controls Eskom's performance. The Minister of Public enterprises appoints members of the council.

Eskom is the largest supplier of electricity in South Africa and accounts for over 95 per cent of all of South Africa's electricity. Eskom's generating

---

83. USEIA DOE, *An Energy Overview of South Africa* (Washington DC, 2003)

capacity of 38,211 MW, which is primarily coal-fired (33,878 MW), also includes one nuclear power station at Koeberg (1,930 MW), two gas turbine facilities (342 MW), six conventional hydroelectric plants (661 MW) and two hydroelectric pumped-storage stations (1,400 MW). Eskom is a vertically integrated public utility and dominates generation and transmission businesses. It supplies electricity directly to commercial farmers and through the National Electrification Program (NEP) to a large number of residential consumers. It also sells 'in bulk' to local municipal authorities who distribute to consumers within their boundaries. South African municipalities own and operate 2,436 MW of generating capacity, of which the majority (1,932 MW) is coal-fired. An additional 836 MW of generating capacity is privately held.

In addition to serving the domestic market, Eskom also exports power to Botswana, Lesotho, Mozambique, Namibia, Swaziland and Zimbabwe. South Africa and other members of the Southern African Development Community (SADC) signed an MoU in August 1995 to establish the Southern African Power Pool (SAPP). Eskom is expanding its involvement across the continent. In October 2000 Nigeria's National Electric Power Authority (NEPA) signed a partnership agreement with Eskom to help improve electricity supply. Eskom would help develop NEPA's repair capabilities, execute transmission line projects and participate in rehabilitating, operate and transfer (ROT) schemes for the running of Nigeria's power stations.

In September 2001 Uganda chose Eskom as one of two entities to bid for two concessions in its power sector. In November 2001 Zimbabwe's state-owned utility, Zimbabwe Electricity Supply Authority (ZESA), awarded Eskom a contract to assist in the management of its main power station. ZESA's Hwange station provides 40 per cent of the country's power. Eskom purchased a 51 per cent interest in Zambia's Lusemfwa Hydropower Company in December 2001.[84]

South Africa's National Electricity Regulator (NER) is responsible for the licensing of electricity generators, transmitters and distributors in the country. The NER regulates Eskom and the rest of the Electric Supply industry. NER's board consists of a chairperson and eight part-time members, who serve in their personal capacities. NER is funded through a cess on generators, which is in turn, borne by the consumers. Its costs are not a part of the general budget.

The NER is also overseeing the restructuring of South Africa's electricity supply industry (ESI) in accordance with existing legislation and the Energy Policy White Paper. The legislation and regulation is crucial to the government's continuing electrification program. The NER licensed Eskom as the National Transmitter for South Africa. The transmission license provides for

---

84. USEIA DOE, *South Africa* (Washington DC, September 2002)

non-discriminatory access by generators being dispatched centrally. It offers a transmission service to parties who are in a position to take supply directly off the transmission system and central dispatch of power stations participating in the National Power Pool. It organizes the exports and imports of electricity to South Africa. A transmission license was issued to a private company, Montraco, to provide a specific transmission service from the National Transmission System to specific supply points in Mozambique and Swaziland. [85]

The NER's main role is the regulation of pricing, tariff and markets, price increases, appropriate costing and accounting systems, contract requirements, financing of electrification effort and ring-fenced licensed activities for the industry. The NER has advised the government that it must work towards ensuring the existence of viable electric utilities, elimination of monopolies in generation and distribution, creating electricity markets, permitting open, non-discriminatory access to transmission systems, encouraging private participation in the industry and creating a level playing field for different participants in the industry.[86]

While Eskom dominates generation, transmission and direct distribution, the distribution is a fragmented activity. Eskom and over 400 municipal corporations distribute electricity to customers across the length and breadth of the country. The municipalities serve about 60 per cent of total customers by number and about 40 per cent by their share of consumption. They normally supply their areas. Consequently, they vary significantly in customer density, size and type of customer base, geographical spread and financial performance.

The fragmented market structure for electricity distribution makes it difficult for the South African government to oversee the sector. The problems are exacerbated by the wide differences in the financial strengths of the municipalities. More than 120 municipalities have less than 1,000 customers and more than 90 municipalities and an additional 18 municipalities account for another 25 per cent of total revenues from electricity sales. Conversely, the lowest 289 municipalities account for less than 1 per cent of the total municipality electricity distribution revenues, while the lowest 25 per cent of municipal distributors all lose money.

The NER's plan for South Africa's electricity distribution is still evolving. Its original plan in 1997 was to merge the distribution assets of Eskom with the country's municipal distributors to form six regional electricity distributors (REDS). Eskom and the municipalities were to own shares in the new distributors based on the assets that each contributed to the REDS. The REDS would come under the umbrella of a newly created government-controlled

85. USEIA DOE, *South Africa, Country Analysis Brief* (Washington DC, December 2003)

86. World Energy Council, *Pricing Energy in Developing Countries* (June 2001), pp.69–75.

holding structure called EDI Holdings (EDI). This plan was changed with the introduction of a new draft Electricity Distribution Industry Restructuring Bill. The new plan, put forth in the spring of 2003, calls for the establishment of EDI and six REDS. Eskom will not hold a stake in the REDS but will still merge its distribution assets into the REDS.

The NER envisions EDI to be a transitional entity with a life-span of 3–5 years. The EDI will be wholly owned by the South African government and would in turn hold a percentage of shares (representing Eskom's contribution of net assets) in the REDS. EDI's functions would include those of project manager and advisor, overseeing and coordinating the implementation of the REDS during the first critical years, providing support as necessary, monitoring and reporting implementation progress to the South African government and reporting on the South African government's financial stake in the REDS. After the transitional period the EDI would be dissolved, leaving a number of nominally independent REDS, their share holders being the South African government and the various municipalities that contributed net assets into the particular RED.

To help finance the REDS, the Electricity Restructuring Inter-Departmental Committee (ERIC) which formulated the REDS proposal has suggested that a tax be placed on electricity charges. This levy would last until the electrification programs are completed. The NER has signed a three-year agreement with the Norwegian Water Resources and Energy Directorate (NWRED) to help the restructuring of the electricity distribution sector. NWRED will also advise NER in the establishment of new tariff and pricing structures.

Energy pricing

South Africa has established a reasonable market basis for pricing energy. Crude oil processed in South Africa's refinery comes from the Middle East and North Sea. The Refinery output is transferred to marketing companies at a nominal in-bond landed cost (IBLC) based on a group of refineries in Singapore and the Middle East. Refinery margins generally follow those in the Far East market. The IBLC formula was introduced in 1950s and was last revised in 1994. Price control in the liquid fuel market is based on keeping parity with imported prices (IBLC) at the refinery gate. The profitability at wholesale and retail levels is controlled through fixing of margins at these levels. The subsidy for synfuel to Sasol financed through a synfuel levy on refineries worth US $150 million was removed in 1999.

On 2 April 2003 a new petroleum pricing mechanism went into effect. The Basic Fuel Price (BFP) formula replaced the IBLC component of the pump price. The formula change became necessary when an investigation by DME, in conjunction with the South African Petroleum Industry Association

(SAPIA), found that the previous formula had become outdated. Under the BFP method, domestic retail prices will still be linked to international crude oil prices but the new benchmark will be based on spot prices published by Platts. The IBLC method combined spot and contract prices. Basic gasoline prices will be based 50 per cent on Platt's spot price assessment in the Mediterranean spot market and 50 per cent on Platts spot price in Singapore. The basic prices of diesel and kerosene will be based 50 per cent on prices in the Persian Gulf and 50 per cent on prices in the Mediterranean refining area. Previously, the government used posted prices from refineries in Singapore and Bahrain and spot prices from Singapore.[87]

The creation of a regulatory authority in 2001 for natural gas was aimed at expanding the use of natural gas. Natural gas regulatory authority is required to determine the basis for natural gas pricing to reflect cost and to increase gas utilization.

The coal industry has operated as a competitive market since 1992. Coal production and beneficiation is completely in the hands of the private sector. The government's role is restricted to monitoring of the industry's performance to determine whether the coal resources are used optimally to meet the national priorities. The advantage of coal prices being determined by market forces is that it does not introduce any distortions in the cost structure of downstream industries like electricity. This is particularly important in view of the fact that over 85 per cent of power generated in South Africa is from coal-based stations.

The cost of service of electric power is determined at different points of value chains in the electricity supply industry. Generation costs are determined by estimating the total revenue requirements (cost of supply plus an appropriate return), including the cost of imported energy. The base costs are adjusted to the time-of-use rates for each period (high, standard, off peak and super peak) and for each season (high demand winter and low demand summer). The time-of-use tariffs are based on the contribution each of the seasons makes to the peak demand periods. Cost of service for transmission is calculated taking into account the capacity costs for each Customer Load Network and the standard energy loss rates.

In the fragmented market of power distribution there is no national standard for determining the cost of service. The cost of supply to the distributors depends on the voltage level and the distance of the supplying substation from Gauteng/ Mpumalanga where most generators are located. As of 2000, Eskom has a national price that is adjusted by a maximum of 3 per cent in the form of transmission charge. The exact transmission charge depends on the distance from Johannesburg. However, the charge does not

87. USEIA DOE, *South Africa: Country Analysis Brief* (Washington DC, December 2003), pp.7–8

exactly reflect the geographical variation in transmission costs.

South Africa has over 2000 different tariffs. The prices consumers are charged for electricity vary greatly across consumer class and are not closely related to the costs associated with servicing those markets. Mining operations in Gauteng province pay from 9–17 cents /kWh, but 23–32 cents /kWh in Mpumalanga province. In some cases, the residential areas adjacent to each other often experience wide variations in tariff structure as well as tariff levels.

Average distribution costs including purchased energy range from 23.9 cents /kWh for distributors less than 1 GWh in annual sales to 13.4 cents /kWh for distributors of more than 1,000 GWh in annual sales, a 46 per cent difference in costs.

There are substantial differences in the financial strength of distributors. Four municipalities earn 50 per cent of the total surpluses being earned by all municipal distributors and an additional 18 earn another 25 per cent of the total surpluses, while the lowest 25 per cent lose money on their electricity sales. Another pricing distortion in distribution tariffs is the practice of monopoly pricing by some of the municipalities for their industrial and commercial consumers. This imposes an unequal burden on these segments, which could inhibit industrial and commercial growth in some of these areas.

Eskom funds subsidies to customers from its own revenue. Eskom offers many specific subsidies, e.g. connection costs and energy prices are subsidized for many poor and low consumption customers. It also offers a voltage level cross-subsidy by charging prices that differ with the voltage level of supply. However, these prices do not reflect the cost of supply for many of the voltage levels. Farms in rural areas also get a subsidy towards cost of network and the cost of its operations. Eskom has invested nearly US $800 million in the electrification program for previously disadvantaged households.

The government is attempting to ensure that cross-subsidies have a minimum negative impact on consumers in the productive sectors of the economy. The government is taking steps to make the cost of subsidies more transparent by recovering specific levies for each of its subsidy programs.

For example, it proposes to recover the past electrification investment through Past Electrification Capital Debt Levy. It proposes a similar method of recovery for future electrification costs and remote rural farm subsidy.

To deal with the varied distribution tariff, Eskom conducted a study along with other distributors to formulate a standard methodology. The study proposed to classify customers into 20 groups, based on the time of use, load factor, geographical location and voltage of supply. The basic categories include industrial, commercial, agricultural and bulk. The total costs are collected under three categories—delivery/ purchase costs, network costs and support costs allocated under energy, demand and customer cost heads for determining the customer charge. The elements affecting cost of service include fuel, operations and maintenance costs, cost of capital, technical and non-technical losses and technical efficiency.

Privatization/private investment

The MME's Energy Policy document of 1998 has outlined changes needed to improve the efficiency in the electricity sector by promoting greater private sector involvement and increasing competition, separating generation and transmission operations, restructuring the distribution system, expanding access to electricity nationwide and supporting expansion of the SAPP.

Coal and petroleum downstream operations are already in the private sector. The first privatization in South Africa's gas distribution sector was Metro Gas Company, the distributor for Johannesburg, in August 2000. A group led by US-based Cinergy and South Africa's Egoli Empowerment Holdings completed the acquisition and renamed the company Egoli Gas.

In August 2000 the Department of Public Enterprise unveiled its Accelerated Program for Restructuring of State-Owned Enterprises to increase competition. Telecommunications, public transport and energy sectors were targeted for restructuring by 2004 and will include opening up the markets to foreign investors. Eskom is to be incorporated with transmission, distribution and generation restructured as separate corporate entities. Transmission being a natural monopoly, state ownership is expected to continue.

As the first step in the restructuring of Eskom, the South African Cabinet has approved the Eskom Conversion Bill which will result in the privatization of Eskom to a limited liability company. Eskom's generation, T&D operations will be unbundled to form separate corporate entities. Privatization of Eskom's generation activity is being planned via Strategic Equity Partners or an IPO. The government has also allowed the introduction of IPPs in power generation. In December 2001 the American Energy Company (AES) completed the acquisition of the Kelvin 'A' and Kelvin 'B' coal-fueled power plants from the city of Johannesburg Metropolitan Municipality. This has created the first IPP project in South Africa.

The Department of Minerals and Energy is also coordinating the design and implementation of the REDs to ensure consolidated localized ownership of electricity distribution. Large customers may be permitted to have direct access from the transmission company. The consolidation of power distributors to REDs involves a number of issues that need to be resolved. These include the contractual or commercial arrangements between the REDs and customers as well as between REDs and the transmission company.

A key issue in the privatization of Eskom in South Africa is to balance the financial viability and competitiveness of energy enterprises with the need to increase access to commercial energy at affordable prices to its vast majority of disadvantaged population. The government wants Eskom's drive to increase rural electrification to continue. The planned privatization of Eskom's generation and distribution activities will need to address the question of how the government would let the privatized Eskom continue to fulfil its policy of increasing access to electricity through its rural electrification program. The establishment of REDS for electric power distribution and restructuring of the power industry requires actions to implement the government's efficiency driven plan to supply energy at competitive prices. Box 5.9 shows the status of energy market transition in South Africa.

Box 5.9 South Africa: Energy Market Transition as of 2003

Energy Pricing

- Coal prices determined by market in a competitive coal market
- Petroleum product prices keeps parity with imported prices. The Basic Fuel Price (BFP) formula replaced IBLC on 2 April 2003
- Power generation costs determined on cost-plus (cost of supply plus appropriate return)
- Highly fragmented distribution tariff (over 2000 distribution tariffs); no national standard for determining the cost of service
- Wide variations in distribution tariffs; cross-subsidies persist.

Regulation

- MME acts as the main regulatory body with jurisdiction on sub-sector regulatory entities
- NER under DME is the regulatory authority over the electricity supply industry
- National Nuclear Regulator and the Council for Nuclear safety are the regulatory agencies for the nuclear industry
- Natural Gas Bill passed in 2001 by the South African Parliament to set up a regulatory system for natural gas

Restructuring, Commercialization/ Corporatization and Privatization

- 1998 White Paper on the Energy Policy of the Republic of South Africa announces restructuring of South Africa's power sector and consolidation of distribution activity into viable and independent REDs
- Introduction of a new draft Electricity Distribution Industry Restructuring Bill in 2003
- Separation of generation and transmission operations
- Privatization of South Africa's Metro Gas distribution company in 2000
- American Energy Company's (AES) acquisition of Kelvin 'A' and Kelvin 'B' coal-fuelled power plants from the city of Johannesburg of Metropolitan Municipality in 2001 and created the first IPP project in South Africa

Future directions

Since the launching of the government's new macroeconomic strategy of reconstruction and development in 1994, the government is making progress in restructuring the economy. Trade and industrial policy reforms, organizational and regulatory changes in the financial markets and the relaxation of exchange control measures have all made South Africa a more attractive place to invest. South Africa's position has enabled it to enter other markets in the Southern African Development Community (SADC). Since 1997 the economic performance has been variable. Economic growth has declined. The current account balance has been unfavourable. The foreign debt by 1999 was around 30 per cent of GDP. However, in 2000 South Africa recovered when growth reached 3.5 per cent—the best performance since 1996. GDP grew at 2.8 per cent in 2001 and 2.6 per cent in 2004. Inflation was 5.5 per cent in 2001 and 1.4 per cent in 2004. Despite these positive trends, FDI inflows remain below expectations. FDI, which averaged US $2.7 billion in the period 1997–2001, fell to US $754 million in 2002.

South Africa's energy sector is being transformed by the 1998 Energy Policy White Paper. It emphasized stimulating black-owned companies in the energy sector referred to as 'empowerment' groups by the industry. In compliance with the South African Law and the objectives stated in the Energy Policy White Paper, large coal corporations have provided through the sale of existing assets, opportunities for emerging black-owned firms. In November 2000 Anglo and Ingwe sold assets for $222 million to the black empowerment group Eyesizwe Coal (Eyesizwe), creating South Africa's fourth largest coal mining company. In November 2001 Eyesizwe initiated talks with Kumba Resources (Kumba) about establishing a strategic partnership in the South African coal sector. The deal is expected to create the second largest provider of coal to South Africa's domestic market.

In July 2001 the black empowerment group, Thebe Investment Corporation, purchased a 25 per cent share of Shell's South African downstream retail and marketing business. Shell, with its Sapref refinery (Durban) partner BP, signed an agreement with black empowerment firm, Southern Tankers, to transport oil from the refinery to other South African locations. Southern Tankers will cover all of the refinery's coastal shipping requirements.

South Africa was one of the first countries in the world to use electric power on a commercial basis, when in 1882, the first electric street lights were lit in the diamond mining city of Kimberly. However, after 112 years, in 1994 more than 20 million people—over 60 per cent of South Africa's population lacked access to electricity and use traditional fuels. The challenge for South Africa's future direction for energy market transition involves using the competitive market as a vehicle to promote economic growth and to increase access to commercial energy at affordable prices.

Continuation of reforms to reconstruct and develop the economy would help lay the groundwork for more broadbased and sustainable growth. Normalization of South Africa's international relations since the 1994 elections and its major role in African affairs extends its position as a springboard for entering other markets in the SADC.

SUB-SAHARAN AFRICA

Sub-Saharan Africa (SSA) as a region, is a net energy exporter. With steady new discoveries of oil reserves and continued investors' interest, African oil accounted for a growing share in global production. In 2000 SSA's net oil exporters were Angola, Cameroon, Congo, Equatorial Guinea, Gabon, Ghana and Nigeria, which together produced over 210 mtoe and accounted for about 5.3 per cent of global production. SSA's commercial energy resources are diverse, with significant reserves of coal, petroleum, and natural gas. Natural gas is becoming more significant to SSA's energy sector as fields in Mozamibque, Namibia, South Africa and Tanzania are developed. The SSA has about 8 per cent of the world's hydro potential, 6 per cent of the world's coal, oil and gas reserves and uranium deposits.

Despite the overall adequacy of commercial energy resource endowment, due to predominantly rural population with low population density SSA's access to commercial energy sources is limited. The energy sector in most SSA countries is characterized by the dominance of the traditional and/ or household fuel sector using mainly wood, waste and dung. About 80 per cent of the primary energy consumption in SSA (excluding South Africa) is of traditional and renewable type. Firewood accounts for 58.5 per cent, followed by 18 percent for wood used for charcoal and 15.5 per cent for petroleum products. Coal, gas and hydroelectricity account for less than 3 per cent each.[88]

With the exception of the SSA net oil exporters (Nigeria, Cameroon, Angola, Congo and Gabon), all SSA countries are net importers of crude oil and petroleum products with related foreign exchange, balance of payments and national security implications. Approximately one-third of the region's hard currency earnings are devoted to the procurement of petroleum. The cost of petroleum and electricity supply servicing a very small percentage of population in SSA remains excessively high, presenting a major obstacle to increasing access to commercial energy and the promotion of economic development.

---

88. WB-ESMAP, 'Report No. 182/96 on Sub-Saharan Africa' (Washington DC, June 1996)

Macro-sector context

With the exception of Mauritius, Gabon and South Africa, SSA countries are in the lower-middle and low income group of countries with increasing rates of growth in population and facing rapid expansion of HIV and other health issues. In the 1990s, many SSA countries experienced low or negative per capita growth with large government budget deficits and high levels of external debt. Energy places considerable pressure on the stability of many SSA economies despite low energy intensity due to the overall low energy consumption and limited access to commercial energy. SSA's net oil importers have serious problems financing high-energy import bills and are exposed to macroeconomic shocks from energy price increases and supply disruptions. SSA's net oil exporters' foreign exchange earnings have been directed mostly towards consumption (utility and refinery subsidies in particular) to protect the poor competitiveness of the domestic industry.[89]

In contrast with the accelerating growth in other regions, GDP growth in SSA slowed to 2.4 per cent in 2003 from 3.3 per cent in 2002. The volatility of domestic performance across Africa is reflected in international capital flows to the region, with the stock of debt fluctuating around US $210 billion, roughly equivalent to two-thirds of GDP. FDI inflows appear to have narrowed slightly from 2.3 per cent of GDP in 2002 to 2.1 per cent in 2003.[90]

The aggregate rate of growth masks divergent trends. The West African energy sector continued to boom due to resilient oil prices and strong investor interests, although linkages to other sectors of these economies remain weak. In many other SSA countries however, adverse weather conditions dampened agricultural production and slowed domestic demand, while a fall off in export growth due to sluggish conditions in Europe caused a compression of imports. Nonetheless, SSA countries excluding oil exporters and South Africa have historically registered a slower rate of GDP, at 2.5 per cent in 2003, compared with 3.8 per cent for SSA oil exporters.

Macroeconomic stability and growth remain threatened by high energy cost and subsidies to cover increasing costs. The financial performance of power utilities is dismal, requiring heavy direct and indirect subsidy. State oil and gas enterprises remain protected monopolies and maintain high prices. Given the income and demographic features of SSA countries, increasing access to commercial energy services is constrained by high up-front costs. The stagnation in access to energy severely hampers efforts to grow beyond a subsistence existence and poverty.

As part of the wave of liberalization sweeping countries in SSA in the

---

89. WB, *A Brighter Future? Energy in Africa's Development* (Washington DC, 2001)

90. WB, *Global Development Finance* (2004), Chapter 1, pp.29–30

1990s, a number of countries such as Cote d'Ivoire, Ghana, Kenya, Zambia and Zimbabwe decided to reform their energy sector. However, over 75 per cent of the SSA countries are undecided about reform. Even countries undertaking the reform process are facing uneven progress. Key elements of energy market transition including pricing and institutional reforms, restructuring, commercialization and promoting competition and private investment need to address the specific issues relevant to the context of SSA's energy sector's prevailing constraints of market size, limited access and high cost of commercial energy and electricity. The SSA countries' energy market transition faces the challenge of increasing access to commercial energy at affordable prices

Energy pricing and institutional arrangements

Pricing of petroleum products

Petroleum products represent 70 per cent of the commercial energy consumption in SSA. In 2003 petroleum consumption in SSA averaged 700,000 b/d. Oil imports account for one-third of foreign exchange earnings and 38 per cent of indirect taxes are obtained from taxes on petroleum products. Prices are set by governments. They do not reflect economic cost and lead to poor efficiency and high cost to consumers. Higher supply inefficiencies occur in those SSA countries where governments have direct involvement in the procurement of oil with inefficient procurement practices or high procurement rent. Often, lack of foreign exchange, poor credit standing, inappropriate bidding procedures and high transit costs result in sub-optimal purchasing procedures and high financial costs.

Many of the pricing distortions and inefficiencies result from inadequate price setting of petroleum products both at the ex-refinery and retail levels. The ex-refinery price (cost of crude plus refining and storage margins) provides a signal to producers. The retail prices to consumers include ex-refinery price plus distribution and marketing margins and consumer taxes. In SSA, all refineries, with the exception of Nigerian and South African refineries are structurally uncompetitive. Refineries in SSA are small topping units and product yields do not match country consumption patterns, leading to imports of expensive light products and exports of discounted fuel oil. High ex-refinery prices in many SSA countries permit the operation of small topping units that are no longer competitive with imports and do not reflect the level of prices in the nearest international market. As a result, SSA refineries produce non-competitive petroleum products *vis-à-vis* direct imports of the large complex refineries in the Gulf, Western Europe and South Africa.

The inability of governments to adjust ex-refinery prices to changes in the international market and to remunerate oil industry commensurately has created severe financial losses as well as delayed investments, reduced production capacity and discouraged new investors.

Distribution inefficiencies result from the extensive use of road instead of rail transport, lack of rational use of storage, need for infrastructure rehabilitation and in general, poor management and inadequate market competition in these activities. Consequently, unattractive investment environments in distribution are excessively raising costs because of dilapidated infrastructure.

Petroleum product pricing is not often transparently linked to economic costs; ex-refinery/ import prices are not adjusted with the movements of international product prices and exchange rates. Transit fees exceed economic costs while wholesale margins are based neither on CIF prices nor on operator's capital employed.

WB's Africa region sponsored a regional study funded by the Ministry of Foreign Affairs, Italy, in the 1990s to focus on the identification of practical measures that could reduce the cost and enhance the reliability of petroleum supply and distribution in Africa. Consultants Cuneo e Associati conducted a three-year study of some key countries in the SSA region. The study estimated the potential annual cost saving of $1.4 billion for 1990 by comparing actual ex-refinery or ex-main depot prices and transport costs with the alternative of procuring finished products under competitive conditions from the international market and using the most efficient internal transport mode.[91]

The study found that in 1994, the average oil supply cost in SSA was $402 /ton compared with the cost in OECD countries of $275 /ton. With changes in pricing and institutional restructuring and privatization policies, the study estimated that savings of $51 /ton could be generated. The process of change in institutional arrangements include privatization of depots, corporatization of the pipeline company and privatization of refineries with elimination of price subsidies and their alignment to import parity for industry privatization. This would require actions to remove supply monopolies that permit the continued operation of inefficient refining units, which no longer ensure the countries with economic and reliable oil supplies. Improvements in procurement practices through the use of international competitive bidding for oil and oil products could lead to significant savings.

Sub-regional cooperation is necessary for the development of practical and efficient supply solutions, especially concerning transit costs. Oil companies have provided inputs to progress towards regional standardization of petroleum product specifications. This could reduce redundant investment and facilitate the development of deregulation and regional trade. Some

91. WB/ Cuneo e Associati, *Petroleum Products Supply and Distribution in Sub-Saharan Africa* (Washington DC, 1994)

SSA countries such as Mali and Kenya are deregulating their markets. Others, such as Ethiopia and Madagascar, are regulating prices but at import parity values with fewer subsidies, a practice established in Southern Africa.

Much remains to be done to reduce the cost of oil products in SSA which averages over 50 per cent /ton compared with the average cost in OECD countries. Closure of the refinery is required in most countries to break the vicious circle of price regulation and to detach government from the downstream operations. Logistical and infrastructure constraints hindering effective deregulation need to be addressed. Improving the transport infrastructure (harbours, jetties, depots, rail facilities, etc.) often require cooperation between different countries to seek feasible sub-regional schemes to reduce transit corridor costs. SSA countries need to reformulate their policies based on the joint efforts of governments as well as commitment from the oil industry to ensure efficient management to secure supplies of oil products at economic costs comparable to international prices.

Electricity tariffs

In the 1990s, on average, only 10 per cent of the population in SSA had access to electricity, which was mainly concentrated in urban and suburban households, while relatively few rural households were electrified. Even with limited access, electricity prices in SSA countries vary widely. In 1994 ten SSA countries (Zaire, Zambia, Malawi, Cameroon, Zimbabwe, South Africa, Ghana, Ethiopia, Nigeria and Mozambique) were paying tariffs below 5 cents /kWh. Five countries (Cote d'Ivoire, Senegal, Gabon, Sierra Leone and Guinea) collected tariffs above 15 cents /kWh. Two countries, Mali and Mauritius, were paying between 10 and 15 cents /kWh. Four others, Kenya, Madagascar, Tanzania and Uganda, were paying 5–10 cents /kWh.[92]

Electricity tariffs in SSA generally cover neither economic nor financial costs of supply. Despite the high level of tariffs in some countries, tariff structures do not meet the economic efficiency objective of reflecting the marginal cost of supply and it also fails to achieve the financial objective of reflecting the average cost. As a result, utilities are unprofitable and rely on government subsidies, and are increasingly unable to increase access to growing population.

A World Bank Operations Evaluation Study (OED)[93] on Lending for Electric Power in Sub-Saharan Africa, 1996, found that with few exceptions, cost recovery in SSA countries has been inadequate and generally below

---

92. WB-ESMAP, Report No. 182/96 (Washington DC, June 1996), p.117

93. WB Operations Evaluation Study (OED), *Lending for Electric Power in Sub -Saharan Africa* (Washington DC, 1996)

that of other regions. The financial performance of the electric power utilities of SSA countries has generally been inadequate due to ineffective billing and collection systems, weak management and lack of penalties or willingness to apply them to delinquent customers. The problem was exacerbated by the government not allowing the power companies to withdraw service from public sector entities for non-payment.

Some of the SSA reforming countries such as Ghana, Cote d'Ivoire, Kenya and Zambia have tried to address the tariff issue by regulatory and institutional reforms to improve operational efficiency. In 1994, Ghana issued a strategic framework for power sector development policy and recognized the need to set up a regulatory body to promote competition and to regulate electricity prices. Key requirements for the power sector regulatory body include institutional reforms to promote competition, private sector participation in power generation through BOOT schemes and transparent market-based procedures to set and adjust electricity prices by establishing a regulatory agency. The regulatory agency also has the authority to prepare, award and monitor compliance with concession agreements with generation with IPPs and to adjust the rate base for distribution companies.

A few other reforming SSA countries (Guinea, Madagascar, Kenya and Zimbabwe) have accepted the need to set up transparent regulatory authorities. Enabling legislation or entity by-laws generally give the utilities the theoretical authority to manage their sectors. In practice, the chairperson and often all of the directors of state-owned utilities and regulatory authorities are government appointed. This arrangement has failed to achieve the separation of responsibilities between regulating authorities and operating companies in the power sectors of all SSA countries.

Wood fuel pricing

Wood fuel represents over 35 per cent of total energy produced and 70 per cent of total energy consumption in SSA. Among rural inhabitants and the urban poor, it is often the sole source of energy. The pricing of wood fuel is complicated because of difficulties to quantify its economic cost. In many SSA countries, the price of wood fuels is comparatively lower than that of its substitute sources of energy—charcoal, LPG and kerosene—mainly because the market cost of wood fuel does not reflect the replacement/ environmental cost. The replanting of trees is not borne by the producer. Reforestation is usually managed by governments and financed through foreign aid, which is in effect a subsidy on the price of wood fuels. Reflecting the economic cost of wood fuel use would entail removal of subsidies that could double or triple the price of wood fuel. Given that wood fuel is often the main energy source for the poorest of the population, this would exacerbate social tensions. Porous borders and significantly differing pricing policies between countries make the contraband of wood fuel both possible and profitable, palliating the impact of government policies.

The collection of wood fuels, generally based upon traditions of free wood gathering, uncertain land tenure and weak agricultural extension services is usually not complemented with replanting, thereby leading to the problems of deforestation, soil erosion and barrenness of previously fertile land. To resolve this crisis, governments have sought to substitute commercial fuels for bio fuels. Efforts to alleviate energy poverty requires creating credit institutions accessible to micro enterprises and building economies of scale to facilitate substitution of wood fuel with more efficient energy sources.

Pricing and institutional arrangements reform in SSA underscores the importance of enhancing the transparency and performance of energy enterprises both at the country and regional levels to overcome the limitations of market size, ownership monopolies, infrastructure and institutional weaknesses, resulting in limited access to efficient energy and high energy supply cost to consumers.

Commercialization, corporatization, privatization and private investment

In the SSA net oil exporting countries, private investors have continued to be interested in upstream oil and gas and a few LNG projects. Angola is developing projects to utilize associated natural gas, which is currently flared or re-injected. Chevron Texaco and a consortium of oil companies, including Exxon Mobil, BP, Total Fina ELF and Norsk Hydro are planning to gather associated natural gas from deep water fields and develop shallow water fields in the Congo Basin as part of the Angola LNG project. In March 2002 participation agreements between the oil companies and Sonangol were signed. The Angola LNG project is expected to come onstream in 2007. The LNG plant is expected to consist of a single train with a capacity of producing 4 million tons per year of LNG. The plant design will include the potential to add a second 4 million ton train.

In December 2003 the WB's private sector arm, the International Finance Corporation (IFC) announced its participation in a US $1 billion venture headed by South Africa's Sasol to develop natural gas fields in Mozambique. The project aims to produce nearly 2.3 tcf of gas over the 25-year expected life of the fields in Mozambique. The IFC is contributing US $18.5 million of the $220 million estimated cost for development of the fields.

With the exception of upstream oil and a few gas/ LNG projects, most of the SSA governments have tended to exercise control on the energy sector through public enterprises and/ or in the petroleum sector through joint ventures that cover even the operational and commercial activities. In many cases, public or mixed enterprises own terminals, refineries and depots and have obtained a monopoly position to procure and distribute petroleum products within a country. As discussed in the foregoing section, petroleum downstream operations continue to be inefficient, resulting in high supply costs.

A common pattern of the SSA countries' energy/ electricity institutional structure in 1990 was state-owned monopoly or near monopoly at all levels of energy supply with limited autonomy from government intervention. In the 1990s several reforming SSA countries, faced with budgetary shortages and growing costs of inefficiency in their state-owned enterprises, have attempted to corporatize their utilities. Many of SSA's utilities have a corporate or similar status and operate in many respects like commercial enterprises. However, they are not financially viable and profit-oriented. Corporatizing public energy enterprises is not proven to assure that energy enterprises will operate as business enterprises without government interference. For example, Kenya's power utility is partly privately owned, yet it was instructed by the government not to comply with its lease agreement for use of the large Kiambere Dam. This led to the financial insolvency of its owner.[94]

Corporatization theories have not been put into the practice of business orientation. A few utilities such as Eskom in South Africa remain autonomous from government interference and ensure that political objectives of increasing access to electricity to the poor are pursued within a reasonable commercial context. In many other SSA countries, governments continue to be in control of investment decisions, tariffs are approved on an *ad hoc* basis, personnel policy is shared between government and utilities, foreign exchange is difficult to obtain for current needs and much improvement is needed in operating performance, financial management and reporting.

Because of the lack of direct incentives built into public sector operation, many SSA governments including Burundi, Ghana, Senegal, Malawi, Zimbabwe and Zambia have developed performance targets for the industry. The WB credits to SSA countries in the early to mid 1990s promoted the use of performance contracts by its borrowers. Performance contracting requires an ability and willingness of the government to set targets, review progress and enforce the terms of contract. These define in greater or lesser detail, the relationship between governments and the management of their public enterprises.

The record of experience with performance contracts in Burundi, Ghana and Senegal shows a disconnection between written contract and theory and their implementation. They have not been proven to be effective mechanisms to help enterprises with achievement of performance targets such as non-payment of bills mainly by other government departments, tariff adjustments and labour productivity. The inadequacy of accounting systems of

94. WB-OED, *Lending for Electric Power in Sub-Saharan Africa* (Washington DC, 1996), p.67

most SSA countries and the staff who operate them and the substantial delay in closing the books fails to perform as control mechanisms by providing the required management information feedback in a timely fashion to improve the performance targets. The major weakness is that these contracts are not legally enforceable and that the government still acts unilaterally and violates agreements. Governments with long traditions of making investment and procurement decisions find it difficult to empower the utilities with autonomy to make these decisions.

Ghana has tried to improve performance by hiring external specialists under a twinning arrangement. Ghana entered into a twinning agreement between Ontario Hydro of Canada and the Volta River Authority (VRA) in Ghana. Under this arrangement, Ghana reorganized its corporate planning and finance function in 1990–1. Improvements in financial management and information systems, corporate planning and reporting have been made following the full computerization of VRA's accounts. The accounting and budgeting systems used by VRA are generally satisfactory and provide timely and reliable financial information. This type of management assistance has worked in Ghana to fill the gap in specializations and train local staff to learn the necessary skills so that they can take over following the completion of the twinning arrangement period. However, the management assistance arrangements have not worked well in other SSA countries like Tanzania and Guinea where there was less support.

Several reform oriented SSA countries have taken an alternative option to privatization to improve the performance of their utilities by contracting out the management of the utility with continued public ownership. Ghana, Cote d'Ivoire, Burundi, Guinea and Mali have taken the management contract option that combines continued public ownership with private operation. Cote d'Ivoire introduced the system in 1990 as part of the power sector reorganization. Its experience with management contract after three years of its signing in 1990 has been positive. Between 1990 and 1994, power losses declined from 19.8 per cent to 17.4 per cent and the average number of hours of power outages from about 50 to 18. Employees per customer were reduced from 9.5 to 6.9 while billing and collection also improved.

Burundi, Guinea, Rwanda, Sierra Leone and Ghana have also allowed the transfer of operations management to private participation through some forms of performance based management contract. In 2003 Zambia was actively seeking foreign investors to refurbish and upgrade its hydroelectric plants.

Management contracts offer responsibility for managing a core function by introducing commercial procedures. However, management contracts do not require operators to finance investments and are no guarantee for efficient cost recovery. Cote d'Ivoire's experience with management contract demonstrates that while efficiency improved and arrears were low, this was not sufficient to finance system expansion. In the Cote d'Ivoire power company, the owner of assets was unable to fund new connections and minor overhauls of the distribution system. The government had to amend management contract to extend contractors' responsibilities to investments, making it evolve toward a concession contract. Cote d'Ivoire also started mobilizing private equity with an IPP contract for gas-based generation.

Ownership of power sector assets by private entrepreneurs has been a touchy political and economic issue in SSA, although privatization of some segments of the operations appears possible. The electricity industry in SSA countries is dominated by small systems with the exception of South Africa. Small size of market at the individual country level raises transaction cost. The right project size requires multi-country political, economic and financial policy coordination and raises project risks. The higher the risk, the private investors expect higher return and shorter payback period. Guarantees also play an important role where the perceived risk is high to raise the expected rate of return. Given that most of the SSA countries have little proven record of enabling investment climate in the power sector, rates of return for deals to be consummated will have to be in excess of 20–24 per cent.

To obtain a better understanding of the factors that are discouraging private participation in Africa's power sectors, Coopers and Lybrand[95] in 1995–6 interviewed 11 banks or financing institutions and six equity investors. Coopers and Lybrand, based on their interviews, identified lack of credible opportunities and a perception of high country risk as the two primary obstacles. While the first concern could be addressed by formulating the right sector reform policies to provide opportunities for private participation in generation, T&D, the perception of high country risk reflect investors' reluctance to commit to the long-term funding required for power projects. Even with commitment to sector reform backed by legislation, commercial lenders would not be interested without solid bilateral/ multilateral and local investors' support.

With the exception of a very few countries, the SSA countries in general are in the starting phase of the energy sector reform process

Regional power interconnection and trade

Given that most SSA countries have small energy sectors and SSA's energy resources of oil, coal, gas and hydro are concentrated in a few countries, economies can be achieved through regional integration by harmonizing technical standards, avoiding duplication of investment and reducing high

95. WB-ESMAP Report, *Financing Africa's Power Sector: Issues and Options*, Report No. 182/96, 'Washington DC, 1996' p.164.

transit costs of supplies.

In the power sector, regional integration and bulk power trading can substantially reduce power system costs. Reserve can be shared. The operating costs of an existing regional network can be minimized. System expansion costs can be reduced through planning on a regional basis. The key constraints to long-term firm power trade are often political. Countries are unwilling to rely on neighbouring countries for a key economic input such as power. They are even more cautious of relying on power being wheeled from more distant sources across one or more neighbouring countries.

One of the main drivers for power trade in SSA has been the availability of hydro—the mismatch between countries which have economic hydro resources and the countries with the greatest load—and the potential for mutual benefits from integration of hydro and thermal systems. As of 2003, the great majority of electricity trade in Africa has been based on hydro capacity. However, gas is playing an increasing role in new power generation.

Africa has four main regional power interconnections. These include East Africa—between Uganda and Rwanda, Kenya and Tanzania; West Africa—with existing interconnections between Cote d'Ivoire, Ghana, Togo and Benin, between Nigeria and Niger and planned interconnections between Cote d'Ivoire and Ghana to Burkina Faso; Central Africa—with interconnections from Zaire to Congo, Rwanda, Burundi and Zambia; and Southern Africa—with interconnection between Zambia, Zimbabwe, Malawi, Mozambique, Botswana, Namibia, South Africa, Lesotho and Swaziland. Despite the history of some regional cooperation, electricity interconnection and bulk energy trade has been limited. In 1995, the 19 SSA countries' interconnection capacity accounted for just 3 per cent of their total installed capacity and their energy trade was about 3.62 per cent of total generation capacity.[96]

Southern Africa remains the most highly interconnected region in Africa. Since the 1990s, the rehabilitation and construction of key T&D links between Southern African countries have allowed a sizeable increase in regional power trade and this activity is likely to expand. Created in 1995, the South African Power Pool (SAPP) aims to link SADC countries into a single electricity grid. The national utilities currently participating in the SAPP are Angola's Empresa Nacional de Electricidade (ENE), the Botswana Power Corporation (BPC), the Democratic Republic of Congo's (DRC) SNEL, the Lesotho's Electricity Corporation (LEC), Malawi's Electricity Supply Commission (MESC), Mozambique's Electricidade de Mocambique (EDM), Namibia's Nam Power, South Africa's Eskom, the Swaziland Electricity Board (SEB), Tanzania Electric Supply Company (Tanesco), Zambia's Zesco, and Zimbabwe's Zesa. SAPP's coordination centre is located in Harare, Zimbabwe.

---

96. WB-ESMAP, Report No. 182/96 (Washington DC, 1996), pp.142–51

South Africa is historically the major driver of regional electricity imports and exports, although other SADC countries, particularly the DRC, Zambia and Zimbabwe have also traded power for decades. In October 1995, a critical link between South Africa and Zimbabwe was established with installation of the 400 kilovolt (kV) Matimba-Insukamini line. Through this line South Africa has the ability to export and import power from DRC, Zambia and Zimbabwe in addition to its already existing capability to supply electricity to Lesotho, Swaziland, Namibia and Mozambique.

The Matimba-Insukamini line was an essential first step to tying the power grids of the northern and southern members of the SAPP together. With this interconnection, power exports expanded from 1,607 GWh in 1990 to a peak of 6,439 GWh in 1997. The reconstruction of the war damaged transmission link from Cahora Bassa in 1998 and the completion of Mozambique Transmission venture (Motraco) in 2000 between South Africa and Mozambique have also facilitated the expansion of energy trade in Southern Africa.

South Africa's massive and reliable coal-fired base load capacity is a good complement to the hydro-based power sectors elsewhere in SADC, where seasonal rains affect water flows and the reliability of electricity generation. As links between the national grids in SADC countries expand, wheeled power exports through third countries becomes the critical new power sourcing option for member countries. Given the severe limits for access to power in many SSA countries, SAPP is striving to raise reliability of supply, improve operational efficiency and reduce costs, all within an increasingly inter-connected system.

Coordinated from Harare, the SAPP has three main generation nodes—South Africa, with its coal fired base load capacity in the South; Mozambique, with the Cahora Bassa dam in the east; and DRC, with the Inga Dam in the west. Zambia and Zimbabwe have sizeable hydropower capacity with the Kariba North and Kariba South.

Restructuring of power sectors in key SADC countries such as South Africa, Zimbabwe and Zambia in particular could spur the internationalization of electricity throughout the region. Eskom has taken a forward leaning position in seeking new power sector ventures with its subsidiary, Eskom Enterprises, and is becoming more involved in regional power sectors that are opening up to outside investment. In October 2000 Nigeria's National Electric Power Authority (NEPA) signed a partnership agreement with Eskom to help improve electricity supply. In September 2001 Uganda chose Eskom as one of two entities to bid for two concessions in its power sector. In November 2001 Zimbabwe's state-owned utility, ZESA, awarded Eskom a contract to assist in the management of its main power station. In December 2001 Eskom purchased a 51 per cent interest in Zambia's Lusemfwa Hydropower Company.

The DRC has extensive energy resources, including hydroelectric potential estimated at 100,000 MW. The Inga dam alone on the Congo river has a potential capacity of 40,000–45,000 MW, sufficient to supply all of Southern Africa's growing electricity needs. Due to continuing political uncertainties and the resulting lack of investor's interest, only a fraction of the potential has been developed at Inga. Total installed generating capacity was estimated at 2,473 MW in 2001. However, actual production is estimated at no more than 650–750 MW, largely because two-thirds of the turbines at Inga are not functioning. South Africa's Eskom has been involved in the rehabilitation of the Inga dam.

SAPP members have started to realize the benefits of sourcing bulk power from existing and new transmission and generation projects across the region. The main constraints to trade have been political and commercial. Political factors constrain the potential for long-term firm power trade in SSA. Most countries in SSA as elsewhere have been unwilling to rely solely on regional interconnection depending on neighbouring countries to meet their power supply requirements. They have been even more cautious of relying on power being wheeled from more distant sources across one or more neighbouring countries.

Commercial factors raise the key issues of pricing bulk supply, transmission pricing and access, policies to be pursued on firm power trade and decisions on developing institutional framework for agreeing trade volumes and pricing principles in promoting regional interconnection and bulk power trading. In February 2004 Eskom of South Africa and HCB of Mozambique announced their refusal to renew contracts with ZESA due to non-payment of previous delivery charges. Failure to agree on pricing systems or to enforce contractual obligations can block trade even when it is in both parties' interest. Power sector reform across SSA countries is fundamental to the full realization of the opportunities for regional interconnection and bulk power trading. The basic reform required to let the utilities operate commercially without political interference remains the first crucial step in the reform process. Equally important is the industry restructuring which allows trade contracts to compete on more equal terms with domestic generation.

Box 5.10 summarizes the status of energy sector reform in SSA countries.

Box 5.10 Energy Market Transition in SSA Countries as of 2003

Energy Pricing

- Petroleum Products pricing on cost-plus basis. High product prices do not reflect competitive international efficiency levels
- Subsidies continue to support inefficient refineries and high transaction costs
- Wide variations in electricity tariffs among SSA countries. Cost range from 5 cents to 30 cents /kWh with limited access to electricity

Regulation and Institutional Reforms

- Reforming SSA countries such as Ghana, Cote d'Ivoire and Guinea are setting up regulatory entities. However, legal and regulatory reform is minimal and weak
- Given the small size of the power systems, several SSA countries have opted for performance and management contracts to improve the efficiency of their power operations. While these options could improve efficiency, they have not been able to generate the required investment of system maintenance and expansion in many SSA countries

Privatization/ Private Investment

- Private investors' continued interest mainly in SSA oil exporting Western African countries in oil and gas upstream and a few LNG projects
- Little privatization of existing energy assets
- Some SSA countries such as Cote d'Ivoire and Ghana are opening up power generation to private participation
- Lack of credible opportunities and high country risk constitute major obstacles for private investment

With few exceptions, energy enterprises of SSA countries remain government owned and integrated monopolies. It has been clearly demonstrated in most SSA countries that public ownership *per se*, does not guarantee adequate public interest and increased access to efficient energy at affordable prices. Whether energy service provision is entrusted to the public or private sector, lack of regulatory capacity to oversee monopoly suppliers constitutes a serious problem of higher energy costs and limited access.

In the 1990s several SSA countries began to introduce pricing, regulatory and institutional reforms to improve efficiency of their energy enterprises. The reform efforts have led to increasing energy prices, setting up of regulatory entities and commercializing of utility operations by performance and management contracts. However, the fundamentals of commercial operations are yet to be practised. Government interference in energy operations continues. Corruption is endemic. Legal and regulatory frameworks are unreliable. On average, over 50 per cent of households in SSA countries lack access to electricity and commercial fuels. The provision of electric power in SSA countries remains unsatisfactory. With prices that are at levels insufficient to cover costs and continued inefficiency in operations, electric utilities are unable to finance system maintenance and expansion. Political and macroeconomic uncertainties and lack of a track record for private participation of many SSA countries continue to be barriers to attract private investment.

Capital markets are clearly underdeveloped in SSA and extensive reliance on foreign borrowing entails exposure to convertibility, transfer and exchange rate risks. The situation is unlikely to improve dramatically without reduced political uncertainty, fiscal discipline and more efficient financial intermediation. However, some signs of progress are noticeable. Stock markets have been developing since 1995 in Africa because of the partial liberalization of rules, which previously prohibited foreign portfolio investment and the introduction of some privatization programs.

In the power sector, signs of change are starting to emerge. Competition is beginning to emerge in varying degrees in the running of even the most integrated power utilities. These include allowing private sector in generation in a few SSA countries, contracting out certain functions of operations and management, etc.

Much of SSA is saddled with higher costs of petroleum products at over 100 per cent of OECD costs. Specific targets for liberalization of oil and gas industry in SSA countries require closure of inefficient refineries and adoption of import parity pricing with rational differential between fuels and refinery subsidies. This will also require investment in the construction of efficient petroleum infrastructure in SSA countries to reduce transit costs.

The small size of power systems and the weakness of the regulatory frameworks of SSA countries make it difficult for these countries to unbundle their power systems to promote competition similar to that of power sectors in Asia and Latin America. Energy market transition in SSA raises, in acute form, special challenges to increase access to efficient energy at affordable cost.

Independent producers might be able to compete with utility based generation in specific circumstances. There is a need to review the barriers to their entry in the market and the rules for pricing their output. Restructuring distribution has attracted less attention than competition in the generation market. In SSA countries, whatever improvements are made in efficiency at the plant and grid levels will be jeopardized if distribution remains grossly overstaffed and unreliable and if utilities fail to collect bills. Management contracts can make a difference but a major issue can be the scarcity of bidders or the dominance of a few. Furthermore, management contracts are not required to finance investments and provide no guarantee for efficient cost recovery. The issue of generating investment to finance system maintenance and expansion will therefore continue to exist. Unbundling of distribution should be accompanied by its decentralization into several service areas designed to make bidding for the franchise attractive.

Whether or not energy enterprises remain vertically integrated, governments need to focus on the changing role of the government from being both the owner and operator to that of facilitator of efficient energy enterprises and promoter of investment opportunities. Transforming the already weak traditional institutional mind-set to manage energy market transition is a daunting challenge for SSA countries. Building effective institutions is of central importance to formulate sector policies, regulatory oversight and promote investment for efficient energy investment at the national and regional level to increase access to energy at affordable prices.

Sector policy should address pricing, regulation and institutional arrangements at the national and regional levels to secure access to efficient energy supplies, sector reform and financial viability of energy enterprises and create an environment to attract investment. Sector reform policy should define clearly the role of private sector and design a realistic and achievable goal to attract private investment.

The first step for SSA countries to attract private participation in energy is careful project preparation. The nature of the private sector participation at the national and regional level and the issues it raises need to be addressed in project preparation, especially since the first private sector commitment is crucial for setting the record. Experience from emerging economies in Asia, the Middle East and Latin America indicate competitive tendering for opportunities is the best approach for an established program of private participation in BOO type generation projects. Government institutions will need to develop standard procedures for soliciting, appraising and negotiating private investment proposals in an open and transparent manner.

Given the political and economic uncertainties, market size, demand growth and lack of track record of private investment in utilities in SSA countries, the first effort of competitive tendering may not generate adequate response. While some form of competitive tendering for private sector opportunities is the best approach, SSA countries in Southern Africa, such as Zimbabwe, Zambia and Botswana have, since 2000, opted to enter into agreements with South Africa's utility, Eskom, on a bilateral basis to attract the first project or contract. The impact of a successful first experience could facilitate an award of subsequent project/contract opportunities on a competitive basis. Given that South Africa is a major player in SSA's regional market, it could further facilitate regional trade and investment in energy to the mutual benefit of SSA countries.

A regional perspective to energy markets and sector reform requires building effective regional institutions to facilitate private investment, increase energy trade and access. Interconnection of national petroleum and power markets will help encourage private investment through expanding market size, thereby helping investors to manage commercial and political risks. Interconnection also encourages global scale projects, which lower supply costs through avoiding investment in redundant supply facilities and decrease strategic and macroeconomic risks by expanding countries' supply options. Furthermore, expanding interconnection opens export opportunities for countries with comparative advantage in energy supply and facilitates growth in those countries.

Despite severe political and operational problems, the SADC region has achieved noticeable progress in regional cooperation in the power sector. Since 1996, the number of interconnections and associated power exchange agreements has increased, in part because of extensions from the Eskom network in South Africa to neighbouring countries. The level of international annual electricity exchanges in the region is doubling about every five years at an approximate growth rate of 15 per cent per year. By 1998 there were about 16 bulk power supply agreements and about eight cross-border power supply agreements in Southern Africa. The new imperative in the region calls for cost-effectiveness based on sound commercial practices and for substantive restructuring efforts targeted towards more rational market approaches in planning and operational procedures.

Given the capital intensive nature of energy investment with high foreign exchange content of investment, the need for a regional approach is crucial to broaden the market base and to address commercial project risks. Areas of regional approach include sector reforms, standards of energy planning and investment in energy and energy infrastructure such as oil and gas pipelines and electricity transmission.

Development of international electricity markets at regional levels is complicated because of limited experience and difficulties of arriving at mutually beneficial arrangements to participating countries. However, experience shows that the trading of electricity is also dependent on several national and regional institutional and organizational factors such as harmonization of sector structures of different national power sectors in a given region and coordination of information at the regional level to maintain stability of the whole interconnected system. This requires the implementation of pooling arrangements with setting up of bulk prices and transmission pricing structures, open access and free transit and an investment climate to attract financing to sustain the increasing power trade in the long run.

Approach to sector reforms, sector structure, standards of planning and institution capabilities vary across the region. Building of effective regional institutions require complementing those institutions that already exist, such as SADC, SAPP UPDEA and the association of power utilities in West Africa. Successful promotion of a regional approach requires reforming the sector across the region, standardizing planning and regulatory requirements and connecting communities of market players through open information flows.

Future directions

SSA has been a late entrant in the wave of globalization and energy market transition. Despite adequate energy resources and being a net exporter of oil, the majority population in SSA countries have little access to commercial energy. Regional per capita income growth has been 0.5 per cent for the previous ten years and per capita energy consumption actually fell from 345 kgoe in 1997 to 337 kgoe in 2000.[97] GDP growth in SSA slowed to 2.4 per cent in 2003. Substantial external debt for individual states remains a major problem. Intractable problems of disease and poor infrastructure persist. According to the WB 2004 Global Development Finance assessment, despite genuine progress in resolving some of the region's most egregious civil conflicts (Angola and Liberia), the situation in the DRC, Somalia, Sudan and Zimbabwe remains unstable.

Finally, SSA oil exporters such as Nigeria and Equatorial Guinea are unable to forge positive linkages between the oil sector and other sectors of their economies even with resilient oil prices and growing oil exports. For example, with the rapid growth of US private investment in Equatorial Guinea's oil industry since 1996, significant offshore discoveries and oil production have made Equatorial Guinea the major driver of its economic growth. However, even with the growing oil exports of over 200,000 b/d, the West African oil exporter Equatorial Guinea has been unable to make positive linkages of oil sector to other sectors of its economy for its small population of just over 500,000. Despite rapid growth in real GDP, there is strong evidence of government misappropriation of oil revenues. While real per capita GDP has doubled since 1998, there has been little positive change in social indicators. Equatorial Guinea's government has been routinely charged with engaging excessively in corruption.

The experience of Equatorial Guinea shows that honest and effective governance remains a major challenge even with strong GDP growth, resilient oil prices, potential for growing exports and the continued interest of private investors. It also underscores the continuing challenge of dealing with mutual suspicion of host country-international oil/ energy company relations. Sector reforms, regulatory provisions, promoting private investment, regional approach to increase energy trade and investment and emerging institutions for market, all require non-corrupt economic governance to connect with the vast population that is without access to commercial energy. SSA has a particular need to address the economic governance issues of serving dispersed rural energy demand. The lack of population density in rural areas requires innovative solutions for electricity and cooking fuels.

Future directions of energy market transition in SSA requires a strategy for efficient economic governance for the twenty-first century by building effective national and regional institutions to reform the energy market, to expand regional energy trade and investment and finally to increase access to efficient energy at affordable cost.

The future direction of SSA's energy market transition raises the special challenge of increasing access to efficient energy at affordable prices. In view of the very high prices that many who are not connected to the public network pay

---

97. UN, *Energy Statistics Yearbook* (2000)

to obtain services from the informal sector or through self-provision, willingness to pay for basic electricity services may be less of a problem. Facilitating private provision and promoting efficiency by lifting the many obstacles to entry and import tariffs on alterative technologies could increase access to efficient energy at affordable prices to a majority of the population. Chapter 6 will focus on the challenge of energy market transition to increase access to efficient energy for the over 2 billion poor, including over 525 million in SSA.

ASSESSING ENERGY SECTOR REFORM EXPERIENCE OF THE 1990S IN CASE STUDY COUNTRIES

Energy sector liberalization in the 1990s in all the case study countries/ regions was part of the general macroeconomic objective towards opening up of the energy market to private investment. It was also a reaction to several factors specific to energy-pricing distortions and growing subsidies, sector inefficiencies/ financial bankruptcy of state-owned energy enterprises, growing energy shortages and the need for mobilizing the required investment in energy for development and the pressures of the energy sector's growing subsidies on the economy.

At the beginning of the 1990s, armed with the facts on deteriorating financial viability of state-owned energy/ power enterprises and the fall of the Berlin Wall signalling the demise of the command and control philosophy of communism, international development institutions and their industrialized member countries shared the conviction that developing countries should reform their energy sectors and open up to private investment. As part of the macroeconomic reform and liberalization program, the energy sector reform agenda of the 1990s ranged from energy price liberalization and transparent regulation to commercialization/ restructuring and privatization/ private sector participation.

Certainly the reforms produced some gains. However, the benefits of the paradigm shift from changing the role of the government from being the owner and operator to that of creator of an enabling environment for private investment in the 1990s were less than expected. The disconnect between expected positive changes in principles of reforming energy pricing, setting up of regulatory institutions, corporatizing/ unbundling and opening up to private investment and realities of implementing required actions to translate reform principles into practices raised questions about the energy liberalization model and the right direction of future energy policy. This section first summarizes the energy sector reform experience of the eight case study countries, discusses the critical factors impacting the outcomes of energy sector reform in case studies in the 1990s and concludes the chapter by bringing out the emerging features of the energy market in the case study countries in shaping their energy future.

The evolution of energy sector liberalization

During the 1990s, practically all case study countries and a few SSA countries embarked in principle on energy sector reforms. However, the shift in policies varied in timing, content and speed from country to country and between countries in the SSA region. Furthermore, despite policy statements made to liberalize energy sector, progress also varied by countries. Broadly, except for South Africa, all case study countries' policy shift to liberalize their energy sectors in the 1990s were made often in the context of stabilization and reform programs supported by the IMF and the WB as the cost of energy subsidies were impacting the fundamentals of macroeconomic stabilization.

The rising tide of global information system technologies and globalization in the 1990s and the prevailing distortions in energy pricing and inefficiencies in the state-owned and operated energy enterprises, particularly in electric power provided the environment for developing countries to transform their energy sectors from plan to market. China, the largest developing economy, continued the reforms as part of its macroeconomic liberalization that began in the late 1970s. After its economic crisis in 1991, India, the second largest developing economy started energy sector reform to deal with growing energy shortages.

Argentina, crippled with hyperinflation, adopted a full-scale 'diving-in' approach to embrace US style capitalism and free market which saw the privatization and opening up of its economy and energy sector. Brazil announced a radical program to open up its economy and energy sector. Egypt, linked to US aid, had to comply with certain conditions to reform its economy and energy sector to qualify for the US-led Paris Club international assistance. Jordan, as importer of all its energy needs adopted a pragmatic approach to energy sector liberalization. Several SSA countries were fed with expectations that liberalization would accelerate growth and access to energy for development. In South Africa, the transition to a multiracial democracy brought to focus the inequities in access to energy despite its high per capita energy consumption and encouraged steps toward reforming the economy/ energy sector along with increasing access to energy for development.

All case study countries/ region made differing policy changes in principle during the 1990s. On balance, despite regional and inter-country disparities during the 1990s, total and per capita commercial energy consumption, total installed electricity capacity and access to electricity improved in all case studies.

The rising energy consumption did not benefit everyone in the case study countries and the population without access to electricity ranged between 13 million people in China to 583 million people in India and 525 million people in SSA. Despite the fact that the SSA region is a net exporter of energy, the SSA population's access to electricity was under 25 per cent. Furthermore, even among those with access to electricity in India and SSA, the quality and reliability of electricity supply continued to be poor. Table 5. 8 shows energy situation in case study countries between 1990–2000.

Table 5.8: Energy for development indicators in case study countries/ regions: 1990 and 2002

(Thousand tons of oil equivalent (1000toe) and kilograms per capita)

Country	*Total energy consumption*	*Total energy consumption*	*Per-capita energy consumption*	*Per-capita energy consumption*	*Per-capita electricity consumption(kwh)*	*Access to electricity(percent of population)*
	1990	2002	1990	2002	2002	2002
Argentina	46,110	56,297	1,428	1,543	2,024	94.6
Brazil	133,531	190,664	902	1,093	1,776	94.9
China	879,923	1,228,574	775	960	987	98.6
Egypt	31,895	52,393	608	789	1,073	93.8
India	366,377	538,305	430	513	380	43.0
Jordan	4,459	5,169	3,610	4,058	1,371	95.0
Sub-Saharan Africa	321,208	418,008	693	667	457	24.7
Of which South Africa	91,229	113,458	2,592	2,502	1,219	66.1

Source: WB, *World Development Indicators* (2005); UN, *Energy Statistics Yearbook* (1990 and 2000); IEA, *WEO* (2005), Chapter 10, 'Energy and Development'

Argentina adopted US style free market liberalizing energy prices and opened up to the private sector. Countries in SSA, with small energy systems already paying high energy prices with little improvement in increasing access to electricity and commercial energy supplies, were unable to attract private investment. China, Brazil, India, Egypt and Jordan made significant progress in eliminating distortions in petroleum prices, to set up regulatory institutions to open up for private investment in offshore petroleum and gas upstream operations and made selective choices to involve private sector in power generation. However, Argentina's economic crisis in 2001, Brazil's 1999 currency crisis followed by drought and energy crisis in 2001 and the 2003 election outcome impacted their energy sectors. These experiences have shaken their expectations of the benefits of the 'Washington Consensus Style' of the free energy market reform model. The gap between the expectations of energy market reform to increase access to energy for development and the realized benefits increased, thus perpetuating energy shortages, black-outs, little improvement in efficiency of existing energy systems and in reliability. The divergences and inequalities in access to energy for development, both across case study countries/ regions and within the countries, underscores the disparity between principles and practices of sector reform in the 1990s.

Critical factors impact outcomes in energy sector reform

The foregoing summary of sector reform experiences and the discussions in Chapter 4 and 5 of the case studies brings out five critical factors impacting the reform outcome. These include reform design, macro-financial and energy sector linkage, market size, reform approach and politics, institutions and reform implementation. The first of these critical factors is the reform design. The energy sector reform agenda of the 1990s was incomplete and deficient in its very design. It was a top-down appendix to the deficient macroeconomic reform agenda. Part of the problem with the design was the expectation generated that reform design elements of pricing, regulation and commercialization would attract private investment, which in turn, would improve efficiency, create competition and increase access to energy for development, with little attention to the details that could adversely affect the reform outcome.

A second critical factor impacting the reform outcome is the macro-financial and energy sector linkage. The fact that few case study countries achieved sound domestic financial systems in the 1990s impacted the systemic banking crises in the 1990s.The reform agenda of the early 1990s often ignored the central role of the financial system for macro stability and financing of investment in energy for development. The 1990s expensive financial crises occurred in the 'East Asia Miracle' countries, Brazil and the African countries. The new millennium began with crises starting in the Latin American showcase model of transition to free market country, Argentina and high non-performing loans in China. Argentina's experience revealed the threat to macroeconomic stability posed by the combination of high debt and the inflexible hard-peg exchange rate with increased capital mobility made its economy vulnerable to sudden shifts in capital flows. By focusing on increasing the role of the market, Argentina in the 1990s introduced a rigid exchange rate without the fiscal and financial conditions and effective institutions for the market that are needed to sustain it.

The East Asian economies and Argentina impacted by the financial crisis of late 1990s and 2001 had high debts and larger current account deficits than usual and were pursuing exchange rate based stabilization policies. The Asian crisis in 1997 and Argentina's crisis in 2001 caused GDP, electricity demand and currency values in foreign exchange markets to fall. As discussed in the Argentina case study in this chapter, net gains from energy sector liberalization up to 1998 in Argentina were reversed, since the 2001 economic/ financial crisis when over-indebted Argentina defaulted. The problems and limited results with energy sector liberalization since the 1990s often reflected macroeconomic and financial sector linkage deficiencies and the overhang of large external debt. Countries such as China and India that managed capital inflows, including through the imposition of restrictions, were able to weather the crises much better than countries that took no such precautions.

The experience of the late 1990s and 2001 financial crises underscored the fact that successful energy market liberalization depends on successful financial liberalization and successful finance depends on macroeconomic stability. An appropriately regulated and supervised domestic financial system is critical to avoid macroeconomic vulnerability arising from the concentration of lending in highly risky activities and/ or the emergence of balance sheet mismatches.

The third critical factor impacting the outcome of energy sector reform in developing countries is the size of the energy market and energy system configuration. Not every case study country/ region is equally well-positioned to benefit from restructuring and privatization. Brazil for example, has a largely hydro based power system with uncertain rainfall and multi-purpose dams precluding substantial gains from privatization. A number of countries in SSA have a system peak below 150 MW with limited opportunities for introducing competition. As discussed in the case study of SSA, these countries could benefit from adopting a regional rather than national approach to regulation, restructuring and private investment. However, the institutional barriers in SSA for effective execution of sector reform at regional levels remains a major deterrent in the reform design.

The fourth critical factor impacting the outcome of energy sector reform is the reform approach followed by countries. Early in the 1990s, when energy sector reform was being launched, there was much discussion about the reform approaches, sequencing and pacing of reforms.

'Diving-in/ shock therapy' or 'wetting the feet/ gradualism/ incrementalism' were a few of the approaches. Argentina opted for the 'diving-in' approach to energy market liberalization, while all other case study countries opted for 'gradualism/ incrementalism' with piecemeal changes, taking start-up conditions into account. China followed a cautious and gradual approach to reform in the energy sector. For example, China was reluctant to take decisions on opening up to private power before understanding the socio-economic-political costs and benefits of making the decision. But India, faced with macroeconomic problems and energy shortages took a 'diving-in' policy decision in 1991 to open up to private power to seize the benefits without following up on building up of the institutions required to translate policy to action on the ground and without understanding the intricacies of how private power works.

With the exception of South Africa, all governments in the case study countries followed the Washington Consensus, liberalized trade, tried to achieve macroeconomic stability, tried to set energy prices right, established regulatory authorities and announced the restructuring and corporatization of their energy enterprises. Discussions on sequencing of reforms gathered momentum. But private investment in energy for development did not follow as strongly as envisaged despite the initially expressed flood of interest from private investors.

While emphasis was placed on setting up of regulatory authorities and changing the organizational structure of energy enterprises, little attention was paid to the capabilities of these institutions to regulate and commercialize energy enterprises. In the absence of an effective regulatory structure, other public objectives such as universal service and increasing access to energy at affordable prices could not be achieved. Consequently, public support for the continuation of reform was undermined. The theories of 'diving-in versus getting wet' and 'sequencing of reform' did not provide guidance for transition from the point of command and control to reach the goal of free market. The reason is, as case studies illustrate, the guidelines evolve with experience and judgment and are shaped by the political economy, commitment and the role and effectiveness of reforming institutions.

The fifth critical factor impacting the reform outcome is the vital role of the government not only in formulating reform design but also in its effective implementation. After 15 years of energy sector reform experience in developing countries, it is now clear that energy sector reform policies can promote energy for development only when combined with the government's political commitment for effective policy implementation. The challenge is to determine what the appropriate approaches are for reform implementation and how to ensure the long-term political commitment to effective economic governance of institutions responsible for translating reform objectives to realities on the ground.

Given the diverse outcome of energy sector reform in the case studies, diverse approaches to reform design and implementation followed underscore the critical role of political philosophy, commitment and effectiveness of reform implementation and outcome. The key question is whether political philosophy, democracy and authoritarianism influence the politics of reform. Democratic developing countries with elected leaders often argue that in a pluralistic democracy, as in the case of India, consensus building for reforms is critical for both adopting the reform agenda and its effective implementation. Although democracy and reform politics are intertwined, the political parties in these countries did agree on the general idea of the need for reform. But politicians, focused on their constituents' agenda to capture votes, failed to agree on the implementation of the required pricing and commercialization policies and often failed to offer voters a credible choice in terms of economic policies and further, even when a policy was offered and adopted, paid little attention to effective policy performance. Consequently, electoral outcomes reflecting the vast majority of disaffected population in India, Argentina and

Brazil impacted the course of the reform process.

In the case of China and Egypt, with no pluralistic democracy, Egypt was a 'pretend reformer', compared with China, which was a 'goal-oriented reformer'. Jordan continued to be 'a willing reformer' of its energy sector. Despite being a net energy exporter, the SSA region's failure to increase access to energy for its development poses the challenge of how to get the goverments and institutions to effectively translate reform principles to operational realities. The success of policy performance/ reform outcome depends on efficient economic governance and the quality of institutions responsible for translating policies to realities on the ground.

The conceptual framework of the impact of critical factors on the diverse outcome of energy sector reforms in the case study countries are summarized in Table 5.9, which also presents several elements of the experience since the 1990s.

Table 5.9: Examples of Impact of Critical Factors on Energy Sector Reform Outcome in Case Study Countries

Country	*Sector reform design-market size*	*Macro-sector linkage*	*Reform approach-political system -governance*	*Reform outcome*
Argentina	Adopted US free market model: medium-size energy market	Dollarization-high-debt /volatile capital flows	Big-Bang/ Dive-in approach	Success in the 1990s followed by economic crisis since 2001 with adverse impact on energy sector
Brazil	Strategic focus; Medium-size energy market with dependency on hydropower	Macro-stabilization with 1990s quasi-fixed exchange-rate policy in 1999 adversely impacted energy sector	Selective-gradual opening –up of energy sector to private investment	Brazil succeeded in reducing oil imports; continued dependence on hydro posed power shortages during drought
China	Socialist-market model: Very big market	Overall macro-sector reform: Two-track system	Communist/ authoritative political system; cautiously-managed incremental transition	Despite inequalities-corruption, crossing the stream of market by groping stones; became net importer of oil in 1994

Country	*Sector reform design-market size*	*Macro-sector linkage*	*Reform approach-political system -governance*	*Reform outcome*
Egypt	'Coerced' reformer' medium-size market	Macro-sector reform linkage as part of IMF-G-8 debt-write-off agreement	Selective/ lagged/ discrete / incremental reform approach/ managed political system	Despite slow/ bureaucratic approach success in reforming oil, gas, and LNG sectors
India	Macroeconomic stabilization-mixed economy model; very big market	Incomplete macro-sector linkage despite cautious monetary policy to ward off capital flow volatilities	Top-down/ selective sector reform. World's largest pluralistic democracy often cited as an excuse for failure to reform power sector	Despite success in reforming macroeconomic fundamentals, failure to reform power sector due to corrupt/ ineffective economic governance and inadequate institutions.
Jordan	'Willing-reformer' small-size market	Classic IMF-WB stabilization model	Democracy-leadership driven reform-process	Despite being a willing reformer and making progress in macro-sector adjustments, popular discontent; Jordan's strategic-position in the Middle-East define the future course of reform
SSA Region	Selective countries such as Ghana/ Uganda/ Mali/ 'Role model' approach; very small individual country market; low population density	Washington-consensus IMF-World Bank model	States' inability to exercise authority/ ineffective economic and political governance	Despite some policy improvements in role model countries and inflow of private investment in oil-exporting West African countries, failure in effective implementation of

Country	*Sector reform design-market size*	*Macro-sector linkage*	*Reform approach-political system -governance*	*Reform outcome*
				reforms to increasing access to energy for development due to geographical/ political/ institutional factors. Consequently, despite the SSA being the net exporter of oil, the region continues to lack the required access to energy for development.
South Africa	Post-1994 reformer; medium-size market	Adopted South-Africa empowerment model	Post-1994 democracy driven reform	Progress in increasing access to energy along with commercial public-private partnership

Source: Author's elaboration.

Emerging features of energy sector in non-OPEC developing countries since 2001

15 years of varied and mixed energy sector reform experience in non-OPEC developing countries coupled with the changing political, economic and energy environment since 2001 are beginning to shape the future of energy sectors in the non-OPEC developing countries. Some of the emerging features of the non-OPEC energy sector in developing countries that could impact energy for development strategies in the coming decades include:

- Diversities in non-OPEC energy markets
- Internationalization of state-owned NOCs
- All options open strategy
- State dominated Energy Policy Model

Diversities in non-OPEC energy markets

Energy sector reforms in developing countries are more complicated because unique country circumstances determine the reform design and its effectiveness in reform implementation. The mixed and varied reform outcome of the last 15 years in developing countries underscores the fact that energy markets in developing countries are diverse. Rising demand for energy, spiking oil prices since 2004 and concerns of security of energy supplies have further accentuated the diverse impacts on the future course of reform strategy. These factors have catalyzed the non-OPEC energy industry to undertake a series of modifications in their reform strategies while seeking access to efficient and reliable energy at affordable prices. The outcome is the emergence of a distinctive three-tiered energy industry structure with each tier of countries facing a variety of challenges.

Tier one countries include mainly India and China, together currently accounting for over one-third of the world's population. With growing energy demand and rising oil imports, China and India are adopting strategies to secure overseas oil supplies to reduce the growing gap between domestic oil production and consumption in order to meet the growing gap between domestic energy production and rising consumption. Tier two countries include all other non-OPEC developing countries with medium size energy markets in Asia, Latin America, the Middle East and South Africa. Tier three non-OPEC developing countries include small size energy markets mainly in SSA and Nepal in South Asia. As discussed earlier in this chapter, more than 60 developing countries, many of which are in SSA have very small energy systems. Tier three countries in SSA with low electrification rate, low population densities and weak institutions and governance face far greater challenges in increasing access to energy for development.

Internationalization of National Oil Companies (NOCs) in non-OPEC developing countries

Faced with the pressure to meet the rising energy demand the leading tier countries, China, India-and medium tier non-OPEC developing countries such as Brazil are taking steps to increase their access to global energy resources by internationalizing their state-owned companies and oil and gas operations. Oil and gas pricing reforms since the 1990s implemented in case study countries such as India, China and Brazil improved the financial viability of the state oil and gas companies and helped increase their profitability, in spite of a setback due to rising oil prices of 2004 when domestic prices failed to reflect market's rising trends. Brazil's PetroBras' main areas of focus are South America and playing to its technical strengths—the deep waters of West Africa and the US Gulf of Mexico (GOM). With contracts signed in Iran and Libya, PetroBras is trying to expand its operations to the Middle East.

The Chinese state-owned oil companies have been particularly active since 2001, with acquisitions of over $40 billion. India's ONGC is a late starter is accelerating its overseas activities of acquisitions. Given the need to bridge the growing gap in energy demand and domestic supply, the Chinese and Indian NOCs are prepared to accept lower rates of return on their international operations than other international oil companies. PetroBras, by contrast, is driven by the need to grow, to satisfy its shareholders and to diversify its portfolio, reducing financing costs and increasing access to hard currency.[98]

The NOCs of Brazil, China and India are also working more closely with other NOCs in OPEC and non-OPEC countries including Nigeria, Libya, Iran, Russia, Indonesia, Saudi Arabia and Venezuela.

The future of internationalization of oil and gas operations by NOCs in China, India and Brazil depends on their skills in operations, their corporate identity and operational independence. Thus far, the NOC's expertise seems to be confined to oil projects although they can form a joint venture with IOCs in their international operations to bring in the required technical skills. The critical factor determining the efficiency of NOCs in their international operations is their autonomy. Political interference in the case of China and Brazil may have helped to build business. However, government interference, as in the case of India's ONGC, where the petroleum Minister was reported in September 2005 to have made attempts to fill the ONGC board with party politicians, if kept unchecked, could erode both efficiency and commerciality of state-owned companies. Forward-thinking NOCs could continue to prosper by transforming their business by playing to the strengths of the changing energy market to keep them technically competent, operationally independent, efficient and financially and commercially viable.

All Options Open Energy Strategy

The new conditions of rising oil prices and concerns of peaking of world oil reserves, security of oil supplies and fears of over-dependence on imported fossil fuels combined with a wave of power cuts experienced worldwide in 2003 have caused developing and developed oil importing countries to address the issue of securing national energy needs, including sourcing of future power supply. Growing fears about energy supply security and the more pressing claims of curbing greenhouse gas emission (GHG) are shaping developed countries' evolving consensus to reconsider their fuel sourcing

98. National Oil Companies, *Petroleum Economist* (April 2005)

options and to allow a stronger role for nuclear energy, despite investors' caution to issues of long lead times and the prohibitively capital intensive nature of building new nuclear plants. Judged on capital costs alone, nuclear plants cost three times more than gas-fired combined cycle plants. Compared with the capital costs for combined cycle gas turbines (CCGTs) ranging between $450 /kW and $900 /kW, capital costs of nuclear plants are $2,000–2,500 /kW for large-scale nuclear plants using the 1980s design range.[99] The financial implications of nuclear plants extend well beyond the initial and construction costs. The social costs of safety regulation to address concerns over the issue of nuclear safety impact the financial risk of nuclear plants. Nonetheless, with rising oil prices and growing fears about the security of fossil fuel supplies, rethinking of the nuclear energy option to permit lifetime extension of existing plants and expectations of building new plants are gathering momentum.

The nuclear industry in the developed world is responding to the changing energy scene by claiming technical advances that could dramatically reduce both the construction and operating costs of new nuclear capacity. The US based Nuclear Energy Institute claims that a well-managed nuclear unit can produce electricity profitably at a total cost of $0.02–0.025 /kWh, compared to a total cost of $0.035–0.045 /kWh assuming that the capital cost of a gas-powered plant is $500–600 /kw and gas prices are $3–4 /mBtu. The nuclear industry also advances the argument of the advent of cheaper reactor models that could reduce the construction cost by more than 50 per cent. However, in the electricity market of a competitive developed country, the perceived financial risks to investors and the requirement of adequate rates of return to overcome the initial financial risks on energy investments impact the decisions on the choice of nuclear options.

Non-OPEC net oil importing countries, while facing similar issues as developed oil importers in the changing global energy situation, also need to address the additional issues of accessing workable efficient technology to reduce capital costs and financing. While all non-OPEC oil importing developing countries are starting to face rising demand for energy, a phase that the developed countries experienced during their rapid industrialization and urban growth, the strategies to narrow the energy deficit gap are increasingly being shaped by the diversified pressures of the three-tier energy sectors. Confronted by rising populations and with inadequate domestic fuel resources, the big and medium size non-OPEC developing countries of Asia are responding to the issues of reducing dependence on imported fossil fuels and sourcing of fuel for power by adopting an 'All Options Open' policy to include the option of nuclear power generation in order to increase their energy supplies. As of 2003, from a total of 27 nuclear stations under con-

99. Nuclear Power, *Petroleum Economist* (April 2005)

struction across the globe, 16 are in China, India, Japan and South Korea.[100]

China and India, the leading tier non-OPEC oil importing countries have started up nine plants since 2000 and plan to build at least ten more. With nine reactors in operation and two under construction, China is well on its way to achieving a more than four-fold increase in nuclear capacity by 2020, to 36 GW. As of 2005, with all 11 units in operation, the nuclear source will provide a capacity of 8.4 GW, although it will still account for less than 3 per cent of the overall electricity generation in China.

Like China, as of 2003, India's share of nuclear energy accounted for just 3 per cent of total capacity in power generation. India expects to increase this to 5 per cent by 2020 by expanding the capacity to 20 GW. South Korea has the region's highest nuclear capacity, with 20 reactors accounting for 40 per cent of its electricity supply. Nuclear capacity is planned to grow to 15 GW by 2015.

State-dominated energy policy model

Despite the diversities of the three-tiered non-OPEC energy sector in developing countries, energy policy in most of the non-OPEC developing countries in Asia, Africa, the Middle East and Latin America is swinging back to a state-dominated model. The trend away from open markets and back towards state domination is gathering momentum since 2001, ranging from Argentina, Bolivia, Brazil, Colombia, Peru and Mexico in Latin America to China and India in Asia. The internationalization of state-owned energy firms and policies on the nuclear energy option discussed above have become a part of state-dominated energy policy models. The retreat from reforms in the energy sector stems from the broader trend in developing countries of a pendulum swing away from the free market agenda of the 1990s. In developing democracies, reforms were sold to the voters as the key to launching an era of growth and prosperity and to lifting millions of people from poverty. However, the gulf between reform principles and the reform outcome of 15 years of the reform experiment failed to deliver the promises made to open up to the private sector to increase access to energy for development.

Many of reformist democracies have been replaced by socialist parties that have committed themselves to generate employment, combat poverty and inequality through state interventions. Newly elected leaders in Argentina, Brazil, India and other developing democracies have targeted controls on the liberalization of energy markets and sought to limit the effect of rising energy prices on their populations. Even the single party communist China

---

100. Nuclear Power, *Petroleum Economist* (April 2005)

is acknowledging the growing inequalities and emergence of dual economy with growing conflicts between the rural and urban, the haves and the have-nots. With the exception of a few countries, non-OPEC developing countries still have poorly developed local capital markets and governments are faced with growing expenditures in social sectors of health, education and basic human needs for clean water, energy poverty and heavy debt burden. Under these circumstances and with the changing twenty-first century scene of rising energy prices, the re-emergence of the state-dominated energy model raises critical issues on the future course of energy sector reform to attract the required public and private investment in energy.

CHAPTER 6

SECTOR REFORM, LIBERALIZATION AND ENERGY FOR THE POOR

After a decade of launching of energy sector reform in developing countries, 1.61 billion people, accounting for over a quarter of world's population, lacked access to electricity. Table 6.1 below shows the number of people without electricity.

Table 6.1. Number of People Without Electricity 2002(million)

Region	*Rural*	*Urban*	*Total*
Africa	416	118	535
Sub-Saharan Africa (SSA)	408	117	526
North Africa	8	1	9
Developing Asia	871	148	1,019
East Asia and China	192	29	221
South Asia	679	119	798
The Middle East	13	7	14
Latin America	39	1	46
Developing Countries	1,339	275	1,623
Organization for Economic Cooperation and Development(OECD) and transition economies	7	<1	7
World	1,347	275	1,623

Source: *WEO* (2004), Chapter 10, Table 10.4

Around two-thirds of people lacking access to electricity are in South Asia and SSA. Over 75 per cent of population in SSA and over 55 per cent of population in South Asia lack access to electricity. Over 80 per cent people without electricity live in the rural areas of South Asia and SSA. Even with slower rate of growth in population in developing Asia and SSA, and if the

IEA's optimistic projected increase in the electrification rates in developing countries, from 66 per cent in 2002 to 78 per cent in 2030, were to be successfully reached, the total number of people without electricity would fall only slightly from 1.6 billion people in 2002 to less than 1.4 billion in 2030. Half the population of SSA and over one-third of the population in South Asia would still be without electricity. Table 6.2 shows projections of Urban and Rural Electrification (RE) Rates by region (per cent).

Table 6.2: Projections of Urban and Rural Electrification Rates by Region (per cent)

Region	2002		2015		2030	
	Urban	*Rural*	*Urban*	*Rural*	*Urban*	*Rural*
Africa	62	19	67	26	75	38
North Africa	99	88	100	96	100	97
Sub-Saharan Africa (SSA)	52	8	58	16	70	30
China and East Asia	96	83	100	88	100	89
South Asia	69	33	77	44	88	50
Latin America	98	61	100	71	100	76
The Middle East	99	78	100	87	100	95
Developing Countries	85	52	89	58	92	61
World	91	58	93	62	94	65
Total: Number of people without electricity (million)	275	1,347	290	1,249	287	1,106

Source: IEA, 2004, World Energy Outlook, Table 10.A4.

As of 2002, 2.4 billion people, accounting for over one-third of the world's population, use traditional biomass, dung, wood and agricultural residue for cooking and heating. Poor people in rural areas of South Asia and SSA, especially women and children are engaged in gathering these traditional fuels. Although governments in South Asia continue to subsidize kerosene and liquefied petroleum gas (LPG), safety concerns, income levels and the front-end cost of using LPG continue to be barriers to access modern energy services.

The number of people relying entirely on traditional fuels is expected to rise from 2.4 billion in 2002 to 2.6 billion in 2030. The share of India and Africa together in the total number of people relying on traditional fuels is expected to grow over to over two-thirds to reach 1.7 billion people.

Table 6.3: Population Relying on Traditional Biomass for Cooking and Heating (in million)

**Region*	*2002*	*2015*	*2030*
Africa	646	805	996
South Asia	746	844	883
(of which) India	595	665	693
East Asia and China	925	829	693
(of which) China	704	618	505
Latin America	79	68	60
Developing Countries	2,398	2,549	2,634

**The Middle East is not included as the numbers are negligible*
Source: IEA, *WEO* (2004), Table 10.6

The IEA/WB[1] acknowledge that projections on electrification rates in developing countries are dependent on increase in incomes, electricity pricing and affordability and making the required investment in electricity-supply-infrastructure and migration of rural–urban migration factors. A number of studies[2] undertaken by the WB-ESMAP, WEC and IEA have underscored the importance of development aid for providing energy services for the poor and have argued for more development aid to eradicate energy poverty.

In September 2000 the member states of the United Nations adopted eight Millennium Development Goals (MDG). These include: eradicating extreme poverty and hunger by reducing the proportion of people living on less than $1 a day by 50 per cent by 2015; achieving universal primary education; promoting gender equality and empowering women; improving maternal health; combating HIV/AIDS, malaria and other diseases, ensuring environmental sustainability; and developing a global partnership for development.

Although MDG do not include eradication of energy poverty, given the strong link between income and access to electricity, increasing the electrification rates and access to modern energy services to the poor are critical yardsticks to achieving the MDG by 2015.

Achieving the objective of MDG to reduce the number of people earning less than $1 per day requires upliftment of over 1 billion poor people in SSA

1. IEA, *'Energy and Development'*, *WEO* (2004), Chapter 10
2. WB, 'Report No. 15912 GLB: Rural Energy and Development' (Washington DC, July 1996)
   WB-ESMAP, *Energy and Development Report* (2000); *Energy Services for the World's Poor* (Washington DC); WEC, The Challenge of Rural Energy Poverty in Developing Countries (London, October 1999); IEA, *WEO* (Paris, 2002)

and South Asia by 2015. Increasing access to electricity and modern energy services for cooking and heating to over 1 billion people require large investment in energy-supply infrastructure in the low income SSA countries and South Asia. Achieving the target of MDG by 2015 would also require that developing countries need to take actions to expand access to modern energy services to cooking and heating such as LPG and kerosene to more than 700 million people by 2015.

Table 6.4 shows additional cumulative investments to meet the MDG of electrification.

Table 6.4: Impact of Meeting MDG Poverty-reduction Target on Investment

	Population without electricity (million)				*Additional cumulative investment ($billion)*
Region	2002	2015 Reference Scenario	2015 MDG case*	Difference	2003–15
Africa	536	601	453	148	46
(of which) North Africa	9	3	1	2	1
(of which) Sub-Saharan Africa	526	598	452	146	45
South Asia	798	773	417	355	104
East Asia and China	221	127	100	28	22
Latin America	46	27	5	22	28
The Middle East	14	9	5	3	3
Total	1,615	1,537	981	557	202

**Assumes that the Millennium Development Goal of reducing by half the proportion of the population living on less than $1 per day is achieved by 2015*
Source: IEA, *WEO* (2004), Table 10.8

IEA WEO (2004) estimates that increasing access to electricity to achieve the MDG would require an additional investment of over $200 billion through 2015, accounting for over 10 per cent of the total cumulative investments in the electricity sector in developing countries. SSA and South Asia with poor existing electricity infrastructure and commercially non-viable power enterprises are estimated to require 75 per cent of this additional investment.

Since the adoption of MDG in 2000, new governments elected in democracies such as India have resolved to take measures to achieve 'electricity for all by 2015'. However, based on the WB's 'Global Monitoring Report', 2004 and policies and actions for achieving the MDG and related outcomes, little progress is being made. The 2004 WB report made little reference to the reform progress on MDG for electricity in its Table 6.5 by just ticking 'yes' for electricity law and independent regulation. With the persisting disconnect between policy statements and concrete measures on the ground on the part of all MDG participants, it is doubtful that the MDG of eradicating energy poverty will be achieved by 2015 unless critical issues of disconnect between targets and results on the ground are identified and actions taken to achieve actual results.

Although the WB report on *Rural Energy and Development* (1996), the WB-ESMAP *Energy and Development Report* (2000), WEC's 1999 report on rural energy development and IEA's 2000 reports recognize the magnitude of the problem, these reports and case studies undertaken by ESMAP focus on data gathering, description of the problems, presentations in energy conferences held for business promotion and isolated best practice prescriptions. None of these studies have linked the main issues of increasing access to efficient energy for poor while staying the course of energy market transition.

The following sections of this chapter therefore, discusses widening access to energy in the context of energy market transition in developing countries. It then focuses on the key issues that developing countries will have to address to formulate policies and options for increasing access to energy to over 2 billion poor, while staying the course of energy sector reform and liberalization.

Energy transition problem

In developing countries 'energy poverty' has been a major problem of the wider 'Energy Market Transition' process. In the pre-1990s the governments were mainly responsible for RE and providing energy services to the poor. The electricity sector has a long history of public involvement in RE. The problems of high cost of RE, and low cash income and affordability were addressed through cross-subsidies between rich and poor, urban and rural and commercial and residential electricity rates. The government programs were supported by international donor agencies, multilateral financial institutions and aid agencies. These programs were supportive of developing countries' efforts to extend electricity supplies to their population. During 1970–90, 1.3 billion people were newly supplied with electricity from national grids, of whom 800 million were in urban areas and 500 million in rural areas. By 1990, practically all major cities and towns had access to some form of electricity service.

However, rural areas where a majority of the population in low income developing countries in South Asia and SSA live continued to lack access to electricity. The high cost of energy supply for low-density, low-demand rural areas and high cost of about 20 cents/kWh and the large subsidies for RE in most countries imposed a heavy financial burden on the utilities. Rural electricity tariffs rarely covered more than 15–30 per cent of estimated costs of supply and contributed to the financial bankruptcy of state electricity enterprises and macroeconomic stability.

The experiment of a decade of energy market transition of the 1990s focusing on reforming the energy sector promoted that market mechanisms supply electricity much more efficiently than the centrally planned governments. Multilateral institutions started to play a catalytic role in improving access to energy for rural and poor people. WB's policy directives of 1992 and 1996 on increasing access to energy for the rural poor replaced pre-1990s supply-driven, top–down programs involving single fuels with little local participation and low local investment. Sector reform required a changed role for the government, from being both owner and operator to becoming the creator of an attractive environment for private investors for energy supply.

Private investment in electric power projects in developing countries increased through 1997 in several countries. It declined following the East Asian financial Crisis in 1998 to recover at lower rates after 2000. While official development assistance declined for SSA and South Asia since 1995, the low level of foreign direct investment in energy did not match the growing demand and expansion requirements. Most of the private investment in IPPs concentrated on power generation and the state electricity companies continue to be responsible for transmission and distribution. Even where distribution is privatized, governments are responsible for expanding access in rural and poorer urban areas.

Despite some progress made in energy market transition in the 1990s to encourage private investment in the electricity industry, the fact remains that private companies supplied electricity mainly to the network and to the state owned electricity companies and preferred to concentrate on more lucrative contracts to supply industrial and urban consumers. Private utilities showed little interest in increasing access by extending electricity supplies to the urban poor and rural areas unless government subsidies made up for financial losses and provided a fair margin of profit. Even connecting to the urban poor where the network exists, private utilities require joint ventures with the state electricity enterprises.

The successful case of Argentina's electricity market transition illustrates this point. Electricity market reform in Argentina resulted in improved supply, quality, grid-extension and connection formalization. However, studies have shown that economic benefits have gone disproportionately to high income and high energy consumers. With growing income inequality and increasing urban poverty even in the pre-2001 period, despite the benefits of electricity sector reform, arguments were advocated for introduction of the social tariff to deal with the issue of increasing urban poverty. In the wake of the 2001 economic crisis and its adverse impact on the majority of Argentina's power companies and soaring unemployment and poverty rates, the need for cross-subsidization of electricity to low income consumers gained momentum. The Argentine government, in the process of restructuring the economy since 2002, began a move towards correcting the imbalances of the reform process by incorporating welfare measures into renegotiation of contracts. The policies for future course of market liberalization began to address issues related to making both public and privately run utilities responsible for welfare by re-reforming utilities towards more equitable outcomes[3].

As shown in Tables 6.1 and 6.2 earlier, the transition from energy poverty to having access at the household level to efficient and affordable energy varies widely among different regions and between countries. The electrification rates in the 1990s decade of market transition varied across regions. East Asia/ China, the Middle East and North Africa recorded about 30 per cent increase in electrification rate. Latin America fell in the middle with 17 per cent increase in electrification rate. SSA and South Asia recorded below 10 per cent increase in electrification rate. However, South Africa since 1994 is making progress to increase access to its urban poor and rural population under its empowerment plan.

The 1990s decade witnessed rapid electrification programs in East Asia. China, in particular, accounted for most of the progress.. China's case illustrates whether reform benefits the poor depends upon the active role of the government in the way in which reform is implemented. The electrification goal was part of China's poverty alleviation campaign in the mid 1980s. Between 1980 and 2000, China secured access to electricity for almost 700 million people enabling it to achieve an electrification rate covering more than 98 per cent of its population. Most Chinese customers pay their bills on time. If they do not, their connections are cut off. Another key factor in China's successful electrification program is the central government's determination and ability to mobilize contribution at the local level.

The electrification program was backed with subsidies and low-interest loans. The program also benefited from government of China's New and Renewable Energy Development Program aimed to raise the efficiency of renewable energy, lower production costs and enlarge its contribution to the energy system. China's policy to attract private investment in renewable energy in joint ventures was aimed at securing technology benefits to lower

---

3. James Haselip, Isaac Dyner, Judith Cherni, 'Electricity Market Reform in Argentina: assessing the impact for the poor in Buenos Aires', *Utilities Policy* (March 2005), Volume 13, No.1

cost. Cheap domestic production ranging from hydro generators to light bulbs and solar panels enabled affordability. Despite unreliable and poor quality of electrical services in rural areas, China's achievement has demonstrated the continued importance of the government's determined role to increase access to the poor while staying on the course of sector reform and price liberalization.

With only 23 per cent of its population electrified, SSA, a net oil exporting region, has the lowest electrification rate in the world with over 525 million people with no access to electricity. In South Asia despite efforts to electrify all villages, technically within reach of 90 per cent of the population, only less than half of the population has access to electricity.

In 2002 over one-third of the world's population was unable to access modern energy services. More than 99 per cent of those who lacked access to modern energy services live in developing Asia and SSA. 80 per cent of those who lack access to electricity live in rural areas. At the 1990s rates of electrification in South Asia and SSA, it would take until 2050 to electrify South Asia and all of the twenty-first century to electrify SSA.

Widening access to electricity

Regional disparities in the future rate of electrification will continue to diverge significantly among regions depending on the rate at which governments can mobilize both private and public investment. Developing countries require investment in electric power sector to install additional generation capacity, to extend the electricity grid in urban areas, to expand transmission and distribution, to install mini-grids in medium-sized settlements, to decentralize installations providing thermal, mechanical and electric power in rural areas and to maintain and upgrade the existing electricity infrastructure.

IEA projections of future electrification rates are based on assumptions that over $70 billion per year through 2030 will be required for new power generation capacity in developing countries of which $7 billion per year is required in SSA and over $10 billion per year in South Asia. If required increases in investment of $20 billion per year to expand capacity were to be actually made, IEA projections indicate that by 2030 it would more than double the electrification rate in SSA. In South Asia, access to electricity is expected to increase to over two-thirds of the population by 2030. Although India as of 2004 has achieved access to electricity to over 80 per cent of its population, recurring and long periods of black-outs, power shutdown and poor reliability in service persist.

Even with mobilizing the required investment of over $17 billion per year to expand capacity and doubling of the electrification rate from 23 per cent in 2000 to over 50 per cent and to 66 per cent in South Asia by 2030, IEA projections as shown in Tables 6.2 and 6.3 above indicate 1.4 billion people in SSA and South Asia will still continue to lack access to electricity.

Mobilizing the required investment in South Asia and SSA will continue to be difficult given the declining trend of multilateral financial institutions funding for government sponsored programs to increase access of energy to the poor. In fact even during 1980–95 when multilateral financial institutions such as the WB group supported governments programs of RE, renewable energy and forestry/ biomass, the WB group funding was $5.5 billion for total project financing of over $30.4 billion. This accounted for WB's average annual funding of less than $600 million for total average annual project financing cost of over $2 billion[4] for energy programs for poor. Between fiscal years 2000 and 2003 the WB's financing of actual operations in electric power and other energy totalled $3.67 billion amounting to less than 5 per cent of total WB lending of over $70.5 billion during this period[5].

Energy access issues

The 1990s changing direction of developing countries from plan to market requires governments in developing countries to reassess their crucial role in promoting greater equity in access to energy for urban and rural poor, while staying the course of energy market transition. In particular, the governments of low-income countries of South Asia and SSA, with low levels of private investment in their power sectors, declining multilateral funding for energy and power/ RE and inadequate public investment even to maintain their existing capacities, need to address the challenge of raising investment to increase access to efficient energy at affordable prices for their rural and urban poor.

Given the scarcity of government resources to extend electricity supplies to large numbers of people and growing markets, developing countries will require financially sound and efficiently managed electricity supply industries. However, despite a six-fold increase in electricity generating capacity and output since 1970 and the rapid increase in the number of customers served by the late 1980s, the financial position and efficiency of electricity supply industries had deteriorated in many countries. As discussed in Chapters 4 and 5, several countries attempting to reform their energy/ electric power sectors are dealing with the issues of electricity tariffs, subsidies, regulation, restructuring of their state owned electricity enterprises as commercial companies and creating a suitable environment for competition to promote private investment.

---

4. WB, 'Report No. 15912 GLB: Rural Energy and Development' (Washington DC, July 1996)
5. WB, *Annual Reports* (2000, 2001, 2002, 2003)

They also need to address the sector reforms' specific implications to increase access to energy for the poor. This requires focusing at macro, sector and household levels on three major issues that impact increasing access to energy for the poor. The first issue comprises pricing and subsidies. The second issue comprises options for increasing both grid-connected and non-grid supplies. The third issue consists of critical factors impacting required financing to increase economically and technically viable grid and off-grid programs to increase access to energy for the poor.

Pricing and subsidies

Given that the majority of the energy poor are in rural areas, policies of increasing access to the energy poor focused on RE and expanding the distribution of petroleum based kerosene and LPG fuels for cooking. Network supply costs to RE were generally based on system wide average LRMC, which were calculated on the basis of annual system load factors that in most cases, were in excess of 60 per cent. RE projects by contrast, have load factors of less than 10 per cent to 25 per cent thereby imposing high and additional peak-load unaccounted costs on generation and transmission facilities. Most RE projects were designed to connect rural areas to a central grid and therefore, included only the capital costs of the distribution system. Total costs which include capital costs of distribution, the LRMC of energy supplied and operating and maintenance costs in the pre-1990 was on average of 20 cents/kWh, ranging from a low of 8.4 cents/kWh to 35 cents/kWh in 1987 dollars. However, in most cases the LRMC of energy supplied was underestimated because it did not take into account low load factors or high losses[6].

The cost of service across customers varied from a high of 31 cents/kWh for a residential consumer with a small load factor and a high peak coincidence to a low of 10 cents/kWh for off-peak irrigation. Average tariffs in most developing countries were lower than even the country's lowest cost. In many cases tariffs have been kept deliberately low because of the belief that rural consumers, particularly irrigation farmers and residential consumers are unable or unwilling to pay more.

In all cases tariffs are significantly below the estimated costs of supply although several countries do at least cover fuel, operating and maintenance costs. Even if minimum tariffs were set to cover only generation, operation and maintenance costs, the minimum tariff would have to be substantially above current rates. This minimum tariff would vary from a low of 5–7 cents/kWh for off-peak irrigation to a high of 18–25 cents/kWh for residential

---

6. WB/ OED, *Rural Electrification in Asia: A Review of Bank Experience* (Washington DC, 1994)

use, most of which coincides with the peak demand system.

The implications of electricity tariff reform to recover costs are crucial for expanding access to electricity for the poor. In countries where electric power utilities are financially weak, such as several state electricity boards in India, their continued subsidization of agriculture and residential customers have prevented commercialization of state electricity boards. The state governments have failed to target the poor farmers with small holdings directly through subsidies for electricity connections. Consequently a great proportion of the high subsidies and free power to agriculture sector in many states in India benefiting mostly the rich farmers demonstrates the political largesse. The loss of revenue has worsened the financial situation of state electricity boards, contributed to the state's budget deficit and has discouraged investment.

On the other hand East Asian countries such as China, Philippines and Thailand exerted a favourable link between electricity tariff reform and increasing access to the poor. China's success in increasing access to energy for the poor illustrates the government's understanding of the realities of market transition and the determined role of the state to increase access to energy for the poor through the path of market socialism entailing a mix of subsidies, low interest rates and use of its potential market size to attract investment.

In countries where the overall financial position of the electric power utility has been sound, RE programs are being implemented with cross-subsidization. Thailand's experience between 1975 and 1994 showed that it achieved more than 75 per cent for the whole country with high participation by the rural poor.

South Africa's Energy policy since 1994 demonstrates the crucial role of the government in formulating policies to achieve the goal of universal access to electricity both through non-grid and grid electrification to the urban and rural poor as part of the energy empowerment program. The 1998 energy policy framework stated in its white paper, 'Government commits itself to implementing reasonable legislative and other measures, within its available resources, to progressively realize universal household access to electricity.' The government's goal is supported particularly by implementing an Electricity Basic Services Tariff (EBST) through providing capital and operational subsidies for all new non-grid connections in the demarcated concession areas for Solar Home Systems (SHS). Although it is questionable whether universal access will be achieved through the provision of electricity through SHS, some increase in access is being made possible to those who have no other source of access to electricity[7].

---

7. M Wentzel, M Pickering, 'The potential impact of an electricity basic services tariff in non-grid electricity', *Journal of Energy in South Africa*, Volume 15, No.1

South Africa's energy policy also requires the restructured and financially viable state owned electric utility ESKOM to continue to increase access to achieve universal access to electricity. ESKOM will continue to divert a percentage of its profits to facilitate investment to increase access to rural and urban poor. An interesting aspect of South Africa's electrification program is that it has demonstrated that for basic services such as electricity, willingness to pay is less of a problem than commonly assumed, in view of the very high prices that many who are not connected to the public network pay to obtain services from the informal sector or through self-provision. In South Africa even the poorest people are connecting to the grid when the service is available. The case of South Africa's Phambili Nombane 'Forward with Electricity'[8] illustates of people's willingness to pay.

The Case of South Africa's Phambili Nombane (Forward with Electricity); Khayelitsha's Township Project

The Phambili Nombane a joint-venture company was formed in 1994 comprising ESKOM, Electricite de France (EDF) and East Midlands Electricity (EME). It acts as an agent for ESKOM in the Khayelitsha project, which is funded by ESKOM and monitored by the National Electrification Forum. By mid-December 1994, within six months, the company achieved its ambitious target of 20,000 connections for 1994, to electrify the township of Khayelitsha, 30 km from Cape Town, with 50,000 dwelling units and 500,000 people.

The Phambili Nombane was successful in supplying electricity at affordable prices. The residents, who used candles, paraffin and gas prior to 1994, were more than willing to pay for connection and supply of electricity. Phambili Nombane involved local community in the electrification process. Sub-contractors were encouraged to use local labour.

Workers trained during the project have the opportunity of applying their skills in similar projects thereby creating sustainable employment and income generation. The labour intensive electrification methods adopted involve replacing machines with people, wherever possible, allowing a large portion of the labour cost to be reinvested in the community.

The Phambili Nombane project shows how a commercial and financially sound state-owned electricity company can complement its sound business and social development objectives to increase access to electricity to the poor at affordable prices in partnership with the private sector and local community. The project also shows how increasing access to electricity becomes the vehicle for employment and income generation.

---

8. R Vedavalli, 'The Beginning of a New South Africa', *Bank's World* (April/ May 1995), Volume 14, No.4/5

Phambili Nombane project illustrates South Africa's state electricity company ESKOM's successful partnership in joint venture with EDF and East Midland Electricity (EME) to increase access to electricity to the urban poor at affordable prices to over 50,000 Khayelishtas homes. South Africa's experiment demonstrates that power to the poor need not be subsidized and public–private partnership brings the desired outcome of increasing access to energy when a government social empowerment program links employment-housing and access to electricity by an innovative payment method.

Critical success factors for any replication of the Khayelishta experiment include: government's commitment to policy design and its effective implementation; public–private and local community partnership adopting a multi-pronged approach of involvement, with poverty alleviation, environmental protection, local participation and economic development by linking employment-housing and access to electricity; financially viable and operationally efficient participating public or private power companies; card and pay or other spot payment methods for purchase of units of electricity; and grid-accessibility. The Khayelishta experiment is however, confined to the grid-accessibility factor.

Although the Khayelishta experiment demonstrates the willingness of the poor to pay for electricity, the theoretical arguments of pricing to reflect full costs of supply because of its accompanying benefits to provide efficient energy supplies to all categories of consumers (including those in remote or difficult to serve areas) may not be automatically realized in practice due to market imperfections, differing country energy market situations and the costs of the transition process. Numerous studies on pricing and subsidies both by the WB and other sources while arguing the ineffectiveness of subsidies acknowledge the need for its continuation in some cases. As discussed in Chapter 5, even a few developing countries which have liberalized petroleum prices, cross-subsidization of petroleum fuels continues for kerosene and LPG used by the poor. In the power sector, while electricity tariffs to consumers are rising they do not reflect competitive and efficient pricing outcomes expected from the transition process because of persisting industry-wide technical, commercial and operational inefficiencies.

In the wake of rising oil prices since 2004 and following the economic crisis in Argentina and election outcomes in Brazil and India, the case for subsidization to the poor is being renewed with lifeline rates for electricity and cross-subsidization of petroleum fuels, such as kerosene and LPG. With rising cost of energy for all categories, charging higher prices for petroleum fuels, such as gasoline and diesel, and higher rates of electricity for above lifeline categories of consumers will continue to be difficult. Governments, therefore, will have to reflect the cost of subsidies as financial transfers from their budgets.

In the next several years for developing countries, staying on the reform course to let their energy enterprises financially and commercially viable and operationally efficient will be critical to expand access to energy for the poor. While general pricing principles as described in Chapter 4 to reflect economic cost of energy and different fuels to be pursued will take more time, effective billing systems, prompt collection of payments, reducing power theft by metering all connections could improve the financial viability of power companies to enable them to make required investment to improve efficiency of their power operations.

In addition, governments need to continue to pursue alternative energy options and focus on addressing the critical factors to raise the required investment to increase access to energy services.

Alternative energy options

Sector reforms in general and power sector reform in particular focus mainly on grid electrification as this is cost effective for high load densities and high load growth near the grid. Following the oil price increases in the seventies, some efforts were made by developing countries, including China, India, Nepal, Indonesia, Jordan and Peru, to promote alternative technologies for both grid-connected and off-grid supplies. Renewable technologies for alternative energy projects in developing countries include wind, solar, biomass, hydro and geothermal.

Declining oil prices since 1986 affected the rapid and continued development of renewable energy. However, with the focus on environment and availability of funding for the renewable energy projects from the Global Environmental Facility (GEF), countries with large segments of dispersed rural population such as China and India continued with the development of renewable energy for environmental considerations and for increasing access to energy for the poor.

Renewable energy consumption in developing countries in 2002, mainly in the form of biomass and other renewables, was 943 Mtoe and accounted for 25 per cent primary energy supply. Biomass providing 922 Mtoe, accounted for 98 per cent of the renewable energy supply in developing countries. Over 2.4 billion people in developing countries, of which 1.9 billion were in China, India and SSA, relied on traditional biomass for cooking and heating. 575 million people accounting for over 80 per cent of the overall SSA population rely primarily on biomass to meet their residential needs. With progress in increasing access to electrification and increased urbanization, the share of traditional biomass use is expected to fall from 24 per cent in 2002 to 16 per cent in 2030 despite modest rates of increase of biomass in total final energy consumption in developing countries between 2002 and 2030.

Modern use of biomass is important in the energy systems of a number of countries. India has installed more than 3 million biomass digesters in villages and produces biogas for cooking. Biomass power projects with an aggregate capacity of 600 Mega Watts (MW) have been commissioned in India as of 2002. Throughout South East Asia the interest in modern bio-energy applications has increased in the 1990s partly because of growing demand for power and because biogas residues from various agricultural systems are plentiful. Modernized biomass use can make a significant contribution to the future energy supply. But they require the development of markets, infrastructure, key conversion technologies and advanced fuel production systems.

Hydropower is the second largest renewable energy source. In 2002, hydro supplied 94 Mtoe of energy in developing countries accounting for 23 per cent of total electricity generation and 98 per cent of power generation from renewables in developing countries. By 2030, hydro is projected to more than double to over 200 Mtoe. However, with rising rates of demand for energy, the share of hydro in power generation in developing countries is projected to fall from 23 per cent in 2002 to 16 per cent in 2030. Large-scale hydro has been a traditional source of generation mix in many developing countries, but is controversial due to ecological and social impacts.

Micro-hydropower provides electricity to rural areas that are too far away from the grid to be connected to it, and can sometimes also supply the grid particularly in China and India where local capacity to manufacture turbines exists. As of 2000, China installed over 20,000 MW of small hydro generating capacity at over 50,000 small hydropower stations. China has a network of local manufacturing facilities and trained personnel, following standard designs and practices.

Despite the demonstrated advantages of micro-hydro in large countries, small countries such as Nepal and countries in SSA who really need urgent access to energy have to consider the cost of imports and transportation of equipment and materials that vary significantly depending on the site and terrain. The development of micro-grids, whatever their primary source of energy, requires a significant level of community consensus and support regarding such factors as billing, service and organization. Local participation is a key factor in the design of such isolated systems.

Non-hydro renewable energies such as wind and solar accounted in 2002 for 1 per cent of power generation in developing countries. Wind farms consist of many turbines clustered together to generate power for the grid. At the beginning of 2000, about 13,500 MW of grid-connected wind-power was in operation. Capacity in developing countries was still small at less than 1300 MW of which India accounted for about 990 MW. However, new capacity additions grew four-fold in India since 2002. By 2005, the grid-connected power generation through wind energy reached 4,228 MW in India.

Although their contribution to total energy supply for the country is negligible, their potential impact on the energy needs of rural and nomadic families is significant.

Direct solar radiation used for concentrating collectors is widespread in the developing world. Photovoltaic (PV) installations already serve thousands of households and include other uses such as water—pumping, communications and leisure. Since the cost of PV electricity is above that of electricity from the grid, photo-voltaic are implemented through market development of commercial high-value applications and stimulating the installation of grid-connected systems. These are generally supported through government and international/ GEF funding programs. Solar Thermal Technologies (STE) concentrate sunlight to heat a fluid and produce electricity. In 1998 operating STE capacity was just 400 MW of electricity.

Geothermal resources have been identified in many developing countries. The growth of total geothermal generating capacity in 1990–8 in developing countries with largest additions in capacity was mainly in Indonesia (445 Mega Watt (MW)) and the Philippines.(957 MW) followed by Mexico(43 MW) and China. The participation of private operators in steam field developments through Build-Operate-Transfer (BOT) and Build-Own-Operate (BOO) contracts and through Joint Operation Contracts (JOC) have speeded up geothermal development in the Philippines. By 2000, geothermal energy accounted for over 20 per cent of its electricity generation. Geothermal energy with its proven technology can make a contribution where the resources are proven. But it requires that the government implement policies to improve the competition of geothermal energy systems with conventional energy systems. Table 6.5 provides the contribution of renewable energy in developing countries in 2002 and their outlook to 2030.

Table 6.5. Renewable Energy Consumption in Developing Countries: 2002–2030

Renewable energy sources	*2002-renewable energy use (mtoe)*	*2002-share of renewables in total demand (per cent)*	*2030-Renewable energy use (mtoe)*	*2030-share of renewables in total demand (per cent)*
Biomass (world)	1,119	11	1,605	10
(of which) :Developing countries	922	24	1,221	16
Hydro (world)	224	2	365	2
(of which) Developing countries	94	2	202	3
Other renewables (world)	55	1	256	2
(of which) Developing countries	21	1	89	1
Total: Developing countries	1,037	27	1,512	19
World Total	1,398	14	2,226	14

Source: IEA, *WEO* (2004), Table 7.1 and Annex A tables.

After three decades of effort since the oil crisis of the 1970s, alternative energy still constitutes a small percentage in the total energy mix. While the oil price increases in the 1970s encouraged development of renewables, declining oil prices since 1985 affected their development.

The confluence of factors since 2003—growing world demand for oil, the post Gulf war 2003 volatility in the Middle East and rising oil prices since 2004 have rekindled the interest to promote renewable energy in the expectation that the post 2003 trends of oil and gas prices will continue. The revival of interest in renewable energy development is also linked to environmental benefits from reducing greenhouse gas emissions and prospects for increasing access to energy for the poor.

With current trends in cost and efficiency, and assuming a continuation of volatility and uncertainty in the Middle East and firming up of oil prices, OECD Europe began pushing for raising the share of renewable energy targets at the global/ regional levels to well over 20 per cent in the total energy mix to help diversify the energy mix and to reduce security of supply concerns. The IEA's WEO (2004) projects that by 2030, 1,113 GW of new renewable capacity will account for 25 per cent of the world's new power generating capacity. The development of renewables-based power generation is expected to require an estimated annual investment of $570 billion through 2030 of which almost 50 per cent is accounted for Hydro. The share of non-hydro renewables in OECD countries is expected to increase from less than 3 per cent in 2002 to 10 per cent in 2030. In developing countries, the share of non-hydro renewables is projected to increase from 1 per cent in 2002 to 3 per cent in 2030.

Some developing countries with rising demand and increasing dependence on imported oil, like China and India are trying to actively promote renewables for electricity generation. As discussed in Chapter 5, India's president, who is also a nuclear scientist, in his annual address on 15 August 2005, to mark India's Independence Day celebrations, called for 'Energy Independence' in electricity generation through alternative energy options to generate electricity. China reaffirmed its renewable energy development policy of 1995 setting the goal of increasing renewable energy supplies to meet 10 per cent of its energy requirement by 2010[9].

Critical factors impacting investment in non-hydro renewables in developing countries

Despite the potential environmental benefits of non-hydro renewables to substantially increase their contribution to electricity generation and possibilities

9. R Vedavalli, *Report on Institutions and Policies for Renewable Energy Development in China* (Washington DC, WB, 1996)

of substitution for petroleum based transport fuels, three decades of experience of renewable energy development in developing countries underscores the fact that several factors are critical for investment in renewables development.

The first critical factor comprises cost-efficiency–reliability considerations

Given that few non-hydro renewable energy technologies can compete with conventional fuels on cost without reflecting environmental costs and other externalities even in some of its niche markets, large-scale development of non-hydro renewables are costly for developing countries. Although the cost of renewables are expected to go on declining in the future, future rates of market deployment to boost capacities in OECD countries and mass production are required to achieve cost reduction to make them more competitive and affordable for developing countries.

Beyond questions of cost, developing countries will need to deal with issues of limits to these technologies with regard to the quality of the energy they produce, and where and when they can be used to determine their share of the future energy mix at least through 2030. Although declining oil prices since 1985 were a major factor affecting the competitiveness of alternative energy development, solar and wind energy technologies face several obstacles in competing with conventional fuels on cost and efficiency considerations. For example, despite heavy investment from major oil companies, such as Exxon Mobil, Arco, Shell and BP in solar energy, the best PV cells despite their suitability for some niche markets, remained a source of intermittent power and not competitive with coal, gas or nuclear power in 2000.

Although renewable electricity may be clean, often the equipment to produce it brings environmental costs. PV cells are essentially semiconductors, the manufacture of which can release cadmium and other toxic pollutants. In addition, both solar cells and wind farms require space and resources. The remoteness of solar and wind locations can actually be a liability, in that any generated power must be transmitted to markets over long distances.

Furthermore, both solar and wind energy sources are not 'dependable' sources of power for 'base load' requirements, compared with year-round, 24 hours a day dependability of conventional energy sources—such as oil, gas, coal and nuclear to deliver maximum power. A 1-MW wind turbine, for example, actually delivers 1 MW only during high winds; its average production will be lower, because average wind speeds are lower. Factoring in this variability, a wind farm's average production or 'capacity' may be just 45 per cent in high-wind regions, but generally closer to 33 per cent—or about a third the capacity of a gas-fired plant.

Thus if a utility wants to add 100 MW of wind capacity to its portfolio, it actually needs to install closer to 250 MW in new turbines, a huge additional expense. Similarly, producing a steady 100 MW of solar power actually requires the installation of 500 MW of PV cells[10]. This extra capacity is called overbuild, and it impacts the economic and financial analysis of both solar and wind projects. Furthermore, both solar and wind power lack qualities of dispatch and reliability. Unlike a coal-fired plant, which can be dependable day or night, regardless of weather, neither wind nor solar is reliable. Solar is simply unavailable at night or on cloudy days and wind is even less dependable despite improvements in weather forecasts. Even if utilities were willing to overbuild, they still have to deal with problems of reliability. Utilities are finding some ways to cope with the wind's unpredictability by computerized scheduling delaying a power delivery from a particular wind farm and/ or taking power from some standby source such as gas and coal-fired plants and maintaining some backup as insurance typically in the form of base-load power plants that are kept idle until needed.

Cost, efficiency and reliability limitations create a natural barrier for expansion of solar and wind. On average, analysts say wind and solar renewables can provide a maximum of 20 per cent of total power mix in a large power system. Beyond 20 per cent, power disruptions from the intermittency factor and the cost of maintaining backup base load could impact both economic and financial viability of the power system. In developing countries, where peak capacity constraints usually persist, financing for maintaining backup base load would be difficult. However, in big developing countries, like India and China, solar and wind could be part of the power system's portfolio mix. China has reaffirmed its policy to promote renewable energy to be 10 per cent of its total power mix by 2010.

Since 2000, falling manufacturing costs and breakthroughs in materials and designs to increase efficiency are improving the competitiveness of solar energy. BP and Shell have made large new investments and the solar market penetration volume has increased.

Given the growing economies of scale, solar is fast approaching a capital cost of $1 per watt of installed power, which in countries with sunny climates with low interest rates worked out to be 8 cents/kWh.

Whereas solar power must wait for both market growth and technological breakthroughs to bring its costs down, the costs for wind power depend almost entirely on economies of scale. Wind has no fuel costs. Its up-front costs, manufacturing, installation, real estate and financing, are its main costs. By 2010, analysts predict that manufacturing costs will have dropped enough to bring wind-generated electricity down to around 3 cents/kWh, at

10. Paul Roberts, *The End of Oil: On the Edge of a Perilous New World* (Boston and New York, Houghton Mifflin, 2004), p.202

which point wind can compete with conventional energy sources[11].

With oil prices reaching US $65 per barrel, substantial research is going on in the area of development of renewables, such as hydrogen and bio fuels as substitute for transportation fuels. Although fuel cells that use hydrogen as a fuel are costly, less efficient in storing hydrogen and do not live up to operating expectations in desired temperatures, research is continuing to evaluate the viability of operating fuel cell buses in varying conditions across the European cities. Shell Hydrogen has been developing its hydrogen and fuel cell demonstration projects in each of its major hydrogen markets: Japan (Tokyo), North America (Washington DC) and Europe[12]. Bio fuels in the form of ethanol or bio diesel are used as transportation fuel. In 2002, global bio fuel consumption was 8 Mtoe, of which Brazil accounted for 70 per cent.

The second critical factor is cost and value determination

For grid-connected electricity systems, the value of renewables can be defined in different ways: avoided fuel, capacity and maintenance costs; avoided electricity consumption costs and buy-back rate and environmental benefits.

The avoided fuel costs in the conventional system usually represent the lowest possible value (typically 2–5 cents/kWh). Renewables also have capacity value though this may be small for intermittent technologies. Avoided costs of electricity consumption refer to the situation where a renewable energy system is connected to the grid by a bi-directional kilowatt hour meter. By definition, the value then becomes equal to the costs (tariffs) of normal electricity. In many countries this is in the range of 10–25 cents/kWh for small users.

In the buy-back rate method, the value of renewables can be lower or higher than that of the energy from the grid. It is lower if the intermediate rate between avoided fuel costs and electricity tariffs is used, as is often the case. It can be higher if a high value is given to the fact it is green electricity. The cost of internalizing environmental costs of mitigating climate change and other environmental costs associated with fossil fuels or external costs could increase the cost of competing fossil fuel.

Finally, the value of renewables depends on the local circumstances. In practice, figures vary between $0.02–1.00 per kWh taking into account the positive externalities of new renewable energy technologies. The WB group has accepted taking account of economic potential and environmental advantages of

11. Paul Roberts, The End of Oil: On the Edge of a Perilous New World (Boston and New York, Houghton Mifflin, 2004), Chapter 8, pp.195–210
12. *Oil and Gas Journal* (27 July 2004)

these technologies in relation to GEF projects. Environmental benefits are valued at the incremental cost of carbon displacement[13].

For off-grid markets with stand-alone systems, the value of renewables is often the value of the services that include lighting, heating, cooling, cooking, pumping, transportation and telecommunication. How this value should be evaluated is determined by the minimum cost of any equivalent alternative energy source or technology.

Off-grid markets pose serious challenges. Distance from the existing lines, dispersion of potential customers and low energy consumption makes access to electricity service through grid extensions more difficult, regardless of the ownership of distribution utilities. Private utilities will not build unprofitable lines unless explicit subsidies or cross-subsidies more than compensate for any financial loss over the life of the project.

Reform programs in the electricity sector to improve access to those who lack electricity regardless of their location with respect to the grid need to be complementary to and consistent with a more competitive market structure, private participation and independent regulation.

The third critical factor comprises regulatory approaches to promote renewables

Regulatory mechanisms to promote renewables include obligations to buy and obligations to supply and complementary regulation and policies in other sectors, such as agricultural policy and land-use planning.

Obligations to buy generally stipulate under what rules independent power producers get access to the grid and the price at which electricity is delivered. This approach is used in monopoly markets to ensure access for IPPs with renewable energy. Regulated access and prices reduce transaction costs. Prices are usually based on avoided costs to the utility. In OECD countries such as the UK, the obligation to buy under the UK Non-Fossil Fuel Obligation (NFFO) has been complemented with a mechanism for reimbursing electricity companies for the extra cost incurred[14].

Obligations to supply entails use of renewable portfolio standards as an alternative to or in combination with system benefit charges to promote renewable electricity. These are mainly practiced in Europe and several states in the USA. A renewable portfolio standard imposes an obligation on all electricity suppliers to include a stipulated fraction of renewable electricity in their supply mix. This obligation is sometimes combined with a system for

13. R Vedavalli, Sri Lanka: Energy Services Delivery Project, *Economic and Financial Analysis for Renewable Energy Sub-Projects* (Washington DC, WB, 1996)
14. UNDP/ WEC, *World Energy Assessment: Energy and the Challenge of Sustainability* (New York, 2000), p.265

renewable energy credits to facilitate trade of renewable electricity between suppliers. Voluntary or negotiated agreements are sometimes used as an alternative to regulation.

Regulations and policies in other sectors such as agriculture and land-use planning need to be consistent with promoting renewable energy sources such as bio energy and for wind concessions. China's reorganization of its energy institutional structure in 1998 by creating a new Ministry for Land and Natural resources consolidates licensing and land management under one authority and is an important step in this direction.

In the 1990s, along with globalization and liberalization, the environment was the topic of the decade. In the 1990s environmental concerns raised the profile of renewable energy technologies and 14 member countries of IEA such as UK, Japan, USA and several European countries applied favourable tariffs for electricity produced from renewable sources. Fixed feed-in tariffs set a predetermined buy-back rate for all electricity produced under certain conditions. In the case of bidding systems, regulatory authorities decide on an amount of electricity to be produced from renewable energy and invite project developers to bid for that capacity. Successful bidders are guaranteed their bid price for a specified period-15 years in the case of the NFFO of the UK. However, the UK has not issued any bids beyond the fifth round of NFFO and has in 2002 introduced a Renewable Obligation combined with Tradable Renewable Energy Certificates (TRCs).

These regulatory approaches to introduce renewable energy in the total electricity mix are being practiced mainly in OECD countries with well-developed power systems. Developing countries embarking on modern use of renewables and competing to serve the unconnected face difficult policy and financial constraints to structure their energy markets with right solutions.

Fourth critical factor is financing and access to credit

Access barriers are common for both commercial and new renewable energy services. The upfront payment of connection fee for accessing electricity service and advance payments, deposit and fee for LPG are beyond the means of poor households who do not have cash reserves for lump-sum upfront payments. The poor who lack access to efficient energy also often spend a significant amount of their time collecting fuel for their household needs and/ or spend a large percentage of their income on energy. Governments in developing countries justify the 'social welfare' objective to provide some form of subsidy to encourage the poorest households to use efficient fuels such as electricity, LPG and kerosene.

While subsidies for access to different types of energy can be justified for economic upliftment when they are rightly targeted and reduce costs in a rural service territory, they are often poorly targeted with political objectives, weaken business incentives, outlive their usefulness and affect the commercial viability of energy companies. Even well designed subsidies constitute only one among many factors involved in enabling access to quality energy services for the poor.

The high up-front cost and availability of long-term credit constitute common barriers to increase access of both conventional and new renewable energy services to the poor. New non-hydro renewable energy technologies account for less than 2 per cent of the primary energy supplies of developing countries. Renewable energy investments also raise issues of risk and uncertainties to move renewable energy technologies to the commercial stage. Programs to extend electricity to rural areas and towns and to establish solar energy programs entail high start-up costs and risks. While most off-grid systems have a long life, their initial capital cost is high and they can only be financed through short terms. Successful penetration of off- or on-grid new renewable technologies as alternatives to conventional power plants and to grid electrification in rural areas face this dual financing problem.

Renewable energy activities in over 20 developing countries in the 1990s were supported by governments and multilateral funding under the GEF following the 1990s rationale of positive externalities and environmental advantages of renewable energy applications.

The GEF financed renewable projects encourage developing countries to address policy, regulatory and financial constraints for developing market-based on- and off-grid renewable energy systems. This includes financing of both absolute level of capital costs and the term of available financing. Small hydroelectric plants may have a life of 40–50 years, PV panels for 25–35 years and wind generation systems of over 25 years. But commercial financing if available for 10–15 years are at market rates—at best—to large PV developers. That contrasts sharply with the 40-year terms and 2 per cent interest rates applied by the RE Administration to develop rural grids in the USA[15].

The commercialization of off-grid technologies requires credit for both suppliers and consumers of off-grid systems, servicing and marketing infrastructure and product certification and quality control. Off-grid system suppliers need credit to expand their markets, to develop sales and service facilities, to improve quality and to lower costs of products.

Limited access to credit by consumers is a barrier to increasing both the average system size and total market potential. Off-grid renewable power systems have a high start-up cost, since the majority of the life-cycle cost is in the purchase price. Without access to credit to spread these costs over time,

15. Eduardo Villagran, 'Key drivers of improved access - off-grid service', *Energy Services for the World's Poor* (Washington DC, WB/ ESMAP, 2000)

the market is limited to those who can afford cash price. The development of innovative financing schemes, including supplier credits, leasing arrangements and developing a mechanism for making subsidies and credit broadly accessible is crucial for renewable energy schemes.

The fifth critical factor is to link policies for successful market deployment mechanism

In OECD countries, governments have traditionally played a decisive role in both framing and funding research and development and market deployment (RD&D) at the national level, in international collaborations and in involving private sector research, development and demonstration. Policies for market deployment pursued by OECD countries address both supply and demand side at capacity and generation levels. Box 6.1 summarizes policy instruments for market deployment in OECD countries.

Box 6.1. Market Deployment Policy Instruments for Renewable Energy Development in OECD Countries

Policy area and type	*Market deployment instruments*	*Outcome*
Supply and Capacity	Investment incentives: Investment tax credits; Property tax exemptions; Government purchase of on-site renewable energy systems at above market rates	Reduces capital costs of deploying renewable energy technologies; Reduces tax-payments to project owners; investment incentive to industry
Supply and generation	Incentive tariffs: Guaranteed price systems; Feed-in tariffs and preferential rates	All terms of tariffs above market rates paid by either consumers or tax payers
	Bidding systems based on competition for contracts to build projects with the lowest generating costs	Competitive bidding are organized separately for different technology categories
	Guaranteed price mechanism with the rate set by competition for the lowest bid based on a function of the power pool wholesale price plus a technology-specific premium paid by consumers	Transparent pricing system
	Production tax credits offered to renewable energy producers at a kilowatt-hour rate	Reduces tax burden
	Obligations/ targets	Encourage the development of renewables at lower cost

Policy area and type	*Market deployment instruments*	*Outcome*
Demand and generation	Voluntary programs, green pricing, net metering and tax measures	Offers choices to producers and consumers; tax measures to capture the externalities associated with energy production and consumption.
Demand and capacity	Investment incentives	Reduces the capital-cost of renewable energy technologies to end-users
	Consumer grants and third-party finance	Government low-interest loans, or buying down the capital cost of renewable technologies
	Tax measures to customer owned systems; a tax credit or system rebate	Allows the owner to recover a portion of the up-front capital costs

Source: IEA, 'Energy Policies of IEA Countries', *Review* (2004)

Given that even in the developed IEA energy markets individual country policy mechanisms in IEA countries are still evolving as countries gain more experience, developing countries continuing on their energy market reform face new challenges for renewable technologies still in the technology development stage. Bilateral aid organizations, non-governmental organizations and the GEF often working in collaboration have been influential in establishing market deployment mechanisms for modern renewable energy pilot schemes and providing education and training to engineers and technicians from developing countries.

New renewable energy technologies are trying to make a way into different markets, often in competition with other options to provide access for energy services. So, the choice of renewable energy systems to increase access to the poor will depend on the successful development and diffusion of competitive renewable technologies to reduce cost, policies to address the key issues of renewable energy development and providing incentive mechanisms for both grid-connected and off-grid applications and governments' effective role in linking policies-financing mechanisms to market deployment at the local, state/ provincial and national levels.

To facilitate market-based development of renewable energy schemes in developing countries, financial incentive mechanisms should conform to three principles. The First involves the determination of the level of financial incentive that reflects the difference between current costs and expected long-run economic value of the power. Second, the financial incentive should be available for a limited time and linked with monitoring of progress toward cost-reduction. And finally, the mechanism should not create market distortions while recognizing the potential economic benefits of renewable sources of energy.

For financing alternative energy options governments have to develop a mechanism that ranges from a small agency for providing access to credit, such as banks, to a more reformed institution than the RE authorities to increase access to energy for the poor by Energy Empowerment Administration (EEA). To be effective such an agency should have capabilities to develop a diverse range of projects, to select the optimum technology and appropriate system designs, to mobilize required technical support, to carry out competitive bidding of goods and services and to follow up on implementation and repairs. International cooperation is critical to build effective partnerships between technology development in developed countries and market deployment in developing countries.

Conclusion

In the context of globalization and the energy market transition of the 1990s, as developing countries review their national policies for increasing access to efficient energy for over 2 billion poor, four imperatives seem clear. The First imperative is that sector reform is necessary to facilitate required investment to bring forth efficient energy supply because of the links between reform and reductions in risks to investors. In addition, energy for development promotes economic growth and employment prospects. So the second imperative is energy development. A third imperative is to frame the right policies complementary to sector reform strategies for the pursuit of equity and welfare objectives that markets, left to their own mechanisms, may not produce. The desired outcome of the right policies is to attract sustainable financing to provide access to efficient energy supplies to billions of the poor.

Finally, the fourth imperative is that beyond questions of cost and efficiency, alternative energy sources have limitations of dependability and reliability. They cannot increase 100 per cent access to energy for the poor. However, the confluence of economic, environmental and geopolitical events since the Iraq 2003 war along with recent technological developments have made renewable energy sources emerge once again as a serious option to be part of energy portfolio mix in the twenty-first century. Since all developing oil importing countries have some form of developable renewable resources, they need to consider using renewable energy to diversify its energy supply, to reduce dependence on oil imports, to provide environment and public health benefits, to enhance domestic energy security, to increase generation reliability and to increase access to energy supply. Increasing access to renewable energy could stimulate local economies, create employment and increase local and state tax revenue bases.

Given that a large percentage of population in developing regions of Asia and SSA remain poor, governments in developing countries need to reconcile these four imperatives in an effective way. Sector reform and effective policies are fundamental for energy development in the changed post 1990s world of global energy finance. With changing traditional patterns of financing for electrification projects, a critical task before developing countries will be to come to a greater understanding of the realities of sustainable financing for energy. Developing countries need to address the lessons learned from the 1990s energy sector reform and liberalization, future challenges of staying the course of market transition while improving the economic prospects for the energy poor. Chapter 7 discusses the lessons of energy market transition in developing countries and twenty-first century challenges for moving forward.

CHAPTER 7

ENERGY SECTOR REFORM AND LIBERALIZATION IN DEVELOPING COUNTRIES: LESSONS AND TWENTY-FIRST CENTURY CHALLENGES

This chapter synthesizes the lessons from the review of experience with energy sector reform in developing countries. The lessons discussed below enable greater understanding of challenges of energy for development at the global and national levels in the twenty-first century. They are examined later in this chapter.

Energy sector reform: 1990–2005: Lessons

Chapters 4–6 and the country studies from Asia, Latin America, the Middle East and SSA show that each area of energy policy reform—pricing, regulation, commercialization and privatization/ private investment is complex as they are interlinked within energy sector and between energy and other sectors and macroeconomic fundamentals. Nonetheless, three cross-cutting lessons emerge.

First, energy sector reforms produced mixed and modest gains. Second. experience from case study situations shows the importance of effective institutions as the key to reform implementation.

And third, the expectations of various energy stakeholders in the energy market about risk-reward trade-off play a crucial role in the success or failure of reforms and the future course of the reform path.

LESSON 1: Energy sector reforms produced mixed and modest gains

Energy sector reform and liberalization was launched in the 1990s to improve sector performance and to attract investment to increase efficient energy for development in developing countries. The conventional wisdom was that moving to market pricing of energy, setting up regulatory institutions to create an environment for competition and private investment and restructuring of energy enterprises by privatization/ private investment would improve efficiency and increase access to energy supply in developing countries.

This model was based on the assumption of an automatic response between reform policies and reform outcome. However, as discussed in Chapter 5, this model failed to explain the disconnect between reform policies and outcomes because of the varying impact of critical factors: market size, reform design, the energy-financial sector and macroeconomic reform interlinkages in the context of developing countries. Sector reform and liberalization is directly dependent on governments' success in sustaining macroeconomic fundamentals. All case study countries launched energy sector reform and liberalization as part of their macroeconomic reform and adjustment.

The results of the decade of energy market transition efforts are mixed not only between developing countries but also between different sub-sectors within a country. While there are encouraging signs of implementation of pricing, regulation, restructuring and investment reforms, the process is yet to achieve the objectives of removal of subsidies and commercialization of energy/ power enterprises to promote efficiency and to attract public–private investment. Restructuring options vary. Some regulatory systems are more efficient than others.

The 1990s showed that gains from energy sector reform actions in the areas of pricing, regulation, restructuring/ commercialization/ privatization/ private investment in terms of its long-run impact on energy investment are mixed and modest. The claims that energy policy reforms would automatically attract private investment to increase access to energy for development were exaggerated. The disappointments with the outcome of energy policy reform reflect the fact that while the conventional wisdom assumed an empirical and causal association between reform elements and private investment in energy, the combination of reform design and approaches advocated could not explain the disconnect between sector reform elements and the outcome in the context of reform implementation in developing countries.

LESSON 2: Successful reform implementation requires effective governance and capable institutions at the federal/ central, state/ provincial and local levels

The reform experience with inter-country and intra-country variations underscores the importance of effective governance and capable institutions for successful reform implementation. The 1990s reforms aimed at changing the role of governments from command and control to create a suitable environment for investors that required successful implementation of market-oriented pricing, regulatory, institutional and investment policies to create a commercial and competitive environment within which energy enterprises should operate. After a decade and a half of experiment with energy sector liberalization approaches of 'Quick dive' vs 'incrementalism' and discussions on sequencing and pacing of reforms, the reality of dynamics of transition is that the weaknesses of governance and institutions are not just technical 'quick-fix' issues. They reflect the difficulty of management and coordination at federal, state and local levels, changing the mind-set of the state-led development system and, more critically in the power sector, its underlying political and economic basis within the time-table set in the policy memoranda. These factors impacted the reform implementation in several ways.

- Electricity tariffs do not reflect cost and cross-subsidization of petroleum products and electricity continue.
- Regulatory institutions are used more as mechanisms for raising tariffs to cover the increasing gaps between revenue and costs of inefficiencies of state monopolies. Regulatory authorities have not been able to regulate industry standard efficiency and promote competition.
- Corporatization of oil and gas enterprises often has failed to separate the government's role as both owner and operator. The Government's continued involvement as majority owner and its right to nominate the majority of board members gives it the controlling voice in state-owned oil and gas corporation boards.
- Unbundling of power sector and privatization of power distributing companies have not improved efficiency and have failed to commercialize power companies.
- Limited private sector participation in downstream oil and gas and power distribution.
- Private investment in power generation through International Private Power Producers (IPPs), Build-Operate-Transfer (BOT) and/or Build-Own-Operate (BOO) mainly engaged in selling power to state power companies and/ or high-income consumers

and not for increasing access to energy poor in urban/ rural areas.

The limited success in energy sector reform implementation reflects to a large extent the continuation of weak governance and ineffective institutions with pre-1990 political and economic power centres. Weak regulation and oversight reflect not just technical problems but also political pressures. It takes time to build effective institutions to successful market transition. A necessary condition for staying the course of the reform process is that the foundations of the market economy rests on good governance and reform institutions capable of translating reform principles to practices and actions on the ground.

Examples include institutional foundations for independent and transparent regulation, rational electricity pricing under the Power Purchase Agreement (PPA), competitive bidding for privatization and private investment. A Country's 'exogenous institutional endowment' is an important determinant of credible sector reform to be put in place. India's case illustrates the institutional weaknesses at the centre-state and enterprise level in policy making, in its decision of quick-fix by not seeking competitive bidding and in failing to formulate a rational pricing formula under the PPA contract which eventually resulted in the closure of the first private investment in power, the Enron power project.

LESSON 3: Expectations of various energy stakeholders in the energy market about risk-reward trade-off play a crucial role in success or failure of reforms and the course of future reform path

The 1990s conventional wisdom was that getting energy policies right, sending right signals and diving-in to market transition would attract private investment in energy. Developing countries expected that government statements on sector reform and liberalization would open the gates for private investment in their energy/ power sectors. The need to reduce government budget deficits forced developing countries to reduce public investment, particularly in the power sector. Developed countries and private investors expected the opportunity to expand their energy business worldwide in profitable operations. Energy consumers in developing countries were told to expect that transition from public to private would release public resources to improve their standards of living by increasing access to education, health and efficient energy.

The great experiment of the 1990s, the transition from command and control to market in energy did not proceed to meet the expectations of quick transformation because it failed to translate expectations of different energy stakeholders to realistic and actionable practices. The 1990s energy market transition experience confirmed that despite the initial flood of interest of private investors in the beginning of the reform process, success is limited in attracting private investment and sustaining the interest of private investors. East Asian and Latin American financial crises have caused the re-evaluation of free market expectations. Countries such as China and India have scaled down their expectations of private sector participation in the power sector to less than 30 per cent of their investment requirements.

Energy sector reform and liberalization of the 1990s, despite its limited success in increasing energy supply failed to meet the expectation of financing investment to provide reliable and efficient energy services to over 2 billion poor who lack access. As discussed in Chapters 5 and 6, governments in Asia and in SSA have started all over again to increase public investment to increase access to energy to their impoverished poor.

The 1990s experience underscores the need for realism about risk-reward trade-off, and short-term transition costs to the economy. The developing host country needs to realize that the greater the risks to be taken by the private sector, the higher will be the returns demanded. A necessary condition for attracting private investment, particularly in the power sector, is that the complementary mechanisms of market fundamentals of pricing and commercial operation of host country power utilities be in place. In the absence of this condition the average rate of return for projects in developing countries with no track record would exceed 20–25 per cent. Developing countries in all case study countries feel that this is almost double that of the rate of return allowed in their countries for public sector projects.

Although private sector financing appeared to be more expensive than public sector finance, part of this apparent expense is due to a reflection of the fact that the cost of risk is not explicitly reflected in publicly financed projects. The additional costs of private sector finance should be outweighed by lower energy prices from least cost competitive bidding, efficiency gains and the benefits of investment that would not otherwise have taken place. Adopting competitive tendering for IPP projects could secure least cost investment and lower price for electricity. Egypt has in 2001 secured the cheapest price for wholesale electricity at less than 3 cents/kWh from its competitive bidding for gas fuelled BOO type IPP project by minimizing the fuel risk by taking the responsibility to supply natural gas for the project. Critics could argue that the low cost does not reflect the economic value of gas. However, Egypt adopted this approach as 'welfare transfer' to increase access to energy for development.

Energy market transition remains work in progress and is far from over. Much of the developing world still has difficulty accessing the international capital markets. Private capital flows remain heavily concentrated in specific countries and regions. Even where private investment is interested in investing in big markets such as China and India, the risk–reward expectations of different energy stakeholders impact the reform outcome. Even countries such as Argentina, considered in the 1990s the show case of successful market transition are facing difficulties to turn back again on their energy market transition path. The promise of governments' policy statements to open up to market to undertake economic transformation to attract quick flows of private investment in energy have proven illusory.

Moving forward

Despite the mixed results and disconnect between expectations and realities of globalization and energy market transition, the fact remains that developing countries remain part of the twenty-first century globalized technology and economic culture. With rising demand for energy and increasing dependence on oil imports, developing net oil importing countries face the daunting challenge of moving forward using energy market transition for promoting development and balancing the market as a vehicle to increase access to efficient energy supplies for development and to increase access of energy to billions of their poor. Moving forward underscores the fact that governments have to adhere to energy market fundamentals to supply energy and cannot go back to the pre-transition period of financing energy through subsidies and multilateral borrowings. Since the beginning of this decade, they are undertaking a balancing act of adopting to market fundamentals while being exposed to high social transition costs. China's path to market is 'market socialism'. India is adapting to market with what it calls a 'Middle Path' and a caring market. South Africa in its quest to empower its vast disadvantaged population is moving forward balancing market transition with energy welfare schemes. The WB, the architect of 1990s energy sector reform and liberalization seems to be following up on this shift by extolling 'Equity and Development' in its 2006 world development report.

The 1990s energy sector reform and liberalization made it clear there is no quick fix for a right institutional and financial formula. Acknowledging the disconnect between expectations and realities, the WB's *Energy and Development Report* (1999) in its foreword summed it up by saying: 'If there is any one message that emerges from this inaugural *Energy and Development Report*, it is that despite encouraging trends in many developing country energy sectors, none of us—energy industry, financiers, NGOs or policy makers—have yet got the institutional and financial formula right'[1].

Moving forward requires that developing countries, energy industry, financiers including multilateral financial institutions need to draw from the few successes and failures of the 1990s energy market liberalization. Governments

1. WB-ESMAP, 'Energy after the Financial Crises', *Energy and Development Report* (Washington DC, 1999)

in developing countries must face the reality that policy statements on sector reform and liberalization without their determination to translate policies into actionable practices in place will not perform the free market miracle to attract private investors. Multilateral financial institutions providing financial and technical assistance to developing countries must realize that arranging annual energy weeks, 'fly-by-night' expert presentations and conferences and publications of repeated analysis of problems are not sufficient to instantaneous paradigm shift to free energy market. Energy investors' and financiers' expectations that they should be compensated with very substantial risk premium and in any and all situations be repaid, fail to increase access to efficient energy for development at affordable prices in the context of today's rising global energy prices.

For moving forward it is critical for developing countries, energy industry, financiers and multilateral financial institutions to learn from the 1990s experience and to come to a greater understanding of twenty-first century challenges at the global and national levels, including security of oil supply, emerging energy portfolios and the direction of energy away from petroleum.

Twenty-first century energy for development policy challenges at the global level: The challenge of dealing with adverse effects of globalization

For developing countries the opening of their economies influenced growth and technology diffusion and investment liberalization conferred benefits of higher output, higher real wages, foreign capital flows, technology transfer and gains in productive efficiency. It is a fact that many irreversible changes including advances in information technology and communications have influenced global economic integration through rising volumes of trade and capital flows in the 1990s. On balance, globalization increased trade, investment and employment. But it also has an effect on economic volatility, and the geographical distribution of economic activity.

It has created a twenty-first century style dual economy of globalized players and marginalized spectators. The class of globalized players are the skilled, mobile and elite population with the strongest trading links and greatest attractiveness to FDI registering the fastest income growth concentrated in urban areas. The spectators—a large proportion of the poor population in semi-urban and rural areas, the under-educated and under-skilled are being left out, marginalized and are out of the global game. The divide between a small proportion of globalized players and a large proportion of marginalized poor spectators is the basic conflict that has generated social discontent and threatened political stability even within the small group of emerging economies perceived to be successful in playing the game of globalization.

For developing economies, while there are forces that bring benefits from economic integration in some sectors, these benefits are limited to information technology linked services in a small group of developing countries. Furthermore, the much emphasized benefits of free flow of goods, capital and ideas were short-lived because of the disconnect between the theory and practice of globalization, free trade, trade barrier practices, international investment and international companies' behaviour and practices. While the benefits of globalization, free flow of goods and capital were emphasized, the implications of the inevitable costs of the disconnect between the theory and practice of globalization and the creativity and commitment at the grass roots level required to connect the poor to the global economy were overlooked.

The 1990s pendulum shift even with the so called miracle economies of East Asia has made it clear that the global economic integration is not a panacea and has raised questions on its effectiveness to address developmental concerns of poverty and increasing access to efficient energy for billions of poor people. The process of globalization is causing a divide between a small segment of the technologically elite population which has the skills and mobility to flourish in global markets and a large percentage of the population which lacks the skills and opportunities and increased the rift between the 'haves' and 'have nots'.

From a development perspective, in the twenty-first century the key challenge for governments/ policymakers is to improve both economic and sector performance by seizing the opportunities created by globalization to benefit the people, particularly the vast majority of the poor from integration into the global economy. Thomas Friedman, discussing globalization in his book 'the Lexus and the Olive tree' emphasized that for the hardware of globalization (technology, telecommunications and transportation systems) to work to confer benefits, the software of globalization is needed to function (a well-educated workforce, the honesty, transparency, legal systems and efficient governance)[2]. This requires focusing on the fundamentals of economic growth—investment, macroeconomic stability, human resource development and good governance to getting the results on the ground.

The twenty-first century pendulum swing would be neither toward the pre-1990s command and control end nor toward the post 1990s globalization and market miracle point as an end in itself. The pendulum shift under way in the twenty-first century acknowledges that many changes that have occurred in the 1990s are irreversible. Developing countries cannot go back to command and control governance and protectionism. Neither can they expect the Market to perform the miracle. The twenty-first century challenge

2. Thomas L Friedman, *The Lexus and the Olive Tree* (New York, Farrar, Strauss, Giroux, 2001)

for governments in developing countries is that while being part of global economy they need to deal with the question of how fairly the benefits are distributed to achieve development objectives with social equity given that a large percentage of their population are yet to realize the promised benefits of reform and liberalization.

The prevailing tension from globalization with increasing inequalities between rich and poor and rural and selected urban centres have exacerbated domestic social unrest and political instability and have influenced changes in elected governments in developing democracies. The case of Argentina since the crisis of 2001, the election of the new president in Brazil in 2003 and the outcome of India's 2004 election illustrate that public patience is often limited for continuation of globalization to benefit a small class of elites while the majority of the poor population are thrown out of the global game. As discussed in Chapter 5, increasing disparities between the urban nouveau riche and the rural poor in China have led to growing social and economic unrest. Acknowledging the need for addressing rising inequalities, China's Politburo, the top policy-making body of the Communist party of China emphasized in October 2005 the need for more equitable distribution of wealth and pledged for balanced and harmonious growth in the eleventh plan period of 2006–11.

Recognizing the obvious adverse outcome of globalization, James D Wolfensohn, President of the WB (the multilateral development institution, which played a key role in the 1990s telling developing countries to globalize and minimize their role to let the market work), remarked in 2003: 'Without social equity, economic growth cannot be sustained. Without enlarging the real opportunities available to all citizens, the market will work only for the elites. This means providing everyone with access to education, health care, decent work, and—as the new Brazilian president Lula has pointed out—with 'at least three meals a day'. The overwhelming experience of the 1990s is that governments' role should go beyond adopting adjustment policies to remove obstacles to growth to become a constructive force in promoting growth with social equity. The twenty-first century challenge for governments in developing countries is that while liberalization and private investment strategy are being part of the global economy, they need to deal with the question of how fairly the benefits are distributed to achieve development objectives with social equity. In the energy sector this involves balancing the requirements of creating a suitable environment for energy investment with increasing access to efficient energy at affordable prices for development.

The challenge of access to global energy financing/ FDI

Establishing a sound financing framework to meet developing countries' growing energy/ infrastructure needs remains a key challenge for policy makers. Estimates by several international organizations including the WB, Regional development banks, UNDP, WEC and IEA point to the substantial investment required in developing countries. IEA's World Energy Investment Outlook (2003) concludes that developing countries, where production and demand increase more rapidly, will require US $7.9 trillion of global investment in the energy sector through 2030. China alone is projected to invest $2.3 trillion or 14 per cent of the world total. Capital needs will be almost as high in the rest of Asia, including India and Indonesia. Investment needs amounts to $1.2 trillion in Africa and $1 trillion in the Middle East, where upstream oil and gas developments account for more than half of total investment. The electricity sector dominates the investment picture accounting for 50 per cent or more of energy investment in all oil importing developing countries. In India and China nearly 85 per cent of investment will be in electricity generation, transmission and distribution sectors.

In the energy sector, since the 1990s wave of globalization all the studies cited on financing energy in Chapters 1–4 conclude that access to global finance has more to do with developing country policy than with the level of world saving. These global energy financing studies[3] argue that global savings for energy financing is adequate and equity investors who want to invest in the developing world have trouble finding suitable projects and developing countries suffering from a shortage of savings and foreign exchange should facilitate the FDI by pursuing sound investor-friendly macroeconomic policies and building effective legal and commercial institutions.

The economic growth in the Asian miracle countries and the post-reform boom in Latin American countries, such as Argentina in the 1990s, are cited as 'proof' that liberal FDI policies benefit the host countries as these countries with open FDI policies have performed better than those with more restrictive policies. It is argued that open trade and FDI policies have given them the access not only to required capital but also to advanced technologies, sophisticated managerial practices and distribution networks in the export markets, thus contributing to their spectacular growth and trade performance.

The 1990s statistics show that net FDI flows to developing countries increased dramatically in the 1990s from $35 in 1991 to reaching their peak of $182 billion in 1999 before declining to $162 billion in 2000, suggesting that more and more countries are benefiting from being drawn into the process of globalization. It is argued that international companies are becoming more and more 'transnational' through the relocation of 'core' activities

3. WEC, *Financing the Global Energy Sector – The Task Ahead* (London, WB, 1997); *The World Bank's Role in the Electric Power Sector* (Washington DC, 1993)

such as R&D and service activities. The emergence of the 'world car' in the automobile industry and the establishment of R&D centres and service centres in information technology and accounting services by US and European companies in developing countries are cited as positive effects globalization of investment opportunities.

Although globally capital is projected to be more than adequate for financing energy investment, access to capital will continue to be a major issue for developing oil importing countries to fill the gap between available domestic savings with limits of domestic financial markets and required investment in the energy sector. During the 1990s, even with the increasing share of the flow in FDI to developing countries, FDI was highly concentrated in a small number of developing countries.

In the developing world, FDI is highly concentrated in the ten largest developing countries, which accounted for over 70 per cent of the flow of all FDI to developing countries. These concentrations of FDI occurred despite the liberal FDI policies that many developing countries introduced during the 1990s liberalization period. Many parts of the developing world and most of Africa with exceptions of Western African oil exporting countries are simply not on the map in corporate board rooms.

The share of energy sector in total FDI flows even in the top ten registered an average of 10 per cent during 1995–2001, peaking at 20 per cent in 1998. For China, the largest recipient of FDI, the manufacturing sector attracted 60 per cent of total FDI, another 35 per cent going to the service sector. In Latin America, the energy sector has accounted for a much higher share of total FDI flows. The upstream oil and gas industries, mainly in Venezuela, Ecuador, Colombia, Chile and Peru, accountrd for 70–80 per cent of FDI inflows into the energy sector. Almost all of the rest went to the electricity and gas utility sectors especially in Argentina, Chile and Colombia.

Since the Asian and Latin American financial crisis, net FDI flows to developing countries declined from $175 billion in 2001 to $147 billion in 2002 and to $135 billion in 2003. As a proportion of developing countries' GDP, FDI continued to decline from 3 per cent in 1999 to 1.9 percent in 2003. Three of the top ten recipients in the 1990s, Argentina, Brazil and Mexico experienced a decline of FDI flows of 12 per cent[4].

While economic recovery is evident in some countries and net private capital flows are expected to reach an all time high since 1997 of $227 billion in 2005, critical uncertainties confronting the global economy including high oil prices, the prospect of rising interest rates and geopolitical developments impact access to financing energy for development.

The collapse of WTO 2003 talks at Cancun underscored the legal and

4. WB, *Global Development Finance* (2004), Chapter 3, p.79

regulatory risks perceived by foreign investors in developing countries and the link between trade and investment. Developing countries were asked to address legal and other issues of concern to foreign investors in exchange for reduction in developed countries' agricultural subsidies.

Investing in energy projects in developing countries, particularly in the gas downstream and power sectors where power is used for domestic consumption and revenues are generated in local currencies, is perceived to be riskier than in OECD countries because of exchange rate and refinancing risks. Moreover, less well-developed institutional, legal and regulatory structures exacerbate investors' perception of economic and political risks. Under these circumstances, as illustrated by case studies in Chapter 5, investors tend to add high-risk premium and consequently high rate of return of over 25 per cent before considering to provide financial resources to energy projects.

Rating agencies attempt to quantify country and political risks by sovereign credit ratings. These ratings are used to help establish the cost of capital for each country. The risk premium demanded by investors and lenders is a function of several variables and is ideally calculated on a project-by-project basis. However, in practice, country ratings serve as a benchmark for risk premium. Energy companies in countries whose credit ratings are at best equivalent to sovereign ratings, can procure funds from foreign investors and lenders only on relatively unfavourable terms. Power companies in many developing countries with poor financial performance will not be able to access funds even at higher costs. Commercial banks have become very reluctant to extend loans to power companies, whether corporate or project finance, unless 'high-risk adjusted' return is assured.

Active macroeconomic management and prudent domestic financial regulation can help to prevent crises created by asset price inflation and excessive short-term borrowing. This may be possible while also leaving markets open to foreign investors, especially longer-term FDI. The rewards of FDI—in the form of increased exports, employment and total factor productivity—are highly attractive for developing countries with shortage of capital and market access. However, given that investors have plenty of choices, they demand market-friendly conditions—a style of governance and incentives comparable to those of the OECD countries. In the energy sector many of the larger investors are giant multinationals with significant power in the market place and choices are influenced by their perception of factors of attractiveness of investment.

The prospects for FDI in energy sector in developing countries will depend on macroeconomic fundamentals, adequacy of return on investments and government policies. Although the external financing environment in developing countries has brightened in 2005, much of the developing world still has difficulty accessing the international capital markets. International investment in energy/ infrastructure has declined since 1997, with the exception of trade finance, private capital flows remain heavily concentrated in specific countries and regions.

Following the East Asian financial crisis of 1998, East Asian developing countries (even those such as Singapore that has heavily relied on FDI) have taken 'strategic' decisions and have deliberately directed FDI toward government designated priority sectors. The experience of the two 'star performers' of East Asia, South Korea and Taiwan possessed a clear understanding of the costs and benefits of FDI and they approved FDI only when they confirmed that there were potential net benefits. FDI in industries supplying critical intermediate inputs using sophisticated technology (e.g. petroleum refinery and synthetic fibres) or labour-intensive export industries generating foreign exchange and employment (e.g. textile and electronic assembly) was encouraged, when compared to domestic market-oriented consumer durable goods industries.

As the case study on China in Chapter 5 demonstrates, China has followed a strategic and cautious approach in allowing FDI in its energy sector and has carefully directed the flow of FDI in power sector by setting up of joint ventures in renewable energy where the benefits of the flow of FDI and technology transfer are clearly identified. China's approach of managed transition to a socialist market economy is a strategic move to use FDI selectively when there are net benefits to the economy.

Even in the top ten developing countries pursuing liberalization policies to attract FDI, there is underlying doubt about the corporate goal of increasing shareholders value. Although with liberalization of energy prices in a number of developing countries, suspicions of some of the practices of international energy companies in the 1960s and 1970s such as the transfer pricing mechanism[5] practiced by international petroleum companies may no longer be appropriate. There is wariness toward multinational corporations and sometimes muted enthusiasm about involving multinationals in the energy development process.

There is a long history of suspicions of multinational energy corporations. Much of it centres on the possibility of multinational companies' undesirable practices leading to overpricing and sharing of excessive risks by host countries. There is also a belief that focuses directly on the central relationship between FDI and the prospects for economic growth, in particular on the role of multinational companies in the power sector of developing countries to increase access to affordable and efficient energy for development and for alleviating energy poverty.

The events since 2000 in the US electric and gas industries have added to

---

5. R Vedavalli, *Private Foreign Investment and Economic Development: A case Study of Petroleum in India* (UK, Cambridge University Press, 1976)

the suspicions of large multinational energy company practices, particularly the revelation of accounting irregularities of companies like Enron which, as of 2005 is under criminal investigation. Year 2002 had been a dark year for the US electric and gas industries. The once high-flying energy corporations including Enron have lost over US $200 billion in market capitalization. The traditional integrated utilities have also had a very bad year. The California energy crisis led to the recall of the governor in October 2003. Over ten companies, many of which were leading marketing companies, have either exited the business entirely, or have limited their business to trading around their assets.

The US Federal Energy Regulatory Commission (FERC) has 50 investigations, including probes into trades during California's energy crisis. Long-standing traditional integrated utilities such as Duke Energy, AEP and Dominion, as well as energy marketing companies including Mirant, NRG, Dynergy and Williams have pulled up stakes in Europe, India, Australia and Latin America. According to Standard and Poor (S&P), in 2002 the US power sector faced more than $590 billion in medium-term debt because of industry underperformance, failed business strategies and in some cases unlawful accounting practices.

The worsening situation since 2001 of the US electric and gas industry reflects partly the 'boom-bust cycle' that characterizes capital-intensive energy industries in competitive markets. The turmoil also reflects the more industry-specific events such as the failed California deregulation experiment, Enron's collapse with weak governance, accounting irregularities and risk management systems and have raised serious doubts about the practices of US energy multinationals and their corporate practices.

The evidence in the case study of India discussed in Chapter 5 of the closure of Enron power plant reflected the conflicts between the host country and the multinational energy corporation's goal of increasing shareholders' value, raised questions of undesirable practices of inflated project cost and tariff agreements leading to overpricing of power. The events since 2001 following the collapse of Enron and the events of the US electric and gas industry reflected the uncertainty of markets and their volatility and have added to the growing suspicions about the benefits of FDI and the market miracle. Consequently, the operating, financial and organizational ramifications of risk and return are significant.

The rewards of globalization of energy market conferring the benefits of access to global financing of energy investments and for achieving global competitiveness need to be weighed against the costs of integration to the global energy market. Developing countries in the twenty-first century face the challenge of attracting FDI in their energy sectors while dealing with the changes in the internal and external conditions that affect it. Ease of access to capital for energy investment is expected to continue to vary widely between energy sub-sectors and the risk-return profiles of individual projects.

National oil companies in major oil importing countries such as China and India, which have liberalized oil prices, will be able to access international financial markets. However, they may face less favourable terms than international oil companies, as indicated by sovereign credit ratings. Furthermore, national oil companies in China and India shifting their investment toward higher cost deep-water and/ or emerging areas as Sudan/ Russia and the Caspian region will have to bear cost of capital that will be higher to reflect higher economic, political and legal risks. Increasing oil price volatility in the post Iraq war period witnessed since 2004 and uncertainties in the post August 2004 developments in the Middle East could raise significantly the 'Terror risk premium' and the cost of capital.

Financing for electricity and downstream gas projects for domestic markets will be more difficult in many developing countries, especially in Africa, South Asia and Latin America because of higher risks perceived from doubts about the effective implementation of reforms in energy sector. Access to global financing will depend on the economic, political, regulatory and legal environment in these countries.

As evidenced during the boom years of globalization in the 1990s, FDI flows concentrated in a few countries and pursuing liberal policies would not guarantee and/ or ensure the flow of FDI as it mainly depends on private investors' behaviour and their perception of the host country's investment climate. As discussed in Chapters 4 and 5, developing countries have traversed the path from the euphoric expectations beginning in the early 1990s of financing most of their energy investments from FDI to financing a realistic 25–30 per cent of their total energy investments. What is needed is a more strategic and balanced approach to FDI, which will require developing countries to establish a good track record of FDI for their long-term energy development. This requires addressing the challenges of financing energy both at the global and national level.

A key lesson from the changing global energy industry, particularly leading to the worsening situation in parts of the US electric and gas industry is that few of the mergers and acquisitions between companies within the same businesses (examples include electricity and gas) created net value for buyers and sellers. Developing countries copying the US model need to distinguish FDI between the different implications of investment in 'greenfield' and 'acquisitions'. FDI in 'greenfield' investments creates net value with immediate investment in physical assets. If the FDI is used to acquire an existing company, while the sale may have supported the macro-economic and budget deficit reduction objectives, the financial investment is merely used to buy part of the existing capital stock without creating net value. Successful cases are characterized neither by a hands-off approach with complete reliance on markets nor by a strategy of command and control. Rather, they share a pragmatic approach built on specific strengths of the domestic economy[6].

The impact of these on the way forward is discussed in Chapter 8.

The challenge of energy security and geopolitics

Since the 1970s oil crisis, energy security (the continuous availability of energy in varied forms, in sufficient quantities and at reasonable prices) has been narrowly viewed as making arrangements for storage of oil for short-term disruptions in the energy market. Dealing with oil shortages of the 1970s also aimed at reducing dependence on oil consumption and imports, particularly in OECD and other major oil importing countries. Following declining prices of oil in the 1980s and the wave of globalization of energy industry and technological advances in the 1990s, global energy industry was reporting abundance of resources and supply which created energy complacency. The UNDP/ WEC World Energy Assessment (2000) discussing energy security concluded: 'All indications point to the gradual but steady improvement in energy security in all parts of the world, thanks to technological advances, adequacy of resources, regional cooperation, energy agencies, treaties and international trade organizations'[7].

In the 1990s global market economy, energy security became a matter of prices, economic growth, investment and technology advances in most OECD countries.

Deregulation and market liberalization were vigorously pursued in OECD power markets to enhance competition, to reduce costs and to spur technological development. When deregulated and liberalized power market pursued short-term objectives, it also posed questions for energy security and the future role of the state with regard to energy security. Black-outs in North America and Europe and other parts of the world in 2003–4 raised serious questions about the adequacy of transmission facilities and whether the right signals were being given to the market to ensure sufficient investment in required power infrastructure. A lack of investment in transmission networks was considered the primary cause of the black-outs in North America and Europe.

According to the Price Waterhouse Coopers' (PWC) report—*Supply Essentials Utilities Global Survey 2004*—which represents the views of 148 leading electricity companies in 47 countries throughout Europe, the underinvestment of the Americas, Asia Pacific, Africa and the Middle East in power infrastructure is causing demand to outstrip supply. The cautious approach to investment in global utility industry were attributed to considerations of

---

6. Rodrik Dani, *The New Global Economy and Developing Countries: Making Openness work* (Washington DC, Overseas Development Council, 1999)
7. UNDP/ WEC, *World Energy Assessment* (New York, 2000), Chapter 4, p.130.

political and market stability, concerns over investment transparency, political unrest and financial failures[8].

The events since 11 September 2001 have brought new dimensions to energy security in the twenty-first century. Oil prices have doubled from $32 per barrel in January 2004 to over $65 by September 2005. Increasing demand for oil mostly by the USA, China and India, terrorism or instability in several oil producing countries, natural disasters shutting down US Gulf Coast oil installations and shortages of US refining capacity were also driving up the prices. The main alternative to the oil, natural gas and electricity market also faced the challenge of security of supplies since the beginning of the twenty-first century. US natural gas prices rose from $2 per million British Thermal Unit (BTU) in the late 1990s to $12.60 in mid September 2005, the highest gas prices in the world.

With the return of the highest oil prices since the energy crisis of the 1970s, there are growing cries of alarm that the world is running out of oil. Petro-pessimist authors such as Paul Roberts and Mathew R Simmons[9] and others citing the 'Hubert Curve' argue that the proven reserves of world oil will last only for a few decades at the current rate of consumption. The Hubert Curve postulates that once more than 50 per cent of reserves are produced output inevitably declines[10]. The world's total oil consumption in 2004 reached 80 million barrels a day and is expected to reach over 110 million barrels a day by 2020. The world's total proven oil reserves in 2004 were estimated to be around 950 billion barrels. At 2004 consumption levels, the proven oil reserves are expected to last for about 30 years, but for significantly less than 30 years if oil consumption rises, as projected by the IEA.

Others who are petro-optimists, such as Adelman of Massachussets Institute of Technology and Daniel Yergin of Cambridge Energy Research Associates, argue that many of today's concerns, including the expectations of running out of oil have been voiced before World War I, assuming a technology freeze. They argue that although the Hubert Curve analysis applies where full commercial exploitation has taken place such as the United States, Canada and the North Sea where production is in decline, this may not apply in most oil rich areas, notably Mexico, Venezuela, Russia and the Middle East where oil may not yet have been fully explored.

Petro-optimists cite increased exploration and technological advances following

---

8. Sian Green, *Security of Supply tops the bill, Power Engineering International* (June 2004)
9. Paul Roberts, *The End of Oil: On the edge of a Perilous New World* (Boston and New York, Houghton Mifflin Company, 2004); Matthew R Simmons, *Twilight in the Desert: The Coming Saudi Oil Shock and the World Economy* (New York, Wiley, 2005)
10. James Jordan, James R Powell, 'After the oil runs out', *The Washington Post* (6 June 2004)

the oil price increases in the 1970s and adding new reserves between 1980 and 1990 of 56 per cent. Adelman notes that in 1971, the non-OPEC countries had about 200 billion barrels of proven reserves. In the next 33 years they produced 460 billion barrels and in 2004 have 209 billion barrels 'remaining'[11]. Yergin argues that based on his company's field-by-field analysis, there will be an additional 20 per cent build-up of oil supply between 2004 and 2010 and capacity to produce oil could grow by 16 million barrels a day—from 85 million barrels per day in 2004 to 101 million barrels per day in 2010[12]. Petro-optimists conclude that oil supply could increase if oil prices remain high long enough to justify the huge investments necessary to encourage new exploration, discovery and development of uneconomical fields and unconventional oil.

Yergin's conclusion based on a field-by-field study of oil production capacity differs from oil experts' discussion of reserves, the amount of oil in the ground. Long-term concerns of energy security reflect adequacy of oil reserves in place. Many oil experts agree that reserve additions in non-OPEC countries have peaked. For every ten barrels of conventional oil consumed, only four new barrels are discovered. In addition 65 per cent of total reserves are in the sensitive Persian Gulf, where Saudi Arabia and Iraq together account for 36 per cent of global oil reserves. Given the declining rate of discovery resulting in modest increase in oil reserves of just 1.4 per cent between 1990 and 2000 with increasingly sophisticated technology around the globe, the 2004–5 energy insecurity differs fundamentally from the situation in 1973 and 1979.

In the initial years of this decade energy security steadily acquired greater urgency and priority in all oil importing countries. Political and social instabilities in oil producing countries such as Saudi Arabia, Venezuela, Nigeria, Indonesia, terrorism and/ or accidents destroying oil pipelines, installations, increased competition among oil importing countries and natural disasters have impacted the supply-demand balance and short and medium term oil and gas security. Although the world will not run out of oil in the short term, the 2004–5 oil price shock has generated good reason for alarm. In the twenty-first century energy security and geopolitics are closely interconnected and the era of cheap oil is over.

Emerging structure of geopolitics since 2001

Some of the emerging features impacting the structure of energy-geopolitics include:

11. George F Will, 'Oil, how badly do you want it?', *The Washington Post* (June 13, 2004)
12. Daniel Yergin, 'It's not the end of the Oil Age', *The Washington Post* (31 July 2005)

Russia as global energy power

With oil prices since 2004 above $60 a barrel and with oil production over 9.5 million barrels a day, two-thirds of which are exported and with rich gas reserves, Russia's political strategy is being shaped to evolve as a major global energy power. In 2005 Russia announced that energy security would be a major topic at the Group of Eight summit that it plans to host in 2006 in St Petersburg by emphasizing that Russia will be a reliable supplier of energy to its industrial partners. As the largest producer of fossil fuels and uranium in 2004–5, Russia provides around one quarter of the European Union's (EU) gas supplies and over one-tenth of its oil supply. Since 2001 there is an ongoing energy dialogue between EU oil and gas importers and Russia to increase energy trade to preserve the long-term contracts for the supply of gas, an important factor in the security of supply. Given Russia's size, its oil and gas resources, its vast nuclear capability and its 'energy alliances' with developing countries including India, China and Iran, Russia is evolving as a major global energy power in the initial years of this century.

Increasing dependence on the Middle East

Despite the increasing role of Russia as global energy power, Russia's proven oil reserves of 60 billion barrels as of 2003 is limited compared with that of the Middle East to continue to supply the growing demand for oil. According to the BP *Statistical Review of World Energy* (2003), major Middle East producers have much larger reserves—Saudi Arabia (261.8 billion barrels), Iraq (112.5 billion barrels), the United Arab Emirates (97.8 billion), Kuwait (96.5 billion) and the Islamic Republic of Iran (89.7 billion)[13]. Even after taking into consideration the global oil companies' success in oil discoveries in non-OPEC West African countries, the total combined proven reserves of oil in West Africa and Russia in 2003 estimated at 120 billion barrels are less than 20 per cent of the Middle East OPEC countries. With growing imbalances between the rising demand for oil and domestic production in oil importing countries, dependence on oil imports from the Middle East will increase. The strategic importance of the Middle East region after the 2003 Iraq war becomes critical for the security of energy supply.

Even with the most optimistic outcome of a democratic Iraq, and success in the US foreign policy to encourage democracy in the Middle East, the Middle East will probably continue to be volatile and disunited in the foreseeable future. The persisting disunity in the Middle East will not diminish for a long time within the region because the transition from terrorism to active participation in the democratic process requires inspiring and unifying leaders

---

13. British Petroleum, *Statistical Review of World Energy* (London, 2003)

and involves sustained efforts to build confidence, trust and consensus among different factions in the long run. In the aftermath of the US policy of the regime change in Iraq, while countries in the Gulf region fear US military strength, they are also apprehensive about reforming their political system to address their internal discontent.

The post Iraq war situation in the Middle East has also prompted Iran's resolve to pursue its national interest to emerge as the region's strong power. Rising oil prices and concerns of energy security have helped Iran's pursuit of the nuclear energy option to leverage its oil and gas resources and rising oil revenue as a quid pro quo in its nuclear technology/ trade and energy alliances linking energy-security and geopolitics. US efforts to isolate Iran by pressuring energy hungry India to vote with the International Atomic Energy Agency's (IAEA) majority in September 2005 on Iran's nuclear program underscores the latent threat of Iran's geopolitical impact in the region. India's vote against Iran's nuclear program may have at least temporarily derailed India's energy alliance plans with Iran to access its oil and gas resources. As long as dependence on oil holding its dominant share as transportation fuel in the total energy mix persists, the Middle East with all its instabilities, will have to continue to be the main source of oil and gas supply along with continued fears of energy insecurity.

United States, energy security and geopolitics

Events from the 2003 Gulf war and the black-out in north eastern US to the 2005 natural disaster in the US gulf coast induced energy shortages spiking the prices of gasoline, crude oil and natural gas to record levels in the USA have pushed energy security to the forefront once again.

Every US President since Richard Nixon vowed to free America from reliance on foreign oil. In 1973, a few weeks after the oil embargo went into effect, President Nixon announced 'Project Independence' to make the US self-reliant in energy. Following the oil crisis of 1973 and 1979 the US and other oil importing countries made efforts to improve efficiency and to reduce oil consumption. However, the US reverted to increased dependence on oil since the 1980s. 30 years later US oil imports have doubled from 30 per cent of its consumption in November 1973 to 60 per cent in 2005.

The market miracle of conventional economic theory continues to be the guiding principle of US energy policy. When oil prices continued to rise in 2005 consumers started to buy small efficient cars, riding bikes and using mass transport systems. US energy policy makers/ Congress responded by finally passing the US Energy Bill in August 2005 after four years of on again-off again debate. The 2005 US Energy Bill did little to reduce the rising cost of energy in the short term and did not address the long-term energy future. It followed the market approach to expand conventional and alternative energy supply in the medium term by providing incentives to investors to expand domestic production of oil and natural gas and greater use of cleaner burning domestic energy sources such as nuclear power, ethanol, renewable energy and LNG by 2025.

The US response to rising prices since 2004 is a continuation of its view of the cyclical nature of the oil markets of the twentieth century years and market response to high oil prices to encourage investment in capacity as in the 1970s and 1980s to increase supply build-up. However, the twentieth century approaches to energy security adopted in the wake of oil price increases in the 1970s, such as expanding the existing system incrementally, no longer address the core of the problem of the inherently insecure oil dependent energy systems in the twenty-first century. The US has assumed the role of a global superpower to shape the long-term future of energy.

With steadily growing appetite for oil, both developed and developing oil importing countries are focusing on developing a more 'diverse portfolio' of oil suppliers. The United States in its role as the largest consumer of oil is working with American oil companies to accelerate development of West African oil fields. US and European funding strategies have shifted to reflect the new realities of energy security by channelling aid dollars strategically to favour regions like the Caspian and West Africa with oil reserves[14]. As discussed in Chapter 5, developing oil importing countries such as China and India are also seeking to diversify their oil supplies with their national oil companies investing in Africa, South East Asia and Russia.

In addition, oil importing countries including the USA are also pursuing other short- and medium-term measures to address their growing supply-demand imbalance. Possible options include: improving fuel economy; ramping up spending on alternative fuels such as bio fuels to an eventual hydrogen alternative to substitute gasoline; renewing commitment to efficiency; seriously considering renewable energy and keeping all options open including clean coal and nuclear power and the electrification of transport.

As the world oil importing countries, both developed and developing steadily become more dependent on oil, the emerging changes in political goals, the relative strengths and weakness of these economies and the linking of their foreign policies to seek alliances with OPEC, non-OPEC developing and transitional oil producing countries to gain access to oil and gas assets worldwide and pursue nuclear energy are impacting the very concept of energy security and its links with geopolitics in the initial years of this decade.

Given that energy security is no longer confined to safeguard continued supply for short-term disruptions of weeks and months but also to shape the

14. Paul Roberts, *The End of Oil: On the Edge of a Perilous New World* (Boston and New York, Houghton Mifflin Company, 2004), Chapter 10, p.244

future of energy, the twenty-first century approach to energy security requires looking beyond short-term requirements to medium- and long-term demand recognizing the obvious fact that the twentieth century addiction to oil cannot be displaced in the short term by radical approaches. Plans for reducing dependence on oil require new technologies, especially for transportation which accounts for over two-thirds of global oil consumption. Whatever non-oil transport technologies prove best, making the transition from present systems will take many years.

If the US record since the mid 1980s is any guide, it is doubtful that tangible progress will be made away from oil as the USA has moved away from using even existing technologies to improve fuel efficiency and taking fiscal measures to raise taxes on gasoline. Even the 2005 Energy Bill passed by the US Congress sticks to increasing domestic energy supply to correct some supply-demand imbalances in the near medium term of ten to 15 years.

The USA has historically embarked decisively on massive programs of longer-term actions whenever its security needs become critical. The Manhattan Project for the development of the atom bomb (1940s), the construction of the national highway system for troop movement (1950s) and the space program for ballistic research (1960s and 1970s) are all examples of such longer-term actions, spanning several administrations. They all addressed immediate security concerns and eventually resulted in vast additional benefits for the economy[15].

Given that the USA is the largest world oil consumer and is the global super power intervening in the oil and gas rich Middle East, there is little doubt that the US energy security and geopolitics linkage is critical to addressing energy security concerns in the short term, developing technologies to make the transition in the medium term and to shape the path for long-term energy future in the twenty-first century. The question is whether the USA in its dual role as world's largest energy consumer and as the global superpower will lead the path through successive administrations to securing the energy future for the twenty-first century.

Energy security concerns in the twenty-first century need to be addressed at several levels: globally, to ensure adequacy of resources; regionally to ensure networking and trade takes place; at the country level, to ensure national security of supply; and at the consumer level, to ensure that consumers demand can be satisfied. Governments are expected to do their part as well when it comes to changing the energy transformation process away from oil. However, political attention of governments is focused mainly on tiding over securing short-term oil requirements. Thus far, governments have not been able to focus on longer-term challenges such as addressing the

---

15. Constantine C Haramis, 'Crude oil, Global Energy Security, and the War in Iraq', www.greekshares.com (20 August 2004)

issue of the future direction of country's energy policy for the twenty-first century given the inherently insecure oil dominated energy mix.

For developing oil importing countries energy security goes beyond focusing political attention on getting access to oil supply at reasonable prices in the short term. They have to focus on designing the direction of energy policies for the twenty-first century. This includes the fundamentals of energy policy in the medium and long term to alleviate energy poverty and to secure adequate supply of efficient energy for sustained high rates of economic growth. The challenges of energy for development faced by developing countries at the national level are discussed below.

Twenty-first century energy for development policy challenges at the national level

As discussed in earlier chapters, a combination of factors, the need for supporting higher rates of economic growth, the rate of growth in population and the political mandate of governments to increase access to energy services by 2010 to over 2 billion poor lacking access will increase the rate of growth in energy demand in developing countries. The challenge of increasing access to efficient energy services to billions of new customers in developing countries cannot be accomplished by market liberalization alone.

The major challenge has been the disconnect between the benefits of the 1990s evolving energy industry in theory and the reality since 2001. Energy sector reform and the liberalization experience discussed in Chapters 4 and 5 show that while technology and management benefits in theory could enhance efficiency, the industry tends to concentrate on the easier and more established markets where demand growth is high. Private investment in the electricity sector in developing countries has so far been concentrated either in new investments in power generation or in the acquisition of assets with relatively little investment in the expansion of distribution.

Furthermore, even successful greenfield investment in generation encountered problems, such as that of Enron's $3 billion Dabhol Power project in India and resulted in its closure.

After the closure of $3 billion Enron's Dabhol Power project in India, few private energy companies are willing to risk billions of dollars building power plants or other energy infrastructure in countries where they cannot recover even their cost of supply. Paul Roberts in his book *The End of Oil* in summarizing the behaviour of private energy companies in 2004, quotes Ira Joseph, a global gas analyst in New York: 'Today, the only energy projects that anyone wants to finance are projects that get energy out of the developing world so it can be sold to the developed world. There is no money in supplying energy to the developing world'[16].

The major challenge of financing growing energy demand in the post 11 September 2001 world requires that developing countries learn from the lessons of their energy sector liberalization experience since the 1990s to understand the key features of the political and economic environment in which the new energy system is evolving. Formulating a policy framework for energy for development in the twenty-first century should begin with facing the facts.

First, energy sector reform and liberalization since the 1990s postulated energy market transition as a panacea for addressing energy financing issues in developing countries. Proponents of market transition upheld the benefits of the competitive market by arguing that it is the most efficient allocater of resources and provider of high levels of consumer service and satisfaction. However, because of market imperfections and market failures it is now clear that the market alone cannot be expected to increase access to energy for the growing and large proportion of vulnerable population, to protect environment and to ensure energy security. Where markets still fail to protect public benefits, targeted government interventions may be required. However, governments need also to face the fact that translating energy sector reform policies into effective implementation takes time and entails transition costs, in particular the costs of inefficiencies of existing government institutions and incapacities of new regulatory institutions. It is therefore, important that developing countries face the hard facts of inefficiencies of governance both with regard to effective implementation of reforms and required market interventions. Effective economic governance is critical to ensure the goals of energy for development.

Second, energy is far more than a sector issue as it is closely linked to the fundamentals of economic growth, environmental issues and security. Energy issues will gain specific importance in the wake of rising oil prices since 2004, supplemented by new challenges of future direction of energy policies and the growing demand for energy in developing oil importing countries. With continued uncertainties in the Middle East, the international energy situation will continue to be complex. International developments, shifting demand patterns, technological innovations and their impact on fuel supply patterns will continue to impact the parameters of decisions and underscore the global nature of energy issues.

Third, driven by political mandate, governments in developing oil importing countries make policy statements promising 'energy for all' in the coming decade. The fact is that the current mix of energy sources, energy infrastructure and energy end-use applications is not efficient and diverse

---

16. Paul Roberts, *The End of Oil: On the Edge of a Perilous New World* (Boston and New York, Houghton Mifflin Company, 2004), Chapter 10, p.244

enough to deliver the energy services required in a sustainable fashion. Given the long lead time of energy investments, decisions on the direction of future energy mix in the medium- and long-term will have to be made now. Governments will have to face the formidable challenge of defining the goals and shaping the direction of their energy policy in the short, medium and long term to blend continuity with change for energy development in the twenty-first century. This requires reformulating energy policies for power, coal, oil and gas, energy efficiency and conservation, the environment and alternative energy supply for rural and urban use taking into account each country's energy resource endowment, demand and investment requirements.

Fourth, as of 2005 developing oil importing countries need to face the hard facts of financing energy for development when it is no longer possible to use multilateral institutions to fund their commercially non-viable state-owned energy/ power companies. The only way to ensure adequate energy supply for development is to attract both public and domestic/ foreign private capital by restructuring their energy/ power companies to operate as commercially and financially viable companies.

Finally, governments in developing countries have to face the fact that political rhetoric and policy statements are not sufficient as the public begin to demand results on the ground. The stresses caused by lack of energy will increase unless tackled with determination as a political priority with long-term commitment. If they are not addressed successfully, the deteriorating longer-term situation could have profound geopolitical consequences as well as severe adverse environmental impacts such as deforestation and soil erosion. Government policies, macroeconomic management, financial sector development, energy policy and effective governance for implementation of policies and projects will continue to play a major role in ensuring that adequate finance for energy is mobilized in a timely fashion.

Based on the above facts, developing countries' challenges to finance energy for development at the national level can be grouped under five areas:

A. Macroeconomic management and energy policy.
B. Financial sector development and project financing.
C. Combating corruption.
D. Changing the role of government in energy for development.
E. Building twenty-first century institutions for effective governance.

A: *Macroeconomic management and energy policy issues*

The macroeconomic environment is the single most important driver of energy demand and therefore, energy investment requirements. As one of the main sources of risk, it affects not only investments needed but also the access of the energy sector to capital. Low sovereign ratings due to poor macroeconomic performance lead to higher risk premium in the cost of capital, which can adversely affect the viability of energy projects in the country concerned. Investors and lenders are more reluctant to provide funds to projects in lower rated countries.

Energy sector reform and liberalization in developing countries discussed in previous chapters and the key lessons of thc reform experience in the 1990s confirm the crucial importance of macroeconomic policies as energy sector reform and liberalization were often launched as part of macroeconomic adjustment programs. Discussions in these chapters also confirm that macroeconomic turbulence leading to East Asian and Argentina's financial crises impacted adversely their demand for energy and their energy companies' performance with far reaching effects on energy investment.

The difficulties that many developing countries face in mobilizing financial resources for energy investment in future will be exacerbated by fragmented, uncoordinated and poorly implemented energy policies. The development and implementation of energy reforms inevitably generate uncertainties. Governments can reduce these uncertainties by minimizing policy-induced risk and clarifying details of planned reform and their effective implementation to reassure investors that energy companies will be able to generate a reasonable rate of return.

Primary energy demand in developing countries as discussed in Chapter 1 is expected to grow at about 2.5 per cent per year and will require investment of about 2.5–3.0 per cent of the GDP of developing countries in the next 25 years. Prior to 1990s government budget allocations, subsidies and multilateral financial institutions financed a major part of energy investments in developing countries and energy price distortions, subsidies and inefficient management of the energy sector persisted.

The 1990s market liberalization of the energy sector emphasized real cost-based pricing, regulatory policies, restructuring, privatization and private investment to improve efficiency and to generate the required financial resources for investment. Key policy components included setting the right framework conditions by removing energy price distortions, setting up of regulatory institutions to set prices and encourage competition in energy markets and creating suitable legal, institutional and financial incentives for attracting private investment.

Although the broad policies of energy sector reform and liberalization were straightforward, achieving the objectives require dealing with the challenges of the political and economic environment in which new energy systems will evolve and also with continued government commitment. The discussions in Chapters 4, the case studies in Chapter 5 and issues related to energy for the poor in Chapter 6 confirm that energy policy is interrelated with macroeconomic development and global financing policy challenges.

For developing countries formulating their energy policies for the twenty-first century, it is important to learn from their lessons of experience in the areas relating to energy sector policy, macroeconomic and development policy, commercialization policy and global energy financing/ private investment policy. Finally, they have to face the realities of the post 11 September 2001 world of uncertainty on their growing dependence on oil in shaping the right direction for their energy policy in the medium- and long-term while ensuring energy security.

Energy sector policies: Common considerations

Energy in 2005 reached centre-stage in two parallel international and national processes. The first process, linked to the security of oil supply, is well known and began in 2001. This includes concerns about the cost of growing dependence on insecure oil supply and mechanisms to ensure energy security at reasonable prices. It has also raised some alarm about the adequacy of oil reserves to meet the growing demand. The second process is just starting up at national levels. Oil importing countries are starting to address the need to diversify their sources of energy supply and keeping all options open to meet their medium- and long-term demand for energy.

For the first time the adequacy of oil reserves at affordable prices to supply the growing demand in the twenty-first century and the cost of growing dependence on inherently insecure oil imports are debated rather than as adjuncts to environment issues. This presents a special opportunity to formulate national energy policy in the right direction to meet the growing demand for energy.

There remains a distinct difference of perspective between OECD and developing countries that has been reflected in the main issues associated with energy for development. While energy use in developing countries has increased three to four times as quickly as that of OECD countries and the share of developing countries in global commercial energy use increased from 13 per cent in 1970 to over 30 per cent in 1998, the per capita energy consumption in developing countries is still below one-tenth that of OECD countries. In addition, despite increased energy use, over 40 per cent of the population in developing countries lack access to energy services. Furthermore, market liberalization over the past two decades and integration of the global economy, expected to promote trade and investment, have also caused the divide between the skilled globally connected higher income class and the hinterland of large impoverished people left behind and intensified inequality, poverty and social conflict in many developing countries.

As the globally connected skilled higher income class in developing countries is emulating industrial countries' living standards, the demand for oil in the transport sector has been growing fast with galloping rates of growth in automobile ownerships. Under these circumstances the underlying concern of developing countries is that a higher rate of economic growth similar to that achieved by the OECD countries based on fossil fuels is critical for development. Consequently, developing countries have thus far focused mainly on securing adequate energy supply at affordable prices in the short term. Energy policy in the last decades of the twentieth century was a collection of general objectives and targets and remained fragmented. However, by 2005 when global discussions on energy are focused on energy security and volatility in oil prices, there is an emerging consensus that the challenges facing energy in the twenty-first century require major, transformative change. The current global energy system suffers from tight oil supply, growing demand, limited capacity and supply disruptions. Although the market has an important role and improved technologies may ease the supply situation, continued uncertainties in the geopolitical world of oil politics entail costs on growing dependence on oil.

Energy policy for development: Critical elements

The many socio-economic and political issues related to energy for development and concerns of the environmental impacts of energy at the local, regional and global level all point to the need for major changes in national and global approaches to energy. Resource abundance and energy complacency of the 1990s have been replaced by tight supply and energy insecurity since 2001. Given that the uncertainties in the post 11 September 2001 global world of oil geopolitics are expected to continue, governments are beginning to debate what should be the right direction for their energy policy in the twenty-first century under alternative rates of growth and energy for development options.

The energy policy challenge for developing countries in the twenty-first century will be to plan for the future while meeting the growing needs in the present at affordable prices by new approaches and by re-examining existing approaches and mechanisms. Energy policies need to consider the country-specific energy market conditions to reflect differences in energy resource endowments, rates of growth in energy demand and investment requirements to increase access to energy supplies. However, despite the differing energy sector features and despite the fact that developing countries are at varying degrees of efforts in reforming their energy sectors, there are eight common energy policy considerations to increase access to efficient energy supplies for development in the twenty-first century.

The common areas of energy policy challenges include (i) energy security, (ii) choice of energy mix/ energy supply-demand, (iii) energy pricing, (iv) energy efficiency and environment considerations, (v) widening access to energy services, (vi) regulation, (vii) restructuring and commercialization and

(viii) finance and investment.

(i) Energy security

Although markets play a dominant role in securing energy supply in OECD countries, their role is modest in some developing countries and absent in others. The security of supply and services in developing countries depends almost solely on government action and multinational companies, which events since the 2001 California energy crisis in the US energy market has shown may not serve the best interests of consumers. For net oil importing developing countries, energy supply could become more vulnerable due to increased dependence on imported oil. The continued spike of oil prices, since August 2004 to reach $65 per barrel in September 2005, underscores the necessity of formulating strategic policy frameworks for energy security.

Policy challenges for energy security framework could include: avoiding excessive dependence on imports, diversifying both suppliers and energy sources and by developing commercially viable domestic energy resources and increasing national strategic reserves of crude oil and finally, fostering greater regional and international trade by development of regional energy sources to increase supply and trade, particularly in South Asia and SSA.

(ii) Choice of Energy, mix/supply-demand

Developing countries' persisting long-term energy/ electricity challenge is to address the issue of growing imbalance between supply and demand. Although some of the large emerging developing oil importing countries with increased dependence on foreign oil such as China and India, have addressed the need for increasing oil and gas supplies by both domestic and foreign sources, this has not been well integrated into a comprehensive national energy policy. In the absence of formulation and adoption of a comprehensive national energy policy, developing countries will continue to feel the effects of shortage of electric capacities, inadequate and inefficient energy infrastructure such as transmission and distribution systems and pipeline systems, insufficient domestic energy supply, a regional imbalance in supply sources and access to energy extension services. It is therefore, important that developing countries formulate a comprehensive national energy policy/ strategy learning from their experience of reform and liberalization that takes a long-term approach to meeting their twenty-first century energy requirements.

Developing countries' pressing challenge is to build enough new generation and transmission capacity along with rehabilitating and maintaining existing capacity to maximize their efficient utilization to generate supplies to meet growing short-/ medium- and long-term demand. Along with increase in adequate generating capacity, developing countries need to have the infrastructure to ensure reliable electricity supply. Investment in new transmission and distribution capacity needs to keep pace with growth in demand and requirements for expanding access and with changes in the industry structure.

Electricity is a secondary source of energy generated through the consumption of primary sources such as coal, natural gas, oil and renewable energy sources such as hydropower, solar wind and geothermal. Developing countries' energy policy should address the issues of diversified energy supply from both fossil and renewable energy resources. Fossil fuels will continue to be required for development in the foreseeable future as commercial energy's share will continue to increase. Despite the potential of renewable energy resources in the long term, the contribution of modern renewable resources will depend on the effectiveness of developing countries' policies to address the issues related to the development of large hydro and commercial viability of technologies of other non-hydro renewable resources.

(iii) Energy pricing

There is general agreement with regard to pricing of internationally traded energy such as oil, gas and coal to reflect their international level of prices plus domestic transport and distribution costs. As discussed in Chapters 4 and 5, it almost took over three decades, since the oil price hikes of the 1970s, for developing oil importing countries to liberalize oil, gas and coal prices as of 2003. Although cross-subsidization of petroleum products such as kerosene and LPG still continue, there is a consensus to progressively reduce subsidies on oil products. However, faced with the rising oil prices of over $60 a barrel in 2005, governments in developing oil importing countries such as India reverted back to partial government intervention in the market by limiting hikes in oil product prices and extending the time for continuation of subsidies. While the governments in oil importing countries have adopted in principle liberalizing energy prices to reflect market prices, in practice, the prospect of staying the course of energy price liberalization once again remains to be determined by the future price of oil and its impact on inflation and socio-political considerations.

Developing countries continue to experience confusion in formulating policy for pricing electricity. In the ongoing set-up of changing electricity sector, the goal of price efficiency to price electricity is expected to reflect the level and structure of the marginal costs of supply, differentiated by time of day, season and voltage levels. Determination of cost-efficiency requires use of international best practice standards, reserve plant margins, electricity losses and plant availability factors. As electricity markets in developing countries are liberalized, price efficiency could reflect the outcome of pool pricing and supply competition. However, as evidenced in Chapter 5 case studies, even in the case of Argentina, which achieved electricity market liberalization in the 1990s, has faced a set-back in electricity pricing.

A major challenge of electricity pricing is the continuation of subsidies to cover cost inefficiencies and failure to recover costs by efficiency pricing. Commercially restructured electric utilities such as the ESKOM in South Africa may be able to finance their expansion through retained earnings and recourse to capital markets. They are able to widen the access to electricity by undertaking empowerment programs. However, even as of 2005, electric utilities particularly in South Asia and SSA are not commercially viable and remain operationally inefficient with poor quality of service. Subsidies continue to cover the widening gap between revenue receipts and real cost of power of public utilities not making them creditworthy enough to raise capital even for the required maintenance and rehabilitation.

Pricing policy should therefore address the issue of subsidies and clearly differentiate between avoidable subsidies for covering cost inefficiencies by failing to meet standard industry practices and social subsidies on a declining level necessary to support 'lifeline' rates for household consumers with low level of consumption, allowances for the higher fixed costs of the extension of service to new areas and investment in R&D projects.

(*iv*) *Energy efficiency and environment considerations*

Since the oil price increases of the 1970s, developed countries have significantly improved their energy efficiency and reduced their energy intensity by developing and expanding the use of energy efficient technologies. In developing countries energy sector inefficiencies have persisted for long periods dating back to the oil price crisis of the 1970s. While energy prices in developing countries are dramatically higher in 2005 than in 1990, high electricity prices in many developing countries do not reflect real efficiency improvements. Many developing countries are still facing rolling black-outs, lack of access to quality energy supplies, persisting electricity subsidies and an uncertain energy policy direction. Continued supply shortages are hurting prospects for increased economic growth and expansion of necessary energy services.

Energy policy for the twenty-first century will need to correct the widening imbalance between supply and growing demand by efficient energy pricing. Economic efficiency provides a good basis for regulation. It points to a range of indicators for assessing an industry's performance. It requires regulators to look at measures of cost and price efficiency, at environmental performance and at the industry's efforts to extend service. Price efficiency for the electricity industry reflects the level and structure of the marginal costs of supply, differentiated by time of day, season and voltage levels. Marginal costs include the costs of compliance with environmental policy.

Economic efficient pricing avoids subsidies that undermine the financial performance of the industry. Exceptions including 'lifeline' rates, allowances for the higher fixed costs of the extension of service to new areas and investments in research and development projects become part of retained earnings and/ or recourse to capital markets. Economic efficiency for electricity industry should compare with the cost and efficiencies of international best practice standards, reserve plant margins, electrical losses and plant availability factors. Probabilities of loss of load and brown-outs are good indicators of service quality.

Energy price liberalization measures along with choice of energy efficient technologies such as combined cycle power plants have helped developing countries to make some progress in energy efficiency and conservation. Given that the rate at which efficiency improvements are made depends on the shifts in the economy and varies over time depending on energy policies, conservation and energy efficiency are crucial components of a national energy plan. Improved energy efficiency and conservation reduces energy consumption and energy costs. For oil importing developing countries energy efficiency helps reduce energy imports, the likelihood of energy shortages and toxic emissions. An increased rate of improvement in energy efficiency can have a large impact on energy supply and infrastructure investment by reducing the need for new power plants, and associated energy supply infrastructure. It could encourage specific industry actions such as load management and policy incentives to promote energy efficient technologies in investment.

Environment considerations

The patterns of energy production and use involving growing reliance on fossil fuels and the continued destruction of forests have a direct effect on the global environment. Fossil fuel combustion and carbon emissions from industry are the main contributors to global greenhouse gas emissions that cause climate change. Industrialized countries have traditionally been the source of these emissions. The long-term cumulative contribution to the increase in atmospheric concentrations has been and will continue to be dominated by the industrialized countries well into 2050[17]. However, developing countries are forecast to account for over half the annual increment of carbon dioxide by 2025, with higher rate of growth in energy demand from

17. Thomas Johansson, Susan McDade, 'Global Warming Post-Kyoto: Continuing Impasse or Prospects for Progress', *Energy and Development Report, Energy After the Financial Crisis* (Washington DC, ESMAP-WB, 1999)

rising per capita income and population growth.

Local and regional pollution from energy production and use in developing countries have high social costs. Diesel powered vehicles and small stoves or boiler-burning coal, wood and oil impose the highest costs per ton of fuel. Environmental costs of fuel use include marginal damage costs per ton of local pollutants affecting local health by increasing lead in blood and sulphur deposition levels per square meter per year.

Given the time required to incorporate the low-polluting options in new investments and to replace the old capital stock, pollution is quite likely to rise before it abates. Furthermore, the increasing use of coal in developing countries such as China and India will also contribute to the rising social cost of the environment in the absence of the use of clean coal technology options. With rising price of oil since 2004 when developing oil importing countries are faced with the problem of meeting the growing demand for energy at affordable prices, reconciling the cost of using clean coal technologies to ameliorate environmental costs becomes a major issue for major coal users such as China and India.

A combination of increased energy efficiency, more utilization of renewable sources of energy and the development and introduction of new, inherently clean technologies for fossil fuel use may address the whole set of issues related to energy for development. As discussed in Chapter 6, the future use of renewable energy will depend on its costs relative to those of using fossil fuels and are currently confined to 'niche markets' in the absence of climate change policies. Even with rising oil prices and innovations in technologies with possibilities of declining relative cost of renewable sources of energy, dependability on renewable sources of energy compared with fossil fuels will continue to be an issue. However, with further innovation and scale of economies in manufacturing and marketing, there is the potential for renewable energy sources to meet up to 20 per cent of the total energy mix in major oil importing developing countries such as China and India.

This requires policies to be formulated to allow prices to reflect the marginal costs of supply, including the costs of pollution control—the central goal of 'internalizing externalities' in market prices.

In the case of electricity generation, the additional costs of pollution control need to be weighed against the benefits that are feasible through reductions in the losses in the distribution networks, the improvements in the efficiency of new power plant, and the improvement in pricing and regulatory policies[18]. But, under a 'business as usual' scenario where energy prices, particularly electricity prices in developing countries do not reflect the marginal cost of supply and subsidization is expected to continue in the foreseeable

18. Dennis Anderson, 'Addressing Pollution Problems in Developing Regions: An Update on Options', *Energy and Development Report* (Washington DC, WB-ESMAP, 1999)

future, it will continue to be difficult for developing countries to pursue policies to reconcile growth objectives with financing sustainable energy alternatives.

Climate change and national development objectives need to be reconciled as they form critical elements of the same energy policies. New forms of arm's length regulation following market liberalization provide opportunities for establishing new forms of incentives for the development and commercialization of environment friendly technologies. Higher rates of economic growth and the required sustainable energy for development can only be achieved with a major reorientation in the production and consumption with a choice of clean technologies based on evaluation of economic/ financial/ environmental cost-benefit analysis.

(v) Widening access to efficient energy

As of 2005, developing countries face the most serious challenge of increasing energy supplies for development and for expanding energy services to over 2 billion or over 40 per cent of their impoverished and poor who lack access to efficient energy at affordable prices. Increasing access to efficient energy supplies for fuelling development and for those who lack access depends on the robustness of development policies.

Energy policy should seek expansion of efficient energy services for development and for expanding access to energy supplies for those who lack them to raise the living standard of the people. This requires integration of energy policy with macroeconomic and development policies. The path of energy development and the rate of change need to be consistent with sustained economic development. Critical policy issues need to address how to widen access to reliable and affordable modern energy supplies. Pricing signals, effective regulatory regime and commercially operated energy enterprises can facilitate energy markets to function better. But markets alone cannot be expected to meet the needs of the poor who lack access.

Targeted government policies and effective regulatory approaches will be required to overcome obstacles and market imperfections and secure important public benefits. Specific policies include: improving access to efficient energy, making electricity available both to satisfy basic needs and to support economic development, addressing the challenge of meeting the energy needs of the growing urban population, increasing access to electricity in rural areas by providing both grid and non-grid options that include financing rural energy, developing new institutional structures and partnerships for providing rural energy services. The success of developing countries' policy of 'Energy for all' depends on governments taking charge to formulate a national comprehensive long-term energy policy/ strategy for the twenty-first century reflecting the costs and benefits of the evolving energy market since the post-2004 oil price increases.

Liberalization of energy markets is fundamental for the growth of the energy industry. However, experience has shown that it is equally important to set out clearly detailed policy goals for pricing, regulation, commercialization, financing and investment and the key policy instruments to achieve these goals taking into consideration their interrelationships.

(vi) Regulation

One major problem facing policy makers in a number of developing countries especially in SSA and developing Asia is that the unbundling of public monopoly often results in substitution by a private monopoly. Despite the setting up of regulatory institutions in a number of countries to encourage competition and regulate public–private monopolies as evidenced in the case studies in Chapter 5, regulatory authorities have not yet been effective in encouraging competition and designing and enforcing economic regulation for efficient electricity pricing.

Examples of economic regulation in India's states include using regulation as an instrument to cover the cost of inefficiencies to close the gap between required and actual revenue receipts. Principles of price efficiency and fair and equal treatment of consumers are not followed with price increases to a certain segment of consumers. The cost-plus pricing regulation practiced in many developing countries does not reflect the international electricity industry's standard costs, reserve margins, transmission and distribution losses and plant availability factors.

It is clear from the reform experience of the 1990s that market reforms involving privatization or commercialization of public utilities are unlikely to advance public benefits and to widen access to the unserved population unless accompanied by specific regulatory objectives and measures to achieve them. Two types of policy initiatives as discussed in Chapter 6 have been introduced mainly in OECD countries in the 1990s to address the public benefit issue. These include: measures to support renewable energy development by obliging utilities to buy or sell a minimum percentage of their energy from renewable sources; and system benefit charges to raise revenue from a 'wires charge' that is then used for public goods programs such as assisting energy use by low income households or promoting energy efficiency, renewable energy and research and development. However, these measures are relatively easy to implement in developed countries with commercially viable utility operations. Some developing countries such as China and India have incorporated some of these policies.

Developing countries still on the learning curve of the reform process need to formulate policies for establishment of a comprehensive, fair and transparent regulatory framework and a system of enforcement. Effective regulation should include: measures to widen competition by guaranteeing independent power producers access to power grids and giving energy service companies opportunities to bid on supply contracts; criteria for economic efficiency as a good basis for regulation with a range of indicators for assessing an industry's performance and establishing performance standards including measures of cost and price efficiency and industry's efforts to extend service.

Economic regulation for pricing electricity should require ground rules for the electricity industry on price efficiency, subsidies, cost efficiency, quality of service and widening access; obligations to serve specific regions with concessionaire arrangements; and reporting requirements to ensure transparency. Regulations could require companies to report on progress in meeting the performance standards including extension of supplies to unserved populations.

Effective regulatory policies could enable the energy industry to mobilize the required financial resources to expand services through a mix of internal cash generation and recourse to financial markets. As the World Energy Council's 1997 report on Financing Energy observed: 'contrary to popular belief, savings rates in many developing countries are double those of the USA and generally one-third greater than those of Europe and Japan'. Given the increasing demand for energy for development, designing a system of arm's length regulatory policies could allow domestic and foreign investors to enter energy markets and to earn good rates of return while enabling the industry to extend service.

(vii) *Restructuring and commercialization policies*

Restructuring policies in developing countries involving unbundling of vertically integrated energy activities is regarded essential for competition and is modelled after the high profile cases of industrialized countries. Examples include some of large middle-income developing countries such as Argentina and Chile, following the UK model of unbundling their power sectors. The restructuring effort resulted in competition among electricity generators and suppliers for large industrial customers, spreading gradually to households. The separation of transmission and distribution networks from providers to ensure access to all suppliers and finally retail competition at the distribution level continue to be part of the restructuring process.

This model of restructuring based on capturing the benefits of competition in the generation sector was promoted in the 1990s to all developing countries irrespective of the size of their power systems. For small countries to achieve real competition from the 'one size fit' restructuring model may be harder to achieve in the short to medium term. Energy sector reform policies will have to address the country-specific situation. Reform objectives need to be flexible and costs and benefits of alternatives need to be evaluated in detail for the system under consideration.

The possibility of introducing competition into generation is critical to a power restructuring strategy. The force of competition will come from new entrants (such as independent power producers). If entry is easy and can take place rapidly, then the threat of entry may be sufficient to induce existing firms to become cost efficient. In large privatized systems such as Chile and Argentina where the generators bid to supply power on a daily or even half-hourly basis the repeated bidding allowed competition to be effective by reducing costs and prices to consumers. Even in the case of Argentina, the benefits of effective competition are short-lived, as Argentina is yet to recover from the macroeconomic crisis of 2001.

Developing countries in general have tried to separate their electricity sectors and in some cases have been successful in attracting IPPs. However, the difficulties of entry and project financing problems have delayed construction and the entry of new firms has not been enough to improve efficiency of the existing utilities. Chapters 4 and 5 show that separation of generation, transmission and distribution has remained more a policy statement on paper and has failed to lead to commercialization of operations. Many of the physical, operational and financial performance measures of restructured energy enterprises differ greatly from the industry standard fundamentals of commercial viability.

Given the complexities and the degree of sophistication required for operation of the de-integrated systems, developing countries will need to formulate restructuring policies taking into consideration the size and structure of their electricity systems. Restructuring policy objectives should be linked with policies and measures for effective commercialization supported by efficient pricing and regulatory policies, application of international accounting standards and incentives for private investment. Energy companies do not always adopt their accounting systems to international standards. Some state-owned energy companies in developing countries, particularly the so-called unbundled electric utilities and natural gas companies do not provide detailed information about their financial cost and profit centres. Uncollected inter-enterprise debts, barter trade, lack of payment discipline and inadequate and non-transparent financial information create uncertainty, which discourages investors and lenders. A restructured and commercially operated energy sector conforming to international operation standards can lower costs and generate the finance required for the expansion and extension of supplies. However, in many developing countries restructuring and reform of electric power sector have remained more as public policy statements than as corporate goals to be pursued effectively.

Examples of case studies in Chapter 5 show that liberalized petroleum and gas operations in India and China since 2001 have increased profitability and generated the finance required for expansion and extension of supplies. However, in restructured energy markets, cross-subsidies will not be available to increase access in areas that are not attractive to investors. Policies of restructuring and commercialization therefore need to include policy measures that specifically address such concerns.

(viii) Financing/ Investment policies

The main objective of the 1990s macro/ sector reform and liberalization policies has been to encourage private investment as developing countries can no longer finance increasing energy supplies through subsidies and government budget allocations for energy operations. With growing and competing demands for public finance, the tightening of international aid budgets and the declining flow of international agency finance to state energy enterprises, the public sector in many developing countries will not be able to finance the investment needed to satisfy their growing energy demand requirements.

Discussions in Chapters 3–5 show the changing pattern of energy financing in developing countries with declining multilateral and official development assistance. Official development assistance fell by about 20 per cent in real terms in the 1990s. In contrast FDI expanded rapidly in the 1990s. However, as discussed in Chapter 4, over 70 per cent of FDI went to the top ten developing countries. In some countries, privatization has led to a high degree of concentration of vested interests in and around the energy sector. A weak jurisdictional system can allow insider-dealing and corruption to develop with increased costs of production and higher prices to consumers.

A decade of energy sector reform experience in developing countries shows that despite the initial interest shown by private investors, many developing countries may not be able to mobilize all the finance they require for energy investment either because of inadequate public resources or because they are unable or unwilling to make fundamental changes required to attract private sector investment. Some energy projects in developing countries have attracted private finance where hydrocarbons can be exported and supplied to established domestic markets. In electricity sector although 62 developing countries have made at least some progress in the 1990s in introducing private participation, the breadth and depth of the private participation remain uneven. More than 60 per cent of memoranda of understanding for energy projects signed in developing countries have failed to secure financing and have failed to materialize.

Advocates of private investment have argued that availability of global savings for financing energy has more to do with developing country policy than with the level of world saving. The WEC study of financing energy (1997) and the IEA study on world energy investment outlook (2003) concluded that global financial resources are more than adequate to meet the vast needs of the energy sector. However, as the experience since 1997 has shown even larger and emerging developing countries with growing domestic market who were able to service international investors' requirements for secure and repatriable returns will increasingly have to be prepared to address the cost of risk premiums of private investment.

Reliable enforcement of legal and regulatory framework is central to bringing energy projects to financial closure. In many developing countries the lack of enforcement, rather than the lack of framework per se, is the more serious concern. Enforcement is particularly critical in project finance, where risks are allocated precisely through agreements and contracts among equity holders, lenders, input suppliers and buyers. An effective mechanism for resolving disputes is an important element.

While there is recognition for the need for interesting private investment in energy, different stakeholders have different opinions about the problems of access to financing energy investment. The experience of the 1990s shows that for developing countries with inefficient state-owned and subsidized energy monopolies, access to international finance will be difficult because of bureaucratic, legal, institutional and implementation barriers and more important, the lack of political will to learn to evaluate the real costs and benefits of investment and commitment to the reform process.

Based on a decade of failed attempts to attract private investors in the state owned bankrupt power sector, some state governments in India, for example, the Chief Minister of the state of Karnataka, concluded in 2003 that private investors overestimated cost, which was double that of the offer he received from the public electricity generating company. There is little doubt that this conclusion reflects the politics of the reform process where politicians fail to acknowledge the barriers to private investors and are unwilling to learn from experience to address the issue of real costs and benefits of public and/ or private investment in making their decisions.

Attracting private investment, particularly in power projects, will increasingly compete with other national and international opportunities where conditions conducive to attracting FDI exist. These include: political and economic stability, a functioning legal framework, including currency convertibility, freedom to repatriate dividends and other investment proceeds and a stable domestic savings and investment regime, an independent regulatory regime protected from arbitrary political intervention, necessary physical infrastructure and availability of technical skills, goods and services and a trained and trainable work force.

Lessons drawn from the liberalization experience since the 1990s including the black-outs of 2003 in the USA and Europe are being debated at open forums. The second World Energy Forum on Energy Regulation held in Rome in October 2003 by the WEC concluded that there was no direct link between the ownership of the electricity infrastructure—whether it is public or private—and quality of service. The issue is often insufficient capacity, in particular, transmission and interconnection infrastructure and the lack of regulatory and other incentives for long-term investment in energy projects[19].

The key elements for attracting finance include: the rule of law and contract enforceability, macroeconomic and energy enterprise creditworthiness, efficiency market pricing, transparent legal and regulatory frameworks to signal pricing/ tariff policies, bankability of investment, the creation of functioning domestic capital markets and effective institutions and government commitment for establishing a sound track record for investment.

Liberalization experience since the 1990s to encourage competition and private investment has had limited success in shifting the mind-set of the poorer regions of South Asia and SSA to develop energy resources to increase supply and regional trade. Examples include the failure of countries in the South Asia region to agree on how to develop the vast hydro and natural gas energy resources, the inability of both Nepal and Bangladesh to develop their large hydro and natural gas resource due to political and national patrimony mind-set barriers to trade to correct the fundamental regional imbalance between supply and demand. In the absence of a shift in the national patrimony mind-set of small and poorer countries, their future will inevitably constrain development and expansion of energy services.

In the final analysis, the experience of developing countries through the decade of transition in the energy sector shows that long-term investment in new capacity and energy infrastructure are crucial for development and governments need to realize that while policy statements to open up for private investment are necessary they are not sufficient to attract investors. The policy challenge in the twenty-first century underscores the need to focus on turning policy talk into action in four priority areas to mobilize required public and private investment: (i) creating business environments conducive to maximizing the contribution of private investment; (ii) restructuring and commercializing the public sector to improve efficiency and to promote services complementary to private investment; (iii) increasing resource mobilization and allocation through financial sector development for energy investors and (iv) fostering public-private partnership for energy development and entrepreneurship for extension of energy services within countries and between countries in the region of South Asia and SSA. In some institutional arrangements, such as joint ventures between public and private owned corporations in China, the Philippines and the state of Andhra Pradesh in India, the combination can increase the political acceptability of conditions to interest public–private investment in energy.

---

19. WEC, *Bi-monthly Commentary on Energy Issues* (London, 15 October, 2003)

Moving the policy agenda forward

In setting policy goals and direction, the governments should incorporate the lessons of energy sector reform and liberalization since the 1990s, both in advanced market economies and market transition developing economies. A careful review of the events of market reform since the 1990s should include the experience of developed countries since 2001, the lessons of the California energy crisis, 2003 power black-outs in the USA and Europe attributed to the restrictive effects of deregulation and liberalization on energy supplies and consequent supply disruptions and price hikes. New approaches to establishing regulatory environments, defining the choice of the future energy mix, use of appropriate technology to stimulate domestic energy supply and rational risk management strategies to encourage public and private investment in energy are required in developing country energy markets. Existing institutional, regulatory and financial mechanisms must be re-evaluated to create suitable conditions to promote energy for development in the twenty-first century.

Energy problems vary among developing countries. For oil importing developing countries strategic themes to effect transition to energy for development include five policy commonalities. First, energy supply enterprises (oil, gas, coal, electricity and renewable energy) should conform to basic business fundamentals of pricing, operational and technical efficiency standards. Second, energy pricing reforms should conform to sound energy price structures, levels and taxation and equitable and economic pricing policies. Pricing policies should specify realistic interim steps to target subsidies without affecting the financial viability of energy enterprises to expand energy services to the poor. Pricing policy reforms are fundamental for improving efficiency and eliminating distortions. Third, linking of energy efficiency policy reforms with pricing reforms, restructuring and commercialization of energy enterprises.

Fourth, energy policy reforms could reduce the cost of imported energy supplies through diversified and increased trade and investment to develop energy resources both at the national and at the regional level mostly for countries in South Asia and SSA. This requires interconnection of regional and inter-regional grids and pipelines (electricity, petroleum fuels and natural gas) and finally, energy policies need to address reducing energy related environmental pollution by restructuring energy producing and consuming sectors, inter fuel substitution for cleaner fuels, introducing clean coal technologies, and improving nuclear safety in developing countries with nuclear energy facilities and policies to promote environmentally friendly technologies through alternative energy development.

Developing countries have to face the fact that achieving the goals of widening access to reliable and affordable energy requires acknowledgement and stronger commitment to face various policy challenges of energy for development. Although energy sector problems and energy sector reform experience vary among developing countries, they do face common challenges related to the issues of project financing, politics of policy reform and implementation, institutional issues and the changing role of governments. The following sections of this chapter discuss common challenges of energy for development.

B: *Financial sector development and energy project financing issues*

The development of financial markets in developing countries will be critical to secure private capital, to mobilize domestic savings and to access international financial resources. Given the large investment requirements for energy development, the participation of the energy sector in the domestic bond and equity markets can contribute to deepening the capital markets. The development of financial markets requires adequate disclosure of information, allowing investors and lenders to monitor debt issuers and to exert corporate control. Lack of transparency and poor information about companies and the financial sector lead to a higher cost of capital and vulnerability to external shocks. Lack of enforcement of international accounting and auditing standards and difficulties of enforcing contracts discourage financial institutions to lend on a long-term basis. Effective coordination of financial and energy sector reforms and policies facilitate channeling of financial resources to energy investment.

The main objective of the 1990s energy sector reform and liberalization program in developing countries was to stimulate domestic and foreign private investment in energy projects. In the 1990s, project finance entered the mainstream of investments in developing markets partly due to the dynamic environment created by the wave of globalization and partly due to policy reforms to privatize and to promote private investment in energy-infrastructure projects that were previously owned by governments. The volume of flows related to project finance expanded dramatically during the 1990s and formed a large part of the overall increase in flows to developing markets. Macroeconomic and energy policy reform in major developing markets increased investor's willingness to support complex energy projects with the active support of official financing agencies. However, as discussed in Chapters 3 through 5, even during the boom years of 1990–6, project finance flow was restricted to a few emerging economies in Asia and Latin America. In 1997, 65 per cent of total gross flow commitments reportedly went to projects in just ten countries, and they were even more concentrated in 1998.

However, even where project financiers expressed initial buoyed interest, more than 60 per cent of sponsored projects did not result in financial closure leading to successful construction and completion of the proposed projects. As the financial crisis that began in East Asia in 1998 and the macroeconomic crisis in Argentina and Brazil since 2001 have shown, the extent to which project finance can be employed in individual countries depends on their sound macroeconomic and sector policy framework.

Project finance techniques were earlier of interest mainly to mining and oil and gas projects aiming to attract foreign currency funding. In general project risks were classified under commercial and political risks. Commercial risks (examples include cost overruns, delays, shortfalls in project revenues caused by uncertain sales and prices) are considered to be under the control of project sponsors, while political risks (examples include expropriation of assets, civil unrest and foreign exchange inconvertibility) are not. With conventional project financing methods, project sponsors and financiers assume and manage the commercial risks and buy insurance against political risks.

In developing countries the political risks also involve the costs of lack of well established legal, institutional and regulatory systems and policies that would make governments control the domestic prices of oil and gas or decide to change the terms of oil and gas taxes and royalties. Even in those developing countries that have established regulatory systems and liberalized petroleum prices, project sponsors are often not confident with the functioning of the new business environment.

The multilateral financing institutions such as the WB Group encouraging developing countries to move to market and to promote private investment in energy instituted a program of providing a partial risk and credit guarantee in 1994 as a way of leveraging private investments mainly in key natural gas infrastructure projects.

The implementation of oil price liberalization in a number of net oil importing developing countries, including China and India has improved the financial performance of the state-owned companies and increased their profitability. As discussed in Chapter 5, case studies China, India and Argentina have continued to finance their oil and gas projects through their own sources and have turned to commercial source of finance, such as commercial bank loans, private bond placements and sales of equity in stock markets. Private investors in oil and gas projects seek to form joint ventures with commercial state companies to enter new markets.

Power project financing issues

Faced with the problems of inefficient public power sectors, declining bilateral/multilateral funds allocated for electric power investment, constrained international concessionary and commercial bank and domestic public finance for investment in power sectors, developing countries in the 1990s were forced to seek the alternative of attracting private investment in power projects. Private power in developing countries seemed to experience a boom between 1994 and 1996 where governments were willing to provide projects with levels of security supported by credit enhancement guarantees provided by multilateral financial institutions.

However, the private power boom, concentrated in a few developing countries of Asia and Latin America seem short-lived. The East Asian financial crisis since mid-1997, the Latin American economic crisis since 2001 beginning with the collapse of Argentina's economy and economic slowdown and political changes in Brazil and Bolivia in 2002 and 2003 have scaled down developing countries' expectations of private power to less than 30 per cent of their total power investment needs.

Economic crisis impact on IPPs

The impact of the East Asian and Latin American financial crisis most severely affected the power sectors of countries such as Indonesia, Malaysia, the Philippines, Thailand and Argentina. All have major IPPs in power generation. Local state-owned utilities are IPPs minority shareholders in Malaysia and majority venture projects in a number of projects in China. IPPs in East Asia generally sell to single state-owned buyers through a PPA. Under the PPA, the single buyer agrees to takes power at specified rates from private power producers for periods ranging from ten to 30 years. In Latin American countries such as Argentina they sell mostly in the short term to many, privately owned off-takers at the going pool price.

The utilities in the crisis-affected countries of East Asia and Argentina with high levels of foreign debt and depreciation have suffered heavy foreign exchange losses in servicing their debt and have eroded their financial positions. Many power projects which are domestically focused sought to mitigate the foreign currency risk funding through PPAs and other off take agreements under long-term government concessions. Many contracts proved unenforceable in the face of catastrophic changes in the underlying assumptions, following the crisis in cases where pricing was linked to a foreign exchange rate, and governments were politically unable to revise tariffs as called for in the agreements.

The financial crisis and the experience of power project finance in several developing countries raise many future challenges for opening up of market for IPPs and project financing. The crisis has dampened growth and investment opportunities in most countries, causing sponsors and governments to reassess the financial and economic viability of proposed power projects, and investors to revaluate the risks, particularly with regard to foreign exchange, market demand, and contract enforcement. Liquidity in the commercial banks and broader securities markets also contracted significantly, reducing access dramatically for most borrowers, including those seeking project finance. Many existing projects, especially those in the process of implementation, came under serious strain and had to be renegotiated or restructured to get back on track. The financial crisis of East Asia, since mid-1997 and in countries of Latin America, since 2001, have exacerbated the adverse impact on private power project financing by increased cost of power, threat of contract defaults and renegotiations and contraction of the market for private power.

Even developing countries such as India and Pakistan that were not directly affected by the East Asian financial crisis faced problems of increased cost of private power, failed contract renegotiations, stalling and/ or abandonment of private power projects and declining interest in the market for private power. The IPP financing experience in developing countries since the 1990s has also raised several questions on IPPs role to increase least cost supplies, risk sharing, cost of power and strengthening of sector institutions.

IPPs and least cost supplies

In the customary approach used by public utilities, capacity and energy requirements are identified first and simulation studies help to identify the least-cost program. With private generation, both capacity requirements and the choice of plant are determined by competitive bidding and licensing. There could be an intermediate case when private generation is allowed to compete with public generation on an essentially public system to invite bids from private producers before undertaking the simulation studies to decide on the least cost investment. In least cost planning in public utility, investments are normally compared on the basis of expected costs, with risks being weighed in the sensitivity analysis. Some allowance for physical and price contingencies (typically 10 per cent) are usually included in the cost estimates. With private investment, risks are provided for in the bids under good contractual arrangements and will have a major impact on investment.

The potential benefits of private generation in electricity supply to reduce costs by improving efficiency was the main argument for promoting private investment in developing countries. In theory, private producers seemed to be more willing to invest in the new efficiency technologies in coal and gas with offer of shorter lead times and less likelihood of slippage in construction and options to reduce costs. Independent power producers are considered to be a force for more commercial pricing policies and for more pro-business practices in public policy to promote energy efficiency. The gains in managerial efficiency including lower losses, improvements in maintenance and the availability of capacity make more capacity available for new demands to be met. In addition, the entry of IPPs could strengthen sector institutions through competition, technology transfer and the introduction of greater transparency and flexibility.

Traditional public utility managers in low-income developing countries such as India argued that under independent regulation and freedom to operate with commercial principles, they could achieve cost effectiveness similar to that of private generators. Public utility managers in India argue that public utilities are not allowed to function on the same level playing field as governments give preferential treatment to private power. In practice, the entry of private suppliers of electricity and privatization of a public monopoly to a private monopoly are not fundamental for achieving cost effectiveness and other benefits associated with private investors. Capacity costs for IPPs are found to vary widely even for similar technologies. IPPs capacity costs are sometimes higher than those achieved by state-owned utilities with WB financing.

In theory, cost efficiency and other associated benefits are achievable through public or private utilities operating under independent regulation and according to the fundamentals of commercial principles. Examples of public utilities in developing countries such as National Thermal Power Corporation of India operating under commercial principles show that this is the case. But given the poor record of government intervention policies actually adopted at state/ provincial and local levels, the case for private power is being promoted with economic policy and by the industry.

Increased cost of private power

The extent of increases in power costs attributable to private power has varied among the countries depending on several factors such as the discount rates used, the origin of the fuel supply, domestic and external debt financing and terms of power purchase contracts including tariffs and currency denomination.

Rate of return

In practice, private investment identified in optimal plans have often not turned out to be least cost owing to the effect on investment from expected risks and high discount rates used by private investors for projects in developing countries. Private investors commonly use discount rates of 20–25 per cent or more compared with 10–12 per cent social opportunity cost of capital on which public investments are commonly appraised in developing countries. High discount rates are used by the private sector to allow for risks in the investments it is financing – cost escalation, slippages, financial risks and country risks. In addition, IPPs expect to be protected against political risks including reform and regulatory risks by explicit government guarantees. High discount rates facilitate realizing high rates of return initially as a benefit to the early risk-takers. Private investors in IPPs such as Enron argued that the high initial rate of return would decline to the levels more commonly achieved and expected in a stable, progressing economy as a good track record is established, risks decline and investments increase in follow-up projects and expansion.

Project financing

IPPs finance most of their debt on commercial terms, with short maturities (8–12 years) and interest rates well above LIBOR. In contrast, state-owned utilities often borrow long or refinance at subsidized interest rates and always with a government guarantee at no charge. Projects attracting high levels of domestic finance are less susceptible to exchange rate volatility although they may be vulnerable to interest rate hikes. Local capital markets have provided a greater share of debt finance in China, Malaysia and Thailand. Equity is held mostly by a few global developers (30 per cent), engineering, procurement, construction contractors (22 per cent) and local industry (22 per cent). Malaysia and Thailand both with high levels of local debt financing for IPPs (90 per cent and 75 per cent) were better able to mitigate the impact of the currency depreciation. In contrast, Indonesia with 14 per cent of domestic financing and the Philippines with just 3 per cent were more exposed to the mismatch between project revenues denominated in local currency and hard currency obligations to project lenders.

Fuel supply

Fuel costs, a pass-through for power off-takers under private power contracts in developing countries can represent about a third of the life-cycle cost of a coal project and about three-quarters of the life-cycle cost of oil and gas projects. IPPs rely mostly on fossil fuels which typically accounts for 50–70 per cent of total operating costs. If fuel is imported, a currency depreciation increases the local currency costs of both public and private power. In the Philippines and Thailand where most private power projects imported fuel, following the 1997 crisis fuel prices rose over 50 per cent in 1998 compared with 1997.

Tariffs and currency

A rational system of wholesale IPP tariffs and retail consumer tariffs is a prerequisite for a successful private power program. The basic tariff formula and subsequent adjustments for inflation and interest rate factors and the currency denomination of payments contribute to the cost of power. In Indonesia and the Philippines, where wholesale electricity tariffs for IPPs have been denominated in hard currency, the local currency cost of utilities' off-take obligations rose sharply following the 1997 crisis. Similarly in Argentina, following the crisis utilities were unable to increase prices to meet their debt obligations after the government's 'Pesofication' of tariffs which fell short of required adjustments following depreciation. The increase in interest costs on foreign debt and in fuel and other costs in the wake of the crisis has further eroded the financial position of Argentina's power utilities. Some of the utilities ratings in East Asia and Argentina have been downgraded as they became technically bankrupt.

The currency collapses have caused power costs to rise sharply because of their foreign exchange content. The economic slowdown and the increased cost of private power and higher construction costs in local currency terms have caused cancellation and delays of several projects. Depreciation poses a greater challenge to countries still in the early phases of IPP development, when construction risks are significant as most equipment and construction costs are in hard currency. The crisis also restricts access to foreign funds and stringent re-evaluation of risks by foreign investors for resuming future investments. IPP financing experiences since the 1990s in developing countries have raised several threats to the future growth in IPP finance.

Threat of contract defaults and renegotiations

A common threat to financing of future IPPs in developing countries is the challenge of contract enforcement. The worsening financial situation of public utilities in many developing countries either affected by the financial crisis and/ or limited progress in commercialization of public utilities has increased pressures to renegotiate PPAs. Governments have also sought to modify contracts for projects already in operation. Indonesia, the most heavily exposed country called for project sponsors to lower power prices and has tried to negotiate lower purchase obligations.

In India, the decision by the Maharashtra state government to question the Government of India's agreement on Enron IPP project led to repudiation and renegotiation of the PPA contract. Even after the Enron private power project went into operation, the state government disputed the terms of PPA refusing to comply with the PPA terms both with regard to power off-take and price and failed to renegotiate the PPA terms for pricing power and other PPA terms. Refusal of the state government to make payments for power off-take and asking Enron to reduce the price led to the closure of the operating Enron private power project as discussed in Chapter 5.

Other developing countries including Argentina and Pakistan have considered a review of essential terms of PPA contracts with regard to price, currency denomination for payments and power off-take requirements. In many developing countries the lack of transparency and competitive bidding have fuelled the public mistrust of foreign private investment to question the governments' decisions on private power projects. Particularly in democratic multilevel governance systems politicians take issues with the political opposition party's private power decisions. The breach of contract by governments and public utilities even if justified hinders establishing a good track record for future private investment and increases the risk premium for future IPP finance in developing countries.

Risk sharing and limits of guarantees

Governments are required to provide multi-level guarantees to provide confidence to private IPP investors for backstopping the obligations of the power purchasing utilities and/ or financial participation in the projects. In the case of India, the Enron private power project was provided guarantees by the central and state governments and the Reserve Bank of India. While direct support to projects in the beginning of the reform process can serve as an indicator of government commitment, excessive liabilities incurred undermined not only the sustainability of the operating phase of the Enron private power project but it also led to default and closure of the project. Furthermore, this has also caused the Government of India and state governments unwilling to provide even partial guarantees for IPP finance. As a result the capacity that has been financed represents only a very small percentage of IPP memorandum of understandings for project development. Many large IPP project sponsors have abandoned their interest on the issue of providing guarantees. Government's unwillingness to provide even partial guarantees remain the chief obstacle to IPP finance in India.

In Malaysia and Thailand, the central government has assumed some risk, but did not provide government guarantees or other forms of official support. In China, government entities have made few or no guarantees for privately owned projects. The Tangshan project sponsors succeeded in finding a creative solution to finance their project without sovereign guarantees. However, this solution required significant commitments from the project's Chinese sponsor and the purchase of costly insurance[20].

In contrast, the government of the Philippines assumed fairly substantial risks through sovereign guarantees, including all fuel supply, inflation and foreign exchange risks. Its willingness to assume these risks was important to the successful financing of several early projects. However, as the market continued to mature, the Philippines reduced the guarantees offered to new projects and some are being financed with no sovereign guarantees.

---

20. WB, *Power Project Finance Experience in Developing Countries* (January 1998), RMC Discussion Paper Series 119

Commercial banks and the capital markets have shown little willingness to take political risks in developing country private power finance. They have provided uncovered finance in only a few, mostly low-risk countries and about 10 per cent of the total debt needed between 1994 and 1996. The prospects for private power in developing countries appears to be more uncertain than before the crisis and investors scrutinize projects more closely. Governments will need to stay the course of reform to attract private power investment by addressing the future challenges of private power by balancing the benefits of private power against the costs of burdensome practices and open-ended commitments.

IPP financing challenges

While the future challenges of financing vary with each country, three main lessons emerge from IPP experience in developing countries since the 1990s.

Competitive bidding

Thailand, Malaysia and Egypt procured new generation projects using competitive bidding with lower wholesale tariffs. In contrast, India's Enron Dabhol power project and many of the earlier IPP projects in Indonesia and the Philippines were concluded through direct negotiation with project sponsors. India's experience with Enron's Dabhol private power project over a decade has shown that governments facing the prospects of increased cost of power are under pressure to renegotiate projects that have not had to undergo the scrutiny of a formal competitive bidding process. Bidding seems to have reduced PPA prices by 25 per cent on average, but exceptions are numerous. Capacity costs were lower in China without bidding than they were in other nine countries, even for imported technologies. Bidding has tended to be neutral on lead times and to reduce corruption allegations[21].

India and the Philippines have since adopted international competitive bidding to increase transparency and lower costs. However, governments still originate requests for IPPs. In India, the multilevel governance bureaucracy, the issues of pricing and guarantees and the vested interest and political considerations at the state level have limited the benefits of selecting the best projects. Governments also often retain control over fuel price and availability. Governments in developing countries need guidance in the preparation of bid packages, competitive bid solicitation, criteria for evaluation, selection of the best offer and award of contracts.

21. WB, *Viewpoint, Note No. 162: The Impact of IPPs in Developing Countries—Out of the Crisis and into the Future* (December 1998)

Contract renegotiations

Governments have resorted to PPA renegotiations mainly related to PPA terms of increasing cost of power and off-take requirements. Competitive bidding if effectively implemented can help developing countries obtain power at reasonable cost. It can also reduce the perception of unfairness and high risk pricing tactics of direct negotiations with a single sponsor that may lead to contract renegotiations. However, sponsors, private investors and institutional lenders are all equally responsible for avoiding power contract renegotiations. Sponsors need to foster professional business relationships that are in the long-term interests of both developing countries and private investors.

Undue risk premiums and conservative allocation of project financing risks could affect financial efficiency. For example, with high-debt-equity ratios, currency depreciation can make borrowing more expensive than internal cash generation and other forms of equity. The IPP experience since the Asian and Argentina's crisis has shown that increased cost of power following depreciation has caused governments to renegotiate PPA contracts. Governments need to recognize that avoiding contract renegotiation is crucial for establishing a good track record of private power. Governments will need to improve their capacities of risk assessment and pricing by lenders and investors, increase the share and lower the cost of equity financing and take steps to increase the share of the local capital market.

While respect for contracts is a critical foundation of private investment, IPPs in trouble may have to be restructured as a last resort by market based solutions of equitable sharing of risks.

Alternatives to sovereign guarantees and commercialization of power distribution companies

An important lesson emerging from private power finance in developing countries and, in particular, in the case study of India is that governments will need to offer a substantial amount of security in the form of government guarantees to private power investors until off-takers become commercially viable to pay for power supplies. Although governments in developing countries offered sovereign guarantees for early private power finance, they have since expressed their unwillingness to continue with the practice of offering sovereign guarantees. Given that many of the state distribution companies in developing countries are not commercially viable, governments have to find alternatives if they want to attract private power finance. However, alternatives such as co-finance from local power finance development banks and opening of escrow accounts offered by India have failed to provide the required comfort to private investors.

The main barrier to private power finance continues to be the inefficient and technically bankrupt state distribution companies who cannot pay for the power supplies. Governments cannot mitigate the market risks as inefficient state-owned distribution utilities with politicized tariffs and collection problems are allowed to remain bankrupt.

Distribution companies need to function as business operations conforming to standard industry technical, operational, financial and commercial practices. The lesson from IPP experience in India (i.e. reforming the distribution segment by conforming to the business fundamentals of the power industry) is crucial for attracting private finance and developing the domestic capital market.

The future of private power finance in developing countries depends on the success of addressing problems of cost recovery, developing local capital markets and optimizing the sector capital structure. Coordinated actions by host country governments, private financiers and project developers are required to find creative solutions to security problems in the interim period until distribution companies are recognized by the industry as commercially viable.

In theory, the entry of IPPs was expected to strengthen sector institutions through competition, technology transfer and the introduction of greater transparency and flexibility. Breaking the monopoly of the state enterprises by the entry of IPPs was considered the first step to sector reform and liberalization. The benefits of efficiency improvements from IPP entry include introducing new technologies for plant regulation and environmental management, improving efficiency with new gas turbines and combined cycles and using low quality coal or gas and accelerating project gestation as in the Philippines to bring forth needed power supplies. However, even excluding the first IPPs in countries that were not prepared for private power financing such as India, Indonesia, Pakistan and Turkey, transaction costs have tended to be high and elapsed times to financial closure generally more than two years. The high transaction cost is partly attributed to the lack of the required institutional capabilities and mainly due to the lack of good governance and corrupt practices.

C. *The challenge of combating corruption*

Attention to corruption as an issue has been reinforced since the 1990s liberalization and growth of international trade and investment. Although good governance is crucial for development it is only since the latter years of the 1990s that the social costs of the lack of good governance and the pervasive impact of corruption on development has been explicitly recognized. For the first time, corruption was selected as one of the critical issues of development in 1997 in the ninth WB's Annual Conference on Development

Economics (ABCDE). Susan Rose-Ackerman of Yale Law School in her paper on 'Corruption and Development' recognized that corruption occurs throughout the world but is of special concern in developing countries, where payers and recipients of bribes can expropriate a nation's limited wealth, leaving little wealth for its poorest citizens. Misgovernance and corruption have increased the fragility of financial sectors and have been linked to the crises in Asian countries and Latin America in the 1990s[22].

The International Finance Corporation (IFC) of the WB Group in its discussion paper 44[23], September 2001, recognized corruption as a pervasive and universal phenomenon affecting democratic and non-democratic countries, rich and poor countries alike. In recent times, industrial countries have drawn the attention of developing countries to the need to eliminate corruption, facilitate private investment and adopt professional business practices through suitable laws under the WTO arrangements. However, these industrial countries themselves experience various forms of corrupt business/ accounting practices and imperfect no-bid government procurement systems. The events since 2000 witnessed corporate accounting frauds, the New York stock exchange and mutual fund insider trading practices, a series of allegations in the media to the effect that US government contracts for work in Iraq and Afghanistan are being awarded in an atmosphere of 'stench of political favouritism and cronyism'—all reflect the fact that corporate accounting and business practices and government procurement systems in developed countries remain imperfect and costly.

Nevertheless, market corrections and constant pressures for better governance force regulatory agencies in developed countries to improve their oversight functions to enforce laws and to take required actions against corporate fraud and corrupt accounting practices. Scores of corporate giants in the USA ranging from Enron's former chief executive to the former chief executive of World Com Inc. and the former financial/ accounting officials have been indicted since 2001 and many of them have been awarded stiff sentences sending signals to the US corporate world to shape up.

Given that corruption as defined by Tanzi (1998)[24] as the abuse of public power for private benefit is universal with varying degrees and forms, the challenge for developing countries is to deal not only with the multilevel public corruption in governance associated with the command and control system of the pre-1990s but also to address new forms of corruption associated with

22. Vinod Thomas, 'Revisiting the Challenge of Development', *Frontiers of Development Economics* (Washington DC, WB, Oxford University Press, 2001)
23. IFC/ WB, 'The Impact on Private Investment of Corruption and the quality of Public Investment', Discussion Paper 44 (Washington DC, September 2001)
24. Vito Tanzi, 'Corruption Around the World: Causes, Consequences and Scope, and Cures', IMF Working Paper WP/98/63 (Washington DC, 1998)

liberalization, privatization and attracting private investors in energy projects.

The energy sector with its complex mix of the public and private sector provides the breeding ground for entrenched political and bureaucratic corruption at all levels from meter reading to the award of contracts for energy projects. Traditional state monopolies controlling oil, gas and electric power as well as government bureaucracies responsible for energy trade such as import of oil and gas and in recent years multilevel government agencies and institutions responsible for private investment in energy projects are prone to corruption. Corruption increases the cost of energy of both imported and domestic supplies. The high cost of imported petroleum products in SSA is partly attributed to corruption involved in import practices and distribution. Padded cost of domestic investment in energy projects translates to high energy prices for consumers.

The development of the IPP market has been accompanied by allegations of corruption, padded project costs and higher wholesale power tariffs. One reason for these allegations is the endemic high-level corruption to contract with multinational companies for excessively expensive and inappropriate projects as a way of extracting large bribes. Evidence that prices have varied widely across and within countries for standard projects in the power sector is cited as one of the reasons supporting the allegations of corruption. Another possibility is the design of the processing steps including the rules for the solicitation, award and close of contracts that have been unclear and onerous and have allowed opportunities for graft. And a third reason has been that politicians taking cover of these allegations continue to perpetuate state power monopolies by awarding construction contracts in return for bribes for their political parties.

The inefficiencies of the state-owned electricity companies, excessive non-technical power loss due to theft and collection problems reflect the prevalence of corruption at different levels. The lower level corruption in electricity and gas systems include bribes for new connections and deal making to avoid required payments.

At the enterprise level in South Asia, on average less than 50 per cent of accounts receivable are collected in the power sector. Even with government subsidies and using the regulatory authority as a vehicle to increase tariffs for selective consumer categories, state-owned power companies are unable to generate revenues to cover cost and finance investment to repair and maintain their systems. Consequently, system reliability continues to worsen with reduced investment.

Even where competitive bidding processes are used corruption practices at the political and bureaucratic levels are carried through bid specifications, bid evaluation criteria, bid evaluation and contract award including design of power purchase formula, required adjustments and method of payments.

Corruption could take several forms including donations to political parties, commission charges for facilitating project implementation, choice of local contractors and consultants for processing payments and obtaining permits. For energy/ power projects with a long time horizon and a multiplicity of logistical, administrative and legal steps, corruption is particularly burdensome as it increases capital costs and leads to overpricing.

Energy/ power projects can be large and the implementation is often carried out by private firms. The incentive for the private enterprise to pay a 'commission' to secure the contract is strong particularly in the case of large power generation projects. When the approval of investment projects is influenced by corrupt politicians holding responsibility for energy/ power the basis for determining least cost alternatives, rates of return and cost benefit analysis become mere exercises to support the government's position rather than forming the basis for decision making. The firm paying the 'commission' is either allowed to pad its project cost and/ or revise it upwards as the project work progresses.

Corrupt management practices lead to increases in supply costs and result in increased tariffs to selective categories of consumers accompanied by substantial revenue loss to the companies. Corrupt bankrupt utilities are unable to provide reliable supply and cannot attract private investors. Interim solutions to hire a private collection agency or import management contract services were tried in several SSA countries and seemed to work in the short term but have failed to transform utilities to operate on a commercial basis. Bangladesh has tried to address the collection problem in rural areas through rural cooperatives which has resulted in higher tariffs than charged by state-owned electric utilities.

Policy distortions and controls, states continued monopoly and involvement in pricing and power tariff decisions through arbitrary application of regulation and lack of competition and transparency are associated with a higher incidence of corruption in the power sector at multilevel governance. Corruption also lowers the quality of public investment and affects the flow of private investment in energy/ power. Policy makers will need to consider the implications of corruption on public and private investment in energy while designing anti-corruption reforms for their countries. One of the recommended approaches is to improve transparency in the power sector by privatization of electricity distribution where most theft occurs, contracting out meter reading and billing, leasing distribution utilities and offering concessions. However, with the prevailing back door commission payments by private companies to secure management contracts and licenses and methods of valuation for privatization, these have had limited success.

Managing the challenge of corruption requires instituting an anticorruption program with several critical elements—an independent judiciary, rule of law, good institutional and public sector management, political and civil liberties, oversight and involvement by civil society, tax and budgetary reforms and financial and procurement reforms. The evidence from analysis of more than 1,500 WB financed projects suggests that civil liberties, participation and institutional capacity are important for protection against corruption and for the achievement of broadly-based development[25]. However, corruption has coexisted with civil liberties, free press and democracy in several developing countries. Although the transaction costs of multiple approval at different levels of government are being addressed by introduction of 'one stop' and/ or single point approval, there still exists an efficient transfer of money to the official or the corrupt politician. In many developing countries the multilevel corruption at the high, middle and low levels generate not only high transaction costs but also a decline in investment as evidenced by the exit of many IPP sponsors.

When top officials and politicians remain corrupt and despite civil liberties, free press and judicial and law enforcement institutions, allegations of corruption are not dealt with, it would be difficult to foster honest behavior at low levels. Even developing countries with a strong civil service tradition remain in the survival mode and have been unable to combat both political and bureaucratic corruption at different levels. Even with a few honest civil service personnel, corrupt politicians continue to enrich themselves and or their political parties. Other cases have shown where a relatively honest set of cabinet level ministers have to deal with multilevel corrupt bureaucracies[26].

Since the beginning of the wave of globalization in the 1990s, the first ethical issue heading towards a global set of rules is corruption. This is because it is one of those areas where international traders and investors are directly involved and have direct responsibility. Although no government or company claims responsibility for corrupt practices they may rationalize and disguise it as inevitable in some circumstances. Corrupt decision-makers are no more acceptable to electorates in any industrial or in any developing countries. The urgency to raise the issue of corruption at the global level was made possible by 'Transparency International'[27] which tried to build a growing consensus among governments and international businesses that corrupt practices are unacceptable and should be curbed.

A variety of embryonic agreements have been reached to formalize collective actions against corruption. These include: an Inter-American Convention

25. Vinod Thomas, 'Revisiting the Challenge of Development', *Frontiers of Development Economics* (Washington DC, WB, Oxford University Press, 2001)
26. Based on author's discussions between 1990 and 2002 with cabinet level ministers and top civil servants in the Middle East, SSA, Latin America and Asia.
27. *Transparency International, Global Corruption Report* (London, Sterling, VA, Pluto Press, 2004)

(signed but not ratified), WTO proposals for creating greater transparency in government procurement, tightened WB procurement guidelines, a voluntary agreement of the International Chamber of Commerce and a proposed OECD treaty to criminalize corrupt payments and to make companies subject to greater disclosure requirements.

While these efforts share common values there are problems of definition and enforcement. It is not always clear when corporate hospitality shades into dishonest inducement; when commission to agents are for bribery rather than genuine incentive payments; when honest dealings with main contractors conceal dishonest practices at the sub-contractor level; when payments to charities or political parties or local community projects are not used for the purposes designated or intended; when a local partner is engaged to secure influence rather than for business expertise or capital.

Corruption is normally defined in terms of inducements to politicians and officials but there is a range of potential abuses within the private sector. Fraud, adulteration, concealment of safety information, collusion—which may be equally or more serious.

Where corruption is alleged, it is often proven difficult to secure evidence sufficiently robust to permit prosecution and conviction in courts whose jurisdiction is accepted by all parties.

Nonetheless, efforts are being made at the global level for expecting and pressing companies involved in trade and international investment to adopt strict internal codes of conduct related to business ethics and for utilizing the various official 'clubs' and institutions—such as the OECD's export credit group and the DAC aid donors as well as the ICC and other private clubs to proscribe corruption and to publicize 'free riders' who condone or encourage it. Peer group pressure and exercises in shame, including Transparency's list of most corrupt countries, is expected to slowly develop a universal set of ethical standard for business[28].

Developing countries still on their path of reform and liberalization promoting competition, separating ownership from operation by regulatory/ institutional reforms and commercialization have to make the sector institutions and practices transparent. Building the required institutions for the market is crucial for transforming the role of government in tandem with anticorruption reforms and liberalization. This requires not only the rule of law under a well-established system but enforcement of the law leading to the detection of those who violate the law and prompt and quick punishment accorded to detectors proven guilty. In the final analysis the changing role of governments and their success in building effective institutions for good governance for the twenty-first century market determines its impact

28. Paul Hirst and Graham Thomson, *Globalization in question: The International Economy and the possibilities of Governance* (Cambridge, Polity Press, 1999)

on corruption.

D. *Changing role of government in energy for development*

The failure of Communism and the centrally planned command and control system of government, the inefficiencies in the state controlled economic system in developing countries and the wave of globalization since the last decade of the twentieth century have raised the issue of the appropriate role for governments in the twenty-first century in economic development. The model of structural adjustment of the 1980s and 1990s, globalization and transition to market economy in developing countries mirror the neoclassical ideology of complete laissez-faire. Structural adjustments, sector reform and liberalization focus on removing the state-sponsored impediments to the private sector driven market economy. As Stiglitz[29] noted, the theoretical foundations for this market oriented perspective rest on Adam Smith's notion of the invisible hand and especially, in the twentieth century rendition, the fundamental theorems of welfare economics.

Developing countries embarking on economic and sector reform and liberalization were advised by multilateral institutions and industrial countries to create a suitable environment for investment and let markets work for development.

As the reform process got under way and serious problems were encountered in the emerging economies of East Asia and Latin America since the financial crisis of 1997, the political leaders and their bureaucrats were more confused about the market miracle. Poorer countries in SSA and South Asia were unable to finance the required investment for development even as they embarked on structural/ sector adjustment reforms and liberalization.

As the twentieth century was closing, the role of the state in economic development remained a contentious issue. At one extreme was the failure of the twentieth-century experience of planned socialism. At the other end was the decade of market transition experience and developing economies' model of structural adjustment of the 1980s and 1990s, sector reform and liberalization focusing on removing the state-sponsored impediments to create private sector driven market economy.

The major lesson of the 1990s reform and liberalization was that while market transition efforts did not meet the expectations of developing countries in promoting development, the command and control system and state-planned socialism of the pre-1990s were no longer viewed as options for promoting development in the twenty-first century.

With the dawn of the twenty-first century, the WB, that was instrumental

---

29. Stiglitz, Joseph E, 'The Role of Government in Economic Development', Keynote Address, WB Annual Bank Conference on Development Economics (ABCDE)

in getting developing countries on structural and sector reforms in the 1990s, and showcased the East Asian and Argentina's market miracle as models to other developing countries, began its hindsight evaluation on the issue of the appropriate role of governments in economic development. A series of WB publications[30] on the *Frontiers of Development Economics* and *Rethinking the East Asian Miracle* debated the issue of the special role of government in economic development as the major development issue of the twenty-first century. The re-evaluation of the role of government to promote economic development in the twenty-first century recognized many 'third ways' between the extremes of total government control of the economy and complete laissez-faire. Stiglitz in his keynote speech on the role of government in economic development to the WB ABCDE conference advocated that at different stages of development or in different situations countries will and should choose different points along the 'Third Way' (ABCDE 1996).

The aggressive roles of East Asian countries between 1960 and 1980 in promoting education and technology transfer, supporting the financial sector, investing in infrastructure and creating and maintaining a social safety net including access to basic health services stimulating outward-oriented growth (Stiglitz, 1996) were cited as model for government's role to promote economic development. The financial crisis of East Asian economies in 1997–9 was attributed to the shifting role of government from collaborative capitalism to a crony capitalism between government and business leading to corruption and the failure of the East Asian governments to take strong actions to ensure good corporate governance to create an effective stock market.

The issue is not whether the state has important role in economic development but how far the state should go to take a more active part in directing economic activity beyond the required limits and how to equip the state with the administrative capacity to perform the changing functions efficiently. There is the realization that neither a total state command and control system nor complete abandonment of the role of state to that of market miracle mechanism would promote economic development with increased growth prospects and raise the living standard for over 2 billion poor in developing countries. Stiglitz (1996) conceded that most economists accept the proposition that markets alone may not succeed in ensuring economic efficiency and may fail to protect some segments of society from abject poverty. The fact of the matter is that 'some segments' of society in developing countries comprise over 2 billion people accounting for over 40 per cent of their

---

30. Joseph E Stiglitz and Shahid Yusuf, ed., *Rethinking the East Asian Miracle* (Washington DC, WB and Oxford University Press, 2001)
Joseph E Stiglitz, *Frontiers of Development Economics* (Washington DC, WB and Oxford University Press, 2001)

population and the evidence of adverse impact of globalization is recognized to contributing to the rising inequality between the 'haves' and 'have-nots' in developing countries.

To realize the development goals of both raising the rate of economic growth at the absolute level and relative growth between segments of the economy, it is critical that the role of government needs to change with the changing economic structure. A relatively honest competent and dynamic government with a well-motivated bureaucracy that can work closely with private and non-governmental entities is fundamental to the success of the reform process.

The government's changing role will continue to include directing macroeconomic policy, providing public goods, supporting macro-sector reforms and liberalization, designing and implementing safety nets, building effective infra structures and effective institutions to create an enabling environment for private-public investment, promoting competition and regulating natural monopolies. The pace at which government builds its administrative capacity to become effective to deal with changing requirements of the reform process determines the outcome.

In the energy/ power sector, governments failed to recognize the necessity for bottom line performance measures by extending the scope for competition. Bureaucratic and cumbersome procurement policies and micromanaging the source of contracting despite moving towards competitive bidding could contribute to higher average costs.

Other sector reform measures including privatization, corporatization and effective regulation require equipping governments with required skills and expertise to effectively implement reform measures to achieve energy development goals. In the case of relatively efficient and profit generating oil enterprises where privatization is possible, governments have not been clear about the objectives and privatization of profitable public oil enterprises undertaken as a means of reducing budget deficit rather than improving economic efficiency. Governments have not been effective in determining the value and incorporating built-in protections including protections against abuse of monopoly power to ensure that the public obtains full value for publicly owned resources.

The changing role of the government from command and control to that of enabler with increasing reliance on market based regulatory policies is more evident in the electricity and gas industries. Here again, the evidence since the 1990s show that while several developing countries have established regulatory authorities, they are yet to function effectively to reflect market realities.

As the centre of focus of development theory and practice is moving forward with the macro-sector reform and liberalization to create competitive market structures, changes in the economic environment are altering the role of governments to become dynamic and performance oriented. Developing countries moving forward with the changing economic structure need to re-examine their risk management strategies as their economies become increasingly open and are more exposed to the vagaries of international markets. Given the relative shallowness of the financial markets in developing countries and the difficulty of constructing appropriate oversight and regulatory regimes by domestic authorities, the tendencies towards exuberant over-borrowing and excessive growth of debt financing could not be prevented in East Asia and Argentina.

The role of government will have to be redefined taking into consideration both macro-sector inter-linkages and national-international linkages. Strengthening of the financial market is fundamental for both macro and sector development. Effective financial market institutional structures in developing countries will have to conform to international standards while adopting them to their special local situations. Strengthening the regulation of the securities market and improved overall legal environment in the area of corporate governance are required to facilitate resource allocation for investment.

Given that government is a large organization operating with a historical institutional matrix, changing the institutional mind-set is difficult and slow as it remains outside the competitive market pressures. However, as Stiglitz (1996) noted, in democracies political competition exercises some discipline. Nonetheless, in democracies, the need to build political consensus with different political parties for the support of reforms including the changing role of government and building effective institutions is time consuming with incremental progress. The inherent weakness of politicians who are prone to corruption and the lack of effective regulatory/ legal enforcement mechanisms to bring to justice corrupt politicians and business have underscored the concern of making government perform better.

The problems of delineating the economic boundaries of the state and of analyzing the structure of incentives and organizations with which it guides economic activity are unique to specific country situations. Nonetheless, the 1990s market transition experience in many of the developing countries in Asia, Africa and the Middle Eastern countries such as Egypt and Jordan represents a consistent model of development which has attempted to blend the neoclassical precepts of market economy with those of highly socialist orientation. The scarcity of resources and fiscal constraints facing developing countries in the early years of the twenty-first century make it imperative that addressing the weaknesses of public and private sectors to complement public-private strengths is crucial for resources to be spent efficiently. The changing role of governments to be a positive and creative force depends on its ability to build effective institutions for good economic governance.

E. *Building twenty-first century institutions for effective governance*

The challenge of institutional development is becoming a dominant theme given the complex interrelations that link institutions, organizations and the process of economic/ sector reform and liberalization. The political changes in the former socialist countries and the difficult process of market transition have introduced a new dimension and further complexities in the already diversified panorama of institutional development. The debt crisis and the painful adjustment processes of the 1980s have contributed to a significant weakening of particular civil services in developing countries. The globalization of trade, production and finance has put pressure on governments to reform institutions in all developing countries.

The rapid change in the role of the state from that of being a main engine of economic and social development accelerated by the collapse of Communism and central planning have created in developing countries political pressures to 'redefine the role of government' to reform institutions to create an appropriate environment for more effective public sector management and to attract private sector participation. The structural and sector adjustment reforms of the 1990s and liberalization efforts requiring decentralization, transparency and increased participation of all stakeholders have created a new emphasis on civil, political, economic, social and cultural rights as key elements of reformed institutional environment[31].

While no dynamic theory of institutions is as yet available, the New Instituitional Economics (NIE) confirms the importance of institutions in furthering economic sector reform/ liberalization and successful transition to the market. The structure that is evolving in the NIE[32] (North 1990 and 1994) takes issue with orthodox neoclassical economists' view of state as either exogenous or as a benign actor in the development process. Given that the neoclassical economists have implicitly assumed that economic and political institutions do not matter and that the static analysis embodied in allocative–efficiency models can be a sufficient guide to policy; that is, 'getting the prices right' by eliminating exchange and price controls. In the neoclassical model of walrasian equilibrium, there is no need for a state since society's

---

31. Alberto Capitani, Douglass C North, 'Institutional Development in Third World Countries: The Role of the World Bank', Working Paper 42 (Washington DC, WB, 1994)
32. WB, World *Development Report, Building Institutions for Market* (Washington DC, WB, 2002); John Harris, Janet Hunter and Colin M Lewis, *The New Institutional Economics and Third World Development* (New York, Routledge, 2000);
North, Institutions, *Institutional Change and Economic Peformance* (New York, Cambridge University Press, 1990)

welfare is maximized. In the strict neoclassical model where Pareto's optimal conditions of welfare are reached no institutions are necessary since exchange is simply driven by utility considerations. In general, once price distortions and other impediments are removed, the private sector driven economy will naturally occur and prosper.

This view limits the role of state and institutions to seeing them as guarantors of the rights of private property and the money supply. The new institutionalists who use the same theoretical precepts as the neoclassicists see institutions for reducing transaction and information costs. The NIE see the key to efficient markets to low costs of transacting. Transaction costs are the costs involved in measuring what is being exchanged and in enforcing agreements. A necessary condition for trade is the ability to measure at low cost multiple valuable attributes of goods and services and performance of agents being exchanged. But a sufficient condition requires in addition that the contracts embodying the exchange process can be enforced at low cost. These conditions are not met in many developing countries and in consequence markets either often do not exist or involve very high costs of transaction. Because transaction costs will influence the technology employed, both transaction and transformation costs will be higher in the factor and product markets of such economies.

The inability to have low cost specification of the attributes being exchanged and effective enforcement of agreements in economic markets is ultimately a function of the political markets of such economies because it is the polity that specifies the property rights and provides the instruments and resources to enforce contracts. The NIE therefore, recognized the vital role of the state in the support and development of markets and other capitalist institutions. States continue to be the primary agents of institutional intervention. Developing countries need to choose their future economic strategy fully informed of the institutional options that exist.

Getting the economic strategy right will not achieve the results until developing countries strengthen their institutions/ organizations. Public bureaucracies in developing countries have a poor track record for encouraging skills in-house and recruiting the skilled personnel required. The institutional environment within which public organizations operate is often resistant to change to improve efficiency and has no accountability and performance standards. Chronic shortage of skills, inadequate management incentives and organization structure and change-resistant institutional structures with no accountability continue to persist[33]. Structural adjustment/ sector reform, privatization/ private investment and liberalization with its neoclassical roots

33. Merilee S Grindle, ed., *Getting Good Government: Capacity Building in the Public Sectors of Developing Countries*. (Cambridge MA, Harvard Institute for International Development, Harvard University Press, 1997)

is rather ill-equipped to meet the challenge of building effective institutions.

The decade of market reform in developing countries has shown that while the reform elements of efficient energy markets were defined in the 1990s, the implementation of these efficient market elements takes time as rules of the game (including competition, independent regulation and efficiency) or institutions need to be structured and their interaction with organizations that are responsible for enforcement pursue the objectives of institutional change. Since the organizations owe their existence to the existing institutional matrix, there is a tendency to perpetuate the institutional structure. Change is typically incremental reflecting ongoing and evolving perceptions of the entrepreneurs of organizations. The fundamental conflict between organizations over institutional change cannot be mediated within the existing institutional framework.

The fundamental character of institutions suggests that the rules of the game, formal and informal norms and their enforcement determines the pace of change in the reform process. While the formal rules can be defined and a formal policy statement can be made overnight, their enforcement to meet the objectives of the rules to conform to efficient performance standards change gradually and these will be different between regions and countries. Countries that adopt the western developed countries' model of regulation in the power sector have very different performance standards from the original country because of differences in both the design of normal/ informal norms and their enforcement features.

Stable political and economic institutions in the western world evolved over hundreds of years. Dornbusch in his *keys to prosperity*[34] commenting on one of the central hypotheses about growth as that of 'catching up', says that the idea that countries that are behind in terms of per capita GDP will grow faster and as a result, get nearly to where advanced countries are seemed tempting and appeared to work when applied to small group of countries in the 1980s. He went on to say that today (as of 2002), stated in an unqualified way it is simply not the case. He further argued that in the full sample of 100+ countries there is no evidence of catching up. The Asian success stories have been catching up, but many poor countries have fallen behind rather than getting relatively ahead. This underscores the challenge of catching up with advanced countries' institutional development.

The WB's World Development Report 2002 on *Building Institutions for Market* recognizes that one size does not fit all in institution building. Multilateral and bilateral institutions have been involved in free-standing technical assistance projects over years in institutional development despite the persisting doubts about the overall effectiveness of these activities.

---

34. Rudy Dornbusch, *Keys to Prosperity: Free market, Sound Money and a bit of luck* (Cambridge MA, MIT Press, 2002), p.43

The lesson is that transferring the formal political and economic rules of successful western market economies to developing countries is not a sufficient condition for good economic performance[35]. This is well demonstrated in the adoption of regulatory reform in the power sector in several developing countries. While in theory, the institutional change of setting up of independent regulatory authority was expected to be independent from government, in practice, in many developing countries regulatory authorities staffed by civil service and state-owned electric power company personnel are neither independent nor effective in promoting efficiency and competition as evidenced in case studies in Chapter 5. The disconnect between adoption of formal elements of sector reform (including energy/ power pricing, institutional/ regulatory reform, commercialization and privatization/ private investment promotion policies) and their effective enforcement to improve energy sector efficiency and attract private investment suggests that it is essential to change both the institutions and the mind-set for successful reform.

Institutional development is a slow and gradual process. Effective institutions can make the difference in the success of market reforms. Without effective regulatory institutions and strong judicial institutions that enforce contracts, investors find energy business activities too risky. Weak institutions with corrupt practices cost the poor more than the rich. Addressing the challenge of building effective institutions is critical to reform the energy sector to generate adequate energy supplies at affordable prices for development. It is important to recognize the interdependence of energy sector institutions with the financial, infrastructure and macroeconomic aspects of development. At the sector and macro levels, policy design requires attention and will need to focus on the political economy of reform. The degree of freedom that policy makers possess to alter the direction of economies is constrained by the historically determined institutional set-up and the mind-set of players in multilevel governance systems. Institutional development will continue to be a slow and gradual process with learning and political/ social leadership committed to making the institutional change.

Case studies of China and Argentina clearly demonstrate the impact of political, economic, social and cultural factors on institutional change. Argentina adopted a 'dive-in' approach to the free market along with dollarization of its currency. Argentina's neoclassical approach to free market was short-lived as the economy collapsed in 2001. One of the main factors contributing to the economic crisis in Argentina remains the inadequacies of institutions for market at the macro and provincial levels responsible for monetary, fiscal and investment policies. Argentina's transition experience

35. Alberto Capitani, Douglass C North, '*Instituional Development in Third World Countries: The Role of the World Bank*', Working Paper 42 (Washington DC, WB, 1994)

underscores the limited knowledge of the working of the capitalist system and the gap between institutions operating under the historical matrix and the realities of market transition.

In contrast with Argentina, China's transition to a market economy has been a carefully planned process over three decades in several stages. In the first stage (1978–93), reformers introduced incentives, hard budget constraints, and competition by decentralizing the government, allowing non-state (mostly local government) enterprise to develop and expand, maintaining financial stability and adopting a dual-track approach to market liberalization. In the second stage starting since 1994, emphasis was placed on co-ordinating various aspects of reforms and appropriate sequencing of reform including a rule-based market system focused on building market-supporting institutions. During the first five years of the second stage (1994–8), it allowed convertibility of the current account, overhauled the fiscal system, reorganized the central bank, downsized the government and began to privatize state-owned enterprises[36]. China's transition experience in the energy sector mirrors its gradual, go as you learn approach in several stages extending over ten to 15 years to set up regulatory institutions, liberalization of energy prices, commercialization, privatization, divesting of stocks and attracting IPPs.

In the energy sector, China's policy on institutional change aimed to maximize economic benefits while retaining control of its political system and philosophy. Regional decentralization of the government, growth of non-state enterprises at the local government level with more power for local governments and absence of collection problems in power distribution companies and efficiency enhancing reforms complemented the efforts of existing institutions. Despite the impressive success story, China no doubt recognizes the problem of growing inequality between the urban and rural population arising out of the weaknesses of the local institutional power base to address the problems of inequity. Major institutional challenges remain in the areas of restructuring state-owned enterprises and corporate governance, establishment of the rule of law and promoting competition.

The experience of a majority of developing countries between China and Argentina's planned and market oriented systems shows lack of basic market-supporting institutions and required skills to enforce the changing rules of the game. Even in countries that have relatively strong judicial/ legal/ financial/ banking institutions, these operate on the historical institutional matrix with weak enforcement. India's case study illustrates that despite India's deep and strong roots in democracy at the local level, strong judicial/

36. Yingyi Qian, 'The Institutional Foundations of China's Market Transition', Paper presented at the World Bank's Conference on Development Economics (Washington DC, 1999)

legal/ accounting/ information technology based institutional systems and English language skills, the multilevel governance/ regulatory/ institutional weak enforcement remains a barrier to commercialization of electricity enterprises at the state and local levels and attracting private investment in the power sector.

The gap between institutions operating under the command and control mind-set and the realities of market transition shows that the knowledge about institutional change and working of the market transition process in developing countries with varying political, social and cultural set-ups impacting the interaction between institutional and organizational change in particular is limited. As Douglass North[37] has clearly recognized: 'While neoclassical theory is focused on the operation of efficient factor and product markets, few western economists understand the institutional requirements essential to the creation of such markets since they simply take them for granted. A set of political and economic institutions that provides low-cost transacting and credible commitment makes possible the efficient factor and product markets underlying economic growth'.

Developing countries' reform experience since the 1990s shows that while the reform objectives and goals are designed and identified, the reform path of rules of the game through changing institutions and their interactions with organizations remains work in progress as it evolves over time reflecting country-specific features. As part of the process of transition policy makers in developing countries need to recognize that effective institutions are crucial for achieving reform objectives and need to pay more attention to institutional development and its interactions with political, judicial and economic institutions/ organizations in the process of economic growth. Policy makers need to integrate the institutional development perspective into development policy framework and reform strategy.

In the energy sector, institutions that affect the governance of energy enterprises are important to promote competition and to regulate how energy enterprises should operate commercially to attract both public and private investment. Inefficiencies of the public sector provision of energy services and financing constraints led developing countries to reform the energy sector to attract private sector since the 1990s. The limited success in developing countries to attract private sector in energy/ power and to reform the public sector power enterprises underscores the importance of institutional factors to achieve the benefits of the reform objectives. In particular, expansion of affordable commercial energy services for 2 billion poor in developing countries is directly linked to successfully addressing the institutional

37. Douglass C North, 'The Contribution of the New Institutional Economics to an Understanding of the Transition Problem', WIDER Annual Lectures (Helsinki, World Institute for Development Economics Research, 1997)

challenge faced by governments in regulating energy service providers to meet both efficiency and distributional goals.

There are often large obstacles to the development of laws and internal governance institutions and to regulatory agencies. New initiatives in institution building need to complement and build on existing institutions. Developing countries' experience in establishing regulatory institutions and their effective functioning shows examples of the wide gap between setting up of regulatory authority and enforcement of regulatory functions. Adopting laws which require regulators to enforce tariff regulation without prior attention to building proper accounting systems and management information systems have failed to provide regulators the required information. The passage of laws is one thing but their effective enforcement through institutional changes requires transformation in belief systems and the general mind-set. For example, the theoretical independence of regulatory authorities remains an enforcement problem as government approvals are still required for the regulator's decisions on tariff.

Building effective institutions requires complementing what already exists, innovating to suit local conditions, promoting open trade and open information exchange and fostering competition[38]. Local, national and international actors, both public and private affect how institutions evolve over time. Many of the institutions that support markets are provided by the state. The ability of the states to change their role from command and control to support building institutions for market, often referred to as governance, is therefore fundamental to reform and liberalization. The changing role of governments is critical to shaping governance for institutional change.

The nature and complexity of the above challenges confronting developing countries in the twenty-first century at the global and national levels are multidisciplinary. In the interlinked world of global information, communication, trade, finance and investment, developing countries will have to accept their ownership for reform policies to be efficiently implemented considering the interplay of the force of challenges between global and national levels. The global nature of the energy industry represents the crucial importance of global-national inter-linkages. The success in attracting the required investment to generate adequate supplies of efficient energy for development and expanding access to energy services to over 2 billion people in the developing world is indeed a challenge for the energy sector. Strategies in which governments and other stakeholders at the national and international level complement and support energy for development are necessary to meet the challenge of energy for development in the twenty-first century.

---

38. WB, *World Development Report, Building Institutions for Market* (Washington DC, 2002)

CHAPTER 8

THE WAY FORWARD

Taking into consideration the lessons of energy sector reform experience since the 1990s and the challenges of energy for development faced by developing countries at the global and national level discussed in earlier chapters, what is the way forward? Three factors influence the way forward for energy future. First, a new era of global energy is emerging in the initial years of the twenty-first century heralded by profound changes in the economic and political systems and policies of a significant part of the world. Second, energy security concerns linked with geopolitics are shaping energy strategies of oil importing countries. Finally, the development paradigm shift envisaged in the energy sector in the 1990s to privatization and free market in energy for development is now being replaced by the shift toward public–private partnership (PPP). It is now clear to all energy stakeholders, governments of developing and developed countries, multilateral development and financial institutions and energy industry that there cannot be strong private sector involvement in energy in developing countries without an effective and strong government.

Given the disconnect between expectations and realities of energy sector reform from the perspective of various energy stakeholders discussed in earlier chapters, key questions about progress could be raised from the perspective of these stakeholders. For developing countries the way forward raises the issue of how policy principles can be translated into effective implementation by improving economic governance and building the required institutions to modernize the state. From the investors' perspective the way forward needs to address the question of how policy action will evolve to address the critical constraints and the disconnect between policy and implementation for energy industry/ private sector participation? In the changing energy world of today, the way forward should also address the question of the adequacy of multilateral development institutions' intervention of the

1990s advocating a 'level playing field' to be an effective means of promoting private enterprise to increase access to energy for development. Because, in many countries experimenting with this approach to energy for development where functioning markets and their effective regulation/ institutions and even more fundamental social, economic and legal preconditions are not in place, the invisible hand of the market needs a helping hand of more direct intervention to address the issues of financing energy for development.

With the ongoing controversy about the appropriate role of the multilateral development institutions in promoting public–private investment in energy for development, should the WB and similar institutions need to reform and redirect their own policies to equip themselves for the task of addressing issues of financing energy for development? Or, are the issues of energy for development since the first years of this decade so different from those faced since the 1970s that the conventional approach is insufficient?

Perhaps the most important and critical lesson of the 1990s is that there is no one right way forward to increase access to energy for development. Given the global nature of the energy industry there is a recognition of the need for common principles to address interconnected global and national challenges in the twenty-first century as part of a comprehensive energy for development framework.

A comprehensive energy for development framework: Key elements

A. Effective economic governance and modernization of the state.
B. Addressing critical constraints for energy industry/ private sector participation.
C. Reforming the role of multilateral institutions.
D. Towards an integrated global institution of energy for development.

A. *Effective economic governance and modernization of the state*

The reform experience has underscored that the fashionable reform packages of the 1990s with strong ideological overtones of moving to the market distracted attention from the fundamental task of modernizing the state for successful management of the market transition process of reform and liberalization.

While developing countries embarked on the reform process in a world where global and local concerns compete, the debate centred on the role of the government. Structural and sector adjustment reforms, liberalization and the creation of a suitable climate for private sector intervention resulted in overextension of state capacities to coordinate myriad rules, standards and setting up of new regulatory institutions to undertake oversight functions. Even governments of developing countries in East Asia which continued to play a crucial role in maximizing the benefits from the 1990s globalization process of 'East Asian Miracle' were not immune from governance deficiencies to manage the market transition. The deficiencies of state governance resulting in crony capitalism subjected to the volatilities of international capital markets led to a financial crisis in 1997 and slowed growth prospects.

Since the 1990s, international organizations sponsoring economic liberalization supported governance reforms ranging from very focused technical reforms of budgetary and civil service systems to setting up of regulatory oversight institutions and overhauling legal and judicial systems. Since getting the reform policies right involves getting the institutions right to implement these policies, changing the role of government actually requires modernizing the capacity of governance to effectively carry forward the reform process.

There is no simple strategy for modernization of the state for successful management of reform for development from the traditional process oriented bureaucracy to modernized economic governance focused on solving problems and getting results. It requires committed leadership to bring about fundamental changes in economic governance at federal, state and local levels. A paradigm shift to market without the required effective institutions to administer the change causes confusion. The transition from centralized and hierarchical government structures to multi-centric and participatory forms of governance is the crux of the challenge for decades to come. The role of government to adopt to the requirements of market economy is increasing in all developing countries. The success of modernizing the state is seen to link closely with the dynamism of leadership at different levels and the strength of the political will of governments to maximize the benefits of the market transition.

China clearly demonstrates the case of dynamic and goal-oriented leadership of modernization of the state for the successful management of its form of socialist-market transition process while at the same time holding the reins of transition to complete liberalization to avoid the costs of exposing its economy to global financial volatilities. China's decision to move cautiously on political reform as its prime minister Wen Jiabao[1] visualized 'in an orderly fashion and in a well-organized manner' underscores the continued goal-oriented role of government in decision-making toward economic liberalization while keeping the lid on participatory politics and a move towards democracy.

---

1. John Pomfret and Philip P. Pan 'Wen defends Chinese system' *The Washington Post* (Washington DC, 23 November 2003)

In contrast, the case of India illustrates the role of government in a fully democratic set-up involved in consensus building among political parties on reform and liberalization. Modernizing of the state for successful management of reform involves reforming institutions where people want to be consulted, involved and taken into confidence. Consequently, transforming an institutional framework for viable participatory policies that can be supported by organizations and resources has proven to be a long drawn process of trial and error along with the cost of delays in creating, monitoring and enforcing rules for successful implementation of the reform effort.

Despite the decline in poverty in many countries, the rise in inequality, the growing gap between the elite and affluent middle and upper classes and a relatively disadvantaged majority that is lagging further and further behind are creating tensions within different regions of the country. The energy sector with 2 billion of energy poor accounting for over 40 per cent of developing countries' population in 2003 illustrates one such development challenge for the changing role of governments. Dealing with cross-regional inequalities and the welfare prospects of a relatively large majority of disadvantaged energy poor who often feel politically marginalized goes beyond temporary fiscal transfers and short-term political compacts.

In the final analysis, the required shift in governance from traditional process oriented bureaucracy to problem-solving and results oriented modernized economic governance is critical in the coming decades to address global, national and local issues of energy for development. What is certain is that as discussed in Chapter 7 energy reform and liberalization policies will continue to be challenges without a clean government and mature and resilient institutions to translate policy goals to actionable results. Examples of two critical areas of energy for development—management of public energy enterprises and building domestic capital market for financing energy—requiring problem-solving and result-oriented effective governance actions are discussed below.

Energy policy priorities

While individual country and sector conditions would vary, the overall policy framework to facilitate energy for development would consist of macro and sector components. The macro component relates to policies and actions necessary to promote overall economic growth and private sector development—both domestic and foreign—in all economic activities including energy in the country is fundamental. These macroeconomic policies are a necessary but not sufficient condition for private sector participation in energy. Specific policies to facilitate private sector participation in energy include: maintaining a stable macroeconomic environment to ensure price and exchange rate stability and permit stable and modest interest rates in real terms; ensuring foreign exchange convertibility, creating a transparent and robust investment code with a reasonable and predictable tax regime; an effective and credible legal and judicial system and a credible, reliable and prompt dispute resolution mechanism.

Major challenges regarding governance and critical elements of energy policies including expanding access to energy and possible approaches to address them were discussed in Chapters 6 and 7. At the sector level, modernizing the role of the state directly related to energy include translating the policy principles to effective actions. The first priority is improving the management of public energy enterprises by commercialization and developing domestic capital markets to channel savings to both public and private energy. Each of these areas is discussed below taking into consideration the lessons of energy reform and liberalization experience in developing countries since the 1990s.

Management of public energy enterprises

Many oil importing developing countries becoming independent since the post World War II period of the twentieth century justified state intervention in energy on grounds of lack of private sector initiative and consideration that energy is of strategic importance to promote development. An equally important factor was that the long gestation period for energy projects with large capital requirements and the state of capital markets and uncertainties prevailing in developing countries made particularly non-tradeable power projects less attractive to the private sector. This expansive view encouraged vertically integrated energy supply systems for protection of public interest by state-owned and operated monopolies. The state-owned energy infrastructure facilities provided expanding access to energy services.

Over the years, because of the monopolistic environment and government interference in day-to-day energy operations many power enterprises were unable to operate as financially viable enterprises. The oil crisis of the 1970s and the debt crisis of the 1980s adversely impacted state energy enterprises. The long drawn and slow pace of adjustment of state energy enterprises to eliminate price distortions led to the proliferation of subsidies. Government restrictions on the freedom of energy enterprises to price energy contributed to the failure to generate adequate revenues to finance required investment. Escalating strains on government budgets and external finance was problematic. The fall of Communism and the emergence of countries in Eastern Europe as transition economies and the 1990s privatization experience of developed countries strengthened arguments against further expansion of the public sector particularly in the energy sector.

The policy of state ownership and operation of energy enterprises were revisited in the 1990s and developing countries were required to restructure and to privatize their energy enterprises to encourage competition and to improve economic efficiency. The major problem that developing countries were facing was that the restructuring, liberalization and privatization experience of power and gas enterprises in industrialized countries could not be transplanted as alternatives to public energy enterprises which had several constraints. The pre-privatized power and gas enterprises in industrialized countries in Europe and USA operated commercially with relative technical and operational efficiency.

Privatization in industrialized countries' electricity and gas was undertaken to further improve efficiency, promote competition and options for consumers. In developing countries, many energy enterprises, in particular power and gas, did not meet the fundamentals of technical and operational industry standards and financial viability. Unbundling of public electric utility monopoly in SSA countries was bound to result in private monopoly. With little competition, private monopolies with limited entrepreneurial and risk taking abilities perpetuated the problems of poor efficiency, poor quality of service and high prices. As illustrated in the case study of India discussed in Chapter 5, state electricity boards despite restructuring require huge subsidies and continue to be inefficient. Privatization of state distribution companies supported by WB financing has not resulted in improving efficiency. Privatization by itself is unlikely to encourage expansion of services, particularly in the rural areas.

The key issue of contemporary energy development policy is how best to manage energy enterprises (public and private) to achieve the objectives of generating efficient and reliable energy supplies for development and to expand access to energy services for those who lack them. The effective implementation of commercialization of state energy enterprises with new ground rules devised for giving autonomy to public energy enterprises without day-to-day interference from government depends on the character of the state. Expecting managers of state enterprises appointed by governments and regulatory authorities set up by governments to be transparent and independent from the government will work only when the ground rules are adhered to and enforced by the state.

The experience of energy sector reform and liberalization shows that the pace of implementation is tedious and slow as governments in developing countries will have to deal with those abusing the reform outcome of the social good for private profit. For example, following the liberalization of petroleum prices and freeing the market the Government of India in November 2003 decided to ban all imports of kerosene by non-government companies to check the rampant adulteration of diesel. One could argue that this is partly due to persisting relative distortion in prices between kerosene still subsidized for poor, and diesel.

The reform experience discussed in Chapters 4 and 5 illustrates that when governments pursued liberalization of petroleum prices, (more than 30 years since the first oil crisis in 1973 and continuation of administered prices) profitability of public petroleum enterprises increased dramatically. Restructured state-owned petroleum enterprises in China and India since price liberalization are financing their investment both at home and abroad by a portion of their profits and through international capital markets.

It took more than three decades to finally enforce oil price liberalization in most of developing countries. It should not be difficult to make a realistic assessment that it might take two to three decades to sustain the reform process in the oil sector and to commercialize the power sector. The multilevel governance problems continue to be a barrier for management of power sector reform in developing countries, particularly in democracies where responsibilities for power sector reform are diffused among central/ state/ provincial/ regional/ local levels.

The effectiveness of reforming of energy sector depends on the institutional safeguards to ensure that the state performs its regulatory functions efficiently and equitably by curbing the manipulative power of vested interests. In this context, it is critical to re-examine the role of levelling the playing field. As part of promoting the private sector, developing countries are required to level the playing field by removing the barriers to promote competition. In the energy sector, inefficient and subsidized public enterprises owning product pipelines and power transmission and distribution networks with monopoly markets were considered to be barriers to private investors.

Pursuit of a level playing field requires policy options of unbundling of the power sector, restructuring and promoting the private sector with financial incentives including 20–25 per cent rate of return, standards, regulations, support for voluntary initiatives and taxes. These policy options were aimed at creating a level playing field for the private sector which mainly served the profitable urban and industrial customers. The public power enterprises in a number of developing countries including India, Egypt and Jordan where both public and private energy enterprises operate argue that they were denied a level playing field similar to that offered to private investors and they were in practice not allowed to operate commercially and were required to serve high cost residential and rural customer categories.

Intervention in public energy enterprises is being justified because the private sector and the liberalized electricity sector are incapable of protecting certain public benefits. These include extending access to supplies and services, maintaining the security of supplies, achieving rapid technology innovation and diffusion, keeping prices affordable and protecting poorer customers. However, public control has not guaranteed public interests. Inadequate investment, poor quality of service, low efficiency, unreliable and inaccessibe service, fuel poverty and continued black-/brown-outs are widespread in many developing countries. The shift towards unbundling of public power enterprises by itself without the state's commitment to effective enforcement of rules will remain on computer-generated unbundling organization charts on paper.

The reform experience has underscored that even in the top ten developing countries receiving private investment, the private sector by itself cannot meet all the required needs for energy services to develop. There is no alternative to proceed with improving the efficiency of public energy enterprises to attract the much needed PPP in energy development. Pursuit of a level playing field in the twenty-first century requires policy options for promoting not only competition in the sector but also fostering PPP. This requires several critical considerations: a strategy to restructure the sector, to open entry to private parties and to create equitable competition between all parties and a firm commitment to enforcement of the strategy by developing effective legal and regulatory frameworks and clear pricing policies. Regulations could require companies to report on progress with the extension of supplies to unserved populations.

Given that both commercialized public energy enterprises and private energy companies are unlikely to protect or advance public benefits, specific regulatory measures need to be designed and enforced to cover the public benefit objectives. As discussed in Chapter 5, South Africa illustrates that commercialization of the power sector facilitates both investment and expansion of access to energy services by energy empowerment policies to expand access to the rural areas and urban poor. System benefit charges (also known as public benefits fund) raise revenue that is used for assisting the expansion of energy services for the poor.

Countries as diverse as Chile, the Republic of Korea, New Zealand, Sweden and the United Kingdom have tried with some success to reform their state-owned enterprises, by imposing on them a common framework of internal and external incentives that applies to successful private corporations. Commercialized state oil, gas and power enterprises in China, India, Malaysia, Philippines and Thailand have been able to develop a financial and regulatory environment and were able to access both domestic and international capital. Debt issues by efficient public energy enterprises can make an important contribution to the development of bond markets. Given the large investment requirements for energy development, the role of state to transform public energy enterprises to become commercially viable is critical for financing both public and private sector energy projects. This role is important to develop the domestic capital market.

Domestic capital markets

The energy sector, particularly, the electric power sector in most large and medium size developing countries can also become an important vehicle for developing the domestic capital market to mobilize the resources for its development. Energy investments are a major part of the asset-base in capital markets particularly for institutional savings, provided the energy enterprises earn reasonable returns and are commercially managed. Chile, Malaysia and Thailand are examples of countries that have effectively used their energy sectors to mobilize domestic funds (e.g. pension and provident funds and insurance companies). Malaysia and Thailand have reached a stage where domestic institutional investors (public and private) and domestic capital markets more generally are becoming an important source of financing for energy and infrastructure.

Developing domestic capital markets require priority attention and specific reform measures in both electricity and financial sectors. Developing country governments have used financial markets as a way of directing resources into the public sector. In many large developing countries, such as India, specific financial institutions such as the power financing corporation of India and ICICI function as financial intermediaries. However, only a small percentage of saving is channelled through these institutions. They are also subject to political influence and funds are often channelled on political feasibility considerations.

The reform experience has also shown that governments have taken positive measures to develop domestic capital market. Even when the state holds a majority control, it can sell a minority ownership in capital markets. It provides the market with needed assets, serves as an independent indicator of value and acts as a brake on excessive political interference in management. This has been done in the republic of Korea and Jordan. Foreign investment with domestic financial partners can also encourage these enterprises as a viable alternative for their savings.

Energy investment needs are massive in developing countries. Most of such investments in power and energy infrastructures (except in net energy exporting countries) generate revenues in domestic currency. An increasing share of the cost is also in domestic currency. Electric power is usually a domestically produced and consumed product in most developing countries. The sector reform experience has shown that the power sector cannot rely exclusively on foreign savings for its financing. For large countries nearly 75 per cent of the sector's financial resources will have to come from the domestic capital market.

The ability to raise a proportion of capital requirements on local markets would eliminate problems related to repatriation of dividends and convertibility of local currencies. It would not be sustainable to finance energy investments primarily by foreign obligations over longer periods as they are likely to produce balance of payments problems similar to those experienced by the Latin American countries in the 1980s, by Argentina since 2001 and by countries in East Asia affected by the financial crisis in 1997. The East

Asian crisis also has shown that domestic financing in countries such as Malaysia and Thailand was a factor in mitigating the effects of the crisis on the cost of power and the sustainability of investment programs.

Although theoretical arguments can be made that additional foreign energy investments would raise the GDP growth of the economy, increase efficiency and thus its capacity to earn foreign exchange, reform experience in practice has shown that local capital markets as one of the sources of project financing for commercially viable public and private power projects is beneficial to the economy and to the sustainability of investments. Sustained economic growth requires development of financial instruments and the market infrastructure to create and tap domestic capital markets to finance energy projects. The long-term objective should be to let domestic capital markets directly finance projects sponsored by autonomous and financially viable public and private energy enterprises without recourse to government guarantee. In this context it is important to note the unwillingness of governments since 1997 to continue to provide sovereign guarantees to enhance private sector/ energy industry participation has created more uncertainty on prospects for private sector investment in energy/ power even in the near/ medium term.

B. *Addressing critical constraints to enhance private sector/ energy industry participation*

The overriding conclusion of the reform experience since 1990 is that in most cases, the original high expectations of the host countries and of private sponsors have not been met. Since the crisis of 1997 in the case of East Asia and Latin America and even in countries not directly affected by the crisis, such as in South Asia and SSA the market for private power appears both smaller and more fraught with uncertainty than before the crisis. While it is necessary for developing countries to stay on the course of reform to attract private sector for energy development, it is critical to focus on what should be the future course of the reform process.

In this context, given that since the 1990s developing countries adopted the models of developed countries to reform their energy sectors, they are now faced with the situation of not only having to continue on the reform path to keep their energy sectors commercially viable, but also in doing this, having to deal with their experience with international energy companies' corporate practices to address the challenge of access to FDI. Determination of the future reform course requires understanding the lessons of reform experience not only in developing countries but also of the advanced countries' experience in energy since 2001, in particular in power and gas such as that of the post-2001 US energy crisis.

Key relevant lessons for developing countries from the post-2001 US energy crisis

The post-2001 US energy crisis, including the California power crisis, the collapse of Enron Corporation, bankruptcies of several US energy companies and the great black-out of 2003, provide several lessons relevant to developing countries adopting a US style of capitalist–corporate management in the energy sector and electricity and gas deregulation. By drawing on these lessons developing countries would be much better equipped to determine what should be the course of future reform in the energy sector and to formulate appropriate strategies.

First, market uncertainty and volatility

The bust of Enron followed by the exit or downsizing of more than ten other energy trading businesses demonstrates that the market is uncertain and volatile and companies are not too big to fail. The period up to the fall of Enron indicated the up-side and the period after has demonstrated the harsh downside with the loss of trust and integrity of market and inadequate oversight agencies. Embarking upon the highly uncertain and unclear path of deregulation could lead to volatility in terms of cash flow, earnings and investor expectations. After a certain point, the increased size became a deterrent for effectively monitoring management and numerous subsidiaries grew increasingly complex and difficult for both internal (boards) and external controls (investors, rating agencies and analysts).

Second, deregulation mirage

The promise of deregulation is that competition among producers will drive electricity rates down. The great black-out in the North East US and Canada in 2003 proved that its possible benefits have been spoiled by Enron-like greedy and dishonest operators that rig the market against consumers. California's energy crisis confirmed the dangers. It raised questions about the benefits of electricity deregulation by opening the debate on whether the public's true interest should be the lowest possible electricity rates or reliable electricity produced at reasonable prices.

Under the old 'regulated' system in the USA, electric power companies had local monopolies, with rates set by state utility commissions. This system was not perfect. There were constant tensions between the regulators who wanted popular low rates and the companies who wanted higher rates and profits to please shareholders. However, this system emphasized reliability. If there were brown-outs and black-outs the blame rested either on regulators for not approving new power plants or keeping rates too low to finance expansion or with companies for not maintaining existing plants or not proposing new ones.

Under the 'deregulated' system in about 22 states in the US, companies were permitted to buy and sell electricity on the open market based on the theory that the cheapest electricity is in many cases out of state. Independent electricity producers were permitted to sell energy to far-away consumers and tap into the local utility's transmission lines to deliver it. Transmission and distribution networks will be open to all. It was expected that competition among power producers would promote efficiency and reduce rates. The up-side for consumers was cheaper energy. The down-side of deregulation resulted in congested transmission lines.

However, under the deregulated competitive electricity system independent electricity producers could earn billions of dollars by selling electricity without any obligation to invest in high-voltage power lines which are still largely owned by local utilities. With multiple power producers and distributors no one is responsible for reliability. No one can ensure that the required plants and distribution systems get built. Companies may sacrifice long-term reliability to maximize short-term profitability.

The idea of electricity 'deregulation' is misleading because despite all the changes electricity production remains regulated. The transmission business remains highly regulated, with built-in returns on investment at about 11 per cent, compared with up to 20 per cent for investment in electricity generation. There is also local opposition to high-voltage lines, triggering NIMBYism—the not-in-my-back-yard sentiment.

Every major decision regarding where plants and transmission lines are built, what fuels — nuclear, coal, natural gas are used and what companies can do, depends on government decisions. Slow approval process for new power plants and construction of new transmission lines created an electricity shortage. As wholesale electricity rates rose, state regulators insulated consumers from the increases and worsened the shortage. California state's major utilities were forced to buy electricity from independent power producers and could not sign long-term contracts and had to pay rising daily prices. As power is increasingly bought and sold across state lines—outside the service areas of old monopolies—day-to-day operational problems also multiply. Reliance on voluntary compliance with standards left the North American Electric Reliability Council—an industry group—little enforcement authority.

The Federal Energy Regulatory Commission's (FERC) efforts to pin down the cause of California's energy crisis in 2000–1 were complicated by the growing evidence of price manipulation by traders, obstacles from competing probes and their own splintered approach to the task. The credibility of FERC was called into question. Federal energy regulators trying to resolve billions of dollars in disputed power charges from the US West Coast energy crisis of 2000–1 opened the possibility of refunds for California holding that energy suppliers that 'gamed' the market by submitting unreasonably high spot market bids would have to surrender excessive profits.

The US Federal Energy Regulatory Commission (FERC) in 2003 was dealing with over 50 investigations in allegations of market misbehaviour, including probes into trade during California's energy crisis. Companies including El Paso and Enron attracted particular attention facing several lawsuits in California alleging market manipulation. FERC commissioners also stripped Enron Corporation and its affiliates of the right to charge unregulated market-based rates on electricity and gas because of its repeated trading deceptions. The FERC action signals that it will not tolerate market manipulations.

The California energy crisis turned out to be one of the critical factors leading to the election for recall of California's governor, Gray Davis, in 2003.

The real issue emerging from the US energy crisis events since 2000 that is relevant to both developed and developing countries is not between 'the market' and 'regulation', because the danger of bad regulation is at least as great as that of bad market behaviour. It is important to seek a rational balance of government regulation and market flexibility. However, for developing countries many of which do not even meet the fundamentals of commercial viability of their energy enterprises, seeking this rational balance is critical as it impacts the key reform elements of regulation, corporate restructuring/ governance and private investment. Strategies for determining the future course of reform should focus on effective institutional mechanisms to deal with the problems of the mirage of deregulation and associated problems of regulatory oversight, bad market behaviour by energy companies and traders and corrupt accounting practices by energy corporations in collusion with the accounting industry.

Third, corporate-industry restructuring

In the pre-2001 period, the US power and gas sector experienced a number of mergers and acquisitions between electric and electric and gas companies in both upstream and downstream. Rather than enhancing shareholders' value, the drivers were often scale and the elusive quest for synergy. Developing countries pursuing the reform course of corporate and industry restructuring need to meet a strict test of commercial viability by creating value as they become exposed to the capital market.

Fourth, corporate governance

In the dynamic business environment of the US, companies often seek out distinguished directors to lend credibility and prestige to their enterprises. Corporate boards are supposed to oversee the executives who run companies on a day-to-day business. They typically include people from outside the company as well as top executives. They meet periodically to review the company's performance and approve major decisions. The audit committees of the boards oversee the work of the outside auditors.

However, following the implosion of several US energy and telecom companies since 2001, investigative reports prepared by the examiner for the bankruptcy court concluded in June 2003 that the board of directors of companies such as Enron and World Com, had become ineffectual and a rubber-stamp for management, thereby, failing to meet their fiduciary duties. At the peak of the boom cycle unsustainable growth expectations helped fuel higher stock prices. At the peak of the boom cycle energy trading companies regularly set targets for annual earnings growth of more than 20 per cent. These targets helped fuel higher stock prices, which created expectations of even higher growth in the form of excessive development and value destroying acquisitions.

Companies scrambling to meet unrealistic earning targets began diversifying away from core business into what were promoted as new more rapidly growing markets. For energy trading companies the decision to fuel growth through high leverage was easy, the capital was readily available, the power plants developed would generate stable future cash flows. Furthermore, for flourishing energy trading operations, revenues from long-term deals could be booked immediately using favourable accounting methods. Even more disturbing was the fact that higher debt equity structures made it more likely that managers could meet the upwardly spiralling earnings expectations by cooking books in questionable deals in collusion with major accounting firms and stock market analysts.

By distracting investors from the fundamentals, the integrity and credibility of corporate management and the industry was damaged.

Following a year of a series of corporate scandals during 2001–2 that rocked Wall Street, the US Congress acted to reform corporate governance by passing the Sarbanes–Oxley law (known for its two principal authors—Senator Paul D Sarbanes and Congressman Michael G Oxley). The law was signed by President Bush in July 2003. The law adopted a multi-tiered approach to ensuring more honest corporate books. At the top, it required a company's chief executive officer and chief financial officer to certify the accuracy of financial statements — on pain of criminal prosecution.

The law beefed up the role of the board of directors' audit committees requiring that they consist of independent directors—including at least one financial expert—and more closely oversee auditor's work. It sought to reduce the conflicts of interest by prohibiting auditors from selling lucrative consulting services to the companies whose books they reviewed. It established a new independent board to oversee auditing firms. On the positive side, the law seems to have spurred corporate directors and audit committees to take their jobs more seriously. They have been empowered to ask questions of management rather than simply rubber-stamping their decisions. However, the law did not address some broader questions such as executives' compensation or shareholders' role in choosing directors. Although the true test of the law will come in the years ahead, the US legislative body acted to repair the erosion of trust in corporate governance.

The critical lesson is the affirmation of market uncertainty and that the boom period exuberance of 1990s was accompanied by corrupt corporate practices in pursuit of unrealistic higher rates of return, which destroyed the confidence of investors and consumers. Even with the advanced oversight institutions corporate mismanagement was left unchecked. However, corrective measures were introduced to repair the damage within a year following a series of corporate scandals. The issues of corporate misconduct and market failures are also being addressed by bringing corrupt corporate accountants and executives to justice.

Within three years of Enron's collapse in 2001, the former assistant treasurer of Enron was proven guilty and sentenced to serve a ten-year prison sentence. Former chief executive and former chairman and founder of Enron, Kenneth Lay was indicted in July 2004. US Federal regulators in 2004 launched an investigation of the Riggs Bank and began an inquiry into four oil companies (Exxon Mobil, Marathon Oil, Amerada Hess, and Chevron Texaco) and their relationship to the government of oil rich Equatorial Guinea in West Africa.

While in the US corporate corrupt practitioners are being investigated and are brought to face justice, in developing countries with corrupt management and heavily subsidized power and fuel rates and weak regulatory and oversight institutions, corrupt corporate practitioners are rarely brought to justice. Developing countries pursuing energy sector restructuring, corporatization and private sector involvement with weak and ineffective institutions are often subject to political influence. Effective corporate governance practices need to deal with strengthening of enforcement institutions to oversee corporate practices of both domestic and foreign energy companies.

Empowering the role of boards of directors

The board of directors of a corporatized energy corporation is in a position to play a pivotal role in defining its strategic direction. The board's responsibility for executive recruitment and for setting compensation policy and rights over dismissal gives it leverage over managers.

The roles and duties of board members depend on national laws as well as on company statutes. These differ among countries. In the USA the board's duty is to shareholders, while in the Netherlands the objective may be to achieve a satisfactory balance of influence of all stakeholders.

The extent to which boards protect the interests of investors and other stakeholders and hold managers accountable depends on the incentives and powers of the board. Board members serve as a weak check on insider authority when insiders appoint and dismiss board members themselves. Voting rules ensure that whoever has the most shares can appoint all the board members. In many developing countries where state energy enterprises are corporatized, governments continue to hold the majority of shares and exert both direct and indirect influence on the choice of board members. Often, public energy corporate boards are dominated by representatives from several government ministries and state energy enterprises. In such circumstances, board members will be more inclined to represent the interests of those who appointed them. If the corporate law mandates, large energy corporations include representatives of labour on the board. Often, pressures to divest the shares have resulted in the transfer of shares to the state financing and banking institutions.

The majority of large private energy corporations in developing countries have concentrated ownership structures with a controlling shareholder, often a member of a business group. The controlling shareholder can dominate the board selection process, particularly when there is no cumulative voting. This makes it unlikely that board members will be independent. In recent years, developing countries are attempting to reform corporate governance by empowering the board members to monitor managers and provide a check on abuses of authority. Drawing from the experience of boards and performance in industrial countries, private sector organizations in over 30 countries have issued codes of 'Best Practice'[2].

Recommendations focus on increasing the percentage of board members not directly tied to management and ensuring that such outside non-executive board members chair subcommittees, including those on financial reporting and compensation, where there are bound to be conflicts of interest between investors and management. However, given the problems of weak information flows in developing countries, the outside board members are often dependent on management for the provision of information. An independent director depending on outside information and selective information provided by the management would have difficulty performing a monitoring role.

Corporate reform governance in developing countries will need to go beyond imposing obligations to conform to standards of best practices by developing effective mechanisms to improve information and enforcement. These could include steps such as the 2003 US corporate reform law empowering

---

2. WB, *World Development Report: Building Institutions for Market* (Washington DC, 2002)

the role of board members as an insider check to management abuses and holding company CEOs and chief financial officers responsible for certifying the accuracy of financial statements on pain of criminal prosecution and swift punishment.

Improving information, accounting and auditing systems

Improving information, accounting and auditing systems has been one of the main objectives of all multilateral and bilateral lending to developing countries for over four decades. The 1990s globalization and adoption of formal corporate governance systems in developing countries further underscored the setting up of an effective information management, accounting and auditing system conforming to the international standard practices to provide timely, accurate and reliable information to prospective investors.

Nonetheless, empirical evidence following the East Asian financial crisis found more than two-thirds of the largest publicly traded banks and corporations produced financial statements with little relation to international accounting standards (IAS).

Weaknesses in accounting standards included lack of disclosure about transactions in which the manager or the entrepreneur had an identifiable conflict of interest, as well as widespread lack of disclosure of liabilities. One of the crucial findings was this lack of disclosure took place despite the involvement of auditing firms affiliated with the top international firms and in many cases was perfectly legal according to national standards[3]. Poor information contributed to the crisis. Investors who relied on publicly available information were in a weak position to identify bad practices and therefore to protect themselves or to distinguish between good and bad investments.

In the energy sector, even with decades of sustained efforts of multilateral financial institutions such as the World Bank requiring under-sector adjustment, project loans and credits and technical assistance to set up an effective information, accounting and auditing system conforming to international standards, the quality of information differed among countries with widespread gaps between national and international accounting and financial reporting. Despite the agreed project loan/ credit conditions, public energy enterprises failed to submit audited annual financial reports on time. Even when reports were submitted after long delays, the audited financial reports failed to reflect conforming to IAS.

As developing countries began corporatization/ privatization of energy enterprises and IPPs were encouraged, international transactions have grown in scope with an increase in demand for the standardization of information across borders by adopting the IAS. For companies seeking to

3. WB, *World Development Report* (2002), p.70

raise capital on the market and especially those seeking foreign investors, conforming to the IAS is now recognized to facilitate the process.

Developing countries such as India where the state has well-established government accounting and auditing standards continue to be responsible for improvement in standard setting and disclosures. In December 2003, India's Comptroller and Auditor General (CAG) in conjunction with the Government Accounting Standards Advisory Board (GASAB) proposed the standard on guarantees by governments, envisaging disclosure requirements and transparency for improving the financial reporting by various state governments and to give incremental information to all stakeholders.

The experience of the industrial countries and the post-2000 US corporate and accounting frauds provides the crucial lesson for effective functioning of oversight institutions of practices of both domestic and foreign energy corporations. Accounting fraud practiced by top international accounting companies such as Arthur Anderson and Ernst and Young since their exposure in the post-2000 period caused an upheaval and public outcry against auditors, a flurry of shareholders lawsuits and regulatory probes. Since then the top seven international accounting firms have reshaped and shrunk to the 'Big Four'. US' passing of the Sarbanes–Oxley act in 2002 created a new system for regulated accountants to transform them into better watchdogs who could prevent massive financial scandals. As of 2002, the 'Big Four' are improving training for auditors, backed away from some types of conflict of interest businesses of mixing consulting and auditing and have started to craft new kinds of relationships with clients.

In most developing countries reforming information, accounting and audit systems requires not only adopting changed international standards but also putting in place effective enforcement mechanisms so that risks of incompetence and possibilities of collusion with management perceived to be great will prevent failures or abuses. As the Asian crisis showed, involving local affiliates of international auditing firms is not sufficient to enhance information quality because the affiliates tend to follow national standards. Furthermore, even where the accounting affiliates follow international standards they are subject to the practices of the foreign investing company.

Formal governance institutions overseeing both domestic and foreign company practices need to be strengthened by new initiatives that complement and build on the existing institutions. Focusing on building information flows such as those which accounting systems provide is important as adopting laws requiring regulators to have extensive information on companies. Tougher internal controls are the best way to detect fraud. Companies with good internal controls have multiple layers for catching financial fraud. Many have computer programs that flag when unusual sums of money are being moved, rules that make it impossible for one person to control a set of books and instructions that tell internal auditors to focus on the highest risk areas. In this context it is important to focus on enforcing mechanisms to keeping the books honest by insulating accountants from pressures to play around the bottom line with alternative interpretations of national and international accounting standards.

Minimizing the cost of private finance and risk management

One basic concern of developing countries as negotiations for the second generation of energy projects start with private foreign investors is the cost of private finance versus sovereign debt. The average nominal cost of private financing—(equity and debt) is clearly higher than the cost of sovereign debt[4]. This is reflected in the rate of return demanded by foreign sponsors. The experience of IPPs in developing countries since the 1990s shows host countries tend to compare the rate of return (or tariff required) demanded by the private sponsors of over 20 per cent to 25 per cent with the usually modest returns allowed to the local public utility of 10 per cent to 12 per cent and conclude that purely on financial terms, the cost of privately financed projects would be higher than those funded through public or publicly guaranteed money.

However, it is important to examine why privately funded projects may still be economically feasible. First is the difference in methodologies for risk assessment and risk sharing between public and private projects and misunderstandings between host governments and private sponsors about the degree of perceived and real risks and mechanisms for risk sharing in a particular project. Host countries tend to perceive much lower risks than do sponsors and lenders in the private sector.

In a typical public sector project, the state assumes most of the associated risks. The nominal rate of return of 10 per cent to 12 per cent is often based on subsidized values. In a well-structured private sector project, the sponsors assume the project completion and commercial risks. To the extent that private financing can be associated with the government offloading important risks to the private sector, the 'economic' (or risk weighted) cost of private financing would be lower than that suggested by a straight comparison of nominal rates. Second, there are often substantial efficiency gains (in terms of project costs and higher operating efficiency) that may more than offset the higher cost of financing. And third, many developing countries need to and would like to limit sovereign debt as a matter of policy. They cannot afford to take on billions of dollars of additional sovereign debt to finance all their energy projects without affecting the macro fundamentals.

It is a fact that private sponsors typically sought high-risk premiums, particularly in the first few ventures in countries with weak financial positions of

---

4. WB, *Infrastructure Development in East Asia and Pacific* (Washington DC, 1995), p.9

some public utilities purchasing the output. As initial project agreements are finalized and implemented effectively, countries could be perceived to have made efforts to establish a good track record. As a result, in many countries, negotiations on the second generation of projects could be started on a more realistic basis between governments and private sponsors.

In the early 1990s, initial projects in most developing countries were handled on a transaction by transaction basis. As discussed in Chapters 4 and 5, most of the independent power projects (IPPs) did not involve open competition and resulted from unsolicited offers. The resulting agreements therefore were on a cost plus or rate of return basis. Such agreements as illustrated by the Enron Dabhol project in India led to a lack of transparency, high transaction costs and questions about whether it was the best possible deal.

In the second stage since the late 1990s, governments are considering ways to increase competition to reduce costs. The latest power projects in a few countries including Egypt have the sponsors after competition and on the basis of delivered cost of power (and not on an agreed minimum rate of return on investment). The cost of power for the first IPP project in Egypt in 1998 was much cheaper at less than 3 US cents kwh. The cost of power from the second-generation projects in the Philippines is about 25 per cent cheaper than the first few projects. With an established track record, open competition can cut the transaction cost of private finance.

The basic approach to risk management should reflect the principle that the party best able to manage a risk at least cost should mitigate it. The private sector sponsors, financiers and insurance companies need to bear commercial and managerial risks. But, in the case of country and policy risks (e.g. currency transfer, policy performance, including commercialization of public power utilities required to buy power from private investor) it may be more economic if the public sector assumes them.

A framework for risk mitigation at the country and sector level will go a long way to encourage a realistic perception of what lies ahead. As risks are mitigated and shared more equitably between the parties, the private sector should be more willing to accept lower returns and assume commercial risks than in the past. However, as long as the private sector is involved in take or pay contracts or BOT-type projects, the risk related to the estimation of demand rests with the public sector.

In the absence of a proper framework, sponsors of individual ventures can try to negotiate mitigation of each and every risk by the state. A competition-oriented approach requires effective institutions to prepare sector 'templates' or standard bidding documents with credible and consistent data. To increase transparency and competition, attempts are being made in a few countries to develop 'templates' specific to the power sector, clarifying ahead of bid competition what are the risks and who will mitigate what risks and how. This way, all potential participants in a given power project would be treated equally and would know the rules of the game before submitting proposals.

Another advantage of preparing a framework for risk management is that it will provide a basis for comparative evaluation of alternative financing options from domestic and international capital markets and between equity and long-term debt financing. As discussed earlier in this chapter, the long-term objective for financing energy/ power projects should be to let domestic private capital markets directly finance projects sponsored by financially viable public and private enterprises without recourse to government guarantees. However, in most countries domestic capital markets are not yet capable of supplying such long-term financing - especially debt financing. For many developing countries private foreign investments and long-term debt would be the primary source to supplement state resources in the foreseeable future.

Mechanisms for long-term debt financing

Lack of appropriate term financing is still the binding constraint. Because of the nature of the assets, most energy projects require long maturity or 15–20 years of debt financing. In developed countries utilities could raise such financing from institutional investors (insurance companies and pension funds) either through the public bond market or through direct placements. Many large international institutional investors were interested in diversifying their portfolios by investing a small proportion of their resources in emerging markets, particularly in East Asia. However, following the East Asian financial crisis in 1998, the future of long-term debt financing for power projects remains uncertain.

One emerging concern about the IPP or any other project-by-project financing approach is the relatively high transaction cost (up to $5–10 million per project for bid preparation plus the cost of raising finance). Countries with a steady flow of private energy projects such as the Philippines considered creation of 'debt funds' to reduce transaction costs and increase the overall flow of long-term debt financing. The idea is to have a privately controlled and managed institution that would raise funds from institutional investors worldwide and invest in a variety of commercially viable energy projects rated high by the market. Through economies of scale and pooling of risks, such funds are expected to provide financing to individual (non-mega) projects at lower costs. However, such funds are likely to be efficient only in countries with potential for a significant number of commercially viable projects.

Experience with investment banks, rating agencies and institutional investors indicate that debt financing from these sources for financially viable and well-structured projects could be resumed provided they can feel comfortable with the 'country policy performance' and transfer (convertibility) risks. Power projects entail additional scrutiny with regard to sector and policy risks. For many countries, potential lenders would prefer additional comfort involving a multilateral institution such as the WB during the transition period. In the power sector sovereign guarantees have often covered contractual obligations of state-owned enterprises in projects such as the PPAs and assured that the host government would maintain a regulatory framework agreed upon.

However, as discussed in Chapters 5 and 7 countries including China and India were reluctant to continue to offer multiple guarantees for second generation projects. They were concerned that sovereign guarantees are contingent liabilities that show up as debt obligations on the government balance sheet. Multilateral financial institutions, export–credit agencies and private sector insurers began scouting ways to plug the holes left by the withdrawal of guarantees. As discussed in Chapters 3 and 4, the WB Group introduced the guarantee mechanisms to provide partial risk guarantee for infrastructure projects during the reform transition period to provide comfort to the private sector and to help provide long-term finance beyond the prevailing market terms for the country. As part of the effort to provide comfort to the private sector, the WB introduced the partial risk guarantee mechanism in the 1990s to foster partnership with the private sector for the benefit of governments, project sponsors and lenders.

The WB's guarantee has been used in two major power projects in Pakistan and the Asian Development Bank's (ADB) in a transmission project, also in Pakistan.

Although the partial risk guarantee will provide coverage for defaults on scheduled debt service payments, the WB requires the host government's counter-guarantees under its charter thereby holding the host government responsible. While guarantees could provide comfort to investors in the transition period, ultimately it remains governments' responsibility to inspire investors confidence to attract private investment in energy.

C. *Reforming multilateral development institutions and energy for development*

As discussed earlier in Chapters 3 and 4, the Multilateral Development Banks (MDBs) such as that of the World Bank's mission of development in general and energy in particular have evolved over the last 60 years from being a lender of the last resort to supporting public sector infrastructure and power projects, to providing direct support to formulate energy policies and technical assistance to build capabilities and to financing project loans and energy sector adjustment operations in the post-1970 oil crisis period.

Following the oil crisis of the 1970s, multilateral financial institutions such as the WB supported developing oil importing countries to help promote oil exploration prospects to private sector and provided financing for some oil and gas projects in developing countries. The WB began to play a prominent role in the oil and gas sector assisting member countries in developing their domestic energy resources.

Three decades ago, in the wake of the first oil price crisis of early 1970s that led to the adverse effects of high oil import bills affecting the economic situation in oil importing developing countries, the global policy circuit buzzed with proposals to address the adjustment problems caused by high oil prices. It was felt that given the interdependent nature of the world economies, appropriate measures need to be taken to correct the global energy situation urgently. The measures considered included direct efforts from multilateral development institutions to provide financial and technical assistance to member countries to reduce their dependence on high-cost energy imports.

A specific proposal was also considered to establish an energy affiliate to finance energy development in member countries. There were considerable discussions on the nature of the affiliate's link to the Bank and the approach it should take in assisting member countries. However, this brainstorming on energy for development weakened with opposition from the oil industry. Direct efforts of financial and technical assistance of multilateral development institutions for energy development declined in the 1990s with the opposition of international oil companies to the WB's financing of oil and gas projects in developing countries and declining oil prices of 1986–7. The debt crisis of the 1980s and its adverse impact on the financial viability of energy companies together with the wave of globalization led to the reassessment of WB's role of financing energy in developing countries. The WB's policy pendulum shifted toward reform and liberalization to promote private investment for energy development.

Since the late 1980s, the MDBs required developing countries to reform and liberalize their energy sectors to create a suitable climate for promoting private investment in energy. Multilateral development institutions' role in the 1990s to influence the path of development in developing countries from plan to market seemed critical to expand trade and investment. There have been structural changes in developing country economic management, progress in stabilization, trade liberalization and flow of private investment. There has also been an explicit redefinition of the role of governments and a recognition of the benefits of improving efficiency and competitiveness from attracting private sector finance for development. Private investors, both domestic and foreign, have responded to the changing environment. Developing countries in 2004 continued to attract capital when FDI increased to over $165.5 billion dollars in 2004, partly offsetting the decline since 2002.

Nonetheless, neither the market-based approach to development nor the inflows of capital to finance energy for development are taking roots in many developing countries. As discussed in earlier chapters, over 80 per cent of capital inflows are accounted for in less than ten developing countries. Even in these countries the capital inflows are mainly in service sectors and in the oil and gas sectors of a few oil exporting African countries such as Angola, Chad, Equatorial Guinea and Sudan.

In the energy sector, of all the MDBs, the WB has been the most influential in setting policy, which then tends to be followed by other regional development banks, including ADB based in Manila, African Development Bank (AfDB) based in Abidjan, and Inter-American Development Bank (IADB) lending for Latin America and the Caribbean. These MDBs have different backgrounds and face different problems. However, in the energy sector, the regional banks have more often followed the WB lead on energy policy and sector reform and adjustment.

This was part of the new direction the WB was taking by changing its role in energy. In reassessing its course, the WB examined in the 1990s deteriorating financial situation of public power enterprises and emphasized the need for reforming the power sector. The four-point reform of the energy sector discussed in Chapters 3 through 5 including liberalization, setting up of regulatory and legal institutional systems, importation of services, commercialization/ privatization and creating a suitable environment for the private sector was required to be pursued by countries as conditions for WB's support. The reassessment was part of the globalization wave to promote the private sector in energy.

As the decade of 1990s was closing, the WB was under attack by longstanding critics and non-governmental organizations for adopting the so-called Washington Consensus—a set of neoclassical economic doctrines that formed the basis for IMF/WB lending policies in the 1990s. Faced by the mixed results of its changing emphasis the WB tried to answer the criticism as part of its effort to face the development challenge in the twenty-first century. A keynote report called 'The Quality of Growth' presented during the WB's 2000 annual meeting tried to answer its critics that it has made a shift from the Washington Consensus. The report emphasized that development is not just about poor countries liberalizing capital markets and opening their borders for trade; it is also about making sure natural resources are not depleted, that corruption must be fought, that impartial judicial and legal systems be established and that there are equal opportunities for education and jobs, greater civil and political liberties and investment in areas like health.

In the energy sector, the WB in 2001 spelt out 'a clarification' of existing policies that have been evolving over time since the 1990s. The energy sector in developing countries, which used to be in the public sector, is now open to the private sector. In the oil and gas sector, the WB's re-examined its strategy in consultation with representatives of the international petroleum industry and other sources of finance emphasized the mitigation of project risks to provide comfort to the private sector by providing a partial risk guarantee and a partial credit guarantee and enable governments to set up effective legal and regulatory institutions.

The level of WB lending to the oil and gas sector has fluctuated substantially since 1980 in response to changes in market conditions as well as shifts in the WB's policy to lend for oil and gas. Bank lending, which initially concentrated on exploration promotion and development of hydrocarbon resources, rose to $1 billion in 1983. The rapid expansion caused concern that the WB might pre-empt private sector. These limitations, combined with the softening of oil prices and perceptions of weakening of future oil demand, caused lending to drop sharply to $300 million in 1986. By 1990, with the changing emphasis on promoting private sector involvement and protecting the environment, WB lending picked up to support the development of natural gas.

In the 1990s, the composition of WB lending in the hydrocarbons sector shifted away from upstream industries to infrastructure, reflecting the changed emphasis that the private sector would invest in upstream projects if the infrastructure for delivering the output was in place. The WB also increased emphasis on technical assistance to facilitate sector restructuring, privatization, private sector development and the establishment of environmental standards and monitoring institutions. This trend is expected to continue.

The WB's official policy as of 2005 is that it will no longer make loans available for upstream projects in the oil and gas sector projects on their own, with the exception of WB funding a minority ownership in the oil pipeline project for the Republic of Chad in Africa at the invitation of Exxon Mobil in the 1990s. The WB supported an oil development project in Chad to support the big private oil companies. The WB assistance focused on designing a plan to ensure that oil revenues would contribute to poverty alleviation and an improved education system.

The decline in types of energy lending includes upstream hydrocarbon project lending, electric power generation and hydropower lending, with the exception of China where the WB has supported some large dam building in the 1990s. The WB may consider lending in power generation only when this simultaneously contributes to either poverty reduction, private sector development or improvements in the governance or macroeconomic stability.

The WB's diminishing involvement in big dam building has coincided with an increase in controversies associated with such lending, especially when large numbers of people have been displaced by the new reservoirs and there are inadequate measures to prevent environmental damage. The

WB unable to address the issues of resettlement, environmental protection, cultural heritage, conservation and the economic and technical feasibility of large hydropower dam projects is withdrawing from financing future large hydropower projects in developing countries.

The IFC, the private sector arm of the WB Group is also changing its emphasis from generation and the IPP market to the distribution side. The basic reasoning is that if distribution is privatized, then IPPs and privately-owned generators can establish contracts directly with distributors and there is no longer a need for government guarantees and PPAs. IFC expects to have a much bigger impact on supplies by reforming the distribution system by reducing high technical and other distribution losses and improving the collection of electricity bills.

Largely as a result of lobbying from the NGOs and others that took place around the time of the Earth Summit in 1992 in the power sector, the change of emphasis has coincided with less WB support for generation projects and more support for improvement in distribution as well as for energy efficiency, renewable energy and rural electrification. In 2000–1, the WB–International Development Association (IDA) total portfolio in renewables projects was $1.4 billion in 26 projects worldwide. Nonetheless, the overriding objective of the WB remains the transfer of these services to the private sector.

The WB Group's changing emphasis on reforming the energy sector and focusing on the privatization of distribution is necessary because distribution companies are poorly managed and suffer from corruption and patronage. However, as discussed in Chapter 5 case studies, simply moving energy utilities from public to private ownership does not solve the problem of corrupt and secretive energy sector management.

With the emphasis on the private sector to pick up investment in energy sector, the overall WB energy sector lending overall has been shrinking from a peak of about $3 billion a year in the pre-1990s to less than $1 billion a year in 2003. In fiscal 2003 (ending June 2003) the WB and its affiliate IDA, which provides credit to the poorest countries of the world on concessionary terms, lent a total of $593 million for the power sector and energy projects in developing countries[5].

In the post September 2001 period, the WB is heading more towards appeasing NGOs and its influential shareholders than focusing on its fundamental development objectives for the early decades of the twenty-first century. The WB's new emphasis on promoting the private sector with respect to energy has yet to demonstrate that it is concerned with extending the delivery of services to the poor people, which is the WB's other declared goal in the sector, in addition to improving the quality of services.

---

5. WB, *Annual Reports* (Washington DC, 1998–2003)

Although ownership and responsibility for successful implementation of the reform program rest with the countries, development encompasses a transformation of both national and international development institutions. The energy sector's size and strategic role in a country's economic development makes it necessary for special attention from the WB.

As many of the WB's critics, including Douglass North of the Hoover Institution, have pointed out that WB is fumbling as it does not know how to promote development. It helps those countries who are doing well but scarcely helps those who are not. Critics argue that the world's top development institution is losing its directing capabilities to the changing needs of energy for development in the twenty-first century. The market-oriented economic reforms introduced since the 1990s throughout the developing world have facilitated some measure of economic recovery and growth, but nowhere near what was anticipated. In the energy sector, as discussed in earlier chapters the WB has admitted to the failure of getting the right formula for financing energy development. Developing countries can no longer depend on the WB to finance their energy projects as the lender of the last resort.

Developing countries require not only private investment in energy but also that the investment helps generate adequate energy supplies at affordable prices for development. Given the large investment requirements for energy in developing countries, the international development institutions such as the WB need to continue to play an important role. Joseph Stiglitz, who served as Chief Economist and Senior Vice-President for the WB from 1997–2000 noted that part of the problem of managing globalization lies with international economic institutions, with the IMF, the WB and the WTO, which help set the rules of the game shaped by a particular vision of the economy and society. Stiglitz advocates that these international institutions should be reshaped and their problems should be fixed[6].

The WB, the chief architect of energy sector reform and liberalization in the 1990s in developing countries admitted:

> If there is any one message that emerges from this inaugural *Energy and Development Report*, it is that despite encouraging trends in many developing country energy sectors, none of us—energy industry, financiers, NGOs or policy makers—have yet got the institutional and financial formula right. The crises exposed this fact starkly.[7]
>
> 'Liberalizing energy markets, however important, may not be the complete an-

---

6. Joseph E Stiglitz, '*Globalization and its discontents*' (London, New York, W W Norton & Company, 2002)
7. WB/ ESMAP, *Energy and Development Report: Energy after the Finanacial Crises* (Washington DC, 1999)

> swer. Despite the progress made in encouraging private investment in the electricity industry since the beginning of the 1990s for example, private companies have shown little interest in extending electricity supplies to rural areas. They have instead preferred to concentrate on more lucrative contracts to generate electricity and to supply industrial and urban consumers'[8].

The direction of development aid since the turn of this century has also moved away from direct support for energy for development. The signing of the Millennium Development Declaration by 189 countries in September 2000, led to the adoption of the Millennium Development Goals (MDG), which set clear targets for reducing poverty and other sources of human deprivation, and promoting sustainable development. A meeting of the world leaders in Monterrey, Mexico, in March 2002, was reported to have ushered in a new compact between developing and developed countries that stressed their mutual responsibilities in the quest for eight development goals. As a result developed countries have now started to link their aid to policies toward the MDG of developing countries they want to support.

The MDG include: eradication of extreme poverty and hunger, achieving universal primary education, promoting gender equality and empowering women, reducing child mortality, improving maternal health, combating HIV AIDS, malaria and other diseases, ensuring environmental sustainability and developing a global partnership for development focusing on debt reduction, technology transfer especially information and communication. While focus on these goals is necessary for poverty alleviation, it is not sufficient to alleviate energy poverty. Energy is not even listed among the eight MDG.

The Joint WB–IMF *Global Monitoring Report*, (2004)[9] devoted two pages in its report on access to electricity in the chapter on infrastructure and its review of reform progress was to answer 'yes' in its Table 6.5 on electricity law and setting up on paper independent regulation. While the report estimated over US $465 billion a year in infrastructure investment in developing countries it left this as a challenge. The report had little to offer as to the role of international development institutions other than stating that the IMF would continue to assist low-income countries to confront macroeconomic challenges, and the WB will continue to support country efforts to deepen the Poverty Reduction Strategy Paper Process (PRSP). The MDG monitoring 'Business as usual' report of 2004 offers little hope for reshaping international financial institutions to promote energy for development. Though

8. WB, *Rural Energy and Development: Improving energy supplies for 2 billion people* (Washington DC, 1996)
9. WB, *'Global Monitoring Report', Policies and actions for achieving the Millennium Development Goals and related outcomes* (Washington DC, 2004), pp.98–9

both industrial and developing countries have endorsed the MDG, as of 2005 little progress has been made to achieve these goals in general and increase access to energy in particular.

With increasing inequity in energy use, continued difficulties in attracting sufficient capital to translate the required demand to meet actual consumption of energy, the overall energy sector reform process led largely by the WB in redefining the role of the state to create suitable conditions for the private sector did not meet the expectation of the pendulum shift to private investment in energy for development. Despite some increase in lending for renewable energy in 2004–5, since the spiking of oil prices in 2004 the WB's diminishing involvement in energy and its continued disseminaton of more of the same knowledge by focusing mainly on undertaking analytical work such as the report on the impact of oil prices on developing countries and providing policy and technical advice to encourage private sector has coincided with an increase in controversies associated with its policy prescriptions and its yet unfulfilled conditions to qualify for any lending in energy.

The energy industry since the 1990s has become more global by the opening up of oil and gas regions in Central Asia, advances in technologies to produce oil, gas and renewable energy, combined-cycle gas power generation and clean coal technologies However, the energy market expansion has also been accompanied since the initial years of this decade by profound changes in the structure and organization of the global energy market, concerns of security of energy supply linking government energy policies and geopolitics of energy supply and the spiking of energy prices since 2004 stoking the fear that the era of cheap energy is over.

What does this mean for the WB? In the changing energy world of today, considering the lessons of reform experience with settings where comprehensive reform has proved politically and institutionally difficult, how will the WB address the pair of issues related to its energy sector reform and market liberalization experience in developing countries to finance the required investment in energy and the unsolved problem of increasing access to efficient and affordable energy to over 2 billion people?

How will the estimated $465 billion a year investment in infrastructure by the joint WB–IMF global MDG monitoring report and an additional annual investment of $250 billion in energy in developing countries be made? Compared with the estimated $250 billion investment in energy required, the WB's average annual lending of $1 billion for energy and minerals even after considering the energy impact of all WB operations in building economies in developing countries including WB's technical assistance activities such as the ESMAP and private sector promotion, hardly makes a positive difference to increase access to energy for development. Should there be a rethinking of the future role of multilateral institutions such as the WB to promote energy for development?

With the emerging features of the non-OPEC developing countries' energy sector discussed in the last section of Chapter 5 and the challenges that developing non-OPEC countries have to face at the national and global levels in the context of rapidly changing energy world since the beginning of this century, how should the WB confront the core issues of energy for development to shape its future.

With rapid expansion in the overall size of the energy market in developing countries absorbing more than 60 per cent of the increase in world primary energy demand since the last three decades, any attempt to address these questions to achieve the goal of secure, efficient and affordable energy for development needs to concentrate on areas of energy supply strategies, reform policies and implementation issues, widening access to energy and technology and energy futures.

Energy supply strategies

Factors affecting strategic energy supply include reliability of reserves, infrastructure adequacy and security, investment and governance. Under the new conditions of security of supply and price of energy, developing and developed oil importing countries need coherent policies to address national energy needs and appropriate strategies to implement them. Such strategies should include critical elements of energy policies discussed in Chapter 7 that will maximize the use of the most efficient energy resources, make more effective use of existing resources, promote conservation, increase knowledge of the country's resource potential and its development and develop and/ or use advancing technologies for using both traditional and new renewable energy fuels more effectively.

In the aftermath of the 1970s oil crisis the WB and other MDBs expanded technical assistance in energy planning and lending for promoting oil and gas exploration and development to private investors and financed more efficient use of traditional fuels to reduce unit costs and expand marketing systems. However, in the changed conditions as of 2005 both with regard to the global energy industry and the magnitude of the energy challenge for development, the MDBs' conventional approach of the post-1970s technical assistance to energy planning is insufficient.

Sector reform policies and implementation

With the spiking of oil prices since 2004 and more than doubling of imported LNG prices in 2005, OIDs are not enthusiastic about the market pricing of energy. Even if higher global energy prices were to recede in the coming years, energy prices reflecting economic and environmental costs in developing countries will have to increase to attract investment. If developing countries were to create suitable conditions for private investment they need to address the issues discussed in the foregoing section on constraints to private investors including the impact of higher rates of return of over 25 per cent expected by private investors on energy prices to their consumers. As discussed in earlier chapters, the WB saddled with the disconnect between expectations of energy sector reform policy goals of pricing, regulation, commercialization and private investment promotion is yet to confront these issues. Even in the aftermath of oil price increases since 2004, the WB continued to confine itself to the pursuit of its 1990s knowledge based ESMAP analytic papers focusing mainly on the need for improving its own understanding of the impact of oil prices on developing countries.

As of 2005 developing countries with mixed experience of energy sector reform and liberalization are passing into varying degrees of an energy-intensive phase which the developed countries experienced during their rapid industrialization and rapid growth. The critical factors impacting the sector reform implementation and the emerging features of non-OPEC energy sector in developing countries discussed in the last section of Chapter 5 underscore the diversity of issues of energy for development in developing countries. Furthermore, the linkages of energy reform policies and strategies of energy supply with the challenging geopolitical issues of capital flows, governance, security, production and consumption practices, sanctions and bilateral and strategic alliances are influencing energy in the beginning years of this decade. Nonetheless, the core issues of energy for development are converging toward more reliable, efficient and secure energy for development at affordable prices. Formulation of the future course of energy reform policies and strategies for their implementation require that development institutions consider lessons and challenges of energy market liberalization in developing countries discussed in Chapter 7 and confront the disparate issues of pricing, regulation, rate of return, investment and project financing. These include:

- How to meet pricing and regulatory objectives in the weak political and institutional settings, while ensuring reliable and efficient energy supply for development at affordable prices?
- How to create a suitable environment for private investment to mobilize the $250 billion annual investment in energy in developing countries, while minimizing the cost of private finance and risk management?
- How to respond to the diversities in energy markets in OIDs and the emerging feature of all options of open energy strategy to enhance security of energy supplies?
- How should the future energy sector reform policies address the unresolved problem of increasing access to efficient, reliable energy

at affordable prices to over 2.4 billion people in developing countries?

Widening access to energy

The UN report of July 2005 entitled *The Energy Challenge for Achieving the Millennium Development Goals,* once again underscored the critical importance of increasing access to modern energy services to 2.4 billion people lacking access to modern fuels in the developing world. The joint WB–UNDP report argued for the need to mobilize investment to expand access to energy services for the poor. It also noted that public sector resources will remain crucial for investing in energy service delivery for the poor due to the private sector's limited appetite for risk in emerging markets.

Despite a stream of analytical reports from the UNDP, WB, IEA and other international organizations, the unserved population has not decreased significantly in absolute numbers of over 2 billion people mainly in the rural areas. Furthermore, the increased demands of the rapidly growing and more influential urban population since the 1990s make it more difficult to address the unresolved problem of energy poverty of the rural poor.

The question raised in an earlier paragraph on how the future reform policies should address the unresolved problem of widening access to over 2.4 billion people in the developing world requires dealing with the critical energy access issues discussed in Chapter 6. These include: cost and value determination of access to energy services, regulatory approaches for pricing of both grid-connected and non grid-connected energy supplies, development and market deployment of right technologies for alternative fuel options, financing mechanisms and access to credit and finally, effective governance with strict enforcement of laws to prevent corruption at federal/ state/ provincial/ local/ village levels by getting on board the required skill-mix of people to put into practice the principles of pricing, regulatory approaches, technology deployment, financing mechanisms and access to credit.

The pressure on the international community to take on a more active role to increase access to energy services as part of the program to reduce poverty resulted in launching the MDG. However, in the absence of confronting the issues discussed in the above paragraph to pave the path of actionable practices to reach the goal of principles, continuation of offering advice on improving policies to developing countries will not by itself resolve the problem of the need for widening access to energy for the poor.

Technology and energy futures

With concerns about the long-term availability of conventional oil and gas resources with known exploration and extraction technologies, there is a growing emphasis on long-term energy trends and technological developments to shape policies for better energy futures. With the rising demand for energy in developing countries, adopting already existing technologies to improve efficient energy use and planning for deployment of new energy technologies are part of shaping better energy futures. Technology developments include: next generation conventional and unconventional fossil fuel technologies, nuclear technologies, renewable energy and their deployment to pave the way for improvements in conservation, efficiency, production and delivery systems and alternative energy futures. Technology developments focusing on development and widespread use of non-oil transportation fuels and improving the reliability of renewable energy resources may contribute to the transition to lesser dependence on oil. Dealing with issues of realizing the potential of technologies to shape better energy futures remains the main challenge of long-term energy for development.

The MDBs operational mission of promoting development has expanded considerably over the past six decades. The concept of energy for development has broadened from financing state owned power projects to lending for oil and gas in the post-1970 oil crisis period to changing the role of governments in developing countries to reform and liberalize their energy sectors to attract private investment. In the 1990s the WB also supported funding 40 per cent of the unique Chad/ Cameroon oil project pipeline with Exxon Mobil to ensure that oil revenues for the governments of Chad and Cameroon would contribute to poverty alleviation and improved education systems. However, in January 2006, the WB suspended disbursements of its loans to Chad for the failure of the Government of Chad to explain how it had spent the money so far.

Following the failed privatization of Senelec, the electric power company in Senegal, the WB Group is also implementing in Senegal an integrated effort of technical assistance, risk mitigation and supply of capital by financing a 67.5 MW thermal generation plant developed by a consortium consisting of Mitsubishi Heavy Industries Europe and Matelec. Since the 1990s, the WB Group has promoted a few PPP to finance a transmission project in India, where the creditworthy state-owned national transmission company, the Power Grid Corporation of India used its own strong balance sheet to act as the off-taker to the project, thereby improving the bankability of the project. The PPP mechanisms are being used as vehicles for promoting some renewable energy technologies to facilitate their market deployment to make them cost competitive with traditional sources of power generation. The WB Group's efforts to foster PPP mechanism through a few specific projects at best serve as models to increase access to energy for development. However, these PPPs still need to address the fundamentally disparate issues of principles and practices of investment. These include:

- Differences in perception of risks between public and private investors. Public power utilities' rate of return ranges between 12 per cent and 16 per cent compared with the private investor's rate of return of over 25 per cent, risk sharing and their impact on power tariffs and affordability.
- Disparate issues of energy sector pricing, regulatory and financial viability of energy enterprises, investment policy objectives and actions required to implement these objectives
- Lack of transparent procedures for bid invitation, evaluation, negotiation and contract award.
- High transaction costs due to the need for engaging legal, contractual and financial experts.
- Weaknesses of the domestic capital market and real interest rates which are barriers to mobilize local financing.

60 years ago, at the Bretton Woods conference in July 1944, the USA and its allies created the International Bank for Reconstruction and Development, (now known as the World Bank Group), believing poverty and hopelessness threatened the world's stability. Six decades later, there are new lessons about what works and what does not. To avoid taking actions to address the unreconciled issues and taking the much needed pro-active role on the scale required is to ignore the lessons of six decades that could hasten a repetition of history. Six decades later, we know now that even when foreign capital has flowed to the top ten emerging economies and several oil rich countries in SSA, unreconciled issues between energy sector reform goals and their implementation persit. These include issues to be addressed with regard to economic governance, capability of institutions, private project financing constraints and the daunting challenge of increasing access to over 2 billion people, where private investment has shown little interest. In the absence of a more pro-active role by the MDBs to address the issues in the areas discussed above, they will continue to offer more of the same knowledge and a few specific pilot projects, tinkering at the edges of the actual challenges.

D. *Towards a one world global energy for development agency*

In the post-2001 world of evolving political economy, efforts to reform will continue to be contested. The reform experience shows that the problem is not reform *per se*. But how it is managed and how the rules of game are set.

Developing countries believed in the early 1990s that they would benefit from reforming their economies. However, in 2005 they had little confidence in the rules of the game of investment reform and liberalization as they perceived that served the interests of investors of advanced countries rather than those of the developing world. Furthermore, in the context of a series of disclosures of corporate corrupt practices of international energy companies since 2001, mobilizing public support to pricing and investment reforms to attract private investment will continue to be difficult. It would put additional pressure on the weak and ineffective government institutions to address issues of acceptable costs of private investment.

As an engine of economic growth, energy will always be of fundamental importance to developing and developed countries. Developing countries' share in global energy demand is expected to double during the first half of the twenty-first century and presents a significant challenge. For developing countries energy is critically linked to poverty and development including investment, finance, foreign exchange, balance of payments, trade impacts and security concerns such as national access to energy supplies.

The future financial investment needed for generating the required energy supplies, due to population increase and economic development and for expanding access to commercial energy supplies for the 2 billion people worldwide without them, are huge. The scale of requirements means that energy systems can only be changed gradually. Twenty-first century systems will take many years to develop and will require implementation of the elements of the framework of energy for development discussed above. Effective implementation of such a framework in the developing world will demand innovative approaches to counteract the negative impacts of globalization now at work in the energy sector.

Implementation will have to deal with several obstacles that stand in the way. First among these obstacles is the clear evidence that the shift towards private sector finance of the energy sector during the 1990s has been selective and not been accompanied by any significant shift towards increasing reliable and adequate supplies of energy. As discussed in earlier chapters of this book most private investments in energy are concentrated in a few developing countries and the 'top ten' (Brazil, China, Argentina, Philippines, Indonesia, India, Pakistan, Malaysia, Colombia and Thailand). Even in these countries, following the 1997 East Asian Financial crisis and 2001 economic crisis in Argentina, the future prospects for private sector investment is expected to be uncertain. Furthermore, 75 per cent of private investment in power projects between 1990 and 1997 in the top ten developing countries has been mainly in new greenfield projects and 25 per cent in transmission and distribution. Access to modern energy services by the rural poor continue to remain marginalized. It is highly questionable whether in the post-2001 period, the private sector will be interested even as selectively as it was between 1990 and 1997 in developing countries.

Second, the 1990s have seen the changing role of the multilateral financing institutions in energy as discussed above and in Chapter 3. While several international agencies' studies including the WB, UNDP, WEC and IEA agree on the large investment required for energy in developing countries, WB's overall energy sector lending has been shrinking, from about $3 billion in 1991 to less than $1 billion in 2003. Attracting private investment when multilateral and bilateral public sector lending has been in decline in the post-1997 crisis period continues to be difficult for many developing countries.

Coinciding with the move towards greater reform and liberalization has been the phenomenon of globalization and its impact on developing countries adopting the rules of this game. The East Asian financial crisis and the economic crisis in Latin America have underscored the volatility of foreign capital flows including commercial bank financing for debt financing of energy projects. Even with substantial reforms such as those related to corporate governance and high savings it will be difficult to efficiently channel the high savings into the corporate sector through equity markets.

A third difficulty that many developing countries have to face even if they were to be successful in moving forward with the reform and liberalization is the negative fallout of inequity in energy use and the longer-term reconciliation of energy for development with environmental protection. With doubling of world population in the twenty-first century, with most of the increase in developing countries, the stresses caused by lack of energy will increase unless tackled with determination.

Failure to mobilize the required investment to generate adequate, reliable and affordable energy for development and to expand access to energy services for over 2 billion energy poor in developing countries will restrict growth prospects and lead to continued increase of energy poor lacking access to energy services with undesirable consequences of perpetuating gender disparity, environment and land degradation. The MDG's approach of linking the flow of aid to reform policies may be necessary, but lessons of experience show that it is not sufficient to translate 'reform talk' to results on the ground.

The challenge of increasing access to energy for development becomes part of decisions on the direction of global energy future in the twenty-first century and must be confronted through political leadership at the global level by fostering effective partnerships of all energy stakeholders. The experience of reform and liberalization since the 1990s has underscored the fact that funding of energy projects has become quite complex involving public and private investors, energy industry sponsors and multilateral financial institutions. Despite thousands of memorandum of understandings (MOUs) signed between energy industry sponsors and developing countries in the 1990s, very few deals reached financial closure. Although the problem may not be that of the concept of reform and liberalization *per se*, it lies in the way it is managed.

With the rapid growth of energy demand in developing countries, the issue is how to make reforms work to meet their growing demand for energy. And if it is to work in the evolving global political economy of the initial years of the twenty-first century, there is a need for an effective vehicle such as an international energy for development agency to help set the rules of energy for development and build effective partnerships of energy stakeholders. In 2005, the world has information, technology and finance, but no partnership between governments, the private sector, international financial institutions and the energy industry to promote the required investment in energy for development.

With the energy sector becoming an increasingly important component of the economy, the combination of events since the initial years of this decade, the tightening world energy market, concerns of security of energy supply and rising energy costs, the energy problems experienced since 2001 are different from the post-1970s oil crisis decade, which was a temporary setback to economic growth in developing countries. Energy for development now appears to be a long-term constraint. This means that OIDs will have to make the politically difficult decision to prepare for shaping a better energy future.

The need for moving forward with structural/ sector reform to let energy enterprises operate as commercially and financially viable enterprises and mobilizing greater domestic financial resources is inescapable. The OIDs, as discussed in Chapters 4 and 5, differ greatly in their ability to reform their energy sectors to mobilize the required investment and to shape their energy future in an era of higher energy costs. This means the poorer and weaker countries will continue to face higher risks of investment viability, higher energy costs and higher prices which affect developing the energy market to increase access to energy for development.

As individual country and sector conditions vary, the supreme challenge is to take a pro-active role first to formulate 'win-win' rules of the actionable game for investment in energy for development. This requires dealing with the issues of access to energy for development to move towards formulating effective partnerships of energy stakeholders both in the emerging developing countries of Asia and Latin America and in the SSA region, which despite being the net energy exporting region has the lowest per capita energy consumption with a large population lacking access to energy.

Mechanisms including PPPs to foster effective partnership of different stakeholders, government, energy industry and energy practitioners need to address common issues to find mutually beneficial outcomes. For the necessary large investments in energy to take place in a sustainable manner, the three main parties must be satisfied. The governments in developing countries need to know that the financing and efficiency objectives are met with fair assessment of risks. The investors, public and private, have to be confident of earning a return consistent with risk. The public must believe that service will be improved and that the cost is justified. Ultimately, the delivery of energy services must have visible benefits through a wide cross-section of society in the developing world. Tariffs and prices for delivery of energy services need to be affordable and acceptable.

Developing countries do not dispute the benefits of foreign investment to improve efficiency and to facilitate the transfer of technology for energy operations. But they do question the rules of multilateral agreements on investments that include the right to unlimited entry, project cost estimates, project financing mechanisms, project risk assessment and risk sharing, premium rates of return, contract enforcement and pricing, particularly for power as it impacts affordability. Formulation of multilateral investment agreements (MAI) aiming to create a fair, transparent and predictable investment regime in partnership with both the transnational energy corporations and developing countries is critical to the future of effective partnerships.

Given the interdependence of the global energy industry and the magnitude of the challenge to energy in the twenty-first century, what is needed is a one-world energy agency to combine the contributions of not only oil importing countries, but the oil/ energy exporters, energy corporations, private investors and energy technology developers to increase access to energy for development in developing countries. The twenty-first century global energy for development agency could create a firm foundation of principles to help formulate mechanisms for multiple effective partnerships of energy stakeholders.

Given the magnitude of the challenge to energy for development in this century, the critical need for promoting effective partnerships between various energy stakeholders and the inability of the MDBs to become the vehicle for fostering such partnerships, there is an urgent need for moving toward a new twenty-first century one-world energy for development agency for a transformed world. Such an agency needs to be shaped by the global energy industry skills of various energy stakeholders addressing the interrelated core issues of strategic energy supply, sector reform and investment strategies, widening access to energy and technology development and deployment. It could serve as an effective vehicle to develop mutually beneficial mechanisms to increase the required scale of access to efficient, reliable energy for development at affordable prices.

Bibliography

Boo Lun, Electricity Demand in the People's Republic of China, *ERD Working Paper Series No. 37* (Manila, ADB, 2003)

Chong Xu Yi, *Powering China: Reforming the Electric Power Industry in China* (Hants, Dartmouth Publishing Company, 2002)

Congress of the United States/ Office of Technology Assessment, *Fueling Development: Energy Technologies for Developing Countries,* (Washington DC, 1992)

Dani Rodrik, *Has Globalization Gone Too Far?* (Washington DC, Institution of International Economics, 1997)

Dani Rodrik, 'The New Global Economy and Developing Countries', *Policy Essay No.24* (Washington DC, Overseas Development Council, 1999)

Dean Baker, Gerald Epstein and Robert Pollin, ed., *Globalization and Progressive Economic Policy,* (Cambridge, Cambridge University Press, 1998, rpt 1999)

Rudy Dornbusch, *Keys to Prosperity, Free Market, Sound Money and A Bit of Luck,* (Cambridge MA, MIT Press, 2002)

William Easterly, *The Elusive Quest for Growth: Economists' Adventures and Misadventures in the Tropics* (Cambridge MA, MIT Press, 2001)

Thomas L Friedman, *The Lexus and the Olive Tree* (New York, Farrar, Strauss and Giroux, 2001)

Dermot Gately, Shane S Strifel, 'The Demand for Oil Products in Developing Countries', *WB Discussion Paper No.359* (Washington DC, 1997)

Gerald M Meier, Joesph E Stiglitz, ed., *Frontiers of Development Economics: The Future In Perspective,* (New York, Oxford University Press, 2001)

Government of India/ Planning Commission, *Annual Report on the Working of State Electricity Boards and Electricity Departments,* (New Delhi, 1999)

Merilee S Grindle, ed., *Getting Good Government: Capacity Building in the Public Sectors of Developing Countries.* (Cambridge MA, Harvard University Press, 1997)

Gudrum Kuchendorfer-Lucius, Boris Pleskovic, *Development Issues in the 21st Century,* Villa Borsig Workshop Series (Berlin, WB/ German Foundation for International Development, 1998)

Pierre Guislain, *The Privatization Challenge: A Strategic, Legal and Instituional Analysis of International Experience,* (Washington DC, WB, 1997)

Donald I Hertzmark, *Financing Power Sector Expansion in Developing Countries: 1980–1993*, Report to the WB (Washington DC, 1994)

Paul Hirst, Graham Thomson, *Globalization in Question—The International Economy and Possibilities of Governance,* (Cambridge, Polity Press, 1999)

IEA, *WEO* (Paris, 2000)

IEA, *WEO* (Paris, 2002)

IEA, *World Energy Investment Outlook* (Paris, 2003)

IEA, *Quarterly Statistics* (Paris, 2000–4)

IEA, *WEO* (Paris, 2004)

IEA, *Energy Policies of IEA Countries, 2004 Review* (Paris, 2004)

IEA/ OECD, *Oil Information* (Paris, 2003)

IFC, *Project Finance in Developing Countries,* Lessons of Experience No.7 (Washington DC, 1999)

IFC, *The Impact on Private Investment of Corruption and the Quality of Public Investment,* (Washington DC, 2001)

IFC, 'Trends in Private Investment in Developing Countries: Statistics for 1970–2000 and the Impact on Private Investment of Corruption and the Quality of Public Investment', *Discussion Paper 44* (Washington DC, 2001)

IIASA-WEC, *Global Energy Perspectives* (Cambridge, Cambridge University Press, 1998)

Keith Lee Kozloff, Roger C Dower, *A New Power Base: Renewable Energy Policies for the Nineties and Beyond,* (Washington DC, World Resources Institute, 1993)

Jochen Kraske, William H Becker, William Diamond, Louis Galambos, *Bankers With A Mission: The Presidents of the World Bank, 1946–1991*, (New York, Oxford University Press, WB, 1996)

Ashoka Mody, ed., *Infrastructure Delivery Private Initiative and the Public Good,* (Washington DC, WB/ EDI Development Studies, 1996)

Theodore H Moran, *Foreign Investment and Development: The New Policy Agenda for Developing Countries and Economies in Transition,* (Washington DC, Institution for International Economics, 1998)

National Energy Policy Development Group, *Reliable, Affordable, and Environmentally Sound Energy for America's Future,* Report from Vice-president Dick Cheney submitted to the President of the USA (Washington DC, 2001)

Petroleum Economist, *World Energy Yearbook* (London, 2000)

Jonathan R Pincus, Jeffrey A Winters, ed., *Reinventing the World Bank* (Ithaca and London, Cornell University Press, 2002)

Govinda M Rao, K P Kalirajan, Ric Shand, *The Economics of Electricity Supply in India,* (Delhi, Macmillan India Limited, 1998)

Hossein Razavi, *Financing Energy Projects In Emerging Economies,* (Tulsa OK, Pennwell Books, 1996)

Paul Roberts, *The End of Oil, on the Edge of a Perilous New World,* (Boston and New York, Houghton Mifflin Company, 2004)

Gabriel Roth, *EDI The Private Provision of Public Services in Developing Countries: EDI Series in Economic Development,* (New York, WB, Oxford University Press, 1987)

Frank Sader, 'Attracting Foreign Direct Investment in to Infrastructure, Why Is It So Difficult?' *Foreign Investment Advisory Service Occasional Paper 12,* (Washington DC, WB, 2000)

Javed Burki Shahid, *Changing Perceptions and Altered Reality: Emerging Economies in the 1990s,* (Washington DC, WB, 2000)

George Soros, *The Crisis of Global Capitalism (Open Society Endangered),* (New York, Public Affairs, 1998)

Joseph E Stiglitz, *Globalization and its Discontents,* (London and New York, W W Norton & Company, 2002)

Lawrence H Summers, 'The Challenges We Face', paper delivered at the Special Session of the G-7 Council in Tokyo (Washington DC, WB, 1991)

Lawrence H Summers, *The Economics of the 1990s: Back to the Future,* (Washington DC, WB, 1991)

William K Tabb, *Economic Governance in the Age of Globalization,* (New York, Columbia University Press, 2004)

Ian Tellam, ed., *Fuel for Change, World Bank Energy Policy: Rhetoric Vs Reality,* (London and New York, Zed Books, 2000; Amsterdam, Both Ends, 2000)

Lester C Thurow, *The Future of Capitalism: How today's Economic Forces Shape Tomorrow's World,* (New York, Penguin, 1996)

UNDP, *World Energy Assessment: Energy and the Challenge of Sustainability* (New York, 2000)

UNDP, *World Energy Assessment 2004 Update,* (New York, WEC, UNDESA, 2004)

UNDP/ESMAP, *The Impact of Higher Oil Prices on Low Income Countries and the Poor, March 2005,* (Washington DC, March 2005)

UN, *Energy Statistics Yearbooks* (New York, 1990-2000)

USEIA, *South Africa, Country Analysis Brief,* (Washington DC, 2002)

USEIA, *Sub-Saharan Africa* (Washington DC, 2003a)

USEIA, *An Energy Overview of the Republic of Egypt* (Washington DC, 2003b)

USEIA, *Egypt's Country Analysis Brief* (Washington DC, 2004)

USEIA, *International Energy Outlook* (Washington DC, 2004a)

USEIA, *China Country Analysis Brief* (Washington DC, July 2004b)

WEC, *Financing the Global Energy Sector—The Task Ahead* (London, 1997)

WEC, *World Energy Assessment 2004 Update,* (UNDESA, UNDP, 2004)

Rangaswamy Vedavalli, *Private Foreign Investment and Economic Development: A Case Study of Petroleum in India* (Cambridge, Cambridge University Press, 1976)

Rangaswamy Vedavalli, 'Domestic Energy Pricing Policies', WB Energy Series Paper 13 (Washington D.C., World Bank, 1989)

Rangaswamy Vedavalli, 'International Energy Financing', *World Energy Council Journal* (London, 1994)

Rangaswamy Vedavalli, 'The Beginnings of A New South Africa', *Bank's World,* Volume 14, No. 415 (Washington DC, April/ May 1995)

Rangaswamy Vedavalli, *Institutions and Policies for Renewable Energy Development in China,* World Bank Report (Washington DC, WB, 1996a)

Rangaswamy Vedavalli, *Sri Lanka Energy Services Delivery Project, Economic and Financial Analysis for Renewable Energy Sub-Projects,* (Washington DC, World Bank, 1996b)

Rangaswamy Vedavalli, 'Regional Energy: The Role of World Energy Council', Paper presented to the WEC (London, 1997)

Jack Welch and John A Byrne, *Jack, Straight From the Gut,* (New York, Warner Books Inc., 2001)

WB, *World Development Report* (Washington DC, 1985)

WB, *Jordan: Energy Sector Study* (Washington DC, 1990), 2 volumes

WB, *Brazil, Energy Pricing and Investment Study* (Washington DC, 1992)

WB, *The World Bank's Role in the Electric Power Sector: A World Bank Policy Paper* (Washington DC, 1993a)

WB, *Energy Efficiency and Conservation in the Developing World: A World Bank Policy Paper* (Washington DC, 1993b)

WB, *World Development Report: Infrastructure for Development* (New York, Oxford University Press, 1994a)

WB, *Reforms and Private Participation in the Power Sector of Selected Latin American and Caribbean and Industrialized Countries*, Report No.33 (Washington DC, 1994b)

WB, *Development in Practice: Private Sector Development in Low Income Countries* (Washington DC, 1995a)

WB, *Lending for Electric Power in Sub-Saharan Africa* (Washington DC, 1995b)

WB, *India, Five Years of Stabilization and Reform and the Challenges Ahead,* (Washington DC, 1996a)

WB, *Rural Energy and Development* (Washington DC, 1996b)

WB, *China, Power Sector, Regulation in a Socialist Economy* (Washington DC, 1997)

WB, 'Power Project Finance Experience in Developing Countries', *RMC Discussion Paper Series 119* (Washington DC, 1998a)

WB, *Rural Energy and Development: Improving Energy Supplies for Two Billion People,* (Washington DC, 1998b)

WB, *Fuel for Thought: A New Environmental Strategy for the Energy Sector* (Washington DC, 1999)

WB, 'The Private Sector and Power Generation in China', *Discussion Paper No.406* (Washington DC, 2000)

WB, *World Development Report* (Washington DC, 2000–1)

WB, *A brighter Future? Energy in Africa's Development* (Washington DC, 2001a)

WB, *Rethinking the East Asian Miracle* (New York, Oxford University Press, 2001b)

WB, *Proceedings of the World Bank Annual Conference on Development Economics (ABCDE)*, (Washington DC, 1989–2001)

WB, *Fostering Competition in China's Power Market* (Washington DC, 2001c)

WB, *Global Development Report* (Washington DC, 2001d)

WB, *World Development Report: Building Institutions for Market* (Washington DC, 2002)

WB, *Global Development Finance* (Washington DC, 1999–2005)

WB, *Annual Reports* (Washington DC, 1976–2004)

WB, *Global Economic Prospects* (Washington DC, 2004a)

WB, *World Development Report: Making Services Work for Poor People* (Washington DC, 2004b)

WB, *World Development Report: A Better Investment Climate for Everyone* (Washington DC, 2005a)

WB, *Global Economic Prospects* (Washington DC, 2005b)

WB, *Economic Growth in the 1990s: Learning from a Decade of Reform* (Washington DC, 2005c)

WB, *At the Frontlines of Development: Reflections from the World Bank* (Washington DC, 2005d)

World Economic Forum, *The Global Competitiveness Report 2004–2005*, (New York, Palgrave Macmillan, 2004)

WB/ Cuneo Association, *Petroleum Product Supply and Distribution in Sub-Saharan Africa* (Rome, Washington DC, 1994)

WB/ ESMAP, *Report on Arab Republic of Egypt: Energy Sector Assessment, Challenges for the Egyptian Energy Sector* (Washington D.C., 1995)

WB/ ESMAP, *Financing Africa's Power Sector: Issues and Options,* Report No.182/96 (Washington DC, 1996)

WB/ ESMAP, *Energy and Development Report: Energy Services for the World's Poor,* (Washington DC, 2000)

WB/ ESMAP, 'Fostering Competition in China's Power Markets', *WB Discussion Paper 416*, (Washington DC, 2001)

WB/ OED, *Rural Electrification in Asia: A Review of Bank Experience* (Washington DC, 1994)

WB/ OED, *Lending for Electric Power in Sub-Saharan Africa* (Washington DC, 1996)

WB/ OED, *Report on Power for Development: A Review of World Bank Experience with Private Sector Participation in the Electricity Sector* (Washington DC, 2003)

WEC, *Energy for Tomorrow's World Acting Now* (London, 2000)

WEC, *Pricing Energy in Developing Countries* (London, 2001)

Energy Periodicals

Developing World Energy
Electrical World
Electricity Journal
Energy Economics
Energy Journal
Financial Times Energy World
Finance and Development

Global Private Power
Independent Energy
International Gas Report
International Journal of Global Energy Issue
International Petroleum Statistics report
International Private Power Quarterly
Journal of Energy Literature Journal of Energy in Southern Africa Journal/World Energy Council (1994–98)
Middle East Energy New Review: The Magazine of New and Renewable Energy
Oil and Gas Journal
Oil Daily
Oil Market Intelligence
Oil Market Report
Oil Week
OPEC Review
Pacific and Asian Journal of Energy
Petroleum Economist
Petroleum Intelligence Weekly
Platt's Oil gram News
Platt's Oil gram Price Report
Power Engineering
Power Engineering International
Power in Asia
Power in Latin America
Project Finance
Public Utilities Fortnightly
Renewable and Sustainable Energy Reviews
Weekly Petroleum Argus
World Oil

Statistical sources

All Energy Sectors

United Nations Energy Statistics Yearbook (New York)
Energy Statistics of Non-OECD Countries (International Energy Agency), (Paris)
Energy Balances of Non-OECD Countries (International Energy Agency) (Paris)
International Energy Outlook (Energy Information Administration) Washington DC

International Energy Statistics Source Book
Survey of World Energy Resources, (World Energy Council) London

Oil, Gas, Coal

BP Statistical Review of World Energy
International Energy Annual (Washington DC)
International Petroleum Encyclopedia (Annual)
World Oil Trends (Annual) Cambridge Energy Associates
Natural Gas Statistics Source Book

Electricity

Energy Balances and Electricity Profiles (for selected developing countries and areas, United Nations)

Electric Utilities Data book for the Asian Pacific Region, Manila, Asian Development Bank

Electricity Information (Annual), Paris

Prices

International Electricity Prices annual (Electricity Council)
Energy Prices and Taxes, International Energy Agency, Paris
Platt's Oil gram Price Report, New York, McGraw Hill (Daily)
Prices of Crude Petroleum Products, Washington, World Bank (Quarterly)

Index